2022

上海统计年鉴

SHANGHAI STATISTICAL YEARBOOK

上　海　市　统　计　局
国家统计局上海调查总队
SHANGHAI MUNICIPAL BUREAU OF STATISTICS
SURVEY OFFICE OF THE NATIONAL BUREAU OF STATISTICS IN SHANGHAI

中国统计出版社
China Statistics Press

图书在版编目（CIP）数据

上海统计年鉴. 2022 = Shanghai Statistical Yearbook 2022 : 汉英对照 / 上海市统计局, 国家统计局上海调查总队编. -- 北京 : 中国统计出版社, 2022.11
ISBN 978-7-5037-9917-4

Ⅰ. ①上… Ⅱ. ①上… ②国… Ⅲ. ①统计资料－上海－2022－年鉴－汉、英 Ⅳ. ①C832.51-54

中国版本图书馆 CIP 数据核字(2022)第 199141 号

上海统计年鉴 2022

作　　者 / 上海市统计局　国家统计局上海调查总队
责任编辑 / 高媛媛
装帧设计 / 方　敏
出版发行 / 中国统计出版社有限公司
地　　址 / 北京市丰台区西三环南路甲6号
邮政编码 / 100073
电　　话 / 邮购 (010) 63376909　书店 (010) 68783171
网　　址 / http://www.zgtjcbs.com
印　　刷 / 上海万卷印刷股份有限公司
经　　销 / 新华书店
开　　本 / 890mm × 1240mm　1/16
字　　数 / 1110千字
印　　张 / 33.5　彩页 1
版　　别 / 2022年11月第1版
版　　次 / 2022年11月第1次印刷
定　　价 / 480.00元　Price: 480.00 yuan(RMB)

本书附同版本CD-ROM一张，光盘内容以书面文字为准。
如有印装差错，由本社发行部调换。

《上海统计年鉴2022》编辑委员会

EDITORIAL BOARD

2021年的上海
Shanghai in 2021

上海市生产总值
43214.85 亿元

人均生产总值
17.36 万元

社会消费品零售总额
18079.25 亿元

全市居民家庭人均可支配收入
78027 元

关区出口总额

11724.29 亿美元

电子商务交易额

32403.60 亿元

外商直接投资实际到位金额
225.51 亿美元

研究与试验发展经费内部支出
1819.77 亿元

金融市场交易总额
2511.07 万亿元

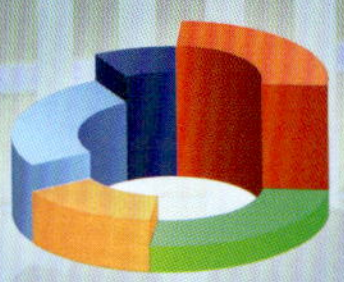

上海市生产总值（亿元）
Gross Domestic Product （100 million yuan）

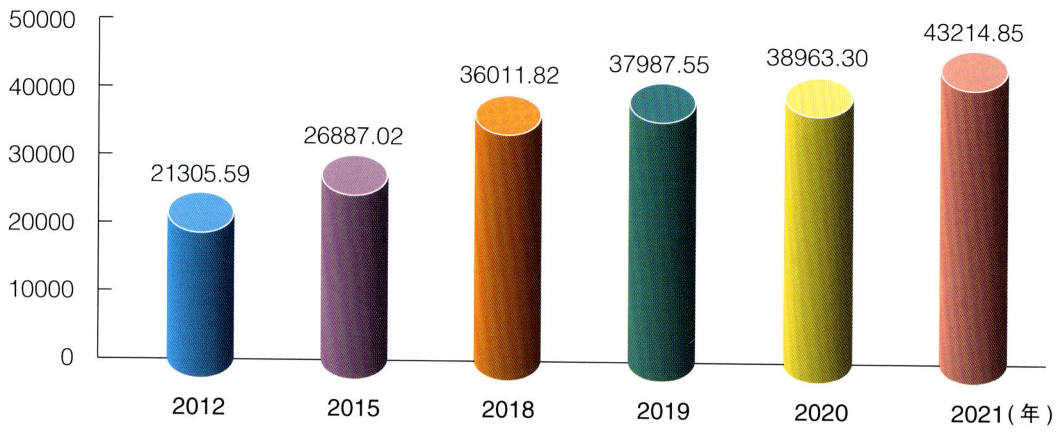

人均生产总值（万元）
Per Capita Gross Domestic Product （10000 yuan）

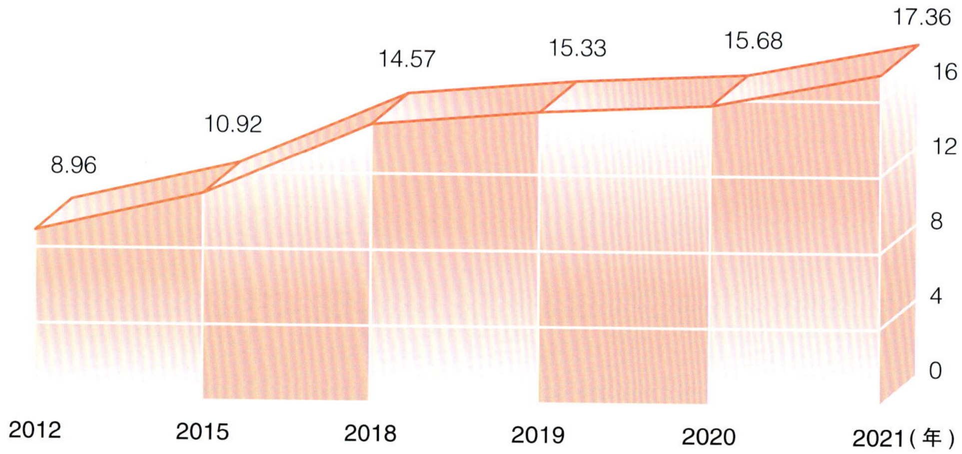

常住人口（万人）
Year-end Resident Population （10000 persons）

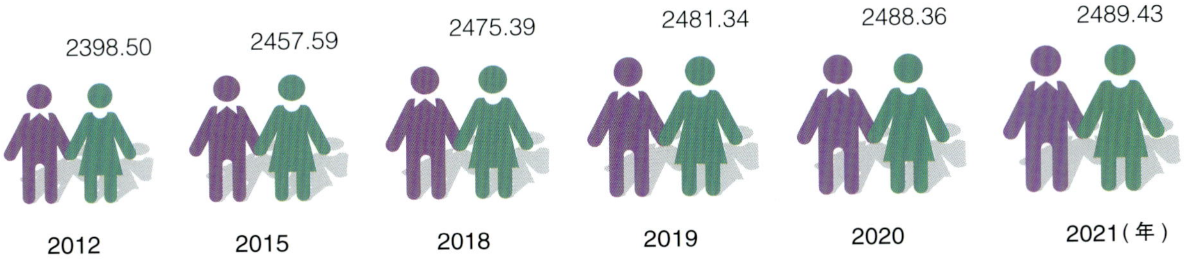

户籍人口期望寿命（岁）
Life Expectancy of Registered Population （year）

居民人均可支配收入和人均消费支出（元）

Per Capita Disposable Income and Per Capita Consumption Expenditure (yuan)

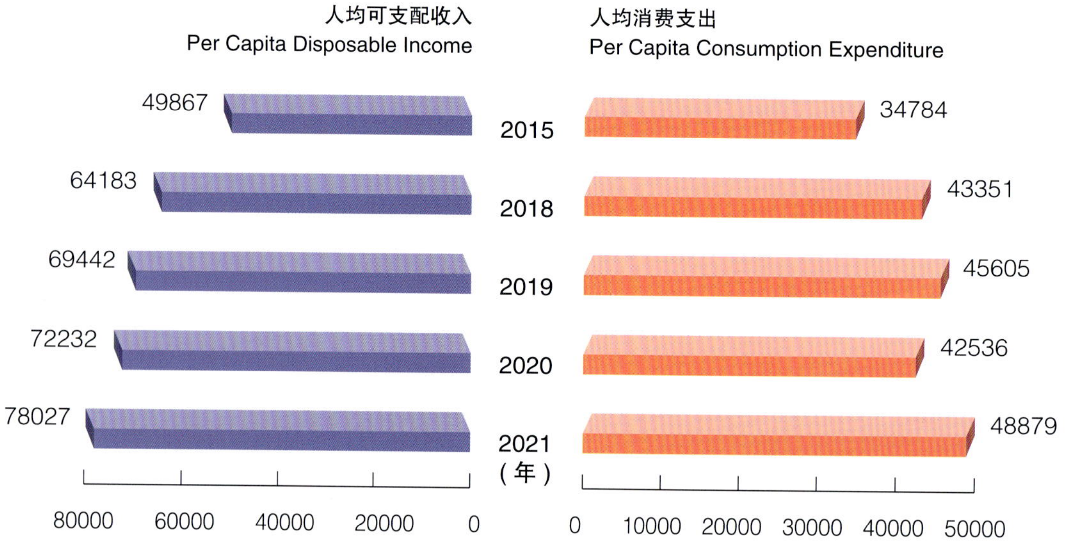

金融市场交易总额（万亿元）

Turnover of Main Financial Market (trillion)

社会消费品零售总额（亿元）

Total Retail Sales of Consumer Goods （100 million yuan）

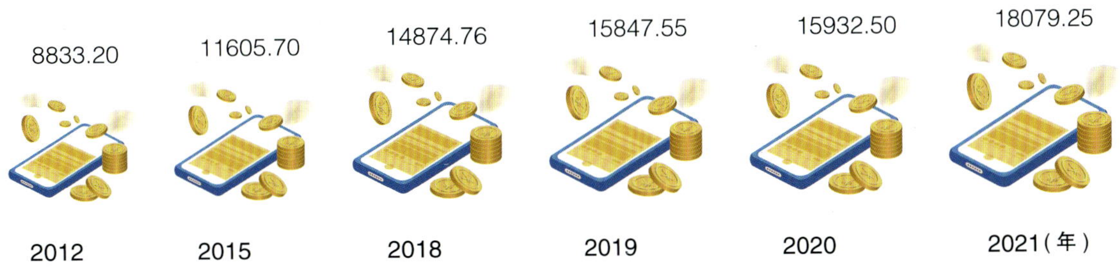

电子商务交易额（亿元）

E-commerce Transaction Volume （100 million yuan）

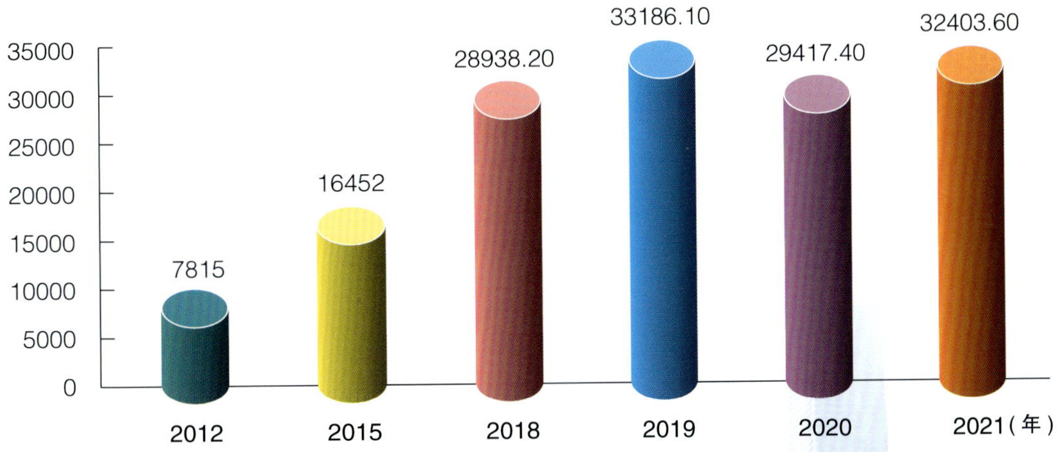

中国国际进口博览会
China International Import Expo

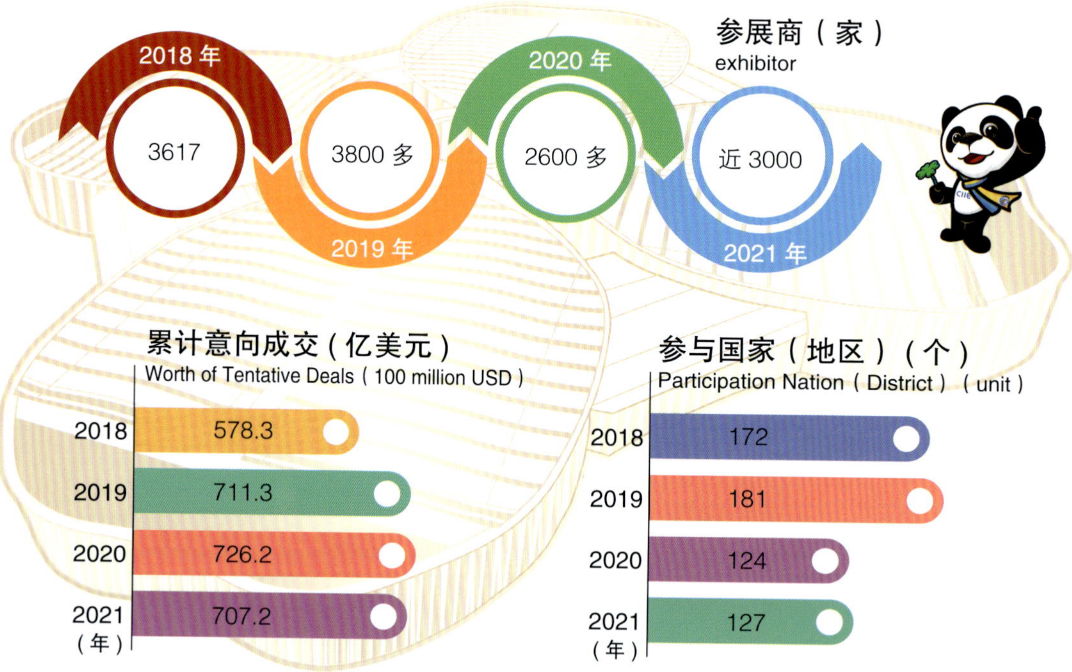

国际标准集装箱吞吐量（万TEU）
International container throughput（10000 TEU）

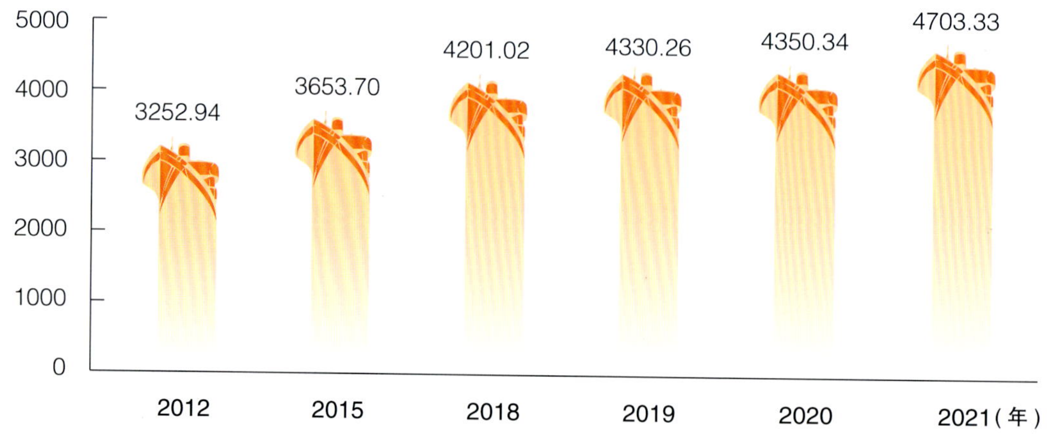

外商直接投资实际到位金额（亿美元）

Actual Amount of Foreign Direct Investment in Place (100 million USD)

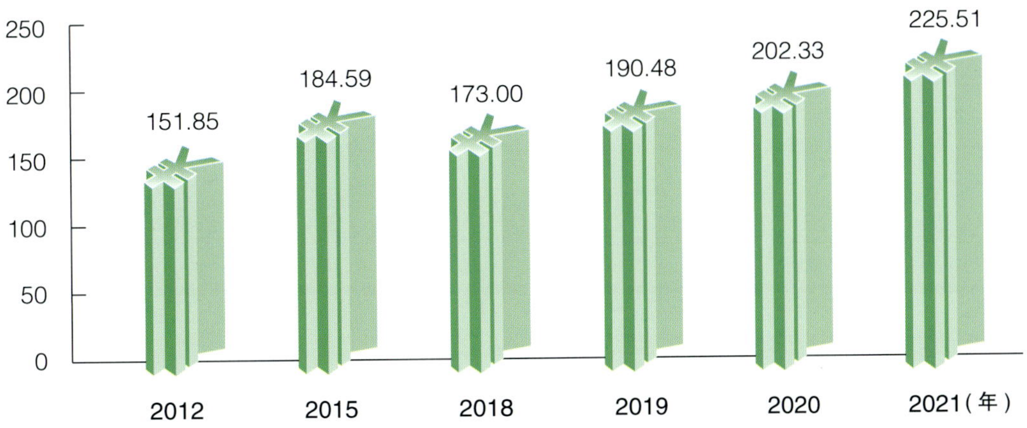

关区进出口总值和服务贸易进出口

Total Import & Export Trade Volume Through Customs and Total Value of Service Trade Imports & Exports

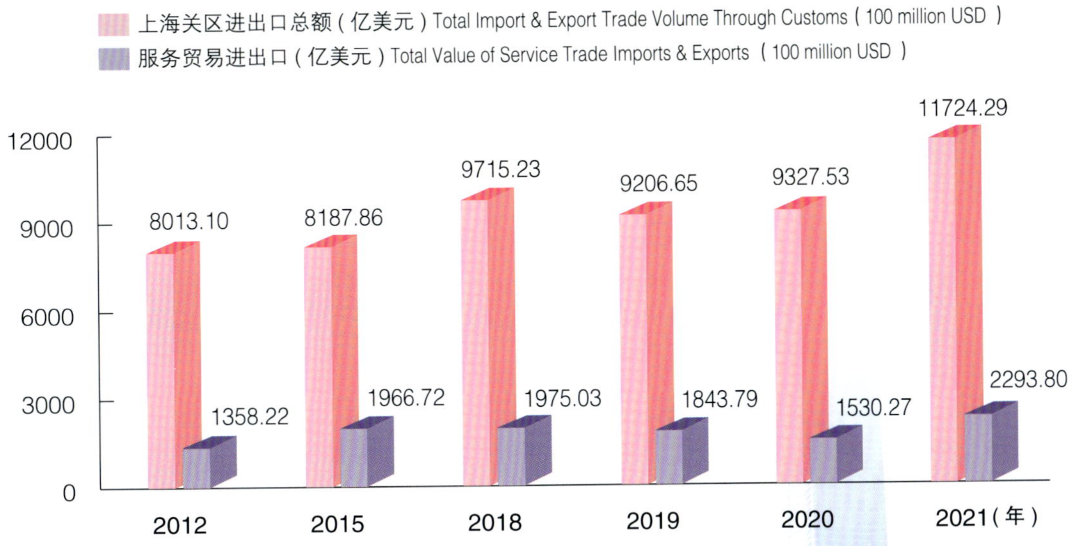

环保类指标（%）
Environmental Protection Indicators （%）

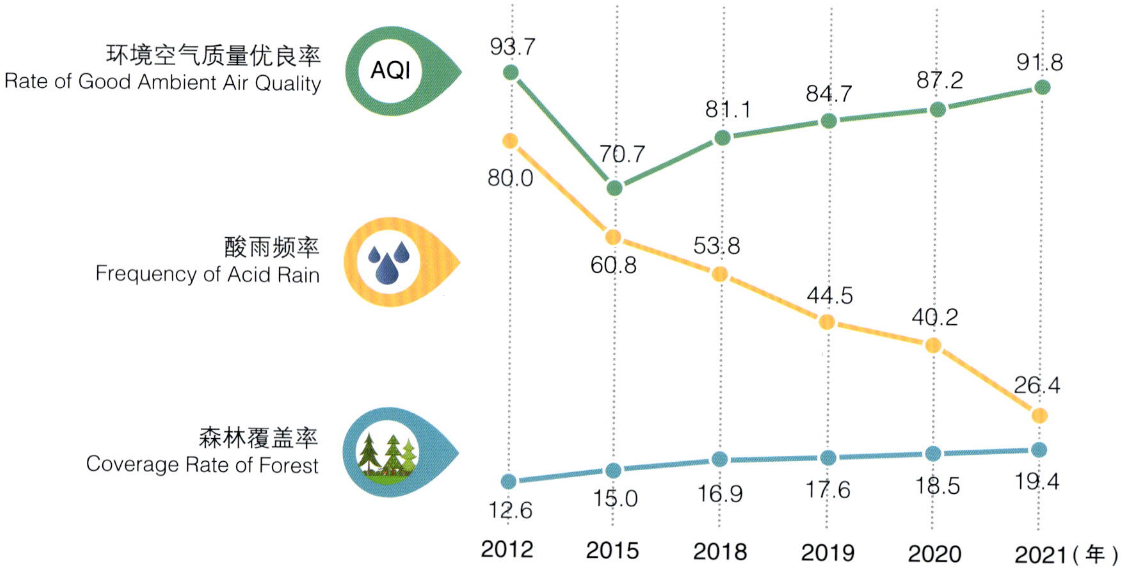

万元地区生产总值能耗（吨标准煤/万元）
Energy Consumption Per 10000 Yuan of GDP （tons of standard coal / 10000 yuan）

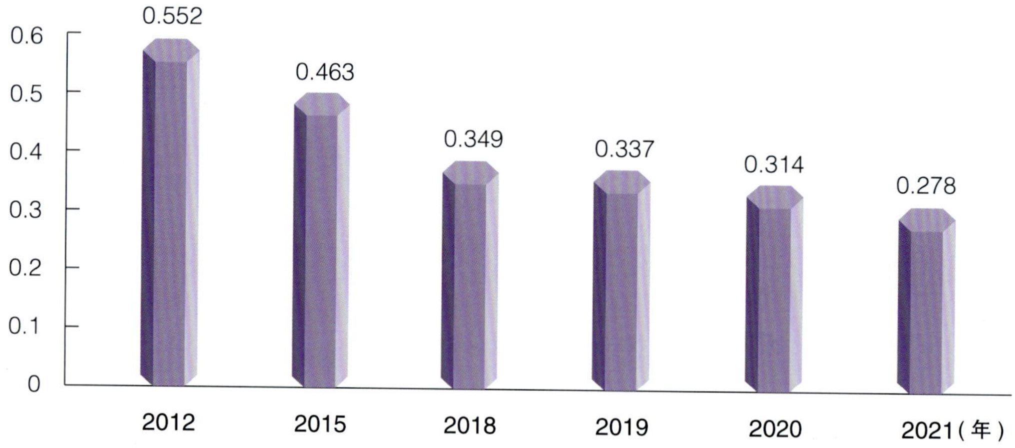

研究与试验发展（R&D）经费内部支出（亿元）

Research and Experimental Development（R&D）Internal Expenditure （100 million yuan）

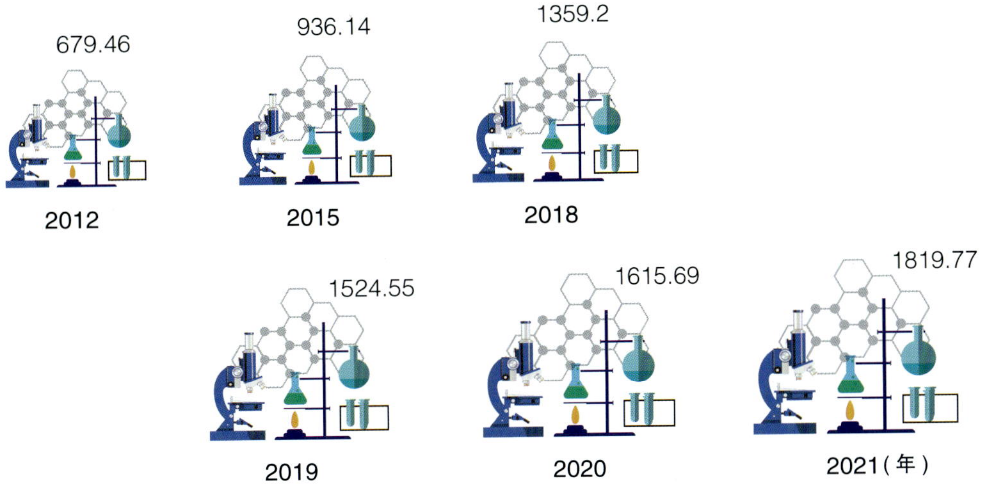

轨道交通运营线路长度和客运总量

Rail Transit Operation Line Length and Passenger Volume

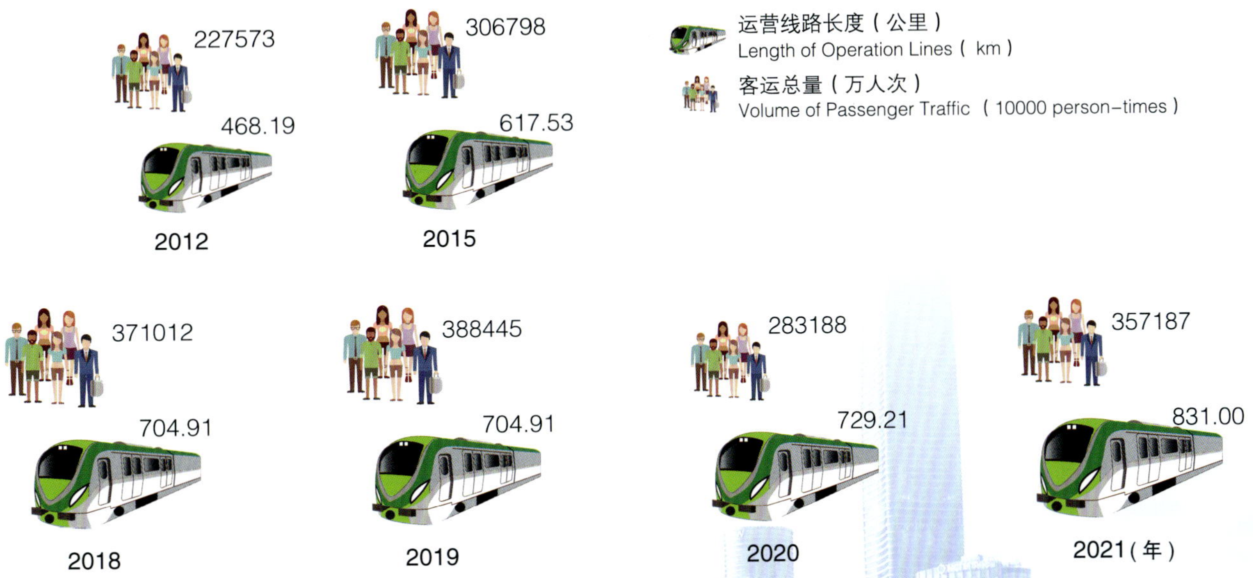

各级各类学校在校学生数（万人）

Number of Students in Various Schools At All Levels （10 000 persons）

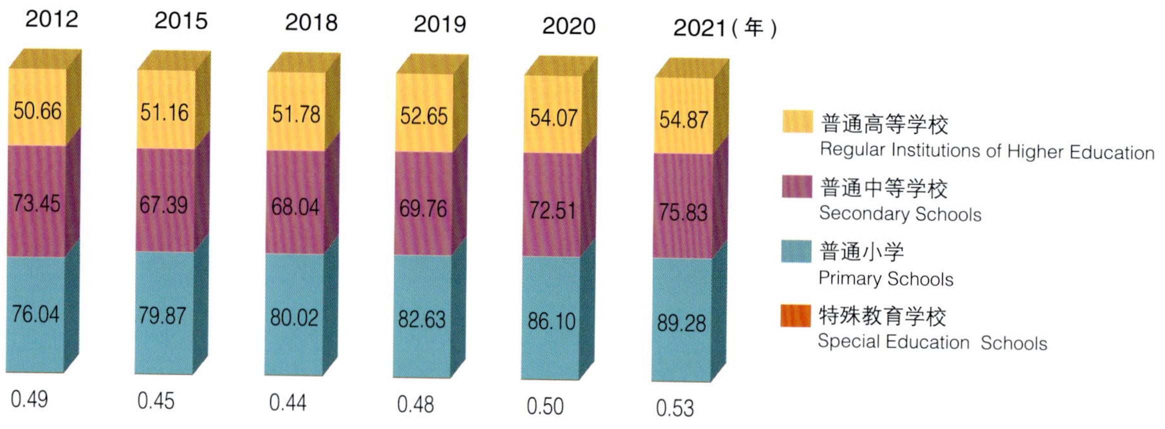

每万人口医生数、每万人口医院床位数

Number of Doctors Per 10000 Population, Number of Hospital Beds Per 10000 Population

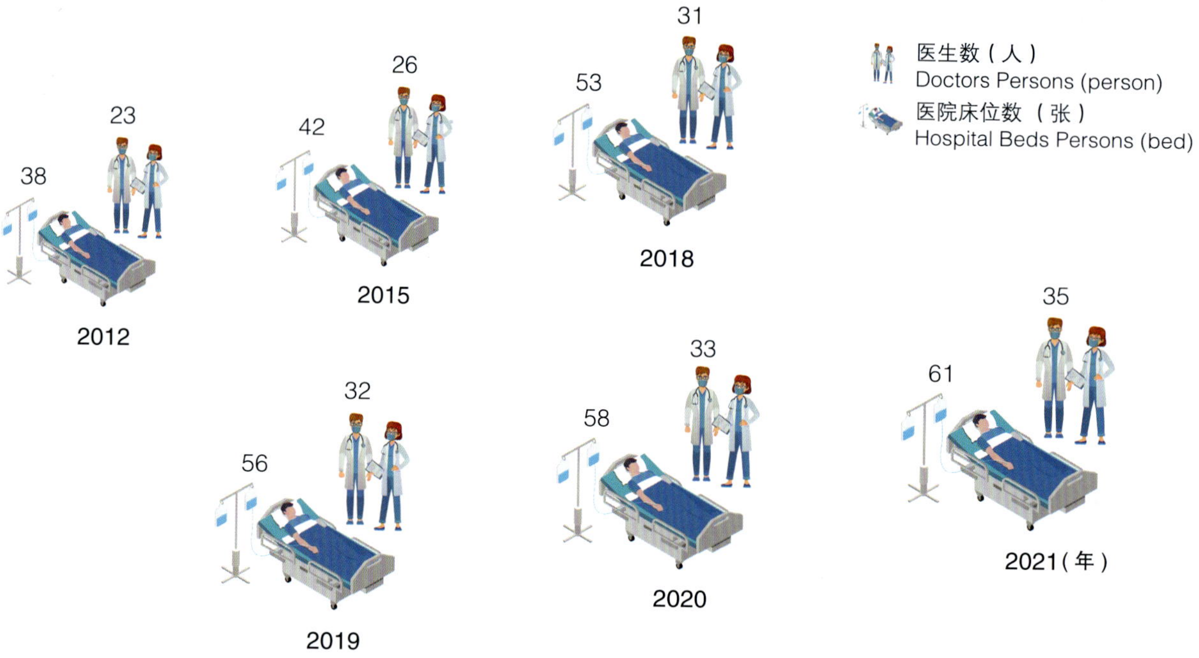

编者说明

一、《上海统计年鉴—2022》是一本信息高度密集的资料工具书。本书收录了2021年上海的经济和社会等各方面的统计数据,以及重要年份和改革开放以来的主要统计数据。

二、全书内容分为23个篇目，即:1. 综合； 2. 人口、就业与工资；3. 国民经济核算；4. 财政收支；5. 能源与环境；6. 固定资产投资；7. 对外经济贸易和旅游；8. 价格水平；9. 人民生活；10. 城市建设；11. 农业；12. 工业；13. 建筑业；14. 服务业；15. 交通运输、邮政和信息传输；16. 批发、零售和住宿、餐饮；17. 金融业；18. 房地产业；19. 科学技术；20. 教育； 21. 卫生、社会保障和社会福利业； 22. 文化和体育；23. 法律、公证和其他。为便于读者正确地使用资料，各篇目还附有简要说明和主要统计指标解释。

三、本年鉴数据除特别说明外,是由上海市统计局和国家统计局上海调查总队通过年报调查收集。本年鉴2021年GDP数据为初步核算数。

四、资料中所使用的度量衡单位均采用国际统一标准计量单位,金额除特别标明外,均以人民币计量。

五、本年鉴总量指标计算所采用的价格均为现行价格。

六、本年鉴部分数据合计数或相对数由于单位取舍不同产生的计算误差均未作机械调整。

七、本年鉴表中的符号使用说明：

“…”表示数据不足本表最小计量单位数；

“空格”表示该项统计数据不详或无该项数据；

“#”表示其中的主要项。

八、《上海统计年鉴》公开出版以来,受到了国内外广大读者的关心和支持,对本年鉴的内容和编辑工作提出了许多宝贵的意见,对此我们深表谢意。限于我们的水平,欢迎读者继续对年鉴的不足之处给予批评和指正,帮助我们进一步改进年鉴的编辑工作,以期更好地为广大读者服务。

EDITOR'S NOTE

Ⅰ. *Shanghai Statistical Yearbook 2022* contains comprehensive statistics of Shanghai's social and economic development in 2021 and selected data of some important years and of the period since China adopted the policy of reform and opening to the outside world.

Ⅱ. The book is composed of 23 parts viz.1. General Survey; 2. Population, Employment and Wages; 3.National Economic Accounting; 4. Fiscal Revenue and Expenditure; 5.Energy and Environment Protection; 6. Investment in Fixed Assets; 7. Foreign Economic Relations, Trade and Tourism; 8.Prices; 9.Living Standards; 10.Urban Construction; 11.Agriculture; 12. Industry; 13. Construction; 14. Serviec; 15. Transportation, Posts and Information Transmission; 16.Wholesale and Retail, Hotels and Catering Services; 17.Finance; 18. Real Estate; 19.Science and Technology; 20.Education; 21.Health, Social Security and Social Welfare; . 22.Culture, Sports; 23.Laws, Notary and others. In order to make readers using materials correctly, brief introduction and explanations of major statistical indicators are attached after every chapter.

Ⅲ. Main part of the data in this yearbook are investigated and collected by Shanghai Municipal Statistical Bureau and Survey Office of the National Bureau of Statistics in Shanghai, except those with special notes. The GDP data of 2021 released in this Yearbook are preliminary calculation figure.

Ⅳ. The international standard unit of measurement is applied in this yearbook. All amounts are denominated in RMB, except those with special notes.

Ⅴ. The prices used for calculating of gross indicators in this yearbook are current prices.

Ⅵ. Statistical discrepancies in this book due to rounding are not adjusted.

Ⅶ. Marks in this book: ··· means not large enough to be rounded into the least unit of measurement; blank space means data are not available; # indicates major item in a category.

Ⅷ. Previous editions of *Shanghai Statistical Yearbook* have won wide acclaim among the readers. In order to get further improvement in the yearbook editing, we welcome all candid comments and criticism from our readers.

目录
CONTENTS

第一篇 CHAPTER 1 综合 GENERAL SURVEY

目录
CONTENTS

第二篇 CHAPTER 2 人口、就业与工资 POPULATION, EMPLOYMENT AND WAGES

第三篇 CHAPTER 3 国民经济核算 NATIONAL ECONOMIC ACCOUNTING

目录
CONTENTS

第五篇 CHAPTER 5 能源与环境 ENERGY AND ENVIRONMENT PROTECTION

目录
CONTENTS

第七篇 CHAPTER 7 对外经济贸易和旅游 FOREIGN ECONOMIC RELATIONS, TRADE AND TOURISM

目录
CONTENTS

第八篇 CHAPTER 8 价格水平 PRICES

第九篇 CHAPTER 9 人民生活 LIVING STANDARDS

目录
CONTENTS

第十篇 CHAPTER 10 城市建设 URBAN CONSTRUCTION

目录
CONTENTS

第十一篇 CHAPTER 11 农 业 AGRICULTURE

第十二篇 CHAPTER 12 工 业 INDUSTRY

目录
CONTENTS

第十三篇 CHAPTER 13 建筑业 CONSTRUCTION

第十四篇 CHAPTER 14 服务业 SERVICE

第十五篇 CHAPTER 15 交通运输、邮政和信息传输 TRANSPORTATION, POSTS AND INFORMATION TRANSMISSION

目录
CONTENTS

第十七篇 CHAPTER 17 金融业 FINANCE

目录
CONTENTS

第十八篇 CHAPTER 18 房地产业 REAL ESTATE

第十九篇 CHAPTER 19 科学技术 SCIENCE AND TECHNOLOGY

目录 CONTENTS

第二十一篇 CHAPTER 21 卫生、社会保障和社会福利业 HEALTH, SOCIAL SECURITY AND SOCIAL WELFARE

目录
CONTENTS

第二十二篇 CHAPTER 22 文化和体育 CULTURE AND SPORTS

目录
CONTENTS

第二十三篇 CHAPTER 23 法律、公证和其他 LAWS, NOTARY AND OTHERS

第一篇

CHAPTER 1

综 合

GENERAL SURVEY

简要说明

本篇主要内容和资料来源

一、综合资料主要包括上海市行政区划、经济和社会发展综合资料两部分。分别由上海市民政局、上海市统计局和国家统计局上海调查总队编辑整理。

二、行政区划资料，由上海市民政局根据上海市政府批准的、截止到上一年末上海市区划变更情况汇总整理并提供。

三、经济和社会发展综合资料是抽取全书的精华，通过对各篇章主要统计指标及其速度、结构、比例和效益等的加工计算，来反映国民经济和社会发展的总体情况。

BRIEF INTRODUCTION

Main Contents and Sources of Data

1. This chapter consists of two parts: divisions of Shanghai administrative areas and summary data on economy and social development, which are compiled by the Shanghai Municipal Civil Affairs Bureau, Shanghai Municipal Bureau of Statistics and the Survey Office of the National Bureau of Statistics in Shanghai.

2. Data on divisions of administrative areas in Shanghai, are prepared and provided by the Shanghai Municipal Civil Affairs Bureau on the basis of the changes in the divisions of administrative areas as approved by the Shanghai municipal government at the end of the previous year.

3. The summary data on the economy and social development reflect on the overall situation of the economy and social development by presenting further processed statistics including growth, structure, ratio, and efficiency data derived from other chapters.

表1.1　行政区划(2021)
ADMINISTRATIVE DIVISION

单位:个（unit）

地　区	District	镇 Towns	乡 Townships	街道办事处 Urban Sub-district Offices	居民委员会 Neighbourhood Committees	村民委员会 Village Committees
全　市	**Total**	**106**	**2**	**107**	**4 576**	**1 556**
浦东新区	Pudong New Area	24		12	1 019	355
黄 浦 区	Huangpu			10	172	
徐 汇 区	Xuhui	1		12	306	
长 宁 区	Changning	1		9	185	
静 安 区	Jing'an	1		13	263	1
普 陀 区	Putuo	2		8	265	7
虹 口 区	Hongkou			8	200	
杨 浦 区	Yangpu			12	288	
闵 行 区	Minhang	9		4	469	114
宝 山 区	Baoshan	9		3	402	103
嘉 定 区	Jiading	7		3	232	141
金 山 区	Jinshan	9		1	112	124
松 江 区	Songjiang	11		6	269	84
青 浦 区	Qingpu	8		3	146	184
奉 贤 区	Fengxian	8		3	159	175
崇 明 区	Chongming	16	2		89	268

注：本表数据由上海市民政局提供。
Note：Data in this table are provided by Shanghai Civil Affairs Bureau.

表 1.2 主要气象指标(2021)
MAIN CLIMATE INDICATORS

指 标	Indicators	2021	指 标	Indicators	2021
平均气温(℃)	Annual Average Temperature(℃)	18.1	蒸发量(毫米)	Evaporation (mm)	1 051.2
极端最高气温(℃)	Utmost Highest Air Temperature(℃)	37.8	降水量(毫米)	Precipitation(mm)	1 388.2
极端最低气温(℃)	Utmost Lowest Air Temperature(℃)	-7.8	降雨日(天)	Annual Rainy Days(day)	140
日照时间(小时)	Annual Sunshine Time(h)	2 056.3			

表 1.3 各月主要气象指标(2021)
MAIN CLIMATE INDICATORS OF EVERY MONTH

月 份	Month	平均气温(℃) Annual Average Temperature(℃)	极端最高气温(℃) Utmost Highest Air Temperature(℃)	极端最低气温(℃) Utmost Lowest Air Temperature(℃)	平均最高气温(℃) Average Maximum temperature(℃)	平均最低气温(℃) Average Minimum temperature(℃)
1月	Jan.	5.5	20.8	-7.8	14.4	-5.0
2月	Feb.	9.8	25.6	-1.8	17.4	4.0
3月	Mar.	12.0	25.3	2.6	18.5	5.8
4月	Apr.	16.5	30.6	6.7	25.0	12.2
5月	May.	22.1	34.8	12.5	28.7	16.6
6月	Jun.	25.2	34.7	16.6	28.0	21.1
7月	Jul.	29.0	37.8	22.6	32.8	25.0
8月	Aug.	28.4	35.6	22.7	30.8	24.3
9月	Sep.	26.7	36.1	19.1	30.8	24.1
10月	Oct.	21.0	32.6	10.5	28.0	13.9
11月	Nov.	13.3	22.9	-0.3	18.6	5.6
12月	Dec.	7.4	17.8	-4.6	12.5	-0.7

表 1.3 续表 continued

月 份	Month	日照时间(小时) Annual Sunshine Time(h)	降水量(毫米) Precipitation (mm)	降雨日(天) Annual Rainy Days (day)	蒸发量(毫米) Evaporation (mm)
1月	Jan.	167.0	20.4	5	48.6
2月	Feb.	145.6	60.6	10	55.3
3月	Mar.	131.0	76.2	15	70.0
4月	Apr.	183.2	44.9	10	89.0
5月	May.	196.6	151.8	17	110.5
6月	Jun.	153.8	77.5	16	94.5
7月	Jul.	196.2	314.2	16	137.5
8月	Aug.	182.9	336.4	19	132.0
9月	Sep.	161.8	165.9	12	94.4
10月	Oct.	154.2	64.6	9	98.3
11月	Nov.	187.9	72.7	8	68.2
12月	Dec.	196.1	3.0	3	52.9

注：本页资料由上海市气象局提供。
Note: Data on this page are provided by Shanghai Meteorological Bureau.

表1.4　中国(上海)自由贸易试验区主要经济指标(2021)
MAIN ECONOMIC INDICATORS OF THE CHINA(SHANGHAI) PILOT FREE TRADE ZONE

指　标	Indicators	单　位 Unit	2021
一般公共预算收入	General Budgetary Revenue	亿元 100 million yuan	763.78
外商直接投资实际到位金额	Foreign Direct Investment Actually Absorbed	亿美元 100 million USD	103.73
全社会固定资产投资总额	Total Investment in Fixed Assets	亿元 100 million yuan	1 688.72
规模以上工业总产值	Gross Output Value of Industry	亿元 100 million yuan	6 877.53
社会消费品零售额	Total Retail Sales of Consumer Goods	亿元 100 million yuan	2 531.94
商品销售总额	Commodity Sales	亿元 100 million yuan	59 819.29
服务业营业收入	Revenue of Service Industry	亿元 100 million yuan	7 427.06
期末监管类金融机构	Regulatory Financial Institutions	个 unit	982
跨境人民币结算总额	Total Cross-border Settlement in RMB	亿元 100 million yuan	54 311.80
跨境人民币境外借款金额	Overseas Borrowing of Cross-border RMB	亿元 100 million yuan	42.40

①自贸区按注册地口径统计，统计范围为120.72平方公里。
②一般公共预算收入按开发区财力结算口径。
❶The statistics of China(shanghai) Pilot Free Trade Zone follow registration place, and statistical range covers 120.72 square kilometers.
❷The statistics of general public budget revenue follow the financial settlement standard of Development Zone.

表 1.5　主要年份社会经济主要指标
MAJOR SOCIAL AND ECONOMIC INDICATORS IN MAIN YEARS

指　标	Indicators	1990	2000	2010	2020	2021
人口与就业	**Population and Employment**					
人　口	**Population**					
年末常住人口(万人)	Year-end Resident Population (10 000 persons)	1 334.00	1 608.60	2 302.66	2 488.36	2 489.43
年末户籍人口(万人)	Year-end Registered Population(10 000 persons)	1 283.35	1 321.63	1 412.32	1 475.63	1 492.92
就　业	**Employment**					
城镇登记失业率(%)	Registered Unemployment Rate in Urban Areas (%)	1.5	3.5	4.2	3.7	2.7
宏观经济	**Macro Economy**					
国民经济核算	**National Economic Accounts**					
上海市生产总值(亿元)	Gross Domestic Product(100 million yuan)	781.66	4 812.15	17 915.41	38 963.30	43 214.85
#第一产业	Primary Industry	34.24	74.76	114.45	107.68	99.97
第二产业	Secondary Industry	505.60	2 215.75	7 434.89	10 258.57	11 449.32
第三产业	Tertiary Industry	241.82	2 521.64	10 366.07	28 597.05	31 665.56
#工　业	Industry	469.83	2 022.53	6 943.93	9 625.53	10 738.80
人均生产总值(万元)(按常住人口计算)	Per Capita Gross Domestic Product(yuan) (Calculated by Resident Population)	0.59	3.00	7.94	15.68	17.36
固定资产投资	**Investment in Fixed Assets**					
全社会固定资产投资总额(亿元)	Total Investment in Fixed Assets (100 million yuan)	227.08	1 869.67	5 317.67		
#房地产开发	Investment in Real Estate	8.16	566.17	1 980.68	4 698.75	5 035.18
财　政	**Public Finance**					
一般公共预算收入(亿元)	General Budgetary Revenue(100 million yuan)	166.99	497.96	2 873.58	7 046.30	7 771.80
一般公共预算支出(亿元)	General Budgetary Expenditure(100 million yuan)	75.56	622.84	3 302.89	8 102.11	8 430.86

表 1.5 续表 1 continued

指　标	Indicators	1990	2000	2010	2020	2021
价　格	**Price**					
居民消费价格指数（上年=100）	Consumer Price Index(preceding=100)	106.3	102.5	103.1	101.7	101.2
商品零售价格指数（上年=100）	Retail Price Index(preceding=100)	104.8	96.4	101.7	100.9	101.3
产　业	**Industries**					
农　业	**Agriculture**					
农业总产值（亿元）	Gross Output Value of Agriculture (100 million yuan)	68.16	216.50	296.24	279.82	268.93
工　业	**Industry**					
工业总产值（亿元）	Gross Output Value of Industry (100 million yuan)	1 642.75	7 022.98	31 038.57	37 052.59	42 013.99
建筑业	**Construction**					
建筑业总产值（亿元）	Gross Output Value of Construction(100 million yuan)	75.62	631.64	4 300.19	8 277.04	9 236.42
交通运输、邮政业和信息传输	**Transportation, Post and Information Transmission**					
货物运输量（万吨）	Freight Transportation Volume (10 000 tons)	22 848	47 954	81 023	139 226	155 212
旅客发送量（万人次）	Passenger Departures (10 000 person-times)	3 835	6 893	13 456	11 973	14 047
港口货物吞吐量（万吨）	Port Cargo Freight Throughput (10 000 tons)	13 959	20 440	65 339	71 670	77 635
国际标准集装箱吞吐量（万 TEU）	International Container Throughput Capacity (10 000 TEU)	45.60	561.20	2 906.90	4 350.34	4 703.33
年末固定电话用户（万户）	Year-end Installed Telephones (10 000 households)	45.69	549.00	931.80	636.48	641.97
批发和零售	**Wholesale and Retail**					
社会消费品零售总额（亿元）	Total Retail Sales of Consumer Goods (100 million yuan)	333.86	1 955.17	6 901.39	15 932.50	18 079.25
批发零售业商品销售总额（亿元）	Sales of Commodities of Wholesale and Retail (100 million yuan)	1 305.41	7 474.81	48 659.55	139 827.92	162 838.66

表 1.5 续表 2 continued

指 标	Indicators	1990	2000	2010	2020	2021
对外经济贸易	**Foreign Trade**					
上海关区进出口总额（亿美元）	Total Trade Value Through Customs (100 million USD)	172.89	1 093.11	6 846.45	9 327.53	11 724.29
进口额	Imports	86.27	477.39	2 613.05	3 906.84	4 962.66
出口额	Exports	86.62	615.72	4 233.40	5 420.69	6 761.63
上海市进出口总额（亿美元）	Total Value of Foreign Trade Imports and Exports (100 million USD)	74.31	547.10	3 688.69	5 031.89	6 286.03
进口额	Imports	21.10	293.56	1 880.85	3 050.82	3 852.90
出口额	Exports	53.21	253.54	1 807.84	1 981.07	2 433.13
外商直接投资	**Foreign Direct Investment**					
合同项目（个）	Number of Contracts (item)	203	1 814	3 906	5 751	6 708
合同金额（亿美元）	Contractual Foreign Capital(100 million USD)	2.14	63.90	153.07	516.54	603.91
实到金额（亿美元）	Foreign Investment Actually Absorbed (100 million USD)	1.77	31.60	111.21	202.33	225.51
国际旅游	**International Tourism**					
国际旅游入境人数（万人次）	Number of Overseas Tourists Through Shanghai Custom (10 000 person-times)	89.30	181.40	851.12	128.62	103.29
国际旅游(外汇)收入（亿美元）	Foreign Exchange Earnings from International Tourism (100 million USD)	2.31	16.13	64.05	37.74	35.85
金 融	**Finance**					
金融机构存款余额（亿元）	Saving Deposits Balance of Financial Institutions (100 million yuan)	851.51	9 349.83	52 190.04	155 865.06	175 831.08
金融机构贷款余额（亿元）	Loan Balance of Financial Institutions (100 million yuan)	1 106.80	7 254.26	34 154.17	84 643.04	96 032.13
有价证券成交总额（亿元）	Total Volume of Priced Securities Trading (100 million)		49 901	398 396	3 667 030	4 611 281
#股 票	Stocks		31 374	304 312	839 861	1 140 006
原保险保费收入(亿元)	Premium of Primary Insurance(100 million yuan)	8.99	127.23	883.86	1 865.00	1 971.00
原保险赔付支出（亿元）	Payment of Primary Insurance (100 million yuan)	2.22	36.44	194.54	631.00	738.00
教育、科技、文化	**Education, Science&Technology and Culture**					
教 育	**Education**					
在校学生数（万人）	Students Enrollment(10 000 persons)					
普通高等学校	Regular Institutions of Higher Education	12.13	22.68	51.57	54.07	54.87
普通中学	Regular Secondary Schools	48.31	79.54	59.44	63.45	67.20
普通小学	Primary Schools	110.19	78.86	70.16	86.10	89.28
每万人拥有大学生（人）	Number of College and University Students Per 10 000 Persons(person)	90	141	224	217	220

表 1.5 续表 3 continued

指　标	Indicators	1990	2000	2010	2020	2021
科　技	**Science and Technology**					
研究与试验发展经费内部支出（亿元）	Expenditures on R&D (100 million yuan)	10.13	76.73	481.70	1 615.69	1 819.77
研究与试验发展经费支出相当于上海市生产总值比例(%)	R&D Expenditure as Percentage of Gross Domestic Product(%)	1.30	1.59	2.69	4.17	4.21
文　化	**Culture**					
出版数量	Number of Publications					
图　书（亿册）	Books (100 million copies)	2.98	2.54	2.89	4.95	4.94
期　刊（亿册）	Periodicals (100 million copies)	1.73	1.85	1.78	0.62	0.59
报　纸（亿份）	Newspapers (100 million copies)	16.16	16.77	15.90	6.94	6.66
家庭、生活、环境	**Family, Living and Environment**					
家　庭	**Household**					
家庭总户数（万户）	Total Households (10 000 households)	415.28	475.73	519.27	560.96	568.27
平均每户家庭人口（人）	Average Persons per Household (person)	3.09	2.78	2.72	2.63	2.63
婚　姻	**Marriages and Divorces**					
登记结婚（万对）	Marriage Registration Permitted (10 000 couples)	10.77	9.31	13.03	9.22	8.98
离　婚（万对）	Divorce (10 000 couples)	1.64	3.18	4.67	6.67	6.57
住　宅	**Housing**					
城镇居民人均住房建筑面积（平方米）	Construction Area per Capita of Urban Residents(sq.m)			32.6	37.3	37.4
生　活	**Living**					
全市居民人均可支配收入(元)	Per Capita Annual Disposable Income of Residents(yuan)	2 008	11 056	30 436	72 232	78 027
全市居民人均消费支出(元)	Per Capita Annual Consumption Expenditure of Residents(yuan)	1 709	8 565	24 758	42 536	48 879
城镇常住居民人均可支配收入(元)	Per Capita Annual Disposable Income of Urban Households(yuan)	2 183	11 718	31 838	76 437	82 429
城镇常住居民人均消费支出(元)	Per Capita Annual Consumption Expenditures of Urban Households(yuan)	1 937	8 868	23 200	44 839	51 295
农村常住居民人均可支配收入(元)	Per Capita Annual Disposable Income of Rural Households(yuan)	1 665	5 565	13 746	34 911	38 521
农村常住居民人均消费支出(元)	Per Capita Annual Consumption Expenditure of Rural Households(yuan)	1 262	4 138	10 225	22 095	27 205
个人存款(住户存款)余额（亿元）	Household Deposits(100 million yuan)		2 627.07	16 249.29	38 302.45	42 652.55

①2012 年起，国家统计局实施了城乡一体化住户调查改革，统一了城乡居民收入名称、分类和统计标准。2015 年起，发布城乡可比的新口径全市居民人均可支配收入及支出。1990 年、2000 年和 2010 年，全市居民人均可支配收入及支出根据历史数据按照新口径推算获得。

②城镇居民人均住房建筑面积由市住房和城乡建设管理委员会提供。

❶Since 2012, the National Bureau of Statistics has implemented the household survey reform of urban and rural integration with unifying the urban and rural income name, classification and statistical standards.Since 2015, the per capita disposable income and expenditure of city's residents have been released.The per capita disposable income and outcome are calculated by new caliber based on historical data in 1990, 2000 and 2010.

❷Construction Area per Capita of Urban Residents data are provided by Shanghai Municipal Housing and Urban-Rural Construction Management Committee.

表 1.5 续表 4 continued

	指 标 Indicators	1990	2000	2010	2020	2021
工 资	**Wages**					
城镇非私营单位就业人员平均工资	Average Wages of Employees in Urban Non-Private Units				171 884	191 844
城镇私营单位就业人员平均工资	Average Wages of Employees in Urban Private Units				80 134	96 011
卫 生	**Health Care**					
医 院（个）	Quantity of Hospitals (unit)	462	459	306	405	432
医 生(万人)	Doctors (10 000 persons)	5.82	4.99	5.13	8.23	8.70
医院床位数（万张）	Quantity of Hospital Beds (10 000 beds)	6.21	7.31	8.48	14.36	15.08
每万人拥有医生（人）	Quantity of Doctors Per 10 000 Persons (person)	44	31	22	33	35
城市建设	**Urban Construction**					
自来水售水量(亿立方米)	Total Quantity of Water Supply(100 million cu.m)	12.25	19.75	24.44	23.59	24.77
用电量(亿千瓦时)	Electricity Power Consumption (100 million kwh)	264.74	559.51	1 295.87	1 575.96	1 749.62
天然气销售总量(亿立方米)	Sales of Natural Gas(100 million cu.m)		2.16	42.66	86.73	92.25
年末出租车运营总数（辆）	Year-end Operating Taxi Vehicles (vehicle)	11 298	42 943	50 007	37 322	35 317
运营公交车辆数（辆）	Total Number of Operating Public Transportation Vehicles (vehicle)	6 264	17 939	17 455	17 668	17 645
道路长度（公里）	Length of Roads (km)	1 631	6 641	16 687	18 453	18 927
人均公园绿地面积（平方米）	Per Capita Park Green Areas(sq.m)	1.0	4.6	13.0	8.5	8.7
森林覆盖率(%)	Coverage Rate of Forest(%)	5.5	9.2	12.6	18.5	19.4
环境保护投资相当于上海市生产总值比例(%)	Investment on Environment Protection as Percentage of Gross Domestic Product (%)	2.06	2.97	2.96	2.80	2.60
环境空气质量优良率(%)	Rate of Good Ambient Air Quality (%)		80.8	92.1	87.2	91.8
火灾、交通事故	**Fires and Traffic Accidents**					
火灾发生数（万起）	Quantity of Fires (10 000 units)	0.21	0.52	0.57	1.05	1.47
火灾损失额（万元）	Loss of Fires (10 000 yuan)	1 868	1 919	22 949	6 546	17 672
交通事故发生数（万起）	Quantity of Traffic Accidents(10 000 units)	0.76	4.13	0.22	43.66	52.29
交通事故损失额（万元）	Loss of Traffic Accidents (10 000 yuan)	1 345	20 391	967	31 495	75 477

注：本表总量指标中的价值量指标均按当年价格计算。从 2018 年起，交通事故统计口径扩大范围，包含走简易程序处理的事故，以前只包含走一般程序处理的事故。

Note: The data in value terms in the table are calculated at current prices.Since 2018, the scope of traffic accident statistics which only including accidents handled by general procedures before has been expanded, and the accidents handled by simple procedures arealso included.

表 1.6 主要年份社会经济主要指标发展速度
GROWTH RATE OF MAJOR SOCIAL AND ECONOMIC INDICATORS IN MAIN YEARS

单位:%

指 标	Indicators	2021 年比下列各年增长 Indicator's Growth Rate Between 2021 and Year Below			
		1990	2000	2010	2020
年末常住人口	Year-end Residnet Population	86.6	54.8	8.1	…
上海市生产总值	Gross Domestic Product	18.6 倍	5.1 倍	1.0 倍	8.1
第一产业	Primary Industry	-28.7	-43.8	-38.6	-6.5
第二产业	Secondary Industry	13.1 倍	3.6 倍	54.1	9.4
第三产业	Tertiary Industry	26.3 倍	6.3 倍	1.4 倍	7.6
全社会固定资产投资总额	Total Investment in Fixed Assets	41.1 倍	4.1 倍	79.6	8.1
城市基础设施投资额	Urban Infrastructure Investment	38.2 倍	3.1 倍	23.6	5.8
一般公共预算收入	General Budgetary Revenue	45.5 倍	14.6 倍	1.7 倍	10.3
一般公共预算支出	General Budgetary Expenditure	110.6 倍	12.5 倍	1.6 倍	4.1
农业总产值	Gross Output Value of Agriculture	-6.5	-41.0	-36.3	-6.7
工业总产值	Gross Output Value of Industry	23.1 倍	4.9 倍	35.9	10.2
货物运输量	Freight Transportation Volume	5.8 倍	2.2 倍	91.6	11.5
旅客发送量	Passenger Departures	2.7 倍	1.0 倍	4.4	17.3
港口货物吞吐量	Port Freight Throughput	4.6 倍	2.8 倍	18.8	8.3
社会消费品零售总额	Total Retail Sales of Consumer Goods	53.2 倍	8.2 倍	1.6 倍	13.5
上海关区进出口总额	Total Trade Value Through Customs	66.8 倍	9.7 倍	71.2	25.7
进口额	Imports	56.5 倍	9.4 倍	89.9	27.0
出口额	Exports	77.1 倍	10.0 倍	59.7	24.8
上海市进出口总额	Total Value of Foreign Trade Imports and Exports	83.6 倍	10.5 倍	70.4	24.8
进口额	Imports	181.6 倍	12.1 倍	1.0 倍	26.0
出口额	Exports	44.7 倍	8.6 倍	34.6	22.9
外商直接投资	Foreign Direct Investment				
合同项目	Number of Contracts	32.0 倍	2.7 倍	71.7	16.6
合同金额	Contractual Foreign Capital	281.2 倍	8.5 倍	2.9 倍	16.9
实到金额	Foreign Investment Actually Absorbed	126.4 倍	6.1 倍	1.0 倍	11.5
全市居民人均可支配收入	Per Capita Annual Disposable Income of Residents	37.9 倍	6.1 倍	1.6 倍	8.0
全市居民人均消费支出	Per Capita Annual Consumption Expenditures of Residents	27.6 倍	4.7 倍	97.4	14.9
城镇常住居民人均可支配收入	Per Capita Annual Disposable Income of Urban Households	36.8 倍	6.0 倍	1.6 倍	7.8
城镇常住居民人均消费支出	Per Capita Annual Consumption Expenditures of Urban Households	25.5 倍	4.8 倍	1.2 倍	14.4
农村常住居民人均可支配收入	Per Capita Annual Disposable Income of Rural Households	22.1 倍	5.9 倍	1.8 倍	10.3
农村常住居民人均消费支出	Per Capita Annual Consumption Expenditures of Rural Households	20.6 倍	5.6 倍	1.7 倍	23.1
医 生	Doctors	49.5	74.3	69.7	5.7
普通高等学校在校学生	Student Enrollment of Institutions of Higher Education	3.5 倍	1.4 倍	4.8	2.7

①本表速度指标中，上海市生产总值及三次产业、工业总产值、农业总产值均按可比价格计算。
②城镇、农村常住居民人均可支配收入及支出增幅同口径累乘计算。
❶The growth rates of the following indicators are calculated by comparable prices: Gross Domestic Product and three industries, gross output value of agriculture and Industry.
❷Per capita disposable income and expenditure of urban and rural permanent resident are calucated by cumulated product.

表 1.6 续表 continued

单位:%

指 标	Indicators	平均每年增长 Indicators' Average Annual Growth Rate 1991~2021	2001~2021	2011~2021
年末常住人口	Year-end Resident Population	2.0	2.1	0.7
上海市生产总值	Gross Domestic Product	10.1	9.0	6.7
第一产业	Primary Industry	-1.1	-2.7	-4.3
第二产业	Secondary Industry	8.9	7.5	4.0
第三产业	Tertiary Industry	11.3	9.9	8.3
全社会固定资产投资总额	Total Investment in Fixed Assets	12.8	8.1	5.5
城市基础设施投资额	Urban Infrastructure Investment	12.6	7.0	1.9
一般公共预算收入	General Budgetary Revenue	13.2	14.0	9.5
一般公共预算支出	General Budgetary Expenditure	16.4	13.2	8.9
农业总产值	Gross Output Value of Agriculture	-0.2	-2.5	-4.0
工业总产值	Gross Output Value of Industry	11.2	9.3	3.1
货物运输量	Freight Transportation Volume	6.4	5.8	6.1
旅客发送量	Passenger Departures	4.3	3.4	0.4
港口货物吞吐量	Port Freight Throughput	5.7	6.6	1.6
社会消费品零售总额	Total Retail Sales of Consumer Goods	13.7	11.2	9.1
上海关区进出口总额	Total Trade Value Through Customs	14.6	12.0	5.0
进口额	Imports	14.0	11.8	6.0
出口额	Exports	15.1	12.1	4.3
上海市进出口总额	Total Value of Foreign Trade Imports and Exports	15.4	12.3	5.0
进口额	Imports	18.3	13.0	6.7
出口额	Exports	13.1	11.4	2.7
外商直接投资	Foreign Direct Investment			
合同项目	Number of Contracts	11.9	6.4	5.0
合同金额	Contractual Foreign Capital	20.0	11.3	13.3
实到金额	Foreign Investment Actually Absorbed	16.9	9.8	6.6
医 生	Doctors	1.3	3.0	5.3
普通高等学校在校学生	Student Enrollment of Institutions of Higher Education	5.3	3.4	0.7

表 1.7 主要年份社会经济发展结构指标
STRUCTURAL INDICATORS OF SOCIAL AND ECONOMIC DEVELOPMENT IN MAIN YEARS

单位:%

指 标	Indicators	1990	2000	2010	2020	2021
户籍人口性别结构	Structure of Sex					
男	Male	50.4	50.4	49.8	49.4	49.4
女	Female	49.6	49.6	50.2	50.6	50.6
上海市生产总值产业结构	Industrial Structure of GDP					
第一产业	Primary Industry	4.4	1.6	0.6	0.3	0.2
第二产业	Secondary Industry	64.7	46.0	41.5	26.3	26.5
第三产业	Tertiary Industry	30.9	52.4	57.9	73.4	73.3
全社会固定资产投资所有制结构	Ownership Structure of Total Investment					
国有经济	State-owned	84.7	44.4	42.0	28.0	28.1
非国有经济	Non-State-owned	15.3	55.6	58.0	72.0	71.9
一般公共预算收入	General Budgetary Revenue					
# 增值税	Value-added Tax		18.8	13.5	32.4	32.0
营业税	Business Tax		30.9	32.5		
企业所得税	Enterprise Income Tax		20.7	21.1	19.8	21.8
个人所得税	Personal Income Tax		12.1	9.1	9.5	11.1
农业总产值结构	Structure of Gross Output Value of Agriculture					
# 种植业	Planting	42.7	41.5	54.0	49.3	53.9
畜牧业	Animal Husbandry	44.4	40.3	22.2	19.7	16.9
渔 业	Fishery	11.8	17.5	18.3	18.2	17.7
货物运输总量结构	Structure of Freight Transportation					
铁 路	Railways	5.5	2.2	1.2	0.3	0.3
公 路	Roadways	38.2	59.1	50.5	33.1	34.1
水 运	Waterways	56.3	38.5	47.9	66.3	65.3
机 场(吞吐量)	Airport	0.1	0.2	0.5	0.3	0.3
社会消费品零售总额结构	Structure of Retail Sales of Consumer Goods					
吃	Food	42.6	39.8	25.9	21.4	21.3
穿	Clothing	15.7	13.4	13.6	23.6	23.0
用	Articles	41.1	46.0	51.9	52.1	52.6
烧	Fuels	0.6	0.8	8.6	2.9	3.1
上海市出口总额结构	Structure of Exports					
# 一般贸易	General Trade		40.1	35.0	46.5	50.3
加工贸易	Processing Trade		58.3	55.5	34.2	30.7
外商直接投资实到金额投资方式结构	Foreign Direct Investment Structure of Foreign Investment Actually Absorbed					
# 合资企业	Joint Ventures	61.0	40.9	16.0	14.7	14.4
合作企业	Cooprative Enterprises	37.9	9.5	1.5	0.2	0.6
独资企业	Sole-foreign Enterprises	1.1	49.6	81.6	84.0	76.7

表 1.7 续表 continued

单位:%

指标	Indicators	1990	2000	2010	2020	2021
金融机构境内存款结构	Structure of Domestic Deposits of Financial Institutions					
住户存款	Household Deposits				25.9	25.6
非金融企业存款	Non Financial Enterprise Deposits				42.8	41.4
财政性存款	Fiscal Deposits				2.7	10.0
机关团体存款	Deposits of Non-profit Institutions				9.9	2.8
非银行业金融机构存款	Deposits of Non Banking Financial Institutions				18.8	20.2
金融机构境内贷款结构	Structure of Domestic Loans of Financial Institutions					
#住户贷款	Household Loans				31.9	31.4
非金融企业及机关团体贷款	Loans of Non Financial Enterprise and Non-profit Institutions				67.6	68.2
非银行业金融机构贷款	Loans of Non Banking Financial Institutions				0.5	0.4
在校学生结构	Structure of Students Enrollment					
大学生	University and College Students	7.1	12.5	28.5	26.5	26.0
中学生	Secondary Students	28.3	43.9	32.8	31.2	31.8
小学生	Primary Students	64.6	43.6	38.7	42.3	42.2
全市居民消费支出构成	Consumption Structure of Residents					
#食品烟酒	Food, Cigarettes and Liquors				26.4	25.8
衣着	Clothing				4.0	4.3
居住	Residence				35.9	33.0
生活用品及服务	Living Goods and Services				4.9	4.6
交通通信	Transportation and Communication				10.7	11.5
教育文化娱乐	Education, Culture and Entertainment				8.6	9.6
城镇常住居民消费支出构成	Consumption Structure of Urban Residents					
#食品烟酒	Food, Cigarettes and Liquors	56.5	44.5	33.5	25.7	25.1
衣着	Clothing	10.7	6.4	7.7	3.9	4.2
居住	Residence	4.7	9.0	9.3	36.7	33.9
生活用品及服务	Living Goods and Services	10.1	7.7	7.8	4.9	4.5
交通通信	Transportation and Communication	3.0	8.6	17.6	10.4	11.2
教育文化娱乐	Education, Culture and Entertainment	11.9	14.5	14.5	8.9	9.9
卫生机构数结构	Structure of Health Care Institutions					
#医院	Hospitals	6.0	10.4	9.4	6.9	6.8
卫生技术人员结构	Structure of Medical Professionals					
#医生	Doctors	49.2	46.6	37.9	36.4	36.3
护士	Nurses	27.6	34.4	41.3	45.5	45.4

①2015 年起，存贷款分类进行了调整，故与往年数据不可比。
②2013 年起，卫生机构数中新增村卫生室数据，故与往年数据不可比。
❶The statistic of deposits and loans has been adjusted since 2015, so the data are not comparable with the previous years.
❷The Number of Health Care Institutions has contained the data of village health rooms since 2013, so it can not be comparable with the previous years.

表 1.8　国民经济主要指标比上年增长(1978~2021)
GROWTH RATE OF MAJOR NATIONAL ECONOMIC INDICATORS OVER PRECEDING YEAR

单位:%

年　份 Year	上海市 生产总值 Gross Domestic Product	一般公共 预算收入 General Budgetary Revenue	一般公共 预算支出 General Budgetary Expenditure	工　业 总产值 Gross Output Value of Industry	全社会固定资产 投资总额 Total Investment in Fixed Assets
1978	15.8	14.6	51.4	12.1	55.1
1979	7.4	2.1	4.0	8.6	27.5
1980	8.4	1.2	-29.1	6.5	27.7
1981	5.6	-0.2	-0.6	3.7	20.2
1982	7.2	-3.6	8.5	4.7	30.7
1983	7.8	-6.9	8.3	7.0	6.5
1984	11.6	4.8	35.4	9.9	21.5
1985	13.4	12.4	51.9	13.5	28.5
1986	4.4	-2.6	28.2	5.5	23.9
1987	7.5	-5.8	-8.9	6.7	26.8
1988	10.1	-4.3	22.3	10.5	31.7
1989	3.0	3.3	11.3	3.0	-12.4
1990	3.5	0.1	3.1	4.0	5.7
1991	7.1	5.1	13.9	14.1	13.7
1992	14.8	5.7	10.4	20.2	38.4
1993	15.1	30.6	36.1	20.1	83.0
1994	14.5	-27.7	52.3	18.2	71.8
1995	15.0	29.6	36.0	17.4	42.6
1996	13.1	26.9	27.9	15.5	21.9
1997	12.8	22.1	25.2	14.5	1.3
1998	10.3	11.3	12.1	7.8	-0.6
1999	10.4	10.1	13.7	10.5	-5.5
2000	11.0	15.3	14.0	13.5	0.7
2001	10.5	24.6	16.6	16.4	6.7
2002	11.4	16.1	20.9	14.6	9.6
2003	12.3	24.9	25.6	31.4	12.1
2004	13.3	24.5	26.6	20.3	25.8
2005	11.5	28.7	19.0	13.9	14.8
2006	12.8	11.6	9.2	13.9	10.8
2007	15.2	31.4	21.4	15.7	13.6
2008	9.7	13.3	18.9	8.1	8.3
2009	8.4	7.7	15.3	3.2	9.2
2010	10.2	13.1	10.5	22.9	0.8
2011	8.3	19.4	18.5	6.6	0.3
2012	7.5	9.2	6.9	-0.3	3.7
2013	7.9	9.8	8.2	4.3	7.5
2014	7.1	11.6	8.7	1.6	6.5
2015	7.0	13.3	19.5	-0.5	5.6
2016	6.9	16.1	11.7	0.7	6.3
2017	7.0	9.1	9.1	6.5	7.3
2018	6.8	7.0	10.7	1.3	5.2
2019	6.0	0.8	-2.1	-0.3	5.1
2020	1.7	-1.7	-0.9	1.6	10.3
2021	8.1	10.3	4.1	10.2	8.1

表 1.8 续表 continued

单位:%

年 份 Year	社会消费品零售总额 Total Retail Sales of Consumer Goods	上海市进出口总额(按美元计算) Total Value of Foreign Trade Import and Export(in USD)	# 出口总额 Export	外商直接投资合同金额 Contracted Foreign Direct Investment	外商直接投资实到金额 Foreign Investment Actually Absorbed	港口货物吞吐量 Port Freight Throughput
1978	9.8	30.4	30.3			30.6
1979	26.2	28.2	27.0			5.0
1980	17.8	16.2	16.1			1.6
1981	10.3	-7.9	-10.8	1.0 倍	…	-1.7
1982	1.2	-6.2	-5.3	1.8 倍	…	7.7
1983	12.1	6.3	1.2	1.8 倍	2.7 倍	2.4
1984	22.9	6.3	-1.7	3.1 倍	1.5 倍	9.5
1985	40.1	17.6	-6.3	56.4	1.2 倍	12.2
1986	13.5	0.6	6.6	-68.9	58.1	11.6
1987	14.4	15.2	16.1	35.8	1.2 倍	1.8
1988	31.3	20.8	10.7	28.7	71.7	3.8
1989	12.0	8.3	9.3	6.6	15.9	9.6
1990	0.7	-5.3	5.7	20.9	-58.1	-4.4
1991	14.4	8.2	7.9	30.4	-1.1	5.2
1992	21.7	21.3	14.2	5.7 倍	6.2 倍	11.0
1993	46.3	30.5	12.6	1.0 倍	84.1	8.0
1994	24.2	24.6	23.0	42.3	39.4	-5.8
1995	26.6	19.9	27.5	0.2	0.6	-0.1
1996	20.4	17.0	14.3	8.4	45.1	-1.0
1997	14.8	11.2	11.2	-8.4	2.0	…
1998	11.7	26.6	8.4	9.9	-24.3	-0.1
1999	8.7	23.2	17.7	-29.8	-16.2	13.7
2000	8.9	41.7	35.0	55.7	3.7	9.7
2001	8.7	11.3	9.0	15.4	39.0	8.1
2002	9.9	19.3	16.0	43.4	14.5	19.4
2003	9.7	54.7	51.2	23.5	30.1	19.8
2004	11.6	42.4	51.6	12.6	11.8	19.8
2005	12.8	16.5	23.4	18.3	4.7	16.9
2006	14.0	22.1	25.2	5.4	3.8	21.3
2007	15.4	24.4	26.7	2.0	11.4	4.5
2008	18.9	13.8	17.7	15.1	27.3	3.6
2009	14.5	-13.8	-16.2	-22.3	4.5	1.8
2010	19.3	32.8	27.4	15.1	5.5	10.4
2011	16.7	18.6	16.0	31.3	13.3	11.4
2012	9.7	-0.2	-1.4	11.1	20.5	1.1
2013	9.7	1.1	-1.2	11.6	10.5	5.5
2014	9.3	5.6	3.0	26.8	8.3	-2.6
2015	9.6	-3.2	-6.3	86.5	1.6	-5.0
2016	8.5	-3.4	-6.4	-13.5	0.3	-2.2
2017	8.8	9.7	5.6	-21.2	-8.1	6.9
2018	8.6	8.3	7.0	16.8	1.7	-2.7
2019	6.5	-4.2	-4.0	7.1	10.1	-1.4
2020	0.5	1.9	-0.4	2.8	6.2	-0.5
2021	13.5	24.8	22.9	16.9	11.5	8.3

表1.9　上海社会经济主要指标占全国比重(2021)
PERCENTAGE OF THE NATIONAL TOTAL OF SHANGHAI'S MAJOR SOCIAL AND ECONOMIC INDICATORS

指　标	Indicators	全　国 Country	上　海 Shanghai	上海占全国比重(%) Percentage of the National Total(%)
生产总值（亿元）	Gross Domestic Product (100 million yuan)	1 143 669.70	43 214.85	3.8
#第一产业	Primary Industry	83 085.50	99.97	0.1
第二产业	Secondary Industry	450 904.50	11 449.32	2.5
第三产业	Tertiary Industry	609 679.70	31 665.56	5.2
#工　业	Industry	372 575.30	10 738.80	2.9
港口货物吞吐量（亿吨）	Port Freight Throughput(100 millions tons)	155.45	7.76	5.0
社会消费品零售总额（亿元）	Total Retail Sales of Consumer Goods (100 million yuan)	440 823.20	18 079.25	4.1
上海关区进出口总额（亿美元）	Total Trade Value Through Customs (100 million USD)	60 514.89	11 724.29	19.4
进口额	Imports	26 875.29	4 962.66	18.5
出口额	Exports	33 639.59	6 761.63	20.1
外商直接投资实到金额（亿美元）	Foreign Direct Investment Actually Absorbed (100 million USD)	1 734.80	225.51	13.0
研究与试验发展经费支出（亿元）	Expenditures on R&D (100 million yuan)		1 819.77	
图书出版量（亿册）	Books Published (100 million copies)		4.94	4.5
期　刊（亿册）	Periodicals (100 million copies)		0.59	3.0
报纸出版量（亿份）	Newspapers Published (100 million copies)		6.66	2.4
医　生（万人）	Doctors (10 000 persons)		8.70	2.0
医院床位数（万张）	Beds in Hospitals (10 000 beds)		15.08	2.0

注：全国港口货物吞吐量为沿海规模以上主要港口货物吞吐量数据。
Note: National Port freight throughput refers to freight throughput of major coastal ports above the set scale.

表 1.10 各时期社会经济主要指标
MAJOR SOCIAL AND ECONOMIC INDICATORS OF EACH PERIOD

时 期	Period	上海市生产总值（亿元）Gross Domestic Product (100 million yuan)	其 中 of which 第一产业 Primary Industry	第二产业 Secondary Industry	第三产业 Tertiary Industry	一般公共预算收入（亿元）General Budgetary Revenue (100 million yuan)
"一五"时期	"First Five-year Plan" Period	293.26	12.56	163.89	116.81	14.93
"二五"时期	"Second Five-year Plan" Period	568.99	21.03	412.70	135.26	304.28
1963～1965		304.94	17.28	220.81	66.85	172.51
"三五"时期	"Third Five-year Plan" Period	657.06	37.64	487.88	131.54	374.19
"四五"时期	"Fourth Five-year Plan" Period	918.76	42.75	708.84	167.17	633.79
"五五"时期	"Fifth Five-year Plan" Period	1 309.61	49.26	1 004.23	256.12	797.56
"六五"时期	"Sixth Five-year Plan" Period	1 871.24	74.20	1 349.98	447.06	846.92
"七五"时期	"Seventh Five-year Plan" Period	3 162.79	132.52	2 105.23	925.04	846.96
"八五"时期	"Eighth Five-year Plan" Period	8 036.26	208.98	4 678.33	3 148.95	1 006.06
"九五"时期	"Ninth Five-year Plan" Period	19 311.48	356.61	9 457.52	9 497.35	1 962.85
"十五"时期	"Tenth Five-year Plan" Period	35 155.40	402.18	16 475.79	18 277.43	4 792.94
"十一五"时期	"Eleventh Five-year Program" Period	71 672.29	527.13	30 441.80	40 703.36	11 499.22
"十二五"时期	"Twelfth Five-year Program" Period	116 676.16	644.89	41 671.90	74 359.37	21 388.10
"十三五"时期	"Thirteenth Five-year Program" Period	175 774.70	544.64	48 909.08	126 320.98	34 367.94

表 1.10 续表 continued

时 期	Period	一般公共预算支出（亿元）General Budgetary Expenditure (100 million yuan)	工业总产值（亿元）Gross Output Value of Industry (100 million yuan)	全社会固定资产投资总额（亿元）Total Investment in Fixed Assets (100 million yuan)	上海市出口总额（亿美元）Total Exports Value (100 million USD)	社会消费品零售总额（亿元）Retail Sales of Consumer Goods (100 million yuan)
"一五"时期	"First Five-year Plan" Period	12.25	512.03	19.29	17.46	121.02
"二五"时期	"Second Five-year Plan" Period	60.79	1 069.50	55.60	31.00	145.82
1963～1965		19.28	596.63	20.29	20.12	79.50
"三五"时期	"Third Five-year Plan" Period	39.41	1 334.94	34.77	43.08	153.86
"四五"时期	"Fourth Five-year Plan" Period	86.78	1 894.01	95.79	92.86	200.62
"五五"时期	"Fifth Five-year Plan" Period	111.30	2 550.91	151.44	150.33	302.07
"六五"时期	"Sixth Five-year Plan" Period	138.52	3 509.15	412.74	180.08	576.32
"七五"时期	"Seventh Five-year Plan" Period	327.68	6 498.13	1 020.34	226.96	1 383.16
"八五"时期	"Eighth Five-year Plan" Period	775.11	17 308.90	3 994.67	403.31	3 441.10
"九五"时期	"Ninth Five-year Plan" Period	2 421.50	29 776.04	9 620.86	880.57	8 166.62
"十五"时期	"Tenth Five-year Plan" Period	5 762.87	59 716.74	13 261.11	2 724.27	13 122.48
"十一五"时期	"Eleventh Five-year Program" Period	12 925.94	124 634.89	23 804.15	7 495.49	25 673.46
"十二五"时期	"Twelfth Five-year Program" Period	23 742.51	168 202.99	28 338.39	10 280.86	48 776.94
"十三五"时期	"Thirteenth Five-year Program" Period	39 099.50	178 165.56		9 813.64	72 942.54

表 1.11　各时期社会经济主要指标平均增长率
GROWTH RATE OF MAJOR SOCIAL AND ECONOMIC INDICATORS OF EACH PERIOD

单位:%

时　期 Period		上海市生产总值 Gross Domestic Product	其　中 of which			一般公共预算收入 General Budgetary Revenue
			第一产业 Primary Industry	第二产业 Secondary Industry	第三产业 Tertiary Industry	
" 一五"时期	"First Five-year Plan" Period	13.8	3.3	18.4	8.3	12.6
" 二五"时期	"Second Five-year Plan" Period	1.5	1.3	4.1	-3.1	57.2
1963~1965		17.0	11.6	21.7	5.6	12.3
" 三五"时期	"Third Five-year Plan" Period	8.7	3.3	9.7	5.7	9.7
" 四五"时期	"Fourth Five-year Plan" Period	6.6	-1.6	7.1	6.2	6.4
" 五五"时期	"Fifth Five-year Plan" Period	8.4	0.9	8.6	8.6	5.1
" 六五"时期	"Sixth Five-year Plan" Period	9.1	4.3	8.3	12.3	1.1
" 七五"时期	"Seventh Five-year Plan" Period	5.7	1.2	5.0	7.9	-1.6
" 八五"时期	"Eighth Five-year Plan" Period	13.3	1.4	14.0	13.0	6.0
" 九五"时期	"Ninth Five-year Plan" Period	11.5	3.4	9.8	15.4	17.0
"十五"时期	"Tenth Five-year Plan" Period	11.8	-1.4	12.9	11.1	23.6
"十一五"时期	"Eleventh Five-year Program" Period	11.2	-0.3	10.1	12.3	14.9
"十二五"时期	"Twelfth Five-year Program" Period	7.6	-0.9	4.2	9.8	13.9
"十三五"时期	"Thirteenth Five-year Program" Period	5.7	-7.2	2.8	6.8	5.0

表 1.11 续表 continued

单位:%

时　期 Period		一般公共预算支出 General Budgetary Expenditure	工　业总产值 Gross Output Value of Industry	全社会固定资产投资总额 Total Investment in Fixed Assets	上海市出口总额 Total Exports Value	社会消费品零售总额 Retail Sales of Consumer Goods
" 一五"时期	"First Five-year Plan" Period	12.3	14.5	23.1	30.6	5.6
" 二五"时期	"Second Five-year Plan" Period	0.6	4.9	26.5	4.2	1.2
1963~1965		25.2	18.8	31.4	11.4	-0.1
" 三五"时期	"Third Five-year Plan" Period	11.2	10.2	-3.6	2.5	3.3
" 四五"时期	"Fourth Five-year Plan" Period	15.5	7.5	19.4	20.7	8.4
" 五五"时期	"Fifth Five-year Plan" Period	-6.3	7.6	-2.4	14.0	11.0
" 六五"时期	"Sixth Five-year Plan" Period	19.2	7.7	20.6	-4.7	16.6
" 七五"时期	"Seventh Five-year Plan" Period	10.4	5.9	18.7	9.6	14.0
" 八五"时期	"Eighth Five-year Plan" Period	28.8	18.0	45.4	16.8	26.2
" 九五"时期	"Ninth Five-year Plan" Period	18.4	12.3	6.2	17.0	12.8
"十五"时期	"Tenth Five-year Plan" Period	21.7	19.2	11.9	29.0	10.6
"十一五"时期	"Eleventh Five-year Program" Period	14.7	12.6	10.0	14.8	16.4
"十二五"时期	"Twelfth Five-year Program" Period	13.4	2.3	3.9	1.7	11.0
"十三五"时期	"Thirteenth Five-year Program" Period	5.5	1.9	6.8	0.1	6.5

表 1.12 长三角三省一市主要指标(2021)
MAJOR INDICATORS IN THREE PROVINCES AND ONE CITY OF THE YANGTZE RIVER DELTA

指标	Indicators	上海 Shanghai 绝对量 Absolute Value	增长(%) Growth Rate(%)
行政区域面积(平方公里)	Administrative Area (square kilometer)	6 341	
年末常住人口(万人)	Year-end Resident Population (10 000 persons)	2 489.43	0.1
地区生产总值(亿元)	Gross Regional Product (100 million yuan)	43 214.85	8.1
第一产业	Primary Industry	99.97	-6.5
第二产业	Secondary Industry	11 449.32	9.4
第三产业	Tertiary Industry	31 665.56	7.6
规模以上工业增加值(亿元)	Industrial Added Value above the Set Scale (100 million yuan)		11.0
规模以上工业利润(亿元)	Industrial Profit above the Set Scale (100 million yuan)	3 052.33	6.3
社会消费品零售总额(亿元)	Total Retail Sales of Consumer Goods (100 million yuan)	18 079.25	13.5
固定资产投资(亿元)	Investment in Fixed Assets (100 million yuan)		8.1
#工　业	Industry		8.2
房地产开发	Investment in Real Estate		7.2
地方一般公共预算收入(亿元)	Local General Budgetary Revenue	7 771.80	10.3
地方一般公共预算支出(亿元)	Local General Budgetary Expenditure	8 430.86	4.1
进出口总额(亿元)	Total Value of Foreign Trade Imports and Exports (100 million yuan)	40 610.35	16.5
进　口	Imports	24 891.68	17.7
出　口	Exports	15 718.67	14.6
金融机构本外币存款余额(亿元)	Balance of Domestic and Foreign Currency Deposits of Financial Institutions (100 million yuan)	175 831.08	
金融机构本外币贷款余额(亿元)	Balance of Domestic and Foreign Currency Loans of Financial Institutions (100 million yuan)	96 032.13	
居民人均可支配收入(元)	Per Capita Annual Disposable Income of Residents	78 027	8.0
城镇常住居民人均可支配收入	Per Capita Annual Disposable Income of Urban Households	82 429	7.8
农村常住居民人均可支配收入	Per Capita Annual Disposable Income of Rural Household	38 521	10.3
全社会用电量(亿千瓦时)	Electricity Power Consumption (100 million kwh)	1 749.62	11.0
#工　业	Industry	851.49	10.7

江　苏 Jiangsu		浙　江 Zhejiang		安　徽 Anhui	
绝对量 Absolute Value	增　长(%) Growth Rate(%)	绝对量 Absolute Value	增　长(%) Growth Rate(%)	绝对量 Absolute Value	增　长(%) Growth Rate(%)
107 217		105 585		140 140	
8 505.40	0.3	6 540.00	1.1	6 113.00	0.1
116 364.20	8.6	73 515.76	8.5	42 959.18	8.3
4 722.42	3.1	2 209.09	2.2	3 360.59	7.4
51 775.39	10.1	31 188.57	10.2	17 613.19	7.9
59 866.39	7.7	40 118.10	7.6	21 985.39	8.7
	12.8		12.9		8.9
9 358.13	25.7	6 789.00	21.0	2 669.89	13.6
42 702.65	15.1	29 210.54	9.7	21 471.16	17.1
	5.8		10.8		9.4
	12.1		17.8		13.5
	2.3		8.5		3.1
10 015.16	10.6	8 262.57	14.0	3 498.19	8.8
14 585.96	6.6	11 016.87	9.3	7 592.14	1.6
52 130.59	17.2	41 429.00	22.4	6 920.21	26.9
19 598.26	14.9	11 308.00	30.3	2 825.43	23.4
32 532.33	18.6	30 121.00	19.7	4 094.78	29.5
196 016.31		170 815.99		66 868.55	
180 538.69		165 755.71		58 669.82	
47 498	9.5	57 541	9.8	30 904	10.0
57 743	8.7	68 487	9.2	43 009	9.0
26 791	10.7	35 247	10.4	18 368	10.5
7 101.16	11.4	5 514.11	14.2	2 715.47	11.9
4 979.99	10.1	3 767.51	14.2	1 721.30	11.0

表 1.13 主要年份人大情况
BASIC STATISTICS OF SHANGHAI MUNICIPAL PEOPLE'S CONGRESS IN MAIN YEARS

类 别	Types	2000	2010	2020	2021
全国人大代表人数(人)	Quantity of National Congress(person)	68	66	59	
#女 性	Female	17	17	14	
全国人大代表提出议案(件)	Proposals Offered by National Congress Representations (case)		21	22	20
市人大代表人数(人)	Quantity of Municipal Congress Representatives(person)	865	864	865	863
#女 性	Female	203	244	285	278
市人大常委会组成人员数(人)	Quantity of Municipal Standing Committee(person)	65	64	64	64
#女 性	Female	13	9	11	11
市人大代表提出议案(件)	Proposals Offered by Municipal Congress Representatives (case)		78	57	57
区人大代表人数(人)	Quantity of District Level Congress Representatives (person)	4 944	4 667	4 475	5 008
#女 性	Female	1 451	1 454	1 727	2 125
区人大常委人数(人)	Quantity of District Level Standing Committee(person)	432	414	518	582
#女 性	Female	67	94	169	256

注：本表数据由市人大代表工作委员会提供。
Note: Data in this Table are provided by Shanghai Committee of People's Congress

表 1.14 主要年份政协情况
BASIC STATISTICS OF SHANGHAI MUNICIPAL PEOPLE'S POLITICAL CONSULTATIVE CONFERENCE IN MAIN YEARS

类 别	Types	2000	2010	2020	2021
全国政协委员人数(人)	Quantity of National Commissary (person)	104	109	110	110
#女 性	Female	20	18	24	24
市政协委员人数(人)	Quantity of Municipal Commissary(person)	729	817	840	839
#女 性	Female	120	168	220	217
市政协常委人数(人)	Quantity of Municipal Standing Committee(person)	121	132	159	154
#女 性	Female	20	24	32	31
市政协委员提出提案(件)	Proposals Offered by Municipal Commissary (case)	1 197	944	902	938
区政协委员人数(人)	Quantity of District Level Commissary(person)	4 802	5 280	4 657	5 012
#女 性	Female	1 230	1 459	1 626	1 912
区政协常委人数(人)	Quantity of District Level Standing Committee(person)	707	709	772	868
#女 性	Female	174	154	285	

注：本表数据由市政协提供。
Note: Data in this table are provided by Shanghai Municipal People's Political Consultative Conference.

上/海/统/计/年/鉴

主要统计指标解释

■ 行政区划

指国家对行政区域的划分。根据宪法规定，我国的行政区域划分如下：(1)全国分为省、自治区、直辖市；(2)省、自治区分为自治州、县、自治县、市；(3)自治州分为县、自治县、市；(4)县、自治县分为乡、民族乡、镇；(5)直辖市和较大的市分为区、县；(6)国家在必要时设立的特别行政区。

■ 气　候

指地球与大气之间长期能量交换与质量交换所形成的一种自然环境状态，它是多种因素综合作用的结果。气候既是人类生活和生产的环境要素之一，又是供给人类生活和生产的重要资源。气温、降水、湿度等气象要素的多年平均值是用来描述一个地区气候状况的主要参数，而各种气象要素某年、某月的平均值(或总量)则可以反映出该时期天气气候状况的重要特征。

■ 气　温

指空气的温度，一般以摄氏度(℃)为单位表示。气象观测的温度表是放在离地面约1.5米处通风良好的百叶箱里测量的，因此，通常说的气温指的是离地面1.5米处百叶箱中的温度。其统计计算方法为：

月平均气温是将全月各日的平均气温相加，除以该月的天数而得。

年平均气温是将12个月的月平均气温累加后除以12而得。

■ 降水量

指从天空降落到地面的液态或固态(经融化后)水，未经蒸发、渗透、流失而在地面上积聚的深度。其统计计算方法为：

月降水量是将全月各日的降水量累加而得。

年降水量是将12个月的月降水量累加而得。

■ 日照时间

指太阳实际照射地面的时间。其统计方法与降水量相同。

■ 国民经济行业分类

本年鉴的行业分类除特别说明外均使用《国民经济行业分类》(GB/T4754-2017)。该分类是由国家统计局组织修订，国家市场监督管理总局和中国国家标准化管理委员会于2017年6月30日发布。这次修订是在2011年分类标准的基础上，结合我国经济活动特点，参照联合国《全部经济活动的国际标准产业分类》(ISIC/Rev.4)进行的。修订后的《国民经济行业分类》(GB/T4754-2017)共有门类20个，大类97个，中类473个，小类1382个。

■ 各个计划时期

表内所用各个“时期”代表的年份如下：恢复时期为1950到1952年；第一个五年计划时期(简称“一五”时期)为1953到1957年；第二个五年计划时期(简称“二五”时期)为1958到1962年;第三个五年计划时期(简称“三五”时期)为1966到1970年;第四个五年计划时期(简称“四五”时期)为1971到1975年;第五个五年计划时期(简称“五五”时期)为1976到1980年;第六个五年计划时期(简称“六五”时期)为1981到1985年;第七个五年计划时期(简称“七五”时期)为1986到1990年;第八个五年计划时期(简称“八五”时期)为1991到1995年;第九个五年计划时期(简称“九五”时期)为1996到2000年；第十个五年计划时期(简称“十五”时期)为2001到2005年；第十一个五年规划时期(简称“十一五”时期)为2006到2010年；第十二个五年规划时期(简称“十二五”时期)为2011到2015年，第十三个五年规划时期(简称“十四五”时期)为2016年到2020年。

■ 指　数

指数是一种表明社会经济现象动态的相对数。运用指数可以测定不能直接相加和直接对比的社会经济现象的总动态；可以分析社会经济现象总变动中各因素变动的影响程度；可以研究总平均指标变动中各组标志水平和总体结构变动的作用。它是在把各个年份的产值换算成可比价格的基础上，根据定基指数等于相应各个环比指数的连乘积这个换算关系计算出来的。

本年鉴所列的上海市生产总值、工业总产值、农业总产值等指标增长速度，就是分别使用上海市生产总值指数、工业总产值指数、农业总产值指数直接计算的。

主要统计指标解释

■ 平均每年增长速度

在我国计算平均增长速度有两种方法。一种是习惯上经常使用的"水平法",又称几何平均法,是以间隔期最后一年的水平同基期水平对比来计算平均每年增长(或下降)速度;另一种是"累计法",又称代数平均法或方程法,是以间隔期内各年水平的总和同基期水平对比来计算平均每年增长(或下降)速度。

在一般正常情况下,两种方法计算的平均每年增长速度比较接近。但在经济发展不平衡,出现大起大落时,两种方法计算的结果差别较大。

本年鉴内所列的平均每年增长速度均用"水平法"计算。从某年到某年平均增长速度的年份,均不包括基期年在内。如1991-2009年平均增长速度是以1990年为基期计算的,余类推。

SHANGHAI STATISTICAL YEARBOOK

EXPLANATORY NOTES TO MAJOR STATISTICAL INDICATORS

□ Administrative Division

Administrative Division refers to the division of administrative areas by the state. The Constitution of the People's Republic of China stipulates that the administrative areas in China are divided as: 1)The whole country is divided into provinces, autonomous regions and municipalities directly under the central government; 2) Provinces and autonomous regions are divided into autonomous prefectures, counties, autonomous counties and cities; 3) Autonomous prefectures are divided into counties, autonomous counties and cities; 4) Counties and autonomous counties are divided into townships, nationality townships and towns; 5) Municipalities and large cities are divided into districts and counties, 6) The state shall, when necessary, establish special administrative regions.

□ Climate

Climate refers to the natural environmental status formed by the long-term exchange of energy and mass between the earth and the air, and is the results of interaction of many factors. Climate is both one of the environment factors and the important resources for the living and production activities of the human being. The average values across several years of meteorological factors such as temperature, rainfall and humidity are used as important parameters to describe the climate of a region, while the average values (or total values) of a given year or month of meteorological factors reflect the key characteristics of climate for that period of time.

□ Temperature

Temperature refers to the air temperature. It often uses centigrade as the unit. The thermometry used for weather observation is put in a breezy shutter, which is 1.5 meters high from the ground. Therefore, the commonly used temperature refers to the temperature in the breezy shutter 1.5 meters away from the ground. The calculation method is as follows:

Monthly average temperature is the summation of average daily temperature of one month divided by the actual days of that particular month. Annual average temperature is the summation of monthly average of a year divided by 12 months.

□ Volume of Precipitation

Volume of Precipitation refers to the deepness of liquid state or solid state (thawed) water falling from the sky to the ground that has not been evaporated, infiltrated or run off. The calculation method is as follows:

Monthly precipitation is the summation of daily precipitation of a month.

Annual precipitation is the summation of 12 months precipitation of a year.

□ Sunshine Hours

Sunshine Hours refer to the actual hours of sun irradiating the earth. The calculation method is the same as that of the precipitation.

□ Classification of the Sectors of the National Economy

Unless otherwise stated, the industry classification used in this yearbook was based on Industrial Classification of the National Economy (GB/T 4754-2017). The revision, based on the 2011 classification, was organized by the National Bureau of Statistics taking into consideration of the characteristics of economic activities in China and the International Standards of the Industrial Classification of All Economic Activities (ISIC/Rev.4) of the United Nations. The new Classification was promulgated by the State Administration for Market Regulation, Inspection and Quarantine and the Standardization Administration of the People's Republic of China on June 30, 2017. The revised version of the Industrial Classification of the National Economy (GB/T 4754-2017) is composed of 20 sections, 97 divisions, 473 groups and 1382 classes.

□ Various Planning Periods

The conventional division of time period in this statistical yearbook is as follows: Rehabilitation Period, 1950-1952; The First Five-Year Plan period (cited as first-five period), 1953-1957; The Second Five-Year Plan period (cited as second-five period), 1958-1962; The Third Five-Year Plan period (cited as third-five period), 1966-1970; The Fourth Five-Year Plan period (cited as fourth-five period), 1971-1975; The Fifth Five-

EXPLANATORY NOTES TO MAJOR STATISTICAL INDICATORS

Year Plan period (cited as fifth-five period), 1976-1980; The Sixth Five-Year Plan period (cited as sixth-five period), 1981-1985; The Seventh Five-Year Plan period (cited as seventh-five period), 1986-1990; The Eight Five-Year Plan period (cited as eighth-five period), 1991-1995; The Ninth Five-Year Plan period (cited as ninth-five period), 1996-2000; The Tenth Five-Year Plan period (cited as tenth-five period), 2001-2005; The eleventh Five-Year Plan period (cited as eleventh-five period), 2006-2010; The twelfth Five-Year Plan period (cited as twelfth-five period), 2011-2015; The Thirteenth Five-Year Plan period (cited as thirteenth-five period), 2016-2020.

□ Index

Index refers to the relative figures indicating social and economic phenomena and developments. Index is used to evaluate the overall development of social and economic phenomena which can not be determined by simple addition or direct comparison. It is also used to analyze the outcome of various changes in the general phenomenon movement of social and economic development, and to study the level of each sub-index in the changes of general average index and the role of the changes of the overall structure. It is calculated at the comparable prices conversed from the output value of each year, using the formula of index number with fixed base period equal to the continuous product of its relative chain index.

The increases of Shanghai Gross Domestic Product, industrial output value and agricultural output value compared with the previous year, which are listed in this yearbook, are calculated according to Shanghai GDP index, industrial output value index and agricultural output value index.

□ Average Annual Growth Rate

Two methods for calculating Average Annual Growth Rate are applied in China, one is often called "level approach" or geometry average, which is derived by comparing the growth rate for the last year of the interval with that of the beginning year; the other is called "accumulating approach" or algebraic average or equation method, which is calculated by comparing the total growth rate of each year for the interval with that of base year .

Usually the results calculated by the two methods are fairly close, but they differ sharply when imbalance occurred in economic development with striking fluctuations in growth.

The Average Annual Growth Rates listed in this statistical yearbook are calculated by "level approach". The base years are not listed when the years are listed for average annual growth rates for instance, the average annual growth rate of 1991-2009 is calculated with the base year 1990, and the analogy of this is also for the rest.

第二篇

CHAPTER 2

人口、就业与工资

POPULATION, EMPLOYMENT AND WAGES

简要说明

一、本篇资料的主要内容

本篇资料反映上海市1978~2021年人口、就业与工资方面的基本情况。

人口方面的基本情况包括全市及各区的主要人口统计数据，如：1978~2021年全市常住人口数和户籍人口数；2021年各区常住人口数和外省市户籍常住人口数；1990~2021年户籍人口自然增长和机械增长变动；2021年各区户籍人口年龄构成等。

就业与工资方面的基本情况包括：规模以上工业、有资质的建筑业、限额以上批发和零售业、限额以上住宿和餐饮业、有开发经营活动的全部房地产开发经营业、规模以上服务业法人单位按职业类型分从业人员期末人数、城镇单位就业人员平均工资、城镇登记失业人数和城镇登记失业率，新增就业岗位，离退休、退职职工人数，及离退休、退职人员养老金情况等。

二、本篇的资料来源

本篇资料由上海市统计局人口和就业统计处整理。

人口统计基本情况资料来源：1982、1990、2000、2010、2020年年末常住人口数据为当年普查数据推算数，其余年份数据为年度人口抽样调查推算数，部分年份数据根据人口普查数据进行了修订。表2.1中除常住人口数据外，其余数据统计范围均为户籍人口，由市公安局提供。表2.2中行政区划面积由市民政局提供，各区年末常住人口数和外省市户籍常住人口数根据上海市2021年度人口抽样调查结果推算。表2.3至表2.6数据统计范围均为户籍人口，由市公安局提供，表2.7由上海市老龄工作委员会办公室提供。

就业与工资方面的基本情况资料来源：

1.本篇从业人员和工资数据是根据国家统计局制定的《劳动工资统计报表制度》整理汇总得到。

2.城镇登记失业人数和城镇登记失业率，新增就业岗位，离退休、退职职工人数，离退休、退职人员养老金情况，由上海市人力资源和社会保障局提供。

三、本篇的统计调查方法

目前由上海市统计局人口和就业统计处实施的人口统计调查方法：

在逢"0"的年份进行全国人口普查；在逢"5"的年份进行全国1%人口抽样调查；其余年份进行全国人口变动情况抽样调查，其样本量约占全市总人口的1.3‰左右。人口抽样调查是以全国为总体，省级单位为次总体，采用分层、多阶段、整群概率比例抽样方法抽取样本。

就业与工资方面的统计调查方法有：对规模以上工业、有资质的建筑业、限额以上批发和零售业、限额以上住宿和餐饮业、有开发经营活动的全部房地产开发经营业、规模以上服务业法人单位采取全面调查；除上述范围以外的法人单位采取抽样调查方法，从2020年起，抽样调查的样本单位由国家统计局统一抽取，统计调查样本中不含村居委会以及从业人员规模在5人及以下的单位。人力资源社会保障的资料采用全面调查方法，由市人力资源社会保障部门收集相关数据资料加工整理取得。

BRIEF INTRODUCTION

I. Main Contents

Data in this chapter reflect the basic conditions of Shanghai´s population, employment and wages between 1978 and 2021.

The basic conditions of Shanghai´s population include data of the city as well as districts under it. For example: there are data of the city´s permanent residents and registered population between 1978 and 2021; permanent residents and residents with household registration in other provinces and cities in districts in 2021; changes of registered population´s natural growth and mechanical growth between 1990 and 2021; registered population age structure in districts in 2020.

The basic conditions of employment and wages reflect the basic conditions of Shanghai´s labor economy, including the number of employed people classified by corporation types of industry enterprises above designated size, qualified construction legal entities, enterprises above designated size of wholesale and retail trades, enterprises above designated size of hotels and catering services, all real estate development business with development and operation activities, service enterprises above designated size, average wages of urban units employed people, the number of urban registered unemployed people and the unemployment rate, the number of new jobs, the number of retired people, and pension situations.

II. Sources of Data

Data in this chapter are collected, prepared, and provided by the Department of Population and Employment Statistics of the Shanghai Statistics Bureau.

Sources of the basic conditions of population: data of permanent residents by the year end for 1982, 1990, 2000, 2010 and 2020 are the census year estimates; the rest of the data are estimates from the annual national sample survey on population changes and data for selected years have been revised according to the census results. Data in table 2.1, provided by Shanghai Public Security Bureau, refer to registered population, with permanent residents in exception. Land area data in table 2.2 are provided by Shanghai Civil Affairs Bureau, and the data on permanent residents in districts, and residents with household registration in other provinces and cities are estimates based on the population sampling survey in Shanghai in 2021. Data in table 2.3 to table 2.6, provided by the Shanghai Public Security Bureau, all refer to registered population. Data in table 2.7, provided by the office of Shanghai Commission on Aging.

Sources of the basic conditions of employment:

Data on basic conditions including the number of employed people and the average wages of employed people are collected, prepared and compiled through The Reporting Form System on Labor Statistics.

Data on the urban registered unemployed people and unemployment rate, the number of new jobs, the number of retired people and pension situations are provided by the Shanghai Human Resources and Social Security Bureau.

III. Survey Methodology

The statistical surveys on population which are conducted by the Department of Population and Employment Statistics of the Shanghai Statistics Bureau are as follows:

The national population census is conducted in the year ending with 0; the national 1 percent population sample survey is conducted in the year ending with 5; sample surveys on population changes are conducted in the rest of the years which cover about 1.3 per thousand of the total population of the city. The sample survey on population change takes the whole nation as the population sample with each province, autonomous region or municipality as sub-populations, and the stratified multi-stage systematic PPS cluster sampling scheme is used.

The statistical survey methodology of employment and wages: data are from comprehensive surveys on industry above designated size, the construction industry, the wholesale and retail industry above the set scale, the accommodation and catering industry above the set scale, all real estate development business with development and operation activities, service industry corporations above the set scale. Data of other legal entities are from sampling surveys. Since 2020, the sample units of the sampling survey have been uniformly selected by the National Bureau of Statistics. The sample of statistical survey does not include the village neighborhood committee and the units with less than 5 employees. The data of human resources and social security are from comprehensive surveys, which collected and processed by Shanghai Human Resources and Social Security Bureau.

表 2.1 户数、人口、人口密度和户籍人口期望寿命(1978~2021)
TOTAL HOUSEHOLDS, POPULATION, DENSITY OF REGISTERED POPULATION AND LIFE EXPECTANCY

年 份 Year	常住人口 (万人) Year-end Resident Population (10 000 persons)	人口密度 (人/平方公里) Density of Population (person/sq.km)	总户数 (万户) Total Households (10 000 households)	平均每户人口 (人) Average Persons Per Household (person)	年末户籍人口 (万人) Year-end Registered Population (10 000 persons)
1978	1 104.00	1 785	291.69	3.77	1 098.28
1979	1 137.00	1 838	296.71	3.82	1 132.14
1980	1 152.00	1 862	303.87	3.77	1 146.52
1981	1 168.00	1 888	314.56	3.70	1 162.84
1982	1 186.00	1 917	321.71	3.67	1 180.51
1983	1 201.00	1 942	330.60	3.61	1 194.01
1984	1 217.00	1 968	340.78	3.54	1 204.78
1985	1 233.00	1 993	351.72	3.46	1 216.69
1986	1 249.00	1 970	364.92	3.38	1 232.33
1987	1 265.00	1 995	380.19	3.29	1 249.51
1988	1 288.00	2 031	394.95	3.20	1 262.42
1989	1 311.00	2 067	406.82	3.14	1 276.45
1990	1 334.00	2 104	415.28	3.09	1 283.35
1991	1 350.00	2 128	425.84	3.02	1 287.20
1992	1 365.00	2 154	431.67	2.99	1 289.37
1993	1 381.00	2 179	438.69	2.95	1 294.74
1994	1 398.00	2 204	444.38	2.92	1 298.81
1995	1 414.00	2 230	450.76	2.89	1 301.37
1996	1 451.00	2 288	457.49	2.85	1 304.43
1997	1 489.00	2 348	461.40	2.83	1 305.46
1998	1 527.00	2 409	465.72	2.81	1 306.58
1999	1 567.00	2 472	470.11	2.79	1 313.12
2000	1 608.60	2 537	475.73	2.78	1 321.63

①户数和年末户籍人口由市公安局提供。2016 年起，年末户籍人口为公安局公布的 11 月底数据(后表同)。户籍人口期望寿命由市卫生和计划生育委员会提供。

②上海取消农业户口和非农业户口性质区分。

❶The figures of household and year-end registered population are provided by Shanghai Municipal Public Security Bureau.From 2016, the figures of year-end registered population refer to the data of the end of November published by Shanghai Municipal Public Security Bureau(same as follows). The figures of life expendency are provided by Shanghai Municipal Health and Family Planning Commission.

❷Shanghai has cancelled the distinction between agricultural and non-agricultural household accounts.

表 2. 1 续表 1 continued

年 份 Year	常住人口 （万人） Year-end Resident Population （10 000 persons）	人口密度 （人/平方公里） Density of Population （person/sq.km）	总户数 （万户） Total Households （10 000 households）	平均每户人口 （人） Average Persons Per Household （person）	年末户籍人口 （万人） Year-end Registered Population （10 000 persons）
2001	1 668.33	2 631	478.92	2.77	1 327.14
2002	1 712.97	2 702	481.77	2.77	1 334.23
2003	1 765.84	2 785	486.06	2.76	1 341.77
2004	1 834.98	2 894	490.58	2.76	1 352.39
2005	1 890.26	2 981	496.69	2.74	1 360.26
2006	1 964.11	3 098	499.54	2.74	1 368.08
2007	2 063.58	3 255	503.29	2.74	1 378.86
2008	2 140.65	3 376	506.64	2.75	1 391.04
2009	2 210.28	3 486	509.79	2.75	1 400.70
2010	2 302.66	3 632	519.27	2.72	1 412.32
2011	2 355.53	3 715	522.01	2.72	1 419.36
2012	2 398.50	3 783	524.31	2.72	1 426.93
2013	2 448.43	3 862	527.52	2.72	1 432.34
2014	2 467.06	3 891	532.55	2.70	1 438.69
2015	2 457.59	3 876	536.76	2.69	1 442.97
2016	2 467.37	3 891	541.62	2.68	1 450.00
2017	2 466.28	3 890	546.13	2.66	1 455.13
2018	2 475.39	3 904	551.95	2.65	1 462.38
2019	2 481.34	3 913	556.23	2.64	1 469.30
2020	2 488.36	3 925	560.96	2.63	1 475.63
2021	2 489.43	3 926	568.27	2.63	1 492.92

①户数和年末户籍人口由市公安局提供。 2016 年起，年末户籍人口为公安局公布的 11 月底数据(后表同)。 户籍人口期望寿命由市卫生和计划生育委员会提供。

②上海取消农业户口和非农业户口性质区分。

❶The figures of household and year-end registered population are provided by Shanghai Municipal Public Security Bureau.From 2016, the figures of year-end registered population refer to the data of the end of November published by Shanghai Municipal Public Security Bureau(same as follows). The figures of life expendency are provided by Shanghai Municipal Health and Family Planning Commission.

❷Shanghai has cancelled the distinction between agricultural and non-agricultural household accounts.

表 2.1 续表 2 continued

年份 Year	按性别分 Grouped by Sex		户籍人口期望寿命（岁） Life Expectancy of Registered Population (year)	其中 of which	
	男性 Male	女性 Female		男性 Male	女性 Female
1978	542.70	555.58	73.35	70.69	74.78
1979	560.40	571.74	73.14	70.64	75.48
1980	569.30	577.22	73.33	71.25	75.36
1981	578.76	584.08	73.38	71.28	75.47
1982	588.82	591.69	74.04	71.77	76.25
1983	596.67	597.34	73.23	71.15	75.26
1984	602.59	602.19	73.90	71.73	76.17
1985	609.70	606.99	74.27	72.14	76.37
1986	618.88	613.45	74.71	72.54	76.85
1987	628.78	620.73	74.46	72.32	76.60
1988	635.82	626.60	74.63	72.50	76.77
1989	643.51	632.94	74.98	72.85	77.12
1990	647.13	636.22	75.46	73.16	77.74
1991	649.03	638.17	75.79	73.58	77.95
1992	649.97	639.40	75.97	74.04	77.91
1993	652.92	641.82	75.97	74.04	77.91
1994	655.14	643.67	76.26	74.29	78.23
1995	656.48	644.89	76.03	74.11	77.97
1996	657.86	646.57	76.11	74.07	78.21
1997	657.93	647.53	77.20	75.18	79.21
1998	658.22	648.36	77.03	75.06	79.02
1999	661.19	651.93	78.44	76.38	80.53
2000	665.51	656.12	78.77	76.71	80.81

表 2.1 续表 3 continued

年 份 Year	按性别分 Grouped by Sex		户籍人口 期望寿命 （岁） Life Expectancy of Registered Population （year）	其 中 of which	
	男 性 Male	女 性 Female		男 性 Male	女 性 Female
2001	668.32	658.82	79.66	77.47	81.83
2002	672.05	662.18	79.52	77.36	81.63
2003	675.47	666.30	79.80	77.78	81.81
2004	680.38	672.01	80.29	78.08	82.48
2005	683.51	676.75	80.13	77.89	82.36
2006	686.66	681.42	80.97	78.64	83.29
2007	691.08	687.78	81.08	78.87	83.29
2008	695.57	695.47	81.28	79.06	83.50
2009	699.25	701.45	81.73	79.42	84.06
2010	703.57	708.75	82.13	79.82	84.44
2011	706.37	712.99	82.51	80.23	84.80
2012	709.62	717.31	82.41	80.18	84.67
2013	711.93	720.41	82.47	80.19	84.79
2014	714.71	723.99	82.29	80.04	84.59
2015	716.37	726.60	82.75	80.47	85.09
2016	719.35	730.65	83.18	80.83	85.61
2017	721.29	733.84	83.37	80.98	85.85
2018	724.14	738.23	83.63	81.25	86.08
2019	726.75	742.55	83.66	81.27	86.14
2020	729.04	746.60	83.67	81.24	86.20
2021	737.54	755.38	84.11	81.76	86.56

表 2.2 各区土地面积、常住人口及人口密度(2021)
LAND AREA, POPULATION AND DENSITY OF POPULATION IN DISTRICTS

地 区 District		行政区域面积（平方公里）Land Area (sq.km)	年末常住人口（万人）Year-end Resident Population (10 000 persons)	其 中 of which 外省市户籍人口 Registered Residence of Other Provinces and Cities	人口密度（人/平方公里）Density of Population (person/sq.km)
全 市	**Total**	**6 340.50**	**2 489.43**	**1 031.99**	**3 926**
浦东新区	Pudong New Area	1 210.41	576.77	242.09	4 765
黄 浦 区	Huangpu	20.46	58.21	24.20	28 451
徐 汇 区	Xuhui	54.76	111.48	33.63	20 358
长 宁 区	Changning	38.30	69.57	22.18	18 164
静 安 区	Jing'an	36.88	96.60	24.50	26 193
普 陀 区	Putuo	54.83	124.36	36.51	22 681
虹 口 区	Hongkou	23.48	71.48	19.49	30 443
杨 浦 区	Yangpu	60.73	123.05	30.57	20 262
闵 行 区	Minhang	370.75	267.32	121.50	7 210
宝 山 区	Baoshan	270.99	225.01	89.15	8 303
嘉 定 区	Jiading	464.20	185.48	102.81	3 996
金 山 区	Jinshan	586.05	81.52	29.93	1 391
松 江 区	Songjiang	605.64	193.88	111.61	3 201
青 浦 区	Qingpu	670.14	129.27	73.16	1 929
奉 贤 区	Fengxian	687.39	114.71	58.76	1 669
崇 明 区	Chongming	1 185.49	60.73	11.90	512

表 2.3 主要年份户籍人口出生率、死亡率、自然增长率
BIRTH RATE, DEATH RATE AND NATURAL GROWTH RATE OF REGISTERED POPULATION IN MAIN YEARS

年 份 Year	出 生 Birth		死 亡 Death		自然增长 Natural Growth	
	人 数 (万人) Population (10 000 persons)	出生率 (‰) Birth Rate (‰)	人 数 (万人) Population (10 000 persons)	死亡率 (‰) Death Rate (‰)	人 数 (万人) Population (10 000 persons)	自然增长率 (‰) Natural Growth Rate(‰)
1990	13.12	10.25	8.63	6.74	4.49	3.51
1995	7.11	5.47	9.79	7.53	-2.68	-2.06
2000	6.95	5.27	9.45	7.17	-2.50	-1.90
2001	5.76	4.34	9.34	7.05	-3.58	-2.71
2002	6.20	4.66	9.67	7.27	-3.47	-2.61
2003	5.73	4.28	10.07	7.52	-4.34	-3.24
2004	8.09	6.00	9.65	7.16	-1.56	-1.16
2005	8.25	6.08	10.23	7.54	-1.98	-1.46
2006	8.12	5.95	9.80	7.19	-1.68	-1.24
2007	10.08	7.34	10.22	7.44	-0.14	-0.10
2008	9.67	6.98	10.70	7.73	-1.03	-0.75
2009	9.23	6.62	10.67	7.64	-1.44	-1.02
2010	10.02	7.13	10.87	7.73	-0.84	-0.60
2011	10.15	7.17	11.11	7.85	-0.96	-0.68
2012	12.11	8.51	11.74	8.25	0.37	0.26
2013	10.89	7.62	11.67	8.16	-0.78	-0.54
2014	12.41	8.64	11.95	8.32	0.46	0.32
2015	10.59	7.35	12.42	8.62	-1.83	-1.27
2016	13.07	9.04	12.35	8.54	0.72	0.50
2017	11.77	8.10	12.64	8.70	-0.87	-0.60
2018	9.84	6.70	12.57	8.60	-2.73	-1.90
2019	9.14	6.24	12.52	8.54	-3.38	-2.31
2020	7.88	5.35	13.06	8.87	-5.18	-3.52
2021	6.91	4.66	13.39	9.02	-6.48	-4.36

表 2.4　主要年份户籍人口迁移
MIGRATION OF REGISTERED POPULATION IN MAIN YEARS

年　份 Year	迁　入 Inflows		迁　出 Outflows		机械增长 Mechanical Increase	
	人　口 （万人） Population （10 000 persons）	迁入率 （‰） Rate of Inflows （‰）	人　口 （万人） Population （10 000 persons）	迁出率 （‰） Rate of Outflows （‰）	人　口 （万人） Population （10 000 persons）	增长率 （‰） Growth Rate （‰）
1990	12.18	9.52	10.72	8.38	1.46	1.14
1995	13.12	10.09	6.47	4.98	6.65	5.11
2000	15.16	11.51	5.32	4.04	9.84	7.47
2001	14.63	11.05	5.56	4.20	9.07	6.85
2002	15.41	11.58	4.38	3.29	11.03	8.29
2003	14.92	11.15	3.69	2.76	11.23	8.39
2004	13.93	10.34	2.74	2.03	11.19	8.31
2005	12.96	9.55	3.46	2.55	9.50	7.00
2006	12.86	9.43	3.50	2.57	9.36	6.86
2007	14.69	10.70	3.95	2.88	10.74	7.82
2008	17.28	12.48	4.29	3.10	12.99	9.38
2009	15.72	11.26	4.77	3.42	10.95	7.84
2010	17.22	12.24	4.97	3.53	12.25	8.71
2011	13.15	9.29	5.33	3.76	7.82	5.53
2012	12.96	8.11	5.89	4.14	7.07	3.97
2013	12.12	8.48	6.06	4.24	6.06	4.24
2014	11.55	8.05	5.78	4.02	5.77	4.03
2015	11.61	8.06	5.32	3.69	6.29	4.37
2016	11.25	7.78	4.64	3.22	6.61	4.57
2017	11.85	8.16	4.17	2.87	7.68	5.29
2018	13.75	9.43	3.92	2.69	9.83	6.74
2019	13.69	9.34	3.41	2.33	10.28	7.01
2020	14.90	10.12	3.41	2.32	11.49	7.80
2021	26.59	17.91	2.84	1.91	23.75	16.00

表 2.5 各区户籍人口迁移(2020~2021)
MIGRATION OF REGISTERED POPULATION IN DISTRICTS

单位:人(person)

地区	District	2020 市外迁入 Inflows from Outside of the City	2020 迁往市外 Outflows To the Outside of the City	2021 市外迁入 Inflows from Outside of the City	2021 迁往市外 Outflows To the Outside of the City
全 市	**Total**	**149 022**	**34 090**	**265 934**	**28 401**
浦东新区	Pudong New Area	40 574	5 243	75 390	4 554
黄 浦 区	Huangpu	3 244	804	4 914	515
徐 汇 区	Xuhui	11 091	4 290	17 273	4 396
长 宁 区	Changning	5 675	1 455	11 183	1 190
静 安 区	Jing'an	5 976	766	9 053	655
普 陀 区	Putuo	6 394	1 053	11 044	659
虹 口 区	Hongkou	4 129	1 087	5 956	995
杨 浦 区	Yangpu	12 009	7 193	19 412	5 684
闵 行 区	Minhang	19 236	3 586	34 809	2 596
宝 山 区	Baoshan	9 414	1 640	16 541	1 407
嘉 定 区	Jiading	9 521	964	18 546	798
金 山 区	Jinshan	1 677	198	4 271	138
松 江 区	Songjiang	12 518	4 586	22 548	3 929
青 浦 区	Qingpu	3 738	638	7 904	552
奉 贤 区	Fengxian	2 305	391	4 830	235
崇 明 区	Chongming	1 521	196	2 260	98

表 2.6 各区户籍人口年龄构成(2021)
AGE STRUCTURE OF REGISTERED POPULATION IN DISTRICTS

单位:万人(10 000 persons)

地区	District	合计 Total	17岁及以下 17 and below	18~34岁 18~34	35~59岁 35~59	60岁及以上 60 and above
全市	**Total**	**1 492.92**	**188.16**	**226.50**	**536.70**	**541.57**
浦东新区	Pudong New Area	320.08	44.99	51.67	118.29	105.13
黄浦区	Huangpu	74.58	7.98	10.61	24.43	31.56
徐汇区	Xuhui	94.01	13.56	15.21	31.33	33.91
长宁区	Changning	57.57	6.45	8.85	19.52	22.74
静安区	Jing'an	90.66	10.65	13.02	30.11	36.88
普陀区	Putuo	89.72	10.61	12.14	29.65	37.32
虹口区	Hongkou	66.58	6.70	9.53	21.62	28.73
杨浦区	Yangpu	104.84	11.91	17.75	33.76	41.41
闵行区	Minhang	123.41	19.86	18.83	45.70	39.02
宝山区	Baoshan	105.31	13.32	14.62	37.74	39.63
嘉定区	Jiading	69.82	9.72	10.04	25.87	24.19
金山区	Jinshan	52.76	5.46	7.61	21.68	18.01
松江区	Songjiang	69.66	10.10	11.79	27.07	20.70
青浦区	Qingpu	51.49	6.18	7.83	20.63	16.85
奉贤区	Fengxian	55.14	5.89	7.92	22.16	19.17
崇明区	Chongming	67.31	4.78	9.08	27.15	26.30

表 2.7 各区户籍老年人口年龄构成(2021)
AGE STRUCTURE OF REGISTERED AGING POPULATION IN DISTRICTS

单位:万人(10 000 persons)

地 区	District	合 计 Total	60~64 岁 60~64	65~79 岁 65~79	80 岁及以上 80 and above
全 市	**Total**	**542.22**	**139.85**	**318.49**	**83.88**
浦东新区	Pudong New Area	105.32	27.11	62.32	15.89
黄 浦 区	Huangpu	31.42	8.67	18.06	4.69
徐 汇 区	Xuhui	33.96	8.36	19.46	6.14
长 宁 区	Changning	22.77	6.00	12.76	4.01
静 安 区	Jing'an	36.94	9.99	21.35	5.60
普 陀 区	Putuo	37.38	10.05	21.94	5.39
虹 口 区	Hongkou	28.66	7.64	16.52	4.50
杨 浦 区	Yangpu	41.44	11.54	23.58	6.32
闵 行 区	Minhang	39.11	9.68	23.31	6.12
宝 山 区	Baoshan	39.76	10.73	23.64	5.39
嘉 定 区	Jiading	24.25	6.08	14.50	3.67
金 山 区	Jinshan	18.03	4.10	11.07	2.86
松 江 区	Songjiang	20.77	4.87	12.69	3.21
青 浦 区	Qingpu	16.88	4.04	10.15	2.69
奉 贤 区	Fengxian	19.21	4.78	11.52	2.91
崇 明 区	Chongming	26.30	6.21	15.60	4.49

表 2.8 主要年份婚姻情况
MARRIAGE STATISTICS IN MAIN YEARS

年份 Year	登记结婚（万对） Marriage Registration (10 000 couples)	初婚（万人） First Marriage (10 000 persons)	再婚（万人） Remarriage (10 000 persons)	其中 of which 女性 Female	离婚（万对） Divorce (10 000 Couples)	其中 of which 民政部门批准 Approved by the Civil Administration	其中 of which 法院调判 Mediated by the Court
1990	10.77	19.49	2.04	1.06	1.64	0.73	0.91
1995	8.40	14.61	2.19	1.09	2.27	0.98	1.29
2000	9.31	15.08	2.89	1.45	3.18	1.76	1.42
2001	9.30	15.23	2.68	1.40	3.15	1.68	1.47
2002	9.10	14.60	3.05	1.40	2.96	1.54	1.42
2003	10.82	17.20	3.97	2.31	3.30	1.98	1.32
2004	12.49	20.27	4.18	2.05	3.63	2.67	0.96
2005	10.27	16.44	4.09	2.05	3.93	3.10	0.83
2006	16.56	27.29	5.83	2.93	4.72	3.78	0.94
2007	12.01	18.10	5.93	2.95	4.69	3.75	0.94
2008	14.16	22.04	6.28	3.17	4.68	3.72	0.96
2009	14.99	23.33	6.65	3.31	4.83	3.92	0.91
2010	13.03	20.10	5.96	2.98	4.67	3.81	0.86
2011	14.89	23.94	5.84	2.90	4.78	3.92	0.86
2012	14.42	22.96	5.88	2.86	5.29	4.42	0.87
2013	14.95	22.17	7.74	3.77	6.96	6.09	0.87
2014	14.19	20.14	8.25	4.06	6.15	5.30	0.85
2015	14.18	19.89	8.47	4.19	6.66	5.83	0.83
2016	12.52	13.79	11.25	4.53	8.26	7.44	0.82
2017	10.87	13.84	7.90	3.92	5.72	5.08	0.64
2018	10.37	14.23	6.51	3.81	5.41	5.18	0.22
2019	9.87	12.01	7.72	3.86	6.17	5.49	0.68
2020	9.22	11.05	7.39	3.75	6.67	6.02	0.65
2021	8.98	11.40	6.57	3.27	6.57	5.81	0.76

表 2.9 主要年份涉外婚姻情况
CHINESE-FOREIGN MARRIAGE IN MAIN YEARS

年 份 Year	涉外婚姻(对) Chinese-Foreign Marriage (couple)	在涉外婚姻中的国内公民(人) In Chinese-Foreign Marriage Chinese Citizens (person)	在国内公民中 Among the Chinese Citizens	
			男 性 Male	女 性 Female
1990	1 345	1 345	136	1 209
1995	3 033	3 030	274	2 756
2000	3 187	3 182	374	2 808
2001	3 447	3 438	399	3 039
2002	2 705	2 690	67	2 623
2003	2 418	2 418	367	2 051
2004	2 636	2 623	417	2 206
2005	2 407	2 385	372	2 013
2006	2 943	2 943	540	2 403
2007	2 495	2 483	109	2 374
2008	2 626	2 553	428	2 125
2009	2 492	2 416	305	2 111
2010	2 231	2 144	414	1 730
2011	2 225	2 125	474	1 651
2012	2 195	2 064	473	1 591
2013	2 054	1 900	430	1 470
2014	1 962	1 817	437	1 380
2015	1 778	1 642	397	1 245
2016	1 684	1 533	433	1 100
2017	1 479	1 347	386	961
2018	1 402	1 269	382	887
2019	1 282	1 246	403	843
2020	723	709	207	502
2021	813	794	245	549

注：本页数据由市民政局和市高级人民法院提供。
Note: This table is provided by Shanghai Civil Affairs Bureau and Shanghai Municipal Senior People's Court.

表 2.10 第七次人口普查常住人口户籍构成
PERMANENT RESIDENTS BY REGISTER FROM THE SEVENTH POPULATION CENSUS

单位:万人(10 000 persons)

地 区	District	合 计 Total	户籍常住 Registered Permanent Residents	外来常住人口 External Permanent Residents
全 市	**Total**	**2 487.09**	**1 439.12**	**1 047.97**
浦东新区	Pudong	568.15	326.15	242.00
黄浦区	Huangpu	66.20	37.67	28.53
徐汇区	Xuhui	111.31	76.87	34.44
长宁区	Changning	69.31	47.17	22.13
静安区	Jing'an	97.57	71.93	25.64
普陀区	Putuo	123.98	87.34	36.64
虹口区	Hongkou	75.75	55.27	20.48
杨浦区	Yangpu	124.25	93.13	31.12
闵行区	Minhang	265.35	141.06	124.29
宝山区	Baoshan	223.52	132.94	90.58
嘉定区	Jiading	183.43	79.73	103.69
金山区	Jinshan	82.28	51.32	30.96
松江区	Songjiang	190.97	79.51	111.46
青浦区	Qingpu	127.14	54.73	72.41
奉贤区	Fengxian	114.09	55.16	58.93
崇明区	Chongming	63.79	49.14	14.65

表 2.11 第七次人口普查常住人口分户籍年龄构成
PERMANENT RESIDENTS BY REGISTER AND AGE FROM THE SEVENTH POPULATION CENSUS

单位:万人(10 000 persons)

项 目	Items	常住人口 Permanent Residents	户籍常住人口 Registered Permanent Residents	外来常住人口 External Permanent Residents
合 计	**Total**	**2 487.09**	**1 439.12**	**1 047.97**
0~4 岁	0-4	85.75	52.14	33.61
5~9 岁	5-9	91.40	59.10	32.30
10~14 岁	10-14	66.48	46.87	19.61
15~19 岁	15-19	71.02	39.50	31.52
20~24 岁	20-24	151.42	44.09	107.33
25~29 岁	25-29	220.58	60.29	160.29
30~34 岁	30-34	274.13	102.67	171.45
35~39 岁	35-39	229.58	121.25	108.33
40~44 岁	40-44	185.75	103.11	82.64
45~49 岁	45-49	177.63	83.98	93.64
50~54 岁	50-54	178.57	89.10	89.47
55~59 岁	55-59	173.24	118.30	54.94
60~64 岁	60-64	176.65	149.92	26.73
65~69 岁	65-69	164.76	143.78	20.98
70~74 岁	70-74	101.40	92.97	8.43
75~79 岁	75-79	55.16	51.60	3.56
80 岁及以上	Above 80	83.59	80.46	3.13

表 2.12 第七次人口普查常住人口分地区年龄构成
PERMANENT RESIDENTS BY DISTRICT AND AGE FROM THE SEVENTH POPULATION CENSUS

单位:万人(10 000 persons)

地 区	District	合 计 Total	0~14 岁 0-14	15~59 岁 15-59	60 岁及以上 Above 60	65 岁及以上 Above 65	80 岁及以上 Above 80
全 市	**Total**	**2 487.09**	**243.63**	**1 661.91**	**581.55**	**404.90**	**83.59**
浦东新区	Pudong	568.15	59.56	385.70	122.89	85.15	16.59
黄 浦 区	Huangpu	66.20	5.74	42.85	17.61	12.24	2.91
徐 汇 区	Xuhui	111.31	10.90	68.45	31.96	22.94	5.59
长 宁 区	Changning	69.31	6.16	42.98	20.17	14.31	3.71
静 安 区	Jing'an	97.57	9.09	57.69	30.80	21.44	4.78
普 陀 区	Putuo	123.98	11.64	74.45	37.89	26.19	5.38
虹 口 区	Hongkou	75.75	6.20	44.39	25.16	17.60	4.08
杨 浦 区	Yangpu	124.25	10.98	73.78	39.49	27.16	6.26
闵 行 区	Minhang	265.35	28.83	182.88	53.64	37.21	7.11
宝 山 区	Baoshan	223.52	22.36	150.06	51.10	34.39	6.32
嘉 定 区	Jiading	183.43	17.99	132.69	32.74	22.13	4.09
金 山 区	Jinshan	82.28	7.58	55.30	19.39	14.01	2.79
松 江 区	Songjiang	190.97	20.46	140.36	30.15	20.83	3.70
青 浦 区	Qingpu	127.14	11.27	94.72	21.16	14.70	2.90
奉 贤 区	Fengxian	114.09	10.59	81.41	22.09	15.70	3.10
崇 明 区	Chongming	63.79	4.27	34.22	25.31	18.90	4.31

表 2.13 第七次人口普查每十万人中各种文化程度人口
VARIOUS EDUCATION ATTAINMENTS POPULATION IN EVERY ONE HUNDRED THOUSAND PEOPLE FROM THE SEVENTH POPULATION CENSUS

单位:人(person)

地 区	District	小 学 Primary Schools	初 中 Junior Secondary Schools	高 中 Senior Secondary Schools	大学及以上 College Students and above
全 市	**Total**	**11 929**	**28 935**	**19 020**	**33 872**
浦东新区	Pudong	11 789	28 904	17 116	35 834
黄 浦 区	Huangpu	9 895	31 052	22 538	32 274
徐 汇 区	Xuhui	8 383	20 509	20 528	45 936
长 宁 区	Changning	7 827	20 996	21 423	45 242
静 安 区	Jing'an	7 873	22 875	23 998	40 541
普 陀 区	Putuo	8 317	22 606	23 229	40 888
虹 口 区	Hongkou	7 685	22 977	24 122	41 023
杨 浦 区	Yangpu	7 792	22 485	23 069	42 009
闵 行 区	Minhang	11 156	26 056	18 273	38 133
宝 山 区	Baoshan	10 573	30 301	20 869	32 488
嘉 定 区	Jiading	12 187	35 537	17 926	27 927
金 山 区	Jinshan	19 038	36 059	15 975	19 948
松 江 区	Songjiang	13 589	29 643	18 220	30 636
青 浦 区	Qingpu	16 658	35 660	16 856	22 803
奉 贤 区	Fengxian	18 895	36 660	15 248	21 268
崇 明 区	Chongming	23 457	41 234	14 493	12 938

表 2.14 第七次人口普查外省市来沪人口主要来源地
MAIN ORIGINS OF EXTERNAL PERMANENT RESIDENTS FROM THE SEVENTH POPULATION CENSUS

单位:万人(10 000 persons)

地区	District	合计 Total	男 Male	女 Female
总计	**Total**	**1 047.97**	**578.91**	**469.06**
北京市	Beijing	3.51	1.91	1.60
天津市	Tianjing	2.26	1.14	1.13
河北省	Hebei	12.55	7.03	5.52
山西省	Shanxi	11.84	6.71	5.13
内蒙古	Inner Mongolia	4.72	2.38	2.33
辽宁省	Liaoning	12.29	5.99	6.31
吉林省	Jilin	10.58	5.16	5.42
黑龙江省	Heilongjiang	16.56	7.95	8.62
江苏省	Jiangsu	179.83	100.92	78.91
浙江省	Zhejiang	51.56	26.44	25.12
安徽省	Anhui	242.65	133.72	108.93
福建省	Fujian	29.48	16.16	13.32
江西省	Jiangxi	50.22	27.66	22.56
山东省	Shandong	50.12	29.34	20.78
河南省	Henan	134.30	80.02	54.28
湖北省	Hubei	41.77	22.04	19.73
湖南省	Hunan	23.75	12.13	11.62
广东省	Guangdong	12.27	6.77	5.50
广西壮族自治区	Guangxi	8.47	4.30	4.16
海南省	Hainan	1.81	0.91	0.91
重庆市	Chongqing	18.91	10.17	8.75
四川省	Sichuan	51.75	27.64	24.10
贵州省	Guizhou	18.87	10.43	8.44
云南省	Yunnan	13.92	7.85	6.07
西藏自治区	Tibet	0.26	0.10	0.17
陕西省	Shaanxi	18.52	10.58	7.94
甘肃省	Gansu	17.81	9.98	7.83
青海省	Qinghai	1.27	0.65	0.63
宁夏回族自治区	Ningxia	1.69	0.90	0.78
新疆维吾尔自治区	Xinjiang	4.42	1.94	2.48

表 2.15 历次人口普查资料
INFORMATION OF PREVIOUS POPULATION CENSUS

指 标	Indicators	第一次普查 (1953 年) First Census	第二次普查 (1964 年) Second Census
人口密度(人/平方公里)	Population Density (person/sq.km.)	1 622	1 749
平均每户人数(人/户)	Average Household Size (person/household)	4.7	4.5
常住人口(万人)	Permanent Residents (10 000 persons)	620.44	1 081.65
#户籍常住人口	Registered Permanent Residents	615.24	1 076.34
外来常住人口	External Permanent Residents		
外省市来沪人口主要来源地(%)	Main Origins of External Permanent Residents(%)		
安 徽	Anhui		
江 苏	Jiangsu		
四 川	Sichuan		
河 南	Henan		
浙 江	Zhejiang		
江 西	Jiangxi		
按性别分(万人)	By gender(10 000 persons)		
男	Male	331.96	536.90
女	Female	288.48	544.74
按年龄构成分(%)	By age(%)		
0~14 岁	0-14	33.0	42.3
15~64 岁	15-64	65.0	54.1
65 岁及以上	Above 65	2.0	3.6
按民族构成分(万人)	By Ethnicity(10 000 persons)		
汉 族	Han		
少数民族	Ethnic Minorities	3.15	4.37
受教育程度(%)	Education attainments(%)		
大专及以上	Junior College and Above		2.2
高 中	Senior Secondary School		5.2
初 中	Junior Secondary School		13.0
小学及以下	Primary School and Below		79.6
就业人口占总人口比重(%)	The Proportion of Employed Population in Total Population (%)		62.7
婚姻状况(%)	Marriage Situation (%)		
未 婚	Single		
有配偶	Married		
离 婚	Divorced		
丧 偶	Widowed		

单位：万人（10 000 persons）

第三次普查（1982 年）Third Census	第四次普查（1990 年）Fourth Census	第五次普查（2000 年）Fifth Census	第六次普查（2010 年）Sixth Census	第七次普查（2020 年）Seventh Census
1 917	2 104	2 588	3 631	3 923
3.6	3.1	2.8	2.5	2.3
1 185.97	1 334.19	1 640.77	2 301.92	2 487.09
1 177.89	1 277.28	1 327.28	1 404.22	1 439.12
		313.49	898	1 047
		34.5	30.2	23.2
		22.4	19.8	17.2
		7.7	7.5	4.9
		4.7	6.4	12.8
		7.2	6.4	4.9
		6.0	5.8	4.8
591.00	680.61	843.03	1 185.49	1 287.52
594.97	653.58	797.75	1 116.43	1 199.57
18.2	18.2	12.2	8.6	9.8
74.4	72.4	76.3	81.3	73.9
7.4	9.4	11.5	10.1	16.3
	1 327.96	1 630.39	2 274.30	2 447.11
4.97	6.22	10.36	27.62	39.98
3.8	7.1	11.4	22.8	35.4
22.0	21.1	23.9	21.8	19.8
30.4	34.2	38.2	38.1	30.2
43.8	37.6	26.5	17.3	14.6
62.2	60.4	51.3	55.6	52.4
30.6	18.1	19.8	21.4	20.2
62.1	74.6	73.4	72.3	72.2
0.6	0.9	1.6	2.0	3.1
6.7	6.4	5.2	4.3	4.5

表 2.16 规模以上工业企业按职业类型分从业人员期末人数(2021)
THE EMPLOYED POPULATION AT THE END OF THE PERIOD BY OCCUPATION TYPE OF INDUSTRIAL ENTERPRISES ABOVE DESIGNATED SIZE

类 别	Types	从业人员期末人数 Number of Employees at the end of the Period
总 计	**Total**	**178.38**
按登记注册类型分	**Grouped by Registration Categories**	
内 资	Domestic Funded	89.37
#国 有	State-owned	1.07
集 体	Collective-owned	0.30
有限责任公司	Companies with Limited Liabilities	23.62
股份有限公司	Share-holding Companies with Limited Liabilities	10.60
私 营	Private	47.26
港澳台商投资	Hong Kong, Macao and Taiwan Funded	27.17
#与港澳台商合资经营	Joint-venture	6.46
港澳台商独资	Sole Funded	18.89
港澳台商投资股份有限公司	Share-holding Companies Ltd.	1.37
外商投资	Foreign Funded	61.84
#中外合资经营	Joint-venture	16.05
外资企业	Sole Funded	41.19
外商投资股份有限公司	Share-holding Companies Ltd.	2.07
按企业规模分	**Grouped by Size of Enterprises**	
大 型	Large	61.20
中 型	Medium	45.92
小 型	Small	71.26
按行业分	**Grouped by Sectors**	
采矿业	Mining Industry	0.17
石油和天然气开采业	Petroleum and Natural Gas Exploiting	0.17
制造业	Manufacture Industry	174.83
农副食品加工业	Farm and Sideline Products Processing	2.38
食品制造业	Food Manufacturing	6.04
酒、饮料和精制茶制造业	Wine, Beverage and Refined Tea Manufacturing	0.91
烟草制品业	Tabacco Manufacturing	0.35
纺织业	Textile	1.70
纺织服装、服饰业	Textiles and Clothing Industry	2.62
皮革、毛皮、羽毛及其制品和制鞋业	Leather, Fur, Wool Products and Shoes Manufacturing	0.91

单位：万人(10 000 persons)

其　中 of which				
中层及以上管理人员 Managers Above Middle level	专业技术人员 Professional and Technical Personnel	办事人员和有关人员 Clerical and Related Personnel	社会生产服务和生活服务人员 Social Production Service and Life Service Personnel	生产制造及有关人员 Manufacturing and Related Personnel
14.73	**30.79**	**23.37**	**6.08**	**103.40**
8.41	17.57	11.56	2.95	48.88
0.07	0.25	0.21	0.03	0.51
0.03	0.04	0.03	…	0.20
1.77	5.96	3.05	0.78	12.06
0.84	3.28	1.49	0.57	4.42
5.23	6.25	5.87	1.31	28.60
1.80	3.74	3.55	0.78	17.30
0.53	1.09	0.74	0.14	3.96
1.08	2.35	2.52	0.50	12.45
0.14	0.25	0.23	0.12	0.63
4.52	9.48	8.27	2.36	37.22
1.14	3.07	2.09	0.60	9.15
3.09	5.54	5.60	1.15	25.81
0.08	0.60	0.26	0.31	0.81
2.91	12.80	7.35	2.17	35.97
3.49	7.97	6.18	1.96	26.32
8.34	10.02	9.85	1.95	41.11
0.02	0.07	0.05		0.04
0.02	0.07	0.05		0.04
14.37	30.21	22.83	5.66	101.76
0.21	0.15	0.34	0.18	1.50
0.44	0.53	1.49	0.54	3.04
0.06	0.08	0.18	0.25	0.34
0.04	0.05	0.04	…	0.22
0.17	0.20	0.20	0.04	1.09
0.23	0.18	0.32	0.12	1.76
0.06	0.03	0.06	0.04	0.72

表 2.16 续表 continued

	类 别 Types	从业人员期末人数 Number of Employees at the end of the Period
木材加工和木、竹、藤、棕、草制品业	Timber Processing and Timber, Bamboo, Rattan, Coir and Straw Products Manufacturing	0.39
家具制造业	Furniture Manufacturing	2.37
造纸和纸制品业	Paper-making and Paper Products Manufacturing	2.08
印刷和记录媒介复制业	Printing and Record Duplicating	2.45
文教、工美、体育和娱乐用品制造业	Culture, Education, Industrial Arts, Sports and Entertainment Goods Manufacturing	1.82
石油、煤炭及其他燃料加工业	Oil, Coal and Other Fuel Processing	1.30
化学原料和化学制品制造业	Raw Chemical Materials and Chemical Products Manufacturing	10.31
医药制造业	Medicine Manufacturing	6.27
化学纤维制造业	Chemical Fiber Manufacturing	0.14
橡胶和塑料制品业	Rubber and Plastic Products Manufacturing	8.21
非金属矿物制品业	Non-metallic Mineral Products Manufacturing	3.92
黑色金属冶炼和压延加工业	Ferrous Metal Smelting and Rolling Processing Industry	2.09
有色金属冶炼和压延加工业	Nonferrous Metal Smelting and Rolling Processing Industry	1.16
金属制品业	Metal Products Manufacturing	8.74
通用设备制造业	General Equipment Manufacturing	21.41
专用设备制造业	Special Purpose Equipment Manufacturing	11.83
汽车制造业	The Automotive Manufacturing	21.26
铁路、船舶、航空航天和其他运输设备制造业	The Railroad, Marine, Aerospace and Other Transportation Equipment Manufacturing	3.99
电气机械和器材制造业	Electric Machinery Equipments and Manufacturing	13.78
计算机、通信和其他电子设备制造业	Computer, Communications and Other Electronic Equipment Manufacturing	28.87
仪器仪表制造业	Instrumentation Manufacturing	3.86
其他制造业	Other Manufacturing	0.74
废弃资源综合利用业	Comprehensive Utilization of Waste Resources	0.20
金属制品、机械和设备修理业	Metal Products, Machinery and Equipment Repair Industry	2.69
电力、热力、燃气及水生产和供应业	**Electricity, Heat, Gas and Water Production and Supply Industry**	**3.38**
电力、热力生产和供应业	Production and Supply of Electricity and Thermal Power	1.82
燃气生产和供应业	Production and Supply of Gas	0.58
水的生产和供应业	Production and Supply of Water	0.97

单位:万人(10 000 persons)

其中 of which				
中层及以上管理人员 Managers Above Middle level	专业技术人员 Professional and Technical Personnel	办事人员和有关人员 Clerical and Related Personnel	社会生产服务和生活服务人员 Social Production Service and Life Service Personnel	生产制造及有关人员 Manufacturing and Related Personnel
0.04	0.02	0.05	0.01	0.27
0.22	0.22	0.37	0.04	1.51
0.20	0.12	0.22	0.02	1.52
0.26	0.26	0.27	0.05	1.61
0.17	0.18	0.28	0.09	1.10
0.05	0.33	0.14	…	0.78
1.21	1.76	1.84	0.42	5.08
0.60	1.40	0.96	0.71	2.60
0.01	0.01	0.01	0.01	0.10
0.77	0.78	0.96	0.18	5.52
0.41	0.48	0.50	0.10	2.43
0.20	0.45	0.08	0.02	1.34
0.12	0.13	0.15	0.01	0.74
0.79	1.00	0.93	0.19	5.83
2.08	4.28	3.49	0.74	10.83
1.21	2.69	1.81	0.41	5.71
1.32	4.29	2.30	0.25	13.11
0.24	1.45	0.54	0.07	1.69
1.22	2.36	1.95	0.50	7.77
1.37	4.48	2.07	0.40	20.55
0.42	0.86	0.66	0.23	1.69
0.07	0.08	0.12	0.02	0.45
0.03	0.03	0.04	0.01	0.10
0.13	1.33	0.46	0.03	0.75
0.35	**0.51**	**0.49**	**0.42**	**1.61**
0.21	0.25	0.28	0.01	1.08
0.04	0.09	0.08	0.30	0.09
0.10	0.18	0.13	0.12	0.45

表 2.17 规模以上服务业企业按职业类型分从业人员期末人数(2021)
THE EMPLOYED POPULATION AT THE END OF THE PERIOD BY OCCUPATION TYPE OF SERVICE ENTERPRISES ABOVE DESIGNATED SIZE

类 别	Types	从业人员期末人数 Number of Employees at the end of the Period
总 计	**Total**	**347.90**
按登记注册类型分	**Grouped by Registration Categories**	
内 资	Domestic Funded	257.30
#国 有	State-owned	9.43
集 体	Collective-owned	1.08
有限责任公司	Companies with Limited Liabilities	89.47
股份有限公司	Share-holding Companies with Limited Liabilities	18.62
私 营	Private	117.79
港澳台商投资	Hong Kong, Macao and Taiwan Funded	46.83
#与港澳台商合资经营	Joint-venture	10.75
港澳台商独资	Sole Funded	30.62
港澳台商投资股份有限公司	Share-holding Companies Ltd.	2.71
外商投资	Foreign Funded	43.77
#中外合资经营	Joint-venture	14.18
外资企业	Sole Funded	25.63
外商投资股份有限公司	Share-holding Companies Ltd.	1.50
按行业分	**Grouped by Sectors**	
交通运输、仓储和邮政业	**Transportation, Warehousing and Postal Service Industry**	**60.03**
铁路运输业	Railway Transportation	3.33
道路运输业	Road Transportation	18.25
水上运输业	Water Transportation	2.72
航空运输业	Air Transportation	8.35
管道运输业	Pipeline Transportation	0.10
多式联运和运输代理业	Multimodal Transport and Ttransport Agency	14.04
装卸搬运和仓储业	Handling and Warehousing	4.79
邮政业	Postal	8.45
信息传输、软件和信息技术服务业	**Information Transmission, Software and Information Technology Service Industry**	**68.15**
电信、广播电视和卫星传输服务	Telecommunications, Radio, Television and Satellite Transmission Service	4.44
互联网和相关服务	Internet and Related Services Service	17.46
软件和信息技术服务业	Software and Information Technology Service	46.25

单位:万人(10 000 persons)

其中 of which				
中层及以上管理人员 Managers Above Middle Level	专业技术人员 Professional and Technical Personnel	办事人员和有关人员 Clerical and Related Personnel	社会生产服务和生活服务人员 Social Production Service and Life Service Personnel	生产制造及有关人员 Manufacturing and Related Personnel
30.92	**94.58**	**80.96**	**119.32**	**22.12**
19.54	66.34	51.51	100.26	19.65
0.46	1.72	2.04	4.68	0.53
0.12	0.05	0.27	0.57	0.08
6.25	24.90	17.13	33.51	7.68
1.44	7.45	2.67	6.51	0.56
9.92	27.60	24.52	46.70	9.05
5.38	13.54	14.40	12.36	1.13
0.94	3.61	1.72	4.11	0.36
3.93	8.97	10.49	6.67	0.56
0.13	0.16	1.80	0.60	0.02
5.99	14.69	15.05	6.70	1.34
1.95	3.01	6.89	1.44	0.89
3.75	9.80	7.64	4.03	0.42
0.11	0.90	0.28	0.19	0.01
4.33	**6.83**	**13.03**	**26.96**	**8.89**
0.02	…	0.15	3.16	
0.94	0.97	1.93	9.04	5.37
0.27	0.65	0.67	0.70	0.42
0.40	3.07	1.11	3.15	0.62
0.01	0.02	0.01	0.03	0.03
1.87	1.54	6.41	3.10	1.12
0.39	0.36	0.70	2.16	1.19
0.42	0.22	2.06	5.61	0.13
5.72	**38.34**	**13.44**	**9.71**	**0.94**
0.27	1.44	0.69	1.90	0.14
1.21	7.37	5.39	3.37	0.12
4.24	29.52	7.36	4.45	0.68

表 2.17 续表 continued

	类 别 Types	从业人员期末人数 Number of Employees at the end of the Period
房地产业(除房地产开发经营外)	**Real Estate Industry (Except for Real Estate Development and Operation)**	**34.84**
租赁和商务服务业	**Leasing and Business Service Industry**	**104.44**
租赁业	Leasing	1.66
商务服务业	Business Service	102.78
科学研究和技术服务业	**Scientific Research and Technical Service Industry**	**40.18**
研究和试验发展	Research and Experimental Development	10.17
专业技术服务业	Professional Technical Service	25.55
科技推广和应用服务业	Science and Technology Promotion and Application Service	4.45
水利、环境和公共设施管理业	**Water Conservancy, Environment and Public Facilities Management Industry**	**10.66**
水利管理业	Water Conservancy Management	0.11
生态保护和环境治理业	Ecological Protection and Environmental Governance	0.82
公共设施管理业	Public Facilities Management	9.67
土地管理业	Land Management	0.06
居民服务、修理和其他服务业	**Residential Services, Repairs and Other Service Industries**	**12.36**
居民服务业	Resident Service	2.11
机动车、电子产品和日用品修理业	Automobile, Electronic Products and Daily Necessities Repair Industry	1.82
其他服务业	Other Services	8.43
教 育	**Education**	**6.25**
卫生和社会工作	**Health and Social Work**	**6.02**
卫 生	Health	5.43
社会工作	Social Work	0.59
文化、体育和娱乐业	**Culture, Sports and Entertainment**	**4.97**
新闻和出版业	Press and publishing	0.68
广播、电视、电影和影视录音制作业	Radio, Television, Film and Television Recording and Production Industry	1.11
文化艺术业	Culture and Art Industry	0.32
体 育	Sports	0.94
娱乐业	Entertainment	1.92

单位:万人(10 000 persons)

其　中　of which				
中层及以上管理人员 Managers Above Middle Level	专业技术人员 Professional and Technical Personnel	办事人员和有关人员 Clerical and Related Personnel	社会生产服务和生活服务人员 Social Production Service and Life Service Personnel	生产制造及有关人员 Manufacturing and Related Personnel
2.93	**3.11**	**7.81**	**20.62**	**0.37**
10.63	**14.61**	**32.95**	**39.30**	**6.95**
0.21	0.15	0.46	0.56	0.29
10.42	14.46	32.49	38.74	6.67
4.39	**23.96**	**6.61**	**2.75**	**2.47**
1.20	6.14	1.59	0.91	0.33
2.62	15.73	3.85	1.48	1.88
0.56	2.10	1.17	0.36	0.26
0.50	**0.72**	**0.83**	**7.26**	**1.34**
0.01	0.05	0.02	…	0.03
0.09	0.19	0.10	0.14	0.30
0.38	0.47	0.69	7.11	1.01
0.02	0.02	0.02	0.01	
0.70	**0.73**	**1.07**	**8.89**	**0.96**
0.22	0.25	0.36	1.17	0.11
0.17	**0.32**	**0.36**	**0.61**	**0.35**
0.31	0.16	0.34	7.11	0.51
0.56	**2.26**	**2.23**	**1.15**	**0.05**
0.60	**2.90**	**1.69**	**0.76**	**0.07**
0.54	2.80	1.58	0.43	0.07
0.06	0.10	0.10	0.33	
0.56	**1.11**	**1.31**	**1.92**	**0.07**
0.14	0.34	0.17	0.02	0.02
0.16	0.41	0.32	0.20	0.02
0.04	0.10	0.10	0.07	0.01
0.10	0.09	0.27	0.47	0.01
0.14	0.17	0.45	1.15	0.01

表 2.18 限额以上批发和零售业企业按职业类型分从业人员期末人数(2021)
THE EMPLOYED POPULATION AT THE END OF THE PERIOD BY OCCUPATION TYPE OF ENTERPRISES ABOVE DESIGNATED SIZE OF WHOLESALE AND RETAIL TRADE

类别	Types	从业人员期末人数 Number of Employees at the end of the Period
总计	**Total**	**111.98**
按登记注册类型分	**Grouped by Registration Categories**	
内资	Domestic Funded	50.68
#国有	State-owned	0.99
集体	Collective-owned	0.10
有限责任公司	Companies with Limited Liabilities	17.23
股份有限公司	Share-holding Companies with Limited Liabilities	3.95
私营	Private	26.80
港澳台商投资	Hong Kong, Macao and Taiwan Funded	25.54
#与港澳台商合资经营	Joint-venture	1.75
港澳台商独资	Sole Funded	22.27
港澳台商投资股份有限公司	Share-holding Companies Ltd.	0.89
外商投资	Foreign Funded	35.76
#中外合资经营	Joint-venture	3.11
外资企业	Sole Funded	31.19
外商投资股份有限公司	Share-holding Companies Ltd.	1.21
按行业分	**Grouped by Sector**	
批发和零售业	Wholesale and Retail	111.98
批发业	Wholesale Trade	72.78
零售业	Retail Trade	39.20

单位：万人（10 000 persons）

其　中 of which				
中层及以上管理人员 Managers Above Middle Level	专业技术人员 Professional and Technical Personnel	办事人员和有关人员 Clerical and Related Personnel	社会生产服务和生活服务人员 Social Production Service and Life Service Personnel	生产制造及有关人员 Manufacturing and Related Personnel
14.45	**13.76**	**44.52**	**34.82**	**4.41**
6.95	5.82	20.80	14.03	3.07
0.13	0.15	0.37	0.30	0.05
0.01	0.01	0.01	0.07	0.01
2.03	2.21	6.19	5.90	0.90
0.45	0.58	1.02	1.34	0.56
4.14	2.69	12.77	5.77	1.44
2.69	2.74	10.49	9.05	0.58
0.25	0.28	0.96	0.21	0.04
2.28	2.28	8.94	8.24	0.53
0.11	0.06	0.39	0.33	…
4.81	5.20	13.24	11.74	0.77
0.32	0.37	1.10	1.14	0.18
4.34	4.43	11.51	10.35	0.56
0.10	0.39	0.49	0.20	0.02
14.45	13.76	44.52	34.82	4.41
11.36	11.38	32.30	14.84	2.90
3.10	2.38	12.22	19.99	1.52

表 2.19 限额以上住宿和餐饮业企业按职业类型分从业人员期末人数(2021)

THE EMPLOYED POPULATION AT THE END OF THE PERIOD BY OCCUPATION TYPE OF ENTERPRISES ABOVE DESIGNATED SIZE OF HOTELS AND CATERING SERVICES

类 别	Types	从业人员期末人数 Number of Employees at the end of the Period
总 计	**Total**	**39.91**
按登记注册类型分	**Grouped by Registration Categories**	
内 资	Domestic Funded	20.30
#国 有	State-owned	0.64
集 体	Collective-owned	0.13
有限责任公司	Companies with Limited Liabilities	5.60
股份有限公司	Share-holding Companies with Limited Liabilities	0.63
私 营	Private	12.33
港澳台商投资	Hong Kong, Macao and Taiwan Funded	8.23
#与港澳台商合资经营	Joint-venture	1.94
港澳台商独资	Sole Funded	5.93
港澳台商投资股份有限公司	Share-holding Companies Ltd.	0.02
外商投资	Foreign Funded	11.39
#中外合资经营	Joint-venture	0.36
外资企业	Sole Funded	10.25
外商投资股份有限公司	Share-holding Companies Ltd.	0.02
按行业分	**Grouped by Sector**	
住宿和餐饮业	Hotels and Catering	39.91
住宿业	Accommodation	7.12
餐饮业	Catering	32.79

单位：万人（10 000 persons）

其　中　of which				
中层及以上管理人员 Managers Above Middle Level	专业技术人员 Professional and Technical Personnel	办事人员和有关人员 Clerical and Related Personnel	社会生产服务和生活服务人员 Social Production Service and Life Service Personnel	生产制造及有关人员 Manufacturing and Related Personnel
3.09	**1.03**	**2.69**	**31.61**	**1.49**
2.26	0.86	2.02	13.79	1.37
0.07	0.02	0.21	0.32	0.02
0.01	0.01	0.01	0.10	
0.54	0.27	0.63	3.96	0.20
0.07	0.03	0.06	0.41	0.06
1.49	0.46	1.00	8.31	1.07
0.56	0.09	0.33	7.17	0.08
0.21	0.02	0.03	1.68	0.01
0.33	0.07	0.27	5.21	0.06
…	…	…	0.01	…
0.26	0.08	0.34	10.66	0.05
0.04	0.01	0.02	0.28	0.01
0.17	0.06	0.30	9.68	0.04
…	…	…	0.02	
3.09	1.03	2.69	31.61	1.49
0.92	0.38	1.19	4.52	0.11
2.17	0.65	1.50	27.10	1.38

表 2.20 有资质的建筑业和房地产开发企业按职业类型分从业人员期末人数(2021)

THE EMPLOYED POPULATION AT THE END OF THE PERIOD BY OCCUPATION TYPE OF QUALIFIED CONSTRUCTION AND REAL ESTATE DEVELOPMENT ENTERPRISES

类别	Types	从业人员期末人数 Number of Employees at the end of the Period
总计	**Total**	**51.72**
按登记注册类型分	**Grouped by Registration Categories**	
内资	Domestic Funded	49.24
#国有	State-owned	0.72
集体	Collective-owned	0.69
有限责任公司	Companies with Limited Liabilities	18.49
股份有限公司	Share-holding Companies with Limited Liabilities	2.51
私营	Private	22.27
港澳台商投资	Hong Kong, Macao and Taiwan Funded	1.59
#与港澳台商合资经营	Joint-venture	0.68
港澳台商独资	Sole Funded	0.64
港澳台商投资股份有限公司	Share-holding Companies Ltd.	0.05
外商投资	Foreign Funded	0.88
#中外合资经营	Joint-venture	0.24
外资企业	Sole Funded	0.55
外商投资股份有限公司	Share-holding Companies Ltd.	…
按行业分	**Grouped by Sector**	
建筑业	Construction Industry	46.17
房屋建筑业	Housing Construction Industry	23.27
土木工程建筑业	Civil Engineering Industry	11.51
建筑安装业	Construction and Installation Industry	5.72
建筑装饰、装修和其他建筑业	Construction and Decoration Industry and Other Construction Industry	5.67
房地产业	Real Estate	5.55

单位：万人(10 000 persons)

其 中 of which				
中层及以上管理人员 Managers Above Middle Level	专业技术人员 Professional and Technical Personnel	办事人员和有关人员 Clerical and Related Personnel	社会生产服务和生活服务人员 Social Production Service and Life Service Personnel	生产制造及有关人员 Manufacturing and Related Personnel
5.36	**16.54**	**9.56**	**2.46**	**17.79**
4.95	15.76	8.81	2.19	17.53
0.10	0.28	0.13	0.01	0.21
0.03	0.41	0.08	…	0.17
1.77	7.04	3.22	0.73	5.72
0.21	1.49	0.36	0.03	0.42
2.24	4.54	3.90	1.25	10.34
0.25	0.44	0.52	0.24	0.14
0.10	0.19	0.23	0.07	0.09
0.11	0.15	0.25	0.10	0.02
0.01	0.01	0.01	0.02	
0.16	0.34	0.23	0.03	0.12
0.04	0.08	0.06	0.02	0.04
0.11	0.22	0.15	0.01	0.06
…		…	…	
4.10	15.20	7.36	1.78	17.73
1.61	8.01	2.86	0.67	10.13
1.20	3.64	1.90	0.79	3.98
0.67	1.77	1.22	0.21	1.85
0.62	1.78	1.37	0.12	1.77
1.26	1.34	2.20	0.68	0.07

表 2.21 主要年份城镇登记失业人数和城镇登记失业率
QUANTITY OF URBAN REGISTERED UNEMPLOYMENT AND URBAN REGISTERED UNEMPLOYMENT RATE IN MAIN YEARS

指标	Indicators	2000	2010	2020	2021
城乡登记失业人数(万人)	Registered Urban Unemployment (10 000 persons)	20.08	27.73	13.54	14.40
城镇登记失业率(%)	Registered Urban Unemployment Rate (%)	3.5	4.2	3.7	2.7

表 2.22 主要年份新增就业岗位
NEWLY ADDED WORKING POST IN MAIN YEARS

指标	Indicators	2003	2010	2020	2021
新增就业岗位(万个)	Newly Added Working Post (10 000 units)	46.20	63.15	57.04	63.51

表 2.23 主要年份离休、退休及退职职工人数
QUANTITY OF RETIRED, RETIRED VETERAN CADRES AND RESIGNED PERSONS IN MAIN YEARS

单位:万人(10 000 persons)

指标	Indicators	2000	2010	2020	2021
总计	**Total**	**234.23**	**352.02**	**521.77**	**528.35**
国有单位	State-owned Units	165.55	166.38	160.69	159.99
离休	Retired Veteran Cadres	3.39	1.82	0.73	0.64
退休	Retired	161.03	160.53	158.23	159.35
退职	Resigned	1.13	4.03	1.73	
集体单位	Collective-owned Units	50.22	46.97	43.88	43.81
离休	Retired Veteran Cadres	0.10	0.04	0.02	0.01
退休	Retired	48.40	45.15	42.82	43.80
退职	Resigned	1.72	1.78	1.04	
其他单位	Other Ownership Units	18.46	138.67	317.20	324.55
离休	Retired Veteran Cadres	0.21	0.68	0.27	0.24
退休	Retired	18.05	132.29	310.24	324.31
退职	Resigned	0.20	5.70	6.69	

注：从 2021 年起，退休职工人数中含退职职工(下表同)。
Note: Since 2021, the quantity of retired person contains resigned person(Same as follows).

表 2.24　城镇单位就业人员平均工资(2019~2021)
AVERAGE WAGES OF EMPLOYEES IN URBAN UNITS

单位:元(yuan)

指　标	Indicators	2019	2020	2021
城镇非私营单位就业人员平均工资	Average Wages of Employees in Urban Non-Private Units	149 377	171 884	191 844
城镇私营单位就业人员平均工资	Average Wages of Employees in Urban Private Units	64 226	80 134	96 011

注：从 2020 起，抽样调查单位的样本由国家统计局统一抽取，样本中不含村居委会以及从业人员规模在 5 人及以下的单位。 从业人员和工资数据由国家统计局反馈。

Note：Since 2020, the samples of sampling survey units are drawn by National Bureau of Statistics.The samples do not include rural residents committees and units with five employees and below. Employees and wages data are refleeted by National Bureau of Statistics.

表 2.25　主要年份离退休(职)人员养老金
PENSION FOR NONWORKING STAFF AND WORKERS IN MAIN YEARS

单位:亿元(100 million yuan)

指　标	Indicators	2000	2010	2020	2021
离退休、退职人员养老金	**Pension for Nonworking Staff and Workers**	**205.14**	**783.42**	**2 882.95**	**3 102.16**
离休人员养老金	Pensions for Retired Veteran Cadres	7.32	11.41	12.46	14.63
退休(职)人员养老金	Pensions for Retired Living Expenses for the Resigned	197.82	772.01	2 870.49	3 087.53

表 2.26　离退休(职)人员养老金(2021)
PENSION FOR NONWORKING STAFF AND WORKERS

单位:亿元(100 million yuan)

指　标	Indicators	合　计 Total	国有单位 State-owned Units	集体单位 Collective-owned Units	其他单位 Other Ownership Units
离退休、退职人员养老金	**Pension for Nonworking Staff and Workers**	**3 102.16**	**1 184.94**	**2 36.77**	**1 680.45**
离休人员养老金	Pensions for Retired Veteran Cadres	14.63	10.05	0.26	4.32
退休(职)人员养老金	Pensions for Retired	3 087.53	1 174.89	236.51	1 676.13

注：本表“其他单位”包括港澳台及外商企业。

Note：“Other Ownership Units” in this table includes foreign invested and HongKong,Macao and Taiwan funded enterprises.

上/海/统/计/年/鉴

主要统计指标解释

■ 人　口

人口数为每年12月31日的年末总人口。根据统计口径的不同，分为户籍人口和常住人口。户籍人口是指在公安部门办理了户籍登记的人口。常住人口是指实际上经常居住在一个地方(住所)的人口，包括：一在调查时点具有上海户籍且实际居住在上海的人口；二在调查时点具有上海户籍且离开上海不足半年的人口；三在调查时点具有上海户籍且在境外工作学习但未定居的人口；四在调查时点实际居住在上海的、离开户籍登记地满半年及以上外省市户籍人口。

■ 出生率

出生率(又称粗出生率)指在一定时期内(通常为一年)一定地区的出生人数与同期平均人数(或期中人数)之比，一般用千分率表示。计算公式：

$$出生率=\frac{年出生人数}{年平均人数}\times 1000‰$$

出生人数是指活产婴儿，即胎儿脱离母体时(不管怀孕月数)，有过呼吸或其他生命现象。年平均人数是年初、年底人口数的平均数，也可用年中人口数代替。

■ 死亡率

死亡率(又称粗死亡率)指在一定时期内(通常为一年)一定地区的死亡人数与同期平均人数(或期中人数)之比，一般用千分率表示。计算公式：

$$死亡率=\frac{年死亡人数}{年平均人数}\times 1000‰$$

■ 人口自然增长率

指在一定时期内(通常为一年)人口自然增加数(出生人数减死亡人数)与该时期内平均人数(或期中人数)之比，一般用千分率表示。计算公式：

人口自然增长率=

$$\frac{本年出生人数-本年死亡人数}{年平均人数}\times 1000‰$$

人口自然增长率= 人口出生率-人口死亡率

■ 户籍人口期望寿命

指在一定年龄组的死亡率水平下，该年龄组人群日后平均可能继续生存的年(岁)数。通常所说的平均期望寿命是指刚出生的一批人平均一生可能存活的年数。

■ 城镇登记失业人员

指有非农业户口，在一定的劳动年龄内(16岁以上及男50岁以下、女45岁以下)，有劳动能力，无业而要求就业，并在当地就业服务机构进行求职登记的人员。

■ 城镇登记失业率

指城镇登记失业人员同城镇单位就业人员、城镇私营企业及个体就业人员(扣除使用的农村劳动力、聘用的离退休人员、港澳台及外方人员)和城镇登记失业人员、城镇单位中的不在岗职工之和的比。计算公式为：

城镇登记失业率=城镇登记失业人员/(城镇单位就业人员－使用的农村劳动力－聘用的离退休人员－聘用的港澳台及外方人员＋不在岗职工＋城镇私营企业及个体就业人员+城镇登记失业人员)× 100%

■ 单位就业人员平均工资

指单位从业人员在报告期内平均每人所得的工资额。

它表明一定时期就业人员工资收入的高低程度，是反映就业人员工资水平的主要指标。计算公式为：

就业人员平均工资=报告期实际支付的全部就业人员工资总额/报告期全部就业人员平均人数。

SHANGHAI STATISTICAL YEARBOOK

EXPLANATORY NOTES TO MAJOR STATISTICAL INDICATORS

□ Population

Population refers to the total population by December 31 every year. According to different statistical approaches, there are two definitions of population named as population with registered residence and population with permanent residence. The former refers to the population with registration in the police while the latter refers to the population that actually reside in a place (residence) permanently, including (1) the population with registered residence in Shanghai at the time of survey and actually live in Shanghai;(2)The population with registered residence in Shanghai but leacing Shanghai less than half a year at the time of investigation;(3)The population with registered residence in Shanghai at the time of investigation and working or studying abroad but not settled down;(4)The population with registered residence in other provinces and cities but actually living in Shanghai at the time of investigation and leaving the registered residence registration place for more than half a year.

□ Birth Rate

Birth Rate (or gross birth rate) means the ratio of the number of births in a certain period (usually a year) to the average population in the same period (or mid-year figure). It is usually calculated in terms of permillage and its calculating formula is:

$$\text{Birth Rate}=\frac{\text{Number of Births}}{\text{Average Number of Population}}\times 1000‰$$

Number of Births refers to live births, when babies have showed any vital phenomena regardless of the length of pregnancy.

Average Number of Population is the average of the number of population at the beginning of the year and, at the end of the year and sometimes is substituted for with mid-year population.

□ Death Rate

Death Rate (or Gross Death Rate) refers to the ratio of number of deaths to the average population (or mid-year population) during a certain period of time (usually a year), which is often presented as permillage. Its calculating formula is:

$$\text{Death Rate}=\frac{\text{Number of Deaths}}{\text{Average Number of Population}}\times 1000‰$$

□ Natural Growth Rate of Population

Natural Growth Rate of Population refers to the ratio of natural increase in population (number of births minus number of deaths) in a certain period of time (usually a year) to the average population (or mid-year population) of the same period, which is often presented as permillage. The following formula are applied:

$$\text{Natural Growth Rate of Population}=\frac{\text{Number of Births}-\text{Number of Deaths}}{\text{Average Number of Population}}\times 1000‰$$

Natural Growth Rate of Population = Birth Rate−Death Rate

□ Life Expectancy of Registered Population

Life Expectancy of Registered Population refers to the average age that an age group may possibly live at a certain mortality rate of the group, in the common knowledge, the average age that a group of new-borns may possibly live.

□ Registered Urban Unemployment

Registered Urban Unemployment refers to those non-agricultural population within working age (16-50 years for male and 16-45 years for females),who are able and willing to work but unemployed and have registered for job in local employment service agencies.

□ Registered Urban Unemployment Rate

Registered Urban Unemployment Rate refers to the ratio of the number of the registered unemployed to the sum of the number of persons employed in various units (minus the rural labour force, retirees, and Hong Kong, Macao, Taiwan and foreign employees they employ) laid-off workers in urban units, urban self-employed individuals and the registered urban unemployed persons . The formula is as follows:

Registered Urban Unemployment Rate = Number of Registered Urban Unemployed Persons ÷ (Number of Persons Employed in Urban Units − rural labour force employed − retirees employed − Hong Kong, Macao, Taiwan and foreign employees + laid-off workers + Self-employed Individuals in Urban Areas + Number of Registered Urban Unemployed Persons) ×

EXPLANATORY NOTES TO MAJOR STATISTICAL INDICATORS

100%

□ Average Wages of the Unit Employees

Average Wages of the Unit Employees refers to the average wage per person during the reporting time.

It indicates the general level of wage income during a certain period of time, which is the main indicator reflecting the wage level of employees, and is calculated as follows:

Average Wages of the Unit Employees = Total Wages of Employees Actually Paid at the Reporting Time / Average Number of Employees at the Reporting Time.

第三篇

CHAPTER 3

国民经济核算

NATIONAL ECONOMIC ACCOUNTING

简要说明

地区生产总值(GDP)是地区所有常住单位在一定时期内生产活动的最终成果。目前,上海地区生产总值由国家统计局统一核算。按照国家统计局最新地区GDP核算和数据发布制度规定,GDP核算分为初步核算和最终核实两个步骤。通常,年度GDP最终核实后,要对季度数据进行修订,称为常规修订;在开展全国经济普查,发现对GDP数据有较大影响的新的基础资料,或计算方法及分类标准发生变化后而对年度GDP历史数据进行修订后,也要对季度GDP历史数据进行相应修订,称为全面修订。

本年鉴所公布的GDP核算数据包括:(1)按照当年价格计算的总量;(2)可比增长及指数。GDP总量变动受到价格变化和物量变化共同影响,在比较不同时期的GDP总量时要剔除价格变化的影响,以反映生产活动成果的实际变动。本年鉴公布的GDP及相关指标的增速为剔除价格变动影响的可比增速,并在此基础上计算指数。本篇GDP核算行业分类标准采用国家标准管理部门2017年颁布的《国民经济行业分类(GB/T 4754-2017)》。

本年鉴中公布的GDP数据中,2021年为初步核算数。

BRIEF INTRODUCTION

Regional GDP is the final outcomes in production activities of all the resident units in a certain period. At present, Shanghai's regional GDP is produced by the National Bureau of Statistics. According to the latest regulations of GDP calculation and data release by the National Bureau of Statistics, GDP calculation includes two parts, preliminary calculation and verified calculation. Generally, quarterly data will be revised after annual GDP calculation, which is called routine revise. During national economic census, when new basic data sources which have significant influence of GDP data are discovered, or when annually historical GDP data are revised after calculation methods and classification criteria change, quarterly data will be revised, which is called comprehensive revise.

GDP data published in this yearbook include: (1) The total output based on the year's prices; (2) Comparable growth and indices. The total output of GDP changes with the prices and volumes, so the comparison of GDP in different periods should exclude the effect of price changes to reflect the actual movement in production activities. Growth of GDP data and related indicators in this yearbook has excluded the effect of price changes and is thus comparable. The indices are based on such comparable data as well. The sector classification criteria of GDP calculation use The Classification of National Economic Sectors (GB/T 4754- 2017) issued in 2017 by Standardization Administration.

According to the results of the fourth national economic census, Shanghai's historical GDP data from 2013 to 2018 are revised comprehensively. Data released in this Yearbook are revised historical data, preliminary figure in 2019.

The GDP data of 2021 released in this Yearbook are preliminary calculation figure.

表 3.1 上海市生产总值（1978~2021）
GROSS DOMESTIC PRODUCT

单位：亿元（100 million yuan）

年 份 Year	上海市 生产总值 Gross Domestic Product	按产业分 Grouped by Industry			按行业分 Grouped by Sector
		第一产业 Primary Industry	第二产业 Secondary Industry	第三产业 Tertiary Industry	#工 业 Industry
1978	272.81	11.00	211.05	50.76	207.47
1979	286.43	11.39	221.21	53.83	216.62
1980	311.89	10.10	236.10	65.69	230.87
1981	324.76	10.58	244.34	69.84	237.12
1982	337.07	13.31	249.32	74.44	240.75
1983	351.81	13.52	255.32	82.97	246.26
1984	390.85	17.26	275.37	98.22	263.19
1985	466.75	19.53	325.63	121.59	311.12
1986	490.83	19.69	336.02	135.12	318.89
1987	545.46	21.60	364.38	159.48	336.54
1988	648.30	27.36	433.05	187.89	399.53
1989	696.54	29.63	466.18	200.73	432.92
1990	781.66	34.24	505.60	241.82	469.83
1991	893.77	34.06	550.64	309.07	514.79
1992	1 114.32	34.16	677.39	402.77	636.68
1993	1 519.23	36.87	895.61	586.75	846.71
1994	1 990.86	46.42	1 139.86	804.58	1 074.37
1995	2 518.08	58.32	1 419.92	1 039.84	1 318.93
1996	2 980.75	67.00	1 598.74	1 315.01	1 466.12
1997	3 465.28	70.23	1 776.81	1 618.24	1 614.13
1998	3 831.00	71.99	1 876.13	1 882.88	1 687.39
1999	4 222.30	72.63	1 990.09	2 159.58	1 807.29

注：2021 年上海市生产总值数据为初步核算数（后表同）。
Note：Data on gross domestic product in 2021 is the initial calculation. The same applies to the following tables.

表 3.1 续表 continued

单位：亿元 (100 million yuan)

年 份 Year	上海市 生产总值 Gross Domestic Product	按产业分 Grouped by Industry 第一产业 Primary Industry	第二产业 Secondary Industry	第三产业 Tertiary Industry	按行业分 Grouped by Sector #工　业 Industry
2000	4 812.15	74.76	2 215.75	2 521.64	2 022.53
2001	5 257.66	76.05	2 413.83	2 767.78	2 194.09
2002	5 795.02	77.69	2 635.28	3 082.05	2 399.07
2003	6 804.04	78.99	3 239.62	3 485.43	3 001.58
2004	8 101.55	81.39	3 872.16	4 148.00	3 621.82
2005	9 197.13	88.06	4 314.90	4 794.17	4 038.67
2006	10 598.86	91.55	4 929.16	5 578.15	4 621.17
2007	12 878.68	99.39	5 677.51	7 101.78	5 357.89
2008	14 536.90	109.37	6 215.45	8 212.08	5 831.99
2009	15 742.44	112.37	6 184.79	9 445.28	5 740.79
2010	17 915.41	114.45	7 434.89	10 366.07	6 943.93
2011	20 009.68	126.44	8 169.34	11 713.90	7 673.28
2012	21 305.59	129.33	8 174.13	13 002.13	7 661.28
2013	23 204.12	131.63	8 286.53	14 785.96	7 765.32
2014	25 269.75	131.96	8 633.25	16 504.54	8 099.89
2015	26 887.02	125.53	8 408.65	18 352.84	7 888.59
2016	29 887.02	114.34	8 570.24	21 202.44	8 045.54
2017	32 925.01	110.78	9 525.89	23 288.34	8 977.41
2018	36 011.82	104.78	10 360.78	25 546.26	9 763.48
2019	37 987.55	107.06	10 193.60	27 686.89	9 565.12
2020	38 963.30	107.68	10 258.57	28 597.05	9 625.53
2021	43 214.85	99.97	11 449.32	31 665.56	10 738.80

注：2021 年上海市生产总值数据为初步核算数(后表同)。
Note：Data on gross domestic product in 2021 is the initial calculation. The same applies to the following tables.

表 3.2 上海市生产总值比上年增长(1978~2021)
GROWTH RATE OF GROSS DOMESTIC PRODUCT RAISED PRECEDING YEAR

单位:%

年 份 Year	上海市 生产总值 Gross Domestic Product	按产业分 Grouped by Industry			按行业分 Grouped by Sector
		第一产业 Primary Industry	第二产业 Secondary Industry	第三产业 Tertiary Industry	#工 业 Industry
1978	15.8	27.0	16.6	10.5	15.8
1979	7.4	-0.7	8.6	3.0	8.8
1980	8.4	-0.6	6.0	22.2	6.1
1981	5.6	0.3	4.9	8.9	4.1
1982	7.2	26.2	4.6	13.4	4.2
1983	7.8	0.0	7.5	9.8	7.5
1984	11.6	25.3	10.0	14.7	9.7
1985	13.4	-22.2	14.9	14.7	15.0
1986	4.4	-0.2	4.0	6.0	3.7
1987	7.5	-2.7	7.4	8.9	6.8
1988	10.1	4.6	9.4	12.6	9.3
1989	3.0	0.3	1.6	7.1	1.9
1990	3.5	4.3	2.8	5.3	2.7
1991	7.1	0.4	6.9	8.6	8.8
1992	14.8	0.4	17.2	12.0	17.7
1993	15.1	-2.7	16.7	13.7	16.9
1994	14.5	2.9	14.2	16.1	14.2
1995	15.0	6.4	15.5	14.7	15.0
1996	13.1	5.0	11.2	17.9	10.4
1997	12.8	4.2	10.6	17.7	10.2
1998	10.3	2.2	8.3	14.7	7.8
1999	10.4	2.1	9.0	13.3	9.7
2000	11.0	3.4	9.8	13.4	10.3

表 3.2 续表 continued

单位:%

年 份 Year	上海市 生产总值 Gross Domestic Product	按产业分 Grouped by Industry			按行业分 Grouped by Sector
		第一产业 Primary Industry	第二产业 Secondary Industry	第三产业 Tertiary Industry	#工　业 Industry
2001	10.5	2.0	12.0	9.5	12.1
2002	11.4	3.0	12.1	10.9	12.7
2003	12.3	2.3	16.0	9.2	17.7
2004	13.3	-4.1	13.8	13.2	15.2
2005	11.5	-9.7	10.5	12.9	10.7
2006	12.8	0.8	11.9	13.8	12.0
2007	15.2	2.9	11.4	18.8	12.2
2008	9.7	0.7	7.5	11.6	7.9
2009	8.4	-0.6	3.4	12.5	3.1
2010	10.2	-5.2	17.0	5.4	17.8
2011	8.3	0.4	6.7	9.6	7.7
2012	7.5	0.4	3.0	10.7	3.1
2013	7.9	-2.2	5.9	9.2	6.2
2014	7.1	1.7	4.4	8.8	4.7
2015	7.0	-4.9	1.1	10.7	1.0
2016	6.9	-12.4	2.2	9.1	2.2
2017	7.0	-0.8	6.7	7.1	7.4
2018	6.8	-9.8	3.5	8.2	3.6
2019	6.0	-4.8	0.5	8.2	0.4
2020	1.7	-7.7	1.1	1.9	1.1
2021	8.1	-6.5	9.4	7.6	9.5

表 3.3 上海市生产总值指数(以 1978 年为 100，1978~2021)
INDEX OF GROSS DOMESTIC PRODUCT(1978=100)

年 份 Year	上海市生产总值 Gross Domestic Product	按产业分 Grouped by Industry 第一产业 Primary Industry	按产业分 Grouped by Industry 第二产业 Secondary Industry	按产业分 Grouped by Industry 第三产业 Tertiary Industry	按行业分 Grouped by Sector #工 业 Industry
1978	100.0	100.0	100.0	100.0	100.0
1979	107.4	99.3	108.6	103.0	108.8
1980	116.4	98.7	115.1	125.9	115.4
1981	122.9	99.0	120.8	137.1	120.2
1982	131.8	124.9	126.3	155.4	125.2
1983	142.1	124.9	135.8	170.7	134.6
1984	158.6	156.5	149.4	195.8	147.7
1985	179.8	121.8	171.6	224.5	169.8
1986	187.7	121.6	178.5	238.0	176.1
1987	201.8	118.3	191.7	259.2	188.1
1988	222.2	123.7	209.7	291.8	205.6
1989	228.8	124.1	213.1	312.6	209.5
1990	236.8	129.4	219.0	329.1	215.1
1991	253.7	129.9	234.1	357.4	234.1
1992	291.2	130.5	274.4	400.3	275.5
1993	335.2	126.9	320.2	455.2	322.0
1994	383.8	130.6	365.7	528.5	367.8
1995	441.3	139.0	422.4	606.1	422.9
1996	499.2	145.9	469.7	714.6	466.9
1997	563.0	152.0	519.5	841.1	514.5
1998	621.0	155.4	562.6	964.8	554.7
1999	685.6	158.7	613.3	1 093.1	608.5
2000	761.0	164.1	673.4	1 239.6	671.2

表 3.3 续表 continued

年 份 Year	上海市 生产总值 Gross Domestic Product	按产业分 Grouped by Industry 第一产业 Primary Industry	 第二产业 Secondary Industry	 第三产业 Tertiary Industry	按行业分 Grouped by Sector #工 业 Industry
2001	841.0	167.3	754.2	1 357.3	752.4
2002	936.8	172.4	845.4	1 505.3	847.9
2003	1 052.1	176.3	980.7	1 643.8	998.0
2004	1 192.0	169.1	1 116.0	1 860.7	1 149.7
2005	1 329.1	152.7	1 233.2	2 100.8	1 272.7
2006	1 499.2	153.9	1 380.0	2 390.7	1 425.4
2007	1 727.1	158.4	1 537.3	2 840.1	1 599.3
2008	1 894.6	159.5	1 652.6	3 169.6	1 725.7
2009	2 053.7	158.5	1 708.7	3 565.8	1 779.2
2010	2 263.2	150.3	1 999.2	3 758.3	2 095.9
2011	2 451.0	150.9	2 133.2	4 119.1	2 257.3
2012	2 634.9	151.5	2 197.2	4 559.9	2 327.2
2013	2 843.0	148.2	2 326.8	4 979.4	2 471.5
2014	3 044.9	150.7	2 429.2	5 417.6	2 587.7
2015	3 258.0	143.3	2 455.9	5 997.2	2 613.6
2016	3 482.8	125.5	2 509.9	6 543.0	2 671.1
2017	3 726.6	124.5	2 678.1	7 007.5	2 868.7
2018	3 980.0	112.3	2 771.8	7 582.2	2 972.0
2019	4 218.8	106.9	2 785.7	8 203.9	2 983.9
2020	4 290.5	98.7	2 816.3	8 359.8	3 016.7
2021	4 638.0	92.3	3 081.0	8 995.1	3 303.3

表 3.4 上海市生产总值构成(1978~2021)
STRUCTURE OF GROSS DOMESTIC PRODUCT

单位:%

年 份 Year	上海市生产总值 Gross Domestic Product	按产业分 Grouped by Industry 第一产业 Primary Industry	第二产业 Secondary Industry	第三产业 Tertiary Industry	按行业分 Grouped by Sector #工 业 Industry
1978	100.0	4.0	77.4	18.6	76.0
1979	100.0	4.0	77.2	18.8	75.6
1980	100.0	3.2	75.7	21.1	74.0
1981	100.0	3.3	75.2	21.5	73.0
1982	100.0	3.9	74.0	22.1	71.4
1983	100.0	3.8	72.6	23.6	70.0
1984	100.0	4.4	70.5	25.1	67.3
1985	100.0	4.2	69.8	26.0	66.7
1986	100.0	4.0	68.5	27.5	65.0
1987	100.0	4.0	66.8	29.2	61.7
1988	100.0	4.2	66.8	29.0	61.6
1989	100.0	4.3	66.9	28.8	62.2
1990	100.0	4.4	64.7	30.9	60.1
1991	100.0	3.8	61.6	34.6	57.6
1992	100.0	3.1	60.8	36.1	57.1
1993	100.0	2.4	59.0	38.6	55.7
1994	100.0	2.3	57.3	40.4	54.0
1995	100.0	2.3	56.4	41.3	52.4
1996	100.0	2.3	53.6	44.1	49.2
1997	100.0	2.0	51.3	46.7	46.6
1998	100.0	1.9	49.0	49.1	44.0
1999	100.0	1.8	47.1	51.1	42.8
2000	100.0	1.6	46.0	52.4	42.0

表 3.4 续表 continued

单位:%

年 份 Year	上海市 生产总值 Gross Domestic Product	按产业分 Grouped by Industry			按行业分 Grouped by Sector
		第一产业 Primary Industry	第二产业 Secondary Industry	第三产业 Tertiary Industry	#工 业 Industry
2001	100.0	1.5	45.9	52.6	41.7
2002	100.0	1.3	45.5	53.2	41.4
2003	100.0	1.2	47.6	51.2	44.1
2004	100.0	1.0	47.8	51.2	44.7
2005	100.0	1.0	46.9	52.1	43.9
2006	100.0	0.9	46.5	52.6	43.6
2007	100.0	0.8	44.1	55.1	41.6
2008	100.0	0.7	42.8	56.5	40.1
2009	100.0	0.7	39.3	60.0	36.5
2010	100.0	0.6	41.5	57.9	38.8
2011	100.0	0.6	40.8	58.6	38.3
2012	100.0	0.6	38.4	61.0	36.0
2013	100.0	0.6	35.7	63.7	33.5
2014	100.0	0.5	34.2	65.3	32.1
2015	100.0	0.4	31.3	68.3	29.3
2016	100.0	0.4	28.7	70.9	26.9
2017	100.0	0.4	28.9	70.7	27.3
2018	100.0	0.3	28.8	70.9	27.1
2019	100.0	0.3	26.8	72.9	25.2
2020	100.0	0.3	26.3	73.4	24.7
2021	100.0	0.2	26.5	73.3	24.8

表 3.5 上海市人均生产总值(1978~2021)
PER CAPITA GROSS DOMESTIC PRODUCT

年 份 Year	上海市 生产总值 (亿元) Gross Domestic Product (100 million yuan)	人均生产总值 (按人民币计算) (万元) Per Capita Gross Domestic Product (10 thousand yuan)	人均生产总值指数 Per Capita Gross Domestic Product Index 以 1978 年为 100 (1978=100)	以上年为 100 (preceding year=100)	人均生产总值 (按美元计算) (万美元) Per Capita Gross Domestic Product (USD 10 thousand)
1978	272.81	0.25	100.0	114.7	0.14
1979	286.43	0.26	105.0	105.0	0.18
1980	311.89	0.27	111.5	106.2	0.18
1981	324.76	0.28	116.2	104.2	0.16
1982	337.07	0.29	122.7	105.6	0.15
1983	351.81	0.29	130.4	106.3	0.15
1984	390.85	0.32	143.7	110.2	0.14
1985	466.75	0.38	160.8	111.9	0.13
1986	490.83	0.39	165.6	103.0	0.11
1987	545.46	0.43	175.7	106.1	0.12
1988	648.30	0.51	190.5	108.4	0.14
1989	696.54	0.54	192.8	101.2	0.14
1990	781.66	0.59	196.1	101.7	0.12
1991	893.77	0.67	207.1	105.6	0.13
1992	1 114.32	0.82	235.1	113.5	0.15
1993	1 519.23	1.11	267.5	113.8	0.19
1994	1 990.86	1.43	302.5	113.1	0.17
1995	2 518.08	1.79	343.9	113.7	0.21
1996	2 980.75	2.08	382.1	111.1	0.25
1997	3 465.28	2.36	419.9	109.9	0.28
1998	3 831.00	2.54	451.4	107.5	0.31
1999	4 222.30	2.73	485.7	107.6	0.33
2000	4 812.15	3.00	520.2	107.1	0.37

表 3.5 续表 continued

年　份 Year	上海市 生产总值 （亿元） Gross Domestic Product （100 million yuan）	人均生产总值 （按人民币计算） （万元） Per Capita Gross Domestic Product （10 thousand yuan）	人均生产总值指数 Per Capita Gross Domestic Product Index		人均生产总值 （按美元计算） （万美元） Per Capita Gross Domestic Product （USD 10 thousand）
			以 1978 年为 100 （1978＝100）	以上年为 100 （preceding year＝100）	
2001	5 257.66	3.18	557.1	107.1	0.39
2002	5 795.02	3.43	607.2	109.0	0.41
2003	6 804.04	3.91	663.1	109.2	0.47
2004	8 101.55	4.50	726.1	109.5	0.54
2005	9 197.13	4.94	782.7	107.8	0.60
2006	10 598.86	5.50	853.1	109.0	0.69
2007	12 878.68	6.40	941.0	110.3	0.84
2008	14 536.90	6.92	989.0	105.1	1.00
2009	15 742.44	7.24	1 036.5	104.8	1.06
2010	17 915.41	7.94	1 101.8	106.3	1.17
2011	20 009.68	8.59	1 155.8	104.9	1.33
2012	21 305.59	8.96	1 217.1	105.3	1.42
2013	23 204.12	9.57	1 287.7	105.8	1.55
2014	25 269.75	10.28	1 359.8	105.6	1.67
2015	26 887.02	10.92	1 452.3	106.8	1.75
2016	29 887.02	12.14	1 551.1	106.8	1.83
2017	32 925.01	13.35	1 656.6	106.8	1.98
2018	36 011.82	14.57	1 765.9	106.6	2.20
2019	37 987.55	15.33	1 864.8	105.6	2.22
2020	38 963.30	15.68	1 890.9	101.4	2.27
2021	43 214.85	17.36	2 040.3	107.9	2.69

表3.6 上海市生产总值(2019~2021)
GROSS DOMESTIC PRODUCT

单位:亿元(100 million yuan)

指　标	Indicators	2019	2020	2021
上海市生产总值	**Gross Domestic Product**	**37 987.55**	**38 963.30**	**43 214.85**
按产业分	**Grouped by Industry**			
第一产业	Primary Industry	107.06	107.68	99.97
第二产业	Secondary Industry	10 193.60	10 258.57	11 449.32
第三产业	Tertiary Industry	27 686.89	28 597.05	31 665.56
按行业分	**Grouped by Sector**			
农、林、牧、渔业	Farming, Forestry, Animal Husbandry and Fishery	113.31	116.67	108.18
工　业	Industry	9 565.12	9 625.53	10 738.80
建筑业	Construction	716.16	714.21	798.49
批发和零售业	Retail and Wholesale Industries	5 023.23	4 980.64	5 554.03
交通运输、仓储和邮政业	Transportation, Warehousing and Post	1 650.44	1 548.03	1 843.46
住宿和餐饮业	Hoteling and Catering	458.86	347.94	399.31
信息传输、软件和信息技术服务业	Information Transmission, Software and IT Services	2 405.12	2 854.31	3 392.88
金融业	Financial Industry	6 535.18	7 216.24	7 973.25
房地产业	Real Estate Industry	3 300.72	3 375.93	3 564.49
租赁和商务服务业	Leasing and Business Services	2 898.56	2 605.68	2 750.66
科学研究和技术服务业	Scientific and Technical Services	1 715.58	1 878.46	2 079.52
水利、环境和公共设施管理业	Water Conservancies, Environment and Public Facilities Management	215.26	225.25	240.12
居民服务、修理和其他服务业	Resident Service and Other Services	326.68	276.03	311.42
教　育	Education	1 285.96	1 357.19	1 450.60
卫生和社会工作	Health and Social Work and Social Welfare	910.08	976.15	1 073.86
文化、体育和娱乐业	Culture, Sports and Entertainment	234.58	202.03	214.83
公共管理、社会保障和社会组织	Public Administration, Social Security and Social Organizations	632.71	663.01	720.95

表 3.7 上海市生产总值比上年增长(2019~2021)
GROWTH RATE OF GROSS DOMESTIC PRODUCT RAISED PRECEDING YEAR

单位:%

指 标	Indicators	2019	2020	2021
上海市生产总值	**Gross Domestic Product**	**6.0**	**1.7**	**8.1**
按产业分	**Grouped by Industry**			
第一产业	Primary Industry	-4.8	-7.7	-6.5
第二产业	Secondary Industry	0.5	1.1	9.4
第三产业	Tertiary Industry	8.2	1.9	7.6
按行业分	**Grouped by Sector**			
农、林、牧、渔业	Farming, Forestry, Animal Husbandry and Fishery	-5.9	-6.7	-5.7
工 业	Industry	0.4	1.1	9.5
建筑业	Construction	2.1	0.5	7.1
批发和零售业	Retail and Wholesale Industries	2.4	-3.1	8.4
交通运输、仓储和邮政业	Transportation, Warehousing and Post	3.6	-7.9	13.5
住宿和餐饮业	Hoteling and Catering	-0.5	-18.7	11.8
信息传输、软件和信息技术服务业	Information Transmission, Software and IT Services	16.2	15.2	12.4
金融业	Financial Industry	11.6	8.6	7.5
房地产业	Real Estate Industry	5.1	1.6	4.8
租赁和商务服务业	Leasing and Business Services	7.4	-10.7	4.9
科学研究和技术服务业	Scientific and Technical Services	9.6	7.1	5.7
水利、环境和公共设施管理业	Water Conservancies, Environment and Public Facilities Management	14.6	2.0	2.3
居民服务、修理和其他服务业	Resident Service and Other Services	6.1	-14.0	9.4
教 育	Education	11.5	3.2	5.0
卫生和社会工作	Health and Social Work and Social Welfare	10.0	5.3	8.0
文化、体育和娱乐业	Culture, Sports and Entertainment	5.0	-10.8	3.1
公共管理、社会保障和社会组织	Public Administration, Social Security and Social Organizations	18.2	4.8	4.5

表 3.8 上海市生产总值收入法项目(1978~2020)
GROSS DOMESTIC PRODUCT(BY INCOME ITEM)

单位:亿元(100 million yuan)

年 份 Year	上海市 生产总值 Gross Domestic Product	劳动者报酬 Compensation of Employees	生产税净额 Net Taxes on Production	固定资产折旧 Depreciation of Fixed Assets	营业盈余 Operating Surplus
1978	272.81	62.03	45.53	10.60	154.65
1979	286.43	68.15	45.61	11.13	161.54
1980	311.89	74.47	49.49	13.05	174.88
1981	324.76	78.99	54.52	14.70	176.55
1982	337.07	85.00	57.09	16.30	178.68
1983	351.81	90.36	57.51	18.73	185.21
1984	390.85	108.79	68.74	20.81	192.51
1985	466.75	125.99	87.36	26.16	227.24
1986	490.83	141.95	86.31	33.42	229.15
1987	545.46	163.88	98.61	40.73	242.24
1988	648.30	197.69	126.95	71.85	251.81
1989	696.54	223.35	136.01	79.79	257.39
1990	781.66	244.03	149.35	92.93	295.35
1991	893.77	302.94	170.42	126.62	293.79
1992	1 114.32	397.72	207.40	160.36	348.84
1993	1 519.23	563.59	257.30	159.93	538.41
1994	1 990.86	692.40	356.32	245.26	696.88
1995	2 518.08	901.83	430.67	352.30	833.28
1996	2 980.75	1 065.85	576.01	392.28	946.61
1997	3 465.28	1 195.63	716.02	442.83	1 110.80
1998	3 831.00	1 341.22	809.04	534.94	1 145.80
1999	4 222.30	1 518.26	902.10	637.83	1 164.11
2000	4 812.15	1 724.29	1 124.30	706.96	1 256.60

表 3.8 续表 continued

单位:亿元(100 million yuan)

年　份 Year	上海市 生产总值 Gross Domestic Product	劳动者报酬 Compensation of Employees	生产税净额 Net Taxes on Production	固定资产折旧 Depreciation of Fixed Assets	营业盈余 Operating Surplus
2001	5 257.66	1 934.27	1 184.62	801.52	1 337.25
2002	5 795.02	2 205.79	1 219.35	886.96	1 482.92
2003	6 804.04	2 426.63	1 296.74	1 023.28	2 057.39
2004	8 101.55	2 723.11	1 311.91	1 313.21	2 753.32
2005	9 197.13	3 188.79	1 457.84	1 523.55	3 026.95
2006	10 598.86	3 826.68	1 664.71	1 814.13	3 293.34
2007	12 878.68	4 593.51	2 110.83	2 104.94	4 069.40
2008	14 536.90	5 566.04	2 611.89	2 343.84	4 015.13
2009	15 742.44	6 125.68	2 881.98	2 501.55	4 233.23
2010	17 915.41	7 018.82	3 235.82	2 588.44	5 072.33
2011	20 009.68	8 028.12	3 612.49	2 664.08	5 704.99
2012	21 305.59	8 833.02	3 945.78	2 930.85	5 595.94
2013	23 204.12	9 852.57	4 412.12	3 076.81	5 862.62
2014	25 269.75	10 975.15	4 669.08	3 220.72	6 404.80
2015	26 887.02	11 818.17	4 852.37	3 410.37	6 806.11
2016	29 887.02	13 213.22	5 314.72	3 724.06	7 635.02
2017	32 925.01	14 997.05	5 224.36	3 923.56	8 780.04
2018	36 011.82	16 610.26	5 291.96	4 261.38	9 848.22
2019	37 987.55	17 527.83	5 517.88	4 209.50	10 732.34
2020	38 963.30	18 517.67	5 131.86	4 592.24	10 721.53

表 3.9 上海市生产总值收入法项目构成(1978~2020)
STRUCTURE OF GROSS DOMESTIC PRODUCT(BY INCOME ITEM)

单位:%

年 份 Year	上海市 生产总值 Gross Domestic Product	劳动者报酬 Compensation of Employees	生产税净额 Net Taxes on Production	固定资产折旧 Depreciation of Fixed Assets	营业盈余 Operating Surplus
1978	100.0	22.7	16.7	3.9	56.7
1979	100.0	23.8	15.9	3.9	56.4
1980	100.0	23.9	15.8	4.2	56.1
1981	100.0	24.3	16.8	4.5	54.4
1982	100.0	25.2	17.0	4.8	53.0
1983	100.0	25.7	16.4	5.3	52.6
1984	100.0	27.8	17.6	5.3	49.3
1985	100.0	27.0	18.7	5.6	48.7
1986	100.0	28.9	17.6	6.8	46.7
1987	100.0	30.0	18.1	7.5	44.4
1988	100.0	30.5	19.6	11.1	38.8
1989	100.0	32.1	19.5	11.5	36.9
1990	100.0	31.2	19.1	11.9	37.8
1991	100.0	33.9	19.1	14.1	32.9
1992	100.0	35.7	18.6	14.4	31.3
1993	100.0	37.1	16.9	10.6	35.4
1994	100.0	34.8	17.9	12.3	35.0
1995	100.0	35.8	17.1	14.0	33.1
1996	100.0	35.8	19.3	13.1	31.8
1997	100.0	34.5	20.7	12.7	32.1
1998	100.0	35.0	21.1	14.0	29.9
1999	100.0	36.0	21.4	15.0	27.6
2000	100.0	35.8	23.4	14.7	26.1

表 3.9 续表 continued

单位:%

年　份 Year	上海市生产总值 Gross Domestic Product	劳动者报酬 Compensation of Employees	生产税净额 Net Taxes on Production	固定资产折旧 Depreciation of Fixed Assets	营业盈余 Operating Surplus
2001	100.0	36.8	22.5	15.3	25.4
2002	100.0	38.1	21.0	15.3	25.6
2003	100.0	35.7	19.1	15.0	30.2
2004	100.0	33.6	16.2	16.2	34.0
2005	100.0	34.7	15.9	16.5	32.9
2006	100.0	36.1	15.7	17.1	31.1
2007	100.0	35.7	16.4	16.3	31.6
2008	100.0	38.3	18.0	16.1	27.6
2009	100.0	38.9	18.3	15.9	26.9
2010	100.0	39.2	18.1	14.4	28.3
2011	100.0	40.1	18.1	13.3	28.5
2012	100.0	41.5	18.5	13.7	26.3
2013	100.0	42.5	19.0	13.2	25.3
2014	100.0	43.4	18.5	12.8	25.3
2015	100.0	44.0	18.0	12.7	25.3
2016	100.0	44.2	17.8	12.5	25.5
2017	100.0	45.5	15.9	11.9	26.7
2018	100.0	46.1	14.7	11.9	27.3
2019	100.0	46.1	14.5	11.1	28.3
2020	100.0	47.5	13.2	11.8	27.5

表 3.10 上海市生产总值(支出法)(1978~2021)
GROSS DOMESTIC PRODUCT(BY EXPENDITURE APPROACH)

年 份 Year	上海市生产总值(亿元) Gross Domestic Product (100 million yuan)	其中 of which 最终消费支出 Final Consumption	资本形成总额 Gross Capital Formation	货物和服务净流出 Net Outflows of Good and Services	最终消费率(%) Final Consumption Rate	资本形成率(%) Capital Formation Rate
1978	272.81	59.06	47.96	165.79	21.6	17.6
1979	286.43	71.34	43.61	171.48	24.9	15.2
1980	311.89	81.24	66.52	164.13	26.0	21.3
1981	324.76	89.73	76.68	158.35	27.6	23.6
1982	337.07	92.90	90.27	153.90	27.6	26.8
1983	351.81	101.19	71.86	178.76	28.8	20.4
1984	390.85	117.25	101.63	171.97	30.0	26.0
1985	466.75	155.15	189.13	122.47	33.2	40.5
1986	490.83	181.74	228.12	80.97	37.0	46.5
1987	545.46	200.74	241.02	103.70	36.8	44.2
1988	648.30	255.42	335.56	57.32	39.4	51.8
1989	696.54	298.62	351.68	46.24	42.9	50.5
1990	781.66	358.45	331.34	91.87	45.9	42.4
1991	893.77	386.06	340.03	167.68	43.2	38.0
1992	1 114.32	476.57	487.63	150.12	42.7	43.8
1993	1 519.23	699.52	744.11	75.60	46.0	49.0
1994	1 990.86	919.83	1 161.49	-90.46	46.2	58.3
1995	2 518.08	1 146.66	1 590.06	-218.64	45.5	63.1
1996	2 980.75	1 344.17	1 984.63	-348.05	45.1	66.6
1997	3 465.28	1 595.59	2 080.68	-210.99	46.0	60.0
1998	3 831.00	1 752.18	2 046.57	32.25	45.7	53.4
1999	4 222.30	1 952.49	2 010.44	259.37	46.2	47.6
2000	4 812.15	2 236.42	2 218.80	356.93	46.5	46.1

表 3.10 续表 continued

年 份 Year	上海市生产总值（亿元）Gross Domestic Product (100 million yuan)	其 中 of which 最终消费支出 Final Consumption	资本形成总额 Gross Capital Formation	货物和服务净流出 Net Outflows of Good and Services	最终消费率（%）Final Consumption Rate	资本形成率（%）Capital Formation Rate
2001	5 257.66	2 466.80	2 413.65	377.21	46.9	45.9
2002	5 795.02	2 775.82	2 596.17	423.03	47.9	44.8
2003	6 804.04	3 225.12	3 177.49	401.43	47.4	46.7
2004	8 101.55	3 791.53	3 864.44	445.58	46.8	47.7
2005	9 197.13	4 377.84	4 276.67	542.62	47.6	46.5
2006	10 598.86	5 087.45	4 992.07	519.34	48.0	47.1
2007	12 878.68	6 233.27	6 027.22	618.19	48.4	46.8
2008	14 536.90	7 253.91	6 512.54	770.45	49.9	44.8
2009	15 742.44	8 060.13	7 257.26	425.05	51.2	46.1
2010	17 915.41	9 620.57	7 936.53	358.31	53.7	44.3
2011	20 009.68	11 025.33	8 324.02	660.33	55.1	41.6
2012	21 305.59	11 888.52	8 415.71	1 001.36	55.8	39.5
2013	23 204.12	13 063.91	9 212.04	928.17	56.3	39.7
2014	25 269.75	14 479.57	9 804.66	985.52	57.3	38.8
2015	26 887.02	15 460.04	10 647.26	779.72	57.5	39.6
2016	29 887.02	17 155.16	11 984.70	747.16	57.4	40.1
2017	32 925.01	18 855.88	12 962.64	1 106.49	57.3	39.4
2018	36 011.82	20 608.94	14 297.37	1 105.51	57.2	39.7
2019	37 987.55	21 895.64	14 927.09	1 164.82	57.6	39.3
2020	38 963.30	21 812.27	15 992.75	1 158.28	56.0	41.0
2021	43 214.85	24 380.95	17 443.76	1 390.14	56.4	40.4

表 3.11 上海市生产总值(支出法)支出项目(1978~2021)
STRUCTURE OF GROSS DOMESTIC PRODUCT(BY EXPENDITURE APPROACH)

单位:亿元(100 million yuan)

年份 Year	最终消费支出 Final Consumption	其中 of which 居民消费支出 Household Consumption	政府消费支出 Government Consumption	资本形成总额 Gross Capital Formation	其中 of which 固定资本形成总额 Gross Fixed Capital Formation	存货变动 Changes in Inventories
1978	59.06	48.25	10.81	47.96	31.69	16.27
1979	71.34	58.80	12.54	43.61	39.05	4.56
1980	81.24	66.31	14.93	66.52	45.57	20.95
1981	89.73	73.69	16.04	76.68	55.10	21.58
1982	92.90	75.02	17.88	90.27	70.49	19.78
1983	101.19	81.64	19.55	71.86	74.51	-2.65
1984	117.25	94.56	22.69	101.63	90.70	10.93
1985	155.15	124.78	30.37	189.13	116.70	72.43
1986	181.74	145.73	36.01	228.12	144.41	83.71
1987	200.74	161.09	39.65	241.02	183.79	57.23
1988	255.42	211.04	44.38	335.56	236.92	98.64
1989	298.62	244.60	54.02	351.68	232.22	119.46
1990	358.45	284.79	73.66	331.34	248.46	82.88
1991	386.06	311.09	74.97	340.03	276.08	63.95
1992	476.57	366.09	110.48	487.63	382.01	105.62
1993	699.52	555.45	144.07	744.11	624.31	119.80
1994	919.83	732.71	187.12	1 161.49	996.48	165.01
1995	1 146.66	926.54	220.12	1 590.06	1 403.19	186.87
1996	1 344.17	1 080.79	263.38	1 984.63	1 739.25	245.38
1997	1 595.59	1 262.12	333.47	2 080.68	1 827.56	253.12
1998	1 752.18	1 379.41	372.77	2 046.57	1 840.63	205.94
1999	1 952.49	1 528.95	423.54	2 010.44	1 841.79	168.65
2000	2 236.42	1 756.27	480.15	2 218.80	1 982.09	236.71

表 3.11 续表 continued

单位:亿元(100 million yuan)

年 份 Year	最终消费支出 Final Consumption	其中 of which 居民消费支出 Household Consumption	其中 of which 政府消费支出 Government Consumption	资本形成总额 Gross Capital Formation	其中 of which 固定资本形成总额 Gross Fixed Capital Formation	其中 of which 存货变动 Changes in Inventories
2001	2 466.80	1 910.44	556.36	2 413.65	2 156.93	256.72
2002	2 775.82	2 132.57	643.25	2 596.17	2 428.11	168.06
2003	3 225.12	2 456.26	768.86	3 177.49	2 742.03	435.46
2004	3 791.53	2 851.75	939.78	3 864.44	3 321.64	542.80
2005	4 377.84	3 274.18	1 103.66	4 276.67	3 844.40	432.27
2006	5 087.45	3 815.59	1 271.86	4 992.07	4 504.52	487.55
2007	6 233.27	4 687.83	1 545.44	6 027.22	5 486.32	540.90
2008	7 253.91	5 378.65	1 875.26	6 512.54	5 974.67	537.87
2009	8 060.13	5 966.39	2 093.74	7 257.26	6 926.67	330.59
2010	9 620.57	7 470.72	2 149.85	7 936.53	6 879.52	1 057.01
2011	11 025.33	8 444.08	2 581.25	8 324.02	7 383.57	940.45
2012	11 888.52	9 054.88	2 833.64	8 415.71	7 733.93	681.78
2013	13 063.91	9 908.15	3 155.76	9 212.04	8 446.30	765.74
2014	14 479.57	10 941.80	3 537.77	9 804.66	9 021.30	783.36
2015	15 460.04	11 642.08	3 817.96	10 647.26	10 082.63	564.63
2016	17 155.16	12 731.88	4 423.28	11 984.70	11 267.41	717.29
2017	18 855.88	13 998.54	4 857.34	12 962.64	12 217.72	744.92
2018	20 608.94	15 415.37	5 193.57	14 297.37	13 441.65	855.72
2019	21 895.64	16 452.13	5 443.51	14 927.09	14 088.83	838.26
2020	21 812.27	16 338.28	5 473.99	15 992.75	15 092.45	900.30
2021	24 380.95	18 528.45	5 852.50	17 443.76	16 375.84	1 067.92

上/海/统/计/年/鉴

主要统计指标解释

■ 生产总值(原国内生产总值)

指按市场价格计算的一个国家(或地区)所有常住单位在一定时期内生产活动的最终成果。生产总值有三种表现形态,即价值形态、收入形态和产品形态。从价值形态看,它是所有常住单位在一定时期内所生产的全部货物和服务价值超过同期投入的全部非固定资产货物和服务价值的差额,即所有常住单位的增加值之和;从收入形态看,它是所有常住单位在一定时期内所创造并分配给常住单位和非常住单位的初次收入之和;从产品形态看,它是所有常住单位在一定时期内最终使用的货物和服务减去货物和服务的进口价值。在实际核算中,生产总值有三种计算方法,即生产法、收入法和支出法。三种方法分别从不同的方面反映生产总值及其构成。根据国务院和国家统计局有关我国GDP核算和数据发布制度的规定,上海国内生产总值自2004年起更名为"上海市生产总值",简称"上海市GDP"。

■ 三次产业

三次产业的划分是国际上常用的产业结构分类。第一产业是指产品直接取自自然界的部门,第二产业是指对初级产品进行再加工的部门,第三产业是指为生产和消费提供各种服务的部门。

第一产业是指农、林、牧、渔业(不含农、林、牧、渔服务业)。

第二产业是指采矿业(不含开采辅助活动),制造业(不含金属制品、机械和设备修理业),电力、热力、燃气及水生产和供应业,建筑业。

第三产业即服务业,是指除第一产业、第二产业以外的其他行业。

■ 旅游产业

指本市与旅游相关的各行业,为境内外旅游者提供旅游服务的产业。这些服务包括:旅行社服务、交通运输服务、住宿服务、电讯服务、娱乐服务、餐饮服务、商品零售服务等。由于旅游产业增加值是依据相关行业的有关资料进行跨行业核算的,因此不宜将其与上海市生产总值中其他行业的增加值进行加总,否则会造成重复计算。

SHANGHAI STATISTICAL YEARBOOK

EXPLANATORY NOTES TO MAJOR STATISTICAL INDICATORS

□ Gross Regional Product(former Gross Domestic Product)

Gross Regional Product refers to the final products at market prices by (of) all resident units of a country (or region) during a certain period of time. Gross product is expressed in three different forms, i.e value, income, and products respectively. The form of value refers to the total value of all products and services produced by all resident units during a certain period of time minus the total value of input of non-fixed-assets products and services or the summation of the value-added of all resident units; the form of income includes all the income items produced by all resident units and distributed primarily to all resident and non-resident units; the form of product refers to all final goods and services minus the value of imports of goods and services. In the practice of national accounting, it is calculated by three approaches, i.e. product approach, income approach, and expenditure approach, respectively, to reflect Gross Product and its composition of different aspects. According to the regulations of GDP national accounting and data release issued by the State Council and National Bureau of Statistics, since 2004 Shanghai Gross Domestic Product has been renamed as Shanghai Gross Product Value, for short Shanghai GDP.

□ Three Industries

Classification of economic activities into three strata of industry is a common practice in the world. Primary industry refers to extraction of natural resources; secondary industry involves processing of primary products; and tertiary industry provides services of various kinds for production and consumption.

Primary industry includes farming, forestry, animal husbandry, fishery industry (not including the service industry for farming, forestry, animal husbandry and fishery).

Secondary industry includes mining (not including mining auxiliary activities), manufacturing (not including metal products, machinery and equipment repair industry), electricity, gas and water production and supply industry and construction.

Tertiary industry refers to all other industries not included in primary or secondary industries.

□ Tourism Industry

Tourism Industry refers to those tourism-related industries that provide tourism services to domestic and overseas tourists, including: travel agency service, transportation service, hostelling service, telecommunication service, entertainment service, catering service and retailing service, etc.. As accounted by referring to relevant cross-industry data of several industries, the value added of the tourism industry shall not be counted together with that of other industries in the Shanghai GDP to avoid repetitive computation.

第四篇
CHAPTER 4

财政收支
FISCAL REVENUE AND EXPENDITURE

简要说明

本篇反映上海市地方财政收支和税收收入情况，资料来源于上海市财政局和国家税务总局上海市税务局。

有关财政收支方面的资料，根据财政收支总表、财政收入明细表、财政支出明细表和各区财政收支完成情况表等的数据加工整理编制，其中，地方财政收支由市本级财政收支和区级财政收支组成。有关税收收入方面的资料，根据全市税收收入情况表的数据加工整理编制。

BRIEF INTRODUCTION

The data in this chapter reflect government revenue, expenditure, and tax income situations. The data are collected, provided and complied by Shanghai Finance Bureau and Shanghai Municipal Tax Service, State Administration of Taxation.

Data on government revenue and expenditure are prepared, collected and compiled on the basis of information from the city's balance sheet of government revenue and expenditures, tables of government revenue and expenditure at city level, and tables of government revenue and expenditure at district level. Among them, local fiscal revenue and expenditure is comprised by revenue and expenditure in the city as well as in districts. The data on tax income is prepared, collected and compiled on the base of information on Shanghai's tax income table.

表 4.1　一般公共预算收支(1978~2021)
GENERAL BUDGETARY REVENUE AND EXPENDITURE

单位:亿元 (100 million yuan)

年　份 Year	一般公共预算收入 General Budgetary Revenue	其　中　of which 税收收入 Taxes	非税收入 Non-taxes	一般公共预算支出 General Budgetary Expenditure
1978	169.22	51.51	117.71	26.01
1979	172.69	53.73	118.96	27.06
1980	174.73	57.59	117.14	19.18
1981	174.35	62.93	111.42	19.06
1982	167.99	65.79	102.20	20.68
1983	156.39	110.05	46.34	22.39
1984	163.96	137.67	26.29	30.32
1985	184.23	185.76	-1.53	46.07
1986	179.46	177.90	1.56	59.08
1987	168.97	167.26	1.71	53.85
1988	161.62	182.42	-20.80	65.88
1989	166.88	190.21	-23.33	73.31
1990	166.99	183.31	-16.32	75.56
1991	175.53	182.88	-7.35	86.05
1992	185.56	188.61	-3.05	94.99
1993	242.34	252.99	-10.65	129.26
1994	175.33	196.60	-21.27	196.98
1995	227.30	240.06	-12.76	267.89
1996	288.49	308.26	-19.77	342.66
1997	352.33	369.23	-16.90	428.92
1998	392.22	406.73	-14.51	480.70
1999	431.85	427.23	4.62	546.38

表 4.1 续表 continued

单位:亿元 (100 million yuan)

年 份 Year	一般公共预算收入 General Budgetary Revenue	其中 of which 税收收入 Taxes	非税收入 Non-taxes	一般公共预算支出 General Budgetary Expenditure
2000	497.96	484.00	13.96	622.84
2001	620.24	589.91	30.33	726.38
2002	719.79	657.70	62.09	877.84
2003	899.29	796.87	102.42	1 102.64
2004	1 119.72	1 036.23	83.49	1 395.69
2005	1 433.90	1 238.40	195.50	1 660.32
2006	1 600.37	1 393.97	206.40	1 813.80
2007	2 102.63	1 975.48	127.15	2 201.92
2008	2 382.34	2 223.43	158.91	2 617.68
2009	2 540.30	2 368.45	171.85	2 989.65
2010	2 873.58	2 707.80	165.78	3 302.89
2011	3 429.83	3 172.72	257.11	3 914.88
2012	3 743.71	3 426.79	316.92	4 184.02
2013	4 109.51	3 797.16	312.35	4 528.61
2014	4 585.55	4 219.05	366.50	4 923.44
2015	5 519.50	4 858.16	661.34	6 191.56
2016	6 406.13	5 625.90	780.23	6 918.94
2017	6 642.26	5 865.51	776.75	7 547.62
2018	7 108.15	6 285.04	823.11	8 351.54
2019	7 165.10	6 216.29	948.81	8 179.28
2020	7 046.30	5 841.88	1 204.42	8 102.11
2021	7 771.80	6 606.74	1 165.06	8 430.86

表 4.2　主要年份一般公共预算收入
GENERAL BUDGETARY REVENUE IN MAIN YEARS

指　标	Indicators	2010	2015	2020	2021
一般公共预算收入(亿元)	**General Budgetary Revenue (100 million yuan)**	**2 873.58**	**5 519.50**	**7 046.30**	**7 771.80**
#增值税	Value-added Tax	388.62	1 012.80	2 285.70	2 485.91
企业所得税	Enterprise Income Tax	606.05	1 104.08	1 394.30	1 694.40
个人所得税	Personal Income Tax	261.20	487.61	670.37	860.78
契　税	Deed	173.58	270.99	380.10	410.45
#市级收入	Revenue at Municipal Level	1 393.23	2 806.13	3 295.06	3 528.04
区级收入	Revenue at District Level	1 480.35	2 713.37	3 751.24	4 243.76
一般公共预算收入构成(%)	**Composition of General Budgetary Revenue (%)**	**100**	**100**	**100**	**100**
#增值税	Value-added Tax	13.5	18.3	32.4	32.0
企业所得税	Enterprise Income Tax	21.1	20.0	19.8	21.8
个人所得税	Personal Income Tax	9.1	8.8	9.5	11.1
契　税	Deed	6.0	4.9	5.4	5.3
#市级收入	Revenue at Municipal Level	48.5	50.8	46.8	45.4
区级收入	Revenue at District Level	51.5	49.2	53.2	54.6

注：2016 年实施“营改增”，增值税收入口径有所调整。
Note: Since the“Business Tax Replaced with VAT” was implemented in 2016, the scope of value-added tax revenue has been adjusted.

表 4.3 主要年份区级一般公共预算收支
GENERAL BUDGETARY REVENUE AND EXPENDITURE OF DISTRICTS IN MAIN YEARS

单位:亿元 (100 million yuan)

地 区	District	一般公共预算收入 General Budgetary Revenue				一般公共预算支出 General Budgetary Expenditure			
		2010	2015	2020	2021	2010	2015	2020	2021
总 计	**Total**	**1 480.35**	**2 713.37**	**3 751.24**	**4 243.76**	**1 955.58**	**3 858.09**	**5 349.53**	**5 587.59**
浦东新区	Pudong New Area	425.40	788.19	1 077.00	1 173.70	524.06	920.22	1 258.70	1 288.49
黄 浦 区	Huangpu	64.36	180.88	229.20	267.03	80.73	207.41	276.67	322.68
卢 湾 区	Luwan	51.30				56.69			
徐 汇 区	Xuhui	90.43	151.08	198.10	220.54	99.29	173.32	306.56	320.92
长 宁 区	Changning	72.08	129.94	129.03	150.33	85.50	143.80	148.39	143.63
静 安 区	Jing'an	65.96	106.24	250.14	278.48	71.43	158.52	295.70	292.71
闸 北 区	Zhabei	46.30	88.13			68.55	129.16		
普 陀 区	Putuo	51.97	96.36	110.63	125.56	78.57	124.41	168.56	176.40
虹 口 区	Hongkou	48.36	90.14	119.39	155.23	74.52	126.82	162.66	195.02
杨 浦 区	Yangpu	50.07	95.77	128.45	143.01	82.65	162.76	201.70	205.80
闵 行 区	Minhang	125.30	214.40	298.29	331.11	156.60	344.25	429.77	402.23
宝 山 区	Baoshan	70.35	127.08	152.97	172.90	114.43	219.23	261.26	278.45
嘉 定 区	Jiading	82.96	191.36	220.40	243.51	112.84	297.24	309.30	336.38
金 山 区	Jinshan	30.75	65.50	126.32	134.32	70.98	145.18	229.85	243.81
松 江 区	Songjiang	77.33	123.11	220.62	250.10	103.55	194.30	319.01	354.68
青 浦 区	Qingpu	58.95	125.33	210.10	231.10	88.40	179.89	336.76	354.97
奉 贤 区	Fengxian	40.43	84.89	161.60	220.80	77.12	168.18	259.22	332.60
崇 明 区	Chongming	28.04	54.98	119.00	146.05	78.21	163.39	385.42	338.82

注：2012 年起，原卢湾区并入黄浦区；2016 年起，原闸北区并入静安区，崇明县改为崇明区。
Note: Former Luwan District has been merged into Huangpu District since 2012; former Zhabei District has been merged into Jing'an District since 2016; Chongming County has been changed to Chongming District since 2016.

表 4.4 主要年份一般公共预算支出
GENERAL BUDGETARY EXPENDITURE IN MAIN YEARS

指 标	Indicators	2010	2015	2020	2021
一般公共预算支出(亿元)	**General Budgetary Expenditure(100 million yuan)**	**3 302.89**	**6 191.56**	**8 102.11**	**8 430.86**
#一般公共服务	General Public Services	226.02	259.84	371.01	382.42
公共安全	Public Security	187.25	269.20	440.82	453.72
教 育	Education	417.28	767.32	1 000.59	1 039.46
社会保障和就业	Social Security and Jobs	362.56	543.16	981.12	1 023.97
卫生健康支出	Health Expenditure	160.07	303.46	544.50	633.13
城乡社区	Urban and Country Community Affairs	475.47	1 173.88	1 419.49	1 431.04
#市级支出	Expenditure at Municipal Level	1 278.76	2 333.47	2 752.58	2 843.27
区级支出	Expenditure at District Level	2 024.13	3 858.09	5 349.53	5 587.59
一般公共预算支出比重(%)	**Percentage of the General Budgetary Expenditure (%)**	**100**	**100**	**100**	**100**
#一般公共服务	General Public Services	6.8	4.2	4.6	4.5
公共安全	Public Security	5.7	4.3	5.4	5.4
教 育	Education	12.6	12.4	12.3	12.3
社会保障和就业	Social Security and Jobs	11.0	8.8	12.1	12.1
卫生健康支出	Health Expenditure	4.8	4.9	6.7	7.5
城乡社区	Urban and Country Community Affairs	14.4	19.0	17.5	17.0
#市级支出	Expenditure at Municipal Level	38.7	37.7	34.0	33.7
区级支出	Expenditure at District Level	61.3	62.3	66.0	66.3

注：自 2014 年开始，计划生育支出从一般公共服务支出中转出，并入原医疗卫生支出，改名为医疗卫生与计划生育支出。 自 2019 年开始，医疗卫生与计划生育支出调整为卫生健康支出。

Note: The government takes the expenditure of family planning from the expenditure of general public services to the expenditure of medical and health care Since 2014. The name of the item has been changed into the expditure expenditure of medical and health care, family planning. The expenditure of medical and health care, family planning has been adjusted to the expenditure of health since 2019.

表 4.5 主要年份全市税收总收入
TAXATION IN MAIN YEARS

单位:亿元(100 million yuan)

指 标	Indicators	2010	2015	2020	2021
全市税收总收入	**Taxation**	**8 003.43**	**13 989.51**	**15 964.85**	**18 703.69**
#证券交易印花税	Stamp Tax of Stock Transaction	305.26	1 344.31	676.65	1 132.28
海关代征	Custom Taxation	2 082.92	2 759.11	2 912.13	3 385.34
国内增值税	Domestic Value Added Tax	1 575.00	2 676.46	4 661.28	5 147.02
国内消费税	Domestic Excise	499.58	825.26	840.52	885.98
企业所得税	Enterprise Income Tax	1 567.31	2 857.32	3 575.56	4 297.40
个人所得税	Personal Income Tax	653.01	1 219.01	1 699.79	2 180.28

上/海/统/计/年/鉴

主要统计指标解释

■ 一般公共预算收入

一般公共预算收入是指根据现行财政管理体制规定，划归地方财政的税收收入和非税收入。

■ 税收收入

一般公共预算收入中的税收收入主要包括房产税、城镇土地使用税、车船税、土地增值税、耕地占用税、契税等固定收入，以及增值税、企业所得税、个人所得税等共享收入部分。

■ 一般公共预算支出

一般公共预算支出是指按照现行中央政府与地方政府事权的划分，经地方人大批准，用于保障地方经济社会发展的各项财政支出。主要包括一般公共服务，公共安全，教育，科学技术，文化体育与传媒，社会保障和就业，卫生健康支出，环境保护，城乡社区，农林水事务，交通运输等支出。

SHANGHAI STATISTICAL YEARBOOK

EXPLANATORY NOTES TO MAJOR STATISTICAL INDICATORS

□ General Budgetary Revenue

General Budgetary Revenue refers to the tax revenue and non-tax revenue collected by the local government as defined by the finance management system.

□ Tax Revenue

Tax Revenue of general budgetary revenue mainly includes, house property tax, urban land use tax, tax on vehicles and boat operation, land appreciation tax, farm land occupation tax, deed tax, etc and the share part of value added tax, corporate income tax, individual income tax, etc.

□ General Budgetary Expenditure

General Budgetary Expenditure refers to the fiscal expenditure demarcated on the basis of the classification of the affairs administration rights between the central government and local government. It is approved by the local people's congress and used for the development of local economy and society. Local fiscal expenditure mainly includes the expenditure for general public services, public security, education, science and technology, culture, sport and media, social safety and employment, health expenditure, environment protection, urban and rural community affairs, agriculture, forestry and water conservancy and transportation, etc.

第五篇

CHAPTER 5

能源与环境

ENERGY AND ENVIRONMENT PROTECTION

简要说明

一、本篇资料的主要内容

本篇主要包含两部分内容:能源生产、消费和环境保护治理。

能源生产、消费的主要内容有能源消耗基本情况,能源消费弹性系数,人均、日均能源消费量,分行业、分主要能源品种的时间序列能源消费量,综合能源平衡表和主要能源品种的单项平衡表,电力建设情况等。

环境保护治理的主要内容有环保投入,工业固体废弃物防治,水环境保护,大气环境保护,环境空气状况、声环境及治理和城市环境卫生情况等。

二、本篇资料的统计范围

本篇资料的统计范围为全社会。

三、本篇的资料来源

能源生产、消费的资料来源:电力建设情况由市电力公司提供,其他表的数据均来自历年能源平衡表。

环境保护治理的资料来源:环保投入、工业固体废弃物防治、大气环境保护、环境空气状况和声环境及治理由上海市生态环境局提供;水环境保护由上海市水务局和上海市生态环境局提供;城市环境卫生情况由上海市绿化和市容管理局提供。

四、关于数据口径与计算方法的说明

环境保护治理

1. 2008年起,工业废气排放量按新排放系数计算。

2. 2011年起,烟尘排放总量统计口径变更为烟(粉)尘排放量。

3. 2011年起,废水排放总量中增加了农业源和集中式治理设施排放的废水。

4. 2013年起,环境空气质量优良率以AQI评价。

BRIEF INTRODUCTION

I. Main Contents

Data in this chapter cover mainly energy production, energy consumption, and environment protection and governance.

Energy production and consumption include basic energy consumption situations, elasticity coefficient of energy consumption, average energy consumption per capita, average daily energy consumption, energy consumption in time series by industry and main energy categories, comprehensive energy balance sheet, single balance sheet of main energy categories and electric power construction.

Environment protection and governance include investment in environment protection, prevention of industrial solid waste, water environment protection, air protection, governance of air and acoustic environment, and management of urban sanitation situations.

II. The Scope of Data

The scope of data in this chapter covers the whole city.

III. Sources of Data

Sources of data on energy production and consumption: Data on electric power construction are provided by the Shanghai Electric Power Company, and the rest are collected from the energy balance sheets over the years.

Sources of data on environment protection and governance: Data on investment in environment protection, prevention of industrial solid waste, air protection, and governance of air and acoustic environment are provided by Shanghai Municipal Bureau of Ecology and Environment; data on water environment protection are provided by Shanghai Water Authority and Shanghai Municipal Bureau of Ecology and Environment; data on urban sanitation situations are provided by the Shanghai Greening & City Appearance Bureau.

IV. Notes on Coverage and Compilation of Data

Environment protection and governance

(a) Industrial emission is calculated on new emission coefficient since 2008.

(b) Coverage of dust discharge changes to dust (smoke) discharge since 2011.

(c) Coverage of wastewater discharge started to include agricultural wastewater and wastewater from centralized treatment facilities from 2011.

(d) Ambient air quality is evaluated by AQI since 2013.

表 5.1 主要年份能源消耗基本情况
ENERGY CONSUMPTION IN MAIN YEARS

年 份 Year	能源消费量 （万吨标准煤） Energy Consumption (10 000 tons SCE)	其中 of which #工 业 Industry	电力消费 （亿千瓦时） Electricity Power Consumption (100 million kwh)	其中 of which #工 业 Industry
1990	3 191.06	2 462.21	264.74	220.97
1995	4 392.48	3 439.11	403.27	307.01
2000	5 413.45	3 687.90	559.42	393.13
2001	5 825.80	3 851.75	592.99	413.33
2002	6 114.47	3 929.31	645.71	447.46
2003	6 658.49	4 245.09	745.97	507.00
2004	7 167.16	4 405.55	821.44	555.12
2005	7 730.66	4 692.65	921.97	617.59
2006	8 355.49	4 987.81	990.15	656.10
2007	9 103.30	5 351.93	1 072.38	705.90
2008	9 608.49	5 544.13	1 138.22	727.13
2009	9 759.35	5 472.16	1 153.38	701.59
2010	10 243.26	5 890.93	1 295.87	786.61
2011	10 489.09	5 946.66	1 339.62	805.76
2012	10 573.00	5 798.02	1 353.45	786.25
2013	10 890.39	5 965.53	1 410.61	799.45
2014	10 639.86	5 796.95	1 369.02	785.64
2015	10 930.53	5 745.55	1 405.56	787.03
2016	11 241.73	5 681.86	1 486.02	798.18
2017	11 381.85	5 537.01	1 526.77	798.22
2018	11 453.73	5 360.68	1 566.66	780.21
2019	11 696.46	5 446.65	1 568.58	748.39
2020	11 099.59	5 304.68	1 575.96	769.46
2021	11 683.02	5 476.23	1 749.62	851.49

表 5.1 续表 1 continued

年　份 Year	单位生产总值能耗 (吨标准煤/万元) Energy Consumption of GDP (ton SCE/10 000 yuan)	单位生产总值电耗 (千瓦时/万元) Electricity Power Consumption of GDP (kwh/10 000 yuan)	工业增加值能耗 (吨标准煤/万元) Energy Consumption of Value Added in Industry (ton SCE/10 000 yuan)	工业增加值电耗 (千瓦时/万元) Electricity Power Consumption of Value Added in Industry (kwh/10 000 yuan)
1990	4.082	3 386.89	5.241	4 703.19
1995	1.757	1 613.45	2.629	2 346.81
2000	1.135	1 172.50	1.845	1 966.67
2001	1.117	1 138.15	1.778	1 907.61
2002	1.074	1 124.73	1.648	1 889.60
2003	1.004	1 114.35	1.435	1 723.76
2004	0.905	1 017.54	1.226	1 544.90
2005	0.862	996.98	1.205	1 529.88
2006	0.825	949.69	1.142	1 453.81
2007	0.780	892.62	1.077	1 394.24
2008	0.751	863.64	1.027	1 334.46
2009	0.704	808.49	0.975	1 251.82
2010	0.678	823.18	0.910	1 194.02
2011	0.589	721.53	0.853	1 146.70
2012	0.552	678.39	0.809	1 089.46
2013	0.528	656.24	0.785	1 044.47
2014	0.482	595.23	0.725	984.30
2015	0.463	517.45	0.725	980.71
2016	0.391	517.25	0.705	990.09
2017	0.370	496.89	0.640	921.97
2018	0.349	477.63	0.597	869.47
2019	0.337	451.35	0.605	830.69
2020	0.314	446.09	0.581	842.69
2021	0.278	415.54	0.519	807.54

注：单位能耗和单位电耗 2005～2010 按 2005 年可比价计算，2011～2015 年按 2010 年可比价计算，2016～2020 年按 2015 年可比价计算，2021～2025 年按 2020 可比价计算。

Note：Energy Intensity and Electricity Intensity by GDP or value added is calculated by comparable prices of 2005 from 2005 to 2010, it is calculated by comparable prices of 2010 from 2011 to 2015, it is calculated by comparable prices of 2015 from 2016 to 2020, it is calculated by comparable prices of 2020 from 2021 to 2025.

表 5.2 能源消费弹性系数(1978~2021)
ELASTICITY OF ENERGY CONSUMPTION

年 份 Year	能源消费 比上年增长 (%) Growth Rate of Energy Consumption over Preceding Year(%)	电力消费 比上年增长 (%) Growth Rate of Electric Power Consumption over Preceding Year(%)	能源消费 弹性系数 Elasticity of Energy Consumption	电力消费 弹性系数 Elasticity of Electric Power Consumption
1978	6.6	10.8	0.42	0.68
1979	1.5	3.0	0.20	0.41
1980	-0.6	3.4		0.40
1981	1.0	6.4	0.18	1.14
1982	2.6	4.4	0.36	0.61
1983	2.5	4.2	0.32	0.54
1984	2.5	4.1	0.22	0.35
1985	4.9	3.9	0.37	0.29
1986	9.0	6.8	2.05	1.55
1987	5.7	4.1	0.76	0.55
1988	1.3	2.5	0.13	0.25
1989	4.4	1.3	1.47	0.43
1990	2.6	5.8	0.74	2.09
1991	8.6	9.0	1.22	1.28
1992	5.5	10.0	0.37	0.67
1993	7.9	9.0	0.52	0.60
1994	5.8	9.1	0.40	0.63
1995	5.2	6.9	0.36	0.48
1996	3.7	6.7	0.28	0.51
1997	3.6	5.5	0.28	0.43
1998	2.5	6.3	0.25	0.61
1999	4.7	3.8	0.46	0.37
2000	6.9	11.6	0.62	1.06
2001	7.6	6.0	0.73	0.57
2002	5.0	8.9	0.43	0.78
2003	8.9	15.5	0.72	1.26
2004	7.6	10.1	0.53	0.71
2005	7.9	12.2	0.68	1.06
2006	8.1	7.4	0.63	0.58
2007	8.9	8.3	0.59	0.55
2008	5.5	6.1	0.57	0.63
2009	1.6	1.3	0.19	0.15
2010	5.0	12.4	0.49	1.22
2011	2.4	3.4	0.29	0.41
2012	0.8	1.0	0.11	0.13
2013	3.0	4.2	0.38	0.53
2014	-2.3	-3.0	-	-
2015	2.7	2.7	0.39	0.39
2016	2.8	5.7	0.42	0.84
2017	1.2	2.7	0.18	0.39
2018	0.6	2.6	0.10	0.39
2019	2.1	0.1	0.36	0.02
2020	-5.1	0.5	-	0.29
2021	5.3	11.0	0.65	1.38

表 5.3 主要年份能源消费总量
FINAL CONSUMPTION OF ENERGY IN MAIN YEARS

单位：万吨标准煤(10 000 tons SCE)

年 份 Year	能源消费总 量 Energy Consumption	能源终端消费量 Final Consumption of Energy	加工转换投入(-)产出(+)量 Processing Conversion Input (-) and Output (+)	损失量 Loss Volume
1990	3 191.06	3 098.82	-52.20	40.04
1995	4 392.49	4 250.44	-1.29	140.75
2000	5 413.45	5 226.81	-3.15	183.49
2001	5 825.80	5 554.41	-60.23	211.16
2002	6 114.47	5 840.35	-55.50	218.62
2003	6 658.49	6 332.88	-82.06	243.55
2004	7 167.16	6 926.24	-22.21	218.71
2005	7 730.66	7 599.84	57.37	188.18
2006	8 355.49	8 196.29	34.47	193.67
2007	9 103.30	8 991.39	96.14	208.05
2008	9 608.49	9 438.48	56.46	226.48
2009	9 759.35	9 649.84	122.71	232.22
2010	10 243.26	10 055.36	60.78	248.69
2011	10 489.09	10 671.97	432.92	250.04
2012	10 573.00	10 715.25	402.53	260.27
2013	10 890.39	10 972.78	355.75	273.37
2014	10 639.86	10 787.07	409.10	261.90
2015	10 930.53	11 034.75	376.62	272.40
2016	11 241.73	11 325.41	366.53	282.85
2017	11 381.85	11 389.41	328.80	321.24
2018	11 453.73	11 477.87	333.68	309.55
2019	11 696.46	11 866.87	338.05	167.64
2020	11 099.59	11 148.20	282.13	233.53
2021	11 683.02	11 738.48	294.46	239.00

表 5.4 平均每人生活用能源(2018~2021)
ANNUAL RESIDENT ENERGY CONSUMPTION PER CAPITA

品 名	Items	2018	2019	2020	2021
生活消费能源总计(千克标准煤)	**Total Resident Energy Consumption (kg of SCE)**	**518.98**	**517.74**	**530.27**	**557.72**
煤 炭(千克)	Coal (kg)	1.62	1.65	1.61	1.41
天然气(立方米)	Natural Gas (cu.m)	64.07	65.08	68.94	68.83
液化石油气(千克)	Liquefied Petroleum Gas (kg)	7.08	7.06	6.34	6.33
电 力(千瓦时)	Electric Power (kwh)	985.70	988.71	1 034.83	1 116.84

注：本表按年平均人口数计算。
Note: Data in this table are calculated by average annual population.

表 5.5 平均每天各种能源消费量(2018~2021)
AVERAGE DAILY ENERGY CONSUMPTION BY VARIETY

能源品种	Items	2018	2019	2020	2021
合计(万吨标准煤)	**Total(10 000 tons of SCE)**	**31.38**	**32.05**	**30.41**	**32.01**
煤 炭(万吨)	Coal(10 000 tons)	9.80	9.33	9.15	10.97
焦 炭(万吨)	Coke(10 000 tons)	1.70	1.74	1.73	1.69
燃料油(万吨)	Fuel Oil(10 000 tons)	1.80	1.80	1.75	1.77
汽 油(万吨)	Gasoline(10 000 tons)	1.35	1.35	1.28	1.33
煤 油(万吨)	Kerosene(10 000 tons)	1.92	2.06	1.37	1.51
柴 油(万吨)	Diesel Oil(10 000 tons)	1.20	1.23	1.21	1.27
天然气(亿立方米)	Natural Gas(100 million cu.m)	0.25	0.27	0.26	0.27
电 力(亿千瓦时)	Electricity(100 million kwh)	4.29	4.30	4.32	4.79

表 5.6 主要年份能源终端消费量
FINAL CONSUMPTION OF ENERGY IN MAIN YEARS

单位：万吨标准煤（10 000 tons SCE）

年 份 Year	能源终端消费量 Final Consumption of Energy	其 中 of which 第一产业 Primary Industry	第二产业 Secondary Industry	第三产业 Tertiary Industry	生活消费 Living Consumption
1980	2 130.56	71.04	1 655.92	194.64	208.96
1990	3 098.82	58.49	2 387.88	403.47	248.98
2000	5 226.81	103.37	3 593.64	1 068.85	460.94
2001	5 554.41	99.12	3 698.17	1 276.89	480.22
2002	5 840.35	79.85	3 790.50	1 481.13	488.86
2003	6 332.88	75.69	4 045.91	1 669.86	541.42
2004	6 926.24	63.72	4 297.68	1 967.59	597.24
2005	7 599.84	53.96	4 717.72	2 159.62	668.54
2006	8 196.29	53.20	4 990.65	2 412.44	740.01
2007	8 991.39	53.09	5 402.14	2 740.20	795.95
2008	9 438.48	56.02	5 564.11	2 953.44	864.91
2009	9 649.84	57.41	5 581.52	3 106.55	904.36
2010	10 055.36	59.56	5 919.84	3 105.60	970.36
2011	10 671.97	58.10	6 359.03	3 255.72	999.12
2012	10 715.25	57.98	6 178.22	3 423.47	1 055.57
2013	10 972.78	59.75	6 295.57	3 488.41	1 129.05
2014	10 787.07	60.21	6 190.79	3 490.06	1 046.00
2015	11 034.75	59.80	6 117.30	3 769.18	1 088.47
2016	11 325.41	63.01	6 046.32	4 033.27	1 182.80
2017	11 389.41	62.16	5 832.40	4 284.04	1 210.82
2018	11 477.87	61.78	5 672.86	4 460.92	1 282.31
2019	11 866.87	59.57	5 917.61	4 606.53	1 283.15
2020	11 148.20	59.30	5 658.82	4 112.44	1 317.64
2021	11 738.48	62.73	5 869.35	4 418.31	1 388.09

表 5.7 主要年份工业能源终端消费量
FINAL CONSUMPTION OF ENERGY OF INDUSTRY IN MAIN YEARS

年 份 Year	工业能源终端消费量 （万吨标准煤） Final Energy Consumption of Industry （10 000 tons SCE）	原 煤 （万吨） Coal （10 000 tons）	焦 炭 （万吨） Coke （10 000 tons）	燃料油 （万吨） Fuel Oil （10 000 tons）	电 力 （亿千瓦时） Electric power （100 million kwh）
1980	1 645.20	535.03	211.52	122.41	136.85
1990	2 369.99	596.14	419.24	136.09	209.21
2000	3 506.07	733.65	676.06	139.67	362.94
2001	3 586.48	790.51	654.79	136.93	381.64
2002	3 662.21	676.60	571.92	112.19	413.61
2003	3 928.44	675.58	573.94	117.11	464.74
2004	4 172.43	731.30	552.68	118.77	510.67
2005	4 577.48	843.73	603.16	80.94	568.29
2006	4 841.96	869.58	617.92	74.80	604.59
2007	5 253.66	790.10	691.38	91.99	649.82
2008	5 393.68	787.01	684.92	74.98	667.59
2009	5 391.00	825.59	658.32	71.92	641.58
2010	5 732.44	854.71	705.21	43.12	718.63
2011	6 165.57	813.06	706.34	62.86	735.27
2012	5 979.74	730.71	673.17	40.23	714.46
2013	6 089.11	800.15	640.30	35.36	723.07
2014	5 983.21	862.92	654.84	21.22	710.70
2015	5 897.69	709.70	630.75	11.86	711.54
2016	5 810.35	635.79	596.95	8.00	718.45
2017	5 591.59	468.97	571.62	7.90	716.29
2018	5 434.91	484.97	607.79	4.59	704.94
2019	5 668.05	510.16	621.82	5.31	715.35
2020	5 395.59	422.24	623.90	3.20	707.17
2021	5 573.98	431.17	611.35	9.86	785.72

表 5.8 能源平衡表(标准量)(2018~2021)
BALANCE SHEET OF ENERGY(STANDARD EQUIVALENT)

单位:万吨标准煤(10 000 tons SCE)

指 标	Indicators	2018	2019	2020	2021
可供本地区消费的能源量	**Volume of Energy Available for Local Consumption**	**11 456.52**	**11 693.41**	**11 096.07**	**11 687.19**
库存差	Inventory Change	-62.52	-11.26	52.18	48.93
一次能源生产量	Primary Energy Production	380.78	385.44	465.26	494.68
外省(市)调入量	Inflow from Other Provinces (Autonomous Region and Municipalities)	15 081.94	14 746.40	15 866.01	14 789.69
进口量	Imports	5 582.76	5 673.14	4 812.94	4 637.98
我轮、机在外国加油量	China Airplanes&ships Refueling in Abroad	954.69	918.63	879.81	622.41
本市调出量(-)	Outflow from Shanghai (Autonomous Region of Municipality)	-9 751.03	-9 292.15	-10 150.59	-8 533.70
出口量(-)	Exports	-451.74	-451.12	-553.87	-372.79
外轮、机在我国加油量(-)	Foreign Airplanes&ships Refueling in China	-278.36	-275.68	-275.68	
加工转换投入(-)产出(+)量	**Processing Conversion Input (-) and Output (+)**	**333.68**	**338.05**	**282.13**	**294.46**
#火力发电	Fuel Power Generation				
供 热	Heating Supply	-32.96	-34.81	-35.52	-39.46
炼 焦	Coke Making	-25.94	-30.28	-33.12	-37.66
炼 油	Oil Refining	26.96	69.14	4.80	-6.39
制 气	Gas Making			-3.63	-3.83
回收能	Recovery of Energy	419.75	425.29	424.35	455.39
损失量	**Loss Volume**	**309.55**	**167.64**	**233.53**	**239.00**
#运输和输配损失	Loss in Transportation and Distribution	309.55	167.64	233.53	239.00
终端消费量	**Final Consumption**	**11 477.87**	**11 866.87**	**11 148.20**	**11 738.48**
第一产业	Primary Industry	61.78	59.57	59.30	62.73
第二产业	Secondary Industry	5 672.86	5 917.61	5 658.82	5 869.35
工 业	Industry	5 434.91	5 668.05	5 395.59	5 573.98
建筑业	Construction	237.95	249.56	263.23	295.38
第三产业	Tertiary Industry	4 460.92	4 606.53	4 112.44	4 418.31
#交通运输、仓储和邮政业	Transportation, Storage and Post	2 520.00	2 618.69	2 196.79	2 307.76
批发、零售贸易业和住宿、餐饮业	Wholesale, Retail Sales and Hotel, Restaurants	534.62	520.53	509.48	547.92
生活消费	Living Consumption	1 282.31	1 283.15	1 317.64	1 388.09
城 镇	Urban	1 151.77	1 157.26	1 189.79	1 256.42
乡 村	Rural	130.54	125.89	127.86	131.67
平衡差额	**Balance**	**2.78**	**-3.05**	**-3.52**	**4.17**
能源消费总量	**Total Energy Consumption**	**11 453.73**	**11 696.46**	**11 099.59**	**11 683.02**

表 5.9 能源终端消费量(2021)
FINAL CONSUMPTION OF ENERGY (QUANTITY EQUIVALENT)

单位:万吨(10 000 tons)

行 业	Sectors	原 煤 Coal	焦 炭 Coke	燃料油 Fuel Oil
总 计	**Total**	**437.60**	**611.35**	**647.02**
生产消费	**Production Consumption**	**434.10**	**611.35**	**647.02**
第一产业	Primary Industry	0.30		1.00
第二产业	Secondary Industry	431.67	611.35	20.55
#工 业	Industry	431.17	611.35	9.86
第三产业	Tertiary Industry	2.13		625.47
#交通运输、仓储和邮政业	Transportation, Storage and Post	0.03		625.29
批发、零售贸易业和住宿、餐饮业	Wholesale, Retail Sales and Hotel, Restaurants	1.10		0.12
生活消费	**Living Consumption**	**3.50**		

表 5.9 续表 1 continued

单位:万吨(10 000 tons)

行 业	Sectors	汽 油 Gasoline	煤 油 Kerosene	柴 油 Diesel Oil
总 计	**Total**	**484.99**	**552.69**	**458.83**
生产消费	**Production Consumption**	**269.49**	**552.69**	**449.93**
第一产业	Primary Industry	13.50		11.00
第二产业	Secondary Industry	39.49	1.00	57.30
#工 业	Industry	14.45	1.00	29.25
第三产业	Tertiary Industry	216.50	551.69	381.63
#交通运输、仓储和邮政业	Transportation, Storage and Post	60.90	551.69	209.93
批发、零售贸易业和住宿、餐饮业	Wholesale, Retail Sales and Hotel, Restaurants	68.00		92.00
生活消费	**Living Consumption**	**215.50**		**8.90**

表 5.9 续表 2 continued

行 业	Sectors	其他石油制品(万吨) Other Petroleum Products (10 000 tons)	热 力(万百万千焦) Thermopower (10 000 million KJ)	电 力(亿千瓦时) Electric Power (100 million kwh)
总 计	**Total**	**158.90**	**9 799.78**	**1 683.85**
生产消费	**Production Consumption**	**158.90**	**9 734.78**	**1 405.88**
第一产业	Primary Industry		55.51	7.21
第二产业	Secondary Industry	158.90	9 353.02	846.17
#工 业	Industry	158.90	9 344.20	785.72
第三产业	Tertiary Industry		326.25	552.50
#交通运输、仓储和邮政业	Transportation, Storage and Post		1.52	58.08
批发、零售贸易业和住宿、餐饮业	Wholesale, Retail Sales and Hotel, Restaurants		63.91	87.52
生活消费	**Living Consumption**		**65.00**	**277.97**

表 5.10 煤炭、石油、电力平衡表（2021）
COAL,PETROLEUM,ELECTRICITY BALANCE SHEET

	指 标 Indicators	煤 炭（万吨）Coal (10 000 tons)	石 油（万吨）Crude Oil (10 000 tons)	电 力（亿千瓦时）Electricity (100 million kwh)
可供本地区消费的能源量	**Total Energy Available for Consumption**	**4 824.20**	**3 190.79**	**1 749.62**
库存差	Inventory Changes in the Year	−112.19	92.59	
生产量	Energy Production		50.94	1 006.75
外省(市)调入量	Inflow from Other Provinces	3 825.90	5 931.92	833.51
进口量	Imports	1 124.94	2 256.14	
我轮、机在外国加油量	China Airplanes&ships Refueling in Abroad		433.32	
本市调出量(−)	Outflow from Shanghai	−14.45	−5 318.57	−90.64
出口量(−)	Exports		−255.55	
外轮、机在我国加油量(−)	Foreign Airplanes&ships Refueling in China			
消费量	**Total Energy Consumption**	**4 826.00**	**3 185.66**	**1 749.62**
按行业分	**Consumption by Sectors**			
农、林、牧、渔业	Farming,Forestry,Animal Husbandry and Fishery	0.30	26.30	7.21
工 业	Industry	4 819.57	962.29	851.49
建筑业	Construction	0.50	85.08	60.45
交通运输、仓储和邮政业	Transport,Storage and Post	0.03	1 465.06	58.08
批发、零售业和住宿、餐饮业	Wholesale,Retail Trade and Hotel,Restaurants	1.10	173.92	87.52
其 他	Others	1.00	221.16	406.90
生活消费	Residential Consumption	3.50	251.85	277.97
按用途分	**Consumption by Usage**			
终端消费	Final Consumption	437.60	3 162.41	1 683.85
#工 业	Industry	431.17	939.04	785.72
用于加工转换	Processing and Conversion	4 380.60	23.25	
损失量	Others Losses	7.80		65.77
平衡差额	**Balanced Difference**	**−1.80**	**5.13**	

表 5.11 规模以上工业分行业能源消费情况(2021)
ENERGY CONSUMPTION BY SECTOR OF INDUSTRIAL ENTERPRISES ABOVE DESIGNATED SIZE

类 别	Types	综合能源消费量(等价值)(万吨标准煤) Energy consumption (equivalence) (10 000 tce)	综合能源消费量(当量值)(万吨标准煤) Energy consumption (calorific) (10 000 tce)
总 计	**Total**	**5 098.48**	**5 385.08**
#五大高载能行业	Five High Energy Consuming Industries	3 959.43	4 760.59
按工业行业分	**Grouped by Scetors**		
制造业	**Manufacture Industry**	**4 736.10**	**3 950.85**
农副食品加工业	Farm and Sideline Products Processing	23.60	16.55
食品制造业	Food Manufacturing	47.16	31.76
酒、饮料和精制茶制造业	Wine, Beverage and Refined Tea Manufacturing	8.84	5.76
烟草制品业	Tabacco Manufacturing	6.30	3.72
纺织业	Textile	13.54	8.23
纺织服装、服饰业	Textiles and Clothing Industry	6.30	4.12
皮革、毛皮、羽毛及其制品和制鞋业	Leather, Fur, Wool Products and Shoes Manufacturing	1.64	0.77
木材加工和木、竹、藤、棕、草制品业	Timber Processing and Timber, Bamboo, Rattan, Coir and Straw Products Manufacturing	3.06	2.06
家具制造业	Furniture Manufacturing	6.02	3.05
造纸和纸制品业	Paper-making and Paper Products Manufacturing	21.27	15.23
印刷和记录媒介复制业	Printing and Record Duplicating	14.10	7.46
文教、工美、体育和娱乐用品制造业	Culture, Education, Industrial Arts, Sports and Entertainment Goods Manufacturing	6.28	3.12
石油加工、炼焦和核燃料加工业	Oil, Coal and Other Fuel Processing	865.15	838.46
化学原料和化学制品制造业	Raw Chemical Materials and Chemical Products Manufacturing	1 466.50	1 297.63
医药制造业	Medicine Manufacturing	52.78	33.67
化学纤维制造业	Chemical Fiber Manufacturing	4.59	2.44
橡胶和塑料制品业	Rubber and Plastic Products Manufacturing	97.53	51.78
非金属矿物制品业	Non-metallic Mineral Products Manufacturing	80.90	57.53
黑色金属冶炼和压延加工业	Ferrous Metal Smelting and Rolling Processing Industry	1 230.61	1 160.24
有色金属冶炼和压延加工业	Nonferrous Metal Smelting and Rolling Processing Industry	27.58	16.07
金属制品业	Metal Products Manufacturing	70.00	39.83
通用设备制造业	General Equipment Manufacturing	82.85	43.20
专用设备制造业	Special Purpose Equipment Manufacturing	37.22	19.14
汽车制造业	The Automotive Manufacturing	184.29	99.47
铁路、船舶、航空航天和其他运输设备制	The Railroad, Marine, Aerospace and Other Transportation Equipment Manufacturing	43.08	26.24
电气机械和器材制造业	Electric Machinery Equipments and Manufacturing	60.91	30.65
计算机、通信和其他电子设备制造业	Computer, Communications and Other Electronic Equipment Manufacturing	249.29	115.75
仪器仪表制造业	Instrumentation Manufacturing	6.18	2.95
其他制造业	Other Manufacturing	5.59	3.33
废弃资源综合利用业	Comprehensive Utilization of Waste Resources	2.77	4.11
金属制品、机械和设备修理业	Metal Products, Machinery and Equipment Repair Industry	10.16	6.53
电力、燃气及水的生产和供应业	**Electricity, Heat, Gas and Water Production an Supply Industry**	**348.96**	**1 421.37**
电力、热力生产和供应业	Production and Supply of Electricity and Thermal Power	316.26	1 406.73
燃气生产和供应业	Production and Supply of Gas	3.98	1.98
水的生产和供应业	Production and Supply of Water	28.72	12.67

表 5.12　电力建设情况（2018～2021）
STATISTICS OF ELECTRIC POWER CONSTRUCTION

	指　标 Indicators	2018	2019	2020	2021
发电量（亿千瓦时）	**Electric Power Generated（100 million kwh）**	**856.59**	**836.70**	**863.74**	**1 006.75**
线损率（%）	Electricity Loss Rate on Lines（%）	5.30	2.23	4.29	4.09
年末发电设备容量（万千瓦）	Power Generating Equipment Capacity（year-end）（10 000kw）	2 524.82	2 664.34	2 669.15	2 785.79
架空线长度（公里）	Length of Overhead Lines（km）	10 096.89	10 307.73	10 321.90	10 506.56
1 000KV（公里）	1 000KV（km）	147.34	147.34	147.34	147.34
750KV（公里）	750KV（km）	106.14	106.14	106.14	106.14
500KV（公里）	500KV（km）	1 151.00	1 151.70	1 151.70	1 151.70
220KV（公里）	220KV（km）	3 716.88	3 868.03	3 893.61	3 972.34
110KV（公里）	110KV（km）	1 028.35	1 159.38	1 202.36	1 259.20
35KV（公里）	35KV（km）	3 592.23	3 520.12	3 465.72	3 514.82
电缆长度（公里）	**Length of Cable（km）**	**14 323.45**	**14 944.29**	**16 507.27**	**16 928.50**
500KV（万千伏安）	500KV（10 000kva）	60.86	60.42	60.42	60.42
220KV（万千伏安）	220KV（10 000kva）	820.07	857.81	891.50	932.43
110KV（万千伏安）	110KV（10 000kva）	2 378.41	2 687.91	2 905.22	3 084.97
35KV（万千伏安）	35KV（10 000kva）	11 064.55	11 338.16	12 650.13	12 850.68
公用变电容量（万千伏安）	**Public Transformer Capacity（10 000kva）**	**18 141.59**	**18 494.43**	**18 778.48**	**19 447.38**
500KV（万千伏安）	500KV（10 000kva）	6 194.64	6 294.84	6 479.64	6 779.64
220KV～35KV（万千伏安）	220KV－35KV（10 000kva）	11 946.95	12 199.59	12 298.84	12 667.74
用电最高负荷（万千瓦）	**Peak Electric Power Consumption Load（10 000kw）**	**3 094.00**	**3 131.90**	**3 311.50**	**3 352.67**

注：本表数据由市电力公司提供。
Note：Data in this table is provided by Shanghai Electric Power Corporation.

表 5.13 主要年份环保投入
INVESTMENT ON ENVIRONMENT PROTECTION IN MAIN YEARS

单位:亿元(100 million yuan)

年 份 Year	环境保护投资 Investment on Environment Protection	其 中 of which: #工业污染源治理投资 Investment on Industrial Pollution Source Control	其 中 of which: #治理废水 Treatment of Wastewater	#治理废气 Treatment of Exhaust Gas	环境保护投资相当于 GDP(%) Investment on Environment Protection as Percentage of Gross Domestic Product(%)
1990					2.06
1995	46.49				1.86
2000	141.91				2.97
2001	152.93				2.94
2002	162.39				2.83
2003	191.53				2.86
2004	225.37				2.79
2005	281.18				3.04
2006	310.85				2.94
2007	366.12				2.93
2008	422.37				3.00
2009	460.42				3.06
2010	507.54				2.96
2011	557.92				2.91
2012	570.49	64.25	4.36	6.59	2.83
2013	607.88	70.40	4.70	17.00	2.81
2014	699.89	260.14	6.84	27.06	2.97
2015	708.83	125.22	3.90	40.93	2.82
2016	823.57	135.29	1.98	50.33	3.00
2017	923.53	146.23	5.81	29.57	3.10
2018	989.19	109.56	8.05	19.30	3.00
2019	1 079.25	130.32	10.38	34.20	2.80
2020	1 087.86	110.11	13.24	26.44	2.80
2021	1 119.86	124.59	15.94	22.34	2.60

表 5.14 主要年份工业固体废弃物防治
PREVENTION AND CURE OF INDUSTRIAL SOLID WASTES IN MAIN YEARS

指 标	Indicators	2000	2010	2020	2021
工业固体废弃物产生量(万吨)	Volume of Industrial Solid Wastes Produced (10 000 tons)	1 354.74	2 448.36	1 808.75	2 072.57
#危险废物	Dangerous Wastes	28.32	51.25	131.89	140.25
工业废弃物综合利用量(万吨)	Volume of Industrial Wastes Treated and Utilized (10 000 tons)	1 515.90	2 366.90	1 701.82	1 947.49
#危险废物	Dangerous Wastes	27.05	28.47	–	–
工业废弃物综合利用率(%)	Ratio of Industrial Wastes Treated and Utilized (%)	93.26	96.16	93.75	93.87
工业固体废物处置量(万吨)	Volume of Industrial Solid Wastes Disposed (10 000 tons)	90.96	93.86	111.40	125.74
#危险废物	Dangerous Wastes	1.08	23.44	–	–

注：本页数据由上海市生态环境局提供。
Note: Data on this page are provided by Shanghai Municipal Bureau of Ecology and Environment.

表 5.15 水环境保护(1995~2021)
WATER ENVIRONMENT PROTECTION

年 份 Year	废水排放总量(亿吨) Total Waste Water Discharged (100 million tons)	其中 of which 工业 Industrial Waste Water	废水化学需氧量排放总量(万吨) Total Emission of Oxygen of Waste Water Needed by Chemistry (10 000 tons)	其中 of which 工业 Industrial Waste Water	污水处理厂数(座) Quantity of Sewage Disposal Plants(unit)	污水处理厂污水处理量(万吨) Volume of Sewage Disposed by Sewage Disposal Plants (10 000 tons)
1995	22.45	11.61		12.29	17	14 665
1996	22.85	11.41	27.46	12.16	20	12 876
1997	21.10	9.99	38.55	11.70	22	14 790
1998	20.81	9.00	36.55	9.63	22	15 605
1999	20.28	8.52	34.98	8.92	22	17 479
2000	19.37	7.25	31.87	6.93	27	23 028
2001	19.50	6.80	30.48	5.27	26	29 487
2002	19.21	6.49	32.96	4.78	27	30 658
2003	18.22	6.11	28.38	4.38	30	39 891
2004	19.34	5.64	29.38	3.76	37	95 301
2005	19.97	5.11	30.44	3.66	42	117 833
2006	22.37	4.83	30.20	3.53	43	155 726
2007	22.66	4.76	29.44	3.38	45	152 886
2008	22.60	4.41	26.67	2.76	47	177 090
2009	23.05	4.12	24.34	2.90	51	171 609
2010	24.82	3.67	21.98	2.16	52	189 654
2011	19.86	4.46	24.90	2.74	53	193 354
2012	22.05	4.77	24.26	2.62	53	200 685
2013	22.30	4.54	23.56	2.55	53	203 222
2014	22.12	4.39	22.44	2.48	53	208 145
2015	22.41	4.69	19.88	2.27	53	213 944
2016	22.08	3.66	14.75	1.44	53	267 954
2017	21.20	3.16	14.18	1.29	52	263 703
2018	20.98	2.91	12.05	1.02	51	265 541
2019	21.42	3.41	10.97	0.93	49	282 575
2020	19.81	3.12	7.29	0.86	46	302 169
2021	20.91	3.21	7.25	0.86	46	306 943

①2011 年起，废水排放总量中增加了农业源和集中式治理设施排放的废水。
②2016 年起，废水化学需氧量排放总量不包括农业源排放量。
❶Since 2011, waste water discharged from the agricultural source and centralized treatment facilities has been added in Total Waste Water Discharged.
❷From 2016 wastewater COD (Chemical Oxygen Demand) emissions do not include agricultural source emission.

表 5.16　大气环境保护(1995~2021)
ATMOSPHERE ENVIRONMENT PROTECTION

年　份 Year	工业废气排放总量(亿标立方米) Industrial Waste Gas Emission (100 million cu.m)	颗粒物排放总量(万吨) Total Emission of Particulate Matter (10 000 tons)	其　中　of which		废气二氧化硫排放总量(万吨) Total Emission of SO_2 (10 000 tons)	其　中　of which	
			工　业 Industrial Sector	生活及其他 Residential Sector and Others		工　业 Industrial Sector	生活及其他 Residential Sector and Others
1995	4 625	20.78	13.33	7.45	53.41	38.15	15.26
1996	4 757	15.78	14.77	1.01	51.00	43.30	7.70
1997	4 755	17.08	13.38	3.70	50.85	43.62	7.23
1998	4 912	15.63	10.74	4.89	48.89	39.09	9.80
1999	4 947	13.57	9.00	4.57	40.31	31.09	9.22
2000	5 755	14.12	8.32	5.80	46.49	32.68	13.81
2001	6 964	13.52	6.23	7.29	47.26	30.00	17.26
2002	7 440	10.74	5.60	5.14	44.66	32.49	12.17
2003	7 799	11.54	4.97	6.57	43.54	30.07	13.47
2004	8 834	12.27	5.25	7.02	47.31	34.95	12.36
2005	8 482	11.52	4.95	6.57	51.28	37.52	13.76
2006	9 428	11.29	4.73	6.56	50.80	37.43	13.37
2007	9 591	10.60	4.04	6.56	49.78	36.44	13.34
2008	10 436	10.63	4.06	6.57	44.61	29.80	14.81
2009	10 059	10.18	3.64	6.54	37.89	23.93	13.96
2010	12 969	10.21	4.18	6.03	35.81	26.32	9.49
2011	13 692	8.98	6.64	2.34	24.01	21.01	3.00
2012	13 361	8.71	6.37	2.34	22.82	19.34	3.48
2013	13 344	8.09	6.72	1.37	21.58	17.29	4.29
2014	13 007	14.17	13.14	1.03	18.81	15.54	3.27
2015	12 802	12.07	11.14	0.93	17.08	10.49	6.59
2016	12 669	7.95	7.28	0.67	7.42	6.74	0.68
2017	13 867	4.70	3.03	1.67	1.85	1.27	0.58
2018	13 780	2.81	1.62	1.19	0.99	0.91	0.08
2019	15 016	1.48	1.33	0.15	0.76	0.66	0.10
2020	15 715	1.05	0.79	0.26	0.54	0.52	0.02
2021	16 408	0.98	0.76	0.22	0.58	0.55	0.02

①2008 年起工业废气排放量按新排放系数计算。
②2022 年起，烟尘排放总量统计口径变更为颗粒物排放总量。
③2014 年工业粉尘排放量统计口径包括无组织排放量。
④2016 年起，废气二氧化硫排放总量不包括非道路移动源排放量。
❶Since 2008, the Volume of Industrial Exhaust Emission is calculated by new emission coefficient.
❷Since 2022, the statistics caliber of Total Emission of Smoke and Dust has been changed to Total Emission of Particulate Matter.
❸The statistics of industrial dust emissions include inorganization emissions in 2014.
❹From 2016 exhaust gas SO_2(sulfur dioxide) emissions do not include non-road moving source emission.

表 5.17 主要年份环境空气状况
AMBIENT AIR CONDITION IN MAIN YEARS

指 标	Indicators	2000	2010	2020	2021
中心城区二氧化硫年日平均值（毫克/立方米）	Annual Daily Mean Concentration of SO_2 in Urban Area (mg/m^3)	0.045	0.029	0.006	0.006
中心城区二氧化氮年日平均值（毫克/立方米）	Annual Daily Mean Concentration of NO_2 in Urban Area (mg/m^3)	0.090	0.050	0.037	0.035
中心城区可吸入颗粒平均浓度（毫克/立方米）	Mean Concentration of Inhalable Particulate in Urban Area (mg/m^3)		0.079	0.041	0.043
降水 PH 平均值	Rain PH Value	5.19	4.66	5.38	5.56
酸雨频率(%)	Frequency of Acid Rain (%)	26.0	73.9	40.2	26.4
环境空气质量优良天数(天)	Quantity of Days with Good Ambient Air Quality (day)	295	336	319	335
环境空气质量优良率(%)	Rate of Good Ambient Air Quality (%)	80.8	92.1	87.2	91.8

注：2013 年起，环境空气质量优良率以 AQI 评价。
Note: Since 2013, rate of ambient air quality is evaluated by AQI.

表 5.18 主要年份声环境及治理
ENVIRONMENTAL NOISE AND TREATMENT IN MAIN YEARS

指 标	Indicators	2000	2010	2020	2021
区域环境噪声平均等效声级	**Average Equivalent Sound Level of Area Ambient Noise**				
昼间时段(LeqdB(A))	Daytime (LeqdB(A))	56.6	55.8	54.2	54.0
夜间时段(LeqdB(A))	Nighttime (LeqdB(A))	49.2	48.3	47.8	47.7
交通环境噪声平均等效声级	**Average Equivalent Sound Level of Traffic Noise**				
昼间时段(LeqdB(A))	Daytime(LeqdB(A))	70.5	69.8	68.2	68.4
夜间时段(LeqdB(A))	Nighttime(LeqdB(A))	64.1	64.3	63.4	63.6

注：本页数据由上海市生态环境局提供。
Note: Data on this page are provided by Shanghai Municipal Bureau of Ecology and Environment.

表 5.19 城市环境卫生情况(1978~2021)
URBAN ENVIRONMENTAL SITUATION

年 份 Year	垃圾产生量 (万吨) Garbage Produced (10 000 tons)	其 中 of which 生活垃圾 Residential Garbage	 建筑垃圾 Construction Garbage	清运粪便 (万吨) Night Soil Disposal Cleared (10 000 tons)
1978	214	108	106	418
1979	250	125	126	374
1980	272	131	141	331
1981	272	146	126	329
1982	296	169	127	325
1983	280	166	113	311
1984	308	185	123	272
1985	305	196	109	252
1986	328	226	102	263
1987	325	229	97	262
1988	329	240	89	249
1989	344	250	94	246
1990	382	279	103	243
1991	393	296	97	229
1992	428	301	127	242
1993	488	335	152	234
1994	558	358	200	240
1995	668	372	296	216
1996	736	419	317	217
1997	755	454	301	227
1998	824	470	353	218
1999	767	500	267	172
2000	858	641	217	256
2001	901	644	257	219
2002	760	467	293	238
2003	800	585	215	251
2004	802	610	192	258
2005	777	622	155	254
2006	805	658	146	247
2007	852	702	150	232
2008	841	678	153	220
2009	870	710	160	221
2010	890	732	158	201
2011	1 142	704	438	207
2012	11 728	716	11 012	200
2013	13 716	735	12 981	222
2014	15 135	743	14 392	200
2015	10 755	790	9 965	173
2016	7 796	880	6 916	160
2017	6 435	900	5 535	158
2018	8 614	984	7 630	137
2019	10 651	1 038	9 613	151
2020	11 109	868	10 241	120
2021	15 188	1 232	13 956	104

①2012 年起，建筑垃圾中增加了工程渣土清运量。
②本页数据由市绿化和市容管理局提供。
❶Since 2012, Construction Garbage Contains Volume of Construction Dregs Clearance.
❷Data on this page are provided by Shanghai Municipal Virescence and Appearance Administration Bureau.

表 5.20 环境卫生设施(1978~2021)
URBAN ENVIRONMENTAL SANITATION

年 份 Year	环卫系统公共厕所(座) Public Lavatories(unit)	生活垃圾收集点(处) Collection Points of Residential Garbage(unit)	废物箱(只) Trash Cans(unit)	倒粪站(座) Excrements Stations(unit)	化粪池(只) Septic Tanks(unit)
1978	706	13 840	2 333	3 303	25 540
1979	696	12 695	3 151	3 382	25 915
1980	713	15 707	3 402	3 445	26 754
1981	740	17 905	2 546	3 464	27 407
1982	760	18 824	2 821	3 484	28 652
1983	778	17 859	2 733	3 467	29 977
1984	798	20 384	3 890	3 481	30 943
1985	952	22 870	5 700	3 470	33 477
1986	950	31 142	5 983	3 537	39 175
1987	978	37 751	6 341	3 587	40 042
1988	992	42 802	5 117	3 342	41 171
1989	1 057	46 149	5 276	3 107	41 349
1990	1 016	46 368	4 921	2 973	43 655
1991	1 033	40 309	4 980	3 006	43 089
1992	1 048	44 752	4 961	2 655	43 694
1993	1 104	46 741	5 756	2 732	43 323
1994	1 100	50 292	6 993	2 739	43 125
1995	1 100	48 563	9 019	2 532	43 151
1996	1 112	51 456	9 522	2 412	38 657
1997	1 120	53 643	12 735	2 207	44 440
1998	1 203	59 498	15 968	2 127	41 760
1999	1 311	66 067	17 326	2 192	44 694
2000	2 215	22 470	23 189	2 045	46 921
2001	2 406	17 694	24 672	1 890	47 500
2002	3 776	26 787	29 517	1 846	49 220
2003	3 468	27 814	31 272	1 709	48 831
2004	3 640	28 649	34 571	1 611	47 579
2005	3 640	28 388	39 539	1 689	47 424
2006	3 746	29 812	44 888	2 253	46 217
2007	5 415	29 538	47 739	2 158	45 841
2008	5 866	29 965	56 485	2 064	45 537
2009	5 633	30 584	67 465	2 257	43 775
2010	6 026	30 645	74 658	1 900	43 170
2011	5 768	30 648	78 213	1 868	42 652
2012	6 340	31 625	82 454	1 837	42 306
2013	6 224	32 018	98 266	1 800	43 887
2014	6 168	32 122	98 857	1 756	43 629
2015	6 197	32 209	94 310	1 729	43 582
2016	6 220	32 257	81 246	1 832	43 983
2017	6 221	32 247	86 246	1 832	43 983
2018	6 128	31 319	80 360	1 627	40 178
2019	6 225	29 811	62 554	1 681	40 439
2020	6 592	28 104	55 309	1 576	37 990
2021	6 799	27 176	40 753	1 539	37 654

上/海/统/计/年/鉴

主要统计指标解释

■ 能源消费总量

能源消费总量指一定时期内全国(地区)物质生产部门、非物质生产部门和生活消费的各种能源的总和,是观察能源消费水平、构成和增长速度的总量指标。能源消费总量包括原煤和原油及其制品、天然气、电力,但不包括低热值燃料、生物质能和太阳能等的利用。能源消费总量分为三部分,即终端能源消费量、能源加工转换损失量和能源损失量。

(1)终端能源消费量指一定时期内全国(地区)物质生产部门、非物质生产部门和生活消费的各种能源在扣除了用于加工转换二次能源消费量和损失量以后的数量。

(2)能源加工转换损失量指一定时期内全国(地区)投入加工转换的各种能源数量之和与产出各种能源产品之和的差额。它是观察能源在加工转换过程中损失量变化的指标。

(3)能源损失量指一定时期内能源在输送、分配、储存过程中发生的损失和由客观原因造成的各种损失量。不包括各种气体能源放空、放散量。

■ 能源消费弹性系数

能源消费弹性系数反映能源消费增长速度与国民经济增长速度之间比例关系的指标:

$$\text{能源消费弹性系数}=\frac{\text{能源消费量年平均增长速度}}{\text{国民经济年平均增长速度}}$$

■ 电力消费弹性系数

电力消费弹性系数反映电力消费增长速度与国民经济增长速度之间比例关系的指标。计算公式为:

$$\text{电力消费弹性系数}=\frac{\text{电力消费量年平均增长速度}}{\text{国民经济年平均增长速度}}$$

■ 能源加工转换效率

能源加工转换效率指一定时期内能源经过加工转换后,产出的各种能源产品的数量与投入加工转换的各种能源数量的比率。它是观察能源加工转换装置和生产工艺先进与落后、管理水平高低等的重要指标。计算公式为:

$$\text{能源加工转换效率}=\frac{\text{加工转换产出量}}{\text{加工转换投入量}}\times 100\%$$

■ 自然保护区

指对有代表性的自然生态系统、珍稀濒危野生动植物物种的天然分布区、水源涵养区、有特殊意义的自然历史遗迹等保护对象所在的陆地、陆地水体或海域,依法划出一定面积进行特殊保护和管理的区域。以县及县以上各级人民政府正式批准建立的自然保护区为准(包括“六五”以前由部门或“革委会”批准且现仍存在的自然保护区)。风景名胜区、文物保护区不计在内。自然保护区分国家级、省级、地市级和县级。按主管部门分属:环保、林业、农业、地矿、海洋、水利和其他部门。

■ 工业固体废弃物产生量

指报告期内企业在生产过程中产生的固体状、半固体状和高浓度废液体状废弃物的总量,包括危险废物、冶炼废渣、粉煤灰、炉渣、煤矸石、尾矿、放射性废物和其他废物等;不包括矿山开采的剥离废石和掘进废石(煤矸石和呈酸性或碱性的废石除外)。酸性或碱性废石指采掘的废石其流经水、雨淋水的pH值小于4或pH值大于10.5者。

■ 危险废物

指列入国家危险废物名录或根据国家规定的危险废物鉴别标准和鉴别方法认定的,具有爆炸性、易燃性、易氧化性、毒性、腐蚀性、易传染疾病等危险特性之一的废物。

■ 工业废弃物综合利用量

指报告期内企业通过回收、加工、循环、交换等方式,从废弃物中提取或者使其转化为可以利用的资源、能源和其他原材料的废弃物量(包括当年利用往年的工业废弃物贮存量),如用作农业肥料、生产建筑材料、筑路等。综合利用量由原产生废弃物的单位统计。

主要统计指标解释

■ 工业废弃物综合利用率

指工业废弃物综合利用量占工业废弃物产生量(包括综合利用往年贮存量)的百分率。计算公式为:

$$工业废弃物综合利用率=\frac{工业废弃物综合利用量}{工业废弃物产生量+综合利用往年贮存量}\times 100\%$$

■ 工业固体废物处置量

指报告期内企业将固体废物焚烧或者最终置于符合环境保护规定要求的场所,并不再回取的工业固体废物量(包括当年处置往年的工业固体废物贮存量)。处置方式有填埋(其中危险废物应安全填埋)、焚烧、专业贮存场(库)封场处理、深层灌注、回填矿井及海洋处置(经海洋管理部门同意投海处置)等。

■ 工业废水排放量

指经过企业厂区所有排放口排到企业外部的工业废水量。包括生产废水、外排的直接冷却水、超标排放的矿井地下水和与工业废水混排的厂区生活污水,不包括外排的间接冷却水(清污不分流的间接冷却水应计算在内)。

■ 工业废水排放达标量

指报告期内废水中各项污染物指标都达到国家或地方排放标准的外排工业废水量,包括未经处理外排达标的,经废水处理设施处理后达标排放的,以及经污水处理厂处理后达标排放的。

■ 工业废水排放达标率

指工业废水排放达标量占工业废水排放量的百分率,计算公式为:

$$工业废水排放达标率=\frac{工业废水排放达标量}{工业废水排放量}\times 100\%$$

■ 工业废气排放量

指企业厂区内燃料燃烧和生产工艺过程中产生的各种排入空气的含有污染物的气体总量,按标准状态〔273K,101 325Pa〕计算。测算公式为:

工业废气排放量 = 燃料燃烧过程中废气排放量 + 生产工艺过程中废气排放量

■ 工业二氧化硫排放总量

指报告期内企业在燃料燃烧和生产工艺过程中排入大气的SO_2总量,计算公式为:

工业二氧化硫排放量 = 燃料燃烧过程中二氧化硫排放量 + 生产工艺过程中二氧化硫排放量

■ 工业烟尘排放量

指企业厂区内燃料燃烧过程中产生的烟气中夹带的颗粒物排放量。

■ 酸雨频率

指酸雨出现的次数占降水出现次数的比例,通常称PH值小于5.6的降水为酸雨。

SHANGHAI STATISTICAL YEARBOOK

EXPLANATORY NOTES TO MAJOR STATISTICAL INDICATORS

□ Total Energy Consumption

Total Energy Consumption refers to the total energy consumption of various forms by material production departments, non- material production departments and households in the country (region) in a given period of time. It is a comprehensive indicator to observe the scale, composition and development of energy consumption. The total energy consumption includes raw coal, crude petroleum and their products, natural gas and electricity, but excludes fuel of low calorific value, bioenergy and solar energy. Total domestic energy consumption can be divided into three parts:

(1) Final Energy Consumption refers to the total energy consumption by material production departments, non-material production departments and households in the country (region) in a given period of time, after deducting the secondary energy consumption and loss during the process of energy conversion.

(2) Loss During the Process of Energy Conversion refers to the total input of various forms for conversion, minus the total output of energy of various forms in the country in a given period of time. It is an indicator to observe the loss that occurs during the process of energy conversion.

(3) Loss refers to the total loss of energy due to mistakes or any objective reasons during the course of energy transport, distribution and storage in a given period of time. The loss of various kinds of gas due to gas discharges and stocktaking is excluded.

□ Elasticity of Energy Consumption

Elasticity Ratio of Energy Consumption is an indicator to show the relationship between the growth rate of energy consumption and the growth rate of the national economy. The formula is:

$$\text{Elasticity of Energy Consumption} = \frac{\text{average annual growth rate of energy consumption}}{\text{average annual growth rate of national economy}}$$

□ Elasticity of Electricity Consumption

Elasticity Ratio of Electricity Consumption is an indicator to show the relationship between the growth rate of electricity consumption and the growth rate of the national economy. The formula is:

$$\text{Elasticity of Electricity Consumption} = \frac{\text{average annual growth rate of electricity consumption}}{\text{average annual growth rate of national economy}}$$

□ Efficiency of Energy Transformation

Efficiency of Energy Transformation refers to the ratio of the total output of energy products after transformation and the total input of energy for transformation in the same reference period .It is an indicator to show the current conditions of energy processing and conversion equipment, production technique and management. The formula is:

$$\text{Efficiency of Energy Transformation} = \frac{\text{output of enery from transformation}}{\text{Input of energy for transformation}} \times 100\%$$

□ Natural Reserves

Natural Reserves refer to all the land, water areas on land and sea areas are under special protection or management due to the possess ion of representative natural ecological system, natural distribution of rare and dying out animal zones, water-resource conservation areas, and natural historical relics. Also included are natural reserves formally approved by people´s governments at various levels at and above county level (including those approved before the Sixth-five-year Program and still active natural reserves).Scenic spots and historical sites and zones for preservation of cultural relics are not included. Natural reserves are classified as national level, provincial level, prefecture level and county level ones. They are under the jurisdiction of different departments, such as: environment protection, forestry, agriculture, geological and mining, oceanic and water conservancy and so on.

□ Industrial Solid Wastes Produced

Industrial Solid Wastes Produced refers to total volume of solid, semi- solid and high concentration liquid residues produced by industrial enterprises from production process in a given period of time, including hazardous wastes, slag, coal ash, gangue, tailings, radioactive residues and other wastes, but excluding stones stripped or dug out in mining (gangue and acid

EXPLANATORY NOTES TO MAJOR STATISTICAL INDICATORS

or alkaline stones not included). A stone is acid or alkaline depending on the pH value of the water below 4 or above 10.5 when the stone is in, or soaked by, the water.

□ Hazardous Wastes

Hazardous Wastes refers to those included in the national hazardous wastes catalogue or specified as any one of the following properties in the national hazardous wastes identification standards: explosive, ignitable, oxidizable, toxic, corrosive or liable to cause infectious diseases or lead to other dangers.

□ Industrial Wastes Utilized

Industrial Wastes Utilized refers to volume of wastes from which useful materials can be extracted or which can be converted into usable resources, energy or other materials by means of reclamation, processing, recycling and exchange (including utilizing in the year the stocks of industrial wastes of the previous year). Examples of such utilizations include fertilizers, building materials and road materials. The information shall be collected by the producing units of the wastes.

□ Ratio of Industrial Wastes Utilized

Ratio of Industrial Wastes Utilized refers to the percentage of industrial wastes utilized over industrial wastes produced (including stocks of the previous years). It is calculated as:

Ratio of industrial wastes utilized=volume of industrial wastes utilized / (industrial wastes produced + stock of previous years) ×100%

□ Industrial Solid Wastes Disposed

Industrial Solid Wastes Disposed refers to quantity of industrial solid wastes which are burnt or placed ultimately in the sites meeting the requirements for environmental protection and not salvaged or recycled (including disposition in the year of those wastes of previous years). The disposition includes landfill (Safe landfills should be conducted for hazardous wastes), incineration, containment spaces, deep underground disposal, backfill in mining pits and disposal at sea.

□ Volume of Industrial Waste Water Discharged

Volume of Industrial Waste Water Discharged refers to the volume of industrial waste water discharged, through all outlets, to the outside of industrial enterprises, including waste water produced, direct-cooling water, underground water from mines that does not meet the standard of discharge, and the domestic sewage mixed up with industrial waste water when discharged, but excluding discharged indirect-cooling water.

□ Industrial Waste Water Meeting Discharge Standards

Industrial Waste Water Meeting Discharge Standards refers to volume of industrial waste water discharge which, with or without treatment, reaches national or local standards with regard to all pollutants.

□ Ratio of Standard Waste Water Discharged to the Total Discharge

Ratio of Standard Waste Water Discharged to the Total Discharge refers to the share of the volume of waste water up to the standard for discharge of the total volume. The formula is as follows:

Ratio of Standard Waste Water Discharged to the Total Discharge

$$\frac{\text{average annual growth rate of electricity consumption}}{\text{average annual growth rate of national economy}} \times 100\%$$

□ Volume of Waste Industrial Gas Emission

Industrial Waste Air Emission refers to discharge into atmosphere of waste air containing pollutants generated from fuel burning and production process in enterprises within a given period of time. It is calculated at standard status (273K, 101325Pa) as:

Industrial waste air emission = emission through fuel burning + emission through production process

□ SO_2 Emission through Industrial Activities

SO_2 Emission through Industrial Activities refers to volume of sulphur dioxide emission from fuel burning and production process by enterprises during a given period of time. It is calculated as:

SO_2 emission through industrial activities = SO_2 emission from fuel burning + SO_2 emission from production process

□ Industrial Soot Emission

Industrial Soot Emission refers to volume of soot in smoke emitted in process of fuel burning in premises of enterprises.

EXPLANATORY NOTES TO MAJOR STATISTICAL INDICATORS

□ Acid Rain Frequency

Acid Rain Frequency refers to the proportion of frequencies of acid rainfall to the total rainfall times. Rainfall is defined as acid rain when the PH value of its rainwater is smaller than 5.6.

第六篇
CHAPTER 6

固定资产投资
INVESTMENT IN FIXED ASSETS

简要说明

一、本篇资料的主要内容

本篇资料通过对一定时期全社会建造和购置固定资产活动的数量方面的描述，反映报告期内固定资产投资的规模、速度和内部结构情况，固定资产投资的资金来源等。

二、本篇资料的统计范围

固定资产投资统计的范围包括：建设项目投资，房地产开发投资及农户投资。

三、本篇的资料来源

建设项目投资的统计资料来自上海市统计局投资建设统计处的固定资产投资统计调查；房地产开发投资的统计资料来自上海市统计局投资建设统计处的房地产开发、经营统计调查；农户投资的统计资料来自国家统计局上海调查总队居民收支调查处的农村住户固定资产投资抽样调查。

四、本篇的统计调查方法

除农户固定资产投资统计采用抽样调查方法外，其他均为全面统计报表。

五、统计口径的变化

自1997年起，固定资产投资项目的统计起点由5万元及以上提高到50万元及以上。

自2011年起，固定资产投资项目的统计起点由计划总投资50万元及以上提高到500万元及以上。

BRIEF INTRODUCTION

I. Main Contents

Statistics in this chapter describe activities on the construction and purchase of fixed assets of the whole society during a given period of time, and reflect the size, growth, internal structure, and financing of the investment in fixed assets during the reference period.

II. Scope of Statistics

Statistics on the investment in fixed assets cover investments in capital construction projects in urban and rural areas, investments in real estate development, and rural household investment.

III. Sources of Data

Data on the investments in construction projects of urban and rural non-farm households are from the surveys of investment in fixed assets from Department of Investment and Construction Statistics of the Shanghai Municipal Bureau of Statistics. Data on the real estate investments are from surveys of real estate development and management conducted by Department of Investment and Construction Statistics of the Shanghai Municipal Bureau of Statistics. Data on the investment of farm households are from surveys of fixed assets investment in rural households conducted by Department of Residents Income and Expenditure Survey of the Survey Office of NBS in Shanghai.

IV. Methodology of Data Collection

All data on investment in fixed assets are collected by the system of reporting form with complete enumeration, except data on individual investments in fixed assets in rural areas, which are collected through sample surveys.

V. Changes in Statistical Scope

Since 1997, the cut-off point of statistics of investment projects in fixed assets is raised from 50000 yuan to 500000 yuan.

Since 2011, the cut-off point of projects covered by statistics of investment in fixed assets is raised from an investment of 500000 yuan to 5000000 yuan.

表 6.1 全社会固定资产投资总额(按投资类别分)(1978~2017)
TOTAL INVESTMENT IN FIXED ASSETS (GROUPED BY TYPE OF INVESTMENT)

单位:亿元(100 million yuan)

年 份 Year	本年完成投资合计 Investment Completed Total	其中 of which				
		建设项目 Construction Project	其中 of which 城镇 Town	其中 of which 农村非农户 Rural Non-agricultural	房地产开发 Investment in Real Estate	农户投资 Farmers' Investment
1978	27.91	26.88	23.92	2.96		0.79
1979	35.58	34.39	32.22	2.17		0.94
1980	45.43	43.45	40.44	3.01		1.41
1981	54.60	49.85	45.20	4.65		3.97
1982	71.34	65.97	61.91	4.06		4.32
1983	75.94	70.21	65.26	4.95		4.48
1984	92.30	83.11	76.04	7.07		7.28
1985	118.56	103.16	96.12	7.04		12.00
1986	146.93	132.44	122.64	9.80		10.30
1987	186.30	167.88	154.04	13.84	0.97	12.66
1988	245.27	219.90	197.71	22.19	1.68	16.90
1989	214.76	194.64	177.70	16.94	1.85	14.32
1990	227.08	199.05	184.67	14.38	8.16	15.96
1991	258.30	232.34	208.72	23.62	7.59	14.17
1992	357.38	318.93	263.51	55.42	12.71	17.00
1993	653.91	610.80	505.98	104.82	22.04	5.33
1994	1 123.29	971.68	830.45	141.23	117.43	10.40
1995	1 601.79	1 097.68	958.11	139.57	466.20	13.10
1996	1 952.05	1 238.85	1 080.53	158.32	657.79	20.00
1997	1 977.59	1 322.92	1 156.76	166.16	614.23	16.80
1998	1 964.83	1 361.41	1 224.01	137.40	577.12	12.76
1999	1 856.72	1 325.84	1 191.51	134.33	514.83	5.54
2000	1 869.67	1 284.08	1 122.47	161.61	566.17	10.36
2001	1 994.73	1 354.22	1 181.09	173.13	630.73	9.28
2002	2 187.06	1 430.69	1 262.77	167.92	748.89	6.87
2003	2 452.11	1 544.38	1 374.38	170.00	901.24	6.49
2004	3 084.66	1 903.33	1 722.51	180.82	1 175.46	5.86
2005	3 542.55	2 288.61	1 984.61	304.00	1 246.86	7.08
2006	3 925.09	2 643.53	2 246.93	396.60	1 275.59	5.96
2007	4 458.61	3 145.87	2 775.81	370.06	1 307.53	5.21
2008	4 829.45	3 459.38	3 044.46	414.92	1 366.87	3.20
2009	5 273.33	3 807.62	3 384.31	423.31	1 464.18	1.53
2010	5 317.67	3 334.95	2 858.56	476.39	1 980.68	2.03
2011	5 067.09	2 893.95	2 519.48	374.47	2 170.31	2.83
2012	5 254.38	2 870.04	2 559.12	310.92	2 381.36	2.98
2013	5 647.79	2 824.54	2 544.99	279.55	2 819.59	3.66
2014	6 016.43	2 806.49			3 206.48	3.46
2015	6 352.70	2 880.45			3 468.94	3.31
2016	6 755.88	3 042.65			3 709.03	4.21
2017	7 246.60	3 384.42			3 856.53	5.66

注：自 2011 年起，全社会固定资产投资由建设项目投资、房地产开发投资和农户投资三部分组成；建设项目投资由城镇投资和农村非农户投资两部分组成，其中城镇投资包括原来的基本建设、更新改造、其他投资和城镇私人建房投资；从 2014 年起建设项目取消“城乡分组”。2018 年以来，国家统计局规定各省市固定资产投资统计对外只发布增速数据，本篇章涉及固定资产投资的指标均为增速(%)数据。

Note: Since 2011, total investment in fixed assets was composed of construction project investment, investment in real estate development and investment of rural households; construction project investment was composed of investment in urban areas and rural non-agricultural investment, in which investment in urban areas was composed of fundamental construction, renovation, other investments and urban private housing investment. Group of urban and rural construction projects was canceled since 2014.

表 6.2 全社会固定资产投资总额(按经济类型分)(1978~2017)
TOTAL INVESTMENT IN FIXED ASSETS (GROUPED BY ECONOMIC TYPES)

单位:亿元(100 million yuan)

年 份 Year	本年完成投资合 计 Investment Completed Total	其 中 of which #国 有 经 济 State-owned	#集 体 经 济 Collective-owned	#股份制 经 济 Share-holding	#外商、港澳台 经 济 Hong Kong, Macao, Taiwan and Foreign Funded
1978	27.91	23.83	3.20		
1979	35.58	32.08	2.42		
1980	45.43	40.27	3.58		
1981	54.60	45.00	5.43		
1982	71.34	61.62	5.11		
1983	75.94	65.01	6.20		
1984	92.30	75.80	8.98		
1985	118.56	95.92	10.44		
1986	146.93	122.46	13.99		
1987	186.30	154.45	18.65		
1988	245.27	198.68	29.03		
1989	214.76	178.81	21.00		
1990	227.08	192.24	18.29		
1991	258.30	215.61	27.82		
1992	357.38	275.67	64.16		
1993	653.91	419.22	124.18	32.83	61.61
1994	1 123.29	721.37	189.75	76.99	101.78
1995	1 601.79	935.92	247.11	150.17	208.30
1996	1 952.05	1 048.27	239.47	165.57	340.18
1997	1 977.59	1 148.69	257.10	118.80	367.50
1998	1 964.83	1 087.94	208.84	203.81	405.17
1999	1 856.72	986.82	227.19	268.68	325.58
2000	1 869.67	829.98	156.34	421.53	319.05
2001	1 994.73	760.58	136.81	580.75	362.25
2002	2 187.06	742.72	101.33	631.70	369.96
2003	2 452.11	811.85	116.63	647.27	468.20
2004	3 084.66	955.12	146.58	667.52	851.39
2005	3 542.55	1 240.27	131.07	916.27	640.31
2006	3 925.09	1 460.09	159.31	910.31	725.85
2007	4 458.61	1 779.43	121.51	1 169.49	711.35
2008	4 829.45	2 295.74	104.86	1 026.67	748.14
2009	5 273.33	2 618.61	132.30	1 174.81	617.90
2010	5 317.67	2 234.12	183.07	1 200.26	686.95
2011	5 067.09	1 875.48	133.33	1 349.65	726.57
2012	5 254.38	1 855.24	112.41	1 417.80	758.08
2013	5 647.79	1 926.89	102.81	1 601.33	894.47
2014	6 016.43	1 796.22	55.07	1 812.77	1 103.04
2015	6 352.70	1 974.08	53.62	2 124.52	1 164.72
2016	6 755.88	1 844.66	33.85	2 611.71	1 153.48
2017	7 246.60	2 192.32	61.35	2 830.73	1 010.74

表 6.3 全社会固定资产投资主要指标比上年增长(2020~2021)
GROWTH RATE OF MAJOR INDICATORS OF TOTAL INVESTMENT IN FIXED ASSETS

单位:%

指 标	Indicators	2020	2021
本年完成投资合计	**Investment Completed Total**	**10.3**	**8.1**
按隶属关系分	**Grouped by Administrative Relationship**		
中央项目	Central Government Projects	-20.2	37.2
地方项目	Local Projects	14.0	5.6
按构成分	**Grouped by Use of Funds**		
建筑安装工程	Construction and Installation	5.1	11.9
设备工器具购置	Purchase of Equipment and Instruments	2.3	2.0
其他费用	Others	21.6	5.4
按建设性质分	**Grouped by Type of Construction**		
#新 建	New Construction	14.5	10.5
扩 建	Expansion	-15.8	55.0
改建和技术改造	Reconstruction and Technical Transformation	20.9	5.8
单纯购置	Simply Purchase	-3.2	-26.0
按产业分	**Grouped by Type of Industry**		
第一产业	Primary Industry	109.8	30.9
第二产业	Secondary Industry	16.5	8.2
第三产业	Tertiary Industry	9.0	8.0
按经济类型分	**Grouped by Economic Types**		
国有经济	State-owned	3.7	8.3
非国有经济	Non-state-owned	13.1	8.0
集体经济	Collective-owned	56.5	36.4
私营经济	Private	2.3	19.3
联营经济	Joint Owned		
股份制经济	Share-holding	17.3	4.9
港澳台商投资经济	Hong Kong, Macao and Taiwan Funded	-11.9	30.3
外商投资经济	Foreign Funded	38.2	-12.4
其他经济	Others	53.4	36.0
新增固定资产(亿元)	**Newly Increased Fixed Assets(100 million yuan)**	**3 427.43**	**3 720.35**

表6.4 全社会固定资产投资按行业分比上年增长(2020~2021)
GROWTH RATE OF TOTAL INVESTMENT IN FIXED ASSETS (GROUPED BY INDUSTRIES) (2020~2021)

单位:%

指 标	Indicators	2020	2021
本年完成投资合计	**Investment Completed Total**	**10.3**	**8.1**
农、林、牧、渔业	Agriculture, Forestry, Animal Husbandry and Fishery	106.5	21.5
工 业	Industry	15.9	8.2
建筑业	Construction	834.9	-62.5
批发和零售业	Wholesale and Retail	-13.5	9.4
交通运输、仓储和邮政业	Transportation, Storage, Postal and Telecommunications	-27.4	20.0
住宿和餐饮业	Hotel and Catering	158.6	-5.4
信息传输、软件和信息技术服务业	Transmission of Information, Software and Information Technology Services	-2.0	31.0
金融业	Finance	-29.9	-63.5
房地产业	Real Estate	11.1	7.4
租赁和商务服务业	Leasing and Business Service	45.9	6.7
科学研究和技术服务业	Scientific Research and Technology Service	18.3	68.6
水利、环境和公共设施管理业	Water Conservancy, Environment and Public Facility Management	31.8	-12.4
居民服务、修理和其他服务业	Residents Service, Repair and Other Services	-23.5	75.8
教 育	Education	1.8	59.9
卫生和社会工作	Health and Social Work	31.3	51.2
文化、体育和娱乐业	Culture, Sports and Entertainment	28.9	8.0
公共管理、社会保障和社会组织	Public Administration and Social Organizations	94.4	-24.9

表6.5 建设项目固定资产投资主要指标比上年增长(2021)
GROWTH RATE OF MAJOR INDICATORS OF INVESTMENT IN FIXED ASSETS OF THE CONSTRUCTION PROJECT

单位:%

指 标	Indicators	全 市 Total	#地 方 Local Projects
本年完成投资合计	**Investment Completed Total**	**9.1**	**3.9**
按建设性质分	**Grouped by Type of Construction**		
#新 建	New Construction	10.5	6.8
扩 建	Expansion	55.0	53.2
改建和技术改造	Reconstruction and Technical Transformation	5.8	7.5
单纯购置	Simply Purchase	-26.0	-51.6
按产业分	**Grouped by Type of Industry**		
第一产业	Primary Industry	30.9	30.9
第二产业	Secondary Industry	8.2	7.2
第三产业	Tertiary Industry	9.5	1.8
按行业分	**Grouped by Economic Sectors**		
#工 业	Industry	8.2	7.3
批发和零售业	Wholesale and Retail	9.4	7.4
交通运输、仓储和邮政业	Transportation, Storage, Postal and Telecommunications	20.0	0.8
住宿和餐饮业	Hotel and Catering	-5.4	-2.8
信息传输、软件和信息技术服务业	Transmission of Information, Software and Information Technology Services	31.0	48.2
金融业	Finance	-63.5	-61.6
房地产业	Real Estate	75.3	75.3
租赁和商务服务业	Leasing and Business Service	6.7	-10.1
科学研究和技术服务业	Scientific Research and Technology Service	68.6	66.9
水利、环境和公共设施管理业	Water Conservancy, Environment and Public Facility Management	-12.4	-14.0
居民服务、修理和其他服务业	Residents Service, Repair and Other Services	75.8	75.8
教 育	Education	59.9	59.6
卫生和社会工作	Health and Social Work	51.2	44.5
文化、体育和娱乐业	Culture, Sports and Entertainment	8.0	7.4
公共管理、社会保障和社会组织	Public Administration and Social Organizations	-24.9	-26.6
新增固定资产(亿元)	**Newly Increased Fixed Assets(100 million yuan)**	**24.1**	**23.6**

表 6.6 工业各行业固定资产投资主要指标(2021)
MAIN INDICATORS OF INVESTMENT IN FIXED ASSETS OF VARIOUS INDUSTRIES

行 业	Sectors	施工项目(个) Projects Under Construction (unit)	本年投产项目(个) Projects Completed and Put into Production (unit)	本年完成投资比上年增长(%) Growth Rate of Construction Transformation Investment (%)
总 计	**Total**	**3 391**	**1 002**	**8.2**
采矿业	**Excavation**			
开采辅助活动	Mining Support Activities			
制造业	**Manufacturing**	**2 310**	**614**	**7.8**
农副食品加工业	Farm and Sideline Products Processing	46	6	145.5
食品制造业	Food Manufacturing	68	14	30.4
酒、饮料和精制茶制造业	Wine, Drinks and Purified Tea Manufacturing	17	7	20.2
烟草制品业	Tabacco Manufacturing	7	2	431.1
纺织业	Textile	24	8	-55.5
纺织服装、服饰业	Textiles and Clothing Industry	17	2	108.8
皮革、毛皮、羽毛及其制品和制鞋业	Leather, Fur, Wool Products, and Shoes Manufacturing	6	1	181.3
木材加工和木、竹、藤、棕、草制品业	Timber Processing and Timber, Bamboo, Rattan, Coir and Straw Products Manufacturing	5	0	-69.0
家具制造业	Furniture Manufacturing	8	3	-54.2
造纸和纸制品业	Paper-making and Paper Products Manufacturing	20	6	11.8
印刷业和记录媒介复制业	Printing and Record Duplicating	42	8	33.8
文教、工美、体育和娱乐用品制造业	Culture, Education, Industrial Arts, Sports and Entertainment Goods Manufacturing	9	2	6.5
石油加工、炼焦和核燃料加工业	Oil Processing, Coking and Nuclear Fuel Processing	62	29	121.0
化学原料和化学制品制造业	Raw Chemical Materials and Chemical Products Manufacturing	178	56	89. 7
医药制造业	Medicine Manufacturing	164	35	87.8
化学纤维制造业	Chemical Fiber Manufacturing	3	1	-44.0
橡胶和塑料制品业	Rubber and Plastic Products Manufacturing	94	21	118.9
非金属矿物制品业	Non-metallic Mineral Products Manufacturing	46	12	-1.3
黑色金属冶炼和压延加工业	Ferrous Metal Smelting and Rolling Processing Industry	242	132	37.5
有色金属冶炼和压延加工业	Nonferrous Metal Smelting and Rolling Processing Industry	7	3	-51.5
金属制品业	Metal Products Manufacturing	85	19	23.8
通用设备制造业	General Equipment Manufacturing	201	68	30.0
专用设备制造业	Special Purpose Equipment Manufacturing	167	29	38.2
汽车制造业	The Automotive Manufacturing	298	59	-10.0
铁路、船舶、航空航天和其他运输设备制造业	The Railroad, Marine, Aerospace and Other Transportation Equipment Manufacturing	52	6	50.5
电气机械和器材制造业	Electric Machinery Equipments and Manufacturing	136	29	32.9
计算机、通信和其他电子设备制造业	Computer, Communications and Other Electronic Equipment Manufacturing	215	30	-11.2
仪器仪表制造业	Instrumentation Manufacturing	35	7	13.2
其他制造业	Other Manufacturing	41	12	-42.9
废弃资源综合利用业	Comprehensive Utilization of Waste Resources	12	6	-9.1
金属制品、机械和设备修理业	Metal Products, Machinery and Equipment Repair Industry	3	1	-78.9
电力、热力、燃气及水的生产和供应业	**Electricity, Heat, Gas and Water Production and Supply Industry**	**1 081**	**388**	**10.3**
电力、热力生产和供应业	Power and Heat Production and Supply	1 006	364	38.7
燃气生产和供应业	Gas Production and Supply	6	4	-87.6
水的生产和供应业	Water Production and Supply	69	20	-16.6

注：单纯购置项目固定资产投资不计算施工项目和本年投产项目个数。
Note: The investment in fixed assets of purchasing and preparatory project doesn't be calculated in projects under construction or projects completed and put into production in this year.

表 6.7 主要年份新增固定资产
NEWLY INCREASED FIXED ASSETS IN MAIN YEARS

年 份 Year	新增固定资产(亿元) Newly Increased Fixed Assets(100 million yuan)	其 中 of which #房地产开发 Investment in Real Estate Development
1990	222.99	4.97
1995	826.94	127.08
2000	1 493.35	477.39
2005	2 547.02	1 054.02
2006	2 680.85	1 058.94
2007	2 466.68	1 048.47
2008	2 773.14	994.10
2009	2 686.43	932.24
2010	3 179.40	964.27
2011	2 816.59	1 250.88
2012	2 911.34	1 388.45
2013	2 664.81	1 354.75
2014	2 739.79	1 583.93
2015	3 281.26	1 890.67
2016	2 958.65	1 558.72
2017	3 957.94	2 110.17
2018	3 599.51	1 955.84
2019	3 834.26	1 951.49
2020	3 427.43	1 946.36
2021	3 720.35	1 881.92

表 6.8 主要年份固定资产投资资金来源
CAPITAL SOURCES OF FIXED ASSETS INVESTMENT IN MAIN YEARS

单位:亿元(100 million yuan)

指 标	Indicators	2010	2015	2020	2021
到位资金合计	**Total Actual Funds This Year**	**7 997.62**	**10 652.67**	**12 840.87**	**15 383.87**
上年末结余资金	Balance at End of Previous Year	1 440.57	2 472.70	4 036.55	5 300.25
本年实际到位资金	Sub-total Actual Funds this Year	6 557.05	8 179.97	8 804.32	10 083.62
国家预算资金	State Budgetary Funds	624.91	501.61	1 092.96	1 190.04
国内贷款	Domestic Loans	1 568.79	2 050.79	1 769.77	2 028.33
债 券	Bonds	10.06	0.50	2.92	
利用外资	Foreign Investment	239.18	130.13	19.70	27.83
#外商直接投资	Foreign Direct Investment	139.72	85.36		
自筹资金	Self-Financed Capital	2 764.91	3 010.99	3 660.11	4 316.41
其他资金	Other Capital	1 349.21	2 485.96	2 258.87	2 521.02
本年各项应付款合计	The Total Payment of This Year	997.93	1 661.63	1 783.57	1 660.90
#工程款	Project Funds	438.19	867.08	674.04	726.69

注：自 2012 年起，国家预算资金和自筹资金统计口径调整，历年指标数据已做相应调整；自 2017 年起，利用外资取消其中外商直接投资指标。
Note: The Statistical caliber of state budget funds and self-financing was adjusted since 2012, and data over the years have been adjusted accordingly. Since 2017, the Foreign Investment has abolished the indicator of Foreign Direct Investment.

表 6.9 全社会房屋施工面积、竣工面积(1985~2019)
TOTAL FLOOR SPACE OF CONSTRUCTION AND COMPLETED BUILDINGS

年份 Year	施工面积(万平方米) Floor Area of Construction (10 000 sq.m)	其中 of which: #住宅 Residential Housing	其中 of which: 占全社会房屋施工面积比重(%) As Percentage of Total Floor Space of Construction(%)	竣工面积(万平方米) Floor Area Completed (10 000 sq.m)	房屋建筑面积竣工率(%) Construction Completion Rate (%)
1985	4 162.15	2 651.52	63.7	2 909.58	69.9
1986	4 874.44	2 469.27	50.7	2 493.93	51.2
1987	4 382.40	2 658.05	60.7	2 700.96	61.6
1988	4 369.20	2 667.00	61.0	2 457.34	56.2
1989	3 683.77	2 048.20	55.6	1 941.80	52.7
1990	3 801.46	2 269.06	59.7	2 138.44	56.3
1991	3 611.53	2 157.46	59.7	1 923.92	53.3
1992	4 709.52	2 463.79	52.3	2 608.20	55.4
1993	4 724.30	2 142.39	45.3	2 031.76	43.0
1994	6 720.70	3 520.27	52.4	2 519.09	37.5
1995	10 566.42	6 195.12	58.6	3 093.93	29.3
1996	10 730.85	5 874.26	54.7	3 254.57	30.3
1997	9 955.21	5 450.13	54.7	3 614.19	36.3
1998	9 364.36	5 113.52	54.6	3 364.43	35.9
1999	8 364.48	4 608.49	55.1	3 257.57	38.9
2000	8 636.31	4 804.12	55.6	3 266.52	37.8
2001	8 588.49	5 236.93	61.0	3 215.12	37.4
2002	9 425.42	5 994.70	63.6	3 102.54	32.9
2003	11 023.24	6 974.27	63.3	3 582.34	32.5
2004	12 291.81	7 873.44	64.1	4 932.57	40.1
2005	14 477.85	8 267.24	57.1	4 873.82	33.7
2006	14 596.49	8 085.28	55.4	4 901.46	33.6
2007	14 979.37	7 789.91	52.0	5 068.46	33.8
2008	14 083.52	7 060.19	50.1	3 828.79	27.2
2009	13 553.64	6 581.16	48.6	2 970.92	21.9
2010	15 020.76	7 344.07	48.9	2 776.21	18.5
2011	16 553.86	8 423.11	50.9	2 913.78	17.6
2012	16 874.72	8 350.83	49.5	2 838.97	16.8
2013	17 180.27	8 188.56	47.7	2 698.35	15.7
2014	18 010.06	8 573.04	47.6	2 682.42	14.9
2015	17 885.94	8 443.82	47.2	2 923.42	16.3
2016	17 733.25	8 157.21	46.0	2 840.03	16.0
2017	18 587.63	8 083.44	43.5	3 832.45	20.6
2018	18 757.71	7 615.04	40.6	3 790.92	20.2
2019	18 032.16	7 513.16	41.7	2 934.85	16.3

注：自 2020 年起，取消施工面积和竣工面积及其中项指标。
Note: Floor area of construction, floor area completed, and indicators of which are cancelled since 2020.

表 6.10 全社会住宅投资(1978~2021)
TOTAL INVESTMENT IN RESIDENTIAL HOUSING

年 份 Year	住宅投资额 (亿元) Investment in Residential Housing (100 million yuan)	其 中 of which #房地产 Real Estate	占全社会固定资产投资总额比重(%) As Percentage of Total Investment in Fixed Asset(%)
1978	2.67		9.6
1979	3.31		9.3
1980	5.82		12.8
1981	10.02		18.4
1982	11.03		15.5
1983	11.18		14.7
1984	15.88		17.2
1985	25.47		21.5
1986	28.24		19.2
1987	36.28		19.5
1988	44.84		18.3
1989	35.82	1.85	16.7
1990	42.94	7.26	18.9
1991	48.92	7.31	18.9
1992	61.23	11.73	17.1
1993	77.14	13.96	11.8
1994	300.65	106.31	26.8
1995	433.76	280.38	27.1
1996	466.99	356.01	23.9
1997	458.22	334.07	23.2
1998	404.96	320.66	20.6

注：1981 年以前住宅投资额不包括城乡私人建房和农村投资，从 1981 年开始为全社会口径。
Note: Before 1981, investment in residential housing in this table didn't cover private-built houses in urban and rural areas and rural investment, the whole society is covered since 1981.

表 6. 10 续表 continued

年 份 Year	住宅投资额 （亿元） Investment in Residential Housing （100 million yuan）	其 中 of which #房地产 Real Estate	占全社会固定资产投资总额比重（%） As Percentage of Total Investment in Fixed Asset(%)
1999	378.82	324.49	20.4
2000	443.90	408.82	23.7
2001	466.71	439.17	23.4
2002	584.51	567.76	26.7
2003	694.30	676.28	28.3
2004	922.61	900.67	29.9
2005	936.36	920.84	26.4
2006	854.15	835.65	21.8
2007	853.13	837.53	19.1
2008	871.52	843.63	18.0
2009	922.81	918.68	17.5
2010	1 232.96	1 229.83	23.2
2011	1 403.13	1 398.75	27.7
2012	1 457.64	1 451.94	27.7
2013	1 626.95	1 615.51	28.8
2014	1 730.81	1 724.65	28.8
2015	1 822.73	1 813.32	28.7
2016	1 979.85	1 965.43	29.3
2017	2 159.07	2 152.40	29.8
2018	2 238.45	2 225.92	
2019	2 329.11	2 318.13	
2020	2 451.84	2 418.79	
2021	2 684.44	2 673.95	

上/海/统/计/年/鉴

主要统计指标解释

■ 全社会固定资产投资

固定资产投资是国民经济再生产活动的一个重要部分。固定资产投资额是以货币形式表现的在一定时期内建造和购置固定资产的工作量以及与此有关的费用总称。它是反映固定资产投资规模、结构和发展速度的综合性指标。按照现行国家统计制度,全社会固定资产投资包括建设项目投资、房地产开发投资和农户投资。

自1997年起,固定资产投资统计起点为50万元(含50万元)以上项目;自2011年起,固定资产投资统计起点为500万元(含500万元)以上项目。

■ 固定资产投资按国民经济行业分

固定资产投资按国民经济行业分是根据建设项目建成投产后的主要产品或主要用途及社会经济活动性质来确定国民经济行业。一般情况下,一个建设项目或一个企业、事业单位只能属于一种国民经济行业。

■ 固定资产投资按隶属关系分

固定资产投资按隶属关系分是按建设单位或企业、事业、行政单位的主管上级机关确定的。

(1)中央:是指中共中央、人大常委会和国务院各部、委、局、总公司以及直属机构直接领导的建设项目和企业、事业、行政单位。这些单位的固定资产投资计划由国务院各部门直接编制和下达,建设中所需物资、主要设备以及建设中的问题都由中央有关部门安排和解决。

(2)地方:是由省(自治区、直辖市)、地区(州、盟、省辖市)、县(旗、县级市)三级政府及业务主管部门直接领导和管理的建设项目、企业、事业、行政单位。地方项目还包括不隶属以上各级政府及主管部门的建设项目和企业、事业单位,如外商投资企业和无主管部门的企业等。

■ 固定资产投资按构成分

固定资产投资按构成分是按其工作内容和实现方式来划分的,主要分为建筑安装工程,设备、工具、器具购置,其他费用三个部分。

(1)建筑安装工程(建筑安装工作量):指各种房屋、建筑物的建造工程和各种设备、装置的安装工程。包括各种房屋建造工程;各种用途设备基础和各种工业窑炉的砌筑工程及金属结构工程;为施工而进行的各种准备工作和临时工程以及完工后的清理工作等;铁路、道路的铺设,矿井的开凿及石油管道的架设等;水利工程;防空地下建筑等特殊工程;列入房屋工程预算内的暖气、卫生、通风、照明、煤气等设备的价值及装设油饰工程;列入建筑工程预算内的各种管道(蒸汽、压缩空气、石油、给排水等管道)、电力、电讯电缆导线等的敷设工程;以及各种机械设备的安装工程;为测定安装工程质量,对设备进行的试运工作;房地产开发单位进行的商品房屋开发建设工程、土地开发工程。

在安装工程中,不包括被安装设备本身的价值。

(2)设备、工具、器具购置:指建设单位或企、事业单位购置或自制的,达到固定资产标准的设备、工具、器具的价值。新建单位及扩建单位的新建车间,按照设计或计划要求购置或自制的全部设备、工具、器具,不论是否达到固定资产标准均计入“设备、工具、器具购置”中。

(3)其他费用:指在固定资产建造和购置过程中发生的,除上述几项内容以外的各种应分摊计入固定资产的费用。

■ 固定资产投资的资金来源

固定资产投资的资金来源是根据固定资产投资的资金来源不同,分为国家预算资金、国内贷款、债券、利用外资、自筹资金和其他资金来源。

(1)国家预算资金:自2011年起,按照全国人大和国务院的要求,各级财政的所有资金,包括税收和非税收入,均必须纳入预算管理,我国已不存在预算外资金的概念,因此各级政府用于固定资产投资的财政资金均为预算资金。旧的国家预算内资金的内容和现中央预算资金的内容基本一致。国家预算包括一般预算、政府性基金预算、国有资本经营预算和社保基金预算。各类预算中用于固定资产投资的资金全部作为国家预算资金填报 。

(2)国内贷款:指报告期内企、事业单位向银行及非银行金融机构借入的用于固定资产投资的各种国内借款。包括银行利用自有资金及吸收的存款发放的贷款、上级主管部门拨入的国内贷款、国家专项贷款(包括煤代油贷款、劳改煤矿专项贷款等)、地方财政专项资金安排的贷款、国内储备贷款、周转贷款等。

(3)债券:是企业(公司)或金融机构通过发行各种债券,筹集用于固定资产投资的资金。包括由银行代理国

主要统计指标解释

家专业投资公司发行的重点企业债券和基本建设债券。

(4)利用外资:指报告期内收到的用于固定资产投资的国外资金,包括统借统还、自借自还的国外贷款,中外合资项目中的外资,以及对外发行债券和股票等。国家统借统还的外资指由我国政府出面同外国政府、团体或金融组织签订贷款协议、并负责偿还本息的国外贷款。

(5)自筹资金:指固定资产投资单位在报告期收到的,由各企事业单位筹集用于固定资产投资的资金,包括各类企事业单位的自有资金和从其他单位筹集的用于固定资产投资的资金,但不包括各类财政性资金、从各类金融机构借入资金和国外资金。

(6)其他资金来源:指在报告期收到的除以上各种资金之外的用于固定资产投资的资金。包括社会集资、个人资金、无偿捐赠的资金及其他单位拨入的资金等。

■ 固定资产投资按建设性质分

建设项目的性质一般分为新建、改建、扩建和单纯建造生活设施。

(1)新建:一般指从无到有"平地起家"开始建设的企业、事业和行政单位或独立的工程。现有企业、事业、行政单位一般不属于新建。但如有的单位原有基础很小,经过建设后新增的固定资产价值超过该企、事业、行政单位原有固定资产价值(原值)三倍以上的也应作为新建。

(2)改建和技术改造:是指现有企业、事业单位对原有设施进行技术改造或更新(包括相应配套的辅助性生产、生活福利设施)的建设项目。改建项目包括现有企业、事业单位为适应市场变化的需要,而改变企业的主要产品种类(如军工企业转民用品等)的建设项目,原有产品生产作业线由于各工序(车间)之间能力不平衡,为填平补齐充分发挥原有生产能力而增建不增加本企业主要产品设计能力的车间的建设项目。技术改造是指企业、事业单位在现有基础上,用先进的技术代替落后的技术,用先进的工艺和装备代替落后的工艺和装备,以改变企业落后的技术经济面貌,实现以内涵为主的扩大再生产,达到提高产品质量、促进产品更新换代、节约能源、降低消耗、扩大生产规模、全面提高社会经效益的目的。技术改造具体包括以下内容:机器设备和工具的更新改造;生产工艺改革、节约能源和原材料的改造;厂房建筑和公共设施的改造;保护环境进行的"三废"治理改造;劳动条件和生产环境的改造等。

(3)扩建:指在厂内或其他地点,为扩大原有产品的生产能力(或效益))或增加新的产品生产能力,而增建主要的生产车间(或主要工程)、分厂、独立的生产线。行政、事业单位在原单位增建业务用房(如学校增建教学用房、医院增建门诊部、病房等)也作为扩建。

现有企、事业单位为扩大原有主要产品生产能力或增加新的产品生产能力,增建一个或几个主要生产车间(或主要工程)、分厂,同时进行一些更新改造工程的,也应作为扩建。

(4)单纯建造生活设施:是指企(事)业及行政单位在不扩建、改建生产性工程和业务用房的情况下,单纯建造职工住宅、托儿所、子弟学校、医务室、浴室、食堂等生活福利设施。

■ 新增固定资产

新增固定资产又称交付使用的固定资产,是指已经完成建造和购置过程,并已交付生产或使用单位的固定资产价值。新增固定资产是表示固定资产投资成果的价值量指标,也是反映建设进度、计算固定资产投资效果的必要数据。

■ 施工项目

指报告期内正式进行过建筑或安装施工活动的建设项目。凡是报告期内施过工的建设项目,不论施工时间长短,均作为施工项目统计。施工项目个数可以反映一定时期固定资产投资的实际规模,与同期建成投产的建设项目个数相比,可以从建设速度的角度反映固定资产投资的效果。根据建设项目施工活动的不同性质,施工项目又分为:本年新开工项目,以前年度开工跨入本年继续施工项目,本年全部投产项目,以前年度全部停缓建在本年恢复施工的项目和本年进行过施工又在本年内全部停缓建的项目。

■ 全部投产项目

指报告期内按设计文件规定建成主体工程和相应配套的辅助设施,形成生产能力或工程效益,经过验收合格,并且已正式投入生产或交付使用的建设项目。

全部投产的工业项目是指设计文件规定形成生产能力的主体工程及其相应配套的辅助设施全部建成,经负荷试运转,证明具备生产设计规定合格产品的条件,并经过验收鉴定合格或达到竣工验收标准,与生产性工程配套的生活福利设施可以满足近期正常生产的需要,正式移交生产的建设项目。

■ 房屋建筑面积竣工率

指一定时期内房屋竣工面积占同期房屋施工面积的比率。该指标从房屋建筑施工速度的角度反映投资效果的指标。

SHANGHAI STATISTICAL YEARBOOK

EXPLANATORY NOTES TO MAJOR STATISTICAL INDICATORS

□ Total Investment in Fixed Assets

Investment in Fixed Assets constitutes an important portion of the national economic reproduction. Fixed assets investment is a general term for both the work volume of production and purchase of fixed assets and relevant expenditure, in the form of currency, during a certain period. It is a comprehensive indicator of scale, structure and development speed of fixed assets investment. As stipulated in the current national statistics regulations, the social fixed assets investment includes the investment into infrastructure and reformation, real estate development, urban and rural collective economic bodies, private house construction in urban and rural areas and other economic bodies.

From 1997, the fixed assets items only include those with investment of 0.5 million yuan and above. From 2011, the fixed assets items only include those with investment of 5 million yuan and above.

□ Investment in Fixed Assets by Sector

Investment in Fixed Assets by Sector refers to determining the classification of construction projects by the major products or the purpose of the projects when they are put into production or use, and by the nature of their social economic activities. In general, one project or one enterprise or institution can only be classified into one sector.

□ Investment in Fixed Assets by Jurisdiction of Management

Investment in Fixed Assets by Jurisdiction of Management refers to the classification of investment by the competent authorities under which investment is made by construction units, enterprises, institutions or administrative units.

(1) Central investment refers to the investment in projects or by enterprises, institutions or administrative units which are under the direct leadership and management of the CPC Central Committee, the NPC Standing Committee, the State Council and of the national commissions, ministries, agencies and state-owned large corporations. Various ministries and departments of the State Council prepare and implement plans for investment in fixed assets by those departments, and arrange and ensure the supply of materials and key equipment required for the projects.

(2) Local investment refers to the investment in projects or by enterprises, institutions or administrative units which are under the direct leadership and management of departments under the provincial, prefecture and county governments. Also included are projects by foreign-invested enterprises and enterprises without competent managing authorities.

□ Investment in Fixed Assets by Structure

Investment in Fixed Assets by Structure is classified by their contents.It is mainly classified into 3 categories, i.e. construction and installation, purchase of equipment and instrument, and other expenses.

(1) Construction and installation (work volume of construction and installation) refers to the construction of various houses and buildings and installation of various kinds of equipment and instruments. They include construction of various houses; equipment foundations, industrial kilns and stoves, and metal structure work; preparation works for project construction, and clearing up works post project construction; pavement of railways and roads, drilling of mines and putting up of oil pipes; construction of projects of water conservancy; construction of underground air-raid shelters and construction of other special projects; value of equipment for heating, sanitation, ventilation, lighting, gas, painting, etc. that are covered by the budget of housing projects; laying out of various pipelines (for steam, compressed air, petroleum, tap water and sewage) and lines for electric power and for communications; installation of various machinery equipment, testing operation for pre-testing the quality of installation projects, and land and other development work conducted by real estate developers for commercial housing. The value of equipment installed is not included in the value of installation projects.

(2) Purchase of equipment and instruments refers to the total value of equipment, tools, and instruments purchased or self-produced which come up to standards for fixed assets by the construction units or investing enterprises or institutions. Equipment, tools and instruments purchased or self-produced for new workshops by newly established or expanded units are catego-

EXPLANATORY NOTES TO MAJOR STATISTICAL INDICATORS

rized as "purchase of equipment and instruments" no matter whether they come up to the standards for fixed assets.

(3) Other expenses refer to expenses occurring during the construction or purchase of fixed assets other than those mentioned above.

□ Sources of Capital for Investment in Fixed Assets

Sources of capital for Investment in Fixed Assets include state budget funds, domestic loans, bond, foreign investment, self-raised funds, and others.

(1) State budget funds. Since 2011, according to the requirement of the NPC and the State Council, all levels of financial resources, including tax and non-tax revenue, must be included in the budget management, extra-budgetary didn't exist any longer, all levels of government for fixing asset investment funds are budget funds. The old state budget funds were basically the same with the central budget funds. State budget includes the general budget, the government fund budget, the state capital budget and the social security fund budget. All kinds of budgets for all funds invested in fixed assets were reported as state budget funds.

(2) Domestic loans refers to various funds borrowed by enterprises and institutions from banks and non-bank financial institutions during the reference period for the purpose of investment in fixed assets, including loans issued by banks from their self-owned funds and deposit, loans appropriated by higher responsible authorities, special loans by government (including loan for replacing petroleum with coal, special loan for reform-through-labour coal mines), loans arranged by local government from special funds, domestic reserve loan, and working loan, etc.

(3) Bond refers to company and finance institutions raising funds for investment in fixed assets by issuing various bond, including keystone enterprise bond and infrastructure bond issued by banks as agency of national professional investment company.

(4) Foreign Investment refers to foreign funds received during the reference period for the purpose of investment in fixed assets, including foreign funds borrowed and managed by the government, by individual units, foreign fund in joint venture program, and issue of bonds and stocks at the international financial markets. The foreign funds borrowed and managed by the government refer to foreign loans borrowed by the government from foreign governments, organizations, or financial institutions under official agreements signed by both parties, under which government is responsible for the repayment of both the principal and interests of the foreign loans.

(5) Self-raised funds refers to the fixed asset investment units received during the reporting period, by the enterprises and institutions to raise funds for investment in fixed assets, including various types of enterprises and institutions of its own funds and from other units raised funds for investment in fixed assets, but does not include all kinds of financial funds, borrowed funds from various financial institutions and foreign capital.

(6) Other sources of funding refers to the reporting period, in addition to all of these funds received outside funding for investment in fixed assets. Including social funds raised from individuals, donations, and funds transferred from other units.

□ Investment in Fixed Assets by Type of Construction

The construction projects in general can be classified, by the type of construction, into new construction, reconstruction and technical transformation, and simply construction establishment for life.

(1) New construction in general refers to newly constructed enterprises, institutions, administrative agencies or independent projects from scratch. Construction in the existing enterprises, institutions or agencies is not considered as new construction. In case the asset of the existing unit is quite small, and the value of newly added fixed assets exceeds the original value of assets by three times, the expansion will be considered as new construction.

(2) Reconstruction and technical transformation refers to construction projects by existing enterprises or institutions in innovation or technical transformation of the old facilities (including auxiliary production equipment and welfare facilities). Also considered as Reconstruction and Technical Transformation is the construction of new workshops by the existing enterprises or institutions to change the variety of products to meet the market demand (such as the production of civil products by defense industries), or to bring the designed production capacity into full play through a more balanced production process on production lines. Technical transformation refers to replacement of old technology and equipment by new technology and equipment, in order to expand the reproduction through improvement of technology contents in production, to improve product quality, to promote new products, to save energy, to reduce consumption, to

SHANGHAI STATISTICAL YEARBOOK

expand the production scale and to improve overall social-economic efficiency. Technical transformation contains the following contents: updating of machinery, equipment and tools; reforming production process by using energy or material saving technology; construction of workshops and transformation of public facilities; improvement of working conditions and environment, etc.

(3) Expansion refers to construction of new major production workshop, branch factory or independent production line within a factory or in other locations, for the purpose of increasing the production capacity (or improving efficiency) of the original products. Newly constructed houses for the operation of institutions and administrative organizations (such as the newly constructed buildings for teaching in schools, buildings for clinics or wards in hospitals, etc.) are also classified as expansion.

Also included in the expansion are investments by existing enterprises or institutions in building major production line(s) or branch factory(ies) along with some work on innovation, for the purpose of expending the production capacity of original products or producing new products.

(4) Simply constructing establishment for life refers to enterprises and administrative unit simply construct the employee 's residence, nursery, children school, infirmary, bathroom and eatery, without expanding or rebuilding the productive engineering and operation houses.

□ Newly Increased Fixed Assets

Newly Increased Fixed Assets, also called fixed assets put into operation, refers to the value of fixed assets that has been put into production or handed over to the production units after the completion of the process of construction and purchase. The newly increased fixed asset is an value indicator of the result of investment. It is also the necessary data for reflecting the construction process and the result of investment in fixed assets.

□ Projects under Construction

Projects under Construction refer to projects with construction and installation activities undertaken in the reference period. All projects that have construction activities undertaken during the reference period are reported as projects under construction irrespective of the length of construction work. The number of projects under construction can reflect the actual size of investment in fixed assets during a given period, and when compared with the number of projects completed and put into use during the same period, it demonstrates the results of investment in fixed assets. Depending on the nature of construction activities, projects under construction can also be classified into projects under construction in current year, winding-up projects in current year and stopped or suspended projects in previous years (with preservation work in current year).

□ Projects Completed and Put into Use

Projects Completed and Put into Use Industrial projects refer to the major projects and accessory facilities completed which result in forming production capacity and have been checked and accepted while the living and welfare facilities have been completed and can ensure normal production and formally put into production. Non-industrial projects refer to the major projects and accessory facilities completed which possess the designed capacity and have been checked, accepted and formally put into production.

□ Completion Rate of Floor Space of Buildings

Completion Rate of Floor Space of Buildings refers to the ratio of the floor space of buildings completed in certain period of time to the floor space of buildings under construction in the same period. This indicator reflects the investment result from the perspective of the speed of construction.

第七篇

CHAPTER 7

对外经济贸易和旅游

FOREIGN ECONOMIC RELATIONS, TRADE AND TOURISM

简要说明

本篇资料综合反映主要年份上海市对外贸易、外商直接投资、对外直接投资、对外经济合作和旅游等方面的概况。

一、货物贸易

货物贸易统计范围是按照联合国国际贸易统计原则，采用专门贸易记录制，对凡能引起区域内物质资源存量增加或减少的进出口货物，除制度另有规定外，均列入统计。在按国别(地区)分的进、出口总额表中，出口货物按中华人民共和国关境外最终目的国(地区)统计，进口货物按中华人民共和国关境外原产国(地区)统计。

主要内容包括：上海关区和上海市货物进出口的金额、国别、贸易方式、企业性质、产品类别等项目。

统计资料来源于上海海关，调查方法是全面调查。

二、服务贸易

服务贸易是根据国际货币基金组织公布的《国际收支手册》中的相关标准进行统计。服务贸易统计范围包括加工服务，运输服务，旅行，建设，保险服务，金融服务，电信、计算机和信息服务，其他商业服务，文化和娱乐服务，别处未涵盖的维护和维修服务、别处未涵盖的知识产权使用费、别处未涵盖的政府货物和服务。统计资料来源于国家外汇管理局上海市分局，调查方法是全面调查。

三、外商直接投资

外商直接投资统计范围是国外及港澳台地区的法人和自然人在中国大陆地区以现金、实物、无形资产、股权等方式投资设立的企业，其中外国投资者在非上市公司中的全部投资及在单个外国投资者所占股权比例不低于10%的上市公司中的投资。

主要内容包括：外商直接投资方式、投资产业和国别地区等情况。

统计资料来源于上海市商务委员会，调查方法是全面调查。

四、对外直接投资

对外直接投资指我国企业、团体等(简称境内投资主体)在国外及港澳台地区以现金、实物、无形资产等方式投资，并以控制国(境)外企业的经营管理权为核心的经济活动。对外直接投资统计范围主要包括境内投资主体通过直接投资在境外设立的各类公司型企业和非公司型企业。

主要内容包括：对外直接投资的项目数、投资总额。

统计资料来源于上海市商务委员会，调查方法是全面调查。

五、对外经济合作

对外经济合作统计范围是经各级商务主管部门批准的从事对外承包和劳务合作业务并具有法人地位的对外承包、劳务合作企业。

主要内容包括:对外承包工程合同金额、完成营业额和对外劳务合作派出人员等。

统计资料来源于上海市商务委员会,调查方法是全面调查。

六、旅游

旅游统计范围是旅行社、星级饭店和旅游者。

主要内容包括:旅行社接待经营情况、旅游景点和星级饭店基本情况、国际旅游入境人数、国内旅游来沪人数和人均消费支出等。

统计调查方法:国内旅游者来沪人数和人均消费支出指标采取抽样调查方法,其余数据均为全面调查。

统计资料来源于上海市文化和旅游局、上海出入境边防检查总站。

BRIEF INTRODUCTION

Data in this chapter reflect Shanghai's foreign trade, foreign direct investment, outbound direct investment, economic cooperation with foreign countries or territories as well as tourism in main years.

I. Goods Trade

The scope of goods trade statistics is in accordance with the United Nations' principles on international trade statistics, i.e.: all imports or exports that will lead to stock changes of material resources with the monitored territory; excluding goods by escape clause. In the table on the total imports and exports classified by countries and regions, the exports are calculated at the Customs of the countries (regions) of destination and the imports are calculated at the Customs of the countries (regions) of origin.

Data on foreign trade include: value of imports and exports through Shanghai ports, imports and exports by countries (regions), mode of trade, nature of trading companies, and product categories.

Sources of data on foreign trade are from the Shanghai Customs through a comprehensive reporting system.

II. Service Trade

Service trade is based on the relative standards in Balance of Payments Manual published by International Monetary Fund. The scope of service trade includes processing services, transportation services, travel, construction, insurance services, financial services, telecommunications, computer and information services, other business services, cultural and entertainment services, other not contained maintenance services, other not contained intellectual property services, other not contained government goods and services.

Sources of data are from Shanghai Branch of State Administration of Foreign Exchange through a comprehensive reporting system.

III. Foreign Direct Investment

The statistics of foreign direct investment cover the enterprises in the mainland established in the form of cash, physical goods, intangible assets or equity by legal and natural persons from foreign countries and Hong Kong, Macao and Taiwan regions, and also cover all investment of foreign investors in non-listed company and investment in listed companies with a share ratio not less than 10% of a single foreign investor.

Foreign direct investment includes: mode of foreign direct investment, investment by industry and countries (regions).

Sources of data are from the Shanghai Commission of Commerce through a comprehensive reporting system.

IV. Outward Direct Investment

Outward Direct Investment refers to the economic activities that Chinese enterprises or groups (referred to as domestic investors) invest in foreign countries and Hong Kong, Macao and Taiwan regions in the form of cash, physical goods and intangible assets, which take the management right of the enterprises both abroad and outside the border controlled as the core. The scope of Outbound Direct Investment mainly includes various types of corporate and non corporate enterprises established by domestic investors through direct investment abroad.

Data on outbound direct investment includes: number of outbound direct investment projects, total investment of outbound direct investment.

Sources of data are from the Shanghai Commission of Commerce through a comprehensive reporting system.

V. Foreign Economic Cooperation

The scope of foreign economic cooperation covers enterprises engaged in contracted projects and labor services cooperation with foreign countries with approvals from the department of commerce at various levels.

Data on foreign economic cooperation include: contracted value of project, its revenue and labor services cooperation.

Data on foreign economic cooperation are from the Shanghai Commission of Commerce through a comprehensive reporting system.

VI. Tourism

The scope of tourism covers travel agencies, star-rated hotels and tourists.

Data on tourism include: operating conditions of the travel agencies, tourist attractions and star-rated hotels, the number of international tourists, the number of domestic tourists to Shanghai and consumption expenditure per capita.

Methodologies: sample survey method is used for domestic tourists to Shanghai and consumption expenditure per capita, and the rest are through a comprehensive reporting system.

Data are from the Shanghai Culture and Tourism Bureau and the Shanghai Entry- Exit Frontier Inspection Station.

表 7.1 主要年份上海关区出口总额
TOTAL EXPORT TRADE VOLUME THROUGH CUSTOMS IN MAIN YEARS

单位:亿美元(100 million USD)

年 份 Year	关区出口总额 Export Trade Volume Through Customs	其中 of which				
		#一般贸易 Ordinary Trade	来料加工装配贸易 Processing and Assembly Trade with Customers' Materials	进料加工贸易 Processing Trade with Imported Materials	对外承包工程货物 Construction Projects in Foreign Countries	出料加工贸易 Outward Processing Trade
1990	86.62	51.39	3.20	30.67	0.41	0.45
1995	256.07	149.16	14.31	90.12	0.63	0.06
2000	615.72	341.02	64.21	205.13	1.25	
2005	2 124.30	1 057.68	195.83	813.26	6.37	0.16
2006	2 665.65	1 319.56	212.77	1 058.07	9.45	0.14
2007	3 284.80	1 659.44	228.77	1 273.71	20.55	0.17
2008	3 936.50	2 050.49	240.91	1 467.78	53.92	0.23
2009	3 251.28	1 647.82	175.38	1 252.87	69.78	0.13
2010	4 233.40	2 183.98	178.52	1 639.70	60.55	0.09
2011	4 999.64	2 691.93	151.78	1 846.59	77.70	0.11
2012	4 911.56	2 722.62	137.52	1 718.06	72.14	0.12
2013	4 991.29	2 857.73	130.46	1 642.18	80.16	0.11
2014	5 232.12	3 112.37	126.18	1 601.78	85.04	0.05
2015	5 005.80	3 016.20	133.26	1 497.66	67.43	0.04
2016	4 798.74	2 978.08	132.05	1 307.63	73.72	0.07
2017	5 166.76	3 256.88	135.63	1 385.12	84.12	0.03
2018	5 624.46	3 666.32	116.73	1 423.57	88.30	0.12
2019	5 402.44	3 583.99	77.63	1 285.17	77.70	0.17
2020	5 420.69	3 692.66	65.72	1 211.66	59.11	0.15
2021	6 761.63	4 768.39	74.81	1 383.16	59.38	0.23

表 7.2 主要年份上海关区进口总额
TOTAL IMPORT TRADE VOLUME THROUGH CUSTOMS IN MAIN YEARS

单位:亿美元 (100 million USD)

年 份 Year	关区进口总额 Import Trade Volume Through Customs	其中 of which				
		#一般贸易 Oridinary Trade	来料加工装配贸易 Processing and Assembly Trade with Customers' Materials	进料加工贸易 Processing Trade with Imported Materials	外商投资企业进口设备 Imported Equipment of Foreign Funded Enterprise	租赁贸易 Leasing Trade
1990	86.27	51.79	2.40	19.70	6.11	
1995	225.30	93.79	13.49	65.96	45.16	0.11
2000	477.39	212.65	44.87	125.13	40.26	2.47
2005	1 382.48	502.49	133.69	409.30	74.76	7.85
2006	1 621.89	574.40	122.52	497.41	73.72	23.74
2007	1 924.29	719.30	154.88	528.03	75.22	24.46
2008	2 129.07	848.23	174.86	525.68	76.91	22.21
2009	1 903.61	883.20	121.40	428.62	38.92	4.36
2010	2 613.05	1 209.42	169.36	552.83	43.81	18.56
2011	3 123.50	1 558.35	135.68	610.32	51.18	13.69
2012	3 101.54	1 516.96	123.06	553.38	33.00	10.79
2013	3 130.08	1 628.68	135.19	524.14	23.58	23.68
2014	3 402.43	1 777.08	164.31	568.61	26.63	40.52
2015	3 182.06	1 616.79	155.92	502.04	13.89	23.12
2016	3 127.25	1 674.22	141.84	452.20	9.00	2.87
2017	3 647.91	2 002.06	93.30	594.74	8.79	1.94
2018	4 090.77	2 234.96	61.41	750.68	6.68	2.94
2019	3 804.21	2 160.22	49.66	617.93	6.94	5.72
2020	3 906.84	2 290.76	46.65	617.69	6.80	3.94
2021	4 962.66	3 081.51	54.09	690.38	3.27	2.14

注：自 2009 年起，原口岸进出口商品总额改为上海关区进出口总额。
Note: Since 2009,Total Value of Port Imports and Exports have been changed to Total Trade Volume through Customs.

表 7.3 主要年份按国别(地区)分的上海关区出口总额
TOTAL EXPORT TRADE VOLUME THROUGH CUSTOMS BY COUNTRIES AND REGIONS IN MAIN YEARS

单位:亿美元 (100 million USD)

国别(地区)	Country(Region)	2010	2015	2020	2021
总　计	**Total**	**4 233.40**	**5 005.80**	**5 420.69**	**6 761.63**
亚　洲	**Asia**	**1 653.96**	**2 145.10**	**2 307.35**	**2 798.61**
#中国香港	Hong Kong, China	210.46	260.67	234.82	267.69
中国台湾	Taiwan, China	112.52	137.00	211.09	247.85
日　本	Japan	442.82	474.49	412.60	458.34
韩　国	Republic of Korea	138.83	212.30	224.01	280.59
新加坡	Singapore	94.80	117.74	110.65	120.90
马来西亚	Malaysia	73.08	78.47	93.40	118.71
泰　国	Thailand	61.18	99.26	108.03	152.49
菲律宾	Philippines	29.43	49.70	57.51	71.38
巴基斯坦	Pakistan	16.12	32.55	45.44	57.32
科威特	Kuwait	4.05	5.48	8.09	5.84
沙特阿拉伯	Saudi Arabia	19.92	34.23	34.11	38.37
阿联酋	United Arab Emirates	44.97	49.20	58.99	62.09
非　洲	**Africa**	**130.79**	**168.00**	**163.49**	**210.47**
#埃　及	Egypt	12.11	16.43	21.07	32.09
苏　丹	Sudan	4.39	3.20	1.99	1.64
欧　洲	**Europe**	**1 095.67**	**1 033.36**	**1 198.21**	**1 522.83**
#德　国	Germany	214.67	186.34	208.96	256.59
法　国	France	110.42	75.35	99.69	114.42
意大利	Italy	118.34	84.83	91.40	113.77
荷　兰	Netherlands	154.89	167.30	157.73	210.84
英　国	United Kingdoms	117.88	142.14	154.36	170.49
瑞　典	Sweden	20.26	19.52	20.30	27.33
俄罗斯	Russia	59.95	55.68	74.84	98.35
美　洲	**America**	**1 234.11**	**1 510.83**	**1 580.46**	**2 017.06**
#美　国	United States	910.54	1 127.24	1 143.08	1 404.09
加拿大	Canada	74.81	75.11	94.92	114.86
巴　西	Brazil	75.44	76.11	91.07	137.46
智　利	Chile	20.47	25.89	31.28	49.86
大洋洲及太平洋岛屿	**Oceanic and Pacific Island**	**118.87**	**148.52**	**171.18**	**212.66**
#澳大利亚	Australia	95.45	118.27	143.00	178.18
新西兰	New Zealand	9.87	13.50	16.63	24.83

表 7.4 主要年份按国别(地区)分的上海关区进口总额
TOTAL IMPORT TRADE VOLUME THROUGH CUSTOMS BY COUNTRIES AND REGIONS IN MAIN YEARS

单位:亿美元(100 million USD)

国别(地区)	Country (Region)	2010	2015	2020	2021
总 计	**Total**	**2 613.05**	**3 182.06**	**3 906.84**	**4 962.66**
亚 洲	**Asia**	**1 477.09**	**1 599.12**	**1 981.30**	**2 436.50**
#中国香港	Hong Kong, China	17.05	8.97	9.18	21.82
中国台湾	Taiwan, China	210.86	225.94	333.29	422.34
日 本	Japan	473.84	393.87	516.79	614.02
韩 国	Republic of Korea	279.87	346.03	356.08	440.45
新加坡	Singapore	51.61	73.92	91.63	104.10
马来西亚	Malaysia	117.63	120.27	133.14	158.45
泰 国	Thailand	63.19	62.99	75.95	105.77
菲律宾	Philippines	36.47	33.81	41.36	46.36
巴基斯坦	Pakistan	3.24	3.81	2.38	3.87
科威特	Kuwait	0.71	0.47	0.21	0.21
沙特阿拉伯	Saudi Arabia	8.28	14.08	13.89	14.85
阿联酋	United Arab Emirates	1.85	5.38	8.25	11.07
非 洲	**Africa**	**41.85**	**37.10**	**64.46**	**126.63**
#埃 及	Egypt	1.31	0.94	0.82	1.03
南 非	South Africa	16.60	14.04	24.61	77.15
欧 洲	**Europe**	**619.42**	**924.88**	**1 154.10**	**1 519.84**
#德 国	Germany	248.28	297.18	371.81	425.99
法 国	France	53.72	80.22	114.87	151.34
意大利	Italy	51.07	70.69	113.65	158.37
荷 兰	Netherlands	15.19	24.85	44.61	49.84
英 国	United Kingdoms	37.69	70.31	64.37	76.46
瑞 典	Sweden	28.75	34.62	42.52	39.52
俄罗斯	Russia	22.93	34.56	56.86	70.92
美 洲	**America**	**420.66**	**509.48**	**591.14**	**680.52**
#美 国	United States	268.76	344.59	348.59	414.89
加拿大	Canada	27.89	25.09	31.02	43.49
巴 西	Brazil	19.03	21.62	48.81	52.77
智 利	Chile	63.82	57.45	74.66	63.22
大洋洲及太平洋岛屿	**Oceanic and Pacific Island**	**53.73**	**110.72**	**113.31**	**196.54**
#澳大利亚	Australia	45.35	96.07	78.93	150.46
新西兰	New Zealand	8.33	14.40	33.63	45.36
其 他	**Others**	**0.30**	**0.74**	**2.54**	**2.63**

注:其他为无国别数(以下同)。
Note: Others refer to regions without sovereignty(Same as follows).

表 7.5　主要年份上海市进出口总额
TOTAL VALUE OF FOREIGN TRADE IMPORTS AND EXPORTS IN MAIN YEARS

年份 Year	上海市进出口总额（亿美元） Total Value of Foreign Trade Imports and Exports (100 million USD)	上海市进口总额（亿美元） Total Value of Foreign Trade Imports (100 million USD)	上海市出口总额（亿美元） Total Value of Foreign Trade Exports (100 million USD)	进出口差额（亿美元） Balance (100 million USD)	进出口总额相当于生产总值的比例(%) Foreign Trade Imports and Export as Percentage of Gross Domestic Product(%)	出口总额相当于生产总值的比例(%) Foreign Trade Export as Percentage of Gross Domestic Product(%)
1990	74.31	21.10	53.21	32.11	47.0	33.6
1995	190.25	74.48	115.77	41.29	63.1	38.4
2000	547.10	293.56	253.54	-40.02	94.1	43.6
2005	1 863.65	956.23	907.42	-48.81	166.0	80.8
2006	2 274.89	1 139.16	1 135.73	-3.43	171.1	85.4
2007	2 829.73	1 390.45	1 439.28	48.83	167.1	85.0
2008	3 221.38	1 527.88	1 693.50	165.62	153.9	80.9
2009	2 777.31	1 358.17	1 419.14	60.97	120.5	61.6
2010	3 688.69	1 880.85	1 807.84	-73.01	139.4	68.3
2011	4 374.36	2 276.47	2 097.89	-178.58	141.2	67.7
2012	4 367.58	2 299.51	2 068.07	-231.44	129.4	61.3
2013	4 413.98	2 371.54	2 042.44	-329.10	117.8	54.5
2014	4 666.22	2 563.45	2 102.77	-460.68	113.5	51.1
2015	4 517.33	2 547.64	1 969.69	-577.95	104.7	45.7
2016	4 338.05	2 503.38	1 834.67	-668.71	96.4	40.8
2017	4 761.23	2 824.42	1 936.81	-887.60	97.6	39.7
2018	5 156.49	3 084.79	2 071.70	-1 013.09	94.7	38.1
2019	4 938.03	2 948.64	1 989.39	-959.25	89.3	36.0
2020	5 031.89	3 050.82	1 981.07	-1 069.75	89.7	35.3
2021	6 286.03	3 852.90	2 433.13	-1 419.77	93.8	36.3

注：1999 年以前外贸进口、出口商品总额为外经贸委统计口径，1999 年以后为海关统计的上海企业进口、出口总额(以下同)。
Note: Before 1999, the figures of Shanghai's Foreign Trade Imports and Exports were based on statistics from Shanghai Foreign Trade and Economic Cooperation Commission. Since 1999, the figures representing imports and exports are made by Shanghai enterprises through Shanghai Custom.Same as follows.

表 7.6　主要年份上海市出口总额
TOTAL VALUE OF FOREIGN TRADE EXPORTS IN MAIN YEARS

单位:亿美元 (100 million USD)

指标	Indicators	2000	2010	2020	2021
出口总额	**Total Value of Exports**	**253.54**	**1 807.84**	**1 981.07**	**2 433.13**
按企业性质分	**Grouped by Different Enterprises**				
#国有企业	State-owned Enterprises	106.78	307.67	235.61	261.71
外商投资企业	Foreign-funded Enterprises	142.61	1 259.74	1 191.79	1 410.54
按贸易方式分	**Grouped by Trade Modes**				
#一般贸易	Original Trade	101.72	632.74	922.09	1 223.42
加工贸易	Processing Trade	147.83	1 003.74	678.16	746.02
按产品类别分	**Grouped by Different Products**				
#机电产品	Electrical and Mechanical Products	121.43	1 311.14	1 369.05	1 671.95
#高新技术产品	High-tech Products		841.11	835.40	937.17

表 7.7 主要年份按国别(地区)分的上海市出口总额
TOTAL VALUE OF FOREIGN TRADE EXPORTS BY COUNTRIES AND REGIONS IN MAIN YEARS

单位:亿美元 (100 million USD)

国别(地区)	Country (Region)	2000	2010	2020	2021
总 计	**Total**	**253.54**	**1 807.84**	**1 981.07**	**2 433.13**
亚 洲	**Asia**	**129.10**	**725.93**	**945.53**	**1 147.29**
#中国香港	Hong Kong, China	23.02	134.09	201.20	246.16
中国台湾	Taiwan, China	5.67	56.54	111.33	119.82
日 本	Japan	60.81	196.46	181.22	202.34
韩 国	Republic of Korea	10.59	58.92	71.61	105.81
新加坡	Singapore	7.88	59.01	66.93	69.35
马来西亚	Malaysia	2.59	42.52	41.70	44.37
泰 国	Thailand	2.48	24.14	36.45	53.04
巴基斯坦	Pakistan	0.55	3.08	9.65	14.73
科威特	Kuwait	0.20	1.53	2.40	1.55
沙特阿拉伯	Saudi Arabia	1.14	5.72	10.65	10.02
阿拉伯联合酋长国	United Arab Emirates	1.79	20.67	19.67	22.47
非 洲	**Africa**	**5.63**	**40.98**	**44.48**	**53.48**
#埃 及	Egypt	0.44	3.28	5.18	7.52
苏 丹	Sudan	0.22	1.21	0.84	0.68
阿尔及利亚	Algeria	0.09	1.29	2.16	1.48
摩洛哥	Morocco	0.20	0.97	1.70	1.53
欧 洲	**Europe**	**45.62**	**450.72**	**391.99**	**523.64**
#德 国	Germany	9.48	86.05	66.50	82.08
法 国	France	4.50	60.97	31.61	38.67
意大利	Italy	4.98	36.99	24.07	30.96
荷 兰	Netherlands	6.16	77.61	68.47	81.25
比利时	Belgium	2.95	16.70	14.56	42.92
英 国	United Kingdoms	7.07	43.11	48.09	64.86
俄罗斯	Russia	0.37	21.15	26.18	32.61
美 洲	**America**	**67.82**	**532.30**	**533.99**	**624.77**
#美 国	United States	56.25	409.91	429.58	478.08
加拿大	Canada	4.04	27.80	24.06	30.73
巴 西	Brazil	1.06	26.95	17.52	25.86
古 巴	Cuba	0.07	0.90	0.37	0.31
大洋洲及太平洋岛屿	**Oceanic and Pacific Island**	**5.37**	**57.91**	**65.09**	**83.95**
#澳大利亚	Australia	4.74	45.59	51.39	68.43

表 7.8 主要年份按国别(地区)分的上海市进口总额
TOTAL VALUE OF FOREIGN TRADE IMPORTS BY COUNTRIES AND REGIONS IN MAIN YEARS

单位:亿美元 (100 million USD)

国别(地区)	Country (Region)	2000	2010	2020	2021
总　计	**Total**	**293.56**	**1 880.85**	**3 050.82**	**3 852.90**
亚　洲	**Asia**	**161.59**	**1 041.98**	**1 459.02**	**1 768.00**
# 中国香港	Hong Kong, China	16.68	12.61	5.93	11.46
中国台湾	Taiwan, China	19.44	150.05	241.30	288.94
日　本	Japan	70.43	308.71	369.96	434.22
韩　国	Republic of Korea	20.63	146.41	189.46	231.15
新加坡	Singapore	9.39	39.42	73.72	73.70
马来西亚	Malaysia	6.49	107.75	119.42	133.90
泰　国	Thailand	4.35	53.09	53.74	75.03
菲律宾	Philippines	1.83	33.44	25.14	31.45
科威特	Kuwait	0.22	0.94	1.26	1.88
沙特阿拉伯	Saudi Arabia	0.78	7.23	12.64	14.84
阿拉伯联合酋长国	United Arab Emirates	0.40	2.11	10.66	14.93
非　洲	**Africa**	**1.89**	**28.19**	**50.87**	**77.50**
欧　洲	**Europe**	**63.36**	**400.75**	**895.74**	**1 142.15**
# 德　国	Germany	26.59	140.61	277.63	308.42
法　国	France	7.95	42.54	95.67	129.26
意大利	Italy	4.81	36.46	91.39	133.73
荷　兰	Netherlands	2.43	11.06	33.83	36.20
比利时	Belgium	2.83	25.08	19.56	22.68
英　国	United Kingdoms	3.76	23.43	55.31	63.46
瑞　士	Switzerland	2.22	29.87	74.45	159.07
瑞　典	Sweden	4.53	15.77	27.06	31.69
美　洲	**America**	**58.60**	**344.63**	**479.07**	**583.14**
# 美　国	United States	40.11	202.75	265.40	308.39
加拿大	Canada	7.03	20.90	33.87	47.17
巴　西	Brazil	4.11	40.89	76.44	102.20
大洋洲及太平洋岛屿	**Oceanic and Pacific Island**	**8.07**	**65.13**	**163.68**	**279.58**
# 澳大利亚	Australia	6.68	56.25	138.10	245.53
新西兰	New Zealand	1.25	7.48	24.15	31.08
其　他	**Others**	**0.05**	**0.17**	**2.44**	**2.55**

表 7.9 服务贸易进出口情况(2021)
TOTAL VALUE OF SERVICE TRADE IMPORTS AND EXPORTS

单位:亿美元 (100 million USD)

指 标	Indicators	进出口 Imports and Exports	其中 of which 出口 Exports	进口 Imports
总 计	**Total**	**2 293.80**	**1 035.70**	**1 258.10**
加工服务	Processing Services	11.40	11.10	0.30
运输服务	Transportation Services	968.60	389.20	579.40
旅 行	Travel	324.10	47.60	276.50
建 设	Construction	15.50	9.70	5.80
保险服务	Insurance Services	26.70	13.60	13.10
金融服务	Financial Services	6.20	4.10	2.10
电信、计算机和信息服务	Telecommunications, Computer and Information Services	190.40	137.00	53.40
其他商业服务	Other Business Services	544.20	394.10	150.10
#法律、会计、广告等专业和管理咨询服务	Law, Accounting, Advertisement and Other Professional and Management Consulting Services	291.30	220.40	70.90
文化和娱乐服务	Cultural and Entertainment Services	8.50	3.20	5.30
#视听和相关服务	Audio Visual and Relevant Services	4.40	1.10	3.30
别处未涵盖的维护和维修服务	Other Not Contained Maintenance Services	24.90	15.50	9.40
别处未涵盖的知识产权使用费	Other Not Contained Intellectual Property Services	170.00	9.00	161.00
别处未涵盖的政府货物和服务	Other Not Contained Government Goods and Services	3.20	1.50	1.70

表 7.10　主要年份服务贸易基本情况
BASIC STATISTICS OF SERVICE TRADE IN MAIN YEARS

单位:亿美元 (100 million USD)

指　标	Indicators	2005	2010	2020	2021
进出口额	**Total of Service Imports and Exports**	**251.40**	**871.42**	**1 530.30**	**2 293.80**
出口额	Total of Exports	122.30	327.96	666.60	1 035.70
进口额	Total of Imports	129.10	543.46	863.60	1 258.10

表 7.11　主要年份总部经济情况
CONDITIONS OF HEADQUARTERS ECONOMY IN MAIN YEARS

单位:家(unit)

指　标	Indicators	2005	2010	2020	2021
跨国公司地区总部	Regional Headquarters of Multinational Corporations	125	305	771	831
外资研发中心	Foreign Research and Development Centers	173	316	481	506

表 7.12　主要年份外商直接投资情况
FOREIGN DIRECT INVESTMENT IN MAIN YEARS

指　标	Indicators	2000	2010	2020	2021
合同项目(个)	**Number of Contracts (item)**	**1 814**	**3 906**	**5 751**	**6 708**
#合资企业	Joint Ventures	441	445	1 119	2 468
独资企业	Sole-foreign Funded Enterprises	1 146	3 443	4 448	3 934
合同金额(亿美元)	**Contracted Foreign Capital (100 million USD)**	**63.90**	**153.07**	**516.54**	**603.91**
实到金额(亿美元)	**Foreign Investment Actually Absorbed (100 million USD)**	**31.60**	**111.21**	**202.33**	**225.51**
#合资企业	Joint Ventures	12.94	17.84	29.75	32.43
合作企业	Cooperative Ventures	2.99	1.69	0.34	1.26
独资企业	Sole-foreign Funded Enterprises	15.67	90.71	169.91	172.91

表 7.13　外商直接投资合同项目和金额(2021)
NUMBER OF CONTRACTS SIGNED AND VALUES OF FOREIGN DIRECT INVESTMENT PROJECTS

类　别	Types	合同项目（个）Number of Contracts (item)		合同金额（亿美元）Contracted Foreign Capital (100 million USD)		实到金额（亿美元）Foreign Investment Actually Absorbed (100 million USD)	
		2021	至2021年底累计 Total by the End of 2021	2021	至2021年底累计 Total by the End of 2021	2021	至2021年底累计 Total by the End of 2021
总　计	**Total**	**6 708**	**116 272**	**603.91**	**6 295.57**	**225.51**	**3 022.72**
按投资方式分	**Grouped by Investment Mode**						
#合资企业	Joint Ventures	2 468	28 298			32.43	641.98
合作企业	Cooperative Ventures		5 151			1.26	123.55
独资企业	Sole-foreign Funded Enterprises	3 934	82 171			172.91	2 167.59
按产业分	**Grouped by Industry**						
第一产业	Primary Industry	11	368	0.42	8.51	0.03	5.00
第二产业	Secondary Industry	167	27 317	25.68	1 147.56	10.18	653.38
#工　业	Industry	81	26 058	23.76	1 115.02	9.86	644.39
第三产业	Tertiary Industry	6 530	88 587	577.81	5 139.50	215.30	2 364.34
按主要国别(地区)分	**Grouped by Country and Region**						
#中国香港	Hong Kong, China	2 098	36 755	436.86	3 495.43	158.63	1 465.03
中国澳门	Macao, China	70	461	0.76	8.60	0.01	2.87
中国台湾	Taiwan, China	1 141	13 782	10.00	123.11	0.24	51.90
日　本	Japan	266	11 478	16.90	327.05	7.32	236.49
韩　国	Republic of Korea	334	5 240	4.08	68.49	1.04	30.39
新加坡	Singapore	329	5 747	43.28	406.86	27.25	217.08
泰　国	Thailand	15	380	0.48	7.38	0.29	4.07
德　国	Germany	154	2 883	4.29	125.32	1.53	90.11
英　国	United Kingdoms	176	2 419	8.62	83.96	1.83	38.03
法　国	France	154	1 654	4.29	59.28	1.53	36.83
意大利	Italy	126	1 575	1.04	18.71	0.12	9.45
美　国	United States	521	10 574	21.46	302.86	6.13	165.55
加拿大	Canada	214	2 170	2.04	34.90	0.39	7.13
澳大利亚	Australia	123	2 128	0.76	20.55	0.06	7.56

表 7.14　主要年份引进技术设备实际到货金额
ARRIVED CAPITAL THROUGH IMPORTED TECHNOLOGY AND EQUIPMENT IN MAIN YEARS

单位:万美元(10 000 USD)

国　别(地区)	Country(Region)	2000	2010	2020	2021
总　计	**Total**	**104 558**	**3 903 807**	**6 812 418**	**17 353 420**
#中国香港	Hong Kong, China	10 746	17 414	5 327	7 465
日　本	Japan	10 069	886 132	1 053 421	2 651 403
德　国	Germany	16 314	814 006	1 317 616	1 963 582
意大利	Italy	622	123 823	177 397	328 754
美　国	United States	49 431	427 275	755 863	1 423 126
瑞　士	Switzerland	1 862	126 605	273 277	552 223
英　国	United Kingdoms	712	85 649	246 805	364 612
瑞　典	Sweden	639	72 594	149 116	225 740
奥地利	Austria	1 162	31 804	79 036	107 013
法　国	France	1 926	98 172	122 925	256 709

表 7.15　对外承包工程和劳务合作(2018~2021)
OVERSEAS CONTRACTED PROJECTS AND LABOR SERVICES COOPERATION

指　标	Indicators	2018	2019	2020	2021
对外承包工程	**Overseas Contracted Projects**				
签订合同金额(亿美元)	Value of Contract (100 million USD)	108.50	118.97	93.13	79.24
实际营业额(亿美元)	Actual Business Volume (100 million USD)	99.30	75.41	96.71	103.78
派出人员(人次)	Dispatched Persons (person-time)	13 902	8 764	7 942	11 768
对外劳务合作	**Overseas Labor Services Cooperation**				
派出人员(人次)	Dispatched Persons (person-time)	18 935	9 808	16 687	18 805

表 7.16 对外直接投资情况(2018~2021)
OUTWARD DIRECT INVESTMENT

指 标	Indicators	2018	2019	2020	2021
投资项目(个)	Number of Projects (unit)	792	845	814	958
对外直接投资中方投资额(亿美元)	Investment Value (100 million USD)	168.72	139.94	151.16	196.20

注：为规范指标名称，本表名原"海外企业情况"调整为"对外直接投资情况"，指标含义和口径不变。
Note: In order to standardize the name of the index, the original name ENTERPRISES ABROAD is adjusted to OUTWARD DIRECT INVESTMENT, but the meaning and statistical coverage of the index remain unchanged.

表 7.17 国际会展(2018~2021)
INTERNATIONAL CONFERENCE AND EXHIBITION

指 标	Indicators	2018	2019	2020	2021
举办国际会展个数(个)	International Exhibit(time)	300	310	181	142
国际会展展出总面积(万平方米)	Total Square of International Exhibit(10 000 sq.m)	1 415.30	1 502.65	873.70	932.80

注：2015 年前，本表数据由上海市会展行业协会提供，2015 年起，本表数据由上海市商务委提供。
Note: Data in this table before 2015 are provided by Shanghai Convention & Exibition Industries Association.Since 2015,data in this table are providede by Shanghai Commossion of Commerce.

表 7.18 主要年份旅行社接待经营情况
TOURISTS RECEIVED BY TOUR AGENCIES IN MAIN YEARS

指 标	Indicators	2010	2015	2020	2021
接待境内外来沪旅游者(万人次)	**Overseas and Domestic Tourists (10 000 person-times)**	**1 239.28**	**816.00**	**190.82**	**365.12**
境外旅游者	Overseas Tourists	158.25	64.16	4.27	0.11
#外国人	Foreigners	147.79	56.15	3.30	0.07
中国香港	Tourists from Hong Kong, China	4.47	3.23	0.29	0.01
中国澳门	Tourists from Macao, China	0.08	1.79	0.10	0.02
中国台湾	Tourists from Taiwan,China	5.91	2.98	0.58	0.01
境内旅游者	Domestic Tourists	1 081.03	751.85	186.55	365.01
出境旅游者(万人次)	**Tourists Going Abroad (10 000 person-times)**	**116.86**	**393.34**	**41.40**	
经营和财务状况	**Operation and Financial Status**				
营业收入(亿元)	Operational Revenues(100 million yuan)	341.88	826.72	805.89	356.15
利润总额(亿元)	Total Profits(100 million yuan)	4.02	0.31	-1.83	-0.44

表7.19 主要年份旅游景点基本情况
BASIC STATISTICS OF SCENIC SPOTS IN MAIN YEARS

指 标	Indicators	2010	2015	2020	2021
A级旅游景点数(家)	Scenic Spots of A Level and above(unit)	61	98	130	134
#5A级景点	AAAAA-Level	3	3	3	4
4A级景点	AAAA-Level	28	51	68	69
红色旅游基地数(个)	Red Travelling Base(unit)	30	34	34	34
#全国红色旅游基地	National Red Travelling Base	8	9	12	12

表7.20 主要年份国内旅游者来沪人数和人均消费支出
NUMBER OF DOMESTIC TOURISTS VISITING SHANGHAI AND PER CAPITA CONSUMPTION EXPENDITURES IN MAIN YEARS

指 标	Indicators	2005	2010	2020	2021
国内旅游者来沪人数(万人次)	**Number of Domestic Tourists Visiting Shanghai (10 000 person-times)**	**9 012**	**22 432**	**23 606**	**29 382**
外省市来沪旅游人数	Number of Tourists from other Provinces Visiting Shanghai	6 805	11 255	11 835	14 228
本市市民在本地旅游人数	Number of Local Tourists	2 207	11 177	11 771	15 154
国内旅游者人均消费支出(元)	**Consumption Expenditure Per Person (yuan)**	**1 452**	**1 175**	**1 190**	**1 204**
#长途交通费	Long-distance Traffic Expenditure	176	139	124	117
住宿费	Accommodation Expenditure	219	168	143	133
餐饮费	Food Expenditure	220	153	166	193
购物费	Shopping Expenditure	553	453	491	464
门票费	Ticket Expenditure	96	131	142	198
娱乐费	Entertainment Expenditure	30	42	17	20
市内交通费	Local Traffic Expenditure	88	53	50	50
邮电通信费	Post and Telecommunications Expenditure	37	14	2	2

注：本表为抽样调查资料。
Note: Data in this table are from the sampling survey.

表 7.21 旅游星级饭店基本情况(2021)
BASIC STATISTICS OF STAR-RATED TOURISM HOTELS

指 标	Indicators	合 计 Total	五星级 Five-Star	四星级 Four-Star	三星级 Three-Star	二星级 Two-Star
饭店数(个)	Number of Hotels(unit)	177	71	56	43	7
客房数(万间)	Number of Rooms (10 000 rooms)	4.55	2.57	1.42	0.50	0.06
床位数(万张)	Number of Beds (10 000 beds)	6.55	3.58	2.06	0.82	0.09
客房平均出租率(%)	Average Occupancy Rate (%)	50.7	52.7	51.3	41.3	44.8
营业收入(亿元)	Business Revenues (100 million yuan)	123.80	83.37	32.85	6.93	0.65
平均房价 (元/间天)	Average Room Rates (yuan/room.day)	629	800	431	334	262

表 7.22 主要年份国际旅游入境人数
NUMBER OF OVERSEAS TOURISTS THROUGH SHANGHAI CUSTOM IN MAIN YEARS

指 标	Indicators	2000	2010	2020	2021
国际旅游入境人数(万人次)	**Number of Overseas Tourists Through Shanghai Custom(10 000 person-times)**	**181.40**	**851.12**	**128.62**	**103.29**
#外国人	Foreigner	139.14	665.63	83.01	56.67
#日 本	Japanese	53.76	152.47	14.17	9.51
新加坡	Singaporean	5.29	23.50	2.97	2.36
德 国	German	7.11	29.52	3.88	3.22
法 国	French	5.39	24.86	2.98	1.83
英 国	Briton	1.69	20.94	3.44	2.58
意大利	Italian	1.88	11.49	1.43	0.91
加拿大	Canadian	2.25	20.97	3.56	3.38
美 国	American	13.78	80.79	11.89	8.37
澳大利亚	Australian	3.23	21.33	2.97	1.94
港澳同胞	Hong Kong and Macao Chinese	17.62	77.47	15.33	19.16
台湾同胞	Taiwanese	19.88	108.02	30.28	27.46
平均每天来沪旅游人数(人次/天)	**Average Number of Tourists Visiting Shanghai Everyday (person-time/day)**	**4 970**	**23 382**	**3 514**	**2 830**
来沪旅游者平均逗留天数(天/人)	**Average Time Tourists Staying in Shanghai (day/person)**	**3.92**	**3.51**	**17.90**	**17.90**
国际旅游(外汇)收入(亿美元)	**Foreign Exchange Earnings from International Tourism(100 million USD)**	**16.13**	**64.05**	**37.74**	**35.85**

上 / 海 / 统 / 计 / 年 / 鉴

主要统计指标解释

■ 关区进出口总额

指在上海海关办理进出口申报手续的进出口商品总额。统计方法依据联合国的国际贸易统计原则,反映进出上海而引起物质资源储备增加或减少的商品运动。按上述原则应具备条件:实际进出上海(海关关境),不仅包括经商业交易行为的进出口货品,也包括援助、捐赠等未发生买卖关系的货品价值。出口按离岸价(FOB)统计,进口按到岸价(CIF)统计。

■ 上海市进出口总额

指海关统计中按经营单位即进出口企业在海关注册地的行政区域口径统计的数据,它反映的是上海行政辖区内各类具有进出口经营权企业(外贸企业)的进出口。它不包含外省市外贸企业途经上海口岸由上海海关结关放行及统计的进出口商品,但包含上海外贸企业经由非上海口岸进出口结关放行及统计的商品。

■ 服务贸易

服务贸易是一国的法人或自然人在其境内或进入他国境内向外国的法人或自然人提供服务的贸易行为。服务提供者在其境内向他国家或地区的服务消费者提供的服务,即服务出口;境外服务提供者从其他国家或地区向他国境内的服务消费者提供的服务,即服务进口。

■ 外商直接投资

指外国企业和经济组织或个人(包括华侨、港澳台胞以及我国在境外注册的企业)按我国有关政策、法规,用现汇、实物、技术等在我国境内开办外商独资企业、与我国境内的企业或经济组织共同设立中外合资经营企业、合作经营企业或合作开发资源的投资(包括外商投资收益的再投资)以及企业投资总额内直接投资者对企业的贷款,即外方股东贷款。

反映外商直接投资状况的指标主要有三个:外商直接投资合同项目、外商直接投资合同金额、外商直接投资实际到位金额。

■ 引进技术

指通过贸易途径从国外获得发展我国国民经济和提高技术水平所需要的技术装备。引进方式有:许可证贸易(技术贸易)、生产线(包括成套设备)、单机(包括关键设备)、软硬件结合(同时引进技术和设备)和其他。

■ 对外承包工程

对外承包工程包括各对外承包公司以招标议标承包方式承揽的下列业务:(1) 承包国外工程建设项目。(2) 承包我国对外经济援助项目。(3) 承包我国驻外机构的工程建设项目。(4) 承包我国境内利用外资进行建设的工程项目。(5) 与外国承包公司合营或联合承包工程项目时我国公司分包部分。(6) 以服务成果向业主收费的技术服务项目(包括承担地形地貌测绘;地质资源勘探与普查;建设区域规划;提供设计文件、图纸、生产工艺技术资料和工程技术经济咨询;工程项目的可行性考察、研究和评估;进行技术指导和培训人员等)。(7) 对外承包兼营的房屋开发业务。对外承包工程的营业额是以货币表现的本期内完成的对外承包工程的工作量,包括以前年度签订的合同和本年度新签订的合同在报告期完成的工作量。

■ 对外劳务合作

指以收取工资的形式向业主或承包商提供技术和劳动服务的活动。上海对外承包公司在境外开办的合营企业,上海公司同时又提供劳务的,其劳务部分也纳入劳务合作统计。劳务合作营业额按报告期内向雇主提交的结算数(包括工资、加班费和奖金等)统计。

■ 国际旅游入境人数

指来上海参观、访问、旅行、探亲、访友、休养、考察、参加会议或从事经济、科技、文化、教育、体育、宗教等活动的外国人、华侨、港澳和台湾同胞的人数。不包括来上海常住1年以上的外国专家、留学生等。上海入境的境外旅游人数包括从上海口岸入境的境外旅游人数和从我国其他口岸入境来沪的境外旅游人数。

■ 国际旅游(外汇)收入

指入境旅游的外国人和华侨港澳台同胞在上海旅游过程中发生的一切旅游支出。

SHANGHAI STATISTICAL YEARBOOK

EXPLANATORY NOTES TO MAJOR STATISTICAL INDICATORS

□ Total Trade Volume Through Customs

Total Trade Volume through Customes refers to the aggregate volume of commodities that are conducted declaration procedure through Shanghai's ports. The statistics method follows the international trade statistics principles set by the United Nations. It reflects the fluctuation of Shanghai's material reserves caused by export or import. Requirements involved in the principle is: the commodities refer to those enter or leave Shanghai's ports, including not only the business trading activities but also the commodities value of the aid and donations that haven't been involved in sales . Exports are calculated according to FOB price, and imports are calculated according to CIF.

□ Total Value of Foreign Trade Imports and Exports of Shanghai

Total Value of Foreign Trade Imports and Exports of Shanghai is offered by Customs authorities, covering the operation units, or the enterprises involved in import and export, that have registered in the administrative regions where the Customs operate. It reflects the import and export of all the enterprises with import and export rights (foreign trade enterprises) under the administration of Shanghai Municipality. It excludes those commodities of foreign trade enterprises from out of town that underwent customs clearance at Shanghai ports but includes commodities of foreign trade enterprises of Shanghai that underwent customs clearance in non-Shanghai ports.

□ Service Trade

Service Trade is the trade behaviour in which a legal person or natural person of a country provides services to a foreign legal person or natural person in its territory or in the territoy of another country. Services provided by service providers to service consumers in other countries or regions in their territory, namely service exprot; services provided by service providers abroad from other countries or regions to service consumers in other countries, namely service import.

□ Foreign Direct Investment

Foreign Direct Investment refers to the investments made inside China by foreign enterprises and economic organizations or individuals (including overseas Chinese, compatriots in Hong Kong, Macao and Chinese enterprises registered abroad), in line with the relevant policies and laws of China, for the establishment of wholly foreign-owned enterprises, and joint ventures or development projects launched in China (including reinvestment of profits from foreign businesses), and the funds that enterprises borrow from abroad in the total investment of projects which are approved by the relevant departments of the governments and the loans from the direct investors within the total investment of the projects, i.e., foreign shareholders' loans.

There are three main indicators that reflect the status of foreign direct investment: signed contracts of foreign direct investment, contracted foreign capital and foreign investment actually absorbed.

□ Import of Technology

Import of Technology refers to technology and equipments obtained through the trade channel from other countries which are needed for advancing China's national economy and improving its technological level. The import form includes: licensing (technological trade), production lines (including complete plant), single machine (including key equipments), combination of hardware and software (importing technology and equipments simultaneously) and others.

□ Overseas Contracted Projects

Overseas Contracted Projects refer to projects undertaken by Chinese contractors (project contracting companies) through bidding process. They include: (1) overseas civil engineering construction projects financed by foreign investors. (2) overseas projects financed by the Chinese government through its foreign-aid programs. (3) construction projects of Chinese diplomatic missions, trade offices and other institutions stationed abroad. (4) construction projects in China financed by foreign investment. (5) sub-contracted projects to be taken by Chinese contractors through a joint umbrella project with foreign contractor(s). (6) technical assistance projects in the form of service results and chargeable to the owners (such as topographic surveying, geological prospecting, development zone programming, provision of documents, blueprint, materials on

EXPLANATORY NOTES TO MAJOR STATISTICAL INDICATORS

production process, technical consultation, project feasibility studies and evaluation, personnel training, etc.). and (7) housing development projects. The business turnover from international contracting is the work of contracted projects completed during the reporting period, expressed in monetary terms, including completed work on project contracts signed in previous years.

□ Overseas Labor Service Cooperation

Overseas Labor Service Cooperation refers to activities of providing technology and labor services to employers or contractors by collecting salaries and wages. Labor services provided by Shanghai ´s international contrasting corporations to their overseas joint ventures shall be included into the statistics of overseas services. The business turn over of overseas labor services is the settlement price (including salaries, overtime pay and bonuses) submitted to the employers during the reporting period.

□ Number of Overseas Tourists to Shanghai

Number of Overseas Tourists to Shanghai refers to the number of foreigners, overseas Chinese, and compatriots from Hong Kong, Macao and Taiwan coming to Shanghai for sightseeing, visits, tours, family reunions, meeting friends, vacations, study tours, attending meetings and other activities of an economic, scientific and technological, cultural, physical culture and religious nature. This does not include foreign experts and students residing in Shanghai for over 1 year. The number of overseas tourists to Shanghai includes those overseas tourists entering China through Shanghai customs and through customs other than Shanghai.

□ Foreign Exchange Earnings from International Tourism

Foreign Exchange Earnings from International Tourism refer to the total expenditures of foreigners, overseas Chinese, Chinese compatriots from Hong Kong, Macao and Taiwan during their stay in Shanghai.

第八篇
CHAPTER 8

价格水平
PRICES

简要说明

一、本篇资料的主要内容

本篇价格指数资料，反映生产、流通、消费、投资与交易等环节的价格变动趋势和变动幅度。主要包括居民消费价格指数、商品零售价格指数、工业生产者出厂价格指数、工业生产者购进价格指数、固定资产投资价格指数。

二、本篇的资料来源

价格指数编制由国家统计局上海调查总队组织实施，依据国家统计局统一制定的价格统计调查制度，由上海调查总队直接或通过区调查队从基层采集原始价格数据汇总后上报。

三、居民消费、商品零售价格指数

编制居民消费、商品零售价格指数的资料采用抽样调查和重点调查相结合的方法取得，即在全市选择不同经济区域和分布合理的商品销售或服务网点，以及有代表性的商品或服务作为样本，对其市场价格进行定期调查，以样本推断总体。目前，居民消费、商品零售价格调查已涉及全市全部16个区。

1. 价格调查网点的抽选方法：对全市消费市场进行摸底调查、掌握市场的基本情况（经营品种、销售额等指标）基础上，将各种类型的商场（店）、超市、农贸市场、服务网点以销售额（成交额或经营规模）为标志，从高到低排队，依据所需调查点的数量进行等距抽样。选择经营品种齐全、销售额大的商场（店）、超市、农贸市场、服务网点作为价格调查网点。

2. 代表规格品根据全市的消费情况确定，必须遵循以下原则：（1）选择消费量较大的消费项目；（2）价格变动趋势和变动程度有较强的代表性，即选中规格品与未选中规格品的价格变动特征愈相关愈好；（3）在市场销售份额大体相等的情况下，同一基本分类的规格品之间，性质差异愈大愈好，价格变动特征的相关性愈低愈好；（4）生产和销售前景较好；（5）选中的工业消费品必须是合格产品，工业产品包装上必须有注册商标、产地、规格等级等标识。

目前，居民消费价格调查分为8大类，268个基本分类，全市每月共调查约1500种的规格品价格；商品零售价格分为16个大类，197个基本分类，全市每月调查约900种的规格品价格。

3. 价格调查方法：居民消费、商品零售价格调查是非全面调查，主要方法是定人、定点、定时直接调查。

4. 权数的确定：居民消费价格指数的权数主要根据全市城镇居民家庭消费支出构成确定；商品零售价格指数的权数主要根据全市社会商品零售额资料确定。

5. 指数计算方法：使用链式拉氏公式计算，每5年更换1次基期，目前固定基期为2020年。

6. 居民消费价格调查分类变化说明

2021年，部分类别结构有所调整，主要是：

（1）调整前“衣着”类包括服装、服装材料、其他衣着及配件、衣着加工服务费和鞋类等5分类，调整后“衣着”类包括服装和鞋类等2分类；

（2）部分分类中文表述有所修改，但分类包含内容没有变化。如“菜”更名为“菜及食用菌”。

四、工业生产者价格指数

工业生产者价格包括工业品第一次出售时的出厂价格和企业作为中间投入的原材料、燃料、动力的购进价格。该项调查采用重点调查的方法调查对象为规模以上工业企业。

1. 选择代表企业的原则：(1)按工业行业选择调查企业，各主要中类行业原则上都要有调查企业；(2)大型企业应尽量都选上（或占相当大比重）；(3)选择生产正常、稳定的企业作为调查对象。根据以上原则上海共选择1000余家工业企业开展工业生产者价格调查。

2. 选择代表产品的原则：(1)按工业行业选择基本分类和代表产品；(2)选择对国计民生影响大的产品；(3)选择生产较为稳定的产品；(4)选择有发展前景的产品；(5)选择具有地方特色的产品。

根据《工业生产者价格调查目录》，上海编制工业生产者出厂价格指数选用470余个基本分类（1000余种产品），工业生产者购进价格指数选用了340余个基本分类（近1000种产品）。

3. 价格调查方式采用企业网上直报形式。

BRIEF INTRODUCTION

I. Main Contents

Data on price indices in this chapter show the changing trends and the changing rates in the prices of production, trade, consumption, investment and transaction, mainly including consumer price indices, retail price indices, producer price indices, producer purchasing price indices, price indices for investment in fixed assets.

II. Sources of Data

Statistics on price indices, organized and compiled by the Survey Office of the National Bureau of Statistics in Shanghai, are collected from the grassroots units or survey offices in districts in accordance with the scheme of price survey system stipulated by the National Bureau of Statistics, and then statistics are tabulated and reported to the higher agencies.

III. Consumer Price Indices and Retail Price Indices

Data for compilation of the consumer price indices and the retail price indices in Shanghai are collected through a combination of sample surveys and surveys of key units. Areas distributed in the city' s economic regions, representative commodities and representative services are selected as samples. Regular surveys are conducted to collect data on their market prices. Population parameters are inferred on the basis of the sample data. At present, 16 districts in Shanghai are all included in the survey of the consumer price indices and the retail price indices.

(1) The selection of sample survey areas: Based on the basic conditions (including product varieties, their sales and etc) the city' s consumer market, the city' s consumer market, shops, supermarkets, wet markets and service outlets of different varieties are ranked by sales (turnover or scales) and then selected on the number of survey areas needed via systematic sampling method schemes. The price survey areas should be shops, supermarkets, wet markets and service outlets with a wide range of products and big sales.

(2) The goods are selected on the city' s consumption conditions, following these principles: (a) goods sold in large quantities; (b) Representative for the price changing trends and the changing rates, which means selected goods are highly relevant with those unselected; (c) Under the conditions of similar market shares, the bigger the differences in nature among goods and the lower the price relevance, the better; (d) Good production and sales outlook; (e) Qualified industrial goods, with registered trademark, origin and grade printed on the packaging.

At present, data are collected on about 1500 specifications each month in the city under 268 basic headings in 8 categories in the consumer price surveys. For the retail price surveys, data are collected on about 900 specifications each month under 197 basic headings in 16 categories.

(3) Method of data collection: Sample surveys are used for the consumer price indices and the retail price indices, with method of direct survey with fixed people, fixed location and fixed time period.

(4) Determination of the weights: The weights of the consumer price indices are determined according to the composition of the consumption expenditures of Shanghai' s urban and rural households. The weights of the retail price indices are determined mainly according to the total retail sales of commodities in the city.

(5) Method of calculation: the approach of the chain Laspyres with base period replaced every 5 years which is 2020 at present.

(6) Classification changes of consumer price survey.

In 2021, there is some minor adjustment in classifications, including:

① The original category of "Clothing" contains 5 categories including Clothes, Clothing Materials, Other Clothing and Fittings, Clothing Manufacturing Service and Shoes. After the adjustment, the category of "Clothing" contains 2 categories including Clothes and Shoes.

②The Chinese expressions of some classifications have been revised, but the contents of classifications have not changed. For example, "Vegetables" is renamed "Vegetables and Edible Fungi".

IV. Producer Price Indices

Producer prices include Producer Prices for Industrial Products, which are the prices of manufactured goods when they are sold for the first time, and Purchasing Prices for Industrial Producers,which are prices paid by industrial enterprises when they purchase productive inputs such as raw materials, fuels and power from the market or from other enterprises. Methologically, this is a survey of the key enterprises, which refer to those industrial enterprises avove set scale.

(1) Principles for the selection of representative enterprises: (a) Enterprises to be covered in the survey are selected by industrial sectors. In principle, every second-level classifacation should have representative enterprises; (b) All (or the majority of) large-scale enterprises should be selected; (c) Enterprises selected should be those with normal and stable production. According to these principles, nearly 1000 enterprises in Shanghai are selected for this survey.

(2) Principle for the selection of representative goods: (a) The goods are selected by industrial sectors; (b) The selected goods should have great importance in the national economy and people's living conditions; (c) The production of the goods selected should be stable; (d) The prospects of the goods selected should be promising; (e) The goods selected should be of local specialties.

According to the catalog of Producer Price Suvey, more than 470 basic categories (over 1000 goods) and more than 340 basic categories (nearly 1000 inputs) in Shanghai are selected for the surveys of Producer Price Index for Industrial Products and Purchasing Price index for Industrial Producers respectively."

(3) Online direct reporting method is used for the data collection of Producer Price survey.

表 8.1 居民消费价格指数和商品零售价格指数(1978~2021)
CONSUMER PRICE INDICES AND RETAIL PRICE INDICES

年 份 Year	居民消费价格指数 Consumer Price Index		年 份 Year	商品零售价格指数 Retail Price Index	
	以上年价格为 100 preceding year = 100	以 1978 年价格为 100 1978 = 100		以上年价格为 100 preceding year = 100	以 1978 年价格为 100 1978 = 100
1978	100.5	100.0	1978	100.1	100.0
1979	100.9	100.9	1979	101.0	101.0
1980	105.9	106.9	1980	106.5	107.6
1981	101.4	108.3	1981	101.5	109.2
1982	100.3	108.7	1982	100.3	109.5
1983	100.2	108.9	1983	100.1	109.6
1984	102.2	111.3	1984	102.2	112.0
1985	115.2	128.2	1985	116.4	130.4
1986	106.3	136.3	1986	106.7	139.1
1987	108.1	147.3	1987	108.8	151.4
1988	120.1	176.9	1988	121.3	183.6
1989	115.9	205.1	1989	116.7	214.3
1990	106.3	218.0	1990	104.8	224.6
1991	110.5	240.9	1991	109.5	245.9
1992	110.0	265.0	1992	109.7	269.8
1993	120.2	318.5	1993	117.5	317.0
1994	123.9	394.6	1994	117.5	372.4
1995	118.7	468.4	1995	113.0	420.9
1996	109.2	511.5	1996	105.0	441.9
1997	102.8	525.8	1997	98.8	436.6
1998	100.0	525.8	1998	95.1	415.2
1999	101.5	533.7	1999	97.3	404.0

表 8.1 续表 continued

年份 Year	居民消费价格指数 Consumer Price Index		年份 Year	商品零售价格指数 Retail Price Index	
	以上年价格为 100 preceding year = 100	以 1978 年价格为 100 1978 = 100		以上年价格为 100 preceding year = 100	以 1978 年价格为 100 1978 = 100
2000	102.5	547.0	2000	96.4	389.5
2001	100.0	547.0	2001	98.6	384.0
2002	100.5	549.7	2002	98.7	379.0
2003	100.1	550.1	2003	99.0	375.4
2004	102.2	561.9	2004	100.9	378.8
2005	101.0	567.3	2005	99.4	376.7
2006	101.2	574.2	2006	100.2	377.3
2007	103.2	592.3	2007	102.4	386.5
2008	105.8	626.5	2008	105.3	407.1
2009	99.6	624.0	2009	99.4	404.8
2010	103.1	643.4	2010	101.7	411.7
2011	105.2	676.7	2011	104.1	428.4
2012	102.8	695.9	2012	101.2	433.6
2013	102.3	711.9	2013	100.2	434.3
2014	102.7	730.7	2014	100.9	438.0
2015	102.4	748.4	2015	101.1	442.8
2016	103.2	772.6	2016	100.8	446.3
2017	101.7	785.7	2017	100.9	450.3
2018	101.6	798.3	2018	101.6	457.5
2019	102.5	818.2	2019	100.4	459.3
2020	101.7	832.3	2020	100.9	463.4
2021	101.2	842.2	2021	101.3	469.6

表 8.2 居民消费价格分类指数(2021，以上年价格为 100)
CONSUMER PRICE INDICES BY CATEGORY(PRECEDING YEAR = 100)

类 别	Types	2021
居民消费价格指数	**Consumer Price Index**	**101.2**
#消费品价格指数	Price Index for Consumer Goods	100.9
服务价格指数	Price Index for Services	101.5
食品烟酒	**Food and Cigarettes and Liquors**	**100.5**
食 品	Food	99.6
粮 食	Grain	99.1
薯 类	Potato	100.9
豆 类	Beans	117.3
食用油	Edible Oil	107.4
菜及食用菌	Vegetables and Edible Fungi	105.2
畜肉类	Meat	86.2
禽肉类	Poultry	89.7
水产品	Aquatic Products	105.4
蛋 类	Eggs	104.5
奶 类	Milk	103.7
干鲜瓜果类	Dried and Fresh Fruits	105.6
糖果糕点类	Sweets and Pastries	102.5
调味品	Flavouring	100.9
其他食品类	Other Food	100.4
茶及饮料	Tea and Drinks	101.0
烟 酒	Cigarettes and Liquors	104.0
在外餐饮	Dining Out	101.8
衣 着	**Clothing**	**99.5**
服 装	Clothes	99.4
鞋 类	Shoes	99.8

注：由于 2021 年居民消费价格分类内容与之前不完全一致，因此在使用历年分类指数时注意数据口径衔接。
Note: Consumer Price Indices by Category has been adjusted in 2021. Please notice the different calibres when using these data.

表 8.2 续表 continued

类 别	Types	2021
居　住	**Housing**	**101.1**
租赁房房租	Renting	101.1
住房保养维修及管理	House Maintenance and Management	102.3
水电燃料	Water, Electric Power and Fuels	101.0
自有住房	Self-owned House	101.0
生活用品及服务	**Living Articles and Services**	**100.7**
家具及室内装饰品	Furniture and Interior Decorations	101.6
家用器具	Household Appliances	102.0
家用纺织品	Home Textiles	97.8
家庭日用杂品	Home Daily Groceries	99.8
个人护理用品	Personal Care Articles	98.8
家庭服务	Family Services	103.4
交通通信	**Transportation and Communication**	**104.0**
交　通	Transportation	104.7
通　信	Communication	101.4
教育文化娱乐	**Education and Culture and Recreation**	**102.7**
教　育	Education	102.3
文化娱乐	Culture and Recreation	103.1
医疗保健	**Medical and Health Services**	**98.9**
药品及医疗器具	Drugs and Medical Devices	94.9
医疗服务	Medical Service	101.7
其他用品及服务	**Other Articles and Services**	**100.9**
其他用品	Other Articles	102.8
其他服务	Other Services	99.1

表 8.3 商品零售价格分类指数(2019~2021，以上年价格为 100)
RETAIL PRICE INDICES (PRECEDING YEAR=100)

类 别	Types	2019	2020	2021
商品零售价格指数	**Retail Price Index**	**100.4**	**100.9**	**101.3**
食 品	Food	105.2	105.9	100.5
#粮 食	Grain	100.7	101.5	99.1
薯 类	Potato	109.6	108.4	100.9
豆 类	Beans	111.3	99.9	117.3
食用油	Edible Oil	100.6	106.6	107.4
菜及食用菌	Vegetables and Edible Fungi	103.5	105.9	105.2
畜肉类	Meat	118.7	131.0	86.2
禽肉类	Poultry	111.3	99.9	89.7
水产品	Aquatic Products	100.3	100.6	105.4
蛋 类	Eggs	105.2	96.7	104.5
奶 类	Milks	101.6	100.7	103.7
干鲜瓜果类	Dried and Fresh Fruits	107.4	94.4	105.6
糖果糕点类	Sweets and Cakes	100.7	101.9	102.5
调味品	Flavoring	100.2	103.6	100.9
其他食品类	Other Food	102.3	100.4	100.4
餐饮业零售	Catering Retail	102.8	103.6	101.8
饮料、烟酒	Beverages, Tobacco and Liquor	101.0	102.6	103.2
服装、鞋帽	Garments, Shoes and Hats	103.1	100.8	99.4
纺织品	Textiles	99.1	100.1	98.3
家用电器及音像器材	Household Appliances and Audio-video Appliances	99.5	97.7	101.9
文化办公用品	Cultural Office Articles	97.8	101.4	101.6
日用品	Daily Use Articles	101.4	100.7	100.6
体育娱乐用品	Sports and Recreation Goods	99.5	100.4	100.3
交通、通信用品	Transportation and Communication Goods	95.6	98.5	101.2
家 具	Furniture	100.9	99.3	101.9
化妆品	Cosmetics	101.7	100.9	98.9
金银饰品	Gold and Silver Ornament	109.6	117.1	102.8
中西药品及医疗保健用品	Traditional Chinese and Western Medicines	103.1	102.4	94.4
书报杂志及电子出版物	Newspapers and Magazines and Electronic Publications	105.8	106.5	99.9
燃 料	Fuels	94.5	88.2	112.9
建筑材料及五金电料	Building Materials and Hardwares	102.3	101.8	104.4

表 8.4 居民消费价格指数(1991~2015，以上年价格为 100)
CONSUMER PRICE INDICES (PRECEDING YEAR=100)

年 份 Year	居民消费价格指数 Consumer Price Index	食 品 Food	烟 酒 Cigarettes and Liquors	衣 着 Clothing
1991	110.5	113.5	103.0	105.7
1992	110.0	113.4	109.7	109.5
1993	120.2	122.1	110.2	118.6
1994	123.9	131.8	112.0	115.7
1995	118.7	126.1	106.9	108.8
1996	109.2	110.5	100.0	108.7
1997	102.8	100.0	90.3	101.1
1998	100.0	97.8	96.0	94.0
1999	101.5	97.4	100.4	98.3
2000	102.5	98.2	97.2	95.3
2001	100.0	100.3	98.9	98.9
2002	100.5	102.9	98.9	97.5
2003	100.1	101.3	99.8	97.5
2004	102.2	108.3	98.3	94.2
2005	101.0	104.5	99.7	92.1
2006	101.2	102.5	100.2	106.4
2007	103.2	109.4	100.7	101.3
2008	105.8	115.3	101.7	101.6
2009	99.6	102.1	100.8	99.3
2010	103.1	107.7	101.1	98.6
2011	105.2	110.8	101.3	104.3
2012	102.8	105.8	101.4	103.0
2013	102.3	104.4	100.1	100.0
2014	102.7	103.2	101.0	103.7
2015	102.4	102.9	104.2	107.8

表 8.4 续表 continued

年 份 Year	家庭设备用品及维修服务 Home Appliances and Repair Service	医疗保健和个人用品 Medicine, Medical Services and Personal Aricles	交通和通信 Transportation and Communication	娱乐教育文化用品及服务 Recreation, Education and Culture Articles	居 住 Residence
1991	112.5	113.1	108.5	96.9	129.3
1992	102.6	117.3	100.4	96.8	119.0
1993	109.5	114.4	117.0	123.4	134.4
1994	110.9	119.2	117.3	117.6	120.6
1995	103.8	110.0	114.7	116.2	120.3
1996	99.1	106.0	106.1	118.6	109.7
1997	91.4	102.1	115.6	109.6	120.6
1998	92.5	101.9	103.7	106.3	113.6
1999	96.4	101.9	112.4	111.7	105.9
2000	95.7	99.9	110.9	121.5	103.3
2001	97.2	97.4	98.1	102.1	102.3
2002	97.7	97.6	96.9	100.8	100.0
2003	98.4	100.0	96.3	100.3	101.1
2004	97.8	100.0	96.5	99.9	101.6
2005	100.8	100.3	97.5	98.3	102.9
2006	102.7	101.1	97.3	98.2	102.9
2007	103.3	100.2	96.9	97.3	104.5
2008	108.3	103.1	97.5	98.2	102.5
2009	101.5	99.4	97.5	98.0	96.6
2010	101.1	103.7	97.4	100.9	103.5
2011	107.1	104.1	100.2	99.2	105.4
2012	103.5	100.6	100.8	99.3	102.8
2013	101.3	100.0	100.4	100.1	103.9
2014	101.8	100.4	100.1	101.8	104.6
2015	102.9	99.3	97.6	100.3	104.6

表 8.5 主要年份居民消费价格指数(以上年价格为 100)
CONSUMER PRICE INDICES IN MAIN YEARS(PRECEDING YEAR = 100)

类 别	Types	2001	2010	2015
居民消费价格指数	**Consumer Price Index**	**100.0**	**103.1**	**102.4**
#消费品价格指数	Price Index for Consumer Goods	98.6	103.5	102.0
服务项目价格指数	Price Index for Services	105.4	102.0	103.2
食 品	**Food**	**100.3**	**107.7**	**102.9**
粮 食	Grain	102.9	112.0	103.0
淀粉及制品	Starch and Its Products	103.6	95.5	103.9
干豆类及豆制品	Dry Beans and Bean Products	95.6	108.7	101.2
油 脂	Oil or Fat	84.5	105.6	98.5
肉禽及其制品	Meat Poultry and Their Products	99.3	104.3	105.3
蛋	Eggs	102.4	106.1	98.0
水产品	Aquatic Products	100.1	116.4	101.3
菜	Vegetables	108.9	111.0	107.5
调味品	Flavoring	99.2	106.5	104.9
糖	Sugars	101.4	103.8	102.2
茶及饮料	Tea and Beverages	98.4	103.9	103.9
干鲜瓜果	Dried and Fresh Fruits	104.3	112.0	96.8
糕点饼干面包	Cakes, Biscuits and Bread	100.5	100.5	101.8
液体乳及乳制品	Milk and Its Products	100.8	102.3	99.2
在外用膳食品	Dining Out	98.0	105.6	104.1
其他食品	Other Food	99.2	105.0	104.2
烟 酒	**Cigarettes and Liquors**	**98.9**	**101.1**	**104.2**
烟 草	Tobacco	99.2	101.0	104.9
酒	Liquors	98.2	101.6	102.5
衣 着	**Clothing**	**98.9**	**98.6**	**107.8**
服 装	Garments	96.4	99.9	107.3
衣着材料	Clothing Materials	98.7	102.9	106.3
鞋袜帽	Shoes, Socks and Hats	106.2	93.6	109.8
衣着加工服务	Garment Processing Service	100.0	107.2	105.5

表 8.5 续表 continued

类 别	Types	2001	2010	2015
家庭设备用品及维修服务	**Home Appliances and Repair Service**	**97.2**	**101.1**	**102.9**
耐用消费品	Durable Consumer Goods	94.7	99.6	101.8
室内装饰品	Interior Decorations	101.0	99.2	102.2
床上用品	Bed Articles	100.5	104.2	103.4
家庭日用杂品	Daily Use Household Articles	98.6	99.4	101.4
家庭服务及加工维修服务	Other Daily Use Articles	100.0	108.8	108.5
医疗保健和个人用品	**Medicine, Medical Services and Personal Aricles**	**97.4**	**103.7**	**99.3**
医疗保健	Medicine and Medical Services	96.5	100.8	100.7
个人用品及服务	Personal Articles and Service	99.8	107.1	98.0
交通和通信	**Transportation and Communication**	**98.1**	**97.4**	**97.6**
交 通	Transportation	102.3	98.7	97.3
通 信	Communications	94.4	95.3	98.2
娱乐教育文化用品及服务	**Recreation, Education and Culture Articles**	**102.1**	**100.9**	**100.3**
文娱用耐用消费品及服务	Durable Consumer Goods for Recreational Use	91.2	89.4	95.9
教 育	Education	109.6	101.2	102.5
文化娱乐类	Recreation and Culture Articles	105.2	101.0	100.7
旅 游	Tourism	96.2	115.9	97.9
居 住	**Residence**	**102.3**	**103.5**	**104.6**
建房及装修材料	Construction and Decoration Materials	97.5	102.1	101.4
住房租金	Rents	111.0	106.8	107.3
自有住房	Self-owned House	99.8	103.0	105.5
水、电、燃料	Water, Electricity and Fuels	101.7	103.8	102.4

表8.6 主要年份商品零售价格指数（以上年价格为100）
RETAIL PRICE INDICES IN MAIN YEARS (PRECEDING YEAR =100)

类别	Types	2001	2010	2015
商品零售价格指数	**Retail Price Index**	**98.6**	**101.7**	**101.1**
食品	Food	98.4	107.6	102.8
#粮食	Grain	100.1	112.0	103.0
淀粉及制品	Starch and Its Products	100.4	95.5	103.9
干豆类及豆制品	Dry Beans and Bean Products	111.3	108.7	101.2
油脂	Oil and Fat	81.4	105.6	98.0
肉禽及其制品	Meat Poultry and Their Products	100.4	104.2	105.3
蛋	Eggs	110.7	106.1	98.0
水产品	Aquatic Products	90.1	116.1	101.3
菜	Vegetables	107.1	111.0	107.5
调味品	Flavoring	99.5	106.5	104.8
糖	Sugars	104.4	103.8	102.2
干鲜瓜果	Dried and Fresh Fruits	107.3	112.1	96.8
糕点饼干面包	Cakes, Biscuits and Bread	99.8	100.5	101.8
液体乳及乳制品	Milk and Its Products	99.8	102.3	99.2
在外用膳食品	Dining Out	100.7	105.6	104.1
其它食品	Other Food	99.5	105.0	104.2
饮料、烟酒	Beverages, Tobacco and Liquors	98.4	101.9	103.9
服装、鞋帽	Garments, Shoes and Hats	107.7	98.4	107.9
纺织品	Textile Products	98.8	103.9	104.1
家用电器及音像器材	Household Appliances and Audio-video Equipment	95.0	92.4	99.3
文化办公用品	Culture and Office Articles	98.7	97.7	99.2
日用品	Daily Use Articles	99.0	100.3	101.5
体育娱乐用品	Sports and Recreation Articles	99.1	95.9	99.4
交通、通信用品	Transport and Communication Products	97.4	94.0	97.8
家具	Furniture	90.4	101.1	101.8
化妆品	Cosmetics	100.7	101.0	100.1
金银珠宝	Jewelry	87.2	111.7	95.2
中西药品及医疗保健用品	Traditional Chinese and Western Medicines, Medical and Health Care Articles	98.7	99.8	100.6
书报杂志及电子出版物	Newspapers and Magazines and Electronic Publications	99.5	103.2	101.7
燃料	Fuels	111.4	112.8	91.2
建筑材料及五金电料	Building Materials and Hardware	101.8	103.3	99.6

表 8.7 工业生产者出厂价格指数（2014~2021，以 2000 年价格为 100）
PRODUCER PRICE INDICES FOR INDUSTRIAL PRODUCTS (2000 = 100)

类 别	Types	2014	2015	2016	2017
工业生产者出厂价格指数	**Producer Price Indices Industrial Products**	**97.8**	**94.0**	**92.9**	**96.2**
按轻重工业分	**Grouped by Light or Heavy Industries**				
轻工业	Light Industry	88.6	87.4	87.2	88.2
以农产品为原料	Using Farm Products as Raw Materials	122.3	120.8	121.3	122.6
以非农产品为原料	Using Non-farm Products as Raw Materials	75.8	74.7	74.1	75.1
重工业	Heavy Industry	108.9	104.0	102.5	106.7
采 掘	Mining and Guarrying	290.1	247.2	229.4	253.9
原 料	Raw Material	181.5	157.5	152.5	174.8
加 工	Manufacturing	89.4	87.3	86.4	87.8
按用途分	**Grouped by Use**				
生产资料	Means of Production	101.1	96.1	94.7	99.3
生活资料	Consumer Goods	92.8	92.2	91.9	92.2
#食 品	Food	138.7	137.7	138.1	139.1
衣 着	Clothing	110.7	110.7	112.0	109.9
一般日用品	Non-Durable Consumer Goods	105.9	104.5	105.4	109.9
耐用消费品	Durable Consumer Goods	63.6	63.3	62.4	61.3

表 8.7 续表 continued

类 别	Types	2018	2019	2020	2021
工业生产者出厂价格指数	**Producer Price Indices for Industrial Products**	**97.8**	**96.6**	**95.0**	**97.0**
按轻重工业分	**Grouped by Light or Heavy Industries**				
轻工业	Light Industry	88.7	89.9	91.2	91.9
以农产品为原料	Using Farm Products as Raw Materials	124.9	127.0	129.0	132.0
以非农产品为原料	Using Non-farm Products as Raw Materials	74.5	75.2	76.1	75.9
重工业	Heavy Industry	108.9	106.8	104.1	106.6
采 掘	Mining and Guarrying	295.9	290.6	243.2	237.4
原 料	Raw Material	188.0	174.7	157.9	180.5
加 工	Manufacturing	88.3	87.8	87.0	86.7
按用途分	**Grouped by Use**				
生产资料	Means of Production	101.6	99.7	97.8	102.5
生活资料	Consumer Goods	92.4	92.8	91.8	88.2
#食 品	Food	140.5	143.2	147.1	151.5
衣 着	Clothing	110.1	113.8	112.8	111.4
一般日用品	Non-Durable Consumer Goods	110.9	115.0	119.5	119.1
耐用消费品	Durable Consumer Goods	61.0	59.5	56.1	51.7

表8.8 工业生产者出厂价格指数(2014~2021，以2000年价格为100)(按国民经济行业分)
PRODUCER PRICE INDICES FOR INDUSTRIAL PRODUCTS(GROUPED BY NATIONAL INDUSTRIES, 2000=100)

类别	Types	2014	2015	2016	2017
工业生产者出厂价格指数	**Producer Price Indices for Industrial Products**	**97.8**	**94.0**	**92.9**	**96.2**
按国民经济行业分	**Grouped by National Economy Industries**				
石油和天然气开采业	Petroleum and Natural Gas Exploiting	290.1	247.2	229.4	253.9
农副食品加工业	Farm and Sideline Products Processing	203.3	187.4	189.1	189.9
食品制造业	Food Manufacturing	143.8	144.8	144.8	148.6
酒、饮料和精制茶制造业	Wine, Beverage and Refined Tea Manufacturing	112.6	110.0	109.6	113.5
烟草制品业	Tabacco Manufacturing	146.3	146.3	146.4	146.4
纺织业①	Textile	103.9	101.7	103.3	111.0
纺织服装、服饰业①	Textile and Garment, Apparel Industry	111.9	111.5	114.1	112.8
皮革、毛皮、羽毛及其制品和制鞋业①	Leather, Fur, Feather and Its Products and Shoemaking Industry	103.7	104.1	102.2	98.5
木材加工和木、竹、藤、棕、草制品业	Timber Processing and Timber, Bamboo, Rattan, Coir and Straw Products Manufacturing	118.0	119.7	118.7	117.5
家具制造业	Furniture Manufacturing	93.0	93.2	94.4	95.0
造纸和纸制品业	Paper-making and Paper Products Manufacturing	97.9	96.9	96.6	102.7
印刷和记录媒介复制业	Printing and Record Duplicating Industry	89.6	88.5	87.9	88.4
文教、工美、体育和娱乐用品制造业①	Stationary, Education ,Industrial Art, Sport and Entertainment Products Manufacturing	98.8	96.3	105.6	109.1
石油加工、炼焦和核燃料加工业	Oil Processing, Coking and Nuclear Fual Processing	311.7	230.3	210.3	240.8
化学原料和化学制品制造业	Raw Chemical Materials and Chemical Products Manufacturing	147.8	129.0	129.3	150.4
医药制造业	Medicine Manufacturing	96.7	98.2	97.7	106.6
化学纤维制造业	Chemical Fiber Manufacturing	114.9	105.4	94.8	109.3
橡胶和塑料制品业	Rubber and Plastic Products Manufacturing	110.3	105.2	102.1	104.1
非金属矿物制品业	Nonmetal Mineral Products	104.4	99.8	96.0	105.2
黑色金属冶炼和压延加工业①	Smelting and Pressing of Ferrous Metals	161.2	138.6	134.2	160.2
有色金属冶炼和压延加工业	Smelting and Pressing of Nonferrous Metals	185.0	168.4	157.8	178.3
金属制品业①	Metal Products Manufacturing	120.8	115.6	115.4	125.1
通用设备制造业①	General Equipment Manufacturing	91.2	90.8	91.4	92.3
专用设备制造业①	Special Purpose Equipment Manufacturing	96.2	98.0	99.7	99.6
汽车制造业	Automotive Industry	94.6	93.7	92.3	90.5
铁路、船舶、航空航天和其他运输设备制造业	Railroads, Ships, Aerospace and other Transportation Equipment Manufacturing Industry	95.8	95.3	94.3	94.6
电气机械和器材制造业①	Electric Machinery Equipments and Manufacturing	89.1	87.2	84.3	83.6
计算机、通信和其他电子设备制造业	Computers, Communications and other Electronic Equipment Manufacturing Industry	47.7	47.4	47.1	47.0
仪器仪表制造业①	Instruments and Meters Manufacturing	81.0	80.7	81.3	82.5
其他制造业①	Other Manufacturing	165.4	168.0	157.2	167.9
废弃资源综合利用业	Comprehensive Utilization of Waste Resources	125.9	93.7	87.0	85.3
金属制品、机械和设备修理业	Metal Products, Machinery and Equipment Repair	97.6	95.2	99.2	104.1
电力、热力生产和供应业	Production and Supply of Electricity and Thermal Power	116.8	115.4	111.8	112.2
燃气生产和供应业	Production and Supply of Gas	148.7	149.0	146.0	140.6
水的生产和供应业	Production and Supply of Water	223.0	225.7	225.0	224.6

①2012年起按新口径编制。
②废弃资源和废旧材料回收加工业以2002年价格为100。
❶These indices have been calaulated according to the new caliber since 2012.
❷The price indices of Waste Resources and Materials Recycling and Processing was 100 in 2002.

表 8.8 续表 continued

类　别	Types	2018	2019	2020	2021
工业生产者出厂价格指数	**Producer Price Indices for Industrial Products**	**97.8**	**96.6**	**95.0**	**97.0**
按国民经济行业分	**Grouped by National Economy Industries**				
石油和天然气开采业	Petroleum and Natural Gas Exploiting	295.5	290.2	242.9	237.1
农副食品加工业	Farm and Sideline Products Processing	193.9	201.3	214.0	248.7
食品制造业	Food Manufacturing	151.4	153.5	154.6	157.2
酒、饮料和精制茶制造业	Wine, Beverage and Refined Tea Manufacturing	122.2	122.7	122.6	123.8
烟草制品业	Tabacco Manufacture	147.1	150.6	155.6	156.4
纺织业	Textile	122.0	119.0	116.4	119.0
纺织服装、服饰业	Textile and Garment, Apparel Industry	112.4	115.8	116.5	115.8
皮革、毛皮、羽毛及其制品和制鞋业	Leather, Fur, Feather and Its Products and Shoemaking Industry	99.8	104.0	100.8	98.4
木材加工和木、竹、藤、棕、草制品业	Timber Processing and Timber, Bamboo, Rattan, Coir and Straw Products Manufacturing	116.4	114.2	108.4	106.2
家具制造业	Furniture Manufacturing	95.9	94.0	93.3	93.4
造纸和纸制品业	Paper-making and Paper Products Manufacturing	107.2	107.6	106.8	
印刷和记录媒介复制业	Printing and Record Duplicating Industry	87.9	89.2	89.9	97.9
文教、工美、体育和娱乐用品制造业	Stationary, Education ,Industrial Art, Sport and Entertainment Products Manufacturing	110.8	126.9	148.2	146.3
石油加工、炼焦和核燃料加工业	Oil Processing, Coking and Nuclear Fual Processing	289.6	277.1	223.9	146.3
化学原料和化学制品制造业	Raw Chemical Materials and Chemical Products Manufacturing	154.6	137.6	130.4	151.1
医药制造业	Medicine Manufacturing	107.0	109.0	111.6	107.2
化学纤维制造业	Chemical Fiber Manufacturing	121.0	109.0	90.8	108.9
橡胶和塑料制品业	Rubber and Plastic Products Manufacturing	105.3	104.0	101.0	103.5
非金属矿物制品业	Nonmetal Mineral Products	119.7	124.7	126.7	134.4
黑色金属冶炼和压延加工业	Smelting and Pressing of Ferrous Metals	165.7	159.7	160.5	207.7
有色金属冶炼和压延加工业	Smelting and Pressing of Nonferrous Metals	182.5	183.6	184.7	218.7
金属制品业	Metal Products Manufacturing	129.7	129.2	128.6	135.5
通用设备制造业	General Equipment Manufacturing	94.9	97.2	97.0	97.9
专用设备制造业	Special Purpose Equipment Manufacturing	99.9	102.4	103.1	99.7
汽车制造业 *	Automotive Industry	89.8	87.3	82.7	78.1
铁路、船舶、航空航天和其他运输设备制造业 *	Railroads, Ships, Aerospace and other Transportation Equipment Manufacturing Industry	94.8	95.9	102.8	97.6
电气机械和器材制造业	Electric Machinery Equipments and Manufacturing	82.4	80.8	78.9	81.1
计算机、通信和其他电子设备制造业	Computers, Communications and other Electronic Equipment Manufacturing Industry	46.2	45.9	46.5	44.4
仪器仪表制造业	Instruments and Meters Manufacturing	82.6	81.9	82.4	82.0
其他制造业	Other Manufacturing	167.4	164.4	155.9	161.7
废弃资源综合利用业	Comprehensive Utilization of Waste Resources	85.9	86.0	86.7	87.1
金属制品、机械和设备修理业 *	Metal Products, Machinery and Equipment Repair	101.8	107.2	111.5	109.5
电力、热力生产和供应业	Production and Supply of Electricity and Thermal Power	111.2	109.5	103.1	103.0
燃气生产和供应业	Production and Supply of Gas	138.5	138.1	135.5	136.3
水的生产和供应业	Production and Supply of Water	220.5	224.0	226.9	235.7

注：* 为以 2011 年价格为 100。
Note: The price index symbled " * " was 100 in 2011.

表8.9 工业生产者出厂价格指数(2014~2021，以上年价格为100)
PRODUCER PRICE INDICES FOR INDUSTRIAL PRODUCTS(PRECEDING YEAR=100)

类别	Types	2014	2015	2016	2017
工业生产者出厂价格指数	**Producer Price Indices for Industrial Products**	**98.9**	**96.1**	**98.8**	**103.5**
按轻重工业分	**Grouped by Light or Heavy Industries**				
轻工业	Light Industry	99.1	98.6	99.8	101.2
以农产品为原料	Using Farm Products as Raw Materials	99.8	98.8	100.4	101.1
以非农产品为原料	Using Non-farm Products as Raw Materials	98.6	98.5	99.2	101.4
重工业	Heavy Industry	98.8	95.5	98.6	104.1
采　掘	Mining and Guarrying	102.2	85.2	92.8	110.7
原　料	Raw Material	98.2	86.8	96.8	114.6
加　工	Manufacturing	99.0	97.7	99.0	101.6
按用途分	**Grouped by Use**				
生产资料	Means of Production	98.7	95.1	98.5	104.9
生活资料	Consumer Goods	99.4	99.3	99.7	100.3
#食　品	Food	100.4	99.3	100.3	100.7
衣　着	Clothing	100.4	100.0	101.2	98.1
一般日用品	Non-Durable Consumer Goods	99.2	98.7	100.9	104.3
耐用消费品	Durable Consumer Goods	98.9	99.6	98.6	98.3

表8.9 续表 continued

类别	Types	2018	2019	2020	2021
工业生产者出厂价格指数	**Producer Price Indices for Industrial Products**	**101.7**	**98.8**	**98.3**	**102.1**
按轻重工业分	**Grouped by Light or Heavy Industries**				
轻工业	Light Industry	100.5	101.3	101.4	100.8
以农产品为原料	Using Farm Products as Raw Materials	101.9	101.7	101.6	102.3
以非农产品为原料	Using Non-farm Products as Raw Materials	99.2	101.0	101.2	99.8
重工业	Heavy Industry	102.0	98.1	97.5	102.4
采　掘	Mining and Guarrying	116.4	98.2	83.7	97.6
原　料	Raw Material	107.5	92.9	90.4	114.3
加　工	Manufacturing	100.6	99.4	99.1	99.7
按用途分	**Grouped by Use**				
生产资料	Means of Production	102.3	98.1	98.1	104.8
生活资料	Consumer Goods	100.2	100.4	98.9	96.1
#食　品	Food	101.0	101.9	102.7	103.0
衣　着	Clothing	100.2	103.4	99.1	98.8
一般日用品	Non-Durable Consumer Goods	100.9	103.7	103.9	99.7
耐用消费品	Durable Consumer Goods	99.4	97.6	94.3	92.2

表8.10 工业生产者出厂价格指数(2014~2021，以上年价格为100)(按国民经济行业分)
PRODUCER PRICE INDICES FOR INDUSTRIAL PRODUCTS(GROUPED BY NATIONAL INDUSTRIES, PRECEDING YEAR=100)

类别	Types	2014	2015	2016	2017
工业生产者出厂价格指数	**Producer Ex-factory Price Indices**	**98.9**	**96.1**	**98.8**	**103.5**
按国民经济行业分	**Grouped by National Economy Industries**				
石油和天然气开采业	Petroleum and Natural Gas Exploiting	102.2	85.2	92.8	110.7
农副食品加工业	Farm and Sideline Products Processing	96.3	92.2	100.9	100.4
食品制造业	Food Manufacturing	102.1	100.7	100.0	102.6
酒、饮料和精制茶制造业	Wine, Beverage and Refined Tea Manufacturing	98.5	97.7	99.6	103.6
烟草制品业	Tabacco Manufacture	100.0	100.0	100.1	100.0
纺织业	Textile	98.5	97.9	101.6	107.5
纺织服装、服饰业	Textile and Garment, Apparel Industry	100.3	99.6	102.3	98.9
皮革、毛皮、羽毛及其制品和制鞋业	Leather, Fur, Feather and Its Products and Shoemaking Industry	101.6	100.4	98.2	96.4
木材加工和木、竹、藤、棕、草制品业	Timber Processing and Timber, Bamboo, Rattan, Coir and Straw Products Manufacturing	102.7	101.4	99.2	99.0
家具制造业	Furniture Manufacturing	100.0	100.2	101.3	100.6
造纸和纸制品业	Paper-making and Paper Products Manufacturing	99.0	99.0	99.7	106.3
印刷和记录媒介复制业	Printing and Record Duplicating Industry	100.1	98.8	99.3	100.6
文教、工美、体育和娱乐用品制造业	Stationary, Education, Industrial Art, Sport and Entertainment Products Manufacturing	95.0	97.5	109.7	103.3
石油加工、炼焦和核燃料加工业	Oil Processing, Coking and Nuclear Fual Processing	95.3	73.9	91.3	114.5
化学原料和化学制品制造业	Raw Chemical Materials and Chemical Products Manufacturing	99.0	87.3	100.2	116.3
医药制造业	Medicine Manufacturing	100.2	101.5	99.5	109.1
化学纤维制造业	Chemical Fiber Manufacturing	97.0	91.7	89.9	115.3
橡胶和塑料制品业	Rubber and Plastic Products Manufacturing	98.0	95.4	97.1	102.0
非金属矿物制品业	Nonmetal Mineral Products	100.5	95.6	96.2	109.6
黑色金属冶炼和压延加工业	Smelting and Pressing of Ferrous Metals	97.7	86.0	96.8	119.4
有色金属冶炼和压延加工业	Smelting and Pressing of Nonferrous Metals	95.9	91.0	93.7	113.0
金属制品业	Metal Products Manufacturing	96.5	95.7	99.8	108.4
通用设备制造业	General Equipment Manufacturing	98.9	99.6	100.7	101.0
专用设备制造业	Special Purpose Equipment Manufacturing	101.0	101.9	101.7	99.9
汽车制造业	Automotive Industry	99.7	99.0	98.5	98.1
铁路、船舶、航空航天和其他运输设备制造业	Railroads, Ships, Aerospace and other Transportation Equipment Manufacturing Industry	99.3	99.5	98.9	100.3
电气机械和器材制造业	Electric Machinery Equipments and Manufacturing	98.4	97.9	96.7	99.2
计算机、通信和其他电子设备制造业	Computers, Communications and other Electronic Equipment Manufacturing Industry	98.5	99.3	99.4	99.8
仪器仪表制造业	Instruments and Meters Manufacturing	99.8	99.6	100.8	101.5
其他制造业	Other Manufacturing	100.1	101.6	93.6	106.8
废弃资源综合利用业	Comprehensive Utilization of Waste Resources	95.0	74.4	92.9	98.0
金属制品、机械和设备修理业	Metal Products, Machinery and Equipment Repair	101.2	97.5	104.2	104.9
电力、热力生产和供应业	Production and Supply of Electricity and Thermal Power	101.4	98.8	96.9	100.4
燃气生产和供应业	Production and Supply of Gas	98.8	100.2	98.0	96.3
水的生产和供应业	Production and Supply of Water	118.0	101.2	99.7	99.8

表8.10 续表 continued

类别	Types	2018	2019	2020	2021
工业生产者出厂价格指数	**Producer Price Indices for Industrial Products**	**101.7**	**98.8**	**98.3**	**102.1**
按国民经济行业分	**Grouped by National Economy Industries**				
石油和天然气开采业	Petroleum and Natural Gas Exploiting	116.4	98.2	83.7	97.6
农副食品加工业	Farm and Sideline Products Processing	102.1	103.8	106.3	116.2
食品制造业	Food Manufacturing	101.9	101.4	100.7	101.7
酒、饮料和精制茶制造业	Wine, Beverage and Refined Tea Manufacturing	107.6	100.4	99.9	101.0
烟草制品业	Tabacco Manufacture	100.5	102.4	103.3	100.5
纺织业	Textile	109.8	97.5	97.8	102.2
纺织服装、服饰业	Textile and Garment, Apparel Industry	99.6	103.0	100.6	99.4
皮革、毛皮、羽毛及其制品和制鞋业	Leather, Fur, Feather and Its Products and Shoemaking Industry	101.3	104.2	96.9	97.6
木材加工和木、竹、藤、棕、草制品业	Timber Processing and Timber, Bamboo, Rattan, Coir and Straw Products Manufacturing	99.1	98.1	94.9	98.0
家具制造业	Furniture Manufacturing	101.0	98.0	99.3	100.1
造纸和纸制品业	Paper-making and Paper Products Manufacturing	104.4	100.4	99.3	100.5
印刷和记录媒介复制业	Printing and Record Duplicating Industry	99.4	101.5	100.8	108.9
文教、工美、体育和娱乐用品制造业	Stationary, Education ,Industrial Art, Sport and Entertainment Products Manufacturing	101.6	114.5	116.8	98.7
石油加工、炼焦和核燃料加工业	Oil Processing, Coking and Nuclear Fual Processing	120.2	95.7	80.8	121.1
化学原料和化学制品制造业	Raw Chemical Materials and Chemical Products Manufacturing	102.8	89.0	94.8	115.9
医药制造业	Medicine Manufacturing	100.4	101.9	102.4	96.1
化学纤维制造业	Chemical Fiber Manufacturing	110.7	90.1	83.3	119.9
橡胶和塑料制品业	Rubber and Plastic Products Manufacturing	101.1	98.8	97.1	102.5
非金属矿物制品业	Nonmetal Mineral Products	113.8	104.2	101.6	106.1
黑色金属冶炼和压延加工业	Smelting and Pressing of Ferrous Metals	103.4	96.4	100.5	129.4
有色金属冶炼和压延加工业	Smelting and Pressing of Nonferrous Metals	102.3	100.6	100.6	118.4
金属制品业	Metal Products Manufacturing	103.7	99.6	99.5	105.4
通用设备制造业	General Equipment Manufacturing	102.8	102.4	99.8	100.9
专用设备制造业	Special Purpose Equipment Manufacturing	100.3	102.5	100.7	96.7
汽车制造业	Automotive Industry	99.1	97.2	94.7	94.4
铁路、船舶、航空航天和其他运输设备制造业	Railroads, Ships, Aerospace and other Transportation Equipment Manufacturing Industry	100.2	101.2	107.2	94.9
电气机械和器材制造业	Electric Machinery Equipments and Manufacturing	98.5	98.1	97.7	102.8
计算机、通信和其他电子设备制造业	Computers, Communications and other Electronic Equipment Manufacturing Industry	98.3	99.3	101.3	95.5
仪器仪表制造业	Instruments and Meters Manufacturing	100.1	99.1	100.6	99.5
其他制造业	Other Manufacturing	99.7	98.2	94.8	103.7
废弃资源综合利用业	Comprehensive Utilization of Waste Resources	100.8	100.1	100.8	100.5
金属制品、机械和设备修理业	Metal Products, Machinery and Equipment Repair	97.8	105.3	104.0	98.2
电力、热力生产和供应业	Production and Supply of Electricity and Thermal Power	99.0	98.5	94.2	99.9
燃气生产和供应业	Production and Supply of Gas	98.5	99.7	98.1	100.6
水的生产和供应业	Production and Supply of Water	98.2	101.6	101.3	103.9

表 8.11 工业生产者购进价格指数(2014~2021，以 2000 年价格为 100)
PRODUCER PURCHASING PRCIE INDICES (2000=100)

类 别	Types	2014	2015	2016	2017
工业生产者购进价格指数	**Producer Purchasing Price Indices**	**144.3**	**130.7**	**127.7**	**139.1**
燃料、动力类	Fuels and Power	257.8	176.1	160.8	195.4
黑色金属材料类	Ferrous Metals	153.7	125.6	127.0	149.5
#钢 材	Rolled-steel	135.2	121.0	122.7	143.4
有色金属材料类	Nonferrous Metals	176.2	156.5	155.9	173.2
化工原料类	Chemical Raw Materials	133.6	119.4	116.1	128.8
木材及纸浆类	Wood and Paper Pulps	98.9	98.2	96.5	101.2
建筑材料类及非金属矿类	Building Materials and Nonmetal Minerals	131.6	124.0	121.6	135.6
其他工业原材料及半成品类	Other Industrial Raw and Processed Materials	99.6	96.6	95.6	97.7
农副产品类	Farm and Sideline Products	168.9	158.9	150.0	156.6
纺织原料类	Textile Raw Material	121.9	122.1	123.1	126.4

表 8.11 续表 continued

类 别	Types	2018	2019	2020	2021
工业生产者购进价格指数	**Producer Purchasing Price Indices**	**146.3**	**144.4**	**139.9**	**150.1**
燃料、动力类	Fuels and Power	228.9	219.1	182.7	229.5
黑色金属材料类	Ferrous Metals	154.3	156.0	159.0	184.8
#钢 材	Rolled-steel	148.6	142.5	141.8	159.8
有色金属材料类	Nonferrous Metals	179.4	192.5	213.3	247.6
化工原料类	Chemical Raw Materials	135.8	127.5	118.3	132.3
木材及纸浆类	Wood and Paper Pulps	105.0	101.6	99.7	105.6
建筑材料类及非金属矿类	Building Materials and Nonmetal Minerals	148.1	151.1	149.1	163.1
其他工业原材料及半成品类	Other Industrial Raw and Processed Materials	98.9	97.9	97.4	97.2
农副产品类	Farm and Sideline Products	157.5	159.5	165.7	191.2
纺织原料类	Textile Raw Material	128.2	130.1	127.4	129.6

表 8.12 工业生产者购进价格指数(2014~2021，以上年价格为 100)
PRODUCER PURCHASING PRICE INDICES(PRECEDING YEAR=100)

类 别	Types	2014	2015	2016	2017
工业生产者购进价格指数	**Producer Purchasing Price Indices**	**95.9**	**90.6**	**97.7**	**108.9**
燃料、动力类	Fuels and Power	93.9	68.3	91.3	121.5
黑色金属材料类	Ferrous Metals	89.7	81.7	101.1	117.7
#钢　材	Rolled-steel	95.5	89.5	101.4	116.9
有色金属材料类	Nonferrous Metals	93.4	88.8	99.6	111.1
化工原料类	Chemical Raw Materials	96.8	89.4	97.2	110.9
木材及纸浆类	Wood and Paper Pulps	99.3	99.3	98.3	104.9
建筑材料类及非金属矿类	Building Materials and Nonmetal Minerals	102.3	94.2	98.1	111.5
其他工业原材料及半成品类	Other Industrial Raw and Processed Materials	98.0	97.0	99.0	102.2
农副产品类	Farm and Sideline Products	97.1	94.1	94.4	104.4
纺织原料类	Textile Raw Material	99.9	100.2	100.8	102.7

表 8.12 续表 continued

类 别	Types	2018	2019	2020	2021
工业生产者购进价格指数	**Producer Purchasing Price Indices**	**105.2**	**98.7**	**96.9**	**107.3**
燃料、动力类	Fuels and Power	117.2	95.7	83.4	125.6
黑色金属材料类	Ferrous Metals	103.2	101.1	101.9	116.2
#钢　材	Rolled-steel	103.6	95.9	99.5	112.7
有色金属材料类	Nonferrous Metals	103.6	107.3	110.8	116.1
化工原料类	Chemical Raw Materials	105.4	93.9	92.8	111.8
木材及纸浆类	Wood and Paper Pulps	103.7	96.8	98.1	105.9
建筑材料类及非金属矿类	Building Materials and Nonmetal Minerals	109.2	102	98.7	109.4
其他工业原材料及半成品类	Other Industrial Raw and Processed Materials	101.2	99.0	99.5	99.8
农副产品类	Farm and Sideline Products	100.5	101.3	103.9	115.4
纺织原料类	Textile Raw Material	101.4	101.5	97.9	101.7

上 / 海 / 统 / 计 / 年 / 鉴

主要统计指标解释

■ 居民消费价格指数

居民消费价格指数是度量一组代表性消费商品及服务项目价格水平随着时间而变动的相对数，反映居民家庭购买的消费品及服务价格水平的变动情况。它是宏观经济分析和决策、价格总水平监测和调控以及国民经济核算的重要指标。其按年度计算的变动率通常被用来作为反映通货膨胀或紧缩程度的指标。

现行的居民消费价格指数按用途分为八个大类，包括食品烟酒、衣着、居住、生活用品及服务、交通通信、教育文化娱乐、医疗保健、其他用品及服务。

■ 商品零售价格指数

商品零售价格指数是反映一定时期内城乡商品零售价格变动趋势和程度的相对数。商品零售价格的变动直接影响城乡居民的生活支出和国家的财政收入，影响居民购买力和市场供需的平衡，影响消费与积累的比例关系。因此，该指数可以从一个侧面对上述经济活动进行观察和分析。

■ 工业生产者出厂价格指数

从2011年起工业品出厂价格指数改为工业生产者出厂价格指数，它是反映一定时期内全部工业产品出厂价格总水平的变动趋势和程度的相对数，包括工业企业售给本企业以外所有单位的各种产品和直接售给居民用于生活消费的产品。该指数可以观察出厂价格变动对工业总产值及增加值的影响。

■ 工业生产者购进价格指数

从2011年起原材料、燃料和动力购进价格指数改为工业生产者购进价格指数，它是反映工业企业作为生产投入，从物资交易市场和能源、原材料生产企业购买原材料、燃料和动力产品时，所支付的价格水平变动趋势和程度的统计指标，是扣除工业企业物质消耗成本中的价格变动影响的重要依据。

SHANGHAI STATISTICAL YEARBOOK

EXPLANATORY NOTES TO MAJOR STATISTICAL INDICATORS

□ Consumer Price Indices

The Consumer Price Indices is an indices that reflects the time-based change of prices of a group of representative consumption commodities and services. It is an important reference factor for macro-economic analysis and strategy, monitoring and adjustment of overall price level and the national economic budgeting. The year-on-year change of the indices is often a norm reflecting the inflation or deflation.

The current CPI covers eight categories of oods and services: Food, Cigarettes and Liquors, Clothing, Housing, Living Articles and Services, Transportation and Communication, Education, Culture and Recreation, Medical and Health Services, Other Articles and Services.

□ Retail Price Indices

Retail Price Indices reflects the trend and degree of change in retail prices of commodities during a given period. The change in retail prices of commodities directly affect the living expenditure of urban and rural residents, government revenue, purchasing power of residents and the equilibrium of market supply and demand, and the ratio of consumption to accumulation. Therefore, the retail price indices is useful to analyze the changes of the above economic activities.

□ Producer Ex-factory Price Indices

Since 2011, Ex-factory Price Indices of Industrial Products has been changed into Producer Ex-factory Price Indices. Producer Ex-factory Price Indices reflects the trend and degree of changes in general ex-factory prices of all industrial products during a given period, including sales of industrial products by an industrial enterprise to all units outside the enterprise, as well as sales of consumer goods to residents. It can be used to analyze the impact of ex-factory prices on gross output value and value-added of the industrial sector.

□ Producer Purchasing Price Indices

Since 2011, Indices of Purchasing Prices of Raw Materials, Fuels and Power has been changed into Producer Purchasing Price Indices which reflects changes in the level and degree of prices paid by industrial enterprises when they purchase production input such as raw materials, fuels and power from the market or from other energy or raw materials producing enterprises. This indices provides important basis for measuring the material consumption of industrial enterprises after removing influence of price changes.

第九篇
CHAPTER 9

人民生活
LIVING STANDARDS

简要说明

第一部分　2015年以来上海居民收支与生活状况调查主要数据(新口径)(见表9.1到表9.17)

一、主要内容

第一部分资料反映2015～2020年上海常住居民收入、消费及其他生活状况。

二、资料来源

上海常住居民生活状况数据来源于国家统计局上海调查总队居民收支与生活状况抽样调查。

三、住户调查对象

上海居民收支与生活状况调查(简称住户调查,下同)对象为“本市常住居民”,既包括本地户籍,也包括外地户籍;既包括以家庭形式居住的户,也包括以集体形式居住的户,即在本市常住的外来务工人员也被纳入调查对象。调查区域扩展到全市16个区的城镇、农村地区。2013年至2017年,全市城镇、农村调查样本量分别为4600户和1400户,合计为6000户。2018年开始,全市城镇、农村调查样本量分别为3390户和610户,合计为4000户。

四、调查内容

调查主要内容包括居民现金和实物收支情况、住户成员及劳动力从业情况、居民家庭食品和能源消费情况、住房和耐用消费拥有情况、家庭经营和生产投资情况、社区基本情况以及其他民生状况等。

五、指标发布的变化

根据国家统计局要求,国家统计局上海调查总队从2015年1季度起,发布城乡一体化住户调查新口径调查数据。主要指标包括:上海居民人均可支配收入、城镇常住居民人均可支配收入、农村常住居民人均可支配收入;上海居民人均消费支出、城镇常住居民人均消费支出、农村常住居民人均消费支出等。

六、数据主要变化情况

根据城乡一体化住户调查改革,2015年起,遵照“统计上的城乡划分标准”,新口径城镇常住居民收入、消费等数据覆盖范围在原有基础上扩大,包括城乡结合部,而农村常住居民范围缩小,不再以行政村划分; 新口径城镇常住居民“人均可支配收入”指标加入了自有住房折算净租金,扣除了财产性支出和转移性支出等。计算城镇和农村常住居民消费支出时,包括了自有住房折算租金。

第二部分　1980~2014年城镇和农村住户调查主要数据（老口径）（见表9.18到表9.28）

一、主要内容

第二部分资料反映1980 ~ 2014年上海市居民生活现状及变化情况，分为城市居民生活和农村居民生活两部分。

二、城镇住户调查资料来源

城镇居民生活状况的数据来源于国家统计局上海调查总队的城镇住户抽样调查。主要内容包括城市居民生活基本情况、收入、生活消费支出、主要消费品消费量等。

三、城镇住户调查方法

上海城镇住户调查以城市常住户为调查对象，2003年及之前，调查样本为500户，2004年至2014年，调查样本增至1000户，分布于黄浦、徐汇、长宁、静安、普陀、闸北、虹口、杨浦、闵行、宝山、浦东等11个区。

城镇住户调查采用分层、多阶段与大小成比例（pps）、随机等距等方法抽选调查样本户，采用日记账与问卷调查相结合的方法取得数据。首先，每月向抽中的调查户发放账本，由调查户采用日记账方式对本住户及每个成员的收支情况进行记录；然后由调查人员每月在规定的时间将账本回收并进行审核、编码和录入；最后由国家统计局上海调查总队进行数据汇总得出人均可支配收入等数据资料。另外，家庭和个人基本情况以及部分调查户的收支情况通过问卷的形式取得数据。

四、农村住户调查资料来源

农村居民生活状况的数据来源于国家统计局上海调查总队的住户收支与生活状况调查。主要内容包括农村居民生活基本情况、收入、生活消费支出、主要消费品消费量等。

五、农村住户调查方法

农村住户调查是以农村常住户为调查对象，农村常住户指长期(半年以上)居住在农村范围内的住户。户口不在本地而在本地居住半年及以上的住户也包括在本地农村常住户范围内。按国家统计局住户收支与生活状况调查方案，采用抽样调查方法在全市郊区抽取约1200户农村居民家庭作为调查样本，分布于浦东、闵行、宝山、嘉定、金山、松江、青浦、奉贤、崇明9个区。

为保证农村住户调查资料的准确性，住户收支与生活状况调查在95%的概率把握程度下要求抽样误差不得超过±3%。调查数据采用农村居民记账与一次性调查相结合的方法取得，调查户按照国家统计局上海调查总队统一编制的账本和要求记账，现金收支账、实物收支账发生一笔记一笔，由区调查员每月收取调查户的账本，录入计算机，通过乡镇、区、总队多级审核确保调查数据真实可靠。

BRIEF INTRODUCTION

Part 1 Main Data from Survey of Income and Expenditure and Living Conditions of Residents in Shanghai Since 2015 (New Statistical Standard)(Table 9.1 to Table 9.17)

I. Main Contents

The data of first part reflect the income and consumption and other living conditions of residents in Shanghai from 2015 to 2020.

II. Sources of Data

Data on the living conditions of Shanghai residents come from the sample survey on residents revenue and expenditure and living conditions, which is conducted by Survey Office of the National Bureau of Statistics in Shanghai.

III. Objects of Household Survey

Respondents of survey on income, expenditure and living conditions of residents in Shanghai (household survey for short) includes household registered and nonlocal registered residence, family household and institutional household in Shanghai. In other words, migrant workers are included. Region of the survey covers all 16 districts of Shanghai, both urban and rural area. From 2015–2017,sample number of urban and rural suvery changes to 4600 and 1400 respectively, a total of 6000 households. Since 2018, sample number of urban and rural suvery changes to 3390 and 610 respectively, a total of 4000 households.

IV. Contents of the Survey

The main contents of the survey include income and expenditure of residents in cash and in kind, employment situation of household members and labor force, food and energy consumption of households, possession of housing and durable goods consumption, situation of household business and production investment, basic situation of the community and other livelihood of people, etc.

V .Changes of Index Releasing

According to the requirements of the National Bureau of Statistics, Survey Office of the National Bureau of Statistics in Shanghai releases the data of household survey of urban and rural integration according to new statistic standard since the first quarter of 2015. The main indicators include: per capita disposable income of Shanghai residents, per capita disposable income of urban residents, per capita disposable income of rural residents, per capita consumption expenditure of Shanghai residents, per capita consumption expenditure of urban residents, and per capita consumption expenditure of rural residents

VI. Main Changes of Data

According to the household survey reform of urban and rural integration, since 2015,following the Statistical Classification of Urban and Rural Areas, coverage of data of new standard on urban resident income and consumption is expanded on the original basis ,including the Urban–Rural Binding Region. But Coverage of rural residents is reduced, and is no longer divided by administrative village. The indicator of Per Capita Disposable Income includes self–ownedhousing converted net rent, and excludes property expenditure and transfer expenditure, etc. The calculation of consumption expenditure of urban and rural residents includes self–owned housing converted net rent.

Part 2　Main Data from Urban and Rural Household Survey from 1980 to 2014 (Old Statistical Standard)(Table 9.18 to Table 9.28)

I. Main Contents

Data in the second part of this chapter reflect the Shanghai people's living conditions and changes from 1980 to 2014, consisting of two parts, on the life of urban and rural households respectively.

II. Sources of Data on the Living Conditions of Urban Residents

Data on the living conditions of urban residents come from the data collected through a sample survey on the urban households conducted by the Survey Office of the National Bureau of Statistics in Shanghai. The main contents of the survey include basic situation of urban residents living, income, consumer spending and the main consumption of consumer goods, etc.

III. Methodology for Urban Household Survey

Data on the survey of urban residents cover long–term residents in urban areas. Shanghai's sample included 500 households before 2003; it increased to 1,000 households between 2004 and 2014, covering 11 districts of Huangpu, Xuhui, Changning, Jing'an, Putuo, Zhabei, Hongkou, Yangpu, Minhang, Baoshan and Pudong.

Samples in urban household survey are selected by systematic sampling method schemes, such as stratifying method, multi –stage method and probability proportional to size (PPS) method, and the data are obtained by method of journal combined with questionnaire. Selected households receive account books each month and keep diaries to record income and expenditure of the household and its individual members. Professional inspectors will then collect, encode and audit the data at fixed time each month, deliver them to the Survey Office of the National Bureau of Statistics to calculate data such as the average disposable income per capita. In addition, data of household and personal basic situation as well as the balance of the selected households are obtained through the form of questionnaire.

IV. Sources of Data on the Living of Rural Residents

Data on the living conditions of rural residents come from data collected through the survey on household revenue and expenditure and living condition, which is organized by the Survey Office of the National Bureau of Statistics in Shanghai. The main contents of the survey include the basic condition of rural households, income, consumption expenditure and consumption of major consumer goods.

V. Methodology for Rural Household Survey

Data on the survey of income and expenditure of rural residents cover long–term residents in rural areas. Long–term residents refer to people living within the administered villages for more than half a year. Households without local registered residence are included given they have lived in the area for more than half a year. According to the scheme of the survey on rural household revenue, expenditure and living condition, the sampling approach is used to select about 1,200 rural households as samples through 9 districts of Pudong, Minhang, Baoshan, Jiading, Jinshan, Songjiang, Qingpu, Fengxian, and Chongming.

To guarantee accuracy of the data on the revenue, expenditure and living condition of rural household, it is required that the sampling error should not exceed ±3%, with a confidence probability as 95%. A combination of diaries kept by rural households and the one-time survey is used for collecting data. The households are keeping diaries on unified requirements compiled by the Survey Office of the National Bureau of Statistics in Shanghai. Income and expenditure of cash and real goods are recorded case by case. Data are collected by inspectors from districts and compiled into computers. Inspectors from townships, districts and the headquarters office will audit the data to make them accurate and reliable.

表 9.1　主要年份全市居民家庭生活基本情况
BASIC STATISTICS OF WHOLE CITY HOUSEHOLDS IN MAIN YEARS

指　标	Indicators	2015	2020	2021
基本情况(人)	Basic Statistics(person)			
户均人口	Population per Household	2.62	2.54	2.54
户均从业人口	Employees per Household	1.29	1.14	1.14
平均每一从业人口负担人数（包括从业者本人）	Persons Supported by Each Employee(person)	2.03	2.24	2.23
家庭收入与支出(元)	Household Income and Expenditure (yuan)			
人均可支配收入	Per Capita Disposable Income	49 867	72 232	78 027
人均消费支出	Per Capita Consumption Expenditure	34 784	42 536	48 879

表 9.2　主要年份城镇常住居民家庭生活基本情况
BASIC STATISTICS OF URBAN HOUSEHOLDS IN MAIN YEARS

指　标	Indicators	2015	2020	2021
基本情况(人)	Basic Statistics(person)			
户均人口	Population per Household	2.64	2.56	2.56
户均从业人口	Employees per Household	1.26	1.12	1.12
平均每一从业人口负担人数（包括从业者本人）	Persons Supported by Each Employee(person)	2.09	2.28	2.28
家庭收入与支出(元)	Household Income and Expenditure (yuan)			
人均可支配收入	Per Capita Disposable Income	52 962	76 437	82 429
人均消费支出	Per Capita Consumption Expenditure	36 946	44 839	51 295

表 9.3　主要年份农村常住居民家庭生活基本情况
BASIC STATISTICS OF RURAL HOUSEHOLDS IN MAIN YEARS

指　标	Indicators	2015	2020	2021
基本情况(人)	Basic Statistics(person)			
户均人口	Population per Household	2.47	2.42	2.32
户均从业人口	Employees per Household	1.54	1.27	1.25
平均每一从业人口负担人数（包括从业者本人）	Persons Supported by Each Employee(person)	1.6	1.9	1.86
家庭收入与支出(元)	Household Income and Expenditure (yuan)			
人均可支配收入	Per Capita Disposable Income	23 205	34 911	38 521
人均消费支出	Per Capita Consumption Expenditure	16 152	22 095	27 205

注：2012 年起，国家统计局实施了城乡一体化住户调查改革，统一了城乡居民收入名称、分类和统计标准。 2015 年起，发布城乡可比的新口径全市居民人均可支配收入以及分城乡常住居民人均可支配收入。

Note: Since 2012, the National Bureau of Statistics has implemented the integrated household survey reform of urban and rural integration with unifying the urban and rural income name, classification and statistical standards. Since 2015, the per capita disposable income of city′s residents and per capita disposable income of urban and rural residents which can be compared by new statistical coverage have been released.

表 9.4 个人存款(住户存款)年末余额(1997~2021)
HOUSEHOLD DEPOSITS AT YEAR-END

年份 Year	个人存款(住户存款)余额 (亿元) Household Deposits (100 million yuan)	其中 of which 活期存款 Current Deposits	定期及其他存款 Time Deposits and Other Deposits	人均个人存款余额 (元) Average Deposits (yuan)
1997	2 109.18	265.93	1 843.25	14 165
1998	2 372.94	355.78	2 017.16	15 540
1999	2 597.12	477.30	2 119.82	16 574
2000	2 627.07	542.86	2 084.21	16 331
2001	3 109.50	808.17	2 301.33	18 638
2002	4 915.54	1 312.49	3 603.05	28 696
2003	6 054.60	1 793.73	4 260.87	34 287
2004	6 960.99	2 056.06	4 904.93	37 935
2005	8 432.49	2 360.66	6 071.83	44 610
2006	9 480.28	2 778.31	6 701.97	48 268
2007	9 326.45	3 140.60	6 185.85	45 195
2008	12 083.66	3 528.02	8 555.64	56 449
2009	14 357.65	4 624.53	9 733.13	64 959
2010	16 249.29	5 396.19	10 853.11	70 567
2011	18 920.43	5 925.39	12 995.04	80 600
2012	21 512.01	6 644.11	14 867.90	90 370
2013	23 097.35	7 251.30	15 846.05	95 635
2014	24 057.05	7 409.90	16 647.15	99 177
2015	23 384.73	8 184.76	15 199.97	96 820
2016	25 112.99	9 416.99	15 696.00	103 786
2017	25 763.20	9 560.65	16 202.54	106 533
2018	28 569.24	10 170.61	18 398.63	117 870
2019	33 295.40	11 354.22	21 941.18	137 123
2020	38 302.45	13 120.93	25 181.52	153 926
2021	42 652.55	14 337.95	28 314.60	171 335

注：本表数据由中国人民银行上海总部提供。1997 年~1999 年，个人存款余额为中资金融机构人民币储蓄存款余额；2000 年~2010 年，个人存款余额为中外资金融机构本外币储蓄存款余额；自 2011 年起，个人存款余额含中外资金融机构本外币活期存款余额、定期存款余额、结构性存款余额、保证金存款余额等。

Note: Data in this table are provided by Shanghai Headquarters of the People's Bank of China. From 1997 to 1999, the household deposits refer to RMB savings deposits in domestic funded financial institutions. From 2000 to 2010, the household deposits refer to all personal savings deposits in foreign and domestic funded financial institutions. Since 2011, the household deposits has included current deposits, time deposits, structured deposits, margin deposit for security and so on.

表 9.5 全市居民收支情况(2018~2021)
BASIC STATISTICS OF INCOME AND EXPENDITURE OF RESIDENTS

单位:元(yuan)

指 标	Indicators	2018	2019	2020	2021
居民人均可支配收入	**Per Capita Disposable Income of Residents**	**64 183**	**69 442**	**72 232**	**78 027**
工资性收入	Wages	37 137	40 025	41 500	48 835
经营净收入	Net Business Income	1 821	2 209	2 052	2 063
财产净收入	Net Property Income	9 666	10 055	9 904	10 209
转移净收入	Net Transferred Income	15 559	17 153	18 776	16 920
居民人均消费支出	**Per Capita Consumption Expenditure of Residents**	**43 351**	**45 605**	**42 536**	**48 879**
食品烟酒	Food,Cigarettes and Liquors	10 728	10 952	11 225	12 604
衣 着	Clothing	2 037	2 072	1 694	2 087
居 住	Residence	14 209	15 046	15 247	16 137
生活用品及服务	Living Goods and Services	2 096	2 123	2 091	2 248
交通通信	Transportation	4 881	5 356	4 558	5 626
教育文化娱乐	Education,Culture and Entertainment	5 049	5 495	3 663	4 710
医疗保健	Medicine and Medical Services	3 070	3 205	3 033	3 878
其他用品及服务	Other Goods and Services	1 281	1 356	1 025	1 589

表 9.6 全市居民收支比上年名义增长(2018~2021)
GROWTH RATE OF INCOME AND EXPENDITURE OF RESIDENTS ON PRECEDING YEAR

单位:%

指 标	Indicators	2018	2019	2020	2021
居民人均可支配收入	**Per Capita Disposable Income of Residents**	**8.8**	**8.2**	**4.0**	**8.0**
工资性收入	Wages	8.1	7.8	3.7	8.9
经营净收入	Net Business Income	18.8	21.3	-7.1	0.5
财产净收入	Net Property Income	7.0	4.0	-1.5	3.1
转移净收入	Net Transferred Income	10.7	10.2	9.5	9.5
居民人均消费支出	**Per Capita Consumption Expenditure of Residents**	**8.9**	**5.2**	**-6.7**	**14.9**
食品烟酒	Food,Cigarettes and Liquors	7.2	2.1	2.5	12.3
衣 着	Clothing	17.5	1.7	-18.2	23.2
居 住	Residence	3.6	5.9	1.3	5.8
生活用品及服务	Living Goods and Services	14.8	1.3	-1.5	7.5
交通通信	Transportation and Communication	20.3	9.7	-14.9	23.4
教育文化娱乐	Education,Culture and Entertainment	7.7	8.8	-33.3	28.6
医疗保健	Medicine and Medical Services	18.0	4.4	-5.4	27.9
其他用品及服务	Other Goods and Services	9.2	5.8	-24.4	55.0

注：因 2020 年样本轮换以及口径调整，2021 年居民人均工资性收入增幅、居民人均转移净收入增幅为同口径测算增幅，不可两年金额直接计算，表 9.8 同。

Note：Because of the sample rotation and caliber adjustment in 2020, the growth of per Capita Wage Income and per Capita Net Transferred Income of Residents in 2021 are measured by the same caliber, which cannot be directly calculated in two years. Same as Table 9.8.

表 9.7 城镇常住居民收支情况(2018~2021)
BASIC STATISTICS OF INCOME AND EXPENDITURE OF URBAN RESIDENTS

单位:元(yuan)

指 标	Indicators	2018	2019	2020	2021
居民人均可支配收入	**Per Capita Disposable Income of Residents**	**68 034**	**73 615**	**76 437**	**82 429**
工资性收入	Wages	39 146	42 328	43 803	51 494
经营净收入	Net Business Income	1 829	2 192	2 063	2 024
财产净收入	Net Property Income	10 653	11 064	10 884	11 204
转移净收入	Net Transferred Income	16 406	18 031	19 687	17 707
居民人均消费支出	**Per Capita Consumption Expenditure of Residents**	**46 015**	**48 272**	**44 839**	**51 295**
食品烟酒	Food,Cigarettes and Liquors	11 104	11 273	11 515	12 878
衣 着	Clothing	2 139	2 162	1 763	2 153
居 住	Residence	15 376	16 253	16 465	17 370
生活用品及服务	Living Goods and Services	2 205	2 215	2 177	2 328
交通通信	Transportation	5 108	5 626	4 677	5 721
教育文化娱乐	Education,Culture and Entertainment	5 491	5 966	3 963	5 090
医疗保健	Medicine and Medical Services	3 222	3 332	3 189	4 063
其他用品及服务	Other Goods and Services	1 370	1 445	1 090	1 692

表 9.8 城镇常住居民收支比上年名义增长(2018~2021)
GROWTH RATE OF INCOME AND EXPENDITURE OF URBAN RESIDENTS ON PRECEDING YEAR

单位:%

指 标	Indicators	2018	2019	2020	2021
居民人均可支配收入	**Per Capita Disposable Income of Residents**	**8.7**	**8.2**	**3.8**	**7.8**
工资性收入	Wages	8.8	8.1	3.5	8.9
经营净收入	Net Business Income	17.9	19.9	-5.9	-1.9
财产净收入	Net Property Income	6.8	3.9	-1.6	2.9
转移净收入	Net Transferred Income	8.8	9.9	9.2	9.4
居民人均消费支出	**Per Capita Consumption Expenditure of Residents**	**8.8**	**4.9**	**-7.1**	**14.4**
食品烟酒	Food,Cigarettes and Liquors	6.2	1.5	2.1	11.8
衣 着	Clothing	17.1	1.0	-18.5	22.1
居 住	Residence	4.3	5.7	1.3	5.5
生活用品及服务	Living Goods and Services	14.4	0.5	-1.7	6.9
交通通信	Transportation and Communication	20.1	10.1	-16.9	22.3
教育文化娱乐	Education,Culture and Entertainment	7.9	8.7	-33.6	28.4
医疗保健	Medicine and Medical Services	17.8	3.4	-4.3	27.4
其他用品及服务	Other Goods and Services	8.0	5.5	-24.6	55.2

表 9.9 全市居民人均可支配收入及构成(2018~2021)
PER CAPITA DISPOSABLE INCOME AND ITS COMPOSITION OF WHOLE CITY RESIDENTS

指 标	Indicators	2018	2019	2020	2021
可支配收入(元/人)	**Disposable Income(yuan/person)**	**64 183**	**69 442**	**72 232**	**78 027**
工资性收入	Wages	37 137	40 025	41 500	48 835
经营净收入	Net Business Income	1 821	2 209	2 052	2 063
财产净收入	Net Property Income	9 666	10 055	9 904	10 209
转移净收入	Net Transferred Income	15 559	17 153	18 776	16 920
可支配收入构成(%)	**Composition of Disposable Income**	**100.0**	**100.0**	**100.0**	**100.0**
工资性收入	Wages	57.9	57.6	57.5	62.6
经营净收入	Net Business Income	2.8	3.2	2.8	2.6
财产净收入	Net Property Income	15.1	14.5	13.7	13.1
转移净收入	Net Transferred Income	24.2	24.7	26.0	21.7

表 9.10 城镇常住居民人均可支配收入及构成(2018~2021)
PER CAPITA DISPOSABLE INCOME AND ITS COMPOSITION OF URBAN RESIDENTS

指 标	Indicators	2018	2019	2020	2021
可支配收入(元/人)	**Disposable Income(yuan/person)**	**68 034**	**73 615**	**76 437**	**82 429**
工资性收入	Wages	39 146	42 328	43 803	51 494
经营净收入	Net Business Income	1 829	2 192	2 063	2 024
财产净收入	Net Property Income	10 653	11 064	10 884	11 204
转移净收入	Net Transferred Income	16 406	18 031	19 687	17 707
可支配收入构成(%)	**Composition of Disposable Income**	**100.0**	**100.0**	**100.0**	**100.0**
工资性收入	Wages	57.5	57.5	57.3	62.5
经营净收入	Net Business Income	2.7	3.0	2.7	2.4
财产净收入	Net Property Income	15.7	15.0	14.2	13.6
转移净收入	Net Transferred Income	24.1	24.5	25.8	21.5

表 9.11 全市居民人均消费支出(2018~2021)
PER CAPITA CONSUMPTION EXPENDITURE OF WHOLE CITY RESIDENTS

单位:元/人(yuan/person)

指 标	Indicators	2018	2019	2020	2021
消费支出	**Consumption Expenditure**	**43 351**	**45 605**	**42 536**	**48 879**
食品烟酒	Food,Cigarettes and Liquors	10 728	10 952	11 225	12 604
#食　品	Food	6 276	6 361	7 239	7 380
在外饮食(不含食堂用餐)	Dining Out(excluding the canteen)	3 207	3 279	2 518	3 424
衣　着	Clothing	2 037	2 072	1 694	2 087
衣　类	Garments	1 665	1 662	1 346	1 708
鞋　类	Shoes	372	410	348	379
居　住	Residence	14 209	15 046	15 247	16 137
#租赁房房租	Rents	1 584	1 447	1 431	1 283
水电燃料及其他	Water,Electricity,Fuel and Others	1 161	1 139	1 173	1 323
生活用品及服务	Living Goods and Services	2 096	2 123	2 091	2 248
#家用器具	Home Appliances	515	475	485	480
家庭日用杂品	Household Daily Groceries	405	418	436	467
交通通信	Transportation and Communication	4 881	5 356	4 558	5 626
交　通	Transportation	3 669	4 183	3 389	4 311
通　信	Communication	1 212	1 173	1 169	1 315
教育文化娱乐	Education,Culture and Entertainment	5 049	5 495	3 663	4 710
教　育	Education	2 263	2 597	2 194	2 991
文化娱乐	Culture and Entertainment	2 786	2 898	1 469	1 719
医疗保健	Medicine and Medical Services	3 070	3 205	3 033	3 878
医疗器具及药品	Medical Devices and Drugs	518	495	514	626
医疗服务	Medical Service	2 552	2 710	2 519	3 252
其他用品及服务	Other Goods and Services	1 281	1 356	1 025	1 589

表 9.12 城镇常住居民人均消费支出(2018~2021)
PER CAPITA CONSUMPTION EXPENDITURE OF URBAN RESIDENTS

单位:元/人(yuan/person)

指 标	Indicators	2018	2019	2020	2021
消费支出	**Consumption Expenditure**	**46 015**	**48 272**	**44 839**	**51 295**
食品烟酒	Food, Cigarettes and Liquors	11 104	11 273	11 515	12 878
#食　品	Food	6 449	6 483	7 391	7 471
在外饮食(不含食堂用餐)	Dining Out(excluding the canteen)	3 428	3 503	2 683	3 645
衣　着	Clothing	2 139	2 162	1 763	2 153
衣　类	Garments	1 754	1 739	1 405	1 766
鞋　类	Shoes	385	423	358	387
居　住	Residence	15 376	16 253	16 465	17 370
#租赁房房租	Rents	1 701	1 551	1 518	1 357
水电燃料及其他	Water, Electricity, Fuel and Others	1 191	1 162	1 198	1 342
生活用品及服务	Living Goods and Services	2 205	2 215	2 177	2 328
#家用器具	Home Appliances	535	493	498	497
家庭日用杂品	Household Daily Groceries	415	429	446	473
交通通信	Transportation and Communication	5 108	5 626	4 677	5 721
交　通	Transportation	3 850	4 413	3 478	4 365
通　信	Communication	1 258	1 213	1 199	1 356
教育文化娱乐	Education, Culture and Entertainment	5 491	5 966	3 963	5 090
教　育	Education	2 452	2 810	2 368	3 238
文化娱乐	Culture and Entertainment	3 039	3 156	1 595	1 852
医疗保健	Medicine and Medical Services	3 222	3 332	3 189	4 063
医疗器具及药品	Medical Devices and Drugs	534	512	538	650
医疗服务	Medical Service	2 688	2 820	2 651	3 413
其他用品及服务	Other Goods and Services	1 370	1 445	1 090	1 692

表 9.13 全市居民人均消费支出及构成(2018~2021)
PER CAPITA CONSUMPTION EXPENDITURE AND ITS COMPOSITION OF WHOLE CITY RESIDENTS

	指 标 Indicators	2018	2019	2020	2021
消费支出(元/人)	**Consumption Expenditure(yuan/person)**	**43 351**	**45 605**	**42 536**	**48 879**
食品烟酒	Food,Cigarettes and Liquors	10 728	10 952	11 225	12 604
衣 着	Clothing	2 037	2 072	1 694	2 087
居 住	Residence	14 209	15 046	15 247	16 137
生活用品及服务	Living Goods and Services	2 096	2 123	2 091	2 248
交通通信	Transportation and Communication	4 881	5 356	4 558	5 626
教育文化娱乐	Education,Culture and Entertainment	5 049	5 495	3 663	4 710
医疗保健	Medicine and Medical Services	3 070	3 205	3 033	3 878
其他用品及服务	Other Goods and Services	1 281	1 356	1 025	1 589
消费支出构成(%)	**Composition of Consumption Expenditure(%)**	**100.0**	**100.0**	**100.0**	**100.0**
食品烟酒	Food,Cigarettes and Liquors	24.7	24.0	26.4	25.8
衣 着	Clothing	4.7	4.5	4.0	4.3
居 住	Residence	32.8	33.0	35.9	33.0
生活用品及服务	Living Goods and Services	4.8	4.7	4.9	4.6
交通通信	Transportation and Communication	11.3	11.7	10.7	11.5
教育文化娱乐	Education,Culture and Entertainment	11.6	12.1	8.6	9.6
医疗保健	Medicine and Medical Services	7.1	7.0	7.1	7.9
其他用品及服务	Other Goods and Services	3.0	3.0	2.4	3.3

注：因指标口径调整，“食品烟酒”占“消费支出”比重与历史数据不可比，表9.14同。

Note：Because of the adjustment of statistical coverage,the proportion of “food,cigarettes and liquors” in the “consumption expenditure” cannot be compared with the historical data.Same as table 9.14.

表 9.14 城镇常住居民人均消费支出及构成(2018~2021)
PER CAPITA CONSUMPTION EXPENDITURE AND ITS COMPOSITION OF URBAN RESIDENTS

指 标	Indicators	2018	2019	2020	2021
消费支出(元/人)	**Consumption Expenditure(yuan/person)**	**46 015**	**48 272**	**44 839**	**51 295**
食品烟酒	Food,Cigarettes and Liquors	11 104	11 273	11 515	12 878
衣 着	Clothing	2 139	2 162	1 763	2 153
居 住	Residence	15 376	16 253	16 465	17 370
生活用品及服务	Living Goods and Services	2 205	2 215	2 177	2 328
交通通信	Transportation and Communication	5 108	5 626	4 677	5 721
教育文化娱乐	Education,Culture and Entertainment	5 491	5 966	3 963	5 090
医疗保健	Medicine and Medical Services	3 222	3 332	3 189	4 063
其他用品及服务	Other Goods and Services	1 370	1 445	1 090	1 692
消费支出构成(%)	**Composition of Consumption Expenditure(%)**	**100.0**	**100.0**	**100.0**	**100.0**
食品烟酒	Food,Cigarettes and Liquors	24.1	23.3	25.7	25.1
衣 着	Clothing	4.7	4.5	3.9	4.2
居 住	Residence	33.4	33.7	36.7	33.9
生活用品及服务	Living Goods and Services	4.8	4.6	4.9	4.5
交通通信	Transportation and Communication	11.1	11.6	10.4	11.2
教育文化娱乐	Education,Culture and Entertainment	11.9	12.4	8.9	9.9
医疗保健	Medicine and Medical Services	7.0	6.9	7.1	7.9
其他用品及服务	Other Goods and Services	3.0	3.0	2.4	3.3

表 9.15 每百户居民家庭年末耐用消费品拥有量(2018~2021)
DURABLE CONSUMER GOODS OWNED BY EACH HUNDRED HOUSEHOLDS AT YEAR-END

指 标	Indicators	2018	2019	2020	2021
家用汽车(辆)	Family Cars(vehicle)	37	39	39	44
助力车(辆)	Moped(vehicle)	68	71	73	77
洗衣机(台)	Washing Machine (unit)	93	95	96	96
电冰箱(柜)(台)	Refrigerators or Freezers(unit)	100	102	102	103
微波炉(台)	Microwave Ovens (unit)	85	86	86	84
彩色电视机(台)	Colour Televisions(unit)	173	177	176	172
空　调(台)	Air-conditioner(unit)	200	207	207	210
热水器(台)	Water Heaters(unit)	95	97	98	99
排油烟机(台)	Range Hoods(unit)	81	83	83	84
固定电话(线)	Fixed Telephones(line)	56	47	45	35
移动电话(部)	Mobile Phones(unit)	220	224	226	230
#接入互联网	Of Which: Access to the Internet	194	203	213	219
计算机(台)	Computers(unit)	99	105	105	98
#接入互联网	Of Which: Access to the Internet	95	101	101	95
照相机(架)	Camera(set)	33	34	33	25
健身器材(套)	Health Equipment(set)	8	8	8	8
空气净化器(含新风系统)(台)	Air Purifier(Fresh Air System Included)	16	18	19	23
吸尘器(台)	Dust Catcher(unit)	33	37	38	40

注：2018 年住户调查进行样本轮换，部分数据可能存在波动。表 9.16 和 9.17 同。
Note: Sample rotation was conducted in household survey in 2018, and some data may fluctuate. Same as table 9.16 and 9.17.

表 9.16 每百户城镇常住居民家庭年末耐用消费品拥有量(2018~2021)
DURABLE CONSUMER GOODS OWNED BY EACH HUNDRED URBAN HOUSEHOLDS AT YEAR-END

指 标	Indicators	2018	2019	2020	2021
家用汽车(辆)	Family Cars(vehicle)	38	39	40	45
助力车(辆)	Moped(vehicle)	61	64	66	70
洗衣机(台)	Washing Machine (unit)	94	96	97	97
电冰箱(柜)(台)	Refrigerators or Freezers(unit)	100	101	102	103
微波炉(台)	Microwave Ovens (unit)	86	87	87	85
彩色电视机(台)	Colour Televisions(unit)	175	178	178	174
空 调(台)	Air-conditioner(unit)	207	213	214	216
热水器(台)	Water Heaters(unit)	96	98	99	100
排油烟机(台)	Range Hoods(unit)	85	87	87	87
固定电话(线)	Fixed Telephones(line)	56	47	46	37
移动电话(部)	Mobile Phones(unit)	223	227	228	233
接入互联网	Of Which: Access to the Internet	201	210	218	224
计算机(台)	Computers(unit)	107	113	113	106
接入互联网	Of Which: Access to the Internet	102	109	109	103
照相机(架)	Camera(set)	36	37	37	28
健身器材(套)	Health Equipment(set)	8	9	9	9
空气净化器(含新风系统)(台)	Air Purifier(Fresh Air System Included)	18	20	21	26
吸尘器(台)	Dust Catcher(unit)	36	40	41	43

表 9.17 每百户农村常住居民家庭年末耐用消费品拥有量(2018~2021)
DURABLE CONSUMER GOODS OWNED BY EACH HUNDRED RURAL HOUSEHOLDS AT YEAR-END

指 标	Indicators	2018	2019	2020	2021
家用汽车(辆)	Family Cars(vehicle)	28	32	35	41
助力车(辆)	Moped(vehicle)	129	130	132	137
洗衣机(台)	Washing Machine (unit)	83	86	85	90
电冰箱(柜)(台)	Refrigerators or Freezers(unit)	101	104	103	104
微波炉(台)	Microwave Ovens (unit)	75	77	74	76
彩色电视机(台)	Colour Televisions(unit)	162	170	161	157
空 调(台)	Air-conditioner(unit)	142	156	152	163
热水器(台)	Water Heaters(unit)	85	90	92	89
排油烟机(台)	Range Hoods(unit)	49	55	53	57
固定电话(线)	Fixed Telephones(line)	50	41	36	21
移动电话(部)	Mobile Phones(unit)	197	203	207	208
#接入互联网	Of Which: Access to the Internet	133	147	169	180
计算机(台)	Computers(unit)	37	40	41	31
#接入互联网	Of Which: Access to the Internet	35	37	38	29
照相机(架)	Camera(set)	7	9	7	4
健身器材(套)	Health Equipment(set)	3	4	4	2
空气净化器(含新风系统)(台)	Air Purifier(Fresh Air System Included)	2	3	3	2
吸尘器(台)	Dust Catcher(unit)	9	13	13	11

表 9.18 主要年份城乡居民家庭人均收入及消费支出
PER CAPITA INCOME AND CONSUMPTION EXPENDITURE OF URBAN AND RURAL HOUSEHOLDS IN MAIN YEARS

年 份 Year	城市居民家庭人均可支配收入（元） Per Capita Disposable Income of Urban Households (yuan)	农村居民家庭人均可支配收入（元） Per Capita Disposable Income of Rural Households (yuan)	城市居民家庭人均消费支出（元） Per Capita Consumption Expenditure of Urban Households (yuan)	农村居民家庭人均消费支出（元） Per Capita Consumption Expenditure of Rural Households (yuan)
1980	637	401	553	323
1985	1 075	806	992	778
1990	2 183	1 665	1 937	1 262
1995	7 172	4 246	5 868	3 368
1996	8 159	4 846	6 763	3 868
1997	8 439	5 277	6 820	4 228
1998	8 773	5 407	6 866	4 207
1999	10 932	5 481	8 248	3 867
2000	11 718	5 565	8 868	4 138
2001	12 883	5 850	9 336	4 753
2002	13 250	6 212	10 464	5 311
2003	14 867	6 658	11 040	5 670
2004	16 683	7 337	12 631	6 329
2005	18 645	8 342	13 773	7 265
2006	20 668	9 213	14 762	8 006
2007	23 623	10 222	17 255	8 845
2008	26 675	11 385	19 398	9 115
2009	28 838	12 324	20 992	9 804
2010	31 838	13 746	23 200	10 225
2011	36 230	15 644	25 102	11 272
2012	40 188	17 401	26 253	12 096
2013	43 851	19 208	28 155	13 425
2014	47 710	21 192	30 520	15 291

表 9.19 城市居民家庭生活基本情况(1980~2014)
BASIC STATISTICS OF URBAN HOUSEHOLDS

年份 Year	调查户数 (户) Number of Households Surveyed (household)	平均每人可支配收入 (元) Per Capita Disposable Income (yuan)	平均每人消费支出 (元) Per Capita Consumption Expenditures (yuan)	可支配收入比上年增长(%) (按当年价格) Growth Rate of Disposable Income on Preceding Year(%) (at Current Price)	消费支出比上年增长(%) (按当年价格) Growth Rate of Consumption Expenditure on Preceding Year(%) (at Current Price)	恩格尔系数 (%) Engel Coefficient (%)
1980	500	637	553	32.5	28.8	56.0
1981	500	637	585	平	5.7	56.8
1982	500	659	576	3.5	-1.5	58.9
1983	500	686	615	4.0	6.9	58.5
1984	500	834	726	21.6	18.0	56.5
1985	500	1 075	992	28.9	36.6	52.1
1986	500	1 293	1 170	20.3	18.0	52.7
1987	500	1 437	1 282	11.1	9.6	54.4
1988	500	1 723	1 648	19.9	28.6	52.7
1989	500	1 976	1 812	14.6	9.9	55.8
1990	500	2 183	1 937	10.5	6.9	56.5
1991	500	2 486	2 167	13.9	11.9	56.9
1992	500	3 009	2 509	21.1	15.8	55.9
1993	500	4 277	3 530	42.2	40.7	53.1
1994	500	5 868	4 669	37.2	32.3	53.5
1995	500	7 172	5 868	22.2	25.7	53.4
1996	500	8 159	6 763	13.8	15.3	50.7
1997	500	8 439	6 820	3.4	0.8	51.7
1998	500	8 773	6 866	4.0	0.7	50.6
1999	500	10 932	8 248	24.6	20.1	45.2
2000	500	11 718	8 868	7.2	7.5	44.5
2001	500	12 883	9 336	9.9	5.3	43.4
2002	500	13 250	10 464	11.5	11.4	39.4
2003	500	14 867	11 040	12.2	5.5	37.2
2004	1 000	16 683	12 631	12.2	14.4	36.4
2005	1 000	18 645	13 773	11.8	9.0	35.9
2006	1 000	20 668	14 762	10.8	7.2	35.6
2007	1 000	23 623	17 255	14.3	16.9	35.5
2008	1 000	26 675	19 398	12.9	12.4	36.6
2009	1 000	28 838	20 992	8.1	8.2	35.0
2010	1 000	31 838	23 200	10.4	10.5	33.5
2011	1 000	36 230	25 102	13.8	8.2	35.5
2012	1 000	40 188	26 253	10.9	4.6	36.8
2013	1 000	43 851	28 155	9.1	7.2	34.9
2014	1 000	47 710	30 520	8.8	8.4	35.0

①本表数据为城市居民家庭收支抽样调查资料，由国家统计局上海调查总队提供。
②2002 年起，人均可支配收入不包括出售财物收入和个人交纳的社会保障支出。 其他年份按原口径计算。
③平均每人可支配收入和平均每人消费支出增长按同口径计算的。
❶Data in this table are obtained from the sample survey of urban households and provided by Survey Office of the National Bureau of Statistics in Shanghai.
❷Incomes from selling properties and social security expenditure are excluded from disposable income since 2002.Other years follow the original caliber.
❸Growth of per Capita Disposable Income and growth of per Capita Consumption Expenditures are calculated by the same caliber.

表 9.20 主要年份城市居民家庭人均可支配收入
PER CAPITA DISPOSABLE INCOME OF URBAN HOUSEHOLDS IN MAIN YEARS

单位:元(yuan)

年 份 Year	人均可支配收入 Average per Capita Disposable Income	工资性收入 Salaries	经营净收入 Net Income from Household Business	财产性收入 Property Income	转移性收入 Transferred Income
1980	637	551			86
1985	1 075	794	1		280
1990	2 183	1 548	1	21	613
1991	2 486	1 780		29	677
1992	3 009	2 138	3	44	824
1993	4 277	3 099	4	37	1 137
1994	5 868	4 224	28	54	1 562
1995	7 172	5 002	69	92	2 009
1996	8 159	5 889	87	61	2 122
1997	8 439	5 969	150	69	2 251
1998	8 773	6 004	98	57	2 614
1999	10 932	7 326	156	68	3 382
2000	11 718	7 832	120	65	3 701
2001	12 883	7 975	119	39	4 750
2002	13 250	7 915	436	94	4 805
2003	14 867	10 097	377	130	4 263
2004	16 683	11 422	507	215	4 539
2005	18 645	12 409	798	292	5 146
2006	20 668	13 962	959	300	5 447
2007	23 623	16 598	1 158	369	5 498
2008	26 675	18 909	1 399	369	5 998
2009	28 838	19 811	1 435	474	7 118
2010	31 838	21 745	1 628	511	7 954
2011	36 230	24 454	1 994	633	9 149
2012	40 188	26 752	2 267	576	10 593
2013	43 851	28 518	2 317	788	12 228
2014	47 710	30 629	2 345	846	13 890

表 9.21 主要年份城市居民家庭人均可支配收入与消费支出
PER CAPITA ANNUAL DISPOSABLE INCOME AND CONSUMPTION EXPENDITURES OF URBAN HOUSEHOLDS IN MAIN YEARS

单位:元(yuan)

指 标	Indicators	2000	2005	2010	2014
人均可支配收入	**Per Capita Disposable Income**	**11 718**	**18 645**	**31 838**	**47 710**
低收入户	Low Income	6 840	7 851	14 996	24 317
中低收入户	Medium-low Income	8 815	11 800	21 780	34 120
中间收入户	Medium Income	10 529	15 668	27 484	40 799
中高收入户	Medium-high Income	12 892	21 313	35 120	52 089
高收入户	High Income	19 959	37 722	62 465	93 901
人均消费支出	**Per Capita Consumption Expenditures**	**8 868**	**13 773**	**23 200**	**30 520**
低收入户	Low Income	6 272	7 698	12 555	17 879
中低收入户	Medium-low Income	7 516	9 807	15 970	20 881
中间收入户	Medium Income	8 555	11 524	21 611	27 974
中高收入户	Medium-high Income	9 445	15 024	26 773	35 904
高收入户	High Income	12 763	25 470	40 744	53 734

表 9.22 主要年份城市居民家庭人均消费支出
PER CAPITA CONSUMPTION EXPENDITURES OF URBAN HOUSEHOLDS IN MAIN YEARS

单位：元（yuan）

年份 Year	消费支出 Total Consumption Expenditures	食品 Food	衣着 Clothing	居住 Residence	家庭设备用品及服务 Household Facilities, Articles and Services	医疗保健 Medicines and Medical Services	交通和通信 Traffic and Communi-cations	教育文化娱乐服务 Education, Culture and Recreation Services	其他商品和服务 Other Commodities and Services
1980	553	310	79	26	50	7	20	49	12
1985	992	517	148	43	131	5	30	91	27
1990	1 937	1 095	208	90	196	11	58	231	48
1995	5 868	3 131	561	401	637	113	321	508	196
1996	6 763	3 429	590	416	614	148	496	827	243
1997	6 820	3 526	552	605	525	197	397	828	190
1998	6 866	3 477	472	674	453	261	406	893	230
1999	8 248	3 731	551	842	772	347	583	1 094	328
2000	8 868	3 947	567	794	683	501	759	1 287	330
2001	9 336	4 056	577	796	579	558	958	1 422	390
2002	10 464	4 120	613	1 189	653	734	1 115	1 668	372
2003	11 040	4 102	751	1 280	792	603	1 259	1 834	419
2004	12 631	4 593	797	1 327	780	762	1 703	2 195	474
2005	13 773	4 940	940	1 412	800	797	1 984	2 273	627
2006	14 762	5 249	1 027	1 436	877	763	2 333	2 432	645
2007	17 255	6 125	1 330	1 412	959	857	3 154	2 654	764
2008	19 398	7 109	1 521	1 646	1 182	755	3 373	2 875	937
2009	20 992	7 345	1 593	1 913	1 365	1 002	3 499	3 139	1 136
2010	23 200	7 777	1 794	2 166	1 800	1 006	4 076	3 363	1 218
2011	25 102	8 906	2 054	2 226	1 826	1 141	3 808	3 746	1 395
2012	26 253	9 656	2 111	1 790	1 906	1 017	4 564	3 724	1 485
2013	28 155	9 823	2 032	2 848	1 706	1 350	4 736	4 122	1 538
2014	30 520	10 677	2 038	3 031	1 779	1 449	4 885	4 931	1 730

表 9.23 主要年份城市居民家庭人均消费支出构成
COMPOSITION OF PER CAPITA CONSUMPTION EXPENDITURES OF URBAN HOUSEHOLDS IN MAIN YEARS

单位：%

年份 Year	消费支出 Total Consumption Expenditures	食品 Food	衣着 Clothing	居住 Residence	家庭设备用品及服务 Household Facilities, Articles and Services	医疗保健 Medicines and Medical Services	交通和通信 Traffic and Communi-cations	教育文化娱乐服务 Education, Culture and Recreation Services	其他商品和服务 Other Commodities and Services
1980	100	56.0	14.3	4.7	9.0	1.3	3.6	8.9	2.2
1985	100	52.1	14.9	4.4	13.2	0.5	3.0	9.2	2.7
1990	100	56.5	10.7	4.7	10.1	0.6	3.0	11.9	2.5
1995	100	53.4	9.6	6.8	10.8	1.9	5.5	8.7	3.3
1996	100	50.7	8.7	6.2	9.1	2.2	7.3	12.2	3.6
1997	100	51.7	8.1	8.9	7.7	2.9	5.8	12.1	2.8
1998	100	50.6	6.9	9.8	6.6	3.8	5.9	13.0	3.4
1999	100	45.2	6.7	10.2	9.3	4.2	7.1	13.3	4.0
2000	100	44.5	6.4	9.0	7.7	5.6	8.6	14.5	3.7
2001	100	43.4	6.2	8.5	6.2	6.0	10.3	15.2	4.2
2002	100	39.4	5.9	11.4	6.2	7.0	10.7	15.9	3.5
2003	100	37.2	6.8	11.6	7.2	5.4	11.4	16.6	3.8
2004	100	36.4	6.3	10.5	6.2	6.0	13.5	17.4	3.7
2005	100	35.9	6.8	10.2	5.8	5.8	14.4	16.5	4.6
2006	100	35.6	6.9	9.7	5.9	5.2	15.8	16.5	4.4
2007	100	35.5	7.7	8.2	5.5	5.0	18.3	15.4	4.4
2008	100	36.6	7.9	8.5	6.1	3.9	17.4	14.8	4.8
2009	100	35.0	7.6	9.1	6.5	4.8	16.7	14.9	5.4
2010	100	33.5	7.7	9.3	7.8	4.3	17.6	14.5	5.3
2011	100	35.5	8.2	8.9	7.3	4.5	15.2	14.9	5.5
2012	100	36.8	8.0	6.8	7.3	3.9	17.4	14.2	5.6
2013	100	34.9	7.2	10.1	6.1	4.8	16.8	14.6	5.5
2014	100	35.0	6.7	9.9	5.8	4.7	16.0	16.2	5.7

表 9.24　农村居民家庭生活基本情况(1990~2014)
BASIC STATISTICS OF RURAL HOUSEHOLDS

年　份 Year	调查户数 (户) Number of Households Surveyed (household)	平均每人 可支配收入 (元) Disposable Income Per Capita(yuan)	平均每人生活 消费支出 (元) Per Capita Consumpition Expenditures (yuan)	平均每人 可支配收入指数 (以 1990 年为 100) Index of Per Capita Disposable Income (1990=100)	平均每人生活 消费支出指数 (以 1990 年为 100) Index of Per Capita Consumption Expenditures (1990=100)	平均每人年底 居住房屋面积 (平方米) Per Capita Living Space Year-end (sq.m)
1990	1 000	1 665	1 262	100.0	100.0	37.08
1991	600	2 003	1 540	120.3	122.0	39.60
1992	600	2 226	1 967	133.7	155.9	42.07
1993	600	2 727	2 200	163.8	174.3	44.22
1994	600	3 437	2 715	206.4	215.1	44.15
1995	600	4 246	3 368	255.0	266.9	43.08
1996	600	4 846	3 868	291.1	306.5	45.47
1997	600	5 277	4 228	316.9	335.0	46.44
1998	600	5 407	4 207	324.7	333.4	47.24
1999	600	5 481	3 867	329.2	306.4	49.00
2000	600	5 565	4 138	334.2	327.9	53.58
2001	600	5 850	4 753	351.4	376.6	54.70
2002	600	6 212	5 311	373.1	420.8	57.08
2003	600	6 658	5 670	399.9	449.3	59.03
2004	600	7 337	6 329	440.7	501.5	59.84
2005	600	8 342	7 265	501.0	575.7	56.56
2006	600	9 213	8 006	553.3	634.4	59.99
2007	600	10 222	8 845	613.9	700.9	61.22
2008	600	11 385	9 115	683.8	722.3	62.30
2009	600	12 324	9 804	740.2	776.9	60.18
2010	600	13 746	10 225	825.6	810.2	59.68
2011	1 200	15 644	11 272	939.6	893.2	58.90
2012	1 200	17 401	12 096	1 045.1	958.5	60.42
2013	1 200	19 208	13 425	1 153.6	1 063.8	58.48
2014	1 200	21 192	15 291	1 272.8	1 211.6	58.92

表 9.25 主要年份农村居民家庭人均可支配收入
PER CAPITA DISPOSABLE INCOME OF RURAL HOUSEHOLDS IN MAIN YEARS

指 标 Indicators	人均可支配收 入(元) Per Capita Disposable Income(yuan)	工资性收入 Wages	家庭经营纯收入 Household Business Income	转移性和财产性收入 Property and Transferred Income	比重(以人均可支配收入为 100) Proportion Per Capita Disposable Income = 100)		
					工资性收 入 Wages	家庭经营纯收入 Household Business Income	转移性和财产性收入 Property and Transferred Income
1990	1 665	1 066	539	60	64.0	32.4	3.6
1995	4 246	2 734	1 183	329	64.4	27.9	7.7
2000	5 565	4 310	934	321	77.4	16.8	5.8
2005	8 342	6 364	811	1 167	76.3	9.7	14.0
2006	9 213	6 892	766	1 555	74.8	8.3	16.9
2007	10 222	7 498	754	1 970	73.3	7.4	19.3
2008	11 385	8 182	711	2 492	71.9	6.2	21.9
2009	12 324	8 721	590	3 013	70.8	4.8	24.4
2010	13 746	9 606	589	3 551	69.9	4.3	25.8
2011	15 644	10 493	877	4 274	67.1	5.6	27.3
2012	17 401	11 496	905	5 000	66.1	5.2	28.7
2013	19 208	12 378	920	5 910	64.4	4.8	30.8
2014	21 192	13 430	1 035	6 727	63.4	4.9	31.7

注：2000 年前平均每人可支配收入按纯收入口径计算。 2011 年起，按可比口径计算，全年家庭经营纯收入增长为 22%；“土地征用补偿收入”不再列入财产性收入中。

Note: The per Capita Annual Disposable Income before 2000 refers to the Net Income. Since 2011, according to the calculation with comparable caliber, the growth rate of annual Household Business Income is 22%.Land Requisition Compensation Income is no longer included in the property income.

表 9.26 主要年份农村居民家庭人均可支配收入和人均生活消费支出
PER CAPITA DISPOSABLE INCOME AND LIVING EXPENDITURES FOR CONSUMPTION OF RURAL HOUSEHOLDS IN MAIN YEARS

单位:元(yuan)

年 份 Year	总平均 Average	低收入户 Low Income	中低收入户 Medium-low Income	中间收入户 Medium Income	中高收入户 Medium-high Income	高收入户 High Income
人均可支配收入	**Average per Capita Disposable Income**					
2000	5 565	2 330	3 906	5 264	6 725	10 405
2005	8 342	3 347	5 594	7 612	9 755	15 309
2006	9 213	3 830	6 194	8 412	10 714	16 843
2007	10 222	4 321	7 098	9 442	11 807	18 443
2008	11 385	4 690	8 065	10 487	13 094	20 748
2009	12 324	5 279	8 785	11 184	14 039	22 465
2010	13 746	5 968	10 107	12 929	16 327	24 536
2011	15 644	7 018	11 772	14 568	18 145	27 227
2012	17 401	7 707	13 071	16 490	20 340	29 180
2013	19 208	8 708	14 415	18 152	22 618	31 196
2014	21 192	10 476	16 375	20 693	25 129	32 631
人均生活消费支出	**Average per Capita Consumption Expenditures**					
2000	4 138	2 390	3 387	3 887	5 487	5 880
2005	7 265	4 618	5 690	6 317	7 059	12 975
2006	8 006	4 788	6 001	6 951	8 015	15 058
2007	8 845	4 890	6 077	7 305	9 541	17 317
2008	9 115	5 024	6 280	9 555	10 700	14 517
2009	9 804	5 472	6 266	9 026	12 843	16 035
2010	10 225	5 026	7 881	8 739	15 103	15 187
2011	11 272	6 979	9 881	11 701	11 654	16 531
2012	12 096	7 784	8 813	10 802	13 725	19 773
2013	13 425	8 011	10 048	12 150	15 793	20 775
2014	15 291	9 629	12 208	13 487	17 909	22 645

表 9.27 主要年份农村居民家庭人均生活消费支出
PER CAPITA CONSUMPTION EXPENDITURES OF RURAL HOUSEHOLDS IN MAIN YEARS

单位:元(yuan)

年 份 Year	生活消费支出 Total Consumption Expenditures	食品 Food	衣着 Clothing	居住 Residence	家庭设备用品及服务 Household Facilities, Articles and Services	交通和通信 Traffic and Communi-cations	文教娱乐用品及服务 Education, Culture and Recreation Articles and Services	医疗保健 Medicines and Medical Services	其他商品和服务 Other Commodities and Services
1990	1 262	586	107	272	129	6	59	33	70
1995	3 368	1 491	233	761	284	159	256	73	111
2000	4 138	1 823	201	724	225	279	559	209	118
2001	4 753	1 915	226	890	294	340	673	265	150
2002	5 311	1 872	226	1 392	281	462	661	280	137
2003	5 670	2 004	250	1 437	297	587	676	333	86
2004	6 329	2 191	280	1 446	344	720	806	425	117
2005	7 265	2 676	367	1 323	458	739	936	562	204
2006	8 006	3 024	418	1 658	481	780	920	549	176
2007	8 845	3 259	476	2 097	452	884	857	571	249
2008	9 115	3 732	467	1 806	504	880	850	697	179
2009	9 804	3 639	496	2 103	481	1 212	943	739	191
2010	10 225	3 807	554	2 070	528	1 459	1 012	585	210
2011	11 272	4 517	644	1 806	649	1 309	1 139	909	299
2012	12 096	4 837	704	1 834	646	1 705	1 088	1 029	253
2013	13 425	5 334	771	2 260	694	1 719	964	1 181	502
2014	15 291	6 188	801	2 747	712	1 891	1 069	1 308	575

表 9.28 主要年份农村居民家庭人均生活消费支出构成
COMPOSITION OF PER CAPITA CONSUMER EXPENDITURES OF RURAL HOUSEHOLDS IN MAIN YEARS

单位:%

年 份 Year	生活消费支出 Total Consumption Expenditures	食品 Food	衣着 Clothing	居住 Residence	家庭设备用品及服务 Household Facilities, Articles and Services	交通和通信 Traffic and Communi-cations	文教娱乐用品及服务 Education, Culture and Recreation Articles and Services	医疗保健 Medicines and Medical Services	其他商品和服务 Other Commodities and Services
1990	100	46.4	8.5	21.6	10.2	0.5	4.7	2.6	5.5
1995	100	44.3	6.9	22.6	8.4	4.7	7.6	2.2	3.3
2000	100	44.0	4.9	17.5	5.4	6.7	13.5	5.1	2.9
2001	100	40.3	4.7	18.7	6.2	7.1	14.2	5.6	3.2
2002	100	35.2	4.3	26.2	5.3	8.7	12.4	5.3	2.6
2003	100	35.4	4.4	25.3	5.2	10.4	11.9	5.9	1.5
2004	100	34.6	4.4	22.9	5.4	11.4	12.7	6.7	1.9
2005	100	36.8	5.1	18.2	6.3	10.2	12.9	7.7	2.8
2006	100	37.8	5.2	20.7	6.0	9.7	11.5	6.9	2.2
2007	100	36.8	5.4	23.7	5.1	10.0	9.7	6.5	2.8
2008	100	40.9	5.1	19.8	5.5	9.7	9.3	7.7	2.0
2009	100	37.1	5.1	21.5	4.9	12.4	9.6	7.5	1.9
2010	100	37.2	5.4	20.2	5.2	14.3	9.9	5.7	2.1
2011	100	40.1	5.7	16.0	5.8	11.6	10.1	8.1	2.6
2012	100	40.0	5.8	15.2	5.3	14.1	9.0	8.5	2.1
2013	100	39.7	5.8	16.8	5.2	12.8	7.2	8.8	3.7
2014	100	40.5	5.2	17.9	4.7	12.4	7.0	8.5	3.8

上/海/统/计/年/鉴

主要统计指标解释

第一部分　2015年以来上海居民收支与生活状况调查主要数据(新口径)(适用表9.1到表9.17)

■ 居民可支配收入(城镇/农村常住居民)

指居民可用于最终消费支出和储蓄的总和，即居民可用于自由支配的收入。既包括现金收入，也包括实物收入。按照收入的来源，可支配收入包含四项，分别为：工资性收入、经营净收入、财产净收入和转移净收入。

■ 居民消费支出(城镇/农村常住居民)

是指居民用于满足家庭日常生活消费需要的全部支出，既包括现金消费支出，也包括实物消费支出。消费支出可划分为食品烟酒、衣着、居住、生活用品及服务、交通通信、教育文化娱乐、医疗保健以及其他用品及服务八大类。

第二部分　1980~2014年城镇和农村住户调查主要数据(老口径)(适用表9.18到表9.28)

■ 城镇居民家庭可支配收入

指城镇居民家庭可用于最终消费支出和其他非义务性支出以及储蓄的总和，即居民家庭可以用来自由支配的收入。它是家庭总收入扣除交纳的所得税、个人交纳的社会保障费以及调查户的记账补贴后的收入。

■ 城镇居民家庭消费支出

指城镇居民家庭用于满足家庭日常生活消费需要的全部支出，包括食品、衣着、居住、家庭设备及用品、交通通信、文教娱乐、医疗保健、其他等八大类。消费支出构成是按照商品或服务的用途进行分类，如果消费支出的目的与用途不一致时，必须按照用途归入相应类内。

■ 农村居民家庭可支配收入

指农村居民家庭获得的经过初次分配与再分配后的收入。可支配收入可用于住户的最终消费、非义务性支出以及储蓄。

农村居民家庭可支配收入=总收入-家庭经营费用支出-税费支出-生产性固定资产折旧-财产性支出-转移性支出。

■ 农村居民家庭生活消费支出

指农村住户用于物质生活和精神生活方面的支出。包括食品，衣着，居住，家庭设备用品及服务，医疗保健，交通和通信，文化教育娱乐用品及服务，其他商品和服务等消费支出。

SHANGHAI STATISTICAL YEARBOOK

EXPLANATORY NOTES TO MAJOR STATISTICAL INDICATORS

Part I Main Data from Survey of Income and Expenditure and Living Conditions of Residents in Shanghai Since 2015(New Statistical Standard,applicable for table 9.1-9.17)

□ Disposable Income of Residents (urban / rural residents)

Disposable Income of Residents refers to the sum of final consumption expenditure and savings of residents, which can be freely allocated by residents. It includes income in cash and in kind. In accordance with the source of income, disposable income includes four parts: wage income, operating income, net income from property and net transfer income.

□ Consumption Expenditures of Residents (urban / rural resident)

Consumption Expenditure of Residents refers to all the expenses that are used to meet the needs of the daily life of the household, including consumption in cash and in kind. Consumption spending can be divided into eight categories: food, alcohol and tobacco, clothing, housing, daily necessities and services, transportation and communication, education culture and entertainment, health care and other goods and services.

Part II Main Data from Urban and Rural Household Survey from 1980 to 2014(Old Statistical Standard,applicable for table 9.18 to 9.28)

□ Disposable Income of Urban Households

Disposable Income of Urban Households refers to the actual income at the disposal of members of the urban households which can be used for final consumption, other non-compulsory expenditure and savings, which is part of the urban households ' income that can be disposed by the urban households themselves. It is the income after deducting personal income tax, social insurance paid by individuals and investigation allowance from the total income of the households. The income from selling properties and borrowing are not included.

□ Consumption Expenditures of Urban Households

Consumption Expenditure of Urban Households refers to all the expenditure paid by urban household for consumption in daily life, including 8 categories as follows: food; clothing; housing; household facilities and articles; traffic and communication; culture, education, and recreation; medical and health care; the others. Consumption expenditure is classified according to the use of goods or services. If the purpose and use of consumption expenditure are inconsistent, it should be included in the appropriate class according to the use.

□ Disposable Income of Rural Households

Disposable Income of Rural Households refers to the actual income at the disposal of rural households after initial distribution and reallocation. Disposal Income can be used for final consumption, non-compulsory expenditure and savings.

Disposal Income of Rural Households=total household income-expenditure for household operations-taxes and fees-depreciation of productive fixed assets-expenses on properties-expenses on transfers.

□ Living Expenditures for Consumption of Rural Households

Living Consumption Expenditure for of Rural Households refers to expenditures of material and culture life of rural household, including expenses on food, clothing, housing, household appliances and service, medical and health care, traffic and communication items, cultural, education and recreation items and service and other commodities and service.

第十篇

CHAPTER 10

城市建设

URBAN CONSTRUCTION

简要说明

一、本篇资料的主要内容

本篇资料反映上海市城市建设的规模、速度及综合水平等基本情况，主要内容包括：市政道路、房屋建筑、供水排水、供气、城市绿化等城市建设情况。

二、本篇资料的来源

城市基础设施建设、公共事业和市政建设投资统计资料依据上海市统计局制定的《固定资产投资统计报表制度》收集整理提供。

房屋建筑统计资料由上海市住房和城乡建设委员会汇总整理提供。

市政工程部分统计资料和供气统计资料由上海市住房和城乡建设管理委员会、上海市交通委员会汇总整理提供。

供水排水统计资料由上海市水务局、上海市生态环境局汇总整理提供。

城市绿化统计资料由上海市绿化和市容管理局汇总整理提供。

三、本篇资料的统计范围

城市基础设施建设、公共事业和市政建设投资的统计资料执行范围同《固定资产投资篇》的执行范围。房屋建筑、市政工程、供水排水、供气、城市绿化的统计资料范围均是全市范围。

BRIEF INTRODUCTION

I. Main Contents

The data in this chapter reflect the basic conditions of the scale, growth rate, and overall level of urban construction of Shanghai. The main contents include municipal roads, house construction, water supply, drainage, gas supply, and urban afforestation.

II. Sources of data

Data on infrastructure construction, public facilities, urban construction investment are collected, prepared and provided by Shanghai Municipal Statistics Bureau in accordance with the Statistics Reporting Form System on the Fixed Asset Investment, which is stipulated by the Shanghai Municipal Statistics Bureau.

Data on house construction are collected, prepared, and provided by Shanghai Municipal Housing and Urban-Rural Construction Management Commission.

Data on urban construction projects and gas supply are collected, prepared, and provided by Shanghai Municipal Housing and Urban-Rural Construction Management Commission and Shanghai Municipal Transportation Commission.

Data on water supply and drainage are collected, prepared, and provided by Shanghai Water Authority, Shanghai Municipal Bureau of Ecology and Enviroment. Data on urban afforestation are collected, prepared, and provided by Shanghai Municipal Afforestation & City Appearance and Environmental Sanitation Administration.

III. Scope and Coverage of Statistics

Coverage of data on urban infrastructure construction, public facilities, and urban construction investment is the same with that in the chapter of Fixed Assets Investment. Data on house construction, urban construction projects, water supply, drainage, gas supply, and urban afforestation cover the whole city.

表 10.1 主要年份城市基础设施投资额
URBAN INFRASTRUCTURE INVESTMENT IN MAIN YEARS

单位:亿元(100 million yuan)

年份 Year	合计 Total	电力建设 Power Generation	运输邮电 Transportation, Postal and Telecommunications	其中 of which: 交通运输 Transportation	其中 of which: 邮电通信 Postal and Telecommunications	公用设施 Facilities for Public Use	其中 of which: 公用事业 Public Utilities	其中 of which: 市政建设 Civil Construction
1950~1978	60.08	19.71	23.25	19.41	3.84	17.12	6.85	10.27
1980	9.55	5.31	2.91	2.31	0.60	1.33	0.64	0.69
1985	23.49	3.97	6.75	5.52	1.23	12.77	7.88	4.89
1986	24.78	5.68	8.40	6.56	1.84	10.70	5.67	5.03
1987	32.64	9.31	12.39	10.02	2.37	10.94	5.36	5.58
1988	37.08	14.18	12.35	8.80	3.55	10.55	4.01	6.54
1989	36.09	11.69	9.96	6.16	3.80	14.44	6.84	7.60
1990	47.22	17.53	10.06	7.17	2.90	19.63	10.83	8.80
1991	61.38	19.79	19.07	14.49	4.58	22.52	9.15	13.37
1992	84.35	19.70	21.44	15.01	6.43	43.21	12.58	30.63
1993	167.94	25.77	46.44	31.75	14.69	95.73	37.91	57.82
1994	238.16	41.57	72.68	36.83	35.85	123.91	26.77	97.14
1995	273.78	57.33	79.36	25.94	53.42	137.09	35.03	102.06
1996	378.78	77.61	147.21	69.66	77.55	153.96	48.31	105.65
1997	412.85	80.24	146.10	85.06	61.04	186.51	52.24	134.27
1998	531.38	89.58	181.46	108.79	72.67	260.34	58.37	201.97
1999	501.39	83.05	166.16	102.24	63.92	252.18	64.20	187.98
2000	449.90	64.61	117.52	48.83	68.69	267.77	104.43	163.34
2001	510.78	72.22	168.42	60.72	107.70	270.14	92.25	177.89
2002	583.49	62.14	171.24	63.01	108.23	350.11	148.42	201.69
2003	604.62	66.00	350.35	273.77	76.58	188.28	36.91	151.36
2004	672.58	89.52	371.35	316.96	54.39	211.71	26.92	184.80
2005	885.74	124.22	443.90	385.58	58.32	317.62	41.33	276.28
2006	1 125.54	116.23	703.24	589.52	113.72	306.07	56.23	249.84
2007	1 466.33	163.30	942.03	840.46	101.57	361.01	60.90	300.11
2008	1 733.18	129.53	947.49	838.91	108.59	656.15	112.81	543.34
2009	2 113.45	253.39	1 100.90	978.24	122.66	759.16	135.95	623.21
2010	1 497.46	148.50	866.20	754.66	111.54	482.76	86.58	396.18
2011	1 157.34	118.81	668.52	595.75	72.76	370.01	54.22	315.80
2012	1 038.61	110.06	570.37	473.43	96.94	358.18	56.45	301.74
2013	1 043.31	110.35	550.42	458.70	91.72	382.54	47.57	334.97
2014	1 057.25	134.22	510.42	422.48	87.94	412.61	32.80	379.81
2015	1 425.08	129.36	854.89	759.23	95.67	440.83	66.73	374.10
2016	1 551.87	145.04	990.18	883.81	106.37	416.66	70.90	345.75
2017	1 705.22	137.85	996.10	903.62	92.48	571.27	97.68	473.60

注：本表各项投资额均不包括住宅建设投资。从2003年起，交通运输投资包括公用设施中市内公共交通投资。2011年始，固定资产投资统计起点为500万元以上(含500万元)项目(下表同)。

Note: All items in this table exclude investment in residential housing. Since 2003, public traffic investment, which is belong to facilities for public use has been included in Transportation Investment. Since 2011, statistics of Investment in Fixed Assets only contain the projects with investment of 5 million yuan and above (same as follows).

表 10.2 用于公用事业和市政建设的投资额(1985~2017)
INVESTMENT IN PUBLIC UTILITIES AND CIVIL CONSTRUCTION

单位:亿元(100 million yuan)

年份 Year	公用事业 Public Utilities	其中 of which		市政建设 Civil Construction	其中 of which			
		自来水 Tap Water	燃气 Gas		园林绿化 Parks and Green Areas	环境卫生 Environmental Sanitation	市政设施 Municipal Facilities	其他 Others
1985	7.88			4.89				
1986	5.67	2.74	1.78	5.03	0.43	0.71	3.84	0.05
1987	5.36	2.53	1.79	5.58	0.30	0.34	4.94	…
1988	4.01	0.72	1.25	6.54	0.24	0.58	5.72	…
1989	6.84	1.52	0.90	7.60	0.01	0.52	7.02	0.05
1990	10.83	1.06	1.81	8.80	0.11	0.37	8.31	0.01
1991	9.15	2.34	2.35	13.37	0.15	0.45	12.77	…
1992	12.58	3.20	3.24	30.63	0.32	0.79	28.45	1.07
1993	37.91	6.90	16.72	57.82	0.52	1.06	56.24	…
1994	26.77	11.49	7.80	97.14	2.42	1.01	93.47	0.24
1995	35.03	13.12	12.97	102.06	4.27	1.26	96.21	0.32
1996	48.31	22.12	14.61	105.65	2.66	1.14	101.80	0.05
1997	52.24	27.08	10.03	134.27	5.11	1.62	127.41	0.13
1998	58.37	14.59	13.15	201.97	9.10	3.35	189.41	0.11
1999	64.20	6.41	9.89	187.98	28.62	2.97	155.73	0.66
2000	104.43	5.35	6.88	163.34	38.76	19.34	102.36	2.88
2001	92.25	5.97	5.83	177.89	32.92	2.97	140.63	1.37
2002	148.42	8.62	6.83	201.69	38.83	1.47	160.64	0.75
2003	36.91	22.89	14.02	151.36	33.85	9.25	107.73	0.53
2004	26.92	16.66	10.26	184.80	16.69	7.01	160.22	0.88
2005	41.33	29.66	11.67	276.28	13.88	15.36	246.58	0.46
2006	56.23	43.79	12.44	249.84	26.41	10.17	213.26	
2007	60.90	50.12	10.78	300.11	34.66	11.26	254.19	
2008	112.81	93.24	19.57	543.34	29.01	20.04	494.29	
2009	135.95	109.79	26.16	623.21	27.96	21.91	573.19	0.15
2010	86.58	61.63	24.95	396.18	35.87	10.80	349.27	0.25
2011	54.22	41.85	12.37	315.80	44.71	23.91	247.15	0.03
2012	56.45	40.75	15.70	301.74	20.99	23.74	256.73	0.26
2013	47.57	24.83	22.74	334.97	27.16	12.52	292.48	2.82
2014	32.80	20.00	12.80	379.81	56.46	9.41	313.94	
2015	66.73	58.63	8.10	374.10	34.84	18.49	320.77	
2016	70.90	58.76	12.14	345.75	29.50	16.37	299.88	
2017	97.68	92.75	4.92	473.60	112.03	20.73	340.83	

表 10.3 主要年份各类房屋构成情况
COMPOSITION OF BUILDING IN MAIN YEARS

单位：万平方米（10 000 sq.m）

指　标	Indicators	2010	2015	2020	2021
总　计	**Total**	**93 591**	**120 390**	**145 431**	**150 808**
居住房屋	Residential Buildings	52 639	63 007	71 152	72 864
花园住宅	Villas	2 064	1 790	1 861	1 864
职工住宅	Staff Dwellings	47 951			
联列住宅	United Columns Residences	1 400	1 400	1 715	1 760
公　寓	Apartments	492	58 308	66 324	68 015
新式里弄	Improved Residential Blocks	527	308	256	254
旧式里弄	Old Residential Blocks	1 237	1 190	987	961
简　屋	Simple Housings	29	11	10	9
其　他	Others	339			
非居住房屋	Non-Residential Buildings	40 952	57 383	74 279	77 944
工　厂	Plants	18 524	25 103	29 837	30 673
学　校	Schools	3 172	3 366	4 235	4 698
仓库堆栈	Warehouses	1 654	1 868	2 128	2 179
办公建筑	Offices	6 365	7 343	9 914	10 381
商场店铺	Stores	5 497	6 773	8 816	9 123
医　院	Hospitals	754	631	873	914
旅　馆	Hotels	931	1 265	1 696	1 804
影剧院	Theatres and Cinemas	75	65	76	82
其　他	Others	3 979	10 970	16 704	18 089

注：根据市住房保障和房屋管理局提供居住房屋分类的调整，2011 年起公寓数据包含职工住宅数据，2012 年起取消其他分类。
Note: According to the adjustment of residential houses classification provided by Shanghai Municipal Housing Security and Building Administration Bureau, since 2011, the apartment data contains data of the staff housing, and since 2012, other classifications are canceled.

表 10.4 主要年份八层以上房屋情况
BUILDINGS OVER EIGHT STOREYS IN MAIN YEARS

类　别	Types	单　位 Unit	2010	2015	2020	2021
总　计	**Total**	**幢（building）**	**20 579**	**40 822**	**51 241**	**53 467**
		万平方米（10 000 sq.m）	21 911	39 652	51 699	54 174
8～10 层	8～10 Storeys	幢（building）	2 744	5 568	7 569	7 923
		万平方米（10 000 sq.m）	2 430	3 903	5 838	6 166
11～15 层	11～15 Storeys	幢（building）	9 672	18 302	21 543	22 204
		万平方米（10 000 sq.m）	6 320	12 712	15 733	16 420
16～19 层	16～19 Storeys	幢（building）	4 247	10 046	13 792	14 665
		万平方米（10 000 sq.m）	4 449	9 640	13 535	14 362
20～29 层	20～29 Storeys	幢（building）	2 936	5 337	6 517	6 811
		万平方米（10 000 sq.m）	5 504	8 917	11 144	11 556
30 层以上	Over 30 Storeys	幢（building）	980	1 569	1 820	1 864
		万平方米（10 000 sq.m）	3 208	4 481	5 449	5 671

注：本页数据按建筑面积计算。
Note: Data on this page are calculated according to floor space of buildings.

表 10.5 各区房屋分布情况(2021)
DISTRIBUTION OF BUILDINGS BY DISTRICTS

单位:万平方米(10 000 sq.m)

地 区	District	全部房屋合 计 Total	其 中 of which 居住房屋 Residential	非居住房屋 Non-Residential
总 计	**Total**	**150 808**	**72 864**	**77 944**
浦东新区	Pudong New Area	35 118	17 142	17 975
黄 浦 区	Huangpu	3 954	1 673	2 281
徐 汇 区	Xuhui	6 633	3 604	3 029
长 宁 区	Changning	4 355	2 429	1 926
静 安 区	Jing'an	6 179	3 147	3 031
普 陀 区	Putuo	6 424	3 823	2 600
虹 口 区	Hongkou	3 914	2 180	1 734
杨 浦 区	Yangpu	6 357	3 459	2 897
闵 行 区	Minhang	16 919	8 481	8 438
宝 山 区	Baoshan	11 760	6 645	5 115
嘉 定 区	Jiading	10 894	4 759	6 135
金 山 区	Jinshan	5 942	2 120	3 822
松 江 区	Songjiang	12 762	5 523	7 240
青 浦 区	Qingpu	8 274	3 109	5 165
奉 贤 区	Fengxian	8 396	3 279	5 117
崇 明 区	Chongming	2 927	1 489	1 438

表 10.6　各区各类房屋分布情况(2021)
DISTRIBUTION OF VARIOUS BUILDINGS BY DISTRICTS

单位:万平方米(10 000 sq.m)

地　区	District	居住房屋 Residential Buildings	其　中 of which		
			花园住宅 Villas	联列住宅 United Columns Residences	公　寓 Apartments
总　计	**Total**	**72 864**	**1 864**	**1 760**	**68 014.90**
浦东新区	Pudong New Area	17 142	377	302	16 309.97
黄 浦 区	Huangpu	1 673	9	2	1 438.24
徐 汇 区	Xuhui	3 604	52	11	3 463.24
长 宁 区	Changning	2 429	58	1	2 347.58
静 安 区	Jing'an	3 147	20	4	2 987.66
普 陀 区	Putuo	3 823	13	23	3 779.62
虹 口 区	Hongkou	2 180	7		2 067.30
杨 浦 区	Yangpu	3 459	4	25	3 352.22
闵 行 区	Minhang	8 481	307	205	7 910.29
宝 山 区	Baoshan	6 645	30	140	6 414.43
嘉 定 区	Jiading	4 759	94	183	4 471.39
金 山 区	Jinshan	2 120	18	46	1 975.12
松 江 区	Songjiang	5 523	395	416	4 641.69
青 浦 区	Qingpu	3 109	332	248	2 500.81
奉 贤 区	Fengxian	3 279	101	100	3 045.23
崇 明 区	Chongming	1 489	46	52	1 310.11

表 10.6 续表 1 continued

单位:万平方米(10 000 sq.m)

地　区	District	其　中 of which 新式里弄 Improved Residential Blocks	旧式里弄 Old Residential Blocks	简　屋 Simple Housings
总　计	**Total**	**254**	**961**	**9**
浦东新区	Pudong New Area		152	1
黄 浦 区	Huangpu	74	148	1
徐 汇 区	Xuhui	51	26	1
长 宁 区	Changning	17	5	0.05
静 安 区	Jing′an	62	73	0.12
普 陀 区	Putuo	3	5	…
虹 口 区	Hongkou	44	60	2
杨 浦 区	Yangpu	3	74	1
闵 行 区	Minhang		59	
宝 山 区	Baoshan	…	61	…
嘉 定 区	Jiading		11	…
金 山 区	Jinshan	…	80	…
松 江 区	Songjiang	…	70	…
青 浦 区	Qingpu	…	28	…
奉 贤 区	Fengxian	1	32	…
崇 明 区	Chongming	…	78	2

表 10.6 续表 2 continued

单位：万平方米(10 000 sq.m)

地　区	District	非居住房屋 Non-Residential Buildings	其中 of which			
			工　厂 Plants	学　校 Schools	仓库堆栈 Warehouses	办公建筑 Offices
总　计	**Total**	**77 944**	**30 673**	**4 698**	**2 179**	**10 381**
浦东新区	Pudong New Area	17 975	6 394	1 000	724	2 420
黄 浦 区	Huangpu	2 281	119	108	17	852
徐 汇 区	Xuhui	3 029	525	353	51	902
长 宁 区	Changning	1 926	189	149	26	669
静 安 区	Jing'an	3 031	435	175	60	874
普 陀 区	Putuo	2 600	340	238	154	607
虹 口 区	Hongkou	1 734	145	131	26	553
杨 浦 区	Yangpu	2 897	701	445	72	651
闵 行 区	Minhang	8 438	3 574	583	257	768
宝 山 区	Baoshan	5 115	1 941	299	328	336
嘉 定 区	Jiading	6 135	2 588	255	170	639
金 山 区	Jinshan	3 822	2 540	151	62	173
松 江 区	Songjiang	7 240	4 539	299	53	312
青 浦 区	Qingpu	5 165	2 807	170	58	293
奉 贤 区	Fengxian	5 117	3 230	231	73	235
崇 明 区	Chongming	1 438	606	111	45	97

表 10.6 续表 3 continued

单位:万平方米(10 000 sq.m)

地 区 District		其 中 of which				
		商场店铺 Stores	医 院 Hospitals	旅 馆 Hotels	影剧院 Theatres and Cinemas	其 他 Others
总 计	**Total**	**9 123**	**914**	**1 804**	**82**	**18 089**
浦东新区	Pudong New Area	1 981	158	453	9	4 836
黄 浦 区	Huangpu	432	69	147	15	522
徐 汇 区	Xuhui	329	124	96	4	644
长 宁 区	Changning	258	41	119	3	472
静 安 区	Jing'an	456	65	167	8	791
普 陀 区	Putuo	474	37	90	3	657
虹 口 区	Hongkou	326	43	105	6	399
杨 浦 区	Yangpu	324	49	50	3	602
闵 行 区	Minhang	965	95	116	3	2 075
宝 山 区	Baoshan	659	35	67	2	1 449
嘉 定 区	Jiading	775	62	99	8	1 539
金 山 区	Jinshan	407	33	31	1	424
松 江 区	Songjiang	627	27	71	3	1 310
青 浦 区	Qingpu	574	31	87	3	1 141
奉 贤 区	Fengxian	389	24	53	8	875
崇 明 区	Chongming	148	22	53	2	354

表 10.7 各区八层以上房屋分布情况(2021)
DISTRIBUTION OF BUILDINGS OVER EIGHT STOREYS BY DISTRICTS

单位:万平方米(10 000 sq.m)

地区 District		合计 Total		8~10 层 8~10 Storeys		11~15 层 11~15 Storeys	
		幢 Building	面积 Floor Space	幢 Building	面积 Floor Space	幢 Building	面积 Floor Space
总计	**Total**	**53 467**	**54 174**	**7 923**	**6 166**	**22 204**	**16 420**
浦东新区	Pudong New Area	12 617	13 029	1 630	1 375	6 133	4 640
黄浦区	Huangpu	1 360	2 542	167	172	182	212
徐汇区	Xuhui	2 264	3 300	334	318	622	623
长宁区	Changning	1 623	2 232	370	318	445	389
静安区	Jing'an	2 412	3 211	340	227	679	544
普陀区	Putuo	2 691	3 223	273	195	811	634
虹口区	Hongkou	1 517	2 086	216	142	365	277
杨浦区	Yangpu	2 286	2 508	324	262	873	724
闵行区	Minhang	6 800	5 870	1 199	1 237	3 938	2 777
宝山区	Baoshan	4 605	3 654	637	368	2 163	1 428
嘉定区	Jiading	4 071	3 715	468	362	1 292	934
金山区	Jinshan	1 495	1 054	239	140	752	459
松江区	Songjiang	4 597	3 448	941	538	2 035	1 387
青浦区	Qingpu	2 325	1 973	402	293	910	686
奉贤区	Fengxian	2 230	1 956	202	140	738	537
崇明区	Chongming	574	374	181	78	266	169

表 10.7 续表 continued

单位:万平方米(10 000 sq.m)

地 区	District	16~19 层 16~19 Storeys 幢 Building	面 积 Floor Space	20~29 层 20~29 Storeys 幢 Building	面 积 Floor Space	30 层以上 Over 30 Storeys 幢 Building	面 积 Floor Space
总 计	**Total**	**14 665**	**14 362**	**6 811**	**11 556**	**1 864**	**5 671**
浦东新区	Pudong New Area	3 264	3 294	1 224	2 208	366	1 513
黄浦区	Huangpu	265	365	493	1 022	253	770
徐汇区	Xuhui	537	674	572	1 125	199	559
长宁区	Changning	285	313	387	729	136	484
静安区	Jing'an	466	495	649	1 184	278	760
普陀区	Putuo	624	681	755	1 153	228	560
虹口区	Hongkou	364	403	381	701	191	562
杨浦区	Yangpu	637	670	395	714	57	138
闵行区	Minhang	1 373	1 366	264	399	26	90
宝山区	Baoshan	1 476	1 374	283	411	46	72
嘉定区	Jiading	1 559	1 431	710	911	42	77
金山区	Jinshan	439	355	55	84	10	16
松江区	Songjiang	1 388	1 180	225	324	8	19
青浦区	Qingpu	877	786	133	205	3	3
奉贤区	Fengxian	986	853	283	380	21	47
崇明区	Chongming	125	121	2	6		

表 10.8 主要年份市政工程设施情况
CIVIL FACILITIES IN MAIN YEARS

指 标	Indicators	2010	2015	2020	2021
道路长度(公里)	Length of Roads(km)	16 687	18 184	18 453	18 927
道路面积(万平方米)	Area of Roads (10 000 sq.m)	25 607	28 567	31 012	32 620
城市桥梁(座)	Bridges (bridge)	11 849	13 677	14 332	14 737
防洪堤长度(公里)	Length of Floodwalls (km)	1 009	1 159	1 146	1 139
城市排水管道长度(公里)	Length of Sewage Pipelines (km)	11 483	23 339	29 053	29 037
污水处理厂污水处理能力(万吨/日)	Capacity of Sewage Treatment(10 000 tons/day)	684	795	840	857
污水处理厂污水处理量(亿吨)	Sewage Disposed Load by Sewage Disposal Plants	18.97	21.39	30.22	30.69

表 10.9 主要年份自来水情况
TAP WATER SUPPLY IN MAIN YEARS

指 标	Indicators	2010	2015	2020	2021
水厂个数(个)	Number of Water Treatment Works (unit)	105	37	38	38
供水能力(万立方米/日)	Water Supply Capacity (10 000 cu.m/day)	1 131	1 137	1 221	1 221
供水管道长度(公里)	Length of Water Supply Mainss (km)	31 182	36 383	39 553	39 690
供水总量(亿立方米)	Total Quantity of Water Supply (100 million cu.m)	30.90	31.22	28.86	30.08
售水总量(亿立方米)	Total Quantity of Water Sales (100 million cu.m)	24.44	24.58	23.59	24.77
工业用水	Industrial Water Consumption	5.80	4.94	3.89	4.05
非工业用水	Comprehensive Domestic Water Consumption	6.02	7.11	6.95	7.89
居民生活用水	Domestic Water Consumption	9.80	9.88	11.37	11.57
其他用水	Others	2.82	2.65	1.14	1.26
人均日居民生活用水量(升)	Per Capita Daily Domestic Water Consumption(liter)	117	112	125.3	126.9

表 10.10 用电量(2018～2021)
ELECTRICITY POWER CONSUMPTION

指 标	Indicators	2001	2010	2020	2021
用电量（亿千瓦时）	Power Consumption（100 million kwh）	1 566.66	1 568.58	1 575.96	1 749.62
农、林、牧、渔业	Farming, Forestry, Animal Husbandry and Fishery	6.37	5.94	6.23	7.21
工 业	Industry	780.21	748.39	769.46	851.49
交通运输、仓储和邮政业	Transportation, Warehousing and Post	54.23	57.00	55.17	58.08
批发和零售业	Retail and Wholesale Industries	73.30	72.48	63.83	70.53
住宿和餐饮业	Hoteling and Catering	15.52	15.25	13.84	16.99
金融业	Financial Industry	18.21	18.04	17.61	16.77
房地产业	Real Estate Industry	167.24	180.72	171.72	201.16
公共服务及管理组织	Public Service and Management Organizations	141.42	148.67	134.47	139.29
居民生活	Residents Living Industry	243.55	245.04	257.14	277.97

注：2018 年起，电力公司对用电量指标的行业分类进行了调整。
Note: Since 2018, Power Companies have Adjusted the Industry Classification of Electricity Consumption Indicators.

表 10.11 主要年份电力建设情况
ELECTRICITY POWER CONSTRUCTION IN MAIN YEARS

指 标	Indicators	2001	2010	2020	2021
年末发电设备容量(万千瓦)	Year-end Capacity of Electricity Generating Equipment(10 000 KW)	1 121.09	1 855.38	2 669.15	2 785.79
架空线长度(公里)	Length of Trolly Wire(k.m.)	6 480.72	8 549.50	10 321.90	10 506.56
#220KV	220KV	1 756.74	2 956.08	3 893.61	3 972.34
电缆长度(公里)	Length of Cable(k.m.)	3 633.00	7 846.98	16 507.27	16 928.50
#220KV	220KV	145.00	516.44	891.50	932.43
公用变电容量(万千伏安)	Public Power Transformation Capacity (10 000 KVA)	4 601.08	11 657.19	18 778.48	19 447.38
#220KV～35KV	220KV-35KV	3 716.68	7 827.75	12 298.84	12 667.74

注：本页数据由市电力公司提供。
Note: Data on this page are provided by Shanghai Electric Power Corporation.

表 10.12 主要年份液化石油气、天然气情况
LIQUEFIED PETROLEUM GAS AND NATURAL GAS IN MAIN YEARS

指　标	Indicators	2010	2015	2020	2021
液化石油气	**Liquefied Petroleum Gas (LPG)**				
液化石油气销售总量(万吨)	Sales of LPG (10 000 tons)	40.05	42.41	27.22	27.6
#家庭用量	Household Consumption	23.62	25.23	15.35	14.83
家庭液化石油气用户数(万户)	Household Users (10 000 households)	316.37	335.50	222.31	223.17
天然气	**Natural Gas**				
天然气销售总量(亿立方米)	Sales of Natural Gas (100 million cu.m)	42.66	69.73	86.73	92.25
#家庭用量	Household Consumption	7.79	13.50	17.38	18.35
天然气管线长度(公里)	Length of Natural Gas Pipelines (km)	17 316	28 601	32 809	33 222
家庭天然气用户数(万户)	Household Users of Natural Gas (10 000 households)	405.89	651.32	753.48	770.48

表 10.13 主要年份公共交通和轮渡情况
PUBLIC TRANSPORTATION AND FERRY IN MAIN YEARS

指　标	Indicators	2010	2015	2020	2021
公共汽电车	**Buses and Trolley Buses**				
公交线路长度(公里)	Length of Public Bus Lines (km)	23 131	24 027	24 932	25 185
公交线路条数(条)	Number of Public Bus Lines (line)	1 165	1 429	1 585	1 596
运营公共汽电车数(辆)	Operating Public Transportation Vehicles (vehicle)	17 455	16 531	17 668	17 645
#公共汽车	Buses	17 038	15 056	4 259	5 752
公交客运总量(亿人次)	Passenger Volume of Pubilc Bus (100million person-times)	28	25	14	15
出租汽车	**Taxi**				
运营车辆(辆)	Operating Vehicles (vehicle)	50 007	49 586	37 322	35 317
#小客车	Small Passenger Car	49 016	48 840	37 312	35 317
载客车次(万次)	Number of Carryings(10 000 times)	63 307	53 974	20 383	20 176
运营里程(亿公里)	Operation Length (100 million km)	65	61	32	34
#载客里程	Transport Lengths of Passengers	40	39	19	20
运营收入(亿元)	Operation Revenues(100 million yuan)	155	166	81	85
运营单位(个)	Operation Unit (unit)	3 301	3 113	3 055	3 184
轮　渡	**Ferry**				
年末轮渡船数(艘)	Year-end Number of Ferry Boats (ship)	67	44	37	35
乘客人数(亿人次)	Passenger Volume (100 million person-times)	0.89	0.53	0.38	0.39

表 10.14　轨道交通、城市快速路、黄浦江大桥和隧道基本情况(2018~2021)
BASIC FACTS OF RAILWAY COMMUNICATION, URBAN EXPRESSWAYS, BRIDGES ACROSS HUANGPU RIVER AND TUNNELS

	指　标 Indicators	2018	2019	2020	2021
轨道交通	**Urban Metro**				
运营车辆(节)	Operating Vehicles(car)	5 302	5 911	7 071	7 393
轨道交通线路条数(条)	Number of Operation Lines (line)	17	17	18	20
运营线路长度(公里)	Length of Operation Lines(km)	704.91	704.91	729.21	831.00
运营里程(万列·公里)	Operation Mileage(10 000 vehicle-km)	9 564	10 394	10 553	11 463
客运总量(万人次)	Volume of Passenger Traffic (10 000 person-times)	371 012	388 445	283 188	357 187
年末从业人数(人)	Year-end Number of Staff and Workers (person)	28 601	30 111	31 298	29 024
城市快速路、大桥和隧道	**Urban Expressways, Bridges and Tunnels**				
城市快速路长度(公里)	Length of Urban Expressways(km)	207	207	207	233
越江大桥数(座)	Number of River-Crossing Bridges(bridge)	11	11	14	14
越江隧道数(条)	Number of River-Crossing Tunnels(tunnel)	15	16	17	18

注：越江大桥、越江隧道是指跨越长江、黄浦江的桥梁和隧道，不含东海大桥。
Note: River-Crossing Bridges and River-Crossing Tunnels refer to the bridges and tunnels which cross the Yangtze River and Huangpu River, and exclude the East China Sea Bridge.

表 10.15　主要年份城市设施水平
LEVEL OF URBAN FACILITIES IN MAIN YEARS

	指　标 Indicators	2010	2015	2020	2021
人均日综合生活用水量(升)	Per Capita Daily Consumption of Water for Life (liter)	223	224	217	227
人均日居民生活用水量(升)	Per Capita Daily Consumption of Water (liter)	117	112	125	127
自来水普及率(%)	Percentage of Population with Access to Tap Water (%)	99.99	99.99	99.99	99.99
拥有道路长度(公里/万人)	Per Capita Length of Roads (km/10 000 persons)	7.25	7.53	7.42	7.60
人均拥有道路面积(平方米)	Per Capita Area of Roads (sq.m)	11.12	11.83	12.47	13.10
每万人拥有城市排水管道长度(公里)	Length of Sewage Pipelines Per 10 000 Persons (km)	4.99	8.83	11.68	11.62
每万人拥有公共汽电车辆(辆)	Number of Public Transportation Vehicles Per 10 000 Persons (vehicle)	7.58	6.84	7.10	7.09
每万人拥有轨道交通运营车辆(节)	Number of Urban Metro Operating Vehicles Per 10 000 Persons (car)	1.23	1.57	2.84	2.97
每万人拥有出租汽车(辆)	Number of Taxi Per 10 000 Persons (vehicle)	21.72	20.53	15.01	14.19
人均公园绿地面积(平方米)	Per Capita Park Green Areas (sq.m)	13.0	7.6	8.5	8.7

注：2000 年起，每万人拥有城市排水管道长度由原先的根据户籍人口计算调整为根据常住人口计算；2010 年起，拥有道路长度和人均拥有道路面积由原先的根据户籍人口计算调整为根据常住人口计算；2014 年起，人均公园绿地面积(平方米)由原先的根据非农户籍人口计算调整为根据常住人口计算；2021 年起，每万人拥有公共交通车辆调整为每万人拥有公共汽电车辆。
Note: Since 2000, the Length of Sewage Pipelines per 10 000 Persons has been adjusted from the original calculation based on the registered population to the calculation based on the permanent population; Since 2010, Per Capita Length of Roads and Per Capita Area of Roads have been adjusted from the original calculation based on the registered population to the calculation based on the permanent population; Since 2014, the Per Capita Park Green Areas(square meters) has been adjusted from the original calculation based on the non-agricultural registered population to the calculation based on the permanent population; From 2021, the Number of Public Transport Vehicles Owned by Every 10 000 Persons will be adjusted to that of Bus and Electric Vehicles Owned by Every 10 000 Persons.

表 10.16 主要年份城市绿地情况
URBAN GREEN SPACE IN MAIN YEARS

单位：公顷（hectare）

年 份 Year	绿地面积 Urban Green Space	其 中 of which			
		公园绿地 Public Green Space	生产绿地 Production Green Space	防护绿地 Environmental Protection Green Space	附属绿地 Sub Green Space
1990	3 570	983	294	37	2 255
1995	6 561	1 793	309	30	4 429
2000	1 2601	4 812	388	55	7 346
2005	28 865	12 038	336	2 743	12 464
2006	30 609	13 307	331	2 869	13 218
2007	31 795	13 899	204	2 025	14 784
2008	34 256	14 777	189	2 039	16 120
2009	116 929	15 406	230	1 877	17 376
2010	120 148	16 053	230	1 936	18 589
2011	122 283	16 446	213	2 081	19 442
2012	124 204	16 848	269	2 087	20 084
2013	124 295	17 142	267	2 089	20 645
2014	125 741	17 789	417	2 152	23 020
2015	127 332	18 395	417	2 108	23 711
2016	131 681	18 957	417	2 203	24 337
2017	136 327	19 805	335	2 238	24 688
2018	139 427	20 578	335	2 277	25 125
2019	157 785	21 425		3 424	27 353
2020	164 611	21 981		3 437	27 792
2021	171 215	22 463		3 749	29 804

表 10.16 续表 continued

年 份	其 中 of which 其他绿地 Other Green Space	公园数（个） Parks (unit)	游园人数（万人次） Visitors to Parks and Zooes (10 000 person-times)	行道树实有数（万株） Roadside Trees (10 000 trees)	新建绿地面积（公顷） Greenlands Newly Created (hectare)
1990		83	8 474	23	186
1995		100	9 064	33	516
2000		122	8 184	57	1 458
2005	1 284	144	13 656	83	2 116
2006	884	144	16 652	86	1 691
2007	884	146	18 342	69	1 629
2008	1 131	147	22 119	73	1 190
2009	82 040	147	21 671	76	1 096
2010	83 340	148	21 794	81	1 223
2011	84 102	153	20 481	93	1 063
2012	84 917	157	22 231	98	1 038
2013	84 152	158	20 574	99	1 050
2014	82 363	161	22 286	103	1 105
2015	82 701	165	22 208	110	1 190
2016	85 767	217	21 797	113	1 221
2017	89 262	243	26 019	115	1 361
2018	91 111	300	25 743	128	1 307
2019	105 580	352	23 893	129	1 321
2020	111 401	406	14 652	132	1 202
2021	115 199	434	17 472	145	1 032

表 10.17　各区绿化情况(2021)
URBAN GREEN AREA IN DIFFERENT DISTRICTS

地　区 District		绿地面积 (公顷) Urban Green Space (hectare)	其　中　of which #公园绿地面积 Park Green Areas	公园数 (个) Quantity of Parks (unit)	公园面积 (公顷) Park Area (hectare)	公园游园人数 (万人次) Visitors to Parks and Zoos (10 000 person-times)
总　计	**Total**	**171 215.20**	**22 463.49**	**434**	**3 650.61**	**17 472.03**
浦东新区	Pudong New Area	34 055.00	7 568.66	61	946.76	3 395.13
黄 浦 区	Huangpu	293.79	182.78	23	71.95	1 061.56
徐 汇 区	Xuhui	1 434.39	607.74	17	152.97	727.13
长 宁 区	Changning	1 132.93	524.89	18	91.98	941.62
静 安 区	Jing'an	821.26	324.74	21	132.96	2 637.78
普 陀 区	Putuo	1 468.49	709.89	30	108.93	1 920.85
虹 口 区	Hongkou	439.88	159.78	21	68.43	1 000.70
杨 浦 区	Yangpu	1 502.03	501.57	22	247.14	1 306.37
闵 行 区	Minhang	10 233.37	2 836.63	58	424.94	1 243.27
宝 山 区	Baoshan	8 059.63	2 561.65	35	509.04	1 669.17
嘉 定 区	Jiading	11 819.70	1 537.18	38	209.13	341.38
金 山 区	Jinshan	12 728.28	757.62	15	36.22	147.32
松 江 区	Songjiang	15 583.53	1 315.56	30	154.06	541.36
青 浦 区	Qingpu	14 964.37	1 258.45	8	172.15	152.60
奉 贤 区	Fengxian	15 681.14	992.44	29	286.30	304.82
崇 明 区	Chongming	40 997.41	623.91	8	37.65	80.97

上/海/统/计/年/鉴

主要统计指标解释

■ 城市基础设施

城市基础设施包括电力建设、交通运输、邮电通信、公用事业和市政建设等。

■ 道路长度

指道路长度和与道路相通的桥梁、隧道的长度，按车行道中心线计算。

■ 绿地面积

指报告期末用作园林和绿化的各种绿地面积。包括公园绿地、防护绿地、附属绿地和其他绿地面积。

其中，公园绿地：指向公众开放的、以游憩为主要功能，有一定的游憩设施和服务设施，同时兼有健全生态、美化景观、防灾减灾等综合作用的绿化用地。它是城市建设用地、城市绿地系统和城市市政公用设施的重要组成部分。

■ 供水管道长度

指从送水泵至用户水表之间所有管道的长度。不包括新安装尚未使用的管道。

■ 供水总量

指报告期供水企业（单位）供出的全部水量。包括有效供水量和漏损水量。

■ 售水总量

指供水企业收费供应的水量，包括工业用水、非工业用水、居民生活用水、其它用水（如消防用水、工房配套水、排管冲洗水等其他用水）。

■ 天然气销售总量

指报告期内燃气供应企业（单位）售给本区域内各类用户的全部燃气量。包括工业企业生产用气量、家庭用气量、商业用气量、燃气汽车用气量和其他用气量。其中，家庭用气量指城市居民日常生活所耗用的燃气数量。

■ 排水管道长度

指所有排水总管、干管、支管、检查井及连接井进出口等长度之和。

■ 运营公交车辆数

指年末公交企业（单位）用于运营业务的全部车辆数。以企业（单位）固定资产台帐中已投入运营的车辆数为准。

■ 污水日处理能力

指城镇污水处理厂（或处理装置）每昼夜处理污水量的设计能力。

SHANGHAI STATISTICAL YEARBOOK

EXPLANATORY NOTES TO MAJOR STATISTICAL INDICATORS

□ Urban Infrastructure Facilities

Urban Infrastructure Facilities include facilities for power generating, transportation, post and telecommunication, public utilities, development of municipal engineering.

□ Length of Roads

The length of roads refers to the length of roads and of the bridges and tunnels connected to the roads, calculated by the center line of the roads.

□ Green Space

Green Space includes all kinds of gardens and green at the end of reporting period. Park green area, sub green area and other green area are all included.

Park green area refers to green areas open to the public for amusement and rest with the facilities of amusement, rest and services. Its function includes perfecting ecology, beautifying landscape, and preventing and reducing disaster. It is an important part of urban construction land, urban green and municipal public infrastructure in city.

□ Length of Water Supply Pipelines

Length of Water Supply Pipelines refers to the total length of all the pipelines between the water pumps and the user′s water meters, excluding pipelines newly installed but not used yet.

□ Volume of Water Supply

Volume of Water Supply refers to the total volume of water supplied by water-works (units) during the reference period, including both the effective water supply and loss during the water supply.

□ Total amount of Water Sold

The total amount of water sold refers to the amount of water charged by water supply enterprises, including industrial water, non-industrial water, residential water and other water (such as firewater, auxiliary water for industrial buildings, flushing water for drainage pipes, etc.).

□ Total amount of Natural Gas Sales

The total amount of natural gas sales refers to the total amount of gas sold by the internal combustion gas supply enterprises(units) to various users in the region during the reporting period. Including industrial production gas consumption, household gas consumption, commercial gas consumption, gas automobile gas consumption and other gas consumption. Among them, household gas consumption refers to the amount of gas consumed by urban residents in daily life.

□ Production Capacity of Gas

Production Capacity of Gas refers to the comprehensive production capacity of the urban gasworks in gas generation, purification and delivery at the end of the reference period, excluding capacity of the reserved facilities. In general, it is determined by the designed capacity, and when actual production capacity is larger than the designed capacity, the capacity is determined by the actual measurement on the weakest link in the production, purification and delivery.

□ Length of Sewage Pipes

Length of Sewage Pipes refers to the total length of general drainage, trunks, branch and inspection wells, connection wells, inlets and outlets, etc.

□ Number of Operating Public Transportation Vehicles

Number of Operating Public Transportation Vehicles refers to the total number of vehicles under operation by public transport enterprises (units) at the end of the year, based on the records of operational vehicles by the enterprises (units).

□ Daily Disposal Capacity of Urban Sewage

Daily Disposal Capacity of Urban Sewage refers to the designed 24 hour capacity of sewage disposal by the sewage treatment works or urban facilities.

第十一篇

CHAPTER 11

农业

AGRICULTURE

简要说明

一、本篇资料的主要内容

本篇资料反映本市农业生产和农村经济的基本情况，内容主要包括农林牧渔业产值、农村户数和人口、农作物播种面积、主要农产品产量、农业机械拥有量、农业技术应用等方面的统计资料。

二、本篇资料的统计范围

农业统计范围为上海市行政区域和上海光明食品(集团)有限公司所属的域外农场。

1. 种植业:指对各种农作物的种植活动。包括谷物、豆类、薯类、棉花、油料、糖料、麻类、烟叶、蔬菜、园艺作物、水果、坚果、饮料和香料作物、中草药及其他作物的种植。

2. 林业:包括林木的栽培(不包括茶园、桑园和果园的栽培、管理和收获等活动),木材和竹材的采运，林产品的采集。

3. 畜牧业:包括牲畜饲养和放牧,家禽饲养以及野生动物的捕猎和饲养。

4. 渔业:包括水生动物和海藻类植物的养殖和捕捞。

5. 农林牧渔服务业:指对种植业、林业、牧业、渔业生产活动进行的各种支持性服务。但不包括各种科学技术和专业性技术服务活动。

农村社会经济统计范围包括除城关镇以外所有乡镇的社会经济活动。

三、本篇的资料来源及统计调查方法

主要由上海市统计局、国家统计局上海调查总队根据《农村统计报表制度》和《农业调查报表制度》的有关资料整理提供。

《农村统计报表制度》包括三部分内容:

一是农林牧渔业统计调查。包括农作物播种面积、主要农作物产量、农产量抽样调查等内容，调查方法由统计部门确定。其中，水果、林业、渔业、农业机械和部分畜牧业数据来源为农委相关部门，调查方法由资料来源相关部门确定。

二是农业产值综合统计。包括农业总产值、农林牧渔业中间消耗等内容，调查方法由统计部门确定。

三是农村社会经济基本情况统计。包括乡镇社会经济基本情况、行政村基本情况等内容。上海参照国家统计局《县域社会经济基本情况统计报表制度》充实部分指标进行调查。

BRIEF INTRODUCTION

I. Main Contents

The data in this chapter reflect the basic conditions of agricultural production and rural economy in Shanghai. The main contents include output of agriculture, forestry, animal husbandry and fishery, number of rural households, rural population, sown area of farm crops, output of major agricultural products, agricultural products export, investment in facilities of water conservancy, electricity consumption in rural areas, ownership of agricultural machinery, application and comprehensive development of rural technology.

II. Scope and Coverage of Statistics

Data on agriculture cover the whole Shanghai Municipality including Minhang, Baoshan, Jiading, Songjiang, Jinshan, Qingpu, Fengxian, Chongming districts, and Pudong New Area(rural area). Included in agriculture statistics are production activities in agriculture by rural production units and by rural households; production activities of farms in counties, villages and rural communities; production activities in agriculture undertaken by Shanghai Bright Food (Group), Shanghai Fisheries (Group) Corporation, the Qingdong Farm, the Qianwei Farm, SIIC Modern Agriculture Park and agricultural production units owned by the central government, municipal government and military agencies.

(1) Agriculture: it refers to cultivation of farm crops, including cereals, beans, tuber crops, cotton, oil-bearing crops, sugar crops, hemp, tobacco leaves, vegetables, gardening plants, fruits, nuts, crops for beverages and spices, medicinal herbs and other farm crops.

(2) Forestry: it includes the planting of trees (excluding activities of planting, managing and harvesting of tea, mulberry fields and fruits), cutting and transport of timber and bamboo and collection of forest products.

(3) Animal husbandry: it includes the raising and grazing of domestic animals and poultry, and the hunting and raising of wild animals.

(4) Fishery: it includes cultivation and catching of aquatic animals and seaweed.

(5) Services in support of agriculture, forestry, animal husbandry and fishery: they include supporting services to production activities in agriculture, forestry, animal husbandry and fishery but do not include activities of science and technology and professional services.

Rural social and economic statistics cover social and economic activities in all townships except towns, where county governments are located.

III. Data Sources and Survey Methodology

Data in this chapter are provided by the Survey Office of the National Bureau of Statistics in Shanghai using data from the Statistical Survey System on Rural Areas.

Statistical Survey System on Rural Areas consists of three parts:

First, it includes statistics on agriculture, forestry, animal husbandry and fishery, including agricultural production area, main crop output and sampling survey of agricultural products, whose survey methodologies are determined by the statistics department. Fruit, forestry, fishery, agricultural machinery and part of animal husbandry data are provided by Shanghai Municipal Agriculture Commission, and survey methodologies are determined by relevant providers of the data.

Second, it includes comprehensive statistics on value of agricultural output, including output of agriculture, intermediate consumption of agriculture, forestry, animal husbandry, and fishery, Survey methodologies are determined by the statistics department.

Third, it includes comprehensive statistics on rural areas. The data include basic conditions of social and economic activities at county, township and rural administrations, and municipal agricultural zones. Data are provided according to Statistical Reporting System on the Basic Condition of Social and Economic Activities of Counties with additional standards supplemented by Shanghai authorities.

表 11.1 农业总产值(1978~2021)
GROSS OUTPUT VALUE OF AGRICULTURE

单位:亿元(100 million yuan)

年 份 Year	农业总产值 Gross Output Value of Agriculture	其中 of which 种植业 Planting	林 业 Forestry	畜牧业 Husbandry	渔 业 Fishery	农林牧渔服务业 Service Industry for Agriculture
1978	18.26	13.49	0.06	3.67	0.86	
1979	20.41	15.10	0.04	4.22	0.90	
1980	18.90	11.40	0.06	6.27	0.97	
1981	20.33	11.91	0.21	6.38	1.23	
1982	23.97	13.80	0.23	7.81	1.56	
1983	22.68	12.59	0.20	7.80	1.29	
1984	26.59	16.41	0.21	8.06	1.40	
1985	31.38	15.63	0.21	12.25	2.82	
1986	33.76	16.83	0.24	12.75	3.45	
1987	38.84	17.69	0.34	15.48	4.79	
1988	53.07	22.47	0.45	22.18	7.43	
1989	60.63	25.53	0.39	26.41	7.88	
1990	68.16	29.09	0.37	30.25	8.04	
1991	73.65	30.51	0.39	33.38	8.97	
1992	80.01	32.80	0.43	37.19	9.18	
1993	96.20	40.52	0.41	42.95	12.31	
1994	140.24	60.19	0.49	62.04	17.52	
1995	182.47	77.71	0.45	81.48	22.83	
1996	200.95	87.64	0.67	85.46	27.18	
1997	204.41	85.20	0.47	88.37	30.37	
1998	206.75	89.10	0.84	87.27	29.54	

①2003 年以前，农业总产值不包括农林牧渔服务业。
②2018 年，根据第三次农业普查结果对 2007 年以后的数据进行了修订，括号内数为 2007 年修订后的数据(后表同)。
❶The Gross Output Value of Agriculture did not include the output value of service industry for planting, forestry, animal husbandry and fishery before 2003.
❷In 2018, the data after 2007 were revised according to the results of the third agricultural census. The figures in brackets are the revised data in 2007 (the same as the table below).

表 11.1 续表 continued

单位：亿元（100 million yuan）

年　份 Year	农业总产值 Gross Output Value of Agriculture	其　中　of which 种植业 Planting	林　业 Forestry	畜牧业 Husbandry	渔　业 Fishery	农林牧渔服务业 Service Industry for Agriculture
1999	206.90	87.86	0.98	86.35	31.71	
2000	216.50	89.81	1.41	87.35	37.92	
2001	227.61	95.53	3.52	88.43	40.13	
2002	233.57	97.21	7.75	83.48	45.13	
2003	247.29	98.17	13.05	81.13	49.21	5.73
2004	248.89	109.32	13.14	70.77	49.90	5.76
2005	233.39	111.25	11.11	54.34	51.64	5.05
2006	237.01	119.99	10.43	46.29	55.25	5.05
2007	255.98	126.74	10.05	58.00	54.19	7.00
(2007)	(257.76)	(128.17)	(10.06)	(58.07)	(54.46)	(7.00)
2008	282.63	139.29	9.13	68.52	57.48	8.20
2009	287.76	151.00	9.02	64.72	54.54	8.49
2010	296.24	159.98	7.58	65.72	54.25	8.71
2011	328.24	169.82	7.73	83.82	57.14	9.73
2012	337.81	176.80	9.77	79.75	60.84	10.66
2013	342.29	177.93	9.80	79.52	63.35	11.69
2014	343.78	175.46	8.83	81.96	66.02	11.50
2015	327.71	167.86	12.30	80.84	55.67	11.04
2016	300.84	146.58	13.21	80.17	50.31	10.57
2017	292.61	146.40	15.31	61.17	58.39	11.34
2018	289.58	150.09	15.80	48.32	56.21	19.16
2019	284.84	145.81	18.27	48.24	54.95	17.56
2020	279.82	138.00	15.16	55.06	50.95	20.65
2021	268.93	144.94	8.68	45.34	47.72	22.24

表 11.2 农业总产值指数(以 1978 年为 100，1978~2021)
GROSS OUTPUT VALUE INDEX OF AGRICULTURE (1978=100)

年　份 Year	农业总产值指数 Index of Gross Output Value of Agriculture	其　中　of which 种植业 Planting	林　业 Forestry	畜牧业 Animal Husbandry	渔　业 Fishery	农林牧渔服务业 Service Industry for Agriculture
1978	100.0	100.0	100.0	100.0	100.0	
1979	101.4	92.9	121.9	128.1	101.6	
1980	92.1	78.6	152.9	115.8	104.1	
1981	100.0	83.9	144.0	140.2	97.3	
1982	117.4	97.4	161.1	170.1	107.3	
1983	109.9	86.0	116.1	167.3	123.6	
1984	124.5	109.0	98.4	167.5	114.7	
1985	113.0	88.2	107.2	181.4	127.6	
1986	119.7	89.5	134.5	201.2	149.5	
1987	122.5	90.6	138.9	206.7	158.1	
1988	130.3	95.3	166.0	227.0	160.0	
1989	132.0	92.3	134.9	245.6	171.8	
1990	139.5	96.3	139.7	271.2	164.3	
1991	146.2	95.6	153.7	299.0	172.7	
1992	154.7	101.3	144.0	322.9	168.8	
1993	147.9	94.1	129.4	313.8	166.8	
1994	159.4	96.0	130.5	336.7	215.0	
1995	177.0	104.0	125.2	363.0	252.4	
1996	191.6	114.5	168.6	389.1	269.6	
1997	202.5	123.1	133.0	404.3	288.4	
1998	207.3	129.4	185.2	412.1	278.6	

注：根据国家统计局方法制度规定，从 2006 年起，农业总产值指数按可比价计算，2006 年以前按不变价计算。
Note: According to the regulation of National Bureau of Statistics, since 2006, index of gross output value of agriculture has calculated by comparable price.

表 11.2 续表 continued

年 份 Year	农业总产值指数 Index of Gross Output Value of Agriculture	其 中 of which				
		种植业 Planting	林 业 Forestry	畜牧业 Animal Husbandry	渔 业 Fishery	农林牧渔服务业 Service Industry for Agriculture
1999	212.6	133.2	258.3	418.0	289.2	
2000	220.9	141.2	414.9	414.6	321.9	
2001	236.5	145.2	629.7	433.7	392.0	
2002	243.6	145.7	1 546.0	416.4	442.6	100.0
2003	246.3	135.3	2 062.4	395.5	544.4	102.6
2004	229.6	144.0	2 070.6	306.5	526.4	103.2
2005	205.5	136.7	1 613.0	221.6	555.4	91.4
2006	206.9	141.1	1 514.6	205.0	587.6	90.3
2007	210.0	142.9	1 458.6	214.2	573.5	121.6
(2007)	(211.6)	(144.5)	(1 460.9)	(214.4)	(576.3)	(121.4)
2008	212.0	149.1	1 188.0	224.1	523.6	134.4
2009	212.5	148.6	1 151.2	239.0	490.9	139.8
2010	204.7	142.6	966.2	242.3	457.0	139.2
2011	205.4	143.2	926.7	256.7	425.4	147.6
2012	207.9	144.1	1 057.7	256.2	434.6	157.4
2013	203.5	138.6	1 092.9	255.7	425.3	168.7
2014	207.3	138.3	1 011.4	269.2	450.7	161.6
2015	196.4	131.0	1 237.8	257.4	407.5	150.3
2016	173.2	113.0	1 345.3	234.7	343.1	137.8
2017	165.8	112.9	1 538.2	178.2	372.2	145.3
2018	162.0	113.6	1 486.5	147.2	346.2	241.5
2019	150.2	104.8	1 656.0	119.1	346.6	216.5
2020	139.7	98.1	1 348.5	108.1	311.9	250.2
2021	130.4	93.7	777.7	106.9	270.4	266.3

表 11.3　主要年份农村户数、人口和从业人员
RURAL HOUSEHOLDS, POPULATION AND EMPLOYEES IN MAIN YEARS

指　标	Indicators	2000	2010	2020	2021
户　数(万户)	**Households (10 000 households)**	**115.17**	**114.22**	**90.77**	**87.77**
人　口(万人)	**Population (10 000 persons)**	**360.71**	**305.68**	**223.38**	**212.74**
农村从业人员(万人)	**Rural Employees(10 000 persons)**	**253.45**	**188.70**	**135.19**	**128.62**
第一产业	Primary Industry	81.45	34.06	31.21	30.00
第二产业	Secondary Industry	119.89	109.84	73.85	69.42
第三产业	Tertiary Industry	52.11	44.80	30.13	29.20

注：根据国家统计制度规定，本表中2010~2012年第一产业从业人员中包括农林牧渔服务业从业人员；从2013年起，农林牧渔服务业从业人员从第一产业中划出，归入第三产业。

Note: According to the provisions of the national statistical system, the first industry employees of 2010~2012 in this table contained the employees in the service industries of farming, forestry, animal husbandry and fishery. Since 2013, employees in the service industries of farming, forestry, animal husbandry and fishery are separated from first industry and merged into third industry.

表 11.4　主要年份农作物总播种面积
TOTAL SOWN AREA OF PLANTING IN MAIN YEARS

年　份 Year	总播种面积(万公顷) Total Sown Area (10 000 hectares)	粮食作物 Grain Crops		经济作物 Cash Crops	
		播种面积 Sown Area	占总播种面积(%) Percentage (%)	播种面积 Sown Area	占总播种面积(%) Percentage (%)
1990	63.11	41.71	66.1	21.40	33.9
1995	54.22	34.40	63.5	19.82	36.5
2000	52.15	25.88	49.6	26.27	50.4
2001	49.09	21.12	43.0	27.97	57.0
2002	47.67	18.77	39.4	28.90	60.6
2003	41.92	14.83	35.4	27.09	64.6
2004	40.44	15.47	38.3	24.97	61.7
2005	40.36	16.61	41.1	23.75	58.9
2006	40.14	16.55	41.2	23.59	58.8
2007	39.07	16.96	43.4	22.11	56.6
(2007)	(40.06)	(17.92)	(44.73)	(22.14)	(55.28)
2008	39.78	18.42	46.3	21.36	53.7
2009	41.72	21.55	51.7	20.17	48.3
2010	41.74	20.12	48.2	21.62	51.8
2011	42.19	20.83	49.4	21.36	50.6
2012	40.33	20.81	51.6	19.52	48.4
2013	39.29	19.05	48.5	20.24	51.5
2014	37.15	18.67	50.3	18.48	49.7
2015	35.17	18.13	51.6	17.04	48.4
2016	30.51	15.85	51.9	14.66	48.1
2017	28.59	13.31	46.6	15.28	53.4
2018	28.53	12.99	45.5	15.54	54.5
2019	26.43	11.74	44.4	14.69	55.6
2020	25.78	11.43	44.3	14.35	55.7
2021	26.68	11.74	44.0	14.94	56.0

表 11.5 主要年份农产品产量
OUTPUT OF MAJOR FARM PRODUCTS IN MAIN YEARS

	指 标 Indicators	2000	2010	2020	2021
农产品	**Farm Products**				
粮 食(万吨)(包括大豆)	Grain (10 000 tons) (Including Soybean)	174.00	132.12	91.44	93.96
棉 花(万吨)	Cotton (10 000 tons)	0.12	0.36	0.00	0.00
油 料(万吨)	Oil Plants (10 000 tons)	16.37	2.45	0.72	0.49
#油菜籽	Rapeseed	15.71	2.14	0.64	0.44
蔬 菜(万吨)	Vegetables (10 000 tons)	377.00	374.52	244.33	244.66
食用菌(万吨)	Edible Fungus(10 000 tons)		8.75	8.53	3.98
西甜瓜(万吨)	Watermelons and Muskmelons (10 000 tons)	49.88	55.49	16.09	12.87
园林水果(万吨)	Garden Fruits (10 000 tons)	22.54	40.83	25.86	17.34
#生 梨	Pear	1.74	3.82	3.42	2.89
柑 橘	Citrus Fruits	10.18	18.88	11.72	5.31
畜禽产品	**Livestock and Poultry**				
生猪出栏量(万头)	Quantity of Sold Hogs(10 000 heads)	471.46	272.92	97.74	90.29
生猪年末圈存量(万头)	Hogs In Pens By Year-end (10 000 heads)	241.60	175.00	82.92	81.90
奶牛年末头数(万头)	Cows In Pens By Year-end (10 000 heads)	5.83	6.97	5.33	5.40
羊年末头数(万头)	Sheep In Pens By Year-end (10 000 heads)	55.44	19.46	12.96	13.83
猪 肉(万吨)	Pork (10 000 tons)	25.96	18.34	7.16	7.15
牛羊肉(万吨)	Beef and Mutton (10 000 tons)	0.79	0.43	0.49	0.51
家禽出栏量(万只)	Quantity of Poultry Sold Birds (10 000 fowls)	17 213	3 994	788.21	606.23
生牛奶(万吨)	Raw Milk (10 000 tons)	25.95	25.08	29.09	29.36
禽 蛋(万吨)	Poultry Eggs (10 000 tons)	16.64	6.01	2.88	2.59
水产品	**Aquatic Products**	**28.87**	**27.28**	**28.29**	**25.91**
海水产品(万吨)	Seawater Aquatic Products (10 000 tons)	12.23	12.15	16.40	16.20
淡水产品(万吨)	Freshwater Aquatic Products (10 000 tons)	16.64	15.13	11.89	9.71

表 11.6 农牧业特色种养产品产量(2020~2021)
OUTPUT OF SPECIAL PRODUCTS IN FARMING AND ANIMAL HUSBANDRY

	指 标 Indicators	2020	2021		指 标 Indicators	2020	2021
桃(万吨)	Peach (10 000 tons)	5.14	4.51	蜂 蜜(吨)	Honey(ton)	722	727
葡 萄(万吨)	Grape (10 000 tons)	4.85	3.93	野 鸭(万只)	Mallard(10 000 fowls)	30	6
草 莓(万吨)	Strawberry (10 000 tons)	1.99	2.41	肉 鸽(万只)	Meat Dove(10 000 fowls)	633	644
枣(吨)	Date(ton)	174	143	鳖(吨)	Soft-shelled Turtle(ton)	330	306
猕猴桃(吨)	Kiwi (ton)	703	1 213	中华绒毛蟹(万吨)	Chinese Hairy Crab(10 000 tons)	0.63	0.55

表 11.7　主要农副产品产量与新中国成立以来最高年产量的比较(2021)
OUTPUT OF MAJOR FARM PRODUCTS IN COMPARISON WITH THE PEAK YEAR SINCE 1949

指　标	Indicators	2021	新中国成立以来最高年 Peak Year Since 1949		2021 年为新中国成立以来最高年份(%) 2021/Peak Year Since 1949
			年　份 Year	产　量 Output	
农产品	**Farm products**				
粮　食(万吨)	Grain (10 000 tons)	93.96	1978	260.88	36.02
油菜籽(万吨)	Rapeseed (10 000 tons)	0.44	1992	21.84	1.99
蔬　菜(万吨)	Vegetables (10 000 tons)	244.66	2002	476.60	51.33
西甜瓜(万吨)	Watermelons and Muskmelons (10 000 tons)	12.87	2003	76.49	16.83
园林水果(万吨)	Garden Fruits (10 000 tons)	17.34	2008	44.34	39.10
畜禽产品	**Animal Husbandry Products**				
猪年末圈存数(万头)	Quantity of Hogs in Pens (year-end) (10 000 heads)	81.90	1978	365.74	22.39
猪　肉(万吨)	Pork (10 000 tons)	7.15	2001	26.40	27.07
奶牛年末头数(万头)	Quantity of Milk Cow (year-end) (10 000 heads)	5.40	2015	8.60	62.78
生牛奶(万吨)	Raw Milk (10 000 tons)	29.36	2015	37.06	79.22
家禽出栏量(万只)	Quantity of Poultry Sold(10 000 fowls)	606.23	1997	17 851	3.40
禽　蛋(万吨)	Poultry Eggs (10 000 tons)	2.59	2001	16.87	15.37
水产品	**Aquatic Products**				
海水产品(万吨)	Seawater Aquatic Products (10 000 tons)	16.20	2019	19.74	82.09
淡水产品(万吨)	Freshwater Aquatic Products (10 000 tons)	9.71	2003	22.13	43.87

注：建国以来最高年年份和产量均是指 2020 及以前的年份和产量，不包括 2021 年在内。
Note: Peak year and output of peak year since 1949 refer to the years before 2020, excluding 2021.

表 11.8 主要年份农业商品产值和商品率
OUTPUT VALUE OF AGRICULTURAL COMMODITY AND COMMODITY RATE IN MAIN YEARS

指 标	Indicators	2000	2010	2020	2021
农业商品产值(亿元)	**Output Value of Agricultural Commodity (100 million yuan)**	**179.79**	**236.15**	**244.13**	**234.73**
#种植业	Planting	61.84	120.22	121.87	127.54
#粮食作物	Grain Crops	10.15	16.43	24.04	25.04
畜牧业	Animal Husbandry	80.75	58.01	52.14	42.20
#生　猪	Hogs	29.82	30.38	30.35	18.80
家　禽	Poultry	33.41	8.95	6.13	5.99
禽　蛋	Eggs	7.94	5.10	2.42	2.74
渔　业	Fishery	36.53	50.42	49.67	46.44
#淡水产品	Freshwater Aquatic Products	25.14	36.62	26.22	25.72
农业商品率(%)	**Agricultural Commodity Rate (%)**	**83.0**	**82.3**	**87.2**	**87.3**
#种植业	Planting	68.8	77.4	88.3	88.0
#粮食作物	Grain Crops	45.4	53.8	85.9	86.8
畜牧业	Animal Husbandry	92.4	92.2	94.7	93.1
#生　猪	Hogs	95.8	94.7	97.3	95.3
家　禽	Poultry	91.9	86.5	92.0	92.7
禽　蛋	Poultry Eggs	82.3	93.3	96.3	97.4
渔　业	Fishery	96.3	95.8	97.5	97.3
#淡水产品	Freshwater Aquatic Products	95.9	95.0	96.0	96.3

注：根据国家统计局方法制度规定，从 2018 年起农业商品产值包括上海市光明(集团)有限公司所属的外地农场。
Note: According to the method system of the National Bureau of Statistics, the output value of agricultural commodities includes the non-local farms of Shanghai Guangming(Group)Co.,Ltd since 2018.

表 11.9 农民专业合作社组织情况(2018~2021)
ORGANIZATION OF FARMER PROFESSIONAL COOPERATIVES

指 标	Indicators	2018	2019	2020	2021
农民专业合作社总数(个)	**Total Number of Farmer Professional Cooperatives (unit)**	**2 865**	**2 757**	**2 506**	**2 538**
种植业	Planting	1 996	2 038	1 771	1 885
畜牧业	Animal Husbandry	119	67	72	65
渔　业	Fishery	347	287	286	242
林　业	Forestry	94	81	76	78
服务业	Service	170	160	163	147
手工业	Handicraft	3	3	3	2
其　他	Others	136	121	135	119
成员总数(人)	Total Members(person)	62 686	58 662	55 317	48 390
带动非成员农户数(户)	Affected Non-member Peasant Households(household)	146 693	133 888	127 074	133 093

表 11.10　主要年份农业机械拥有量
POSSESSION OF AGRICULTURAL MACHINERY IN MAIN YEARS

机械名称	Name of Machinery	2000	2010	2020	2021
农业机械总动力（万千瓦）	**Total Power of Agricultural Machinery (10 000 kw)**	**142.50**	**104.15**	**123.36**	**125.22**
耕作机械动力合计（万千瓦）	Total Power of Farming Machinery (10 000 kw)	37.60	29.54	43.19	43.13
# 大、中型拖拉机（台）	Large and Medium Tractors (set)	7 844	5 796	7 431	7 299
（万千瓦）	(10 000 kw)	29.30	24.21	40.77	40.79
小型拖拉机（台）	Small Tractors (set)	9 253	5 788	2 214	2 089
（万千瓦）	(10 000 kw)	8.30	5.34	2.42	2.34
收获机械动力合计（万千瓦）	Total Power of Harvest Machinery (10 000 kw)	33.30	12.19	14.29	14.13
# 联合收割机（台）	Combined Harvesters (set)	4 991	2 230	2 193	2 083
（万千瓦）	(10 000 kw)	2.70	8.52	14.29	13.58
机动植保机械动力合计（万千瓦）	Total Power of Plant Protecting Machine (10 000 kw)	3.07	5.34	5.97	5.95
# 机动喷雾器（万台）	Motorized Nebulizers (10 000 sets)	2.07	2.11	1.98	2.02
（万千瓦）	(10 000 kw)	3.07	4.72	5.97	5.95
渔业机械动力合计（万千瓦）	Total Power of Fishery Machinery (10 000 kw)	23.40	23.23	21.14	20.28
# 机动渔船（艘）	Motorized Fishing Boats (ship)	2 905	1 788	537	481
（万千瓦）	(10 000 kw)	20.50	18.74	15.12	14.16

注：本表农业机械化统计范围 2018 年以前（含 2018 年）未包括上海光明食品（集团）有限公司所属的域外农场（下表同）。

Note: The statistical scope of Agricultural Mechanization in this table before 2018 (including 2018) does not include the farms outside Shanghai territory of Shanghai Guangming Food (Group) Co., Ltd. (same as next table)

表 11.11 主要年份农业技术应用和综合开发情况
TECHNOLOGY APPLICATIONS AND INTEGRATIVE EXPLOITATION IN AGRICULTURE IN MAIN YEARS

指 标	Indicators	2000	2010	2020	2021
机耕面积(万公顷)	Areas of Motorized Cultivation (10 000 hectares)	23.46	39.47	25.52	26.43
粮食机种面积(万公顷)	Areas of Motorized Planting (10 000 hectares)	6.08	5.30	10.19	10.77
占粮食播种面积(%)	Percentage in Total Planting Area of Grain (%)	23.5	29.6	91.3	93.2
粮食机收面积(万公顷)	Areas of Motorized Harvesting (10 000 hectares)	16.42	16.57	11.08	11.44
占粮食收获面积(%)	Percentage in Total Harvesting Area of Grain (%)	63.4	92.5	99.3	99.8
机械植保面积(万公顷)	Areas of Mechancial Protecting (10 000 hectares)	41.10	30.41	25.26	26.17
化肥施用量(实物量)(万吨)	Chemical Fertilizer Consumption (real) (10 000 tons)	82.54	47.05	19.97	19.03
化肥施用量(折纯量)(万吨)	Chemical Fertilizer Consumption (convert to pure amount) (10 000 tons)	19.33	12.76	6.89	6.59
农药施用量(万吨)	Farm Pesticides Consumption (10 000 tons)	1.10	0.76	0.26	0.24
农用塑料薄膜使用量(万吨)	Agricultural Plastic Film Consumption (10 000 tons)	2.13	2.11	1.29	1.17
地膜覆盖面积(万公顷)	Areas Covered by Plastic Film (10 000 hectares)	2.05	2.62	1.22	1.19

表 11.12　域外市属农场农业生产情况(2018~2021)
AGRICULTURAL PRODUCTION OF EXTERNAL MUNICIPAL FARM

指　标	Indicators	2018	2019	2020	2021
农业总产值(亿元)	**Gross Output Value of Agriculture(100 million yuan)**	**31.52**	**32.16**	**42.33**	**33.30**
#种植业	Planting	6.29	6.59	7.53	6.76
林　业	Forestry	0.11			0.03
牧　业	Animal Husbandry	18.92	20.50	28.10	19.87
渔　业	Fishery	4.90	4.88	4.78	4.58
主要农产品产量	**Output of Major Farm Products**				
粮食(万吨)	Grain(10 000 tons)	16.27	16.51	15.51	15.91
夏　粮	Summer Grain Crops	6.32	5.03	4.66	4.79
秋　粮	Autumn Grain Crops	9.95	11.48	10.85	11.12
油菜籽(吨)	Rapeseed(ton)	1 433	1 275	1 630	1 699
蔬　菜(吨)	Vegetables(ton)	4 761	3 973	10 031	5 043
园林水果(吨)	Fruits(ton)	207		29	110
西　瓜(吨)	Watermelon(ton)	33 339	29 474	53 058	31 029
茶　叶(吨)	Tea-leaves(ton)	2.50	67.35	58.13	9.84
生猪出栏(万头)	Quantity of Sold Hogs(10 000 heads)	72.61	60.37	66.27	48.76
生牛奶(万吨)	Raw Milk(10 000 tons)	16.23	16.26	15.42	15.76
水产品(万吨)	Aquatic Products(10 000 tons)	4.42	4.44	3.55	2.87

注：域外市属农场是指上海光明食品(集团)有限公司所属的外地农场。
Note: External municipal farm refers to the nonlocal farms owned to Shanghai bright food (Group) Co., Ltd..

上 / 海 / 统 / 计 / 年 / 鉴

主要统计指标解释

■ 农村从业人员

指乡村人口中16岁以上实际参加生产经营活动并取得实物或货币收入的人员，既包括劳动年龄内实际参加劳动人员，也包括超过劳动年龄但实际参加劳动的人员，但不包括户口在家的在外学生、现役军人和丧失劳动能力的人，也不包括待业人员和家务劳动者。劳动者年龄为16岁以上。

■ 农业总产值

农业总产值是以货币表现的农、林、牧、渔业全部产品的总量和对农林牧渔生产活动进行的各种支持性服务活动的价值。它反映一定时期内农业生产的总规模和总成果。

农、林、牧、渔业的统计范围是：

(1) 种植业　包括谷物、豆类、薯类、棉、油料、糖料、麻类、烟叶、蔬菜、药材、瓜类和其他农作物的种植，以及茶园、桑园、果园的生产经营。

(2) 林业　包括林木的栽培(不包括茶园、桑园和果园的栽培、管理和收获等活动)、林产品的采集和村及村以下合作经济组织和农户的竹木采伐。

(3) 牧业　包括除渔业养殖以外的一切动物饲养和放牧，以及野生动物的捕猎和饲养。

(4) 渔业　包括水生动物和海藻类植物的养殖和捕捞。

(5) 农林牧渔服务业　包括农林牧渔业生产活动进行的各种支持性服务活动。但不包括各种科学技术和专业技术服务活动。

农业总产值的计算方法通常是按农林牧渔业产品及其副产品的产量分别乘以各自单位产品价格求得，少数生产周期较长、当年没有产品或产品产量不易统计的，则采用间接方法匡算其产值，然后将四业产品产值和服务业产值相加即为农业总产值。

1957年以前的农业总产值中包括了厩肥和农民自给性手工业(如农民自制衣服、鞋、袜，自己从事粮食初步加工等)。1958年及以后的农业总产值，林业中增加了村及村以下竹木采伐产值；牧业中取消了厩肥产值；副业中取消了农民自给性手工业产值，增加了村及村以下办的工业产值；渔业中增加了海洋捕捞水产品产值。1980年及以后的农业总产值，在副业中增加了农民家庭兼营工业商品部分的产值。从1984年起村及村以下办工业产值划归工业。从1993年起，取消副业。将野生动物的捕猎划入牧业，野生植物采集和农民家庭兼营商品性工业划归农业。从2003年起，农业总产值中包括了农林牧渔服务业产值。

■ 农业机械总动力

指用于农、林、牧、渔业生产的各种动力机械的动力总和。动力机械包括耕作、排灌、种植、植物保护、收获、农产品加工、运输、畜牧、渔业、农田水利等各种机械。不包括专门用于乡办工业、基本建设、非农业运输、科学试验和教学等非农业生产方面用的动力机械与作业机械的数量。

■ 农作物播种面积

指报告期内收获农产品的作物的实际播种或移植有农作物的面积。凡是实际种植农作物的面积，不论种植在耕地上还是种植在非耕地上，均包括在农作物播种面积中。在播种季节基本结束后，因遭灾而重新改种和补种的农作物面积，也包括在内。

■ 粮食产量

指全社会的产量。包括国有经济经营的、集体统一经营的和农民家庭经营的粮食产量，还包括工矿企业办的农场和其他生产单位的产量。粮食除包括稻谷、小麦、玉米、高粱、谷子及其他杂粮外，还包括薯类和豆类。其产量计算方法，豆类按去豆荚后的干豆计算；薯类(包括甘薯和马铃薯，不包括芋头和木薯)1963年以前按每4公斤鲜薯折1公斤粮食计算，从1964年开始改为按5公斤鲜薯折1公斤粮食计算。城市郊区作为蔬菜的薯类(如马铃薯等)按鲜品计算，并且不作粮食统计。其他粮食一律按脱粒后的原粮计算。1989年以前粮食产量数据主要靠全面报表取得，1989年开始使用抽样调查数据。

■ 棉花产量

指全社会的产量。包括春播棉和夏播棉。产量按皮棉计算。3公斤籽棉折1公斤皮棉，不包括木棉。

■ 油料产量

指全部油料作物的生产量。包括花生、油菜籽、芝麻、向日葵籽、胡麻籽(亚麻籽)和其他油料。不包括大

主要统计指标解释

豆、木本油料和野生油料。花生以带壳干花生计算。

■ 水产品产量

指人工养殖的水产品和天然生长的水产品的捕捞量。包括海水的鱼类、虾蟹类、贝类和藻类以及内陆水域的鱼类、虾蟹类和贝类,不包括淡水生植物。水产品产量是通过各级水产和统计部门逐级上报取得数据。1995年及以前,贝类中牡蛎按鲜肉计算;蚶、蛤、蛙按5斤鲜品折1斤计算。1996年以后则统一按鲜品计算。

■ 猪、牛、羊肉产量

指当年出栏并已屠宰、除去头蹄下水后带骨肉(即胴体重)的重量。包括全社会范围内的产量。1996年前为各级逐级上报数据。1996年第一次农业普查以后,由于畜牧业产品年报数据与普查数据之间存在一定的差距,国家统计局农调总队对畜牧业年报数据与普查数据进行衔接。上海仍使用各级统计部门逐级上报数据。

SHANGHAI STATISTICAL YEARBOOK

EXPLANATORY NOTES TO MAJOR STATISTICAL INDICATORS

□ Employees in Rural Areas

Employees in Rural Areas refers to people in rural areas who are older than 16 years and engaged in production and business activities that generate incomes in cash or in practicality. It includes all working laborers, no matter whether they are within the working age or not, whereas students studying outside but with their registered residence at home, active serviceman, people who lost their ability to work, unemployed people, and those engaged in housework are not included. The working age is defined as older than 16 years.

□ Gross Output Value of Agriculture

Gross Output Value of Agriculture refers to the total volume of products of farming, forestry, animal husbandry and fishery expressed in the monetary terms and output value of all kinds of service activities that support farming, forestry, animal husbandry and fishery production. It reflects the overall scale and achievements of agricultural production during a given period of time.

The scope of statistics on farming, forestry, animal husbandry, and fishery are as follows:

(1) Farming includes cultivation of grain crops, legume crops, tuber-crops, cotton, oil-bearing crops, sugar crops, bastfiber plants, tobacco, vegetables, medicinal herbs, melon crops, and cultivation and management of tea plantations, mulberry fields and orchards.

(2) Forestry refers to planting trees of various kinds (excluding tea plantations, mulberry fields and orchards), collection of forestry products and cutting and felling of bamboo and trees by villages and other cooperative organizations under village level.

(3) Animal husbandry refers to raising and grazing of all kinds of farm animals except fishing and aquatic cultivating, and hunting and rising of wild animals.

(4) Fishery refers to cultivation and catching of fish and other aquatic products and cultivation and collection of seaweed and other aquatic plants.

(5) Service Industry for Farming, Forestry, Animal Husbandry and Fishery refers to all kinds of service activities that support farming, forestry, animal husbandry and fishery production, whereas activities of science, technology and professional service are not included.

Gross output value of agriculture is obtained by first multiplying the output of products or by-products by their unit price. For a small number of products, annual output of which is not available or difficult to get due to the long production/growing process involved, the output value will be estimated through an indirect approach. The sum of output value of all products of farming, forestry, animal husbandry and fishery and output value of service activities will then and together to form gross output value of agriculture.

Before 1957, China´s gross agricultural output value included the value of barnyard manure and handicraft products for self- consumption (clothes, shoes, stockings, and initial grain processing under-taken by peasants). After 1958, the output value of cutting and felling of bamboo and trees by villages and other cooperative organizations under villages have been included in forestry; value of barnyard manure has been excluded from animal husbandry; the value of self- consumed handicrafts has been excluded from sideline occupations, while output value of industries run by villages and cooperative organizations under village level has been included in sideline occupations and output value of fish catches by motor fishing boats has been added to fishery. Since 1980, the output value of handicraft products made for sale by farmer households has been added to sideline occupations. From 1984, industries run by villages and cooperative organizations under village level have been included in the sector of industry. After 1993, the category of sideline occupations has been canceled and hunting of wild animals has been classified into husbandry, and harvesting of wild vegetation and commodity industry run by rural households have been grouped into the category of agriculture. Since 2003, the output value of service industry for farming, forestry, animal husbandry and fishery is included in the gross output value of agriculture.

□ Total Power of Agricultural Machinery

Total Power of Agricultural Machinery refers to the total mechanical power of machinery used in farming, forestry animal husbandry and fishery, including machines used for ploughing, irrigation and drainage, crop growing, plant protection, harvesting, farm product processing, transport, stock breeding, fishery

EXPLANATORY NOTES TO MAJOR STATISTICAL INDICATORS

and water conservancy. Machinery employed for non-agricultural purposes such as township industry, capital construction, non-agricultural transport, scientific experiments and for teaching is excluded.

□ Sown Area of Planting

Sown Area of Planting refers to area of land sown or transplanted with crops that have been harvested during report period, regardless of being in cultivated area or non-cultivated area. Area of land re-sown due to natural disasters is also included.

□ Grain Output

Grain Output refers to the total output in the whole country including grains produced by state farms, collective units, rural households, as well as by farms affiliated to industrial and mining enterprises and other production units. Grain includes rice, wheat, corn, sorghum, millet and other miscellaneous grains as well as tubers and bean. Output of beans refers to dry beans without pods. The output of tubers (sweet potatoes and potatoes, not including taros and cassava) was converted into that of grain at the ratio 4:1, i.e. 4 kilograms of fresh tubers was equivalent to 1 kilogram of grain up to 1963. Since 1964 the ratio for conversion has been 5:1. Tubers supplied as vegetables (such as potatoes) in cities and suburbs are calculated as fresh vegetables and their output is not included in the output of grain. Output of all other grains refers to husked grain. Data on grain production before 1989 were obtained through Comprehensive Statistical Reporting System. Since 1989, data from sample surveys are used.

□ Cotton Output

Cotton Output refers to the cotton production in the whole country including cotton sown in spring and in autumn. Output is measured as the weight of ginned cotton. Three kilograms of seed-cotton are equivalent to 1 kilogram of ginned cotton, excluding ceiba.

□ Output of Oil-bearing Crops

Output of Oil-bearing Crops refers to the total production of oil-bearing crops of various kinds, including peanuts, (dry, in shell) rapeseeds, sesame, sunflower seeds, flax seeds, and other oil- bearing crops. Soybeans, oil- bearing woody plants, and wild oil-bearing crops are not included.

□ Output of Aquatic Products

Output of Aquatic Products refers to catches of both artificially cultured and naturally grown aquatic products, including fish, shrimps, crabs and shellfish in sea and inland water as well as seaweed. Freshwater plants are not included. Data on output of aquatic products are reported by aquatic product and statistical agencies level by level. Before 1995, among the shellfish, the oyster was counted as fresh meat; 5 kilograms of ark shell, clams and frogs are equivalent to 1 kilogram of fresh aquatic products; they are all counted as fresh aquatic products since 1996.

□ Output of Pork, Beef, and Mutton

Output of Pork, Beef, and Mutton refers to the meat of slaughtered hogs, cattle, sheep and goats with head, feet, and offal taken away. Data refers to the production of the whole country. The first agriculture census of China in 1996 revealed some discrepancy between the production of animal products from the annual reports and that from the census. Efforts were made by the Rural Socio-economic Survey Organization of NBS to adjust the output value of animal husbandry to make the figures from the annual reports consistent with the census data. Data of Shanghai are still reported by statistical agencies level by level.

第十二篇

CHAPTER 12

工 业

INDUSTRY

简要说明

一、本篇资料的主要内容

本篇资料反映上海市工业经济方面的基本情况，主要内容包括：

1. 上海工业经济概况。规模以上工业企业主要经济指标，以及按地区、隶属关系、企业登记注册类型、企业规模和工业行业大类分组的主要经济指标；按隶属关系、企业规模分组和国有控股的主要经济效益指标。

2. 国有控股主要经济指标及其占全市比重。

3. 高技术产业（制造业）主要经济指标。

4. 都市型工业按企业规模、登记注册类型和行业分组的主要经济指标。

5. 历年主要工业产品产量及2021年主要工业产品产、销量。

6. 大中小型工业企业按隶属关系、工业总产值、行业分组的主要经济指标。

7. 国家级、市级工业园区主要经济指标。

二、本篇资料的统计范围

本篇资料除表12.1为全市工业企业以外，其余工业数据的统计范围如下：1998年至2006年为全部国有和年主营业务收入500万元及以上的非国有工业企业；2007至2010年为年主营业务收入500万元及以上的工业企业（即规模以上工业企业）；从2011年开始，为年主营业务收入2000万元及以上的工业企业（即规模以上工业企业）。

本篇资料中工业行业分类按2017年《国民经济行业分类（2017版）》标准划分；企业大中小微型划分按《统计上大中小微型企业划分办法（2017）》标准执行。

本篇资料中税金总额包含的应交增值税指标从2015年年报起，负数不做替零处理。

三、本篇的资料来源和统计调查方法

本篇工业企业统计数据根据工业统计年度报表整理汇总。

BRIEF INTRODUCTION

I. Main Contents

The Data in this chapter reflect the basic conditions of the industrial sector in Shanghai. Major contents include:

(1) Basic conditions of industrial sectors in Shanghai; major economic indicators of industrial enterprises above designated sizes; as well as major economic indicators classified by regions, by subordination, by types of registration, by size of enterprise, and by branch of industry; and major economic efficiency indicators classified by subordination, by sizes of enterprise, and on state–controlled industrial enterprises.

(2) Major economic indicators of state–controlled industrial enterprises and their proportions of the city's total.

(3) Major economic indicators of high technology industries (manufacturing).

(4) Major economic indicators of urban industries classified by sizes of enterprise, by type of registration, and by industrial sectors.

(5) Output of major industrial products in recent years, as well as output and sales of major industrial products in 2021.

(6) Major economic indicators of large–, medium–, and small–size industrial enterprises classified by subordination, by gross output value of industry.

(7) Major economic indicators of municipal and national industrial zones.

II. Scope and Coverage of Statistics

Except for table 12.1, which covers all industrial enterprises in the city, the scopes of industrial statistics were all state–owned industrial enterprises and non–state–owned industrial enterprises whose annual revenue from principal business was more than 5 million yuan from 1998 to 2006. For 2007 to 2010, the scopes of industrial statistics were all industrial enterprises whose annual revenue from principal business was more than 5 million yuan, (i.e., the industrial enterprises above designated size). Since 2011, the scope is adjusted to all industrial enterprises whose annual revenue from principal business was more than 20 million yuan (i.e. industrial enterprises above designated size).

Branches of industry in this chapter are based on the 2017's National Industrial Classification of all Economic Activities, and data by size of enterprise are based on 2017 Standards of Enterprises by Size.

In this chapter, the negative numbers of value added tax payable included in the total amount of tax needn't do zero treatment since annual report of 2015.

III.Sources of Data and Methodology of Survey

The data of industrial enterprises statistics in this Chapter are collected mainly from the relevant data in the annual industrial statistics reporting forms.

表 12.1 工业总产值及指数(1978~2021)
GROSS OUTPUT VALUE OF INDUSTRY AND INDICES

年 份 Year	工业总产值 (亿元) Gross Output Value of Industry (100 million yuan)	工业总产值指数 (以 1978 年为 100) Indices of Gross Output Value of Industry (1978=100)	年 份 Year	工业总产值 (亿元) Gross Output Value of Industry (100 million yuan)	工业总产值指数 (以 1978 年为 100) Indices of Gross Output Value of Industry (1978=100)
1978	514.01	100.0	1999	6 213.24	805.1
1979	556.30	108.6	2000	7 022.98	913.7
1980	598.75	115.7	2001	7 806.18	1 063.8
1981	620.12	120.0	2002	8 730.00	1 219.1
1982	634.65	125.6	2003	11 708.49	1 601.9
1983	663.53	134.4	2004	14 595.29	1 927.1
1984	728.12	147.7	2005	16 876.78	2 195.0
1985	862.73	167.7	2006	19 631.23	2 500.1
1986	952.21	177.0	2007	23 108.63	2 892.6
1987	1 073.84	188.9	2008	25 968.38	3 126.9
1988	1 304.66	208.8	2009	24 888.08	3 227.0
1989	1 524.67	215.0	2010	31 038.57	3 966.0
1990	1 642.75	223.6	2011	33 834.44	4 227.8
1991	1 947.18	255.2	2012	33 186.41	4 215.1
1992	2 429.96	306.7	2013	33 899.38	4 396.3
1993	3 327.04	368.2	2014	34 071.19	4 466.7
1994	4 255.19	435.3	2015	33 211.57	4 444.3
1995	5 349.53	510.9	2016	33 079.72	4 475.4
(1995)	(4 547.47)		2017	36 094.36	4 766.3
1996	5 126.22	590.1	2018	36 451.84	4 828.3
1997	5 649.93	675.7	2019	35 487.05	4 813.8
1998	5 763.67	728.5	2020	37 052.59	4 890.8
			2021	42 013.99	5 389.7

注：从 1996 年开始，工业总产值按新规定计算，括号内数为 1995 年新规定数(以下同)。
Note: Since 1996, new regulations have been adopted in calculating total industrial gross output value of industry. The figures of 1995 in brackets are calculated in line with the new regulations(same as follows).

表 12.2　各区工业企业主要指标(2021)
MAJOR INDICATIORS OF INDUSTRIAL ENTERPRISES IN DISTRICTS

单位:亿元(100 million yuan)

地　区	District	工业总产值 Gross Output Value of Industry	年末资产总计 Total Assets (year-end)	营业收入 Operating Revenue	利润总额 Total Pre-tax Profits
总　计	**Total**	**39 975.01**	**53 642.41**	**45 402.33**	**3 164.63**
#浦东新区	Pudong New Area	12 515.15	18 314.53	13 633.46	836.99
黄 浦 区	Huangpu	45.97	93.33	77.41	17.14
徐 汇 区	Xuhui	783.89	909.44	1 136.16	59.68
长 宁 区	Changning	153.93	307.84	159.58	8.48
静 安 区	Jing'an	55.05	143.02	62.01	4.63
普 陀 区	Putuo	160.80	313.43	199.93	10.74
虹 口 区	Hongkou	58.35	178.73	79.01	5.57
杨 浦 区	Yangpu	741.12	2 251.64	1 378.64	233.93
闵 行 区	Minhang	3 735.55	4 866.87	4 200.87	367.22
宝 山 区	Baoshan	2 645.26	4 155.46	3 577.23	200.73
嘉 定 区	Jiading	5 510.12	5 682.42	6 033.43	418.03
金 山 区	Jinshan	2 504.42	2 775.05	2 754.26	133.58
松 江 区	Songjiang	4 612.55	4 196.58	4 965.05	256.96
青 浦 区	Qingpu	1 793.71	2 433.32	2 029.25	139.71
奉 贤 区	Fengxian	2 427.47	3 046.03	2 616.04	234.94
崇 明 区	Chongming	489.58	1 103.92	532.14	0.17

表 12.3 规模以上工业企业主要指标(2021)
MAJOR INDICATORS OF INDUSTRIAL ENTERPRISES ABOVE THE SET SCALE

类 别	Types	工业总产值 Gross Output Value of Industry
总 计	**Total**	**39 975.01**
按隶属关系分	**Grouped by Subordination**	
中央工业	Central Government	6 558.26
地方工业及其他	Local Government and others	33 416.75
按登记注册类型分	**Grouped by Registration Categories**	
内 资	Domestic Funded	17 869.77
#国 有	State-owned	174.94
集 体	Collective-owned	21.79
有限责任公司	Companies with Limited Liabilities	8 401.94
股份有限公司	Share-holding Companies with Limited Liabilities	2 678.80
私 营	Private	6 554.78
港澳台商投资	Hong Kong, Macao and Taiwan Funded	6 585.19
#与港澳台商合资经营	Joint-venture	1 630.28
港澳台商独资	Sole Funded	4 577.36
港澳台商投资股份有限公司	Share-holding Companies Ltd.	336.37
外商投资	Foreign Funded	15 520.05
#中外合资经营	Joint-venture	6 965.75
外资企业	Sole Funded	7 844.79
外商投资股份有限公司	Share-holding Companies Ltd.	374.48
按企业规模分	**Grouped by Size of Enterprises**	
大 型	Large	19 050.58
中 型	Medium	8 903.99
小 型	Small	12 020.44
按工业行业分	**Grouped by Sectors**	
采矿业	**Mining Industry**	**55.70**
石油和天然气开采业	Petroleum and Natural Gas Exploiting	55.70
制造业	**Manufacture Industry**	**38 053.04**
农副食品加工业	Farm and Sideline Products Processing	391.41
食品制造业	Food Manufacturing	818.48
酒、饮料和精制茶制造业	Wine, Beverage and Refined Tea Manufacturing	119.44
烟草制品业	Tabacco Manufacturing	981.32

单位:亿元(100 million yuan)

年末资产总计 Total Assets (year-end)	流动资产合计 Current Assets	年末负债合计 Total Liabilities (year-end)
53 642.41	**31 683.76**	**26 192.09**
11 609.59	5 460.30	5 264.79
42 032.82	26 223.47	20 927.30
32 427.24	17 996.00	14 885.32
294.72	213.16	188.09
38.79	29.25	18.48
14 686.25	7 905.76	7 257.33
8 866.86	3 689.40	3 244.66
8 523.56	6 143.85	4 171.70
5 489.04	3 373.69	2 777.40
1 848.16	957.91	752.30
2 985.27	2 029.39	1 786.55
602.55	353.40	217.15
15 726.13	10 314.07	8 529.37
6 840.10	4 140.17	3 918.38
7 369.04	5 326.70	3 754.78
1 190.17	581.31	717.73
26 943.81	13 886.46	13 176.59
12 143.04	7 577.55	5 874.43
14 555.56	10 219.75	7 141.08
308.83	**123.36**	**183.40**
308.83	123.36	183.40
48 698.88	**30 794.39**	**23 965.51**
352.13	235.21	191.67
915.60	565.39	486.61
166.27	109.84	89.64
1 738.47	1 333.36	266.32

表 12.3 续表 1 continued

类 别	Types	工业总产值 Gross Output Value of Industry
纺织业	Textile	192.05
纺织服装、服饰业	Textiles and Clothing Industry	225.64
皮革、毛皮、羽毛及其制品和制鞋业	Leather, Fur, Wool Products and Shoes Manufacturing	124.33
木材加工和木、竹、藤、棕、草制品业	Timber Processing and Timber, Bamboo, Rattan, Coir and Straw Products Manufacturing	45.56
家具制造业	Furniture Manufacturing	314.05
造纸和纸制品业	Paper-making and Paper Products Manufacturing	271.49
印刷和记录媒介复制业	Printing and Record Duplicating	213.31
文教、工美、体育和娱乐用品制造业	Culture, Education, Industrial Arts, Sports and Entertainment Goods Manufacturing	549.16
石油、煤炭及其他燃料加工业	Oil, Coal and Other Fuel Processing	1 297.27
化学原料和化学制品制造业	Raw Chemical Materials and Chemical Products Manufacturing	3 771.69
医药制造业	Medicine Manufacturing	1 097.33
化学纤维制造业	Chemical Fiber Manufacturing	22.31
橡胶和塑料制品业	Rubber and Plastic Products Manufacturing	1 015.74
非金属矿物制品业	Non-metallic Mineral Products Manufacturing	914.77
黑色金属冶炼和压延加工业	Ferrous Metal Smelting and Rolling Processing Industry	1 549.44
有色金属冶炼和压延加工业	Nonferrous Metal Smelting and Rolling Processing Industry	500.74
金属制品业	Metal Products Manufacturing	1 171.19
通用设备制造业	General Equipment Manufacturing	3 468.96
专用设备制造业	Special Purpose Equipment Manufacturing	1 724.99
汽车制造业	The Automotive Manufacturing	7 452.66
铁路、船舶、航空航天和其他运输设备制造业	The Railroad, Marine, Aerospace and Other Transportation Equipment Manufacturing	867.80
电气机械和器材制造业	Electric Machinery Equipments and Manufacturing	2 652.32
计算机、通信和其他电子设备制造业	Computer, Communications and Other Electronic Equipment Manufacturing	5 429.34
仪器仪表制造业	Instrumentation Manufacturing	486.94
其他制造业	Other Manufacturing	61.54
废弃资源综合利用业	Comprehensive Utilization of Waste Resources	49.82
金属制品、机械和设备修理业	Metal Products, Machinery and Equipment Repair Industry	271.94
电力、热力、燃气及水生产和供应业	**Electricity, Heat, Gas and Water Production and Supply Industry**	**1 866.27**
电力、热力生产和供应业	Production and Supply of Electricity and Thermal Power	1 314.27
燃气生产和供应业	Production and Supply of Gas	456.11
水的生产和供应业	Production and Supply of Water	95.90

单位：亿元（100 million yuan）

年末资产总计 Total Assets (year-end)	流动资产合计 Current Assets	年末负债合计 Total Liabilities (year-end)
183.67	138.81	74.08
197.63	157.57	111.43
264.14	241.54	57.48
54.60	36.97	24.24
357.12	269.00	242.30
291.02	195.50	130.71
278.14	177.65	114.76
399.94	318.92	197.86
864.32	388.10	379.18
3 745.14	2 296.15	1 537.44
2 203.03	1 194.06	763.50
23.58	14.58	11.68
1 268.83	823.41	488.32
1 230.89	990.99	817.66
2 631.22	1 063.84	1 009.87
322.93	248.49	167.88
1 380.98	954.55	760.04
5 141.77	3 668.21	2 977.03
2 874.52	2 163.83	1 390.17
8 971.41	4 622.11	4 707.96
2 184.47	1 621.80	1 628.41
3 072.77	2 279.01	1 655.12
6 491.53	3 891.08	3 170.30
606.51	485.65	240.92
75.51	52.06	36.45
64.81	36.91	27.74
345.91	219.78	208.73
4 634.70	**766.01**	**2 043.18**
2 932.31	430.66	1 353.94
521.48	220.74	219.18
1 180.91	114.62	470.07

表 12.3 续表 2 continued

类 别	Types	年末所有者权益 Owners' Equity (year-end)
总 计	**Total**	**27 450.16**
按隶属关系分	**Grouped by Subordination**	
中央工业	Central Government	6 344.80
地方工业及其他	Local Government and others	21 105.36
按登记注册类型分	**Grouped by Registration Categories**	
内 资	Domestic Funded	17 541.92
#国 有	State-owned	106.63
集 体	Collective-owned	20.31
有限责任公司	Companies with Limited Liabilities	7 428.92
股份有限公司	Share-holding Companies with Limited Liabilities	5 622.20
私 营	Private	4 351.84
港澳台商投资	Hong Kong, Macao and Taiwan Funded	2 711.64
#与港澳台商合资经营	Joint-venture	1 095.85
港澳台商独资	Sole Funded	1 198.72
港澳台商投资股份有限公司	Share-holding Companies Ltd.	385.40
外商投资	Foreign Funded	7 196.60
#中外合资经营	Joint-venture	2 921.72
外资企业	Sole Funded	3 614.11
外商投资股份有限公司	Share-holding Companies Ltd.	472.44
按企业规模分	**Grouped by Size of Enterprises**	
大 型	Large	13 767.23
中 型	Medium	6 268.61
小 型	Small	7 414.32
按工业行业分	**Grouped by Sectors**	
采矿业	**Mining Industry**	**125.43**
石油和天然气开采业	Petroleum and Natural Gas Exploiting	125.43
制造业	**Manufacture Industry**	**24 733.21**
农副食品加工业	Farm and Sideline Products Processing	160.46
食品制造业	Food Manufacturing	428.99
酒、饮料和精制茶制造业	Wine, Beverage and Refined Tea Manufacturing	76.63
烟草制品业	Tabacco Manufacturing	1 472.15

单位:亿元(100 million yuan)

营业收入 Operating Revenue	利润总额 Total Pre-tax Profits	税金总额 Total Tax and Duties	成本费用总额 Total Cost and Expenses
45 402.33	**3 164.63**	**1 892.32**	**41 990.84**
7 769.00	463.16	1 073.33	6 578.34
37 633.33	2 701.47	818.98	35 412.51
21 335.87	1 521.65	1 230.97	19 695.32
186.86	25.67	7.05	178.80
25.76	0.97	0.67	25.15
9 561.59	549.06	989.88	8 432.03
4 190.23	437.72	61.87	4 123.17
7 332.17	508.15	170.52	6 896.70
6 767.17	362.82	206.91	6 318.93
1 780.13	117.95	168.61	1 545.13
4 582.75	193.42	30.05	4 393.49
360.84	47.27	7.11	340.16
17 299.29	1 280.16	454.44	15 976.60
7 588.83	534.46	308.70	6 977.76
8 906.90	690.69	135.14	8 235.74
429.41	24.75	2.20	417.17
21 868.72	1 437.66	1 413.74	19 957.46
10 138.54	812.67	190.51	9 430.88
13 395.07	914.30	288.06	12 602.50
54.34	**7.30**	**5.41**	**45.22**
54.34	7.30	5.41	45.22
43 252.79	**3 139.28**	**1 841.48**	**39 813.75**
506.15	27.35	6.50	486.99
963.31	93.98	37.15	879.98
132.97	11.08	6.23	121.89
1 075.50	227.25	752.15	234.93

表 12.3 续表 3 continued

类 别	Types	年末所有者权益 Owners' Equity (year-end)
纺织业	Textile	109.60
纺织服装、服饰业	Textiles and Clothing Industry	86.20
皮革、毛皮、羽毛及其制品和制鞋业	Leather, Fur, Wool Products and Shoes Manufacturing	206.66
木材加工和木、竹、藤、棕、草制品业	Timber Processing and Timber, Bamboo, Rattan, Coir and Straw Products Manufacturing	30.35
家具制造业	Furniture Manufacturing	114.82
造纸和纸制品业	Paper-making and Paper Products Manufacturing	160.31
印刷和记录媒介复制业	Printing and Record Duplicating	163.38
文教、工美、体育和娱乐用品制造业	Culture, Education, Industrial Arts, Sports and Entertainment Goods Manufacturing	202.08
石油、煤炭及其他燃料加工业	Oil, Coal and Other Fuel Processing	485.14
化学原料和化学制品制造业	Raw Chemical Materials and Chemical Products Manufacturing	2 207.70
医药制造业	Medicine Manufacturing	1 439.53
化学纤维制造业	Chemical Fiber Manufacturing	11.90
橡胶和塑料制品业	Rubber and Plastic Products Manufacturing	780.51
非金属矿物制品业	Non-metallic Mineral Products Manufacturing	413.23
黑色金属冶炼和压延加工业	Ferrous Metal Smelting and Rolling Processing Industry	1 621.36
有色金属冶炼和压延加工业	Nonferrous Metal Smelting and Rolling Processing Industry	155.05
金属制品业	Metal Products Manufacturing	620.95
通用设备制造业	General Equipment Manufacturing	2 164.74
专用设备制造业	Special Purpose Equipment Manufacturing	1 484.35
汽车制造业	The Automotive Manufacturing	4 263.45
铁路、船舶、航空航天和其他运输设备制造业	The Railroad, Marine, Aerospace and Other Transportation Equipment Manufacturing	556.06
电气机械和器材制造业	Electric Machinery Equipments and Manufacturing	1 417.49
计算机、通信和其他电子设备制造业	Computer, Communications and Other Electronic Equipment Manufacturing	3 321.22
仪器仪表制造业	Instrumentation Manufacturing	365.59
其他制造业	Other Manufacturing	39.06
废弃资源综合利用业	Comprehensive Utilization of Waste Resources	37.07
金属制品、机械和设备修理业	Metal Products, Machinery and Equipment Repair Industry	137.18
电力、热力、燃气及水生产和供应业	**Electricity, Heat, Gas and Water Production and Supply Industry**	**2 591.52**
电力、热力生产和供应业	Production and Supply of Electricity and Thermal Power	1 578.38
燃气生产和供应业	Production and Supply of Gas	302.30
水的生产和供应业	Production and Supply of Water	710.84

单位：亿元（100 million yuan）

营业收入 Operating Revenue	利润总额 Total Pre-tax Profits	税金总额 Total Pre-tax and Duties	成本费用总额 Total Cost and Expenses
216.12	13.15	3.16	203.42
275.48	9.87	2.96	270.04
107.34	4.69	-0.20	102.91
51.89	3.05	1.61	48.49
345.57	37.91	8.65	328.67
335.66	21.91	7.62	314.94
231.19	8.07	7.39	225.03
764.51	59.85	8.03	725.26
1 329.24	64.09	238.56	1 081.47
4 290.60	444.32	92.26	3 856.98
1 119.11	190.40	51.85	958.25
23.71	1.05	0.47	22.78
1 163.61	99.80	23.75	1 075.38
1 035.42	60.37	25.77	978.36
2 277.25	124.41	8.33	2 193.05
577.92	14.49	4.04	563.21
1 394.17	99.37	17.59	1 304.72
3 848.53	278.22	73.74	3 580.35
1 911.13	184.03	44.07	1 749.79
8 554.33	594.34	295.70	8 162.73
960.26	8.13	16.49	962.47
3 124.57	194.03	53.63	2 939.67
5 704.05	181.14	27.44	5 583.13
539.06	68.88	13.81	481.92
62.46	5.69	2.17	56.62
49.80	7.10	2.51	44.03
281.91	1.27	8.02	276.28
2 095.20	**18.05**	**45.43**	**2 131.87**
1 456.80	-3.84	36.46	1 487.56
494.79	14.87	4.58	503.08
143.61	7.02	4.40	141.23

表 12.4 工业企业经济效益指标(2021)
ECONOMIC EFFICIENCY INDICATORS OF INDUSTRIAL ENTERPRISES

类　别	Types	营业收入利润率(%) Operating Revenues Profit Ratio (%)	每百元营业收入中的成本(元) Cost of Revenues per hundred yuan (yuan)	每百元营业收入中的费用(元) Expenses of Revenues per hundred yuan (yuan)
总　计	**Total**	**6.97**	**81.72**	**10.76**
#国有控股企业	Enterprises with the State Holding Major Shares	6.34	81.86	9.12
按隶属关系分	Grouped by Subordination			
中央工业	Central Government	5.96	79.53	5.14
地方工业及其他	Local Government and others	7.18	82.18	11.92
按企业规模分	Grouped by Size of Enterprise			
大　型	Large	6.57	82.00	9.26
中　型	Medium	8.02	80.80	12.22
小　型	Small	6.83	81.98	12.10

表 12.4 续表 continued

类　别	Types	每百元资产实现的营业收入(元) Operating Revenues from per hundred yuan of Asserts (yuan)	资产负债率(%) Debt Assets Ratio (%)	产成品存货周转天数(天) Days Sales of Finshed Goods Inventory (day)
总　计	**Total**	**84.64**	**48.83**	**20.18**
#国有控股企业	Enterprises with the State Holding Major Shares	69.07	48.59	14.88
按隶属关系分	Grouped by Subordination			
中央工业	Central Government	66.92	45.35	11.76
地方工业及其他	Local Government and others	89.53	49.79	21.86
按企业规模分	Grouped by Size of Enterprise			
大　型	Large	81.16	48.90	14.39
中　型	Medium	83.49	48.38	23.91
小　型	Small	92.03	49.06	26.86

表 12.5 国有控股企业主要指标占全市比重(2021)
PROPORTION OF THE MAJOR INDICATORS OF ENTERPRISES WITH THE STATE HOLDING MAJOR SHARES

单位:亿元(100 million yuan)

指　标	Indicators	合　计 Total	国有控股企业 Enterprises with the State Holding Major Shares	占全市比重(%) Proportion of City(%)
工业总产值	Gross Output Value of Industry	39 975.01	14 151.91	35.4
年末资产总计	Total Assets (year-end)	53 642.41	24 610.40	45.9
流动资产合计	Current Assets	31 683.76	11 718.77	37.0
年末负债合计	Total Liabilities (year-end)	26 192.09	11 957.38	45.7
年末所有者权益	Owners Equity (year-end)	27 450.16	12 653.02	46.1
营业收入	Operating Revenue	45 402.33	16 999.19	37.4
税金及附加	Sales Tax and Addition	1 101.94	1 025.21	93.0
利润总额	Total Pre-Tax Profits	3 164.63	1 078.54	34.1
税金总额	Total Tax and Duty	1 892.32	1 418.97	75.0
亏损企业亏损额	Total Losses Made by Enterprises-in-red	397.93	179.64	45.1

表 12.6 高技术产业(制造业)主要指标(2021)
MAJOR INDICATORS OF HIGH TECHNOLOGY INDUSTRY

单位:亿元(100 million yuan)

类　别	Types	工业总产值 Gross Output Value of Industry	年末资产总计 Total Property (year-end)
总　计	**Total**	**7 996.28**	**11 101.16**
占全市比重(%)	**Proportion (%)**	**20.0**	**20.7**
按技术领域分	**Grouped by Technology Areas**		
医药制造业	Medical and Pharmaceutical Product Manufacturing	1 097.33	2 203.03
航空航天器及设备制造业	Aviation, Aircraft and Equipments Manufacturing	314.98	606.87
电子及通信设备制造业	Electron and Communicate Equipments Manufacturing	3 860.02	6 344.98
计算机及办公设备制造业	Electronic Computers and Office Equipments Manufacturing	1 937.70	764.67
医疗仪器设备及仪器仪表制造业	Medical Treatment Instrument and Meter Manufacturing	775.32	1 174.56
信息化学品制造业	Information Chemical Product Manufacturing	10.93	7.04

表 12.6 续表 1 continued

单位:亿元(100 million yuan)

类 别	Types	营业收入 Operating Revenue	营业成本 Operating Costs
总 计	**Total**	**8 411.33**	**6 958.92**
占全市比重(%)	**Proportion (%)**	**18.5**	**18.8**
按技术领域分	**Grouped by Technology Areas**		
医药制造业	Medical and Pharmaceutical Product Manufacturing	1 119.11	593.16
航空航天器及设备制造业	Aviation, Aircraft and Equipments Manufacturing	329.66	277.52
电子及通信设备制造业	Electron and Communicate Equipments Manufacturing	4 097.65	3 562.86
计算机及办公设备制造业	Electronic Computers and Office Equipments Manufacturing	1 989.51	1 945.05
医疗仪器设备及仪器仪表制造业	Medical Treatment Instrument and Meter Manufacturing	864.93	570.83
信息化学品制造业	Information Chemical Product Manufacturing	10.49	9.50

表 12.6 续表 2 continued

单位:亿元(100 million yuan)

类 别	Types	利润总额 Total Pre-tax Profits	税金总额 Total Tax and Duties
总 计	**Total**	**546.46**	**116.83**
占全市比重(%)	**Proportion (%)**	**17.3**	**6.2**
按技术领域分	**Grouped by Technology Areas**		
医药制造业	Medical and Pharmaceutical Product Manufacturing	190.40	51.85
航空航天器及设备制造业	Aviation, Aircraft and Equipments Manufacturing	-4.63	6.38
电子及通信设备制造业	Electron and Communicate Equipments Manufacturing	215.40	29.06
计算机及办公设备制造业	Electronic Computers and Office Equipments Manufacturing	17.51	3.42
医疗仪器设备及仪器仪表制造业	Medical Treatment Instrument and Meter Manufacturing	127.19	26.10
信息化学品制造业	Information Chemical Product Manufacturing	0.59	0.02

表 12.7　都市型工业主要指标(2021)
MAIN INDICATORS OF URBAN INDUSTRIES

单位:亿元(100 million yuan)

类　别	Types	工业总产值 Gross Output Value of Industry	年末资产总计 Total Assets (year-end)	营业收入 Operating Revenue
总　计	**Total**	**4 001.02**	**4 325.82**	**4 771.43**
按企业规模分	**Grouped by Size of Enterprises**			
大　型	Large	820.38	978.31	1 010.36
中　型	Medium	1 431.15	1 366.46	1 738.12
小　型	Small	1 749.50	1 981.05	2 022.94
按登记注册类型分	**Grouped by Registration Categories**			
内　资	Domestic Funded	2 205.46	2 478.61	2 703.49
#国　有	State-owned	108.67	135.23	119.74
集　体	Collective-owned	1.01	6.69	4.00
有限责任公司	Companies with Limited Liabilities	844.25	710.68	1 096.41
股份有限公司	Share-holding Companies with Limited Liabilities	141.89	316.77	240.71
私　营	Private	1 106.83	1 307.94	1 239.76
港澳台商投资	Hong Kong, Macao and Taiwan Funded	508.71	597.69	562.60
#与港澳台商合资经营	Joint-venture	102.25	137.88	119.13
港澳台商独资	Sole Funded	362.78	354.87	390.20
外商投资	Foreign Funded	1 286.85	1 249.52	1 505.34
#中外合资经营	Joint-venture	165.29	150.73	173.73
外资企业	Sole Funded	992.82	966.88	1 188.98
按行业分	**Grouped by Sectors**			
服装服饰业	Garment and Trappings	212.25	217.76	266.13
食品加工制造业	Food Processing	1 229.73	1 340.67	1 497.03
包装、印刷业	Packaging and Printing	315.67	374.58	344.54
室内装饰用品制造业	Indoor Decoration Materials and Equipments Manufacturing	671.08	734.51	746.45
化妆品及清洁洗涤用品制造业	Cosmetics and Cleaning Manufacturing	559.55	725.10	650.23
工艺美术品、旅游用品制造业	Art Crafts and Tourism Equipments Manufacturing	634.86	500.12	854.62
小型电子信息产品制造业	Small Electronic Information Products Manufacturing	377.89	433.08	412.43

表 12.7 续表 continued

单位:亿元(100 million yuan)

类 别	Types	营业成本 Operating Costs	利润总额 Total Pre-tax Profits	税金总额 Total Tax and Duties
总 计	**Total**	**3 750.56**	**377.01**	**112.19**
按企业规模分	**Grouped by Size of Enterprises**			
大 型	Large	683.54	115.07	31.66
中 型	Medium	1 392.36	149.23	39.72
小 型	Small	1 674.66	112.70	40.80
按登记注册类型分	**Grouped by Registration Categories**			
内 资	Domestic Funded	2 252.73	198.57	54.44
#国 有	State-owned	93.13	24.03	2.88
集 体	Collective-owned	2.49	0.93	0.17
有限责任公司	Companies with Limited Liabilities	981.45	56.11	14.94
股份有限公司	Share-holding Companies with Limited Liabilities	179.09	36.39	5.74
私 营	Private	993.94	81.17	30.68
港澳台商投资	Hong Kong, Macao and Taiwan Funded	419.08	27.97	14.29
#与港澳台商合资经营	Joint-venture	93.44	4.61	3.93
港澳台商独资	Sole Funded	283.40	15.54	8.85
外商投资	Foreign Funded	1 078.75	150.46	43.45
#中外合资经营	Joint-venture	138.51	12.65	3.00
外资企业	Sole Funded	838.99	123.94	36.24
按行业分	**Grouped by Sectors**			
服装服饰业	Garment and Trappings	225.31	11.91	3.60
食品加工制造业	Food Processing	1 096.58	125.41	47.10
包装、印刷业	Packaging and Printing	285.49	11.76	9.55
室内装饰用品制造业	Indoor Decoration Materials and Equipments Manufacturing	606.26	59.00	16.04
化妆品及清洁洗涤用品制造业	Cosmetics and Cleaning Manufacturing	454.30	66.87	20.72
工艺美术品、旅游用品制造业	Art Crafts and Tourism Equipments Manufacturing	750.99	67.80	10.45
小型电子信息产品制造业	Small Electronic Information Products Manufacturing	331.62	34.25	4.72

表 12.8　主要年份工业产品产量
OUTPUT OF INDUSTRIAL PRODUCTS IN MAIN YEARS

年　份 Year	精制食用植物油 (万吨) Refined Vegetable Oil (10 000 tons)	啤　酒 (亿升) Beer (100 million litres)	服　装 (亿件) Garments (100 million cases)	机制纸及纸板(万吨) Machine-Made Paper and Paperboards (10 000 tons)
1978	7.32		0.73	27.34
1980	6.77		1.19	29.57
1985	11.13		2.33	41.29
1990	13.42		2.43	46.49
1995	39.94		6.30	39.97
2000	11.55	3.04	4.45	43.54
2005	45.11	7.05	6.72	35.73
2006	72.86	7.17	6.73	85.87
2007	85.24	7.30	6.60	83.76
2008	96.88	7.27	6.10	80.46
2009	92.27	6.74	3.91	71.03
2010	85.31	6.54	5.72	86.94
2011	84.56	5.09	5.06	87.28
2012	101.70	5.95	5.04	91.46
2013	104.24	4.92	4.78	85.30
2014	109.85	6.11	5.00	92.14
2015	111.45	6.11	4.49	65.79
2016	98.76	6.08	4.04	62.08
2017	90.91	5.64	4.00	46.25
2018	83.10	5.00	3.38	16.79
2019	69.60	4.42	3.71	50.40
2020	59.73	2.89	3.05	42.33
2021	55.95	2.79	2.90	40.59

表 12.8 续表 1　continued

年　份 Year	硫酸(折 100%) (万吨) Sulfuric (100% Pure) (10 000 tons)	乙　烯 (万吨) Ethylene (10 000 tons)	化学药品原药 (万吨) Raw Chemicals (10 000 tons)	化学纤维 (万吨) Chemical Fibers (10 000 tons)
1978	34.49	12.69	0.69	11.59
1980	38.76	13.59	0.62	15.15
1985	35.22	14.02	0.59	22.49
1990	40.04	21.95	1.51	25.74
1995	31.03	40.83	3.47	37.83
2000	34.22	59.05	1.98	47.15
2005	33.32	160.44	1.27	49.78
2006	30.37	193.83	1.34	50.60
2007	30.46	187.24	1.65	51.48
2008	26.06	182.03	1.74	43.00
2009	27.02	180.30	2.57	37.91
2010	28.66	226.72	2.80	49.00
2011	27.98	197.53	2.61	51.34
2012	18.15	195.57	2.71	48.24
2013	19.47	212.00	2.90	47.76
2014	18.10	188.53	3.31	45.35
2015	19.38	210.76	4.33	45.85
2016	17.32	209.32	5.00	43.34
2017	19.02	201.20	3.89	43.44
2018	15.92	172.88	3.55	39.70
2019	8.62	211.12	5.16	41.01
2020	5.53	206.09	5.17	37.93
2021	5.89	194.87	5.00	32.47

表 12.8 续表 2 continued

年　份 Year	橡胶轮胎外胎（万条） Rubber Tires (10 000 tires)	水　泥（万吨） Cement (10 000 tons)	生　铁（万吨） Pig Iron (10 000 tons)	粗　钢（万吨） Steel (10 000 tons)
1978	149.59	139.47	149.86	476.52
1980	174.85	161.28	171.12	521.61
1985	219.00	219.31	215.37	570.16
1990	318.78	230.30	526.90	914.62
1995	639.09	433.22	1 048.38	1 454.11
2000	830.66	311.69	1 473.00	1 778.70
2005	932.27	719.97	1 582.89	1 927.96
2006	1 055.47	818.28	1 639.13	1 902.82
2007	932.54	786.24	1 790.00	2 081.58
2008	866.65	765.46	1 735.87	1 992.09
2009	849.07	754.19	1 787.48	2 032.24
2010	915.22	670.80	1 901.39	2 214.27
2011	908.26	805.56	1 947.48	2 225.48
2012	1 004.37	794.71	1 800.44	1 970.91
2013	1 079.57	750.31	1 637.58	1 811.08
2014	1 045.49	685.97	1 643.29	1 774.55
2015	971.00	433.59	1 686.66	1 783.77
2016	894.75	418.42	1 587.21	1 709.14
2017	806.03	415.73	1 447.72	1 607.70
2018	649.37	409.08	1 476.75	1 630.10
2019	625.00	429.99	1 490.07	1 640.25
2020	624.43	389.54	1 411.33	1 575.60
2021	729.75	434.97	1 390.97	1 557.06

表 12.8 续表 3 continued

年　份 Year	成品钢材（万吨） Rolled-Steel Products (10 000 tons)	汽　车（万辆） Motor Vehicles (10 000 vehicles)	其　中 of which #轿　车 Cars	发电机组（发电设备）（万千瓦） Generator Set (Power Generating Equipments) (10 000 kw)
1978	360.08	1.04	0.26	109.80
1980	412.63	1.47	0.53	58.20
1985	451.18	1.22	0.86	133.00
1990	609.59	2.81	2.46	210.20
1995	1 185.89	16.27	16.07	496.50
2000	1 544.46	25.29	25.15	179.00
2005	1 964.16	48.45	48.09	2 138.05
2006	2 129.78	65.28	64.47	2 944.71
2007	2 144.16	82.12	81.15	2 845.59
2008	2 074.95	80.65	80.00	2 831.10
2009	2 181.37	125.03	122.46	2 440.70
2010	2 475.95	169.89	159.77	2 555.60
2011	2 482.81	191.57	174.20	2 889.59
2012	2 340.76	202.43	180.68	2 886.30
2013	2 322.76	226.89	201.03	2 538.84
2014	2 309.14	247.45	214.22	3 632.46
2015	2 202.72	242.97	203.91	2 080.69
2016	2 080.14	260.77	207.39	2 561.00
2017	2 056.04	291.32	195.94	3 458.46
2018	1 983.32	297.76	194.77	3 235.62
2019	1 819.69	274.90	161.96	2 113.79
2020	1 879.61	264.68	144.49	1 882.25
2021	1 941.43	283.32	145.16	1 537.47

表 12.8 续表4 continued

年　份 Year	家用电冰箱（万台）Household Refrigerators (10 000 units)	房间空气调节器（万台）Household Airconditioners (10 000 units)	家用洗衣机（万台）Household Washing Machines (10 000 units)	家用燃气热水器（万台）Gas Water Heaters (10 000 units)
1980	0.42	0.10	0.81	
1985	20.49	0.74	113.85	
1990	53.36	1.83	101.29	
1995	128.72	62.46	144.80	34.45
2000	43.12	186.08	62.11	32.27
2005	42.68	358.57	183.26	65.64
2006	101.08	410.60	288.74	69.89
2007	100.66	395.21	289.68	80.46
2008	123.21	387.12	234.63	67.89
2009	189.15	317.78	207.79	59.35
2010	218.55	400.41	216.57	103.70
2011	185.19	619.91	218.96	104.44
2012	151.63	584.10	197.12	106.49
2013	153.93	410.00	184.23	126.22
2014	153.98	403.53	181.93	171.47
2015	148.18	327.33	160.27	173.62
2016	56.38	349.00	163.21	185.88
2017	54.74	389.74	148.76	200.58
2018	46.08	382.84	140.07	178.93
2019	33.81	314.20	147.75	173.51
2020	21.15	231.23	133.96	155.89
2021	0	261.04	129.88	207.17

表 12.8 续表5 continued

年　份 Year	微型计算机设备（万部）Personal Computers (10 000 units)	彩色电视机（万台）Color TV Set (10 000 units)	集成电路（万块）Semi-conduct IC (10 000 units)	发电量（亿千瓦时）Electric Power Generation (100 million kwh)
1978		0.24		199.32
1980		0.55		206.41
1985		71.75		256.25
1990	0.77	81.48	1 167	284.10
1995	4.07	111.77	15 290	403.42
2000	42.04	147.97	239 330	553.09
2005	2 176.17	145.46	677 003	728.74
2006	2 670.09	251.67	640 483	710.96
2007	4 478.78	158.37	891 138	737.80
2008	5 767.97	185.78	830 487	773.54
2009	7 320.15	195.51	722 883	778.20
2010	9 388.44	254.03	1 134 629	876.19
2011	10 162.53	224.63	1 663 143	946.96
2012	9 804.83	142.87	1 602 978	886.19
2013	8 101.30	99.38	1 613 762	959.51
2014	6 295.42	155.28	2 233 261	792.30
2015	3 651.98	135.39	2 173 552	792.70
2016	3 083.95	115.41	2 380 730	872.29
2017	2 487.32	136.12	2 331 854	830.26
2018	1 448.81	144.38	2 334 807	824.66
2019	1 121.69	135.75	2 075 941	792.65
2020	1 799.51	158.74	2 886 703	819.01
2021	3 093.27	153.50	3 649 451	956.78

表 12.9 主要工业产品生产、销售总量(2021)
OUTPUT AND SALES OF MAIN INDUSTRIAL PRODUCTS

产品名称	Product	单 位 Unit	生产量 Output	销售量 Sales
精制食用植物油	Refined Vegetable Oil	万吨（10 000 tons）	55.95	60.94
糖 果	Candy	万吨（10 000 tons）	20.31	20.49
乳制品	Dairy Product	万吨（10 000 tons）	54.43	54.30
啤 酒	Beer	亿升（100 million liters）	2.79	2.81
饮 料	Beverage	万吨（10 000 tons）	302.49	293.09
卷 烟	Cigarettes	亿支(100 million pieces)	875.22	882.34
纱	Yarn	万吨（10 000 tons）	1.30	1.29
布	Cloth	亿米（100 million m）	0.65	0.65
服 装	Garments	亿件（100 million cases）	2.90	2.92
皮革鞋靴	Leather Shoes	万双（10 000 pairs）	321	324
复合木地板	Flooring	万平方米(10 000 sq.m)	1 313.81	1 346.78
机制纸及纸板	Paperboard	万吨（10 000 tons）	40.59	35.05
汽 油	Gasoline	万吨（10 000 tons）	541.60	544.65
柴 油	Diesel Oil	万吨（10 000 tons）	552.58	551.75
焦 炭	Coke	万吨（10 000 tons）	540.86	95.70
硫 酸(折 100%)	Sulphuric Acid(100% Pure)	万吨（10 000 tons）	5.89	5.91
烧 碱(折 100%)	Caustic Soda(100% Pure)	万吨（10 000 tons）	76.37	71.25
乙 烯	Ethylene	万吨（10 000 tons）	194.87	41.79
化学农药原药(折有效成分 100%)	Chemical Pesticide Technical (100% Pure)	万吨（10 000 tons）	1.37	1.39
涂 料	Coating	万吨（10 000 tons）	268.13	267.68
初级形态塑料	Primary Form Plastic	万吨（10 000 tons）	345.81	345.19
合成橡胶	Synthetic Rubber	万吨（10 000 tons）	28.64	25.22
合成洗涤剂	Synthetic Detergents	万吨（10 000 tons）	61.36	60.79
化学药品原药	Raw Chemicals	万吨（10 000 tons）	5.00	4.66
化学纤维	Chemical Fibers	万吨（10 000 tons）	32.47	31.04
橡胶轮胎外胎	Outer Cover of Rubber Tyre	万条（10 000 tires）	729.75	701.82
水 泥	Cement	万吨（10 000 tons）	434.97	427.64

表 12.9 续表 continued

产品名称	Product	单　位 Unit	生产量 Output	销售量 Sales
生　铁	Pig Iron	万吨（10 000 tons）	1 390.97	0.93
粗　钢	Steel	万吨（10 000 tons）	1 577.06	25.80
成品钢材	Rolled-steel Products	万吨（10 000 tons）	1 941.43	1 945.05
铜　材	Copper Materials	万吨（10 000 tons）	41.88	41.66
金属集装箱	Metal Container	万立方米（10 000 cu.m）	2 337.15	2 269.36
发动机	Engines	万千瓦（10 000 kw）	27 884.34	19 382.81
金属切削机床	Metal-cutting Machines	台(unit)	4 564	4 640
#数控金属切削机床	Digital Machine Tools	台(unit)	1 433	1 463
汽　车	Motor Vehicles	万辆（10 000 vehicles）	283.32	282.64
#轿　车	Cars	万辆（10 000 vehicles）	145.16	145.57
#新能源汽车	New Energy Vehicles	万辆（10 000 vehicles）	63.19	63.19
民用钢质船舶	Civil Steel Ships	万载重吨（10 000 syn-tons）	553.97	553.97
两轮脚踏自行车	Bicycles	万辆（10 000 vehicles）	113.39	113.39
发电机组(发电设备)	Generator Set(Power Generating Equipments)	万千瓦（10 000 kw）	1 537.47	1 502.49
电力电缆	Electric Cable	万公里（10 000 km）	285.54	308.16
房间空气调节器	Household Air-conditioners	万台（10 000 units）	261.04	260.89
家用吸排油烟机	Range Hoods	万台（10 000 units）	8.68	10.48
电饭锅	Electric Rice Cookers	万个（10 000 units）	4.52	4.52
微波炉	Microwave Oven	万台（10 000 units）	253.54	254.90
家用洗衣机	Household Washing Machines	万台（10 000 units）	129.88	130.03
家用吸尘器	Vacuum Cleaners	万台（10 000 units）	112.34	108.33
家用燃气热水器	Gas Water Heaters	万台（10 000 units）	207.17	203.89
微型计算机设备	Personal Computers	万台（10 000 units）	3 093.27	3 149.98
移动通信手持机(手机)	Mobile Phone	万台（10 000 units）	2 892.24	3 006.04
彩色电视机	Color Television Sets	万台（10 000 units）	153.50	154.49
集成电路	Integrated Circuits	亿块（100 million units）	364.95	360.29
集成电路圆片	Wafer	万片（10 000 units）	1 117.30	1 097.27
光学仪器	Optical Instruments	万台（10 000 units）	128.23	128.27

表 12.10 大型工业企业主要指标(2021)
MAJOR INDICATORS OF LARGE SIZED INDUSTRIAL ENTERPRISES

类别	Types	工业总产值 Gross Output Value of Industry	年末资产总计 Total Assets (year-end)
总计	**Total**	**19 050.58**	**26 943.81**
按隶属关系分	**Grouped by Subordination**		
中央工业	Central Government	5 532.69	9 411.60
地方工业及其他	Local Government and others	13 517.89	17 532.22
按工业总产值分	**Grouped by Gross Output Value of Industry**		
10 亿元及以上	1000 million yuan and above	18 845.51	26 501.19
5~9.99 亿元	500~999 million yuan	174.37	369.81
5 亿元以下	Below 500 million yuan	30.71	72.82
按工业行业分	**Grouped by Sectors**		
制造业	**Manufacture Industry**	**18 063.57**	**24 345.23**
农副食品加工业	Farm and Sideline Products Processing	26.12	29.21
食品制造业	Food Manufacturing	249.11	300.87
酒、饮料和精制茶制造业	Wine, Beverage and Refined Tea Manufacturing	50.43	47.84
烟草制品业	Tabacco Manufacturing	975.59	1 733.64
纺织业	Textile	16.52	23.63
纺织服装、服饰业	Textiles and Clothing Industry	10.83	12.89
皮革、毛皮、羽毛及其制品和制鞋业	Leather, Fur, Wool Products and Shoes Manufacturing	80.57	202.05
家具制造业	Furniture Manufacturing	112.32	140.09
造纸和纸制品业	Paper Making and Paper Products Industry	4.95	3.14
印刷和记录媒介复制业	Printing and Record Duplicating	30.36	36.23
文教、工美、体育和娱乐用品制造业	Culture, Education, Industrial Arts, Sports and Entertainment Goods Manufacturing	81.28	111.02
石油、煤炭及其他燃料加工业	Oil, Coal and Other Fuel Processing	1 231.39	831.69

单位：亿元(100 million yuan)

年末负债合计 Total Liabilities (year-end)	营业收入 Operating Revenue	营业成本 Operating Costs	利润总额 Total Pre-tax Profits	税金总额 Total Tax and Duties	成本费用总额 Total Costs and Expenses
13 176.59	**21 868.72**	**17 931.56**	**1 437.66**	**1 413.74**	**19 957.46**
4 014.17	6 536.75	5 036.08	451.00	1 044.36	5 332.14
9 162.42	15 331.97	12 895.48	986.66	369.39	14 625.32
12 949.93	21 615.61	17 746.70	1 435.95	1 404.18	19 694.26
153.98	202.36	145.91	22.40	7.57	191.08
72.68	50.74	38.96	-20.69	1.99	72.12
12 212.85	**20 769.35**	**16 866.86**	**1 428.41**	**1 385.27**	**18 859.04**
12.32	23.14	16.36	3.25	0.92	22.41
180.66	373.35	251.09	17.58	9.39	358.61
29.73	55.53	35.16	3.27	1.92	52.06
264.18	1 069.48	184.94	227.25	751.86	228.89
2.30	15.79	9.83	2.72	0.61	13.07
6.34	13.03	9.54	0.72	0.38	12.93
27.51	59.96	53.37	3.26	-0.21	56.70
109.08	118.89	89.68	27.66	3.29	110.59
1.89	5.84	5.05	0.27	0.03	5.59
4.87	29.05	23.46	1.18	1.05	27.80
35.01	86.67	57.56	16.35	2.32	71.67
361.60	1 246.77	973.95	60.60	236.85	1 002.84

表 12.10 续表 continued

	类别 Types	工业总产值 Gross Output Value of Industry	年末资产总计 Total Assets (year-end)
化学原料和化学制品制造业	Raw Chemical Materials and Chemical Products Manufacturing	844.59	844.50
医药制造业	Medicine Manufacturing	218.08	411.24
橡胶和塑料制品业	Rubber and Plastic Products Manufacturing	119.43	116.46
非金属矿物制品业	Non-metallic Mineral Products Manufacturing	31.64	57.28
黑色金属冶炼和压延加工业	Ferrous Metal Smelting and Rolling Processing Industry	1 050.33	2 286.41
金属制品业	Metal Products Manufacturing	148.79	111.60
通用设备制造业	General Equipment Manufacturing	1 212.49	2 207.09
专用设备制造业	Special Purpose Equipment Manufacturing	399.10	603.42
汽车制造业	The Automotive Manufacturing	5 519.81	6 846.56
铁路、船舶、航空航天和其他运输设备制造业	The Railroad, Marine, Aerospace and Other Transportation Equipment Manufacturing	685.44	1 856.47
电气机械和器材制造业	Electric Machinery Equipments and Manufacturing	881.86	966.90
计算机、通信和其他电子设备制造业	Computer, Communications and Other Electronic Equipment Manufacturing	3 864.78	4 335.73
仪器仪表制造业	Instrumentation Manufacturing	62.22	43.52
其他制造业	Other Manufacturing	20.38	20.49
金属制品、机械和设备修理业	Metal Products, Machinery and Equipment Repair Industry	135.20	165.28
电力、热力、燃气及水生产和供应业	**Electricity, Heat, Gas and Water Production and Supply Industry**	**987.01**	**2 598.59**
电力、热力生产和供应业	Production and Supply of Electricity and Thermal Power	919.42	1 754.97
燃气生产和供应业	Production and Supply of Gas	39.51	97.97
水的生产和供应业	Production and Supply of Water	28.08	745.65

单位:亿元(100 million yuan)

年末负债合计 Total Liabilities (year-end)	营业收入 Operating Revenue	营业成本 Operating Costs	利润总额 Total Pre-tax Profits	税金总额 Total Tax and Duties	成本费用总额 Total Costs and Expenses
323.58	1 029.74	796.29	142.19	24.33	887.91
184.33	244.86	132.82	7.93	12.24	238.68
46.48	121.37	83.51	17.87	4.68	102.99
42.03	38.33	30.28	3.78	0.52	34.27
818.13	1 702.30	1 572.86	101.63	3.29	1 639.05
66.75	161.13	120.13	28.87	-2.86	132.35
1 521.43	1 349.14	1 117.66	71.14	17.27	1 273.57
295.09	455.89	332.43	55.63	8.90	408.74
3 530.67	6 409.12	5 314.97	478.41	260.36	6 117.95
1 445.90	757.50	703.34	-2.55	11.23	768.43
617.74	1 152.94	971.98	55.79	19.76	1 096.90
2 169.92	4 015.55	3 798.96	89.82	10.67	3 973.38
17.71	68.91	55.65	6.78	0.20	61.87
6.10	20.56	13.21	3.17	1.15	17.28
91.51	144.51	112.79	3.85	5.09	142.50
963.74	**1 099.37**	**1 064.70**	**9.25**	**28.47**	**1 098.42**
625.48	995.66	974.84	5.75	26.07	992.09
67.59	47.66	38.91	2.07	0.98	48.85
270.67	56.05	50.95	1.43	1.43	57.48

表 12.11 中型工业企业主要指标(2021)
MAJOR INDICATORS OF MEDIUM SIZED INDUSTRIAL ENTERPRISES

类 别	Types	工业总产值 Gross Output Value of Industry	年末资产总计 Total Assets (year-end)
总 计	**Total**	**8 903.99**	**12 143.04**
按隶属关系分	**Grouped by Subordination**		
中央工业	Central Government	531.45	1 481.66
地方工业及其他	Local Government and others	8 372.54	10 661.38
按工业总产值分	**Grouped by Gross Output Value of Industry**		
10 亿元及以上	1 billion yuan and above	5 674.14	6 540.33
5~9.99 亿元	500~999 million yuan	1 965.43	3 100.62
1~4.99 亿元	100~499 million yuan	1 249.59	2 425.29
5000~9999 万元	50~99.99 million yuan	13.83	63.82
5000 万元以下	Below 50 million yuan	1.0	12.98
按工业行业分	**Grouped by Sectors**		
采矿业	**Mining Industry**	**49.34**	**272.96**
石油和天然气开采业	Petroleum and Natural Gas Exploiting	49.34	272.96
制造业	**Manufacture Industry**	**8 738.82**	**10 973.27**
农副食品加工业	Farm and Sideline Products Processing	104.31	75.58
食品制造业	Food Manufacturing	328.79	335.76
酒、饮料和精制茶制造业	Wine, Beverage and Refined Tea Manufacturing	12.78	17.53
纺织业	Textile	46.58	30.96
纺织服装、服饰业	Textiles and Clothing Industry	45.88	35.16
皮革、毛皮、羽毛及其制品和制鞋业	Leather, Fur, Wool Products and Shoes Manufacturing	12.97	8.53
木材加工和木、竹、藤、棕、草制品业	Timber Processing and Timber, Bamboo, Rattan, Coir and Straw Products Manufacturing	20.59	35.90
家具制造业	Furniture Manufacturing	64.58	78.12
造纸和纸制品业	Paper-making and Paper Products Manufacturing	81.76	110.73
印刷和记录媒介复制业	Printing and Record Duplicating	68.54	96.05

单位:亿元(100 million yuan)

年末负债合计 Total Liabilities (year-end)	营业收入 Operating Revenue	营业成本 Operating Costs	利润总额 Total Pre-tax Profits	税金总额 Total Tax and Duties	成本费用总额 Total Costs and Expenses
5 874.43	**10 138.54**	**8 191.65**	**812.67**	**190.51**	**9 430.88**
873.85	653.08	612.53	-8.76	14.22	678.98
5 000.58	9 485.46	7 579.12	821.43	176.30	8 751.90
3 454.25	6 388.38	5 302.75	532.86	108.27	5 912.82
1 335.33	2 213.92	1 708.90	199.45	44.18	2 048.66
1 046.27	1 472.45	1 136.55	76.90	35.22	1 409.06
36.58	56.52	39.50	3.52	2.66	52.99
2.0	7.27	3.95	-0.07	0.19	7.35
174.62	**47.37**	**34.0**	**6.97**	**4.53**	**38.80**
174.62	47.37	34.0	6.97	4.53	38.80
5 111.97	**9 899.52**	**7 948.87**	**828.80**	**184.57**	**9 155.28**
36.37	128.91	102.89	11.76	1.88	117.81
163.90	322.73	193.30	57.18	19.01	271.81
6.67	14.20	9.50	0.32	1.12	13.47
9.76	47.64	41.85	2.24	0.66	45.59
15.32	51.96	43.45	1.71	0.86	50.59
3.59	12.60	10.11	0.65	-0 .02	11.94
13.49	23.78	18.78	1.90	0.85	21.52
47.00	75.61	63.19	4.29	1.91	72.72
44.23	123.07	81.07	15.85	3.97	107.23
35.35	81.72	64.0	4.40	2.54	78.35

表 12.11 续表 continued

类别	Types	工业总产值 Gross Output Value of Industry	年末资产总计 Total Assets (year-end)
文教、工美、体育和娱乐用品制造业	Culture, Education, Industrial Arts, Sports and Entertainment Goods Manufacturing	372.65	177.98
化学原料和化学制品制造业	Raw Chemical Materials and Chemical Products Manufacturing	1 225.82	1 210.80
医药制造业	Medicine Manufacturing	539.12	1 178.76
橡胶和塑料制品业	Rubber and Plastic Products Manufacturing	246.15	437.35
非金属矿物制品业	Non-metallic Mineral Products Manufacturing	239.67	402.03
黑色金属冶炼和压延加工业	Ferrous Metal Smelting and Rolling Processing Industry	258.86	135.03
有色金属冶炼和压延加工业	Nonferrous Metal Smelting and Rolling Processing Industry	194.98	148.24
金属制品业	Metal Products Manufacturing	325.10	410.05
通用设备制造业	General Equipment Manufacturing	897.76	1 151.97
专用设备制造业	Special Purpose Equipment Manufacturing	577.31	1 039.63
汽车制造业	The Automotive Manufacturing	1 008.26	1 219.71
铁路、船舶、航空航天和其他运输设备制造业	The Railroad, Marine, Aerospace and Other Transportation Equipment Manufacturing	74.90	163.82
电气机械和器材制造业	Electric Machinery Equipments and Manufacturing	740.06	859.72
计算机、通信和其他电子设备制造业	Computer, Communications and Other Electronic Equipment Manufacturing	976.68	1 246.21
仪器仪表制造业	Instrumentation Manufacturing	151.07	195.64
其他制造业	Other Manufacturing	20.17	26.45
废弃资源综合利用业	Comprehensive Utilization of Waste Resources	5.73	11.02
金属制品、机械和设备修理业	Metal Products, Machinery and Equipment Repair Industry	97.73	134.52
电力、热力、燃气及水生产和供应业	**Electricity, Heat, Gas and Water Production and Supply Industry**	**115.82**	**896.81**
电力、热力生产和供应业	Production and Supply of Electricity and Thermal Power	59.80	603.60
燃气生产和供应业	Production and Supply of Gas	24.43	68.72
水的生产和供应业	Production and Supply of Water	31.60	224.50

单位:亿元(100 million yuan)

年末负债合计 Total Liabilities (year-end)	营业收入 Operating Revenue	营业成本 Operating Costs	利润总额 Total Pre-tax Profits	税金总额 Total Tax and Duties	成本费用总额 Total Costs and Expenses
112.58	566.60	537.54	27.63	4.23	548.40
557.19	1 367.76	1 100.30	128.94	26.10	1 247.83
365.03	520.05	276.41	101.64	22.71	429.48
152.65	320.66	261.52	33.75	4.63	295.90
254.66	282.39	236.98	22.50	4.83	263.37
61.06	273.11	252.34	11.68	2.41	263.22
70.77	246.86	228.18	6.22	1.23	240.16
240.86	404.74	337.15	26.59	5.17	377.19
529.16	1 019.15	821.70	86.10	22.54	940.78
478.71	650.32	497.27	59.99	14.73	595.57
660.62	1 143.24	954.01	71.82	17.13	1 081.88
97.87	86.57	71.51	3.36	2.30	84.53
434.0	829.09	666.38	74.79	13.37	757.56
537.40	1 020.09	861.43	48.58	4.35	975.11
71.14	169.41	116.11	29.35	4.40	148.23
14.38	19.80	14.86	1.02	0.41	18.78
4.42	5.74	2.50	2.68	0.29	3.28
93.78	91.71	84.55	-8.15	0 .95	92.96
587.84	**191.66**	**208.77**	**- 23.09**	**1.42**	**236.81**
440.50	116.69	144.25	-21.26	-0.96	157.60
35.68	29.89	23.09	1.28	0.65	30.27
111.66	45.08	41.43	-3.12	1.73	48.94

表 12.12 小型工业企业主要指标(2021)
MAJOR INDICATORS OF SMALL SIZED INDUSTRIAL ENTERPRISES

类别	Types	工业总产值 Gross Output Value of Industry	年末资产总计 Total Assets (year-end)
总计	**Total**	**12 020.44**	**14 555.56**
按隶属关系分	**Grouped by Subordination**		
中央工业	Central Government	494.12	716.33
地方工业及其他	Local Government and others	11 526.32	13 839.23
按工业总产值分	**Grouped by Gross Output Value of Industry**		
5 亿元及以上	500 million yuan and above	4 586.60	4 178.28
1~4.99 亿元	100~499 million yuan	4 833.79	6 250.41
5000~9999 万元	50~99.99 million yuan	1 621.34	2 324.79
5000 万元以下	Below 50 million yuan	978.70	1 802.07
按工业行业分	**Grouped by Sectors**		
采矿业	**Mining Industry**	**6.35**	**35.88**
石油和天然气开采业	Petroleum and Natural Gas Exploiting	6.35	35.88
制造业	**Manufacture Industry**	**11 250.64**	**13 380.38**
农副食品加工业	Farm and Sideline Products Processing	260.98	247.33
食品制造业	Food Manufacturing	240.57	278.97
酒、饮料和精制茶制造业	Wine, Beverage and Refined Tea Manufacturing	56.22	100.90
烟草制品业	Tabacco Manufacturing	5.73	4.83
纺织业	Textile	128.96	129.07
纺织服装、服饰业	Textiles and Clothing Industry	168.92	149.59
皮革、毛皮、羽毛及其制品和制鞋业	Leather, Fur, Wool Products and Shoes Manufacturing	30.79	53.57
木材加工和木、竹、藤、棕、草制品业	Timber Processing and Timber, Bamboo, Rattan, Coir and Straw Products Manufacturing	24.97	18.70
家具制造业	Furniture Manufacturing	137.15	138.90
造纸和纸制品业	Paper-making and Paper Products Manufacturing	184.78	177.15
印刷和记录媒介复制业	Printing and Record Duplicating	114.42	145.87

单位：亿元（100 million yuan）

年末负债合计 Total Liabilities (year-end)	营业收入 Operation Revenue	营业成本 Operating Costs	利润总额 Total Pre-tax Profits	税金总额 Total Tax and Duties	成本费用总额 Total Costs and Expenses
7 141.08	**13 395.07**	**10 981.35**	**914.30**	**288.06**	**12 602.50**
376.76	579.18	530.14	20.91	14.76	567.21
6 764.31	12 815.89	10 451.21	893.39	273.30	12 035.29
2 158.52	5 047.05	4 367.89	357.44	83.77	4 706.88
2 874.22	5 290.92	4 210.65	409.37	119.0	4 935.03
1 136.35	1 813.92	1 417.63	110.15	49.74	1 730.55
971.99	1 243.17	985.17	37.34	35.56	1 230.05
8.79	**6.97**	**6.04**	**0.34**	**0.88**	**6.42**
8.79	6.97	6.04	0.34	0.88	6.42
6 640.69	**12 583.93**	**10 207.89**	**882.08**	**271.64**	**11 799.44**
142.98	354.09	317.33	12.34	3.70	346.77
142.05	267.22	208.50	19.22	8.75	249.57
53.25	63.24	43.27	7.50	3.19	56.36
2.14	6.02	4.09		0.29	6.04
62.02	152.69	126.88	8.19	1.89	144.77
89.77	210.49	184.68	7.44	1.72	206.51
26.38	34.77	29.77	0.78	0.03	34.27
10.75	28.11	23.59	1.14	0 .77	26.96
86.23	151.07	124.64	5.96	3.45	145.36
84.58	206.76	180.58	5.79	3.62	202.11
74.55	120.42	99.05	2.49	3.79	118.88

表 12.12 续表 continued

	类 别 Types	工业总产值 Gross Output Value of Industry	年末资产总计 Total Assets (year-end)
文教、工美、体育和娱乐用品制造业	Culture, Education, Industrial Arts, Sports and Entertainment Goods Manufacturing	95.23	110.94
石油、煤炭及其他燃料加工业	Oil, Coal and Other Fuel Processing	65.88	32.63
化学原料和化学制品制造业	Raw Chemical Materials and Chemical Products Manufacturing	1 701.28	1 689.84
医药制造业	Medicine Manufacturing	340.13	613.03
化学纤维制造业	Chemical Fiber Manufacturing	22.31	23.58
橡胶和塑料制品业	Rubber and Plastic Products Manufacturing	650.15	715.03
非金属矿物制品业	Non-metallic Mineral Products Manufacturing	643.46	771.58
黑色金属冶炼和压延加工业	Ferrous Metal Smelting and Rolling Processing Industry	240.24	209.79
有色金属冶炼和压延加工业	Nonferrous Metal Smelting and Rolling Processing Industry	305.76	174.69
金属制品业	Metal Products Manufacturing	697.29	859.33
通用设备制造业	General Equipment Manufacturing	1 358.72	1 782.72
专用设备制造业	Special Purpose Equipment Manufacturing	748.58	1 231.47
汽车制造业	The Automotive Manufacturing	924.60	905.14
铁路、船舶、航空航天和其他运输设备制造业	The Railroad, Marine, Aerospace and Other Transportation Equipment Manufacturing	107.47	164.18
电气机械和器材制造业	Electric Machinery Equipments and Manufacturing	1 030.41	1 246.15
计算机、通信和其他电子设备制造业	Computer, Communications and Other Electronic Equipment Manufacturing	587.88	909.59
仪器仪表制造业	Instrumentation Manufacturing	273.66	367.35
其他制造业	Other Manufacturing	20.99	28.57
废弃资源综合利用业	Comprehensive Utilization of Waste Resources	44.08	53.79
金属制品、机械和设备修理业	Metal Products, Machinery and Equipment Repair Industry	39.02	46.11
电力、热力、燃气及水生产和供应业	**Electricity, Heat, Gas and Water Production and Supply Industry**	**763.44**	**1 139.30**
电力、热力生产和供应业	Production and Supply of Electricity and Thermal Power	335.05	573.75
燃气生产和供应业	Production and Supply of Gas	392.17	354.79
水的生产和供应业	Production and Supply of Water	36.22	210.76

单位:亿元(100 million yuan)

年末负债合计 Total Liabilities (year-end)	营业收入 Operation Revenue	营业成本 Operating Costs	利润总额 Total Pre-tax Profits	税金总额 Total Tax and Duties	成本费用总额 Total Costs and Expenses
50.28	111.24	92.75	15.86	1.47	105.20
17.58	82.48	73.36	3.49	1.71	78.63
656.67	1 893.10	1 526.93	173.18	41.82	1 721.24
214.13	354.20	183.93	80.83	16.89	290.09
11.68	23.71	20.93	1.05	0.47	22.78
289.19	721.57	588.00	48.18	14.43	676.49
520.98	714.69	618.61	34.10	20.42	680.72
130.68	301.83	279.08	11.10	2.63	290.78
97.11	331.05	307.56	8.27	2.80	323.05
452.42	828.30	700.88	43.90	15.28	795.17
926.43	1 480.24	1 148.34	120.98	33.93	1 365.99
616.37	804.92	594.19	68.42	20.45	745.48
516.67	1 001.97	861.45	44.10	18.21	962.89
84.64	116.19	90.10	7.32	2.97	109.51
603.38	1 142.55	934.90	63.44	20.50	1 085.21
462.98	668.42	545.78	42.74	12.42	634.64
152.08	300.74	211.47	32.76	9.21	271.82
15.97	22.10	15.89	1.50	0.62	20.55
23.32	44.05	35.93	4.42	2.22	40.76
23.44	45.69	35.43	5.57	1.99	40.83
491.60	**804.17**	**767.43**	**31.89**	**15.54**	**796.65**
287.96	344.45	320.99	11.66	11.35	337.87
115.90	417.24	416.94	11.51	2.95	423.97
87.74	42.48	29.50	8.72	1.24	34.81

表 12.13 国家级、市级工业园区主要经济指标(2021)
MAJOR ECONOMIC INDICATORS OF MUNICIPAL AND NATIONAL INDUSTRIAL ZONE

指 标 Indicators		国家级开发区 National Level Develop Zone	其 中 of which	
			上海张江高新技术产业开发区 Zhangjiang High and New Technical Industrial Development Zone	上海外高桥保税区 Shanghai Waigaoqiao Free Trade Zone
工业总产值	Gross Output Value of Industry	12 446.43	1 728.26	501.40
年末资产总计	Total Assets (year-end)	16 667.18	5 790.22	458.81
流动资产合计	Total Current Assets	8 946.83	2 650.42	358.51
年末负债合计	Total Liabilities (year-end)	7 213.28	1 811.14	216.17
年末所有者权益	Owners' Equity (year-end)	9 453.90	3 979.08	242.64
营业收入	Operating Revenue	14 177.49	2 160.17	572.54
营业成本	Operating Costs	11 888.05	1 719.38	486.93
利润总额	Total Pre-tax Profits	1 123.90	320.04	36.06
税金总额	Total Tax and Duties	307.36	50.74	4.54
亏损企业亏损额	Total Losses Made by Enterprises-in-red	79.55	36.04	1.23

表 12.13 续表 1 continued

指 标 Indicators		其 中 of which		
		上海松江综合保税区 Shanghai Songjiang Comprehensive Bonded Zone	青浦综合保税区 Qingpu Comprehensive Bonded Area	上海化学工业经济技术开发区 Chemical Industry Economic and Technological Development Zone
工业总产值	Gross Output Value of Industry	1 660.51	73.81	1 319.52
年末资产总计	Total Assets (year-end)	596.63	67.51	1 183.65
流动资产合计	Total Current Assets	512.21	47.95	589.74
年末负债合计	Total Liabilities (year-end)	455.32	40.48	528.51
年末所有者权益	Owners' Equity (year-end)	141.31	27.03	655.14
营业收入	Prime Operating Revenue	1 680.07	75.82	1 431.65
营业成本	Operating Costs	1 656.62	65.99	1 147.83
利润总额	Total Pre-tax Profits	9.16	4.29	221.13
税金总额	Total Tax and Duties	0.52	0.24	28.62
亏损企业亏损额	Total Losses Made by Enterprises-in-red	0.45	0.23	11.44

单位：亿元(100 million yuan)

其　中　of which						
虹桥经济技术开发区 Hongqiao Economic and Technological Development Zone	洋山特殊综合保税区 Yangshan Special Comprehensive Bonded Zone	闵行经济技术开发区 Minhang Hi-tec Park	漕河泾综合保税区 Caohejing Comprehensive Bonded Zone	上海紫竹高新技术产业开发区 Zizhu High and New Technical Industrial Development Zone	上海陆家嘴金融贸易区 Lujiazui Financial Trade Zone	上海金桥经济技术开发区 Jinqiao Economic and Technological Development Zone
0.92	2.45	899.30	269.03	170.57	1 097.74	2 548.27
0.79	1.63	1 059.92	170.95	174.21	2 159.81	2 307.67
0.78	1.47	774.55	152.51	104.19	381.55	1 531.17
0.41	0.24	631.78	119.55	70.32	841.93	1 296.80
0.38	1.39	428.13	51.40	103.88	1 317.88	1 010.87
1.01	2.83	997.10	301.20	152.76	1 287.64	3 081.17
0.84	2.57	745.58	295.46	75.15	1 237.75	2 538.95
0.04	0.17	96.77	3.42	38.70	16.84	178.12
0.01	0.03	22.60	1.15	10.20	31.64	110.93
		3.78	1.70	0.56	0.44	5.15

单位：亿元(100 million yuan)

其　中　of which			市级开发区 Municipal Level Development Zone	其　中　of which		
奉贤综合保税区 Fengxian Comprehensive Bonded Zone	漕河泾开发区浦江高科技园 Pujiang Hi-Tech Park of Caohejing Development Zone	上海松江经济技术开发区 Songjiang Economic and Technological Development Zone		上海新杨工业园区 Xinyang Industrial Park	上海未来岛高新技术产业园区 Weilai Island High and New Technical Industrial Park	上海市市北高新技术服务园区 Shibei Hi-Tech Park
73.32	149.79	1 951.52	9 422.81	11.16	40.36	7.67
54.22	258.52	2 382.64	12 306.47	37.89	71.03	13.94
48.69	178.94	1 614.15	8 085.25	15.68	54.01	10.31
36.99	123.69	1 039.94	6 019.78	10.41	30.86	5.83
17.23	134.83	1 342.69	6 286.53	27.48	40.17	8.11
72.94	160.71	2 199.87	10 628.61	17.40	54.37	9.59
64.89	104.30	1 745.82	8 438.32	15.01	40.81	7.43
1.47	22.48	175.20	896.12	0.82	7.64	0.83
0.04	5.51	40.58	214.88	0.36	2.18	0.13
	5.45	13.06	72.07	0.26	1.78	

表 12.13 续表 2 continued

指 标	Indicators	其 中 of which		
		上海市莘庄工业园区 Xinzhuang Industrial Park	上海宝山工业园区 Baoshan Industrial Park	上海月杨工业园区 Yueyang Industrial Park
工业总产值	Gross Output Value of Industry	1 224.76	516.36	313.49
年末资产总计	Total Assets (year-end)	1 672.58	867.71	374.59
流动资产合计	Total Current Assets	1 204.91	546.05	246.83
年末负债合计	Total Liabilities (year-end)	841.86	501.40	184.22
年末所有者权益	Owners' Equity (year-end)	830.73	366.31	190.37
营业收入	Operating Revenue	1 389.32	672.47	335.04
营业成本	Operating Costs	1 082.91	548.39	272.32
利润总额	Total Pre-tax Profits	141.08	43.02	24.12
税金总额	Total Tax and Duties	28.59	11.11	6.66
亏损企业亏损额	Total Losses Made by Enterprises-in-red	7.21	10.73	3.39

表 12.13 续表 3 continued

指 标	Indicators	其 中 of which		
		上海松江经济开发区 Songjiang Economic Development Zone	上海青浦工业园区 Qingpu Industrial Park	上海西郊工业园区 Xijiao Economic Development Zone
工业总产值	Gross Output Value of Industry	313.05	1 044.43	211.56
年末资产总计	Total Assets (year-end)	331.00	1 393.45	260.55
流动资产合计	Total Current Assets	249.83	915.93	180.19
年末负债合计	Total Liabilities (year-end)	169.93	612.95	122.78
年末所有者权益	Owners' Equity (year-end)	161.08	780.35	137.78
营业收入	Operating Revenue	327.49	1 183.72	246.70
营业成本	Operating Costs	267.58	903.66	204.80
利润总额	Total Pre-tax Profits	18.80	92.32	14.39
税金总额	Total Tax and Duties	4.78	29.13	5.06
亏损企业亏损额	Total Losses Made by Enterprises-in-red	2.83	8.18	0.77

单位：亿元(100 million yuan)

其中 of which						
上海嘉定工业园区 Jiading Industrial Park	上海嘉定汽车产业园区 Jiading Automobile Industrial Park	上海浦东空港工业园区 Pudong Konggang Industrial Park	上海浦东合庆工业园区 Pudong Heqing Industrial Park	上海朱泾工业园区 Zhujing Industrial Park	上海枫泾工业园区 Fengjing Industrial Park	上海金山工业园区 Jinshan Industrial Park
1 637.17	871.01	227.69	239.26	50.75	145.51	1 121.56
2 043.10	734.17	281.10	328.38	81.53	178.45	1 609.83
1 451.62	545.48	192.00	220.18	44.21	128.40	904.72
1 072.47	424.15	126.47	151.31	53.79	70.83	770.19
970.62	310.03	154.63	177.06	27.74	107.62	839.63
1 843.41	946.19	239.56	264.05	54.94	145.97	1 328.10
1 461.24	792.65	183.18	212.48	43.04	117.46	1 129.13
159.18	51.63	25.59	25.46	3.95	13.36	68.46
35.93	12.81	4.32	4.16	1.45	2.70	22.84
7.36	1.98	1.48	0.52	0.32	0.38	15.48

单位：亿元(100 million yuan)

其中 of which						
上海浦东康桥工业园区 Pudong Kangqiao Industial Park	上海南汇工业园区 Nanhui Industrial Park	上海奉城工业园区 Fengcheng Industrial Park	上海星火工业园区 Xinghuo Industrial Park	上海奉贤经济开发区 Fengxian Economic Development Zone	上海崇明工业园区 Chongming Industrial Park	上海富盛经济开发区 Fusheng Economic Development Zone
346.69	175.60	128.64	212.67	550.61	17.17	15.64
353.44	280.02	129.60	252.87	955.79	21.77	33.68
259.95	182.58	97.63	151.35	462.07	16.03	5.30
205.45	175.11	68.39	98.56	286.78	12.50	23.55
148.00	104.90	61.21	154.30	669.01	9.27	10.13
381.75	196.35	124.11	229.80	604.58	18.08	15.60
290.50	158.98	98.18	197.33	383.13	15.21	12.91
61.05	14.89	8.42	13.35	106.96	0.44	0.35
11.67	3.12	3.46	2.75	21.19	0.46	0.02
0.57	1.46	1.00	3.09	3.12	0.15	

上 / 海 / 统 / 计 / 年 / 鉴

主要统计指标解释

■工　业

为了满足国民经济核算、统计和管理的需要，将《国民经济行业分类》中的采矿业，制造业，电力、热力、燃气及水生产和供应业三个门类归并为“工业”。

■工业总产值

(1)定义：工业总产值指工业企业在报告期内生产的以货币形式表现的工业最终产品和提供工业劳务活动的总价值量。

(2)计算原则：

工业生产的原则，即凡是企业在报告期内生产的最终产品和提供的劳务，均应包括在内。其中的最终产品，不管是否在报告期内销售，只要是报告期内生产的，就应包括在内。凡不是工业生产的产品，均不得计入工业总产值。

最终产品的原则，即企业生产的成品价值必须是本企业生产的，经检验合格不需再进行任何加工的最终产品。企业对外销售的半成品也应视为最终产品计入工业总产值。而在本企业内各车间转移的半成品和在制品只能计算其期末期初差额价值。

“工厂法”原则，即以法人工业企业作为一个整体计算工业总产值，是其报告期内生产的最终产品和提供劳务的总价值量。

(3)内容及计算方法：

工业总产值包括三部分内容：即生产的成品价值、对外加工费收入、自制半成品在制品期末期初差额价值三部分。

成品价值：指企业在报告期内生产，并在报告期内不再进行加工，经检验合格、包装入库的已经销售和准备销售的全部工业成品（包括半成品）价值合计。成品价值包括企业生产的自制设备及提供给本企业在建工程、其他非工业部门和生活福利部门等单位使用的成品价值，但不包括用订货者来料加工的成品（半成品）价值。

工业总产值是按现行价格计算的。成品价值按成品实物量乘以报告期不含应交增值税（销项税额）的产品实际销售平均单价计算。会计核算中按成本价格转账的自制设备和自产自用的成品，按成本价格计算成品价值。

对外加工费收入：指企业在报告期内完成的对外承做的工业品加工（包括用订货者来料加工生产）的加工费收入和对外工业品修理作业所收取的加工费收入和对内非工业部门提供的加工修理、设备安装等收入。对外加工费收入按不含应交增值税（销项税额）的价格计算。

对于以对外加工生产为主，对外加工费收入所占比重较大的企业，如果对外加工费收入出现跨报告期支付的情况，为保证总产值生产口径计算的准确性，则应将对外加工费收入按实际情况调整，记录本报告期应实际收取的对外加工费收入。

自制半成品在制品期末期初差额价值：为了使工业总产值与工业中间投入中的物耗价值一致，以便同口径地计算工业增加值，规定本指标的计算原则是：凡是企业会计产品成本核算中计算半成品、在制品成本，则工业总产值中必须包括自制半成品在制品期末期初差额价值。反之则不包括。

自制半成品在制品期末期初差额价值等于自制半成品在制品期末价值减去期初价值后的余额，如果期末价值小于期初价值，该指标为负值，企业在计算产值时，应按负值计算，不能作为零处理。

(4)工业总产值统计范围变化和计算方法修订情况：

1984年以前工业总产值不包括村办工业，村办工业总产值划归农业。1984年以后工业总产值包括村办工业。

1995年工业普查对工业总产值计算方法做了修订，即从1995年始按新修订(新规定)方法计算工业总产值。新规定与原规定的区别如下：

全价与加工费的计算原则不同：新规定为凡自备原材料，不论其生产繁简程度如何，一律按全价计算工业总产值；凡来料加工，允许按加工费计算工业总产值。原规定则视生产加工的繁简程度不同，规定哪些行业按全价，哪些行业按加工费计算工业总产值。

自制半成品、在产品期末期初差额价值的计算原则不同：新规定要求，凡会计产品成本核算时计算了成本的差额价值，总产值中就应包括，否则可不包括；原规定则按生产周期六个月的界限区分，凡生产周期六个月以上的企业，总产值计算中应包括这部分差额价值，否则可不包括。

计算价格不同：新规定按不含增值税(销项税额)的价格计算；原规定则按含增值税(销项税额)的价格计算。

主要统计指标解释

■ 工业大、中、小、微型企业

工业大中小微型划分按《统计上大中小微型企业划分办法(2017)》标准执行。即对于工业企业来说,大型企业必须同时达到从业人员1000人、主营业务收入40000万元;中型企业必须同时达到从业人员300人、主营业务收入2000万元;小型企业必须同时达到从业人员20人、主营业务收入300万元;其余的均为微型企业。

■ 利润总额

指企业在生产经营过程中各种收入扣除各种耗费后的盈余,反映企业在报告期内实现的盈亏总额。

■ 营业收入

指企业从事销售商品、提供劳务和让渡资产使用权等生产经营活动形成的经济利益流入。包括主营业务收入和其他业务收入。

■ 营业成本

指企业从事销售商品、提供劳务和让渡资产使用权等生产经营活动发生的实际成本。包括主营业务成本和其他业务成本。营业成本应当与营业收入进行配比。

■ 资产总计

指企业过去的交易或者事项形成的、由企业拥有或者控制的、预期会给企业带来经济利益的资源。

■ 负债合计

指企业过去的交易或者事项形成的,预期会导致经济利益流出企业的现时义务。

■ 所有者权益

指企业资产扣除负债后由所有者享有的剩余权益。

■ 应收账款

指资产负债表日以摊余成本计量的,企业因销售商品、提供服务等经营活动应收取的款项。

财政部在《关于修订印发2019年度一般企业财务报表格式的通知》(财会〔2019〕6号)中,对一般企业财务报表格式进行了修订,企业《资产负债表》不再列示"应收票据及应收账款"项目,改为分别列示"应收票据""应收账款"项目。为与企业财务报表一致,从2020年起,停止发布月度"应收票据及应收账款"数据,改为发布"应收账款"数据。相关指标相应调整。

■ 产成品存货

指企业报告期末已经加工生产并完成全部生产过程,可以对外销售的制成产品。

SHANGHAI STATISTICAL YEARBOOK

EXPLANATORY NOTES TO MAJOR STATISTICAL INDICATORS

□ Industry

The three classes in the National Industrial Classification of all Economic Activities, which are mining, manufacturing, production and supply of electricity, heating, gas and water, are merged as industry in order to meet the requirements of national accounts, statistics and management.

□ Gross Output Value of Industry

(1)Definition: Gross output value of industry is the total volume of final industrial products produced or industrial services provided during the reporting period.

(2)Principles for calculation:

Statistics on industrial production follow the principle that all final products produced and industrial services provided by the enterprises during the reporting period are to be included. Final products are to be included if they are produced during the reporting period no matter whether they are sold or not during the reference period. Products which are not produced by industry shall not be counted into gross output value of industry.

Determination of final products follow the principle that all products that are included in the calculation of value of finished products are the final products of the enterprise which have been accepted through quality check and require no further processing. If an enterprise has intermediate (semi-finished) products to sell, these intermediate products are considered as the final products to be counted into gross output value of industry. The semi-finished products transferred within workshops of the enterprise can only calculate the value of change at the end and at the beginning of the reference period.

Gross industrial output value is calculated following the principle of factory approach, i.e. industrial enterprise is used as the basic accounting unit in calculating the gross industrial output value. By this approach, value of the same product is not to be double counted, and the output value of different workshops (branch factories) should not be added. However, this approach does not exclude the possibility of double counting between enterprises.

(3)Content and calculation method:

The definition of gross industrial output value consists of 3 components: value of the finished products income from external processing, and value of change in self-made semi-finished products at the end and at the beginning of the reference period.

Value of the finished products: refers to the value of all finished (semi-finished) industrial products sold of ready to sell that are produced during the reporting period without the need for further processing, checked for acceptance, packed and put into the warehouse of the enterprise, including the value of own-produced equipment and the value of products provided to the projects under construction of the enterprise, and to other non-industrial or welfare units. Value of finished products does not include the value of finished products (semi-finished products) that are produced using the materials from the clients who make the orders.

Gross industrial output value is calculated with current price. Value of finished products is calculated by the quantity of products multiplied by the average unit prices at which products are sold (excluding value-added tax). Own-produced equipment and products produced for own use are value at cost prices as in the case of enterprise accounting.

Income from external processing: refers to income from contracted external processing of industrial products (including processing of industrial products using materials from the clients), and the income from industrial repairing work provided to other units, and the income from services such as processing, repairing and installation of equipment provided to non-industrial units within the enterprise. Income from external processing is calculated at the prices excluding value-added tax.

For enterprises where external processing production is major business or the income from external processing takes major proportion, if the income from external processing is paid over the reference period, the income from external processing should be adjusted by actual situation and should be recorded as the actual receivable income in the reference period in order to ensure the calculation accuracy of the production caliber of gross output value.

Value of change in semi-finished products at the end and at the beginning of the reference period: in order to conform gross output value and the material consumption of intermediate input in industry, so that industry added value will be calculated in the same caliber, the calculation principle of this indica-

EXPLANATORY NOTES TO MAJOR STATISTICAL INDICATORS

tor is as follows: when calculating the cost of semi-finished products in the costing of accounting products, gross industrial output value must include the value of change in self-made semi-finished products at the end and at the beginning of the reference period, not vice versa.

The value of change in self-made semi-finished products at the end and at the beginning of the reference period equals the balance of the ending value minus the beginning value in self-made semi-finished products. If the ending value is less than the beginning value, the indicator will be minus. The enterprise should take the minus value rather than zero to calculate output value.

(4)Changes in the coverage and method of calculation of gross industrial output value

Prior to 1984, the value of rural industry run by villages was classified into agriculture instead of industry. Since 1984, it has been included in the gross industrial output value.

Method of calculation for the gross industrial output value was modified in the industrial census in 1995. The difference in the new method as compared with the old one is outlined below:

Principle in using full value vs. processing fee: The new method stipulates that all products produced using own materials are to be calculated with full value in reporting the gross industrial output value irrespective of sophistication of production, and for external processing, it allows calculation using processing fee. In the old method, however, the use of full value or processing fee was determined by the degree of sophistication of production in different branches of industries.

Principle in determining the value of change in semi-finished products: The new method requires that value of the change in semi-finished products should be included in the gross industrial output value if it is included in the accounting record of the enterprise, otherwise it should not be included. By the old method, it is determined by the type of enterprises in terms of production cycle. If the production cycle is over 6 months, the value of change in semi-finished products is included in the gross industrial output value, otherwise it is excluded.

Difference in prices: The new method uses prices excluding value-added tax in the calculation of gross industrial output value, while the old method used prices including value-added tax.

□ Large, Medium, Small and Micro Industrial Enterprises

Large, Medium, Small and Micro Industrial Enterprises division criteria is in accordance with the Method for the Division of Large, Medium, Small and Micro Enterprises in Statistics (2017). Under the new classification criteria, an industrial enterprise could be entitled Large Enterprise only when it has more than 1000 employees, its principle business revenue exceeds 400 million yuan, simultaneously. An enterprise could be entitled Medium Enterprise only when it has more than 300 employees, its principle business revenue exceeds 20 million yuan, simultaneously. An enterprise could be entitled Small Enterprise only when it has more than 20 employees, its principle business revenue exceeds 3 million yuan, simultaneously. All other enterprises should be entitled Micro Enterprise.

□ Total Profits

Total profits refer to the balance of various incomes minus various spendings in the course of operation, reflecting the total profits and losses of enterprises in reference period.

□ Business Revenue

Business revenue refers to the inflow of economic benefits through production and operation activities of enterprises, such as selling commodities, providing labor services and transferring the right to use of assets. It includes "revenue from principal business" and "revenue from other business".

□ Business Cost

Business cost refers to the actual costs incurred by the enterprises in such production and operation activities as selling commodities, providing labor services and transferring the right to use of assets. It includes "cost from principal business" and "cost from other business". Business cost should be matched with business revenue.

□ Total Assets

Total Assets refer to economic resources which are gained from past transactions or events by enterprise, owned or controlled by enterprise, and are expected to bring economic benefits to enterprise.

□ Total Liabilities

Total Liabilities refer to the current obligations which are created from business transactions or events in the past and expected to result in an outflow of economic benefits from the enterprise.

EXPLANATORY NOTES TO MAJOR STATISTICAL INDICATORS

□ Creditors' Equity

Creditors' equity refers to the creditors' residual equity which is equal to the total assets of the enterprise minus its total liabilities.

□ Accounts Receivable

Accounts receivable refer to the receivable payments from operating activities such as selling commodities and providing services. It is computed by amortized cost on the date of balance sheet.

In the Notification of Revise and Issue Annual Format of Financial Statements for General Enterprises in 2019 (Accounting〔2019〕No.6) by Ministry of Finance, the format of financial statements for general enterprises was revised. The item of "notes and accounts receivable" was changed to "notes receivable" and "accounts receivable" respectively. In order to confirm the financial statements of enterprises, the monthly data of "notes and accounts receivable" would not be released from 2020, and would release the data of "accounts receivable" instead. Relevant indicators were adjusted accordingly.

□ Finished Goods Inventories

Finished goods inventories refer to the selling- allowed products which has been processed and has finished the entire productive process at the end of reference period.

第十三篇

CHAPTER 13

建筑业

CONSTRUCTION

简要说明

一、本篇资料的主要内容

本篇资料反映上海市建筑业概况和发展情况。包括建筑业企业基本情况和生产经营情况。主要指标有企业个数、从业人员数、建筑业签订的合同额、建筑业总产值、房屋建筑面积和劳动生产率指标等。此外,还包括本市各区主要建筑业指标完成情况。

二、本篇资料的统计范围

根据建筑业发展的实际情况,建筑业统计范围从2019年年报起由原具有建筑业资质的独立核算建筑业企业调整为具有总承包或专业承包建筑业资质的独立核算的建筑业企业。

三、本篇的资料来源及统计调查方法

本篇建筑业企业统计数据是根据国家统计局制定的《建筑业统计报表制度》整理汇总的。建筑业统计报表是上海市统计局根据企业实际情况采取全面调查的方法布置、收集,由具有总承包或专业承包资质的建筑业企业通过联网直报上报的全面报表。

BRIEF INTRODUCTION

I. Main Contents

Data in this chapter show a general situation and development of the construction industry in Shanghai. They cover the situation of production and management of the construction enterprises, including the number of enterprises; number of employed persons; construction contracts signed; gross output value of construction industry; floor space of buildings under construction and labor productivity etc. They also cover the performance of main construction indicators in districts.

II. Scope of Statistics

In view of the development of the construction industry, since 2019, the scope of construction statistics has been adjusted to include all the construction enterprises of various types of ownership with general contracting or professional contracting qualification and independent accounting systems, replacing all the construction enterprises of various types of ownership with qualification certificates and independent accounting systems.

III. Sources of Data and Methods of Survey

Data on construction enterprises are collected in accordance with the Reporting Form System of Construction Statistics stipulated by the NBS. The annual reporting forms on construction statistics are designed by the Shanghai Municipal Statistics Bureau in accordance with local situations for comprehensive collection by the construction enterprises with general contracting of professional contracting qualification.

表 13.1 建筑业主要指标(1978~2021)
MAJOR INDICATORS OF CONSTRUCTION INDUSTRY

年 份 Year	年末从业人员 (万人) Year-end Employees (10 000 persons)	总产值 (亿元) Output Value (100 million yuan)	房屋竣工面积 (万平方米) Floor Space of Buildings Completed (10 000 sq.m)	人均房屋竣工面积 (平方米/人) Area of Completed Buildings Per Employee(sq.m/person)	全员劳动生产率 (按总产值计算) (元/人) Overall Labor Productivity (In Term of Output Value) (yuan/person)
1978	10.07	5.55	234.03	26.32	6 005
1979	23.35	13.98	564.62	26.10	6 226
1980	27.27	17.07	607.91	24.13	6 513
1981	30.21	18.03	649.93	22.28	5 941
1982	30.73	21.56	684.61	22.90	6 928
1983	33.35	24.64	736.34	22.46	7 189
1984	32.94	30.62	799.40	23.10	8 402
1985	33.35	36.73	819.24	23.78	10 070
1986	35.53	49.91	867.08	22.87	12 147
1987	35.83	59.45	872.25	22.66	14 455
1988	36.70	68.83	836.73	21.26	16 251
1989	34.43	74.75	758.34	19.70	18 053
1990	34.01	75.62	747.88	20.01	18 569
1991	34.62	84.30	775.63	20.14	21 022
1992	36.33	117.68	860.49	19.92	26 221
1993	36.90	193.00	1 144.16	26.10	44 020
1994	39.95	309.68	1 557.87	29.33	58 305
1995	41.10	391.42	1 485.87	25.44	67 023
1996	36.19	450.41	1 514.58	26.95	80 161
1997	37.40	564.37	1 777.41	29.60	93 995
1998	40.88	593.11	1 913.55	33.08	102 531

表 13.1　续表 continued

年　份 Year	年末从业人员（万人）Year-end Employees (10 000 persons)	总产值（亿元）Output Value (100 million yuan)	房屋竣工面积（万平方米）Floor Space of Buildings Completed (10 000 sq.m)	人均房屋竣工面积（平方米/人）Area of Completed Buildings Per Employee(sq.m/person)	全员劳动生产率（按总产值计算）（元/人）Overall Labor Productivity (In Term of Output Value) (yuan/person)
1999	39.01	573.06	1 950.76	33.86	99 473
2000	35.91	631.64	1 909.11	33.02	109 244
2001	35.52	730.33	2 434.73	39.55	118 641
2002	41.97	822.27	2 596.95	42.23	133 698
2003	50.52	1 195.80	3 609.20	71.44	153 910
2004	74.26	1 724.40	4 672.53	62.92	168 719
2005	72.23	1 889.25	5 648.85	78.21	182 299
2006	73.44	2 285.38	6 506.41	88.59	208 368
2007	69.33	2 524.18	6 090.22	87.84	228 710
2008	80.79	3 245.77	5 723.90	70.85	293 520
2009	88.88	3 830.53	5 719.93	64.36	312 360
2010	96.09	4 300.19	6 217.15	64.70	344 720
2011	96.86	4 586.28	5 984.74	61.79	359 232
2012	88.08	4 843.44	6 476.07	73.52	451 564
2013	81.54	5 102.84	6 274.25	76.95	417 313
2014	77.65	5 499.94	7 580.77	97.63	416 002
2015	69.19	5 652.47	7 258.69	104.91	445 768
2016	65.45	6 046.19	7 481.15	114.30	477 994
2017	60.07	6 426.42	8 066.54	134.29	531 442
2018	58.28	7 112.32	7 886.31	135.36	577 007
2019	52.64	7 812.65	9 231.95	175.37	617 090
2020	46.44	8 277.04	8 150.76	175.51	665 878
2021	44.75	9 236.42	9 232.42	206.31	759 246

表 13.2 建筑业主要指标(2021)
MAJOR INDICATORS OF CONSTRUCTION INDUSTRY

类别	Types	企业数(个) Quantity of Enterprises (unit)	年末从业人员(万人) Year-end Employees (10 000 persons)	竣工产值(亿元) Output Value of Construction Completed (100 million yuan)
总 计	**Total**	**2 550**	**44.75**	**5 100.51**
按登记注册类型分	**By Registration Categories**			
内 资	Domestic Funded	2 462	43.77	5 031.63
#国 有	State-owned	7	0.29	10.13
集 体	Collective Owned	10	0.18	8.12
股份合作	Stock-holding Cooperative	10	0.04	4.94
联 营	Joint Owned	2	0.04	1.27
有限责任公司	Limited Liability Companies	541	20.79	3 145.91
股份有限公司	Stock-holding Companies Ltd.	50	1.95	673.75
私 营	Private	1 842	20.47	1 187.50
港澳台商投资	Hong Kong, Macao and Taiwan Funded	45	0.39	27.77
外商投资	Foreign Funded	43	0.59	41.10
按行业分	**By Sectors**			
房屋建筑业	Housing Construction Industry	729	22.33	3 543.11
土木工程建筑业	Civil Engineering Industry	627	11.37	769.66
建筑安装业	Construction and Installation Industry	581	5.50	362.87
建筑装饰和其他建筑业	Construction and Decoration Industry and Other Construction Industry	613	5.56	424.86
按资质标准分	**By Qualification Standard**			
施工总承包	Chief Construction Contract	1 395	35.43	4 518.33
专业承包	Professional Contract	1 155	9.33	582.17

总产值（亿元）Output Value (100 million yuan)	其中 of which		房屋建筑面积(万平方米) Floor Space of Buildings (10 000 sq.m)	
	#建筑工程 Construction	安装工程 Installation	施工面积 Under Construction	竣工面积 Completed
9 236.42	**7 914.87**	**1 123.15**	**54 802.86**	**9 232.42**
9 082.67	7 826.67	1 071.87	54 390.92	9 079.73
23.32	22.48	0.82	82.79	13.73
12.51	11.99	0.34	51.50	0.04
5.72	5.47	0.24		
1.27	1.27		5.73	5.73
6 681.72	5 850.70	698.17	40 057.75	5 620.57
357.29	296.15	59.91	6 002.98	1 774.82
2 000.86	1 638.61	312.39	8 190.17	1 664.84
71.89	42.89	25.51	299.11	109.27
81.86	45.31	25.77	112.82	43.42
5 100.02	4 635.65	334.77	53 604.88	8 994.87
2 527.09	2 277.60	205.36	848.57	126.09
687.57	165.48	510.37	273.45	98.79
921.75	836.14	72.66	75.96	12.67
8 117.82	7 100.20	837.50	54 455.11	9 140.52
1 118.61	814.68	285.65	347.75	91.90

表 13.3 各区建筑业主要指标(2021)
MAIN CONSTRUCTION INDICATORS OF DISTRICTS

地　区	District	企业数(个) Quantity of Enterprises (unit)	年末从业人员(万人) Year-end Employees (10 000 persons)	总产值(亿元) Output Value (100 million yuan)
总　计	**Total**	**2 550**	**44.75**	**9 236.42**
浦东新区	Pudong New Area	506	10.37	2 651.53
黄 浦 区	Huangpu	96	1.26	253.45
徐 汇 区	Xuhui	146	3.15	969.45
长 宁 区	Changning	106	1.47	289.22
静 安 区	Jing'an	138	4.89	823.73
普 陀 区	Putuo	172	3.29	539.53
虹 口 区	Hongkou	94	3.14	647.11
杨 浦 区	Yangpu	162	2.52	314.23
闵 行 区	Minhang	210	3.05	716.74
宝 山 区	Baoshan	193	3.64	1 176.86
嘉 定 区	Jiading	122	1.68	152.41
金 山 区	Jinshan	126	1.69	135.85
松 江 区	Songjiang	177	1.78	217.94
青 浦 区	Qingpu	66	1.12	148.67
奉 贤 区	Fengxian	148	1.14	150.02
崇 明 区	Chongming	88	0.57	49.69

表 13.3 续表 Continued

地 区 District		房屋施工面积（万平方米）Floor Space of Buildings Under Construction (10 000 sq.m)	房屋竣工面积（万平方米）Floor Space of Buildings Completed (10 000 sq.m)	其中 of which #住宅房屋 Residence
总 计	**Total**	**54 802.86**	**9 232.42**	**4 967.06**
浦东新区	Pudong New Area	21 137.38	2 482.75	1 076.96
黄浦区	Huangpu	172.41	27.27	18.44
徐汇区	Xuhui	673.10	68.39	25.00
长宁区	Changning	4 436.66	1 156.25	641.35
静安区	Jing'an	858.72	56.81	40.25
普陀区	Putuo	4 910.74	1 108.26	779.18
虹口区	Hongkou	4 408.59	1 063.31	577.14
杨浦区	Yangpu	553.80	162.11	101.80
闵行区	Minhang	7 176.15	944.66	593.66
宝山区	Baoshan	6 875.09	1 286.47	588.03
嘉定区	Jiading	878.05	406.70	364.94
金山区	Jinshan	433.18	67.28	24.27
松江区	Songjiang	870.64	239.65	73.37
青浦区	Qingpu	255.53	67.93	20.16
奉贤区	Fengxian	1 098.07	85.80	41.83
崇明区	Chongming	64.74	8.78	0.69

表 13.4 建筑业主要财务指标(2021)
MAJOR ACCOUNTING INDICATORS OF CONSTRUCTION ENTERPRISES

指标	Indicators	合计 Total	内资 Domestic Investment
施工企业单位数(个)	Quantity of Construction Enterprises (unit)	2 550	2 462
固定资产原价(亿元)	Fixed Assets (Original Value) (100 million yuan)	834.36	817.00
总产值(亿元)	Output Value(100 million yuan)	9 236.42	9 082.67
资产合计(亿元)	**Assets at Year-end (100 million yuan)**	**13 730.81**	**13 372.27**
#流动资产	Current Assets	11 371.17	11 078.66
无形资产	Intangible Assets	32.20	30.67
负债合计(亿元)	Total Liabilities at Year-end (100 million yuan)	10 704.07	10 457.84
流动负债	Current Liabilities	10 318.82	10 090.51
非流动负债	Non-current Liabilities	288.54	273.15
所有者权益(亿元)	Total Owners Equity (100 million yuan)	3 026.74	2 914.43
企业总收入(亿元)	Total Revenue of Enterprises (100 million yuan)	12 446.81	12 130.93
主营业务收入	Prime Operating Revenue	12 301.24	11 988.55
其他业务收入	Other Revenue	145.56	142.38
房屋施工面积(万平方米)	Floor Space of Buildings Under Construction (10 000 sq.m)	54 802.86	54 390.92
房屋竣工面积(万平方米)	Floor Space of Buildings Completed (10 000 sq.m)	9 232.42	9 079.73
利润总额(亿元)	Total Profits (100 million yuan)	225.12	210.99
全员劳动生产率(元/人)(按总产值计算)	**Overall Labor Productivity (yuan/person) (In Term of Output Value)**	**759 246**	**764 934**
房屋建筑面积竣工率(%)	Rate of Buidings Completed (%)	16.8	16.7
产值利润率(%)	Ratio of Profit/Gross Output Value (%)	2.4	2.3

其 中 of which					
# 国 有 State-owned	集 体 Collective Owned	股份合作 Stock-holding Cooperation	联 营 Joint Owned	有限责任公司 Companies With Limited Liabilition	股份有限公司 Stock-holding Companies Liabilities
7	10	10	2	541	50
8.06	0.94	0.29	0.13	546.63	31.23
23.32	12.51	5.72	1.27	6 681.72	357.29
205.84	**10.32**	**2.57**	**1.72**	**9 137.55**	**905.87**
189.54	9.69	2.18	1.62	7 298.17	787.20
0.85	0.01	0.03	0.00	20.70	1.14
176.18	6.60	1.64	0.77	7 320.45	768.92
170.52	6.60	1.64	0.77	7 058.36	758.24
5.66	0.00	0.00	0.00	211.11	10.22
29.66	3.71	0.92	0.95	1 817.10	136.96
116.84	14.78	2.52	2.52	8 206.60	1 130.59
116.77	14.72	2.44	2.52	8 171.07	1 124.17
0.07	0.05	0.08	0.00	35.53	6.42
82.79	51.50	0.00	5.73	40 057.75	6 002.98
13.73	0.04	0.00	5.73	5 620.57	1 774.82
1.99	0.12	0.02	0.02	146.83	16.43
590 437	**420 502**	**329 668**	**333 520**	**903 393**	**514 866**
16.6	0.1	0.0	100.0	14.0	29.6
8.5	1.0	0.3	1.6	2.2	4.6

表 13.4 续表 Continued

指标	Indicators	其中 of which 私营 Private	港澳台商投资 Hong Kong, Macao and Taiwan Funded	外商投资 Foreign Funded
施工企业单位数（个）	Quantity of Construction Enterprises (unit)	1842	45	43
固定资产原价（亿元）	Fixed Assets (Original Value) (100 million yuan)	229.73	12.89	4.47
总产值（亿元）	Output Value(100 million yuan)	2 000.86	71.89	81.86
资产合计（亿元）	**Assets at Year-end (100 million yuan)**	**3 108.41**	**220.53**	**138.01**
# 流动资产	Current Assets	2 790.26	165.65	126.86
无形资产	Intangible Assets	7.94	1.43	0.11
负债合计（亿元）	Total Liabilities at Year-end (100 million yuan)	2 183.28	148.62	97.61
流动负债	Current Liabilities	2 094.38	135.60	92.71
非流动负债	Non-current Liabilities	46.16	12.42	2.97
所有者权益（亿元）	Total Owners Equity (100 million yuan)	925.13	71.91	40.40
企业总收入（亿元）	Total Revenue of Enterprises (100 million yuan)	2 657.07	158.87	157.00
主营业务收入	Prime Operating Revenue	2 556.85	155.78	156.91
其他业务收入	Other Revenue	100.23	3.09	0.10
房屋施工面积（万平方米）	Floor Space of Building Under Construction (10 000 sq.m)	8 190.17	299.11	112.82
房屋竣工面积（万平方米）	Floor Space of Building Completed (10 000 sq.m)	1 664.84	109.27	43.42
利润总额（亿元）	Total Profits (100 million yuan)	45.57	4.68	9.45
全员劳动生产率（元/人）（按总产值计算）	**Overall Labor Productivity (yuan/person) (In Term of Output Value)**	**541 764**	**782 722**	**410 083**
房屋建筑面积竣工率（%）	Rate of Buiding Completed (%)	20.3	36.5	38.5
产值利润率（%）	Ratio of Profit/Gross Output Value (%)	2.3	6.5	11.5

表 13.5 建筑业签订合同情况(2021)
SITUATION OF CONSTRUCTION CONTRACTS

单位:亿元(100 million yuan)

类别	Types	签订的合同额 Signed Contract Value	上年结转合同额 Value from Contracts Signed Last Year	本年新签合同额 Value from New Contracts Signed This Year
总计	**Total**	**32 678.55**	**17 856.29**	**14 822.26**
按经济类型分	**Grouped by Registration Categories**			
内资	Domestic Funded	32 275.33	17 688.73	14 586.60
#国有	State-owned	83.11	11.77	71.35
集体	Collective Owned	29.43	17.49	11.94
股份合作	Stock-holding Cooperation	6.40	1.38	5.02
联营	Joint Owned	2.14	0.70	1.44
有限责任公司	Limited Liability Companies	26 672.34	14 730.70	11 941.63
股份有限公司	Stock-holding Companies Ltd.	2 065.92	1 292.23	773.69
私营	Private	3 415.99	1 634.47	1 781.52
港澳台商投资	Hong Kong, Macao and Taiwan Funded	144.85	54.73	90.12
外商投资	Foreign Funded	258.37	112.83	145.54
按隶属关系分	**Grouped by Subordination**			
#中央属	Central Government	16 805.58	8 872.95	7 932.62
地方属	Local Government	8 470.50	5 035.59	3 434.91
其他属	Others	7 402.47	3 947.75	3 454.72
按资质等级分	**Grouped by Quarlification Level**			
#特级	Special Grade	23 497.14	13 525.80	9 971.34
一级	First Grade	6 734.17	3 364.38	3 369.79
二级	Second Grade	1 618.36	677.58	940.78
三级	Third Grade	814.13	282.97	531.15
按行业类别分	**Grouped by Sector**			
房屋建筑业	Housing Construction Industry	19 033.21	10 882.00	8 151.21
土木工程建筑业	Civil Engineering Industry	10 989.16	5 917.99	5 071.16
建筑安装业	Construction and Installation Industry	1 379.38	560.17	819.21
建筑装饰和其他建筑业	Construction and Decoration Industry and Other Construction Industry	1 276.80	496.13	780.67
按资质标准分	**Grouped by Qualification**			
施工总承包	Chief Construction Contract	30 978.57	17 126.28	13 852.29
专业承包	Professional Contract	1 699.97	730.01	969.96

表 13.6 建筑业承包工程完成情况(2021)
COMPLETION OF CONTRACTED PROJECTS BY CONSTRUCTION ENTERPRISES

单位:亿元(100 million yuan)

类别	Types	直接从建设单位承揽工程完成产值 Completed Output Value of Projects Contracted Directly from Investors	其中 of Which 自行完成施工产值 Own-completed Output Value	其中 of Which 分包出去工程的产值 Output Value of Out-sourced Projects	从建设单位外承揽工程完成产值 Completed Output Value of Projects Contracted from Non-investors
总计	**Total**	**9 793.12**	**7 786.83**	**2 006.29**	**1 449.60**
按经济类型分	**Grouped by Registration Categories**				
内资	Domestic Funded	9 595.41	7 655.55	1 939.86	1 427.12
#国有	State-owned	24.19	16.17	8.02	7.15
集体	Collective Owned	13.61	12.23	1.39	0.28
股份合作	Stock-holding Cooperation	5.31	5.24	0.07	0.48
联营	Joint Owned	1.65	1.27	0.38	0.00
有限责任公司	Limited Liability Companies	6 989.15	5 753.79	1 235.36	927.93
股份有限公司	Stock-holding Companies Ltd.	759.24	169.41	589.83	187.88
私营	Private	1 802.26	1 697.44	104.82	303.41
港澳台商投资	Hong Kong, Macao and Taiwan Funded	71.88	60.88	11.00	11.01
外商投资	Foreign Funded	125.83	70.40	55.44	11.47
按隶属关系分	**Grouped by Subordination**				
#中央属	Central Government	3 670.89	3 497.49	173.4	467.33
地方属	Local Government	2 984.09	1 817.70	1 166.39	358.86
其他属	Others	3 138.14	2 471.64	666.50	623.40
按资质等级分	**Grouped by Qualification Level**				
#特级	Special Grade	5 440.54	3 923.87	1 516.67	450.88
一级	First Grade	2 960.47	2 605.91	354.56	749.30
二级	Second Grade	889.11	801.59	87.51	152.43
三级	Third Grade	492.44	445.40	47.04	93.15
按行业类别分	**Grouped by Sector**				
房屋建筑业	Housing Construction Industry	5 599.51	4 384.83	1 214.68	715.18
土木工程建筑业	Civil Engineering Industry	2 835.61	2 184.74	650.87	342.35
建筑安装业	Construction and Installation Industry	695.67	593.21	102.47	94.36
建筑装饰和其他建筑业	Construction and Decoration Industry and Other Construction Industry	662.33	624.06	38.28	297.69
按资质标准分	**Grouped by Qualification**				
施工总承包	Chief Construction Contract	8 904.48	6 949.70	1 954.78	1 168.11
专业承包	Professional Contract	888.65	837.13	51.52	281.48

上 / 海 / 统 / 计 / 年 / 鉴

主要统计指标解释

■ 建筑业总产值

建筑业总产值是以货币表现的建筑业企业在一定时期内生产的建筑业产品和服务的总和。建筑业总产值包括:

(1)建筑工程产值: 指列入建筑工程预算内的各种工程价值。

(2)安装工程产值: 指设备安装工程价值,不包括被安装设备本身价值。

(3)其他产值:建筑业总产值中除建筑工程、安装工程以外的产值。包括房屋构筑物修理产值、非标准设备制造产值、总包企业向分包企业收取的管理费以及不能明确划分的施工活动所完成的产值。

a.房屋构筑物修理产值:指房屋和构筑物修理所完成的产值,但不包括被修理房屋、构筑物本身价值和生产设备的修理产值。

b.非标准设备制造产值:指加工制造没有定型的非标准生产设备的加工费和原材料价值(如化工厂、炼油厂用的各种罐、槽,矿井生产统一使用的各种漏斗、三角槽、阀门等)以及附属加工厂为本企业承建工程制作的非标准设备的价值。

■ 按建筑业总产值计算的全员劳动生产率

即平均每个从事建筑业生产活动的人员的建筑业总产值,计算公式为:

按建筑业总产值计算的全员劳动生产率=建筑业总产值/计算建筑业劳动生产率的平均人数

计算建筑业劳动生产率的平均人数指建筑业企业报告期实际拥有的、与建筑施工活动有关的人员的平均人数,包括参加本企业建筑施工活动的非本企业人员,但不包括企业内部社会服务性机构的人员以及由本企业支付工资但所从事的工作与本企业生产基本无关的人员。

■ 房屋建筑面积

指房屋全部平面面积的总和。它从房屋的外墙线算起,包括可供使用的有效面积和墙柱等结构占用面积。多层房屋按各层(包括地下室)面积总和计算。旧房加层或改造,只计算增加的建筑面积;旧房拆除重建,计算其全部面积;临时房屋不计算建筑面积。

■ 房屋施工面积

指报告期内施工的全部房屋建筑面积,包括本期新开工的房屋面积、上期跨入本期继续施工的房屋面积、上期停缓建在本期恢复施工的房屋面积、本期竣工的房屋面积及本期施工后又停缓建的房屋面积。

■ 房屋竣工面积

指在报告期内房屋建筑按照设计要求已全部完工,达到了使用条件,经检查验收鉴定合格,正式移交使用单位的房屋建筑面积。

SHANGHAI STATISTICAL YEARBOOK

EXPLANATORY NOTES TO MAJOR STATISTICAL INDICATORS

□ Gross Output Value of Construction

Gross Output Value of Construction refers to total of construction products and services, expressed in money terms, produced of rendered by construction and installation enterprises during a given period of time. It includes:

(1)Output value of construction projects: the value of projects covered by the project budgets;

(2) Output value of installation projects: the value of the installation of equipments, excluding the value of the equipment to be installed;

(3) Other output values: the output value of construction industry apart from that of construction projects and installation projects. It includes: output value of repair of buildings and structures; output value of non-standard equipment manufacturing; overhead expenses received by contracted enterprises from the sub-contracted enterprises and the complete output value of construction activities for which there is no clear definition.

a. Output value of repair of buildings and structures: the value created through the repair of buildings and structures. It doesn't include the value of buildings or structures being repaired and the value of the repair of production equipment;

b. Output value of manufactured non-standard equipment: the value of non-standard production equipment, including raw materials and manufacturing cost, made for the project (i.e., chemical plant; kettles or tanks used by refineries; various fillers, triangle tanks, valves used by mines). It also includes the output value of equipment manufactured by subsidiary workshops.

□ All-personnel Labor Productivity Calculated by Gross Output Value of Construction Industry

All-personnel labor productivity calculated by gross output value of construction industry refers to the average gross output value of construction industry by every personnel engaged in production activities in the construction industry.

All-personnel labor Productivity Calculated by Gross Output Value of Construction Industry = Gross Output Value of Construction Industry / Average Number of Construction Industry

Average Number of Construction Industry refers to average number of persons that construction enterprises actually have and related to construction activities, includes those engaged in the construction activities of the enterprises but belong to other enterprises, and excludes those work for the social service institutions inside the enterprise and those paid by the enterprise but whose work has nothing to do with the construction.

□ Floor Space of Buildings

Floor Space of Buildings under Construction refers to total floor space of the horizontal section of outer walls above the plinth of the building, including the effective area and the area occupied by the structure. Multi-storey building refers to the sum of each storey, including the basement. The old buildings with storey added or rebuild only calculate the floor space added. The old buildings after dismantling and reconstruction calculate the total floor space. The tabernacle calculates no floor space.

□ Floor Space of Buildings Under Construction

Floor Space of Buildings under Construction refers to floor space of buildings under construction during the reference period, including newly started buildings, buildings started earlier and continued during the reference period, and buildings suspended earlier but restarted during the reference period, buildings completed during the reference period, and buildings under construction and then suspended during the reference period.

□ Floor Space of Buildings Completed

Floor Space of Buildings Completed refers to the floor space of buildings that are completed in the reference period in accordance with the requirements of the design, up to the standard for putting them into use, and have been checked and accepted by concerned departments as qualified ones.

第十四篇
CHAPTER 14

服务业
SERVICE

简要说明

一、本篇资料的主要内容

本篇资料反映上海服务业经济概况。包括规模以上服务业企业主要经济指标，以及按隶属关系、企业登记注册类型、地区和服务业行业大类分组的主要经济指标。

二、本篇资料的统计范围

本篇资料统计范围为达到规模以上服务业统计标准的服务业企业。包括交通运输、仓储和邮政业，信息传输、软件和信息技术服务业，租赁和商务服务业，科学研究和技术服务业，水利、环境和公共设施管理业，居民服务、修理和其他服务业，教育，卫生和社会工作，文化、体育和娱乐业，公共管理、社会保障和社会组织；以及物业管理、房地产中介服务、房地产租赁经营和其他房地产业等国民经济行业。

三、本篇的资料来源及统计调查方法

本篇服务业企业统计数据根据国家统计局制定的《服务业统计报表制度》整理汇总得到。

BRIEF INTRODUCTION

I. Main Contents

This data reflects the general situation of Shanghai´s service industry economy. It includes the main economic indicators of service enterprises above Designated Size, and the main economic indicators grouped by affiliation, enterprise registration type, region and service industry.

II. Statistical Scope

The statistical scope of the data in this article is service enterprises that have reached the statistical standard of service industry above designated size. Including national economic industries of transportation, warehousing and postal services, information transmission, software and information technology services, leasing and business services, scientific research and technology services, water conservancy, environment and public facilities management, residential services, repair and other services, education, health and social work, culture, sports and entertainment, public management, social security and social organizations; and Property management, real estate intermediary services, real estate leasing and other real estate industries.

III. Data Sources and Statistical Investigation Methods

The statistical data of service industry enterprises in this part are collected according to the service industry statistical report system formulated by the National Bureau of Statistics.

表 14.1 规模以上服务业企业资产总计(2020~2021)
TOTAL ASSETS OF SERVICE ENTERPRISES ABOVE THE SET SCALE

单位:亿元(100 million yuan)

类别	Type	2020	2021
总 计	**Total**	**232 512.98**	**259 395.35**
批发和零售业	Retail and Wholesale	51 338.53	56 922.82
交通运输、仓储和邮政业	Transportation, Warehousing and Post	24 213.90	27 501.36
住宿和餐饮业	Hotels and Catering	1 918.96	2 118.23
信息传输、软件和信息技术	Information Transmission, Software and IT Services	16 013.72	20 869.12
房地产业	Real Estate	78 265.35	84 575.14
租赁和商务服务业	Leasing and Business Services	47 419.35	51 618.29
科学研究和技术服务业	Scientific and Technical Services	6 524.22	8 599.03
水利、环境和公共设施管理业	Water Conservancies, Environment and Public Facilities Management	2 674.58	3 208.48
居民服务、修理和其他服务业	Resident Service and Other Services	737.56	463.42
教 育	Education	423.28	430.13
卫生和社会工作	Health and Social Work	385.77	474.01
文化、体育和娱乐业	Culture, Sports and Entertainment	2 597.77	2 615.31

注：本表含批发和零售业、住宿和餐饮业，和房地产业中的房地产开发经营。
Note: This table includes Retail and Wholesale, Hotels and Catering, Real Estate Development and Operation.

表 14.2 规模以上服务业企业营业收入(2020~2021)
OPERATING REVENUE OF SERVICE ENTERPRISES ABOVE THE SET SCALE

单位:亿元(100 million yuan)

类别	Type	2020	2021
总 计	**Total**	**162 974.11**	**198 415.84**
批发和零售业	Retail and Wholesale	119 158.99	143 311.71
交通运输、仓储和邮政业	Transportation, Warehousing and Post	11 626.75	17 959.94
住宿和餐饮业	Hotels and Catering	1 093.76	1 404.44
信息传输、软件和信息技术	Information Transmission, Software and IT Services	8 785.97	11 237.30
房地产业	Real Estate	7 280.21	7 365.27
租赁和商务服务业	Leasing and Business Services	9 440.95	9 774.70
科学研究和技术服务业	Scientific and Technical Services	3 678.82	5 059.14
水利、环境和公共设施管理业	Water Conservancies, Environment and Public Facilities Management	524.59	635.15
居民服务、修理和其他服务业	Resident Service and Other Services	333.21	378.88
教 育	Education	256.75	316.08
卫生和社会工作	Health and Social Work	254.70	359.50
文化、体育和娱乐业	Culture, Sports and Entertainment	539.44	613.72

注：本表含批发和零售业、住宿和餐饮业，和房地产业中的房地产开发经营。
Note: This table includes Retail and Wholesale, Hotels and Catering, Real Estate Development and Operation.

表 14.3 规模以上服务业企业利润总额(2020~2021)
TOTAL PROFITS OF SERVICE ENTERPRISES ABOVE THE SET SCALE

单位:亿元(100 million yuan)

类 别	Type	2020	2021
总 计	**Total**	**7 455.41**	**9 199.05**
批发和零售业	Retail and Wholesale	2 762.98	3 663.40
交通运输、仓储和邮政业	Transportation, Warehousing and Post	248.51	1 238.30
住宿和餐饮业	Hotels and Catering	-35.00	1.63
信息传输、软件和信息技术	Information Transmission, Software and IT Services	959.31	937.71
房地产业	Real Estate	1 532.89	1 344.31
租赁和商务服务业	Leasing and Business Services	1 663.10	1 591.23
科学研究和技术服务业	Scientific and Technical Services	257.79	353.72
水利、环境和公共设施管理业	Water Conservancies, Environment and Public Facilities Management	37.10	40.45
居民服务、修理和其他服务业	Resident Service and Other Services	34.37	33.24
教 育	Education	-4.27	-6.77
卫生和社会工作	Health and Social Work	-18.13	-13.31
文化、体育和娱乐业	Culture, Sports and Entertainment	16.75	15.15

注：本表含批发和零售业、住宿和餐饮业，和房地产业中的房地产开发经营。
Note: This table includes Retail and Wholesale, Hotels and Catering, Real Estate Development and Operation.

表 14.4 规模以上服务业企业从业人员(2020~2021)
QUANTITY OF EMPLOYEES OF SERVICE ENTERPRISES ABOVE THE SET SCALE

单位:万人(10 000 persons)

类 别	Type	2020	2021
总 计	**Total**	**487.31**	**505.33**
批发和零售业	Retail and Wholesale	105.97	111.98
交通运输、仓储和邮政业	Transportation, Warehousing and Post	59.48	60.03
住宿和餐饮业	Hotels and Catering	36.95	39.91
信息传输、软件和信息技术	Information Transmission, Software and IT Services	58.65	68.15
房地产业	Real Estate	37.76	40.39
租赁和商务服务业	Leasing and Business Services	118.73	104.44
科学研究和技术服务业	Scientific and Technical Services	35.61	40.18
水利、环境和公共设施管理业	Water Conservancies, Environment and Public Facilities Management	6.88	10.66
居民服务、修理和其他服务业	Resident Service and Other Services	12.16	12.36
教 育	Education	5.46	6.25
卫生和社会工作	Health and Social Work	4.89	6.02
文化、体育和娱乐业	Culture, Sports and Entertainment	4.78	4.97

注：本表含批发和零售业、住宿和餐饮业，和房地产业中的房地产开发经营。
Note: This table includes Retail and Wholesale, Hotels and Catering, Real Estate Development and Operation.

表 14.5 分类型规模以上服务业企业主要指标(2021)
MAIN INDICATORS OF SERVICE ENTERPRISES ABOVE DESIGNATED SIZE BY SECTORS

单位:亿元(100 million yuan)

类别	Types	资产总计 Total Assets	营业收入 Operating Revenue	利润总额 Total Profits	税金总额 Total Tax and Duties
总计	**Total**	**125 816.93**	**48 137.24**	**4 450.41**	**978.22**
按隶属关系分	**Grouped by Subordination**				
中央	Central Government	21 004.25	6 352.24	1 085.91	107.66
地方	Local Government	38 552.34	4 744.77	593.48	106.67
其他	Others	66 260.33	37 040.23	2 771.03	763.89
按登记注册类型分	**Grouped by Registration Categories**				
内资	Domestic Funded	91 951.56	32 661.21	3 334.63	703.01
#国有	State-owned	3 496.30	815.13	59.15	16.99
集体	Collective-owned	435.14	50.54	12.81	2.89
有限责任公司	Companies with Limited Liabilities	35 166.17	12 160.39	1 380.82	261.21
股份有限公司	Share-holding Companies with Limited Liabilities	14 617.32	2 773.97	385.82	54.32
私营	Private	18 113.27	15 105.52	1 083.85	312.75
港澳台商投资	Hong Kong, Macao and Taiwan Funded	19 735.80	9 854.43	419.05	144.59
外商投资	Foreign Funded	14 129.57	5 621.60	696.73	130.62
按行业分	**Grouped by Sectors**				
交通运输、仓储和邮政业	Transportation, Warehousing and Postal Service Industry	27 501.36	17 959.94	1 238.30	149.89
铁路运输业	Railway Transportation	6 014.95	1 143.58	20.30	51.20
道路运输业	Road Transportation	6 427.37	1 767.09	16.50	32.00
水上运输业	Water Transportation	5 145.61	2 915.82	998.52	26.77
航空运输业	Air Transportation	5 105.04	1 049.24	-115.50	6.93
管道运输业	Pipeline Transportation	127.98	25.31	8.61	1.35
多式联运和运输代理业	Multimodal Transport and Ttransport Agency	2 621.69	8 416.44	264.81	11.74
装卸搬运和仓储业	Handling and Warehousing	711.46	439.09	42.77	9.90
邮政业	Postal	1 347.27	2 203.37	2.29	10.00
信息传输、软件和信息技术服务业	Information Transmission, Software and Information Technology Service Industry	20 869.12	11 237.30	937.71	282.52
电信、广播电视和卫星传输服务	Telecommunications, Radio, Television and Satellite Transmission Service	2 283.87	956.52	81.22	15.66
互联网和相关服务	Internet and Related Services Service	8 034.43	4 978.52	38.41	106.82
软件和信息技术服务业	Software and Information Technology Service	10 550.81	5 302.26	818.09	160.04

表 14.5 续表 continued

单位：亿元(100 million yuan)

类别	Types	资产总计 Total Assets	营业收入 Operating Revenue	利润总额 Total Profits	税金总额 Total Tax and Duties
房地产业(除房地产开发经营外)	**Real Estate Industry (Except for Real Estate Development and Operation)**	**10 037.77**	**1 802.82**	**260.70**	**105.42**
租赁和商务服务业	**Leasing and Business Service Industry**	**51 618.29**	**9 774.70**	**1 591.23**	**276.37**
租赁业	Leasing	1 663.56	338.82	18.90	15.10
商务服务业	Business Service	49 954.73	9 435.88	1 572.33	261.27
科学研究和技术服务业	**Scientific Research and Technical Service Industry**	**8 599.03**	**5 059.14**	**353.72**	**117.82**
研究和试验发展	Research and Experimental Development	2 515.31	1 027.24	16.67	18.23
专业技术服务业	Professional technical Service	4 518.41	3 124.15	239.75	76.23
科技推广和应用服务业	Science and Technology Promotion and Application Service	1 565.31	907.75	97.30	23.37
水利、环境和公共设施管理业	**Water Conservancy, Environment and Public Facilities Management Industry**	**3 208.48**	**635.15**	**40.45**	**16.49**
水利管理业	Water Conservancy Management	155.42	20.40	-1.43	0.07
生态保护和环境治理业	Ecological Protection and Environmental Governance	301.61	106.38	16.27	3.20
公共设施管理业	Public Facilities Management	1 313.20	452.91	17.37	12.02
土地管理业	Land Management	1 438.25	55.45	8.25	1.20
居民服务、修理和其他服务业	**Residential Services, Repairs and Other Service Industries**	**463.42**	**378.88**	**33.24**	**9.15**
居民服务业	Resident Service	288.10	159.18	29.92	1.41
机动车、电子产品和日用品修理业	Automobile, Electronic Products and Daily Necessities Repair Industry	101.35	108.72	2.44	3.72
其他服务业	Other Services	73.97	110.98	0.89	4.03
教　育	**Education**	**430.13**	**316.08**	**-6.77**	**6.07**
卫生和社会工作	**Health and Social Work**	**474.01**	**359.50**	**-13.31**	**1.63**
卫　生	Health	391.46	341.45	-12.58	1.02
社会工作	Social Work	82.55	18.05	-0.73	0.60
文化、体育和娱乐业	**Culture, Sports and Entertainment**	**2 615.31**	**613.72**	**15.15**	**12.86**
新闻和出版业	Press and publishing	439.27	83.73	19.22	2.99
广播、电视、电影和影视录音制作业	Radio, Television, Film and Television Recording and Production Industry	1 316.43	287.82	25.44	3.96
文化艺术业	Culture and Art Industry	47.46	19.29	2.21	0.54
体　育	Sports	253.63	80.34	-11.87	2.07
娱乐业	Entertainment	558.53	142.55	-19.86	3.30

表 14.6 各区规模以上服务业企业主要指标(2021)
MAJOR INDICATIORS OF SERVICE ENTERPRISES ABOVE DESIGNATED SIZE IN DISTRICTS

单位:亿元(100 million yuan)

地 区	Districts	资产总计 Total Assets	营业收入 Operating Revenue	利润总额 Total Profits	税金总额 Total Tax and Duties
总 计	**Total**	**125 816.93**	**48 137.24**	**4 450.41**	**978.22**
黄浦区	Huangpu	14 055.35	3 879.53	175.62	66.19
徐汇区	Xuhui	14 533.41	3 991.41	661.47	113.12
长宁区	Changning	14 602.06	5 473.58	57.32	96.19
静安区	Jing'an	13 046.06	5 039.92	308.03	135.81
普陀区	Putuo	3 438.49	1 746.14	-9.79	29.67
虹口区	Hongkou	8 258.35	5 506.43	971.68	42.59
杨浦区	Yangpu	3 135.67	2 213.14	-20.41	35.48
闵行区	Minhang	9 089.06	2 649.77	365.38	62.25
宝山区	Baoshan	1 754.07	1 231.50	60.23	31.96
嘉定区	Jiading	3 044.58	1 451.77	278.90	36.81
浦东新区	Pudong New Area	33 208.96	10 836.08	1 383.79	262.59
金山区	Jinshan	444.25	179.03	14.43	3.73
松江区	Songjiang	2 043.47	619.82	77.04	20.18
青浦区	Qingpu	3 886.95	3 022.89	89.08	33.87
奉贤区	Fengxian	1 116.10	249.24	37.99	5.45
崇明区	Chongming	160.09	46.98	-0.36	2.33

上 / 海 / 统 / 计 / 年 / 鉴

主要统计指标解释

■ 营业收入

指企业经营主要业务和其他业务所确认的收入总额。营业收入包括“主营业务收入”和“其他业务收入”。

■ 利润总额

指企业在一定会计期间的经营成果，是生产经营过程中各种收入扣除各种耗费后的盈余，反映企业在报告期内实现的盈亏总额。利润总额为营业利润加上营业外收入，减去营业外支出后的金额。

■ 营业外收入

指企业发生的除营业利润以外的收益，主要包括与企业日常活动无关的政府补助、盘盈利得、捐赠利得等。

■ 营业外支出

指企业发生的除营业利润以外的支出，主要包括公益性捐赠支出、非常损失、盘亏损失、非流动资产毁损报废损失等。

■ 税金合计

税金是指企业发生的除企业所得税和允许抵扣的增值税以外的各项税金及其附加。税金合计=税金及附加+应交增值税。

■ 税金及附加

指企业因从事生产经营活动按税法规定应缴纳的消费税、城市维护建设税、资源税、教育费附加及房产税、土地使用税、车船使用税、印花税等相关税费。

■ 应交增值税

指按照税法规定，以销售货物、服务、无形资产、不动产或提供加工、修理修配劳务的增值额和货物进口金额为计税依据而课征的一种流转税。按照权责发生制核算本期应负担的增值税额。

■ 资产总计

指企业过去的交易或者事项形成的、由企业拥有或者控制的、预期会给企业带来经济利益的资源。资产一般按流动性（资产的变现或耗用时间长短）分为流动资产和非流动资产。其中流动资产可分为货币资金、交易性金融资产、应收票据、应收账款、预付款项、其他应收款、存货等；非流动资产可分为长期股权投资、固定资产、无形资产及其他非流动资产等。包括企业拥有的土地、办公楼、厂房、机器、运输工具、存货等实物资产和现金、存款、应收账款和预付账款等金融资产。

SHANGHAI STATISTICAL YEARBOOK

EXPLANATORY NOTES TO MAJOR STATISTICAL INDICATORS

□ Operating Income

Operating income refers to the total amount of revenue recognized by the main business and other businesses of the enterprise. Operating Income includes "Prime Operating Income" and "Other Operating Income".

□ Total Profit

Total Profit refers to the operating results of an enterprise in a certain accounting period. It is the surplus of various incomes after deducting various expenses in the process of production and operation, reflecting the total profit and loss realized by the enterprise in the reporting period. The Total Profit is the operating profit plus non operating income minus non operating expenditure.

□ Non Operating Income

Non Operating Income refers to the income other than operating profit of an enterprise, mainly including government subsidy, inventory profit, donation profit, etc. unrelated to the daily activities of an enterprise.

□ Non Operating Expenses

Non Operating Expenses refers to expenditure other than operating profit incurred by an enterprise, mainly including public welfare donation expenditure, extraordinary loss, inventory loss, non current assets damage and scrap loss, etc.

□ Total Tax

Total Tax refers to all taxes and surcharges except enterprise income tax and value-added tax that can be deducted. Total tax = tax and surtax + VAT payable.

□ Taxes and Surcharges

Taxes and Surcharges refers to the consumption tax, urban maintenance and construction tax, resource tax, education surtax, real estate tax, land use tax, vehicle and ship use tax, stamp tax and other related taxes that an enterprise shall pay due to its production and operation activities in accordance with the tax law.

□ VAT Payable

VAT Payable refers to a kind of turnover tax levied on the basis of the value-added value of goods, services, intangible assets, real estate or the provision of processing, repair and replacement services and the import amount of goods in accordance with the tax law. The VAT payable in the current period shall be accounted for on the accrual basis.

□ Total Assets

Total Assets refers to the resources formed by the past transactions or events of the enterprise, owned or controlled by the enterprise and expected to bring economic benefits to the enterprise. Assets are generally divided into current assets and non current assets according to liquidity (the time of realization or consumption of assets). Among them, current assets can be divided into monetary capital, trading financial assets, notes receivable, accounts receivable, prepayment, other receivables, inventory, etc.; non current assets can be divided into long-term equity investment, fixed assets, intangible assets and other non current assets, etc. It includes physical assets such as land, office building, factory building, machinery, means of transport, inventory and financial assets such as cash, deposit, accounts receivable and prepayment owned by the enterprise.

第十五篇

CHAPTER 15

交通运输、邮政和信息传输

TRANSPORTATION, POSTS AND INFORMATION TRANSMISSION

简要说明

一、本篇资料的主要内容

本篇资料反映上海市交通运输、仓储和邮政业及信息传输业发展的基本状况。

交通运输、仓储和邮政业资料主要包括：运输线路长度、旅客发送量、旅客周转量、货物运输量、货物周转量、港口码头情况、港口货物吞吐量、集装箱吞吐量、邮轮经济、经营性停车场、民用车辆拥有量、邮政业务主要指标等内容。

信息传输业资料主要包括：电信业务开展情况、邮电通信水平、信息化基础设施情况等方面资料。

二、本篇资料的统计范围和统计方式

1. 铁路资料：包括国家铁路（含控股合资）、地方铁路和非控股合资铁路运营情况，不含军用铁路及由厂矿企事业单位自建的铁路专用线和专用铁道。

2. 公路、水路、港口资料：(1)公路、水路运输量统计包括全面调查和非全面调查两种方式，统计范围为在上海市交通运输主管部门登记注册的从事公路、水路客、货运输的营业性的车辆和船舶所完成的运输量；(2)港口统计采用全面调查方式，统计范围为上海市全部沿海港口和内河港口。

3. 民用车辆拥有量资料：民用车辆拥有量由民用汽车拥有量和民用拖拉机拥有量组成。

4. 民航运输资料：统计范围为在上海市注册从事民用航空运输飞行和通用飞行的航空运输企业和定期航班通航机场，不包括在上海市从事运输飞行的外省市和外国航空公司。

5. 邮电业务量按业务种类分为邮政业务量和电信业务量：邮政业务量统计范围是上海市邮政业企业和取得快递业务经营许可的快递企业及其备案分支机构；邮政业基础设施资料统计范围是上海市境内提供国家邮政服务的机构和设施。

三、本篇的资料来源

本篇资料中的交通运输、仓储和邮政业资料由上海市统计局服务业统计处负责整理、编辑。有关交通运输资料分别来源于中国铁路上海局集团有限公司、上海市交通委员会、上海机场（集团）有限公司、上海市公安局车辆管理所、上海市农业机械化管理办公室、上海市邮政公司、上海市邮政管理局、上海各航空公司。

本篇资料中的信息服务业资料由上海市统计局服务业统计处负责采集、整理和编辑。相关电信业务资料由上海市通信管理局提供，信息化基础设施等方面资料由上海市经济和信息化委员会提供。

BRIEF INTRODUCTION

I. Main Contents

Data in this chapter reflect the basic conditions of transportation, warehousing, postal services and telecommunications industries in Shanghai.

Data on the transportation, warehousing and postal services industries cover mainly the length of the traffic lines, passenger departing volume, turnover volume of passenger traffic, freight traffic volume, turnover volume of freight traffic, conditions of ports, port freight throughput, container throughput, yacht economy, parking lots operation, civil motor vehicles, and postal services.

Data on the telecommunications industry cover mainly conditions of telecommunications services, telecommunications level, infrastructure of informatization.

II. Scope and Methodology of Statistics

(1)Data on railway transportation: They include the operation and management of the national (including state-controlled joint ventures), local and non state- controlled joint- venture railways but exclude railways for military purpose, lines built by industrial and mining enterprises and special railways.

(2) Data on highways, waterways and ports: (a) Data on highway and waterway transportation are collected through both comprehensive reporting system and non- comprehensive reporting system. The statistical scope encompasses all the vehicles and ships registered with the transportation authorities in Shanghai and engaged in highway or waterway freight or passenger transportation business. (b) Data on ports are collected through comprehensive reporting system. The statistical scope encompasses all ports along the sea and the rivers.

(3)Data on civil motor vehicles: They include the numbers of civil automobiles and tractors.

(4)Data on civil aviation transportation: The targets of statistical collection are enterprises registered in Shanghai for engagement in civil aviation transportation flights and flights for general purposes and general aviation airports with scheduled flights. They exclude foreign companies and companies registered in other provinces and cities, which operate flights within the Shanghai territory.

(5)By types of business, the business volumes of postal and telecommunications sectors are divided into those of postal services and telecommunication services: Data on postal businesses include postal enterprises and express delivery companies and its filing branches with express business license. Data on postal infrastructure include institutions and facilities in Shanghai that provide state postal services.

III. Sources of Data

Data on transportation, warehousing and postal services in this chapter are collected, processed and compiled by the Department of Service Industry, Shanghai Municipal Statistics Bureau. Data on transportation are from China Railway Shanghai Group Co.,Ltd, Shanghai Municipal Transportation Commission, Shanghai Airport Group, Shanghai City Public Security Bureau vehicle management, Shanghai Civil Agricultural Mechanization Management Office, Shanghai Post Corporation and Shanghai Municipal Postal Administration, airlines companies in Shanghai.

Data on information service industry in this chapter are collected, processed and complied by Department of Service Industry, Shanghai Municipal Statistics Bureau. Data on telecommunication businesses are provided by Shanghai Communications Administration. Data on infrastructure of informatization, information are provided by Shanghai Municipal Economic and Informatization Commission.

表 15.1 主要年份运输线路长度
LENGTHS OF TRAFFIC LINES IN MAIN YEARS

	指 标 Indicators	2000	2010	2020	2021
铁路运输	**Railway**				
营业里程(公里)	Operation Mileage (km)	257	414	491	491
正线延展里程(公里)	Mainline Railway Length Extended (km)	397	697	890	890
公路运输	**Roadway**				
通车里程(公里)	Operation Mileage(km)	5 970	11 974	12 917	13 083
#高速公路	High Speed Highways	98	775	845	851
内河航道	**Navigable Inland Waterways**				
航道里程(公里)	Length of Navigable Inland Waterways (km)	2 100	2 110	1 589	1 665

表 15.2 主要年份交通运输主要指标
MAJOR INDICATORS OF TRANSPORTATION IN MAIN YEARS

	指 标 Indicators	2000	2010	2020	2021
公路运输	**Roadway Transportation**				
营运汽车拥有量(辆)	Operating Vehicles (vehicle)	155 860	185 531	256 770	303 679
载客汽车	Passenger Vehicles	30 757	20 386	55 083	59 054
载货汽车	Freight Trucks	125 103	165 145	201 687	244 625
载客汽车客位数(客位)	Seat of Passenger Vehicles(seat)	309 834	523 564	675 318	653 265
载货汽车吨位数(万吨)	Tonnage of Freight Trucks(10 000 tons)	48.36	132.59	284.31	356.10
港　口	**Harbor**				
船舶平均在港停泊时间(天)	Average Days of Vessel Berthed at Harbor (day)	0.90	0.40	0.41	0.43
机　场	**Aviation**				
起降航班数(万架次)	Aircraft Movements(10 000 sortie-times)		55.11	54.51	58.08
进出港旅客人次(万人次)	Passenger Turnover(10 000 person-times)		7 187.74	6 164.21	6 541.41
国内航线	Domestic Flight		5 106.96	5 644.24	6 373.62
国际及地区航线	International and Regional Flight		2 080.78	519.97	167.79

表 15.3 主要年份旅客发送量
PASSENGER DEPARTING IN MAIN YEARS

单位:万人次(10 000 person-times)

年 份 Year	旅客发送量 Passenger Departures	其中 of which 铁 路 Railway	公 路 Roadway	港 口 Harbor	机 场 Airport
1990	3 835	2 476	605	555	199
1995	5 265	2 929	1 257	512	567
2000	6 893	2 980	2 482	539	892
2005	9 487	4 313	2 468	626	2 080
2006	9 619	4 458	2 784	68	2 309
2007	10 371	4 795	2 872	95	2 609
2008	10 927	5 343	2 934	89	2 565
2009	11 136	5 161	2 995	90	2 890
2010	13 456	6 095	3 634	85	3 642
2011	13 519	6 198	3 477	78	3 766
2012	14 547	6 758	3 748	66	3 974
2013	15 933	7 972	3 720	68	4 173
2014	17 560	9 194	3 754	90	4 522
2015	18 571	9 692	3 766	113	5 000
2016	19 564	10 609	3 402	172	5 381
2017	20 855	11 617	3 419	176	5 644
2018	21 497	12 267	3 151	158	5 921
2019	22 238	12 834	3 168	115	6 121
2020	11 973	7 605	1 332	15	3 021
2021	14 047	9 284	1 479	10	3 273

①2000 年前旅客发送量是专业运输部门的数字，2001 年开始改为跨省市旅客运输的行业统计数字。
②港口旅客发送量从 2006 年起口径不包含海港到内河部分。
❶The passenger departures volume before 2000 is based on the figures for special traffic departments and the volume since 2001 is based on the figures for the inter-provincial passenger transport industries.
❷The Volume of Passenger Departures excludes those from seaports to freshwater since 2006.

表 15.4 主要年份旅客周转量
TURNOVER VOLUME OF PASSENGER TRAFFIC IN MAIN YEARS

单位:亿人·公里 (100 million persons·km)

年 份 Year	旅客周转量 Turnover Volume of Passenger Traffic	其中 of which 铁 路 Railway	公 路 Roadway	水 运 Waterway	民用航空 Civil Aviation
1990	113.94	26.85	8.42	40.84	37.84
1995	170.98	34.18	8.23	31.71	96.86
2000	234.72	35.40	16.44	6.77	176.11
2005	663.93	48.86	75.06	4.52	535.48
2006	742.87	51.23	86.85	4.52	600.28
2007	883.25	51.34	94.02	6.10	731.79
2008	869.07	53.22	94.07	6.73	715.09
2009	1 002.59	51.12	99.57	6.38	845.52
2010	1 214.25	60.16	115.44	3.69	1 034.96
2011	1 307.56	63.11	106.74	1.02	1 136.69
2012	1 223.05	68.38	112.72	0.99	1 040.97
2013	1 343.73	75.26	108.71	0.82	1 158.95
2014	1 427.10	84.46	124.34	1.04	1 217.26
2015	1 661.03	88.95	125.45	0.81	1 445.81
2016	1 903.39	98.73	114.98	0.71	1 688.97
2017	2 130.55	107.34	116.67	0.78	1 905.75
2018	2 325.82	112.09	105.81	0.79	2 107.12
2019	2 561.11	117.69	108.49	0.76	2 334.18
2020	1 348.77	69.59	44.47	0.50	1 234.21
2021	1 398.91	84.27	49.68	0.71	1 264.25

表 15.5 主要年份货物运输量
FREIGHT TRAFFIC VOLUME IN MAIN YEARS

单位:万吨(10 000 tons)

年 份 Year	货物运输量 Freight Traffic Volume	其 中 of which				
		铁 路 Railway	公 路 Roadway	水 运 Waterway	其 中 of which #远洋运输 Ocean Shipping	机 场 Airport
1990	22 848	1 257	8 714	12 864	2 246	13
1995	22 531	1 376	6 273	14 845	2 778	37
2000	47 954	1 055	28 369	18 442	7 022	88
2005	68 741	1 278	32 684	34 557	10 091	222
2006	72 617	1 223	33 799	37 342	11 766	253
2007	78 108	1 143	35 634	41 041	12 575	290
2008	84 347	1 012	40 328	42 729	12 197	305
2009	76 967	941	37 745	37 983	11 916	298
2010	81 023	959	40 890	38 803	15 172	371
2011	93 318	888	42 685	49 389	16 044	356
2012	94 376	825	42 911	50 302	17 491	338
2013	91 535	694	43 809	46 697	15 255	335
2014	90 341	549	42 848	46 583	16 541	361
2015	91 239	471	40 627	49 770	18 145	371
2016	88 689	461	39 055	48 787	18 912	387
2017	97 257	472	39 743	56 619	23 871	423
2018	107 387	468	39 595	66 906	28 213	418
2019	109 609	472	38 750	69 981	30 650	406
2020	139 226	478	46 051	92 294	88 127	403
2021	155 212	496	52 899	101 380	95 443	437

①2005 年起民航货物吞吐量不包括旅客行李。
②2008 年，公路货运量为交通部公路运输专项调查数据。
③2020 年起，公路货运量为交通部调查数据；水运货运量为行业统计数字。
❶The Freight Traffic Volume of Civil Aviation in 2005 doesn't include the freight transportation volume.
❷The Roadway Freight Traffic Volume of 2008 refers to the result of highway transportation special investigation hold by Ministry of Communications.
❸Since 2020, the Roadway Freight Traffic Volume is the result of highway transportation special investigation; and the Waterway Freight Traffic Volume is based on the figures from the waterway industries.

表 15.6 主要年份货物周转量
TURNOVER VOLUME OF FREIGHT TRAFFIC IN MAIN YEARS

单位:亿吨·公里(100 million tons · km)

年 份 Year	货物周转量 Turnover Volume of Freight Traffic	其 中 of which				
		铁 路 Railway	公 路 Roadway	水 运 Waterway	其 中 of which #远洋运输 Ocean Shipping	民用航空 Civil Aviation
1990	3 359	111	11	3 236	1 957	1
1995	4 187	143	9	4 030	2 259	5
2000	6 620	122	56	6 430	5 285	12
2005	12 132	47	73	11 986	9 285	27
2006	13 837	55	80	13 683	10 817	19
2007	15 949	35	85	15 789	12 039	40
2008	16 031	29	253	15 712	11 529	37
2009	14 436	25	244	14 118	10 596	49
2010	16 173	26	266	15 818	14 535	63
2011	20 367	21	284	20 005	15 654	57
2012	20 427	18	288	20 067	16 086	54
2013	17 868	14	299	17 497	13 562	57
2014	18 691	12	301	18 320	14 487	57
2015	19 553	11	290	19 196	15 150	57
2016	19 376	10	282	19 026	15 473	58
2017	25 058	10	298	24 691	20 276	60
2018	28 362	10	299	27 991	23 019	62
2019	29 801	14	297	29 429	24 515	61
2020	32 847	16	685	32 095	31 871	52
2021	34 146	19	1 037	33 018	32 670	71

①2004 年起，上海铁路分局改为上海铁路局，货物周转量数据有所调整。
②2006 年，民航货物周转量未包括中国货运航空公司的数据。
③2008 年，公路货物周转量为交通部公路运输专项调查数据。
④ 2020 年起，公路货物周转量为交通部调查数据；水运货物周转量为行业统计数字。
❶Since 2004, Shanghai Railway Branch Bureau has been change into Shanghai Railway Bureau, the turnover volume of freight has been adjusted accordingly.
❷In 2006, the date of China Cargo Airlines wasn't included in the Turnover Volume of Fright of Aviation.
❸The Roadway Freight Turnover Volume of 2008 refers to the result of highway transportation special investigation hold by Ministry of Communications.
❹Since 2020, the Roadway Freight Turnover Volume is the result of highway transportation special investigation; and the Waterway Freight Turnover Volume is based on the figures from the waterway industries.

表 15.7 主要年份港口码头情况
PORTS IN MAIN YEARS

年 份 Year	沿海码头长度（万米） Length of Harbor (10 000 m)	沿海泊位（个） Berths (unit)	其 中 of which #生产用万吨级 10 000 Tons for Production	其 中 of which #集装箱泊位 Container Berths
1990	1.77	122	64	7
1995	1.90	140	68	12
2000	7.64	1 098	111	18
2005	8.95	1 181	124	28
2006	9.16	1 140	131	32
2007	10.15	1 155	133	37
2008	11.49	1 203	137	42
2009	11.68	1 145	153	38
2010	11.92	1 218	157	45
2011	11.97	1 226	160	43
2012	12.29	1 245	162	43
2013	12.40	1 253	170	43
2014	12.60	1 282	170	42
2015	12.69	1 300	174	42
2016	10.92	1 152	172	42
2017	10.61	1 078	172	42
2018	10.72	1 097	181	51
2019	10.70	1 075	185	55
2020	10.58	1 024	185	55
2021	10.92	1 037	185	59

注：1997 年以前，沿海码头长度、沿海泊位为原港务局数据，从 1998 年后，为全港数据。
Note：Before 1997, the figures of length of harbor and berths were from the ports belonged to Port Administration Bureau, and after 1998, data have been collected from all types of ports.

表 15.8 主要年份港口货物吞吐量
PORT FREIGHT THROUGHPUT IN MAIN YEARS

单位：万吨（10 000 tons）

年 份 Year	港口货物吞吐量 Port freight Throughput	其中 of which 内 贸 Internal Trade	外 贸 Foreign Trade	进 港 Entry	其中 of which 内 贸 Internal Trade	外 贸 Foreign Trade	出 港 Departure	其中 of which 内 贸 Internal Trade	外 贸 Foreign Trade
1990	13 959	11 366	2 593	9 461	7 592	1 869	4 498	3 774	724
1995	16 567	12 481	4 086	12 097	9 492	2 605	4 470	2 989	1 481
2000	20 440	12 807	7 633	13 791	9 242	4 549	6 649	3 565	3 084
2005	44 317	25 825	18 492	27 539	17 441	10 098	16 778	8 384	8 394
2006	53 748	32 480	21 268	34 600	23 613	10 987	19 148	8 867	10 281
2007	56 144	30 574	25 570	35 479	22 619	12 860	20 665	7 956	12 709
2008	58 170	30 793	27 377	36 481	22 782	13 699	21 689	8 012	13 677
2009	59 205	33 394	25 811	39 000	24 920	14 080	20 205	8 474	11 731
2010	65 339	35 114	30 225	41 549	25 083	16 466	23 791	10 032	13 759
2011	72 758	38 980	33 778	45 525	27 173	18 352	27 233	11 807	15 426
2012	73 559	37 734	35 825	45 151	25 233	19 918	28 408	12 501	15 907
2013	77 575	39 869	37 706	46 978	25 657	21 321	30 597	14 213	16 384
2014	75 529	37 297	38 232	44 663	23 654	21 009	30 866	13 643	17 223
2015	71 740	33 943	37 797	41 907	21 447	20 460	29 833	12 495	17 337
2016	70 177	32 164	38 012	40 295	20 039	20 256	29 882	12 126	17 756
2017	75 051	34 008	41 043	43 315	21 182	22 133	31 736	12 826	18 910
2018	73 048	32 842	40 206	41 931	21 445	20 486	31 117	11 397	19 720
2019	72 031	32 372	39 659	41 500	21 584	19 916	30 531	10 788	19 743
2020	71 670	32 753	38 917	42 810	23 489	19 321	28 860	9 264	19 596
2021	77 635	36 146	41 489	45 774	26 172	19 602	31 861	9 974	21 887

表 15.9 主要年份国际集装箱吞吐量(按进出港分)
INTERNATIONAL CONTAINERS AND CARGO THROUGHPUT OF FOREIGN TRADE IN MAIN YEARS

年 份 Year	国际标准集装箱吞吐量重量(万吨) Weight of International Containers (10 000 tons)	国际标准集装箱吞吐量(万 TEU) International Containers (10 000 TEU)	其 中 of which	
			进 港 Entry	出 港 Departure
1990	446	45.6	22.4	23.2
1995	1 389	152.6	69.3	83.3
2000	5 170	561.2	266.1	295.1
2005	16 250	1 808.4	887.2	921.3
2006	19 595	2 171.9	1 064.4	1 107.5
2007	23 850	2 615.2	1 276.3	1 338.9
2008	25 992	2 800.6	1 397.8	1 402.8
2009	24 619	2 500.2	1 222.9	1 277.3
2010	27 992	2 906.9	1 436.1	1 470.8
2011	31 220	3 173.9	1 555.1	1 618.9
2012	32 480	3 252.9	1 605.1	1 647.9
2013	34 243	3 361.7	1 652.2	1 709.5
2014	35 335	3 528.5	1 732.3	1 796.2
2015	35 850	3 653.7	1 818.7	1 835.0
2016	36 736	3 713.3	1 825.2	1 888.1
2017	39 759	4 023.3	1 980.3	2 043.0
2018	41 126	4 201.0	2 064.6	2 136.4
2019	42 314	4 330.3	2 149.1	2 181.1
2020	43 473	4 350.3	2 146.7	2 203.7
2021	45 691	4 703.3	2 325.0	2 378.3

注：TEU 是“折合 20 英尺标准箱”英文缩写语。
Note: TEU is the abbreviation, which refers to 20-feet equivalent unit.

表 15.10 经营性停车场(库)营运情况(2018~2021)
STATISTICS OF PARKING LOTS (GARAGES) OPERATION

指 标	Indicators	2018	2019	2020	2021
计时停放(万辆次)	Time Parking (10 000 vehicletimes)	33 600.63	37 385.42	40 804.29	45 681.60
包月停放(万辆次)	Monthly Parking (10 000 vehicletimes)	8 083.70	9 433.70	10 567.62	14 756.13
车辆停放车次合计(万辆次)	Quantity of Parking Times (10 000 vehicletimes)	49 318.26	55 361.08	59 359.97	69 754.00
经营车辆停放收入(亿元)	Revenue of Parking Lots (100 million yuan)	35.64	47.78	40.02	49.93

表 15.11 民用车辆拥有量(2018~2021)
CIVIL MOTOR VEHICLES

单位:万辆(10 000 vehicles)

指 标	Indicators	2018	2019	2020	2021
总 计	**Total**	**423.13**	**442.55**	**471.39**	**501.48**
#汽 车	Civil Automobile	393.42	413.86	442.38	465.84
载客汽车	Passenger Vehicles	358.37	378.50	408.14	429.39
#轿 车	Cars	235.85	241.96	254.79	258.13
载货汽车	Freight Trucks	32.87	33.07	31.79	33.58
其他汽车	Other Automobile	2.18	2.30	2.45	2.87
摩托车	Motorcycle	20.57	19.17	18.48	24.41
拖拉机	Tractors	1.00	1.00	0.96	0.56

①本表不包括军用车辆和码头、机场等专用特种车辆。
②从 2012 年起，民用车辆拥有量的数据不含强制报废量(下表同)。
❶This table doesn't include the quantity of military vehicles and special vehicles for port and airport.
❷Since 2012, the civil vehicle ownership data does not contain mandatory retirement amount (the same as the following table).

表 15.12 个人民用车辆拥有量(2018~2021)
INDIVIDUAL CIVIL MOTOR VEHICLES

单位:万辆(10 000 vehicles)

指 标	Indicators	2018	2019	2020	2021
总 计	**Total**	**322.14**	**339.90**	**365.56**	**386.76**
#汽 车	Civil Automobile	302.17	321.29	347.61	362.93
载客汽车	Passenger Vehicles	301.26	320.27	346.68	362.07
#轿 车	Cars	209.53	215.53	226.08	226.48
载货汽车	Freight Trucks	0.65	0.74	0.64	0.56
其它汽车	Other Automobile	0.25	0.28	0.29	0.30
摩托车	Motorcycle	19.94	18.58	17.90	23.77

表 15.13 现代航运服务业营业收入(2019~2021)
OPERATING INCOME OF MODERN SHIPPING SERVICE INDUSTRY

单位:亿元(100 million yuan)

指标	Indicators	2019	2020	2021
现代航运服务业营业收入	**Operating Income of Modern Shipping Service Industry**	**11 018.12**	**12 153.93**	**18 486.09**
交通运输	Transportation	5 112.63	4 555.07	6 359.75
铁路运输	Railway Transportation	1 292.13	1 040.74	1 216.53
道路运输	Highway Transportation	777.94	942.01	1 236.46
水上运输	Waterway Transportation	1 533.62	1 672.28	2 849.91
航空运输	Civil Aviation Transportation	1 508.93	900.03	1 056.85
多式联运和运输代理	Multimodal Transport and Ttransportation Agency	2 920.11	4 245.89	8 029.14
装卸搬运和仓储	Handling and Warehousing	381.20	429.08	478.61
快　递	Express delivery	1 333.84	1 607.48	2 086.95
信息传输、软件和信息技术服务	Information transmission,software an IT services			229.07
金　融	Financial	468.36	489.50	499.26
租赁和商业服务	Leasing and Commercial Services	517.07	506.53	440.63
科学研究和技术服务	Scientific Research and Technical Services	268.80	301.53	339.76
教　育	Education	16.11	18.85	22.90

表 15.14 邮政主要指标(2018~2021)
MAIN INDICATORS OF POST

指标	Indicators	2018	2019	2020	2021
邮电局、所(个)	Post Office (unit)	536	536	536	536
报刊图书销售点(个)	Publications Sales Outlet (unit)	26	12	12	
邮政信筒信箱(个)	Mail Boxe (unit)	3 013	2 651	2 557	2 555
集邮品销售点(个)	Stamps Sales Outlet (unit)	254	297	288	365
邮政储蓄网点(个)	Postal Savings Office (unit)	380	380	382	383
邮路条数(条)	Number of Mail Route (route)	281	295	379	1 122
邮路总长度(万公里)	Total Length of Mail Routes (10 000 km)	5.29	5.64	6.53	12.94
农村投递路线总长度(万公里)	Length of Rural Delivery Routes (10 000 km)	0.16	0.12	0.08	0.20

注：由于经营调整，邮政速递物流公司的邮路并入邮政公司经营。
Note: As business needs, mail route of Shanghai Post Express and Logistics are co-operated with Shanghai Post Corporation.

表 15.15　主要年份邮政业务主要指标
MAJOR INDICATORS OF POSTAL BUSINESS IN MAIN YEARS

指标	Indicators	2000	2010	2020	2021
邮政业务总量(亿元)	Volume of Postal Business (100 million yuan)	22.40	49.48	848.14	1 691.92
函　件(亿件)	Mails (100 million units)	4.61	11.66	3.14	2.09
国内快递(万件)	Domestic Express delivery (10 000 pieces)	709.90	25 708.85	322 446.43	358 885.14
国际及港澳台快递(万件)	International and Hong Kong、Macao and Taiwan Express delivery (10 000 pieces)	52.10	3 088.01	13 884.25	15 252.77
邮政储蓄期末余额(亿元)	Postal Saving Deposit Balance (100 million yuan)	153.50	545.64	1 292.17	1 344.10
报纸、杂志累计订销数(亿份)	Total Copies of Newspapers and Magazines Subscribed and Sold (100 million pieces)	11.30	11.99	7.02	6.81
集邮业务(万枚)	Stamp Collection Business (10 000 stamps)	9 467	5 156	3 365	1 389

注：2012 年起，"邮政业务总量"包括国家邮政业务总量和非国家邮政业务总量。
Note: Since 2012, Volume of Postal Business contains volume of national postal business and volume of non-national postal-business.

表 15.16　主要年份电信业务主要指标
MAJOR INDICATORS OF TELECOM BUSINESS IN MAIN YEARS

指标	Indicators	2010	2015	2020	2021
电信业务总量(亿元)	Volume of Telecom Business (100 million yuan)	373.00	778.80	2 822.91	574.58
电信业务收入(亿元)	Income of Telecom Business (100 million yuan)	440.49	535.68	595.75	633.56
年末固定电话用户 (万户)	Year-end Installed Telephones (10 000 households)	931.80	797.29	636.48	641.97
移动电话用户 (万户)	Mobile Phone Subscribers Users (10 000 households)	2 361.55	3 132.41	4 277.62	4 398.83
#4G 移动电话用户	4G Mobile Phone Users		1 219.90	3 246.21	2 730.08
5G 移动电话用户	5G Mobile Phone Users			859.67	926.31
固定电话通话时长(亿分钟)	Installed Telephone Call Lasting Time(100 million minutes)	340.05	193.36	84.29	82.75
移动电话通话时长 (亿分钟)	Mobile Calls (100 million minutes)	1 011.00	1 238.20	841.77	830.81
移动短信业务量(亿条)	Volume of Mobile Short Messages (100 million pieces)	396.00	211.86	840.39	819.58
IPTV 用户(万户)	IPTV Users (10 000 households)	130	177	564.96	559.53
有线数字电视用户(万户)	Digital Cable TV Users (10 000 households)	220	662	750	754
固定互联网宽带接入用户(万户)	Fixed Broadband Internet Access Users (10 000 households)	545.00	568.76	918.96	995.43
移动互联网用户(万户)	Mobile Internet Users (10 000 households)	1 355.00	2 569.29	3 365.70	3 616.60
移动互联网接入流量(万 G)	Mobile Internet Access Traffic (10 000G)	1 153.70	10 818.80	309 548.10	421 262.08

①2010 年起，固定互联网宽带接入用户的统计口径从基础电信企业的用户调整为所有宽带驻地网企业的用户。
②电信业务总量是指以货币形式表示的电信企业为社会提供的各类电信服务的总数量。包括固定话音业务总量、固定数据及互联网业务总量、固定增值及其他业务总量、移动话音业务总量、移动数据及互联网业务总量、移动增值及其他业务总量，2021 年起年电信业务总量调整为按照上年不变单价计算。
❶The Indicator "Fixed Broadband Internet Access Users" was calculated by all local business users since 2010.
❷Volume of Telecom Business refers to the total number of telecommunication services provided by telecommunication enterprises for the society in the form of money, including the total volume of fixed voice services, fixed data and total Internet services, fixed value-added and other services, mobile voice services, mobile data and Internet services, mobile value-added and other services, the total amount of telecom business was calculated according to the constant unit price of last year since 2021.

表 15.17　主要年份邮电通信水平
POSTAL AND TELECOM LEVEL IN MAIN YEARS

指　标	Indicators	2010	2015	2020	2021
固定电话普及率(%)	Popularity Rate of Telephone Line(%)	48.5	33.0	26.2	25.8
移动电话普及率(%)	Popularity Rate of Mobile Telephone(%)	122.9	129.7	176.2	176.9
平均每一邮政局所服务面积（平方公里）	Average Area Served by One Post Office (sq.km)	10.69	11.81	11.83	11.83
平均每一邮政局所服务人口(万人)	Average Population Served by Every Post Office (10 000 persons)	3.86	4.50	4.64	4.64
人均每年发函件数(件)	Average Number of Letters Mailed (piece)	50.89	37.56	12.63	8.39
人均每年购报刊数(份)	Average Number of Newspaper and Magazine Purchased (piece)	50.50	40.46	28.22	27.34

注：固定电话普及率及移动电话普及率为根据第六次人口普查调整后的数据。
Note: Data of Popularity Rate of Telephone Line and Popularity Rate of Mobile Telephone have been adjusted according to the sixth census.

表 15.18　主要年份信息化基础设施情况
INFRASTRUCTURE OF INFORMATIZATION IN MAIN YEARS

指　标	Indicators	2010	2015	2020	2021
信息通信管线长度(沟公里)	Length of Information Communication Pipelines (channel km)	5 821	9 975	11 574	11 959
光缆线路长度(公里)	Length of Optical Cable Line(km)	4 670	475 024.56	697 996.85	713 201.79
移动电话交换机容量(万户)	Mobile Phone Exchange Capacity (10 000 households)	3 995	4 424	6 464	7 099

上 / 海 / 统 / 计 / 年 / 鉴

主要统计指标解释

铁路运营里程

铁路运营里程又称营业长度(包括正式营业和临时营业里程),指办理客货运输业务的铁路正线总长度。凡是全线或部分建成双线及以上的线路,以第一线的实际长度计算;复线、站线、段管线、岔线和特殊用途线以及不计算运费的联络线都不计算营业里程。铁路营业里程是反映铁路运输业基础设施发展水平的重要指标,也是计算客货周转量、运输密度和机车车辆运用效率等指标的基础资料。

内河航道里程

内河航道里程也称内河通航里程,指在一定时期内,能通航运输船舶及排筏的天然河流、湖泊水库、运河及通航渠道的长度。包括全年季节性通航累计三个月以上的航道,不包括仅供零散流放竹、木排的河道。该指标可以反映内河水运网的规模、水平和发展情况。

货物(旅客)周转量

指在一定时期内,由各种运输工具运送的货物(旅客)数量与其相应运输距离的乘积之总和,是反映运输业生产总成果的重要指标,也是编制和检查运输生产计划,计算运输效益、劳动生产率以及核算运输单位成本的主要基础资料。通常以吨公里和人公里为计算单位。计算货物周转量通常按发出站与到达站之间的最短距离,也就是计费距离计算。

货(客)运量

指在一定时期内,各种运输工具实际运送的货物(旅客)数量。它是反映运输业为国民经济和人民生活服务的数量指标,也是制定和检查运输生产计划、研究运输发展规模和速度的重要指标。货运按吨计算,客运按人计算。货物不论运输距离长短、货物类别,均按实际重量统计。旅客不论行程远近或票价多少,均按一人一次客运量统计;半价票、小孩票也按一人统计。

港口货物吞吐量

指经由水路进出港区范围,并经过装卸的货物数量。按货物流向分为进港吞吐量和出港吞吐量,按货物贸易性质分为内贸和外贸吞吐量。按货物的类别分,可根据现行的交通行业标准《运输货物分类和代码》分类。

国际标准集装箱吞吐量

凡经过水运进出港区范围,并经过装卸的集装箱箱数和重量(含集装箱自重),通常是按进港和出港分别统计。

TEU是"折合20英尺标准箱"的英文缩写。它是指各种尺寸的国际标准集装箱的自然箱数,按各自的换算比例,折算为20英尺标准箱的换算箱数。其换算比例为:40英尺箱 1∶2;35英尺箱 1∶1.75;20英尺箱 1∶1;10英尺箱 1∶0.5。

民用车辆拥有量

指报告期末,在公安交通管理部门按照《机动车注册登记工作规范》,已注册登记领有民用车辆牌照的全部汽车数量。汽车拥有量统计的主要分类:根据汽车结构分为载客汽车、载货汽车及其他汽车;根据汽车所有者不同分为个人(私人)汽车、单位汽车;根据汽车的使用性质分为营运汽车、非营运汽车和特种汽车;根据汽车大小规格不同载客汽车分为大型、中型、小型和微型,载货汽车分为重型、中型、轻型和微型。

邮政业务总量

指以货币表现的邮政部门用于邮政服务的总数量。它综合反映了一定时期邮政工作的总成果,是研究邮政业务量构成和发展趋势的重要指标。它用各种邮政分类业务量,如函件件数、电报份数、订销报刊累计份数等,分别乘以相应的平均单位(不变价),加总后再加上其他业务收入求得。

移动电话用户

指通过移动电话交换机进入移动电话网、占用移动电话号码的电话用户。用户数量以报告期末在移动电话营业部门实际办理登记手续进入移动电话网的户数进行计算,一部移动电话统计为一户。

主要统计指标解释

电信业务总量

是指以货币形式表示的电信企业为社会提供的各类电信服务的总数量。包括固定话音业务总量、固定数据及互联网业务总量、固定增值及其他业务总量、移动话音业务总量、移动数据及互联网业务总量、移动增值及其他业务总量。

SHANGHAI STATISTICAL YEARBOOK

EXPLANATORY NOTES TO MAJOR STATISTICAL INDICATORS

□ Operation Mileage of Railways

Operation Mileage of Railways refers to the total length of the trunk line under passenger and freight transportation (including both full operation and temporary operation). The calculation is based on the actual length of the first line even if this line has a full or partial double track or more tracks, excluding double tracks, station sidings, tracks under the charge of stations, branch lines, special-purpose lines and the non-payable connecting lines. The length of railways in operation is an important indicator to show the development of the infrastructure for the railway transport, and also the essential data to calculate volume of passenger freight transport, traffic density and utilization efficiency of the locomotives and carriages.

□ Length of Navigable Inland Waterways

Length of Navigable Inland Waterways it is an indicator reflecting the size and development of inland water network, it refers to the length of the natural rivers, lakes, reservoirs, canals, and ditches open to navigation during a given period, which enables the transport by ships and rafts. It includes the channels open to navigation for over an accumulative 3 months in a year, yet this does not include the river courses, which are only used to float odd logs and bamboo rafts. This indicator can reflect the scale, level and development situation of the inland waterway network.

□ Freight (Passenger) Turnover Volume

Freight (Passenger) Turnover Volume refers to the total of the product of the physical volume of transported cargo (passenger) by the transport distance, usually using ton/kilometer and person/kilometer as calculating units. Normally, the shortest distance between the departure point and the destination is the basis to calculate the freight turnover volume, that is to say, the payable distance. This is an important indicator to show the total results of the transport industry, to prepare and examine the transport plan and to measure the efficiency, the labor productivity and the unit cost of transport.

□ Freight (Passenger) Traffic

Freight (Passenger) Traffic refers to the volume of freight (passenger) transported with various means. The freight (passenger) traffic provides a quantitative measure to show how the transport industry serves the national economy and people, and is also an important indicator for planning the transport industry and for studying the development scale and speed of the transport industry. Freight transport is calculated in tons and passenger traffic is calculated in the number of persons. Despite the type of freight and travelling distance, the freight transport is calculated in the actual weight of the goods: and despite the travelling distance and ticket price, the passenger traffic is calculated by the principle that one person can be counted only once in one travel. The passenger who travels with a half price ticket or a child ticket is also calculated as one person.

□ Volume of Freight Handled in Ports

Volume of Freight Handled in Ports refers to the volume of cargo passing in and out of the harbour area of the major coastal ports and having been loaded and unloaded. The volume of freight handled may be classified by direction of flow as freight for import and freight for export, or by nature of cargo as freight for domestic trade and freight for foreign trade. The volume of freight handled maybe classified by the classification of cargo, or the current transport standard of The Classification and Code of Cargo Type.

□ International Container Throughput Capacity

International Container Throughput Capacity refers to number and weight of containers which are loaded or unloaded within port area via water carriage. It is often calculated by entering and leaving port, respectively. TEU was the abbreviation of twenty foot equivalent unit, which refers to converted number of all kinds of containers. The conversion method is based on respective conversion ratio and the number of all kinds of container is converted to the standard number of twenty foot equivalent unit. The conversion ratio is: 40 feet container 1∶2, 35 feet container 1∶1.75, 20 feet container 1∶1, 10 feet container 1∶0.5.

□ Individual Civil Motor Vehicles

Individual Civil Motor Vehicles refers to the total numbers of vehicles that are registered and received vehicles′ license

EXPLANATORY NOTES TO MAJOR STATISTICAL INDICATORS

tags according to the Work Standard for Motor Vehicles Registration formulated by transport management office under department of public security at the end of reference period.They are divided into following categories according to the structure of motor vehicles: passenger vehicles, trucks and others; and private vehicles and vehicles for units use according to ownerships; working vehicles, non-working vehicles and special motor vehicles according to kind of usage; large passenger vehicles, medium passenger vehicles and small passenger vehicles, heavy trucks, light-heavy trucks and light trucks according to sizes of vehicles.

□ Volume of Post Business

Volume of Post Business refers to the total amount of post services provided by the post department, which reflects the total achievements by the post departments during a given period of time in a comprehensive way, and is an important indicator to study the composition and development of the post business. It is arrived by first multiplying the business volume of different types, such as number of letters, telegrams and accumulated number of newspaper and journals subscribed and sold, etc. by their respective average unit price (fixed price) and then adding these products together, plus the income from other business revenues.

□ Mobile Phone Subscribers

Mobile Phone Subscribers refer to the persons who own mobile telephone numbers and are connected with the mobile telephone communication network through the mobile telephone switchboards. The number of subscribers is calculated by the subscribers who have completed registration at mobile communication business centers and entered into the mobile telephone network. One mobile telephone is taken as a user.

□ Total Amount of Telecommunication Services

Total Amount of Telecommunication Services refers to the total amount of various types of telecommunications services in the form of money provided by telecommunications companies for society. It includes the total amount of fixed voice services, fixed data and Internet services, fixed value-added business and other services, mobile voice services, mobile data and internet services, mobile value-added business and other services.

第十六篇
CHAPTER 16

批发、零售和住宿、餐饮
WHOLESALE AND RETAIL, HOTELS AND CATERING SERVICES

简要说明

一、本篇资料的主要内容

本篇资料主要反映上海市批发和零售业、住宿和餐饮业的发展与经营状况，同时反映国内商品流通、商品消费、市场运行态势。主要内容包括：限额以上批发和零售业产业活动单位和从业人员、经营状况、财务状况；限额以上住宿餐饮业经营状况、财务状况；连锁经营情况；商品交易市场成交情况；社会消费品零售总额；商品销售总额等。

二、本篇资料的统计范围

批发和零售业、住宿和餐饮业的法人企业、产业活动单位、个体户，批发和零售业、住宿和餐饮业连锁集团，商品交易市场。

三、本篇的资料来源

本篇资料根据《批发和零售业统计报表制度》、《住宿和餐饮业统计报表制度》整理汇总。

四、本篇的统计调查方法

本篇资料中限额以上批发和零售业、住宿和餐饮业法人企业、个体户、其他行业附营的限额以上批发和零售业、住宿和餐饮业产业活动单位资料，以及批发和零售业、住宿和餐饮业连锁集团，商品交易市场采用全面调查的方法；限额以下企业及个体户等资料采用抽样调查方法推算。

BRIEF INTRODUCTION

I. Main Contents

Data in this chapter reflect the development and operation of Shanghai´s wholesale and retail trade, hotels and catering service. Data also reflect domestic commodity circulation, consumption, and market operation. Main contents include the basic conditions, employment, business situation, and financial status of wholesale and retail trades above the set scale; business situation, and financial status of hotels and catering services above the set scale; chain business conditions, transactions of commodities market, retail sales of main consumer goods, and total sales of consumer goods.

II. Scope of Statistics

Included in this chapter are the registered enterprises and self-employed individuals of wholesale and retail trade, hotels and catering service; chain enterprises in retail, hotels, and catering businesses; and commodities markets.

III. Sources of Data

Data in this chapter are collected and processed in accordance with The Statistical Reporting Form System on Wholesale and Retail Trades and The Statistical Reporting Form System on Hotel and Catering.

IV. Survey Methodology

Data on basic conditions for all corporate enterprises and self-employed individuals above the set scale of wholesale and retail trades, hotel, and catering businesses; affiliating establishments above the set scale of other industries involved in the wholesale and retail trades, hotels and catering businesses; chain enterprises of wholesale and retail trades; and commodities markets data are collected through comprehensive reporting system. Data on enterprises and self-employed individuals below the set scale are collected by sample surveys.

表 16.1 限额以上批发业产业活动单位和从业人员(2021)
QUANTITY OF BUSINESS UNITS AND EMPLOYEES OF WHOLESALE ABOVE THE SET SCALE

类 别	Types	法人企业（个）Quantity of Corporations (unit)	产业活动单位数（个）Quantity of Business Units (unit)	从业人员（人）Quantity of Employees (person)
总 计	**Total**	**13 715**	**23 743**	**728 311**
按登记注册类型分	**Grouped by Registration Categories**			
内 资	Domestic Enterprises	10 140	14 019	320 210
#国 有	State-owned	3	25	171
集 体	Collective-owned	7	10	128
股份合作	Share Holding Cooperative Enterprises	2	2	37
联 营	Joint-Owned Enterprises	1	1	18
有限责任公司	Companies with Limited Liabilities	2 213	3 363	107 109
股份有限公司	Share Holding Companies with Limited Liabilities	115	699	23 452
私 营	Private	7 787	9 907	189 175
其 他	Others	12	12	120
港澳台商投资	Hong Kong, Macao and Taiwan Funded	1 095	3 615	143 991
外商投资	Foreign Funded	2 480	6 109	264 110
按行业分	**Grouped By Sectors**			
农、林、牧产品批发	Agriculture, Forestry and Animal Husbandry Products	174	215	4 152
食品、饮料及烟草制品批发	Food, Beverage and Tabacco	1 234	2 632	83 197
#米、面制品及食用油批发	Rice, Flour and Cooking Oil	153	245	14 950
烟草制品批发	Tabacco	25	208	4 099
纺织、服装及日用品批发	Textile Products, Garments and Commodity	1 749	5 078	165 714
#服装批发	Garments	407	1 785	49 513
文化、体育用品及器材批发	Culture & Sports Articles and Equipments	476	914	31 433
医药及医疗器材批发	Medicines and Special Appliances of Medicines	811	1 367	94 241
矿产品、建材及化工产品批发	Mineral Products, Materials of Construction and Chemical Products	5 100	6 549	114 453
#煤炭及制品批发	Coal	118	123	2 113
石油及制品批发	Petroleum	442	931	10 901
金属及金属矿批发	Metal Products and Metal Minerals	1 934	2 180	28 204
建材批发	Building Materials	441	542	14 155
机械设备、五金产品及电子产品批发	Mechinery Equipments, Hardwares, Electric Appliances and Eletronic Products	3 680	6 282	214 061
#汽车及零配件批发	Automobiles and Spare Parts	468	680	28 243
电气设备批发	Electrical Equipment	244	379	13 374
计算机、软件及辅助设备批发	Computers, Softwares and Accessorial Equipments	337	568	26 027
贸易经纪与代理	Trade Broker and Agent	250	358	7 040
其他批发	Others	241	348	14 020

表 16.2　限额以上零售业产业活动单位和从业人员(2021)
QUANTITY OF BUSINESS UNITS AND EMPLOYEES OF RETAIL ABOVE THE SET SCALE

类　别	Types	法人企业(个) Quantity of Corporations (unit)	产业活动单位数(个) Quantity of Business Units (unit)	从业人员(人) Quantity of Employees (person)
总　计	**Total**	**2 910**	**25 218**	**391 925**
按登记注册类型分	**Grouped by Registration Categories**			
内　资	Domestic Funded	2 426	14 655	191 733
#国　有	State-owned	9	16	112
集　体	Collective-owned	10	79	677
股份合作	Share Holding Cooperative Enterprises	7	44	148
联　营	Joint-Owned Enterprises	12	13	183
有限责任公司	Companies with Limited Liabilities	850	6 106	84 627
股份有限公司	Share Holding Companies with Limited Liabilities	22	561	10 959
私　营	Private	1 516	7 836	95 027
港澳台商投资	Hong Kong, Macao and Taiwan Funded	279	4 912	109 367
外商投资	Foreign Funded	205	5 651	90 825
按行业分	**Grouped By Sectors**			
综合零售	Comprehensive Retail Sale	280	5 917	87 403
#百货零售	Articles For Daily Use	123	399	16 378
超级市场零售	Retail Sale of Supermarket	109	1 344	60 909
食品、饮料及烟草制品专门零售	Food, Beverage and Tabacco	212	3 427	27 271
纺织、服装及日用品专门零售	Textile, Garments and Articles for Daily Use	475	8 974	145 875
#服装零售	Garments	276	5 929	102 518
文化、体育用品及器材专门零售	Culture & Sports Articles and Equipments	180	1 836	20 330
#体育用品及器材零售	Sporting Goods and Equipment	23	221	3 288
图书、报刊零售	Books, Newspapers and Periodicals	23	268	3 645
医药及医疗器材专门零售	Medicines and Special Appliances of Medicines	169	1 882	13 165
#西药零售	Western Medicine	117	1 619	10 599
中药零售	Chinese Medicine	24	172	1 867
汽车、摩托车、零配件和燃料及其他动力设备零售	Automobiles, Motocycles, Spare Parts and Fuels and other Power Equipments	829	1 323	44 834
#汽车新车零售	New Automobiles	611	847	38 031
家用电器及电子产品专门零售	Household Electrical Appliances and Electronic Products	215	747	11 900
#家用视听设备零售	Home Audio-visual Equipment	6	12	104
日用家电零售	Household Appliances	70	200	3 108
计算机、软件及辅助设备零售	Computers, Softwares and Accessorial Equipments	65	195	5 258
通信设备零售	Telecommunication Appliances	39	249	1 944
五金、家具及室内装饰材料专门零售	Hardwares, Furnitures and Materials of Decoration	132	298	6 948
货摊、无店铺及其他零售业	Stall, Non-store and Other Retailing	418	814	34 199
#互联网零售	Internet	373	603	31 449
邮购及电视、电话零售	Mail Order and TV, Telephone Sales	4	11	501

表 16.3 社会消费品零售总额(1978~2021)
TOTAL RETAIL SALES OF CONSUMER GOODS

单位:亿元(100 million yuan)

年 份 Year	社会消费品零售总额 Total Retail Sales of Consumer Goods	按商品用途分 by Use			
		食品类 Foods	衣着类 Clothing	用品类 Articles	燃料类 Fuels
1978	54.10	26.51	11.60	15.16	0.83
1979	68.28	30.05	16.07	21.28	0.88
1980	80.43	34.30	19.75	25.44	0.94
1981	88.73	38.78	21.27	27.73	0.95
1982	89.80	40.72	19.57	28.52	0.99
1983	100.68	44.20	22.31	33.18	0.99
1984	123.72	50.18	27.71	44.81	1.02
1985	173.39	64.08	35.51	72.70	1.10
1986	196.84	76.99	39.38	79.31	1.16
1987	225.25	91.01	42.52	90.41	1.31
1988	295.83	119.36	53.66	121.17	1.64
1989	331.38	140.03	51.95	137.70	1.70
1990	333.86	142.15	52.33	137.23	2.15
1991	382.06	162.82	52.91	163.30	3.03
1992	464.82	190.70	67.04	202.83	4.25
1993	679.91	261.46	101.90	311.09	5.46
1994	844.64	329.29	125.36	383.34	6.65
1995	1 069.67	414.69	156.48	490.54	7.96
1996	1 287.96	502.66	183.06	592.91	9.33
1997	1 478.23	581.48	206.61	679.30	10.84
1998	1 650.52	663.87	220.50	754.39	11.76

①根据全国第四次经济普查数据，按国家统计局有关规定，对 1993 年~2018 年的社会消费品零售总额及相应分组进行修订。
②1997 年以前私营经济为合营。
❶According to the regulations of NBS, the Total Value of Retail Sales of Consumer Goods and the corresponding groups between 1993 and 2018 have been revised based on The Fourth National Economic Census.
❷The figures of Private Owned before 1997 refer to these of Joint Owned.

表 16.3 续表 1 continued

单位:亿元(100 million yuan)

年 份 Year	社会消费品零售总额 Total Retail Sales of Consumer Goods	按商品用途分 By Use			
		食品类 Foods	衣着类 Clothing	用品类 Articles	燃料类 Fuels
1999	1 794.74	723.21	237.77	820.73	13.03
2000	1 955.17	779.13	260.94	899.69	15.41
2001	2 126.01	846.17	280.79	981.64	17.41
2002	2 337.44	927.77	306.97	1 083.76	18.94
2003	2 565.20	1 002.09	330.41	1 211.17	21.53
2004	2 863.17	1 124.25	367.77	1 344.23	26.92
2005	3 230.66	1 113.25	363.56	1 694.92	58.93
2006	3 681.66	1 221.44	414.32	1 931.53	114.37
2007	4 250.23	1 321.94	478.30	2 229.82	220.17
2008	5 053.35	1 527.55	568.67	2 651.18	305.95
2009	5 786.83	1 563.89	794.73	2 985.50	442.71
2010	6 901.39	1 788.10	941.31	3 581.22	590.76
2011	8 052.21	1 997.79	1 047.74	4 293.02	713.66
2012	8 833.20	2 078.58	1 195.08	4 801.12	758.42
2013	9 693.15	2 222.96	1 300.10	5 383.35	786.74
2014	10 592.68	2 386.41	1 517.01	6 019.40	669.86
2015	11 605.70	2 676.74	1 753.46	6 603.38	572.12
2016	12 588.21	2 778.63	2 057.85	7 186.37	565.36
2017	13 699.52	2 949.06	2 568.89	7 652.23	529.34
2018	14 874.76	3 031.05	3 052.97	8 192.26	598.48
2019	15 847.55	3 441.80	3 500.10	8 346.62	559.03
2020	15 932.50	3 406.35	3 767.67	8 302.26	456.22
2021	18 079.25	3 852.41	4 161.15	9 507.63	558.06

表 16.3 续表 2 continued

单位：亿元(100 million yuan)

年 份 Year	按经济类型分 By Type of Ownership				
	国有经济 State-owned	集体经济 Collective-owned	私营经济 Private-owned	个 体 Individual	其 他 Others
1978	39.50	14.41		0.19	
1979	46.47	21.32		0.20	0.29
1980	54.01	25.31		0.24	0.87
1981	56.57	30.28	0.04	0.29	1.55
1982	56.48	31.39	0.03	0.32	1.58
1983	63.17	34.55	0.02	0.70	2.24
1984	75.63	43.80	0.02	1.68	2.59
1985	102.59	59.49	0.18	6.42	4.71
1986	111.73	69.06	0.67	8.47	6.91
1987	123.05	80.38	0.88	11.46	9.48
1988	161.65	103.84	1.72	14.56	14.06
1989	176.07	119.97	1.76	16.16	17.42
1990	179.37	115.59	2.05	16.17	20.68
1991	200.25	135.30	2.72	18.70	25.09
1992	247.68	157.56	5.75	22.88	30.95
1993	252.45	203.24	0.51	41.69	182.02
1994	252.22	200.91	0.65	65.77	325.09
1995	251.50	196.47	0.88	77.80	543.02
1996	244.22	187.87	30.82	94.85	730.20
1997	232.08	179.04	22.48	118.31	926.32
1998	218.50	167.51	61.62	131.50	1 071.39

表 16.3 续表 3 continued

单位:亿元(100 million yuan)

年 份 Year	按经济类型分 By Type of Ownership				
	国有经济 State-owned	集体经济 Collective-owned	私营经济 Private-owned	个 体 Individual	其 他 Others
1999	187.91	147.79	65.41	147.09	1 246.54
2000	157.32	123.96	520.80	160.97	992.12
2001	143.07	111.66	628.63	182.05	1 060.60
2002	139.90	108.38	742.15	202.21	1 144.80
2003	142.28	109.54	857.47	222.39	1 233.52
2004	144.88	110.76	1 008.06	251.10	1 348.37
2005	171.29	55.98	882.96	480.68	1 639.75
2006	195.21	63.79	1 006.22	547.78	1 868.66
2007	225.35	73.64	1 161.61	632.38	2 157.25
2008	267.93	87.56	1 381.11	751.87	2 564.88
2009	431.98	32.16	1 407.38	812.30	3 103.01
2010	502.63	36.47	1 697.39	968.76	3 696.14
2011	496.18	39.79	1 851.23	1 130.31	4 534.70
2012	531.05	51.66	1 970.56	1 239.93	5 040.00
2013	532.72	43.97	1 977.73	1 360.64	5 778.09
2014	283.23	27.60	2 130.33	1 304.79	6 846.73
2015	263.18	23.49	2 094.10	1 224.86	8 000.07
2016	102.96	22.53	2 162.81	1 184.91	9 115.00
2017	80.39	21.50	2 374.31	1 142.18	10 081.14
2018	65.33	18.60	2 560.29	1 083.40	11 147.14
2019	62.10	17.85	2 782.44	1 154.25	11 830.91
2020	57.02	14.82	3 086.09	1 160.44	11 614.13
2021	23.38	9.53	3 289.27	1 347.45	13 409.62

表 16.3 续表 4 continued

单位:亿元(100 million yuan)

年 份 Year	社会消费品零售总额 Total Retail Sales of Consumer Goods	按行业分 By Sectors			
		批发零售业 Wholesale and Retail	住宿餐饮业 Hotels and Catering	制造业 Manufacturing	其他行业 Others
1978	54.10	47.55	2.39	1.65	2.51
1979	68.28	59.02	2.82	2.54	3.90
1980	80.43	70.28	3.41	4.24	2.50
1981	88.73	77.53	3.68	4.61	2.91
1982	89.80	77.31	3.76	5.44	3.29
1983	100.68	84.93	4.26	7.72	3.77
1984	123.72	103.27	4.90	10.60	4.95
1985	173.39	150.03	7.58	8.41	7.37
1986	196.84	170.12	9.54	8.79	8.39
1987	225.25	193.50	11.09	10.47	10.19
1988	295.83	254.99	14.48	11.90	14.46
1989	331.38	265.87	15.66	16.84	33.01
1990	333.86	265.67	17.08	15.15	35.96
1991	382.06	300.26	20.91	17.70	43.19
1992	464.82	362.03	25.92	20.25	56.62
1993	679.91	562.86	35.68	29.41	51.96
1994	844.64	692.92	43.25	33.14	75.33
1995	1 069.67	879.39	53.55	38.73	98.00
1996	1 287.96	1 057.38	80.37	40.79	109.42
1997	1 478.23	1 208.99	96.28	45.70	127.26
1998	1 650.52	1 345.05	100.05	47.04	158.38

表 16.3 续表 5 continued

单位:亿元(100 million yuan)

年 份 Year	社会消费品零售总额 Total Retail Sales of Consumer Goods	按行业分 By Sectors			
		批发零售业 Wholesale and Retail	住宿餐饮业 Hotels and Catering	制造业 Manufacturing	其他行业 Others
1999	1 794.74	1 449.56	119.76	49.21	176.21
2000	1 955.17	1 565.09	140.58	51.53	197.97
2001	2 126.01	1 707.17	156.98	53.54	208.32
2002	2 337.44	1 863.23	205.42	55.85	212.94
2003	2 565.20	2 048.58	240.93	57.47	218.22
2004	2 863.17	2 272.28	301.13	60.66	229.10
2005	3 230.66	2 859.60	371.06		
2006	3 681.66	3 258.80	422.86		
2007	4 250.23	3 762.07	488.16		
2008	5 053.35	4 472.95	580.40		
2009	5 786.83	5 118.19	668.64		
2010	6 901.39	6 129.56	771.83		
2011	8 052.21	7 223.86	828.35		
2012	8 833.20	7 930.50	902.70		
2013	9 693.15	8 739.35	953.80		
2014	10 592.68	9 580.86	1 011.82		
2015	11 605.70	10 443.51	1 162.19		
2016	12 588.21	11 354.96	1 233.25		
2017	13 699.52	12 359.08	1 340.44		
2018	14 874.76	13 469.24	1 405.52		
2019	15 847.55	14 381.34	1 466.21		
2020	15 932.50	14 754.23	1 178.27		
2021	18 079.25	16 623.32	1 455.93		

表 16.4 商品交易市场成交情况(2021)
DEALS IN MERCHANDISE EXCHANGE MARKET

分　类	Types	年末出租摊位数(个) Quantity of Year-end Booth Lent (unit)	成交额(亿元) Transaction Volume (100 million yuan)
总　计	**Total**	**103 245**	**10 843.48**
#粮油、食品类	Grain and Oil, Foodstuff	47 338	1 296.90
饮料类	Beverage	2 342	9.05
烟酒类	Tobacco and Liquor	676	3.71
服装、鞋帽、针纺织品类	Garments, Shoes and Hats, Textile Products	16 027	56.03
化妆品类	Cosmetics	511	0.66
金银珠宝类	Jewelry	311	0.85
日用品类	Articles for Daily Use	2 472	15.01
五金、电料类	Hardware and Electrical Appliances	4 117	21.56
体育、娱乐用品类	Recreation and Sports Articles	131	0.27
书报杂志类	Books, Newspapers and Magazines	19	0.26
电子出版物及音像制品类	Electronic Publications and Audio-video Products	58	0.06
家用电器和音像器材类	Household Appliances and Audio-video Equipments	235	3.80
中西药品类	Medicines	200	1.90
文化办公用品类	Culture and Office Articles	995	7.10
家具类	Furnitures	2 647	18.81
通讯器材类	Telecommunication Appliances	1 183	2.61
木材及制品类	Woods and Woods Product	991	34.38
石油及制品类	Oil and Oil Product	319	1 252.02
化工材料及制品类	Chemical Material and Chemical Product	72	0.62
金属材料类	Mental and Mental Product	1 861	7 531.46
建筑及装潢材料类	Construct and Decorate Material	7 816	132.84
机电产品及设备类	Mechanical and Electrical Product and Equipments	852	16.68
汽车类	Automobile	2 844	387.97

表 16.5 主要年份批发零售业销售、库存总额
PURCHASE, SALES AND INVENTORY OF WHOLESALE AND RETAIL IN MAIN YEARS

单位：亿元（100 million yuan）

指 标	Indicators	2000	2010	2015	2020	2021
商品销售总额	**Sales of Commodities**	**7 474.81**	**48 659.55**	**100 145.37**	**139 827.92**	**162 838.66**
零 售	Retail	1 723.31	5 090.26	9 697.73	14 748.14	16 594.31
批 发	Wholesale	5 751.50	43 569.29	90 447.64	125 079.78	146 244.35
年末库存总额	**Year-end Inventory**	**262.50**	**1 913.49**	**4 682.69**	**7 416.59**	**8 026.52**

表 16.6 批发零售业商品销售、库存总额（2021）
PURCHASE, SALES AND INVENTORY OF WHOLESALE AND RETAIL

单位：亿元（100 million yuan）

类 别	Types	商品销售总额 Sales of Commodities	商品库存总额 Year-end Inventory
总 计	**Total**	**162 838.66**	**8 026.52**
限额以上单位	Above the Set Scale	162 209.34	7 995.50
限额以下单位	Below the Set Scale	629.32	31.02

表 16.7 住宿餐饮业营业额（2021）
TURNOVER OF HOTELS AND CATERING SERVICES

单位：亿元（100 million yuan）

类 别	Types	总 计 Total	其 中 of which	
			限额以上单位 Above the set scale	限额以下单位 Below the Set Scale
营业额	**Turnover**	**1 704.46**	**1 440.29**	**264.17**
客房收入	Room Revenue	215.91	182.45	33.46
餐费收入	Catering Service Revenue	1 346.52	1 137.82	208.70
商品销售额	Commodity Sales	56.27	47.55	8.72
其他收入	Other Revenue	85.76	72.47	13.29

表 16.8　汽车交易情况(2018~2021)
DISTRIBUTION OF AUTOMOBILE

单位:万辆(10 000 vehicles)

指　标	Indicators	2018	2019	2020	2021
小型客车及轿车(本市上牌量)	Domestic Small Passenger Cars(Number of New Car Licences)	46.87	43.22	48.82	58.07
#国产小型汽车	Domestic Small Passenger Cars	20.65	19.67	22.48	29.42
国产轿车	Domestic Cars	20.03	17.35	20.91	22.96
进口小型客车及轿车	Small Passerger Cars Imported(including cars)	6.19	6.20	5.43	5.70
二手车交易量	Dealing Number of Secondhand Cars	48.61	53.80	53.35	53.60
#轿　车	Saloon Cars	31.07	33.81	31.76	31.05

表 16.9　限额以上零售企业主要业态零售额(2018~2021)
RETAIL SALES OF MAJOR PATTERNS OF RETAIL ENTERPRISES ABOVE THE SET SCALE

单位:亿元(100 million yuan)

指　标	Indicators	2018	2019	2020	2021
有店铺零售	**Store-based Retailing**				
便利店	Convenience Store	161.41	201.41	167.38	169.02
超　市	Supermarket	88.04	51.27	59.32	48.34
大型超市	Hypemarket	493.33	448.97	486.27	493.21
仓储会员店	Warehouse Club	235.83	257.43	279.96	282.05
百货店	Department Store	640.02	689.09	660.46	758.84
专业店	Speciality Store	1 026.44	1 383.60	1 348.10	1 513.59
专卖店	Franchiesd Store	2 840.06	2 949.73	3 440.95	4 411.46
无店铺零售	**Non-store retailing**				
电视购物	Television Shopping	78.52	101.36	80.96	58.93
网上商店	Online Store	1 083.95	1 404.20	1 778.39	3 138.30

表 16.10 限额以上零售业商品购、销、存总额(2021)
PURCHASE, SALES AND INVENTORY OF RETAIL ABOVE THE SET SCALE

单位:亿元(100 million yuan)

类 别	Types	商品购进总额 Purchase of Commodities	商品销售总额 Sales of Commodities	商品库存总额 Year-end Inventory
总　计	**Total**	**9 492.83**	**12 111.85**	**1 209.17**
按登记注册类型分	**Grouped by Type of Registration**			
内　资	Domestic Funded	5 432.32	6 260.45	542.62
#国　有	State-Owned Enterprises	7.05	8.45	1.74
集　体	Collective-Owned Enterprises	3.21	5.45	0.63
股份合作	Share Holding Cooperative Enterprises	1.86	2.27	0.08
联　营	Joint-Owned Enterprises	9.00	10.05	0.32
有限责任公司	Companies with Limited Liabilities	2 902.03	3 433.10	216.12
股份有限公司	Share Holding Companies with Limited Liabilities	258.42	285.65	46.11
私　营	Private Enterprises	2 250.75	2 515.48	277.62
港澳台商投资	Hong Kong, Macao and Taiwan Funded	2 654.14	3 498.21	361.08
外商投资	Foreign Funded Enterprises	1 406.37	2 353.19	305.47
按行业分	**Grouped by Sector**			
#综合零售	Comprehensive Retail Sale	1 502.44	1 636.95	91.81
食品、饮料及烟草制品专门零售	Food, Beverage and Tabacco	180.69	240.64	19.82
纺织、服装及日用品专门零售	Textile Products, Gaments and Commodity	1 957.04	3 569.76	544.94
文化、体育用品及器材专门零售	Culture & Sports Articles and Equipments	308.76	461.44	128.57
医药及医疗器材专门零售	Medicines and Special Appliances of Medicines	128.90	154.93	14.72
汽车、摩托车、零配件和燃料及其他动力销售	Automobiles, Motocycles, Spare Parts and Fuels and other Power Equipments	2 450.50	2 546.81	200.08
家用电器及电子产品专门零售	Household Electrical Appliances and Electronic Products	564.26	594.26	48.65
五金、家具及室内装饰材料专门零售	Hardwares, Furnitures and Materials of Decoration	100.70	142.50	21.87

表 16.11 限额以上批发业商品购、销、存总额(2021)
PURCHASE, SALES AND INVENTORY OF WHOLESALE ABOVE THE SET SCALE

单位:亿元(100 million yuan)

类 别	Types	商品购进总额 Purchase of Commodities	商品销售总额 Sales of Commodities	商品库存总额 Year-end Inventory
总 计	**Total**	**140 490.90**	**150 097.49**	**6 786.33**
按登记注册类型分	**Grouped by Type of Registration**			
内 资	Domestic Funded	95 683.70	98 365.67	3 105.90
#国 有	State-Owned Enterprises	78.61	81.95	2.05
集 体	Collective-Owned Enterprises	3.45	4.03	0.48
股份合作	Share Holding Cooperative Enterprises	2.05	2.13	0.04
联 营	Joint-Owned Enterprises	0.48	0.54	…
有限责任公司	Companies with Limited Liabilities	47 623.42	48 873.28	1 645.12
股份有限公司	Share Holding Companies with Limited Liabilities	6 615.06	6 874.97	171.36
私 营	Private Enterprises	41 343.59	42 511.36	1 286.54
其 他	Oehters	17.04	17.41	0.31
港澳台商投资	Hong Kong, Macao and Taiwan Funded Enterprises	13 131.80	15 439.33	1 248.77
外商投资	Foreign Funded Enterprises	31 675.40	36 292.49	2 431.66
按行业分	**Grouped by Sector**			
农、林、牧产品批发	Agriculture, Forestry and Animal Husbandry products	2 333.65	2 302.76	168.72
食品、饮料及烟草制品批发	Food, Beverage and Tabacco	7 987.82	9 076.01	605.02
#米、面制品及食用油批发	Rice, Flour and Cooking Oil	2 279.56	2 514.65	111.06
烟草制品批发	Tabacco	658.52	783.43	16.71

表 16.11 续表 continued

单位:亿元(100 million yuan)

类　别	Types	商品购进总额 Purchase of Commodities	商品销售总额 Sales of Commodities	商品库存总额 Year-end Inventory
纺织、服装及家庭用品批发	Textile, Clothing and Household Goods	6 930.98	9 237.07	1 082.36
#服装批发	Garments	1 247.57	1 610.43	312.85
文化、体育用品及器材批发	Culture & Sports Articles and Equipments	2 822.15	3 243.91	333.14
医药及医疗器材批发	Medicines and Special Appliances of Medicines	4 636.59	5 567.61	770.20
矿产品、建材及化工产品批发	Mineral Products, Materials of Construction and Chemical Products	87 294.01	89 008.86	2 072.69
#煤炭及制品批发	Coal	3 469.40	3 571.64	31.94
石油及制品批发	Petroleum	7 829.71	8 026.13	147.09
金属及金属矿批发	Metal Products and Metal Minerals	61 222.71	61 703.86	1 305.42
建材批发	Building Materials	1 840.34	1 928.29	65.35
机械设备、五金产品及电子产品批发	Mechinery Equipments, Hardwares, Electric Appliances and Eletronic Products	26 568.94	29 562.51	1 638.82
#汽车及零配件批发	Automobiles and Spare Parts	8 773.55	9 729.34	468.53
电气设备批发	Electrical Equipment	701.91	758.52	57.43
计算机、软件及辅助设备批发	Computers, Softwares and Accessorial Equipments	5 522.97	6 136.20	273.22
贸易经纪与代理	Trade Broker and Agent	1 028.82	1 060.31	42.44
其他批发业	Others	887.94	1 038.45	72.94

表 16.12 限额以上批发零售业主要商品分类销售额(2021)
TOTAL SALES OF ENTERPRISES ABOVE THE SET SCALE IN WHOLESALE AND RETAIL BY CATEGORY OF MAIN COMMODITIES

单位:亿元(100 million yuan)

类 别	Types	合 计 Total	批发额 Wholesale	零售额 Retail
粮油、食品类	Grain and Oil, and Food	7 991.06	6 835.30	1 155.76
#粮油类	Grain and Oil	3 291.12	3 046.61	244.51
肉禽蛋类	Meat, Poultry and Eggs	1 053.83	881.41	172.42
水产品类	Aquatic Products	318.23	234.00	84.23
蔬菜类	Vegetables	207.89	113.74	94.15
干鲜果品类	Dry and Fresh Fruits	596.21	484.15	112.06
饮料类	Beverages	773.23	587.00	186.23
烟酒类	Tobacco and Liquor	1 986.19	1 688.56	297.63
#烟 类	Tobacco	849.84	759.90	89.94
酒 类	Liquor	1 129.65	922.26	207.39
服装、鞋帽、针纺织品类	Clothing, Shoes, Hats and Textiles	6 214.10	3 367.12	2 846.98
#服装类	Clothing	3 817.72	1 706.26	2 111.46
鞋帽类	Shoes and Hat	1 221.67	587.91	633.76
针、纺织品类	Knitwear and Textiles	1 174.71	1 072.95	101.76
化妆品类	Cosmetics	2 627.13	1 446.26	1 180.87
金银珠宝类	Gold, Silver and Jewelry	1 673.53	1 244.61	428.92
日用品类	Articles for Daily Use	3 646.03	2 584.81	1 061.22
五金、电料类	Hardware and Electrical Materials	1 262.23	1 249.13	13.10
体育、娱乐用品类	Sports and Recreation Articles	414.48	277.06	137.42
#照相器材类	Photographic Equipment	49.43	35.04	14.39
书报杂志类	Newspapers and Magazines	97.94	41.78	56.16
电子出版物及音像制品类	E-journal and Video Products	9.59	7.11	2.48
家用电器和音像器材类	Household Appliances and Video Appliances	1 262.30	815.32	446.98
中西药品类	Traditional Chinese and Western Medicines	2 367.14	2 228.46	138.68
#西药类	Western Medicines	1 840.57	1 760.82	79.75
中草药及中成药类	Traditional Chinese Medicines	216.37	180.70	35.67
文化办公用品类	Cultural and Official Goods	4 450.18	3 976.54	473.64
#计算机及其配套产品	Computer and Its Supporting Producrs	2 458.09	2 264.38	193.71
家具类	Furniture	500.64	378.10	122.54
通讯器材类	Communication Appliances	4 448.98	3 851.65	597.33
煤炭及制品类	Coal and Related Product	3 345.17	3 345.17	
木材及制品类	Lumber and Related Product	946.45	946.45	
石油及制品类	Oil and Related Product	7 784.76	7 226.70	558.06
化工材料及制品类	Chemical Material and Related Product	12 482.40	12 482.40	
#化肥类	Fertilizer	230.67	230.67	
金属材料类	Metal Material	58 905.48	58 905.48	
建筑及装潢材料类	Building and Decoration Materials	1 281.62	1 168.37	113.25
机电产品及设备类	Mechanical and Electrical Products	8 888.79	8 847.26	41.53
#农机类	Agriculture Machinery	64.69	64.69	
汽车类	Automobile	11 205.48	9 163.36	2 042.12
#新能源汽车类	New Energy Automobile	679.35	308.89	370.46
种子饲料类	Seed and Feedstuff	526.06	526.06	
棉麻类	Cotton and Hemp	229.26	229.22	0.04
其他类	Others	8 737.78	8 473.21	264.57

表 16.13　限额以上批发零售业主要财务指标(2017~2021)
MAIN ACCOUNTING INDICATORS OF WHOLESALE AND RETAIL SALES ABOVE THE SET SCALE

单位:亿元(100 million yuan)

指　标	Indicators	2017	2018	2019	2020	2021
流动资产	Current Assets	25 147.91	26 580.96	33 473.76	41 251.61	45 662.20
#存　货	Inventory	4 591.24	5 248.68	6 120.77	6 872.28	7 677.07
固定资产原价	Fixed Assets Original Value	1 798.39	1 888.91	2 231.06	2 431.05	2 598.54
累计折旧	Accumulative Depreciation	841.51	893.66	1 077.46	1 221.06	1 324.79
#本年折旧	Depreciation	111.12	112.56	162.87	180.73	189.56
资产总计	Total Assets	32 023.04	33 231.91	41 778.17	51 338.53	56 922.82
负债合计	Total Liabilities	22 726.53	23 382.30	29 282.69	35 997.30	39 800.03
所有者权益合计	Total Owner's Equities	9 297.24	9 857.75	12 497.62	15 319.09	17 007.65
实收资本	Paid-up Capital	4 910.93	5 525.51	7 232.31	7 237.73	7 541.97
#国家资本	State Capital	783.95	893.89			
港澳台资本	Hong Kong, Macao and Taiwan Capital	661.11	723.49			
外商资本	Foreign Capital	1 109.56	1 125.59			
营业收入	Operating Revenues	83 621.52	88 350.97	108 125.96	119 158.99	143 311.71
营业成本	Operating Costs	76 936.49	80 789.53	99 163.38	109 464.26	131 532.34
税金及附加	Sales Taxes and Extra Charges	148.86	152.27	164.69	186.76	232.90
销售费用	Selling Expenses	3 712.62	4 183.58	5 065.22	5 206.72	6 119.88
管理费用	Management Expenses	1 354.41	1 549.84	1 897.29	2 058.96	2 359.00
财务费用	Financial Expenses	165.07	237.97	257.02	165.16	207.05
营业利润	Operating Profits	1 657.51	1 732.88	2 047.56	2 614.48	3 529.88
利润总额	Total Profits	1 773.72	1 860.60	2 195.21	2 762.98	3 663.40
应付职工薪酬	Payroll Payable	1 254.29	1 376.82	1 815.19	1 842.43	2 244.06

表 16.14 限额以上批发零售业主要财务指标(2021)
MAIN FINANCIAL INDICATORS OF WHOLESALE AND RETAIL ENTERPRISES ABOVE THE SET SCALE

类别	Types	流动资产 Current Assets	固定资产原价 Fixed Assets Original Value	资产总计 Total Assets
总计	**Total**	**45 662.20**	**2 598.54**	**56 922.82**
按登记注册类型分	**Grouped by Type of Registration**			
批发业	**Wholesale Trade**	**41 257.31**	**1 790.96**	**50 860.77**
内资	Domestic Funded Enterprises	22 822.98	867.00	29 043.84
#国有	State-Owned Enterprises	43.81	3.51	52.16
集体	Collective-Owned Enterprises	2.57	0.23	2.68
股份合作	Share Holding Cooperative Enterprises	0.71	0.04	0.71
联营	Joint-Owned Enterprises	0.02	0.06	0.04
有限责任公司	Companies with Limited Liabilities	10 255.24	360.85	13 253.21
股份有限公司	Share Holding Companies with Limited Liabilities	1 808.13	137.97	3 212.45
私营	Private Enterprises	10 711.02	364.08	12 520.99
其他	Others	1.48	0.26	1.60
港澳台商投资	Hong Kong, Macao and Taiwan Funded Enterprises	5 647.44	287.30	6 794.94
外商投资	Foreign Funded Enterprises	12 786.89	636.66	15 021.99
零售业	**Retail Trade**	**4 404.89**	**807.58**	**6 062.05**
内资	Domestic Funded Enterprises	2 186.08	413.44	3 090.58
#国有	State-Owned Enterprises	5.61	1.05	6.33
集体	Collective-Owned Enterprises	8.79	1.51	15.64
股份合作	Share Holding Cooperative Enterprises	1.61	0.05	1.85
联营	Joint-Owned Enterprises	1.15	0.80	1.60
有限责任公司	Responsibility Co.Ltd.	1 001.01	236.41	1 503.49
股份有限公司	Share Holding Co.Ltd.	201.93	79.34	367.36
私营	Private Enterprises	965.98	94.28	1 194.31
港澳台商投资	Hong Kong, Macao and Taiwan Funded Enterprises	1 276.27	215.79	1 712.35
外商投资	Foreign Funded Enterprises	942.54	178.35	1 259.12

单位:亿元(100 million yuan)

负债合计 Total Liabilities	所有者权益合计 Total Owner's Equity	实收资本 Paid-up Capital	营业收入 Operating Revenues	营业成本 Operating Costs	利润总额 Total Profits
39 800.03	**17 007.65**	**7 541.97**	**143 311.71**	**131 532.34**	**3 663.40**
35 293.77	**15 456.08**	**6 449.23**	**132 279.20**	**123 343.79**	**3 195.22**
20 754.76	8 184.12	4 038.16	86 072.14	83 482.33	1 013.07
28.32	23.84	2.72	372.70	347.14	5.01
1.58	1.09	0.22	3.60	3.21	0.18
0.57	0.15	0.03	1.89	1.83	0.02
-0.01	0.05	0.02	0.48	0.42	0.02
9 478.46	3 694.48	1 979.53	42 915.98	41 859.27	575.05
1 658.72	1 552.83	470.75	6 083.45	5 903.61	103.36
9 586.02	2 911.28	1 584.74	36 678.77	35 351.90	329.30
1.10	0.40	0.15	15.27	14.95	0.13
4 365.24	2 430.66	818.95	12 821.04	10 941.86	622.40
10 173.77	4 841.30	1 592.12	33 386.02	28 919.60	1 559.75
4 506.26	**1 551.57**	**1 092.74**	**11 032.51**	**8 188.55**	**468.18**
2 330.11	757.89	542.44	5 684.10	4 800.79	46.18
2.04	4.28	0.20	7.70	6.48	0.33
1.99	13.64	0.50	5.19	3.95	0.11
0.96	0.88	0.11	2.06	1.69	0.38
0.71	0.89	0.08	8.91	7.90	0.44
1 140.71	360.32	332.42	3 029.55	2 618.32	40.33
115.30	252.06	30.98	257.93	209.27	8.78
1 068.40	125.82	178.15	2 372.76	1 953.18	-4.19
1 290.04	412.95	322.52	3 216.46	2 168.29	226.08
886.11	380.73	227.78	2 131.95	1 219.47	195.92

表 16.14 续表 continued

类 别	Types	流动资产 Current Assets	固定资产原价 Fixed Assets Original Value	资产总计 Total Assets
按行业分	**Grouped by Sector**			
批发业	**Wholesale Trade**	**41 257.31**	**1 790.96**	**50 860.77**
农、林、牧产品批发	Agriculture, Forestry and Animal Husbandry Products	834.50	20.06	985.36
食品、饮料及烟草制品批发	Food, Beverage and Tabacco	3 275.39	221.90	4 216.01
纺织、服装及家庭用品批发	Textile, Clothing and Household Goods	4 004.08	373.54	5 002.64
文化、体育用品及器材批发	Culture & Sports Articles and Equipments	1 306.12	48.95	1 507.41
医药及医疗器材批发	Medicines and Special Appliances of Medicines	3 293.16	315.48	4 355.23
矿产品、建材及化工产品批发	Mineral Products, Materials of Construction and Chemical Products	15 902.10	427.65	19 808.05
机械设备、五金交电及电子产品批发	Mechinery Equipments, Hardwares, Electric Appliances and Eletronic Products	11 763.83	340.10	13 860.89
贸易经纪与代理	Trade Broker and Agent	424.84	13.59	550.65
其他批发	Others	453.29	29.69	574.53
零售业	**Retail Trade**	**4 404.89**	**807.58**	**6 062.05**
综合零售	Comprehensive Retail Sale	679.02	319.84	1 256.62
食品、饮料及烟草制品专门零售	Food, Beverage and Tabacco	111.57	20.40	158.35
纺织、服装及日用品专门零售	Textile Products, Garments and Commodity	1 537.27	197.07	1 980.47
文化、体育用品及器材专门零售	Culture & Sports Articles and Equipments	253.69	41.57	322.63
医药及医疗器材专门零售	Medicines and Special Appliances of Medicines	51.93	6.94	80.48
汽车、摩托车、零配件和燃料及其他动力销售	Automobiles, Motocycles, Spare Parts and Fuels and other Power Equipments	613.78	128.12	823.61
家用电器及电子产品专门零售	Household Electrical Appliances and Electronic Products	240.20	10.12	287.75
五金、家具及室内装饰材料专门零售	Hardwares, Furnitures and Materials of Decoration	103.11	40.92	172.22
货摊、无店铺及其他零售业	Stall, Non-store and Other Retailing	814.32	42.60	979.92

单位:亿元(100 million yuan)

负债合计 Total Liabilities	所有者权益合计 Total Owner's Equity	实收资本 Paid-up Capital	营业收入 Operating Revenues	营业成本 Operating Costs	利润总额 Total Profits
35 293.77	**15 456.08**	**6 449.23**	**132 279.20**	**123 343.79**	**3 195.22**
790.31	192.17	149.62	2 105.95	2 036.83	20.31
2 762.35	1 447.49	574.98	8 259.58	7 239.61	228.86
3 194.66	1 808.45	662.08	8 444.07	6 245.76	474.69
1 016.96	490.19	201.45	2 895.33	2 518.76	179.06
2 757.52	1 596.20	385.44	5 186.53	4 185.73	276.47
14 452.60	5 293.62	2 874.42	76 310.17	74 783.38	844.60
9 571.20	4 251.82	1 464.86	27 138.24	24 578.15	1 110.03
343.81	205.83	36.18	990.25	920.87	32.73
404.36	170.31	100.20	949.08	834.70	28.47
4 506.26	**1 551.57**	**1 092.74**	**11 032.51**	**8 188.55**	**468.18**
965.69	297.38	301.71	1 451.71	1 157.17	15.02
121.38	37.97	24.54	235.03	157.00	4.79
1 340.92	639.72	299.52	3 205.31	1 686.81	420.71
220.10	102.79	52.69	419.32	249.48	13.26
61.75	18.53	11.52	146.71	115.90	3.34
577.65	245.13	145.81	2 388.40	2 194.31	45.49
237.91	49.84	34.21	539.11	482.62	-2.32
134.03	27.11	36.35	126.18	93.21	0.78
846.83	133.10	186.39	2 520.74	2 052.05	-32.89

表 16.15 限额以上住宿和餐饮业经营情况(2021)
OPERATING CONDITIONS OF HOTELS AND CATERING INDUSTRY ABOVE THE SET SCALE

单位:亿元(100 million yuan)

类 别	Types	营业额 Turnover	其 中 of which 客房收入 Room Revenue	餐费收入 Catering Service Revenue	商品销售额 Commodity Sales	其他收入 Other Revenue
总 计	**Total**	**1 440.29**	**182.45**	**1 137.82**	**47.55**	**72.47**
住宿业	**Accommodation**	**309.11**	**180.59**	**68.06**	**9.54**	**50.92**
按登记注册类型分	**Grouped by Type of Registration**					
内资企业	Domestic Funded Enterprises	244.22	150.74	52.79	1.84	38.85
国有企业	State-Owned Enterprises	1.32	0.46	0.42	0.12	0.32
集体企业	Collective-Owned Enterprises	1.07	0.28	0.67		0.12
有限责任公司	Companies with Limited Liabilities	131.50	67.56	32.02	1.45	30.47
股份有限公司	Share Holding Companies with Limited Liabilities	0.92	0.30	0.57		0.05
私营企业	Private Enterprises	109.35	82.12	19.09	0.27	7.87
其他企业	Others	0.06	0.02	0.02	…	0.02
港、澳、台商投资企业	Hong Kong, Macao and Taiwan Funded Enterprises	34.20	15.83	9.90	0.27	8.20
外商投资企业	Foreign Funded Enterprises	30.69	14.02	5.37	7.43	3.87
按星级分组	**Grouped by Star Level**					
五 星	Five-Star	89.89	38.64	29.68	0.43	21.14
四 星	Four-Star	28.78	14.53	7.93	0.38	5.94
三 星	Three-Star	10.60	6.53	1.42	0.02	2.63
二 星	Two-Star	1.24	0.77	0.18	…	0.29
一 星	One-Star					
其 他	Others	178.60	120.12	28.85	8.71	20.92
餐饮业	**Catering**	**1 131.18**	**1.86**	**1 069.76**	**38.01**	**21.55**
按登记注册类型分	**Grouped by Type of Registration**					
内资企业	Domestic Funded Enterprises	602.72	1.86	575.64	11.76	13.46
国有企业	State-Owned Enterprises	1.60		1.46		0.14
集体企业	Collective-Owned Enterprises	0.81	0.04	0.75		0.02
联 营	Joint-Owned Enterprises	0.81	0.01	0.66		0.14
股份合作企业	Share Holding Cooperative Enterprises	0.03		…		0.03
有限责任公司	Companies with Limited Liabilities	138.22	0.33	131.02	2.81	4.06
股份有限公司	Share Holding Companies with Limited Liabilities	19.17		14.72	3.66	0.79
私营企业	Private Enterprises	440.88	1.43	426.33	4.95	8.17
其他企业	Others	1.20	0.05	0.70	0.34	0.11
港、澳、台商投资企业	Hong Kong, Macao and Taiwan Funded Enterprises	253.51		235.03	12.77	5.71
外商投资企业	Foreign Funded Enterprises	274.95		259.09	13.48	2.38
按行业分	**Grouped by Sectors**					
正餐服务	Restaurant	691.79	1.84	662.64	14.85	12.46
快餐服务	Fast Food	175.66	0.02	167.46	3.11	5.07
饮料及冷饮服务	Beverages and Cold Drinks	178.96		158.31	16.95	3.70
茶馆服务	Teahouse	0.42		0.41	0.01	…
咖啡馆服务	Café	139.08		122.28	15.04	1.76
酒吧服务	Bar	1.13		1.13		…
其他饮料及冷饮服务	Others	38.33		34.49	1.90	1.94
餐饮配送及外卖送餐服务	Food and Beverage Distribution and Delivery Service of Takeout Food	53.56		50.82	2.62	0.12
餐饮配送服务	Food and Beverage Distribution	52.70		49.96	2.62	0.12
外卖送餐服务	Delivery Service of Takeout Food	0.86		0.86		
其他餐饮业	Others	31.21		30.53	0.48	0.20
小吃服务	Refreshment	10.30		9.99	0.19	0.12
其他未列明餐饮业	Others	20.91		20.54	0.29	0.08

表 16.16 限额以上住宿餐饮业主要财务指标(2017~2021)
MAIN FINANCIAL INDICATORS OF HOTELS AND CATERING ENTERPRISES ABOVE THE SET SCALE

单位:亿元(100 million yuan)

指 标	Indicators	2017	2018	2019	2020	2021
流动资产	Current Assets	610.26	647.35	819.49	997.51	1 044.32
#存 货	Inventory	31.34	30.15	23.88	30.12	33.74
固定资产原价	Fixed Assets Original Value	700.12	732.57	872.57	928.47	961.31
累计折旧	Accumulative Depreciation	353.45	381.44	431.26	478.51	490.89
#本年折旧	Depreciation	36.42	32.92	36.76	40.91	36.54
资产总计	Total Assets	1 339.11	1 351.55	1 626.83	1 918.96	2 118.23
负债合计	Total Liabilities	845.62	826.81	1 068.59	1 375.54	1 535.90
所有者权益合计	Total Owner's Equities	493.48	525.37	558.35	549.17	587.35
实收资本	Paid-up Capital	523.05	880.89	530.91	608.51	611.96
#国家资本	State Capital	137.57	133.67			
港澳台资本	Hong Kong, Macao and Taiwan Capital	63.60	73.71			
外商资本	Foreign Capital	58.72	59.18			
营业收入	Operating Revenues	961.35	1 016.31	1 231.31	1 093.76	1 404.44
营业成本	Operating Costs	383.06	406.92	529.88	519.45	647.00
税金及附加	Sales Taxes and Extra Charges	7.78	6.28	6.51	6.11	6.78
销售费用	Selling Expenses	346.38	373.63	452.39	416.56	515.39
管理费用	Management Expenses	165.41	174.70	207.77	196.32	230.33
财务费用	Financial Expenses	10.98	12.05	15.56	21.32	23.81
营业利润	Operating Profits	61.79	48.01	34.06	-43.50	-5.64
利润总额	Total Profits	68.75	48.55	37.67	-35.00	1.63
应付职工薪酬	Total Payable Welfare Involved in Major Business	185.54	198.51	249.80	264.99	322.71

表 16.17 主要年份连锁零售业和餐饮业经营情况
BASIC STATISTICS OF CHAIN RETAIL AND CATERING SERVICES IN MAIN YEARS

指 标	Indicators	2010	2015	2019	2020	2021
门店总数(个)	Quantity of Stores(unit)	20 969	21 918	30 926	28 901	29 040
营业面积(万平方米)	Operational Area(10 000 sq.m)	937.97	1 190.96	1 351.00	1 386.47	1 356.36
从业人数(万人)	Number of Persons Employed(10 000 person)	37.17	33.86	44.34	39.91	39.74
零售业商品购进总额(亿元)	Purchase of Commodities of Retail(100 million yuan)	2 249.57	2 805.36	3 582.57	3 225.38	3 520.59
零售业商品销售总额(亿元)	Sales of Commodities of Retail (100 million yuan)	3 071.67	3 174.58	4 304.76	3 679.81	4 004.14
#零售额	Retail Sales	2 241.97	2 456.26	3 450.47	3 127.72	3 273.51
餐饮业营业额(亿元)	Total Operating Revenue of Catering Services (100 million yuan)	104.18	209.48	420.89	378.92	450.21

表 16.18 限额以上住宿餐饮业主要财务指标(2021)
MAIN FINANCIAL INDICATORS OF HOTELS AND CATERING ENTERPRISES ABOVE THE SET SCALE

类 别	Types	流动资产 Current Assets	固定资产原价 Fixed Assets Original Value	资产总计 Total Assets
总 计	**Total**	**1 044.32**	**961.31**	**2 118.23**
按登记注册类型分	**Grouped by Type of Registration**			
住宿业	**Accommodation**	**563.46**	**802.51**	**1 373.05**
内 资	Domestic Enterprises	347.45	493.08	858.81
#国 有	State-Owned Enterprises	14.09	11.48	33.10
集 体	Collective-Owned Enterprises	0.75	3.36	1.83
有限责任公司	Companies with Limited Liabilities	189.84	348.93	513.03
股份有限公司	Share Holding Companies with Limited Liabilities	0.26		0.26
私 营	Private Enterprises	142.47	129.31	310.55
其 他	Others	0.04	…	0.04
港澳台商投资	Hong Kong, Macao and Taiwan Funded	145.29	173.68	330.52
外商投资	Foreign Funded Enterprises	70.72	135.75	183.72
餐饮业	**Catering**	**480.86**	**158.80**	**745.18**
内 资	Domestic Enterprises	253.72	60.13	346.76
国 有	State-Owned Enterprises	1.64	0.18	1.93
集 体	Collective-Owned Enterprises	0.29	0.73	0.98
联 营	Joint-Owned Enterprises	0.32	0.14	0.45
股份合作	Share Holding Cooperative Enterprises	0.05	0.04	0.05
有限责任公司	Responsibility Co.Ltd.	41.92	11.86	62.56
股份有限公司	Share Holding Co.Ltd.	22.48	2.63	32.74
私 营	Private Enterprises	186.18	43.13	246.18
其 他	Others	0.84	1.42	1.87
港澳台商投资	Hong Kong, Macao and Taiwan Funded	108.98	60.64	209.83
外商投资	Foreign Funded Enterprises	118.16	38.03	188.59

单位：亿元（100 million yuan）

负债合计 Total Liabilities	所有者权益合计 Total Owner's Equity	实收资本 Paid-up Capital	营业收入 Operating Revenues	营业成本 Operating Costs	利润总额 Total Profits
1 535.90	**587.35**	**611.96**	**1 404.44**	**647.00**	**1.63**
991.10	**384.06**	**441.75**	**311.25**	**133.88**	**-18.49**
652.87	208.05	246.30	240.48	102.88	-14.39
7.92	25.09	13.91	3.26	0.63	-0.69
0.08	1.74	0.29	1.02	0.40	-0.13
327.83	185.98	183.08	128.55	56.41	-5.46
0.39	-0.13		0.86	0.20	-0.13
316.63	-4.65	49.01	106.74	45.21	-7.99
0.02	0.02	0.01	0.05	0.03	0.01
217.20	113.32	99.21	33.49	15.59	-4.98
121.03	62.69	96.24	37.28	15.41	0.88
544.80	**203.29**	**170.21**	**1 093.19**	**513.12**	**20.12**
290.45	58.01	56.45	584.37	304.45	-1.17
1.78	0.15	0.11	1.49	0.73	-0.11
0.47	0.51	0.11	0.79	0.38	0.04
0.21	0.24	0.04	0.78	0.30	0.02
…	0.05	0.02	0.03	0.02	…
64.05	-0.83	11.99	132.57	65.34	-4.46
16.60	16.14	4.30	19.28	10.40	2.59
206.52	40.71	38.95	428.26	226.54	0.74
0.82	1.04	0.93	1.17	0.74	0.01
144.46	66.64	66.12	242.77	104.91	-2.15
109.89	78.64	47.64	266.05	103.76	23.44

表 16.18 续表 continued

类别	Types	流动资产 Current Assets	固定资产原价 Fixed Assets Original Value	资产总计 Total Assets
按行业分	**Grouped by Sector**			
住宿业	**Accommodation**	**563.46**	**802.51**	**1 373.05**
旅游饭店	Tiyrust Hotel	443.61	707.46	1 127.41
一般旅馆	Fonda	116.50	93.13	240.83
经济型连锁酒店	Economic Chain Hotel	56.82	35.53	116.89
其他一般旅馆	Other Fonda	59.68	57.60	123.94
民宿服务	Homestay	0.30	0.09	0.55
露营地服务	Campsite	0.04	0.05	0.04
其他住宿业	Others	3.01	1.78	4.22
餐饮业	**Catering**	**480.86**	**158.80**	**745.18**
正餐服务	Restaurant	287.12	100.04	441.56
快餐服务	Fast Food	47.33	28.86	114.85
饮料及冷饮服务	Beverages and Cold Drinks	112.15	24.11	148.63
茶馆服务	Teahouse	0.55	0.06	0.57
咖啡馆服务	Café	91.62	20.25	121.70
酒吧服务	Bar	0.22	0.04	0.27
其他饮料及冷饮服务	Others	19.76	3.76	26.09
餐饮配送及外卖送餐服务	Food and Beverage Distribution and Delivery Service of Takeout Food	22.04	3.49	25.18
餐饮配送服务	Food and Beverage Distribution	21.67	3.47	24.80
外卖送餐服务	Delivery Service of Takeout Food	0.37	0.02	0.38
其他餐饮业	Others	12.22	2.30	14.96
小吃服务	Refreshment	5.13	1.60	7.19
其他未列明餐饮业	Others	7.09	0.70	7.77

单位:亿元(100 million yuan)

负债合计 Total Liabilities	所有者权益合计 Total Owner's Equity	实收资本 Paid-up Capital	营业收入 Operating Revenues	营业成本 Operating Costs	利润总额 Total Profits
991.10	**384.06**	**441.75**	**311.25**	**133.88**	**-18.49**
789.67	338.78	378.03	204.26	84.87	-16.23
194.36	47.54	61.35	102.58	46.56	-1.84
93.12	24.07	29.37	49.16	22.41	-1.21
101.24	23.47	31.98	53.42	24.15	-0.63
0.56	-0.01	0.55	0.33	0.29	-0.02
0.01	0.03	0.07	0.12	0.12	0.01
6.50	-2.28	1.75	3.96	2.04	-0.41
544.80	**203.29**	**170.21**	**1 093.19**	**513.12**	**20.12**
358.05	86.19	106.07	665.57	313.12	-5.40
89.17	25.68	35.32	170.02	80.83	3.25
68.68	79.96	16.82	175.71	61.17	21.29
0.65	-0.09	0.08	0.40	0.23	-0.03
45.61	76.09	15.28	134.06	44.36	18.88
0.45	-0.18	0.06	1.07	0.38	0.04
21.97	4.14	1.40	40.18	16.20	2.40
16.59	8.56	6.45	51.76	41.64	0.77
16.55	8.23	6.44	50.94	41.35	0.66
0.04	0.33	0.01	0.82	0.29	0.11
12.31	2.90	5.55	30.13	16.36	0.21
5.76	1.69	3.93	9.87	4.38	-0.23
6.55	1.21	1.62	20.26	11.98	0.44

上/海/统/计/年/鉴

主要统计指标解释

■ 社会消费品零售总额

指企业(单位、个体户)通过交易直接售给个人、社会集团非生产、非经营用的实物商品金额,以及提供餐饮服务所取得的收入金额。个人包括城乡居民和入境人员,社会集团包括机关、社会团体、部队、学校、企事业单位、居委会或村委会等。

■ 商品购进总额

指从本企业以外的单位和个人购进(包括从国外直接进口)作为转卖或加工后转卖的商品金额(含增值税)。本指标反映批发和零售业从国内外市场上购进商品的总价。商品购进包括:(1)从工农业生产者、批发和零售业、住宿和餐饮业、出版社或报社的出版发行部门和其他服务业等企事业单位和个体经营户购进的商品;(2)从机关、社会团体购进的商品;(3)从海关、市场管理部门购进的缉私和没收的商品;(4)从居民收购的废旧商品等。

■ 商品销售总额

指对本单位以外的单位和个人出售的商品金额(包括售给本单位消费用的商品,含增值税),在批发和零售业中,本指标反映在国内市场上销售商品以及出口商品的总价。商品销售包括:(1)售给个人和社会集团消费用的商品;(2)售给农业、工业、建筑业、服务业等国民经济各行业用于生产、经营用的商品,包括售予批发和零售业作为转卖或加工后转卖的商品;(3)对国(境)外直接出口的商品。

■ 主营业务收入

指企业经营主要业务所实现的收入。

■ 营业成本

指企业从事销售商品、提供劳务和让渡资产使用权等生产经营活动发生的实际成本。

■ 连锁总店(总部)

负责连锁企业资源(商号、商誉、经营模式、服务标准、管理模式等)的开发、配置、控制或使用等功能的企业核心管理机构。连锁经营是指经营同类商品或服务,使用统一商号的若干店铺,在同一总店(总部)的管理下,采取统一采购或特许经营等方式,实现规模效益的组织形式,包括直营连锁、特许连锁和自愿连锁三种形式。系统内企业,如新华书店、烟草公司、石油公司等,应注意是否具备连锁经营特征,如果不具备连锁经营特征,则不能纳入连锁统计范畴。

■ 商品交易市场

指经有关部门和组织批准设立,有固定场所、设施,有经营管理部门和监管人员,若干市场经营者入内,常年或实际开业三个月以上,集中、公开、独立地进行生活消费品、生产资料等现货商品交易以及提供相关服务的交易场所,包括各类消费品市场、生产资料市场等。

SHANGHAI STATISTICAL YEARBOOK

EXPLANATORY NOTES TO MAJOR STATISTICAL INDICATORS

□ Total Retail Sales of Consumer Goods

Total Retail Sales of Consumer Goods refer to the revenue received by enterprises (units, self-employed individuals) through direct sales of non-production and non-business physical commodities to individuals and social institutions, and revenue from providing catering services. Individuals include rural and urban households, population from abroad, social institutions include government agencies, social organizations, military units, schools, institutions, neighbourhood (village) committees, etc.

□ Total Purchase of Commodities

Total Purchases of Commodities refer to the total value of purchases of commodities by enterprises (establishments) from other establishments or individuals (including direct import from abroad) for the purpose of re-selling, either with or without further processing of the commodities purchased. The commodities include: (1) commodities purchased from agricultural and industrial producers, wholesalers, retailers, hotels and catering services, publishing houses and other enterprises, institutions and individual operators of service business; (2) commodities purchased from institutions and government departments; (3) smuggled or confiscated goods purchased from the customs authorities or market regulation agencies; (4) second-hand goods purchased from households.

□ Total Sales of Commodities

Total Sales of Commodities refer to value of commodities sold by the establishments to other establishments and individuals (including goods sold for self consumption, including VAT). The commodities include: (1) commodities sold to individuals and social groups for their consumption; (2) commodities sold to establishments in all industries for their production and operation, including agriculture, industry, construction, and catering services, including commodities sold to wholesale and retail establishments for re-selling, with or without further processing; (3) commodities for direct export to abroad.

□ Prime Operating Revenue

Prime Operating Revenue refers to the revenue from prime business.

□ Operating Cost

Operating Cost refers to the cost a corporation paid to producing and operating activities such as selling goods, providing services and delivering the permission of assets.

□ Chain Head Stores (Headquarters)

Chain Head Stores (Headquarters) refer to the core leading stores responsible for development, allocation, administration and utilization of resources (name of stores, brand of stores, operation model, service standard, management way, etc.) of chain stores. Chain stores refer to the stores engaged in providing homogeneous commodities or services, with the central leadership of the head stores (headquarters) and guided by common policies, conduct centralized purchase and distributed selling of commodities, in order to gain better efficiency through standardized operation. The chain stores include regular chain stores, franchise chain stores and voluntary chain stores. Corporations in systems, such as Xinhua Bookstore, Tobacco Corporation, Petroleum Corporation, etc, should have the characteristics of chain stores, otherwise can not be counted in chain stores.

Regular Chain store refers to chain stores that are invested or controlled by the headquarters. They operate under direct and unified management from the headquarters.

□ Commodity Markets

The commodity markets refer to markets approved and managed by related departments, where there are fixed sites, facilities, managers and administrative offices, where there are a certain number of traders to operate for at least three months or all the year, where the commodities, including articles for daily consumption and capital goods and services, are traded in a centralized, independent and open way. Such markets include markets for daily goods, markets of capital goods, etc.

第十七篇

CHAPTER 17

金融业

FINANCE

简要说明

本篇反映上海市金融业发展情况。由以下四部分组成:一是保费收支情况,数据由中国银行保险监督管理委员会上海监管局提供;二是金融机构存贷款余额情况,数据由中国人民银行上海总部和上海公积金管理中心提供;三是金融市场运行情况,数据由上海证券交易所、上海期货交易所、中国金融期货交易所、全国银行间同业拆借中心和上海黄金交易所提供。

BRIEF INTRODUCTION

Data in this chapter reflect the development of Shanghai´s financial industries. The data consit of four parts: (1) Premium of primary insurance and payment. Data are provided by the China Banking and Insurance Regulatory Commission Shanghai Bureau. (2) The situations regarding the changes of deposit and loan balance. Data are provided by the Shanghai Headquarters of People´s Bank of China and the Shanghai Provident Fund Administration Center. (3) Data on the activities of financial institutions. Data are provided by the Shanghai Stock Exchange, the Shanghai Futures Exchange, the China Financial Futures Exchange, the National Interbank Funding Center, and the Shanghai Gold Exchange.

表 17.1 主要年份原保险保费收入和赔付支出
PREMIUM OF PRIMARY INSURANCE AND PAYMENT IN MAIN YEARS

单位:亿元(100 million yuan)

年 份 Year	原保险保费收入 Premium of Primary Insurance	其 中 of which		原保险赔付支出 Payment of Primary Insurance	其 中 of which	
		人身保险 Liability Insurance	财产保险 Property Insurance		人身保险 Liability Insurance	财产保险 Property Insurance
1978	0.17			0.17		
1980	0.70			0.13		
1990	8.99			2.22		
1991	11.16			4.47		
1992	18.20			4.23		
1993	25.91			5.89		
1994	39.48			11.91		
1995	44.04	17.08	26.96	12.75		
1996	58.10	28.64	29.46	15.00		
1997	87.72	58.13	29.59	19.10		
1998	102.92	70.50	32.42	28.67		
1999	115.28	81.53	33.75	39.46		
2000	127.23	92.14	35.09	36.44	20.56	15.88
2001	180.25	140.30	39.95	38.82	19.61	19.21
2002	237.61	193.30	44.31	49.97	28.38	21.59
2003	289.93	232.50	57.43	61.97	34.87	27.10
2004	307.11	231.30	75.81	70.86	36.79	34.07
2005	333.62	245.76	87.86	87.46	40.20	47.26
2006	407.04	305.72	101.33	91.31	46.14	45.17
2007	482.64	363.22	119.43	139.82	86.79	53.03
2008	600.06	468.27	131.79	184.09	104.57	79.52
2009	665.03	513.22	151.81	176.74	98.24	78.50
2010	883.86	686.68	197.18	194.54	110.28	84.26
2011	753.11	519.71	233.39	260.71	156.39	104.32
2012	820.64	564.26	256.38	255.79	117.16	138.63
2013	821.43	536.18	285.25	301.95	139.62	162.33
2014	986.75	666.39	320.36	378.66	201.42	177.24
2015	1 125.16	769.77	355.40	473.59	282.22	191.38
2016	1 529.26	1 158.11	371.15	528.77	306.22	222.55
2017	1 587.10	1 158.49	428.61	548.93	315.11	233.81
2018	1 405.79	920.70	485.09	581.56	309.93	271.62
2019	1 720.01	1 195.12	524.90	654.90	348.78	306.12
2020	1 865.00	1 356.00	509.00	631.00	352.00	278.00
2021	1 971.00	1 447.00	524.00	738.00	451.00	287.00

注：2010 年原保险保费收入为按财产险公司和寿险公司分类。
Note：Data of Premium of Primary Insurance of 2010 are classified by Property Insurance Company and Liability Insurance Company.

表 17.2 中外资金融机构存贷款年末余额(2019~2021)
DEPOSIT AND LOAN BALANCE OF FINANCIAL INSTITUTIONS AT YEAR-END

单位:亿元(100 million yuan)

指 标	Indicators	2019	2020	2021
中外资金融机构存款余额	**Saving Deposit Balance of Financial Institutions**	**132 820.27**	**155 865.06**	**175 831.08**
中资金融机构	Chinese Financial Institutions	124 387.21	146 293.07	165 804.76
人民币	RMB	116 633.41	137 624.46	155 629.84
外汇(折人民币)	Foreign Currencies(Converting into RMB)	7 753.80	8 668.61	10 174.92
外资金融机构	Foreign-funded Financial Institutions	8 488.05	9 621.68	10 091.13
外汇(折人民币)	Foreign Currencies (Converting into RMB)	1 736.44	1 870.30	1 838.44
人民币	RMB	6 751.61	7 751.38	8 252.69
中外资金融机构贷款余额	**Loan Balance of Financial Institutions**	**79 843.01**	**84 643.04**	**96 032.13**
中资金融机构	Chinese Financial Institutions	74 834.35	80 003.85	90 491.74
人民币	RMB	70 167.21	74 413.63	84 281.24
外汇(折人民币)	Foreign Currencies (Converting into RMB)	4 667.14	5 590.22	6 210.50
外资金融机构	Foreign-funded Financial Institutions	6 070.55	5 821.86	6 842.86
外汇(折人民币)	Foreign Currencies (Converting into RMB)	1 575.79	1 256.99	1 710.30
人民币	RMB	4 494.76	4 564.87	5 132.56

注：自 2015 年起，中资和外资金融机构存贷款统计口径有所不同，外资金融机构各项存贷款包含对银行业非存款类金融机构的存放和拆放款项。
Note：Since 2015, the diposits and loan balance of foreign-funded financial institutions include the deposits and borrowings with non deposit financial institutions in the banking industry.

表 17.3 中外资金融机构存款年末余额(2021)
DEPOSITS OF FINANCIAL INSTITUTIONS AT YEAR-END

单位:亿元(100 million yuan)

指 标	Indicators	2021	比 2021 年初增加 Increase from the Beginning of 2021
中外资金融机构本外币各项存款余额	**All Deposits of Chinese and Foreign-funded Financial Institutions**	**175 831.08**	**19 966.51**
境内存款	Domestic Deposits	166 742.74	18 698.75
住户存款	Household Deposits	42 652.55	4 342.68
活期存款	Current Deposits	14 337.95	1 213.17
定期及其他存款	Time Deposits and Other Deposits	28 314.60	3 129.51
非金融企业存款	Non Financial Enterprise Deposits	68 894.07	6 056.15
活期存款	Current Deposits	20 382.84	2 119.87
定期及其他存款	Time Deposits and Other Deposits	48 511.23	3 936.29
机关团体存款	Deposits of Non-profit Institutions	16 702.86	1 521.80
财政性存款	Fiscal Deposits	4 737.36	802.77
非银行业金融机构存款	Deposits of Non Banking Financial Institutions	33 755.90	5 975.35
境外存款	Foreign Deposits	9 088.34	1 267.75

表 17.4 中外资金融机构贷款年末余额(2021)
LOAN BALANCE OF FINANCIAL INSTITUTIONS AT YEAR-END

单位:亿元(100 million yuan)

指标	Indicators	2021	比 2021 年初增加 Increase from the Beginning of 2021
中外资金融机构本外币各项贷款余额	**All Loans of Chinese and Foreign-funded Financial Institutions**	**96 032.13**	**11 390.73**
境内贷款	Domestic Loans	90 979.20	10 674.92
住户贷款	Household Loans	28 557.72	2 958.69
短期贷款	Short-term Loans	3 235.65	358.45
中长期贷款	Mid and Long-term Loans	25 322.06	2 600.25
非金融企业及机关团体贷款	Loans of Non Financial Enterprise and Non-profit Institutions	62 031.76	7 730.61
#短期贷款	Short-term Loans	17 594.14	864.03
中长期贷款	Mid and Long-term Loans	34 566.20	5 208.99
票据融资	Notes Finacing	4 440.37	1 058.89
非银行业金融机构贷款	Loans of Non Banking Financial Institutions	389.72	-14.39
境外贷款	Foreign Loans	5 052.94	715.82

表 17.5 个人消费贷款及公积金贷款年末余额(2019~2021)
PERSONAL CONSUMPTION LOAN AND ACCUMULATION FUND LOAN AT YEAR-END

指标	Indicators	2019	2020	2021
中外资金融机构人民币个人消费贷款余额(亿元)	**Personal Consumption Loan of Chinese and Foreign-funded Financial Institutions (100 million yuan)**	**22 393.43**	**22 146.92**	**24 100.29**
#个人住房贷款	Housing Mortgage Loan	14 351.73	15 377.03	16 672.74
汽车消费贷款	Car Consumption Loan	4 227.64	3 075.67	3 399.33
个人住房贷款占金融机构人民币个人消费贷款额比重(%)	**Housing Mortgage Loan Percentage of Personal Consumption Loan(%)**	**64.1**	**69.4**	**69.2**
公积金贷款余额(亿元)	**Accumulation Fund Loan(100 million yuan)**	**4 450.05**	**4 978.75**	**5 580.86**

表 17.6 主要金融市场成交额(2019~2021)
TURNOVER OF MAIN FANANCIAL MARKET

单位:亿元(100 million yuan)

指 标	Indicators	2019	2020	2021
上海证券交易所成交额	Turnover of Shanghai Stock Exchange	2 834 818.77	3 667 030.13	4 611 280.67
上海期货交易所成交额	Turnover of Shanghai Future Exchange	1 125 219.99	1 528 015.13	2 145 779.20
中国金融期货交易所成交额	Turnover of China Financial Futures Exchange	696 210.17	1 154 350.96	1 181 651.64
银行间市场成交额	Turnover of Interbank Market	14 543 054.67	16 182 301.37	17 069 348.38
上海黄金交易所成交额	Turnover of Shanghai Gold Exchange	143 775.38	216 609.20	102 639.71

注：银行间市场成交额包括银行间本币市场和外汇市场成交额。本表中成交额数据均按单向计算。
Note: The turnover of Interbank Market has included turnover of Interbank RMB market and turnover of foreign exchange trading market. The turnover data in the table are calculated by buy or sell.

表 17.7 上海证券交易所上市公司股本结构和市价总值(2021)
CAPITAL STOCK STRUCTURE AND MARKET CAPITALIZATION OF PUBLIC COMPANIES IN SHANGHAI STOCK EXCHANGE

单位:亿元(100 million yuan)

类 别	Types	发行总股本 Issued Volume	市价总值 Market Capitalization
A 股总股本	Total Equity of A Shares	46 054.51	518 800.13
A 股非限售股本	Non-restricted Equity of A Shares	40 263.10	434 682.14
A 股限售股本	Restricted Equity of A Shares	5 791.42	84 117.99
B 股总股本	Total Equity of B Shares	182.51	898.20
B 股非流通股本	Non-tradable Equity of B Shares	23.25	11 404.00

表 17.8 上海证券交易所市场概况(2019~2021)
SHANGHAI STOCK EXCHANGE MARKET

指 标	Indicators	2019	2020	2021
上市公司数(个)	Quantity of Public Company (unit)	1 572	1 800	2 037
上市证券数(个)	Quantity of Negotiable Securities(unit)	17 623	22 922	26 989
上市股票数(个)	Quantity of Listed Stock(unit)	1 615	1 843	2 079
股票发行股数(亿股)	Shares of Stocks Issued (100 million shares)	40 199.42	42 600.52	46 237.03
A 股	A Shares	39 795.01	41 798.36	44 843.02
B 股	B Shares	162.72	160.57	182.51
科创板	Sar Market	241.69	641.59	1 211.50
股票市价总值(亿元)	Aggregate Value of Stocks in Market Price (100 million yuan)	355 519.70	455 321.60	519 698.34
A 股	A Shares	346 094.57	421 151.69	462 494.58
B 股	B Shares	787.49	679.19	898.20
科创板	Sar Market	8 637.64	33 490.72	56 305.56
流通股数(亿股)	Shares in Circulation (100 million shares)	35 170.22	37 501.49	40 422.35
A 股	A Shares	34 971.59	37 170.90	39 849.19
B 股	B Shares	162.72	160.57	159.26
科创板	Sar Market	35.91	170.02	413.90
流通市值(亿元)	Value in Circulation (100 million yuan)	301 254.52	380 013.00	435 466.30
A 股	A Shares	299 178.99	369 331.70	412 091.27
B 股	B Shares	787.49	679.19	784.16
科创板	Sar Market	1 288.04	10 002.11	22 590.87
市场筹资额(亿元)	Financing Market (100 million yuan)	42 681.82	57 375.40	58 575.10
普通股	Common shares	5 145.33	8 981.73	8 335.93
首次发行	IPO	1 843.93	3 477.06	3 654.26
再次发行	Additional Issued	3 301.40	5 504.67	4 681.67
优先股	Preferred shares	2 550.00	170.00	
债 券	Bond	34 986.49	48 223.67	50 239.17

表 17.9 上证各类指数概况(2021)
ALL KINDS OF INDEX OF SHANGHAI

指 标	Indicators	最 高 High	日 期 Date		最 低 Low	日 期 Date		收 盘 Close
上证综指	SSE Composite Index	3 731.69	2 月 18 日	18,Feb	3 312.72	7 月 28 日	28,Jul	3 639.78
科创 50 指数	SSE Star 50 Index	1 639.19	8 月 6 日	6,Aug	1 212.34	3 月 16 日	16,Mar	1 398.19
上证 180	SSE 180 Index	11 935.97	2 月 18 日	18,Feb	9 513.03	7 月 28 日	28,Jul	10 130.47
上证 50	SSE 50 Index	4 110.18	2 月 18 日	18,Feb	3 044.88	8 月 20 日	20,Aug	3 274.32
上证 380	SSE 380 Index	6 922.79	9 月 14 日	14.Sep	5 488.50	3 月 9 日	9,Mar	6 768.87
红利指数	Dividend Index	3 333.21	9 月 13 日	13.Sep	2 457.67	2 月 4 日	4,Feb	2 792.70
治理指数	Governance Index	1 240.02	2 月 22 日	22,Feb	1 038.02	7 月 28 日	28,Jul	1 148.94
A 股指数	A-Share Index	3 911.92	2 月 18 日	18,Feb	3 471.89	7 月 28 日	28,Jul	3 814.30
B 股指数	B-Share Index	287.32	12 月 13 日	13,Dec	235.05	2 月 4 日	4,Feb	285.86
基金指数	Fund Index	7 832.23	2 月 18 日	18,Feb	7 065.52	3 月 25 日	25,Mar	7 572.49
国债指数	T-Bond Index	191.63	12 月 31 日	31,Dec	183.79	1 月 4 日	4,Jan	191.57

表 17.10 主要年份上证综合指数
THE SSE COMPOSITE INDEX IN MAIN YEARS

年份 Year	开盘 Open	最高 High	日期 Date		最低 Low	日期 Date		收盘 Close
1990	96.05	127.61	12月31日	31, Dec	95.79	12月19日	19, Dec	127.61
1995	637.72	926.41	5月22日	22, May	524.43	2月7日	7, Feb	555.29
1996	550.26	1 258.69	12月11日	11, Dec	512.83	1月19日	19, Jan	917.02
1997	914.06	1 510.18	5月12日	12, May	870.80	2月20日	20, Feb	1 194.10
1998	1 200.95	1 422.98	6月4日	4, June	1 043.02	8月18日	18, Aug	1 146.70
1999	1 144.89	1 756.18	6月30日	30, June	1 047.83	5月17日	17, May	1 366.58
2000	1 368.69	2 125.72	11月23日	23, Nov	1 361.21	1月4日	4, Jan	2 073.48
2001	2 077.08	2 245.44	6月14日	14, June	1 514.86	10月22日	22, Oct	1 645.97
2002	1 643.49	1 748.89	6月25日	25, June	1 339.20	1月29日	29, Jan	1 357.65
2003	1 347.43	1 649.60	4月16日	16, Apr	1 307.40	11月13日	13, Nov	1 497.04
2004	1 492.72	1 783.01	4月7日	7, Apr	1 259.43	9月13日	13, Sep	1 266.50
2005	1 260.78	1 328.53	2月25日	25, Feb	998.23	6月6日	6, June	1 161.06
2006	1 163.88	2 698.90	12月29日	29, Dec	1 161.91	1月4日	4, Jan	2 675.47
2007	2 728.19	6 124.04	10月16日	16, Oct	2 541.53	2月6日	6, Feb	5 261.56
2008	5 265.00	5 522.78	1月14日	14, Jan	1 664.93	10月28日	28, Oct	1 820.81
2009	1 849.02	3 478.01	8月4日	4, Aug	1 844.09	1月5日	5, Jan	3 277.14
2010	3 289.75	3 306.75	1月11日	11, Jan	2 319.74	7月2日	2, July	2 808.08
2011	2 825.33	3 067.46	4月18日	18, Apr	2 134.02	12月28日	28, Dec	2 199.42
2012	2 212.00	2 478.38	2月27日	27, Feb	1 949.46	12月4日	4, Dec	2 269.13
2013	2 289.51	2 444.80	2月18日	18, Feb	1 849.65	6月25日	25, jun	2 115.98
2014	2 112.13	3 239.36	12月31日	31, Dec	1 974.38	3月12日	12, Mar	3 234.68
2015	3 258.63	5 178.19	6月12日	12, June	2 850.71	8月26日	26, Aug	3 539.18
2016	3 536.59	3 538.69	1月4日	4, Jan	2 638.30	1月27日	27, Jan	3 103.64
2017	3 105.31	3 450.50	11月14日	14, Nov	3 016.53	5月11日	11, May	3 307.17
2018	3 314.03	3 587.03	1月29日	29, Jan	2 449.20	10月19日	19, Oct	2 493.90
2019	2 497.88	3 288.45	4月8日	8, Apr	2 440.91	1月4日	4, Jan	3 050.12
2020	3 066.34	3 474.92	12月31日	31, Dec	2 646.81	3月19日	19, Mar	3 473.07
2021	3 649.15	3 731.69	2月18日	18, Feb	3 312.72	7月28日	28, Jul	3 639.78

表 17.11 上海证券交易所有价证券成交总额(2018~2021)
TOTAL VOLUME OF PRICED SECURITIES TRADING IN SHANGHAI STOCK EXCHANGE

单位:亿元(100 million yuan)

指 标	Indicators	2018	2019	2020	2021
总 计	**Total**	**2 646 248.80**	**2 834 818.77**	**3 667 030.13**	**4 611 280.67**
股 票	Stocks	403 184.38	543 844.01	839 860.86	1 140 006.47
#A 股	A Shares	401 575.27	530 150.00	773 240.15	1 034 173.29
B 股	B Shares	389.75	380.21	390.55	411.29
债 券	Bond	2 169 458.16	64 086.87	114 501.45	169 107.14
回 购	Repurchase		2 154 518.87	2 596 872.07	3 137 998.19
基 金(含 ETF)	Fund	71 651.49	68 589.58	107 526.84	153 405.84

注：自 2019 年开始，债券仅含政府债和信用债，不再包含债券回购；股票成交额不再包含股票回购；回购包括股票回购和债券回购。
Note: Since 2019, bonds include government bonds and credit bonds only, not including bond repurchase any more; repurchase includes stock repurchase and bond repurchase.

表 17.12 上海证券交易所股票账户开户情况(2018~2021)
ACCOUNT-OPENING BY INVESTORS IN SHANGHAI STOCK EXCHANGE

单位:万户(10 000 households)

指 标	Indicators	2018	2019	2020	2021
累计开户总数	**Total Accounts Accumulated**				
总 数	Total	21 447.87	23 600.27	26 608.07	29 945.58
个 人	Private	21 379.04	23 524.76	26 524.98	29 852.70
机 构	Institution	68.83	75.51	83.09	92.88
A 股累计户数	**A Shares Accounts Accumulated**				
总 数	Total	21 279.91	23 431.88	26 438.98	29 775.98
个 人	Private	21 213.67	23 359.01	26 358.56	29 685.82
机 构	Institution	66.24	72.87	80.42	90.16
B 股累计户数	**B Shares Accounts Accumulated**				
总 数	Total	167.96	168.39	169.09	169.60
个 人	Private	165.37	165.75	166.42	166.88
机 构	Institution	2.59	2.64	2.67	2.72
当年新开户总数	**Newly Opened Accounts During the Year**				
总 数	Total	1 947.76	2 152.40	3 007.80	3 337.51
个 人	Private	1 943.24	2 145.72	3 000.22	3 327.72
机 构	Institution	4.52	6.68	7.58	9.79
A 股新开户数	**Newly Opened Accounts of A Shares**				
总 数	Total	1 947.27	2 151.97	3 007.10	3 337.00
个 人	Private	1 942.82	2 145.34	2 999.55	3 327.26
机 构	Institution	4.45	6.63	7.54	9.74
B 股新开户数	**Newly Opened Accounts of B Shares**				
总 数	Total	0.49	0.43	0.70	0.51
个 人	Private	0.42	0.38	0.66	0.46
机 构	Institution	0.07	0.05	0.04	0.04

上/海/统/计/年/鉴

主要统计指标解释

存 款

机构或个人在保留资金或货币所有权的条件下，以不可流通的存款凭证为依据，暂时让渡或接受资金使用权所形成的债权或债务。

贷 款

机构或个人在保留资金或货币所有权的条件下，以不可流通的借款凭证或类似凭证为依据，暂时让渡或接受资金使用权所形成的债权或债务。

上证综合指数

以在上海证券交易所上市的全部股票（A股和B股）作为样本计算的股票价格指数。

市场筹资额

企业在上海证券交易所通过发行股票和债券所筹集的资金总额。

原保险保费收入

指保险人与投保人之间直接签订的原保险合同中确认的保费收入，不包括再保险保费收入。

原保险赔付支出

指保险企业根据保险人与投保人之间直接签订的原保险合同中确认的赔付款项，不包括再保险赔付支出。

SHANGHAI STATISTICAL YEARBOOK

EXPLANATORY NOTES TO MAJOR STATISTICAL INDICATORS

□ Deposit

Deposit refers to the creditor's rights or debt formed by temporary lending or receiving funds in condition of institutions or individuals to retain the ownership of funds or monetary and based on the non-negotiable certificates of deposits.

□ Loan

Loan refers to the creditor's rights or debt formed by temporary lending or receiving funds in condition of institutions or individuals to retain the ownership of funds or monetary and based on the non-negotiable certificates of loan or similar certificates.

□ SSE Composite Index

SSE Composite Index is a stock price index, which is calculated by the price of all stocks (including A stocks and B stocks) in Shanghai Stock Exchange.

□ Market Financing

Market Financing refers to the total amount of fund which enterprises raise by issuing shares or bonds in Shanghai Stock Exchange.

□ Premium of Primary Insurance

Premium of Primary Insurance includes the insurance premium which is entered into the original insurance contract signed directly between the insurer and the insured, and reinsurance premium is excluded.

□ Payment of Primary Insurance

Payment of Primary Insurance includes the insurance payment which is entered into the original insurance contract signed directly between the insurer and the insured, and reinsurance payment is excluded.

第十八篇

CHAPTER 18

房地产业

REAL ESTATE

简要说明

一、本篇资料的主要内容

本篇资料反映上海市房地产业生产经营和发展情况。主要指标有房地产开发投资额、房屋施工面积、商品房销售面积、房屋征收户数、存量房成交面积等。

二、本篇的资料来源

本篇中房地产开发投资和到位资金情况、房屋建筑面积、商品房销售和出租情况根据上海市统计局制定的《房地产开发统计报表制度》调查汇总提供。

本篇中房屋征收情况、存量房交易情况由上海市住房和城乡建设管理委员会提供。

本篇中土地使用权出让情况由上海市规划和自然资源局提供。

三、本篇资料的统计调查方法

本篇中涉及房地产开发统计资料采用全面调查的方法,由全市房地产开发经营法人企业通过联网直报的方式上报取得。

BRIEF INTRODUCTION

I. Main Contents

Data in this chapter reflect business operation and development of real estate industry in Shanghai. Main indicators include investment in real estate development, floor area of construction, sold area of commodity, quantity of expropriation (resettlements), and registration areas traded of second-hand houses.

II. Sources of statistics

Data on real estate development investment and capital in place, construction area, commodity housing sold and leased are compiled in accordance with Statistical Reporting System on Real Estate Development and Operation made by Shanghai Municipal Statistics Bureau.

Data on buildings resettlement and the registration of second-hand houses transaction are provided by Shanghai Municipal Housing and Urban and Rural Construction Management Committee

Data on lease of land plot tenure are provided by Shanghai Municipal Bureau of Planning and Natural Resources.

Ⅲ. Survey Methodology

Data on development and operation of real estate adopt comprehensive reporting system, being collected from data directly reported by the city′s real estate development and operation enterprises with legal person status through the Internet.

表 18.1 主要年份房地产开发企业投资和到位资金情况
INVESTMENT IN REAL ESTATE DEVELOPMENT ENTERPRISES AND AVAILABILITIES OF CAPITALS IN MAIN YEARS

单位:亿元(100 million yuan)

指 标	Indicators	2010	2015	2020	2021
房地产开发投资额	**Total Investment**	**1 980.68**	**3 468.94**	**4 698.75**	**5 035.18**
按开发用途分	**By use**				
住 宅	Residence	1 229.83	1 813.32	2 418.79	2 673.95
办公楼	Office Building	224.46	654.54	833.08	767.63
商业营业用房	Commercial Building	244.70	467.67	559.85	511.52
其 他	Others	281.69	533.41	887.03	1 082.08
本年新增固定资产	**Newly Increased Fixed Assets This Year**	**964.27**	**1 890.67**	**1 946.36**	**1 811.92**
到位资金合计	**Total Capital in Place This Year**	**4 443.85**	**7 483.72**	**9 027.52**	**10 465.80**
上年末结余资金	Balance at End of Previous Year	1 214.56	1 951.86	3 511.38	4 541.41
本年实际到位资金	Capital in Place This Year	3 229.29	5 531.86	5 516.14	5 924.39
国内贷款	Domestic Loans	819.57	1 516.59	1 345.92	1 358.88
利用外资	Foreign Capital Utilized	96.05	33.92	5.76	6.78
自筹资金	Self-Financed Capital	1 070.88	1 519.99	1 975.50	2 232.84
其他资金	Other Capital	1 242.78	2 461.36	2 188.97	2 325.89

表 18.2 主要年份房地产开发企业房屋建设情况
CONSTRUCTION STATUS OF REAL ESTATE DEVELOPMENT ENTERPRISES IN MAIN YEARS

指标	Indicators	2010	2015	2020	2021
房屋施工面积（万平方米）	**Floor Area of Construction (10 000 sq.m)**	**11 295.03**	**15 095.33**	**15 740.34**	**16 627.90**
住宅	Residence	7 313.85	8 372.12	7 712.25	7 603.14
办公楼	Office Building	1 103.18	1 978.49	2 282.65	2 615.02
商业营业用房	Commercial Building	1 292.96	1 944.02	1 820.52	1 866.67
其他	Others	1 585.04	2 800.70	3 924.91	4 543.07
房屋新开工面积（万平方米）	**Floor Space of Newly-started Buildings (10 000 sq.m)**	**3 030.59**	**2 605.08**	**3 440.62**	**3 845.97**
住宅	Residence	2 111.11	1 560.28	1 756.37	1 682.49
办公楼	Office Building	147.39	304.87	421.09	629.45
商业营业用房	Commercial Building	298.10	307.57	331.70	347.73
其他	Others	473.99	432.36	931.45	1 186.30
房屋竣工面积（万平方米）	**Floor Area Completed (10 000 sq.m)**	**1 941.25**	**2 647.18**	**2 877.78**	**2 739.55**
住宅	Residence	1 396.05	1 588.95	1 627.61	1 421.43
办公楼	Office Building	150.69	219.23	259.14	342.11
商业营业用房	Commercial Building	176.41	306.45	286.38	294.05
其他	Others	218.09	532.55	704.64	681.96
房屋竣工价值(亿元)	**Value of Building Completed (100 million yuan)**	**779.93**	**1 488.32**	**1 875.14**	**1 794.16**
住宅	Residence	536.66	881.17	1 089.20	853.33
办公楼	Office Building	74.23	174.90	206.65	328.83
商业营业用房	Commercial Building	87.13	176.58	211.94	240.87
其他	Others	81.91	255.67	367.35	371.13

表 18.3 主要年份房地产开发企业商品房销售和出租情况
COMMODITY HOUSING SOLD AND LEASED OF REAL ESTATE DEVELOPMENT ENTERPRISES IN MAIN YEARS

指　标	Indicators	2010	2015	2020	2021
商品房销售面积（万平方米）	**Sold Area of Commodity Housing (10 000 sq.m)**	**2 055.53**	**2 431.36**	**1 789.16**	**1 880.45**
住　宅	Residence	1 685.35	2 009.17	1 434.07	1 489.95
办公楼	Office Building	162.89	197.41	101.68	90.89
商业营业用房	Commercial Building	125.56	113.70	83.74	79.87
其　他	Others	81.72	111.08	169.68	219.75
商品房销售额（亿元）	**Sales Volume of Commodity Housing (100 million yuan)**	**2 959.94**	**5 093.55**	**6 046.97**	**6 788.73**
住　宅	Residence	2 395.35	4 319.93	5 268.85	6 104.95
办公楼	Office Building	307.67	488.68	469.57	338.93
商业营业用房	Commercial Building	197.57	227.89	198.57	214.28
其　他	Others	59.34	57.05	109.97	130.57
商品房出租面积（万平方米）	**Commodity Housing Leased (10 000 sq.m)**	**1 262.47**	**1 202.42**	**2 053.33**	**2 074.37**
住　宅	Residence	85.72	120.59	134.27	141.95
办公楼	Office Building	516.18	501.86	775.87	774.63
商业营业用房	Commercial Building	373.34	367.02	751.08	734.76
其　他	Others	287.23	212.95	392.10	423.04

表 18.4 房屋征收情况(2000~2021)
BUILDINGS EXPROPRIATION

年 份 Year	征收户数（户） Quantity of Expropriation (unit)	其中 of which #居民住宅 Residence	征收面积（万平方米） Floor Area Expropriated (10 000 sq.m)	其中 of which #居民住宅 Residence
2000	70 606	68 293	365.77	288.35
2001	73 728	71 909	515.65	386.66
2002	101 097	98 714	644.53	485.00
2003	80 858	79 077	584.93	475.47
2004	42 415	41 552	308.40	232.52
2005	75 857	74 483	1 222.53	851.85
2006	81 126	76 874	1 516.85	848.35
2007	51354	49 092	825.00	690.00
2008	53583	51 288	1 028.53	753.71
2009	68 286	65 439	927.63	612.56
2010	39 721	38 441	585.70	389.87
2011	23 112	22 349	333.83	182.83
2012	21 910	21 262	219.42	127.27
2013	30 921	30 322	159.57	123.18
2014	26 799	26 334	118.58	95.81
2015	23 062	22 801	78.52	69.83
2016	28 426	27 063	136.47	86.00
2017	19 148	18 456	76.60	64.38
2018	16 763	16 215	62.77	52.46
2019	35 780	35 052	145.77	112.67
2020	43 318	42 652	161.36	133.92
2021	57 415	56 506	264.55	225.12

表 18.5 各区房屋征收情况(2021)
BUILDINGS EXPROPRIATION IN DIFFERENT DISTRICTS

地 区	District	征收户数（户） Quantity of Expropriation (unit)	其中 of which #居民住宅 Residence	征收面积（平方米） Floor Area Expropriated (sq.m)	其中 of which #居民住宅 Residence
总 计	**Total**	**57 415**	**56 506**	**265**	**225**
#浦东新区	Pudong New Area	224	168	31	21
黄 浦 区	Huangpu	29 157	28 806	91	89
徐 汇 区	Xuhui	180	166	3	1
长 宁 区	Changning	12	12	0	0
静 安 区	Jing'an	905	788	37	24
普 陀 区	Putuo	40	40	0	0
虹 口 区	Hongkou	14 713	14 612	50	50
杨 浦 区	Yangpu	12 147	11 909	45	40
闵 行 区	Minhang	7	3	0	0
宝 山 区	Baoshan	2	0	0	0
嘉 定 区	Jiading	2	2	0	0
松 江 区	Songjiang	17	0	5	0
青 浦 区	Qingpu	1	0	0	0
奉 贤 区	Fengxian	1	0	0	0
崇 明 区	Chongming	7	0	1	0

表 18.6 土地使用权出让情况(2021)
LEASE OF LAND PLOT TENURE

指 标	Indicators	出让地块(幅) Leased Plot (piece)	出让面积(万平方米) Leased Area (10 000 sq.m)
总 计	**Total**	**464**	**1 889.40**
商业服务	Commercial Service	53	137.04
住 宅	Residence	182	915.83
工业仓储	Storage of Industry	222	830.87
公共建筑	Public Buildings	7	5.65

表 18.7 存量房交易情况(1994~2021)
EXCHANGE OF SECOND-HAND HOUSES

年 份 Year	成交套数(套) Houses Traded (set)	成交面积(万平方米) Areas Traded (10 000 sq.m)	其 中 of which		
			#住 宅 Residence	办公楼 Office	商业营业用房 Commerce
1994	2 821	31.76	10.59		
1995	4 176	60.87	19.70		
1996	4 689	82.29	25.09		
1997	9 180	162.40	87.68	23.95	14.95
1998	24 501	315.23	197.56	21.49	18.28
1999	44 234	510.84	336.69	37.63	14.61
2000	96 348	778.52	648.23	39.48	21.65
2001	164 598	1 422.43	1 031.48	56.99	57.24
2002	204 239	1 790.50	1 341.60	65.70	91.80
2003	263 297	2 306.28	1 807.57	105.14	114.28
2004	303 291	2 726.70	2 222.24	117.12	121.39
2005	189 896	1 971.50	1 608.20	88.10	78.00
2006	184 194	1 706.81	1 375.22	67.35	46.53
2007	213 733	1 992.59	1 715.05	49.73	36.34
2008	142 224	1 413.41	1 107.17	40.61	42.04
2009	312 857	2 809.45	2 490.58	48.19	43.59
2010	202 511	1 966.86	1 522.21	68.31	70.61
2011	146 151	1 398.67	1 058.71	62.87	51.21
2012	157 585	1 446.77	1 136.17	57.34	46.71
2013	291 176	2 575.70	2 228.02	65.59	47.18
2014	177 083	1 586.14	1 324.18	52.61	40.90
2015	303 414	2 647.83	2 351.30	52.27	41.62
2016	347 667	3 219.80	2 225.42	450.89	261.04
2017	179 385	1 563.53	1 264.13	80.75	60.26
2018	175 061	1 549.12	1 229.01	77.45	58.47
2019	242 254	2 028.93	1 733.15	69.65	54.19
2020	303 244	2 495.43	2 246.23	69.40	48.83
2021	316 020	2 547.09	2 290.40	98.20	58.43

上/海/统/计/年/鉴

主要统计指标解释

房地产开发投资

指房地产开发企业本年完成的全部用于房屋建设工程、土地开发工程的投资额以及公益性建筑和土地购置费等的投资。

施工面积

指房地产开发企业本年施工的全部房屋建筑面积。包括本期新开工的面积和上期开工跨入本期继续施工的房屋面积,以及上期已停建在本期恢复施工的房屋面积。本期竣工和本期施工后又停缓建的房屋,其建筑面积仍计入本期房屋施工面积中。

新开工面积

指房地产开发企业本年新开工建设的房屋建筑面积,以单位工程为核算对象。不包括在上期开工跨入报告期继续施工的房屋建筑面积和上期停缓建而在本期复工的建筑面积。房屋的开工以房屋正式开始破土刨槽(地基处理或打永久桩)的日期为准。

竣工面积

指房地产开发企业本年按照设计要求已全部完工,达到住人和使用条件,经验收鉴定合格或达到竣工验收标准,可正式移交使用的各栋房屋建筑面积的总和。

商品房销售面积

指房地产开发企业本年出售新建商品房屋的合同总面积(即双方签署的正式买卖合同中所确认的建筑面积)。

商品房销售额

指房地产开发企业本年出售商品房屋的合同总价款(即双方签署的正式买卖合同中所确定的合同总价)。该指标与商品房销售面积同口径。

商品房出租面积

指年末房地产开发企业可供出租的商品房屋的全部面积。

SHANGHAI STATISTICAL YEARBOOK

EXPLANATORY NOTES TO MAJOR STATISTICAL INDICATORS

□ Investment in Real Estate Development

Investment in Real Estate Development refers to investment entirely used for building construction project and land development project by real estate development enterprises, and investment in public buildings and purchase costs of land.

□ Floor Area of Construction

Floor Area of Construction refers to total floor space of all buildings constructing by real estate development enterprises during the reference period, including floor space of newly started buildings during the reference period, floor space of construction extended from the previous period to the current period, and floor space of construction suspended during the previous period and resumed in the current period. Floor space of construction completed in the current period, and floor space of construction started and then suspended in the current period are also included in the floor space under construction of the current year.

□ Floor Area of Newly-started Buildings

Floor Area of Newly- started Buildings refers to the floor space of buildings newly started to construct by real estate development enterprises during the reference period, one unit project was considered as a calculating unit. Excluding the floor space of buildings started in last period or stopped or delayed in last period and restarted in this period. The date of start construction refers to the beginning of breaking gouging (foundation treatment or permanent pile).

□ Floor Area Completed

Floor Area Completed refers to the floor space of all buildings completed in the reference period, which have been appraised and accepted (or come up to the designed standards) and have been transferred to the owners for use.

□ Sold Area of Commodity Housing

Sold Area of Commodity Housing refers to the total area of new commodity housing sold by real estate development enterprises in the reference period (the construction area confirmed by formal contracts).

□ Sales Volume of Commodity Housing

Sales Volume of Commodity Housing refers to the total sales volume of new commodity housing sold by real estate development enterprises in the reference period (the sales volume confirmed by formal contracts). The caliber of this index is same to Sold Area of Commodity Housing.

□Commodity Housing Leased

Commodity Housing Leased refers to the total area of commodity housing leased by real estate development enterprises at the end of the reference period.

第十九篇

CHAPTER 19

科学技术

SCIENCE AND TECHNOLOGY

简要说明

一、本篇资料的主要内容

科技统计资料主要内容包括:全社会以及工业企业、政府部门属研究机构、高校的研究与试验发展(R&D)活动情况;技术市场交易情况;科技成果情况;科协系统科技活动情况;专利申请和授权情况等。

二、本篇资料的统计范围

科技活动统计资料范围为全社会有研究与试验发展(R&D)活动的企事业单位,具体包括工业企业、政府部门属研究机构、普通高等学校以及研究与试验发展(R&D)活动相对密集行业(包括农、林、牧、渔业,建筑业,交通运输、仓储和邮政业,信息传输、软件和信息技术服务业,金融业,租赁和商务服务业,科学研究和技术服务业,水利、环境和公共设施管理业,卫生和社会工作,文化、体育和娱乐业等)中从事研究与试验发展(R&D)活动的企事业单位。

三、本篇的资料来源

全市综合资料、企业及有关行业企事业单位的研究与试验发展(R&D)活动情况资料由上海统计局调查提供;政府部门属研究机构资料由上海市科学技术委员会、上海市经济和信息化委员会调查提供;技术市场资料、科技成果由上海市科学技术委员会调查提供;高校资料由上海市教育委员会调查提供;科协系统科技活动资料由上海市科学技术协会调查提供;专利资料由上海市知识产权局调查提供。

四、本篇的调查方法

研究与试验发展(R&D)活动情况采用全面调查取得;科协、专利资料采用抽样等多种调查方法取得。

五、统计资料口径变化

2000年以前科技活动统计资料只包括大中型工业企业、政府部门属研究机构、普通高等学校,2000年及以后年份扩大到了全社会范围。

BRIEF INTRODUCTION

I. Main Contents

Data on science and technology mainly include: data on scientific and technological activities, R&D activities all over the country, including industrial enterprises, scientific and technological institutions under government departments, universities and colleges; data on technological markets; data on science and technology achievements; data on the scientific and technological activities in the system of associations for science and technology; patents application accepted and granted.

II. Statistical Range

Data on science and technology include research and development (R&D) activities of enterprises and institutions all over the country, mainly including industrial enterprises, scientific and technological institutions under government departments, universities, colleges and relatively R&D-intensive industries (such as agriculture, forestry, animal husbandry, fisher, construction, transport, storage and post, information transmission, software industry and information technology service, financial intermediation, leasing and business services, scientific research and technical service management of water conservancy, environment and public facilities, health and social work, culture, sports and entertainment).

III. Data Sources

Data on citywide aggregates and R&D activities of various enterprises and institutions are from Shanghai Municipal Statistics Bureau; data on scientific and technological institutions under government departments are from Science and Technology Commission of Shanghai Municipality、Shanghai Municipal Commission of Economy and Informatization; data on technological markets, scientific and technical payoffs are from Science and Technology Commission of Shanghai Municipality; data on scientific and technological activities in universities and colleges are from Shanghai Municipal Education Commission; data on the scientific and technological activities of associations for science and technology are from Science and Technology Commission of Shanghai Municipality; Shanghai Intellectual Property Administration provides data on patents.

IV. Statistical Methodology

Data on R&D activities are collected through complete surveys. Data on scientific and technological associations and patent applications are through sample surveys and other surveys.

V. Changes of the statistical coverage of data

Before 2000, data only included large and medium-sized industrial enterprises, scientific research institutions under government departments, and universities and colleges. Since 2000 (inclusive), data have covered all industries.

表 19.1　主要年份科技活动主要指标
MAIN INDICATORS OF SCIENTIFIC AND TECHNOLOGICAL ACTIVITIES IN MAIN YEARS

年　份 Year	研究与试验发展(R&D)人员全时当量(万人年) Full-time Equivalent of R&D Personnel (10 000 person-years)	研究与试验发展(R&D)经费内部支出(亿元) Expenditures on R&D (100 million yuan)	研究与试验发展经费支出相当于上海市生产总值比例(%) R&D as Percentage of Gross Domestic Product (%)	地方财政科技经费支出(亿元) Local Fiscal Expenditures on Scientific and Technological Research (100 million yuan)	科技经费支出占地方财政支出比重(%) Percentage of Expenditures on Scientific and Technological Research in Local Fiscal (%)
1990		10.13	1.30	2.44	3.2
1995		32.60	1.29	5.12	2.0
2000	6.31	76.73	1.59	10.08	1.6
2001	5.20	88.08	1.68	12.39	1.7
2002	5.02	102.36	1.77	15.25	1.7
2003	5.62	128.92	1.89	19.84	1.8
2004	5.73	170.28	2.10	39.32	2.8
2005	7.07	213.77	2.32	79.34	4.8
2006	8.01	258.84	2.44	94.89	5.2
2007	9.03	307.50	2.39	105.77	4.9
2008	9.75	362.30	2.49	120.27	4.6
2009	13.29	423.38	2.69	215.31	7.2
2010	13.50	481.70	2.69	202.03	6.1
2011	14.85	597.71	2.99	218.50	5.6
2012	15.34	679.46	3.19	245.43	5.9
2013	16.58	776.78	3.35	257.66	5.7
2014	16.82	861.95	3.41	262.29	5.3
2015	17.18	936.14	3.48	271.85	4.4
2016	18.39	1 049.32	3.51	341.71	4.9
2017	18.35	1 205.21	3.66	389.90	5.2
2018	18.81	1 359.20	3.77	426.37	5.1
2019	19.86	1 524.55	4.01	389.54	4.8
2020	22.86	1 615.69	4.15	406.20	5.0
2021	23.55	1 819.77	4.21	422.70	5.0

①本表部分数据由上海市财政局等部门提供。
②2021 年“研究与试验发展经费支出相当于上海市生产总值比例”根据 2021 年上海市生产总值快报数计算。
❶Data in this table are mainly provided by Shanghai Municipal Finance Bureau.
❷In 2021, the R&D as Percentage of Gross Domestic Product is calculated according to the 2021 Shanghai GDP express report.

表 19.2 主要年份研究与试验发展(R&D)活动情况
BASIC STATISTICS OF RESEARCH AND DEVELOPMENT (R&D) ACTIVITIES IN MAIN YEARS

指标	Indicators	2000	2010	2020	2021
有 R&D 活动单位数(个)	**Quantity of Science and Technology Institutions (unit)**	**1 070**	**1 782**	**3 990**	**4 312**
科研机构	Research Institutions	125	113	116	114
高等院校	Institutions of Higher Education	41	68	125	124
企　业	Enterprises	820	1 453	3 686	3 998
其　他	Others	84	148	63	76
R&D 人员投入情况	**Personnel Investment on R&D**				
R&D 人员(万人)	R&D Personnel(10 000 persons)		17.75	32.04	34.50
R&D 人员全时当量(万人年)	Full-time Equivalent of R&D Personnel(10 000 person-year)	6.31	13.50	22.86	23.55
基础研究	Basic Research	0.60	1.42	3.30	3.53
应用研究	Applied Research	1.92	2.29	3.49	3.63
试验发展	Experimental Development	3.79	9.79	16.07	16.38
R&D 经费投入情况	**Expenditure on R&D**				
R&D 经费内部支出(亿元)	Intramural Expenditure on R&D (100 million yuan)	76.73	481.70	1 615.69	1 819.77
按活动类型分	By Activity Types				
基础研究	Basic Research	4.98	31.05	128.28	177.73
应用研究	Applied Research	18.18	68.99	190.90	190.09
试验发展	Experimental Development	53.57	381.67	1 296.51	1 451.95
按经费来源分	By Source of Funds				
政府资金	Government Funds	24.22	142.78	526.54	570.63
企业资金	Self-raised Funds by Enterprises	33.76	318.28	1 026.75	1 181.23
境外资金	Offshore Funds	4.79	6.80	23.73	15.64
其　他	Others	13.96	13.83	38.67	52.27
R&D 项目(课题)情况	**R&D project**				
项目(课题)数 (万项)	Quantity of Projects (10 000 item)	2.07	5.56	10.34	11.64
项目(课题)参加人员(万人年)	Personnel Engaged in Projects (10 000 persons year)	5.42	11.89	11.73	24.07
项目(课题)经费内部支出(亿元)	Inner Expenditure on Projects (100 million yuan)	54.31	379.37	1 564.16	1 691.93
科技活动产出情况	**Output of Science and Technic Activities**				
新产品销售收入(亿元)	Sales Revenue of New Product(100 million yuan)	1 398.54	6 543.07	10 159.22	10 574.88
专利授权数(万件)	Patents Granted(piece)	4 050	48 215	139 780	179 317
#发明专利	Invention Patents	304	6 867	24 208	32 860
有效发明专利数(件)	Effective Invention Patents(piece)		23 843	145 604	171 972
发表科技论文数(篇)	Quantity of Science and Technic Papers Published(case)	37 216	87 971	127 215	147 479
出版科技著作(种)	Science and Technic Works Published(piece)	2 614	3 329	3 078	3 139
商标申请注册数(万件)	Register Applications for Trade Marks (case)	0.95	6.02	50.53	55.94
商标核准注册数(万件)	Registration approved for Trade Marks (case)	0.62	7.04	30.74	42.10
科技成果登记数(项)	Quantity of Achievements Registered in Scientific and Technological Activities(item)	1 102	2 318	1 172	849

注：本表部分数据由市知识产权局和市科学技术委员会提供。
Note: Data in this table are partly provided by Shanhgai Intellectual Property Service Center, and Shanghai Municipal Science and Technology Commission.

表 19.3 主要年份各类技术合同项目
VARIOUS TECHNOLOGICAL CONTRACTS IN MAIN YEARS

单位：项(item)

年份 Year	项目 Item	其中 of which 技术开发 Technological Development	技术转让 Technological Transfer	技术咨询 Technological Consulting	技术服务 Technological Service
1991	25 023	3 038	1 992	3 203	16 790
1995	21 213	1 915	775	3 672	14 851
2000	20 974	1 561	888	3 905	14 620
2001	23 816	2 385	1 294	5 012	15 125
2002	26 010	2 984	1 156	4 983	16 887
2003	27 292	3 512	2 112	5 306	16 362
2004	27 327	4 398	2 453	4 814	15 662
2005	30 290	5 256	2 444	4 753	17 837
2006	28 191	6 165	2 172	3 592	16 262
2007	27 742	6 425	2 133	3 086	16 098
2008	28 713	7 154	1 749	3 873	15 937
2009	27 109	8 071	1 549	3 034	14 455
2010	26 185	8 894	1 370	2 685	13 236
2011	29 332	10 771	1 317	3 277	13 967
2012	27 998	10 974	1 170	3 026	12 828
2013	26 297	10 057	1 102	3 094	12 044
2014	25 238	10 187	1 201	2 876	10 974
2015	22 513	9 579	1 050	2 458	9 426
2016	21 203	9 141	1 041	2 211	8 810
2017	21 559	9 498	912	1 819	9 330
2018	21 630	10 694	1 203	1 140	8 593
2019	36 324	14 685	1 161	3 417	17 061
2020	26 811	14 087	1 099	1 215	10 410
2021	36 998	17 856	1 743	2 309	15 090

表 19.4 主要年份各类技术合同成交金额
TOTAL CONTRACTED VALUE IN VARIOUS TECHNOLOGICAL CONTRACTS IN MAIN YEARS

单位：亿元(100 million yuan)

年份 Year	成交金额 Contracted Value	其中 of which 技术开发 Technological Development	技术转让 Technological Transfer	技术咨询 Technological Consulting	技术服务 Technological Service
1991	9.33	2.15	1.90	0.55	4.72
1995	23.04	4.14	1.57	2.12	15.21
2000	73.90	9.96	36.44	3.51	23.99
2001	106.16	28.24	50.71	4.63	22.58
2002	120.22	45.40	46.18	4.63	24.01
2003	142.78	50.96	50.79	6.11	34.92
2004	171.70	61.31	42.32	6.00	62.07
2005	231.73	87.47	110.08	6.42	27.76
2006	344.43	142.79	165.18	7.60	28.86
2007	432.64	181.50	212.49	5.50	33.15
2008	485.75	213.24	229.53	6.41	36.57
2009	489.86	266.30	174.34	5.39	43.83
2010	525.45	264.68	213.86	4.93	41.98
2011	550.32	328.25	164.49	5.40	52.18
2012	588.52	297.14	223.48	5.17	62.73
2013	620.87	267.33	230.15	7.40	115.99
2014	667.99	299.83	221.99	5.95	140.22
2015	707.99	321.49	296.99	5.32	84.20
2016	822.86	309.39	338.00	9.69	165.78
2017	867.53	513.91	271.59	5.35	76.68
2018	1 303.20	683.16	311.57	3.44	305.03
2019	1 522.21	1 012.54	251.71	7.06	250.90
2020	1 815.27	1 145.87	314.38	3.57	351.45
2021	2 761.25	1 622.82	367.26	11.46	759.71

注：本页数据由市技术市场管理办公室提供。
Note: Data on this page are provided by Shanghai Technology Market Administrative Office.

表 19.5 科技成果（2000~2021）
ACHIEVEMENTS IN SCIENTIFIC AND TECHNICAL RESEARCH

单位:项(item)

年 份 Year	科技成果 Achievements in Science and Technology	按成果水平分 By Level of Achievements			
		#国际领先 Being First Created in the World	国际先进 Attaining Advanced World Levels	国内领先 Being First Created in China	国内先进 Attaining Advanced Domestic Levels
2000	1 102	45	462	452	117
2001	1 338	78	542	444	116
2002	1 418	65	603	463	106
2003	1 508	71	532	481	155
2004	1 629	147	669	480	155
2005	1 701	123	629	588	189
2006	1 953	250	675	655	191
2007	2 396	180	761	938	254
2008	1 866	125	664	663	226
2009	2 166	260	651	831	247
2010	2 318	188	698	724	202
2011	2 388	211	598	568	158
2012	2 415	177	572	596	142
2013	2 490	125	462	548	164
2014	2 384	108	423	531	149
2015	2 356	125	367	467	155
2016	2 245	122	364	438	189
2017	2 028	102	349	437	131
2018	1 618	101	298	330	106
2019	1 348	76	295	338	124
2020	1 172	57	148	230	95
2021	849	15	64	127	80

注：科技成果数指项目完成单位(人)自愿登记数。
Note: The number of Achievements in Science and Technology refers to the number of projects voluntarily registered by units(persons).

表 19.5 续表 continued

单位:项(item)

年 份 Year	按成果分 By Type of Achievements				
	基础理论成果 Fundamental Theory Research Results	应用技术成果 Application of Technological Achievements	其中 of which		软科学成果 Soft Scientific Achievements
			已推广应用 Been Popularized	未应用 Not Been Popularized	
2000	79	953	809	144	70
2001	81	1 196	940	256	61
2002	110	1 250	961	289	58
2003	97	1 281	1 045	236	130
2004	70	1 488	1 204	284	71
2005	61	1 555	1 261	294	85
2006	52	1 799	1 506	293	102
2007	139	2 162	1 724	438	95
2008	115	1 695	1 337	358	56
2009	94	2 009	1 747	262	63
2010	152	2 104	1 824	280	62
2011	182	2 137	1 943	194	69
2012	218	2 112	1 914	198	85
2013	248	2 152	1 872	280	90
2014	263	2 023	1 798	225	98
2015	239	2 040	1 764	276	77
2016	272	1 909	1 654	255	64
2017	181	1 788	1 638	150	59
2018	190	1 357	1 219	138	71
2019	102	1 199	1 264	84	47
2020	105	988	877	111	79
2021	83	717	607	110	49

表 19.6 高等学校科技活动人员(2021)
SCIENTIFIC AND TECHNOLOGICAL PERSONNEL OF INSTITUTIONS OF HIGHER EDUCATION

单位:人(person)

指 标	Indicators	合 计 Total	其中 of which 自然科学 Natural Science	工程与技术 Engineering and Technology	医学科学 Medical Science	农业科学 Agriculture Science	其 他 Others
总 计	**Total**	**73 607**	**8 194**	**19 007**	**43 611**	**564**	**2 231**
#科学家和工程师	Scientists and Engineers	70 790	7 966	18 532	41 638	556	2 098
按职称分	**By Professional Title**						
高 级	Senior	24 797	4 710	8 985	10 563	231	308
中 级	Medium	30 352	2 823	7 744	18 504	219	1 062
初 级	Junior	18 458	661	2 278	14 544	114	861

表 19.7 高等学校研究机构和课题情况(2021)
RESEARCH INSTITUTIONS AND PROJECT OF HIGHER EDUCATION

指 标	Indicators	合 计 Total	其中 of which #自然科学 Natural Science	工程与技术 Engineering and Technology	医学科学 Medical Science	农业科学 Agriculture Science
课题数(个)	Quantity of Projects of R&D (unit)	59 039	9 421	27 797	20 971	850
课题投入人员(人年)	Project Personnel(person-year)	29 647	3 691	10 550	15 050	357
课题投入经费(亿元)	Project Funding(100 million yuan)	172.84	33.11	95.78	41.80	2.16
课题经费支出(亿元)	Project Expenditure(100 million yuan)	126.78	24.46	73.58	27.19	1.56

注:本页统计范围是指高等学校中理工农医类口径。
Note: Figures of this page refer to those of science, engineering, agriculture and medicine of higher education.

表 19.8 主要年份专利申请量和授权量
PATENT APPLICATIONS AND CERTIFIED IN MAIN YEARS

单位：件(item)

指 标	Indicators	2000	2010	2020	2021
专利授权量	Patent Certified	4 050	48 215	139 780	179 317
#发 明	Inventions	304	6 867	24 208	32 860
有效发明专利	Effective Invention Patents		23 843	145 604	171 972
PCT 国际专利受理	PCT International Patent Application Accepted		735	3 558	4 830

表 19.9 科协系统出版物和科技服务情况(2021)
PUBLICATIONS AND CONSULTATIVE ACTIVITIES OF SCIENCE AND TECHNOLOGY ASSOCIATIONS

指 标	Indicators	合 计 Total	其中 of which: 市级科协 Municipal Level Associations	区级科协 District Level Associations	市级学会 Municipal Level Societies
出版物	Publications				
主办科技期刊(种)	Scientific Journals (sort)	60	1		59
科技期刊总印数(万册)	Total Printed (10 000 copies)	222.95	0.12		222.83
编著科技图书(种)	Science and Technology Books (sort)	37		1	36
科技图书总印数(万册)	Total Printed of Science and Technology Books (10 000 copies)	81.27		0.45	80.82
主办科技报纸(种)	Technology Newspaper (sort)	4	1		3
科技报纸总印数(万份)	Total Printed of Technology Newspaper(10 000 copies)	222.76	219.36		3.40
咨 询	Consultation				
提供决策咨询报告(篇)	Decision Consultation Reports (sheet)	324	9	35	280
#获上级领导批示报告(篇)	Marking by Superiors (sheet)	249		1	248
举办决策咨询活动(次)	Decision Consultation Activities (time)	424	10	22	392
参加决策咨询活动专家数(人次)	Experts Participating in Decision Consultation Activities (person-time)	3 680	130	48	3 502

表 19.10 科协系统科普活动和科技培训情况(2021)
PROMOTING SCIENCE ACTIVITIES AND TRAINING PROGRAM ORGANIZED BY SCIENCE AND TECHNOLOGY ASSOCIATIONS

指标	Indicators	合计 Total	其中 of which 市级科协 Municipal level Associations	区级科协 District Level Associations	市级学会 Municipal Level Societies
举办科普宣讲活动(次)	Science Propaganda Activities (time)	4 537	27	2 036	2 474
科普宣讲活动参加人次(万人次)	Participants in Science Propaganda Activities (10 000 person-times)	1 992.81	9.03	228.78	1 755.00
举办实用技术培训(次)	Practical Technical Training (time)	594		269	325
实用技术培训参加人数(万人次)	Trainees of Practical Technical Training (10 000 person-times)	5.13		1.79	3.34
举办青少年科技竞赛(次)	Youth Science Competition (time)	227	4	182	41
青少年科技竞赛参加人数(万人次)	Competitors of Youth Science Competition (10 000 person-times)	191.23	33.78	147.01	10.43
青少年科技竞赛获奖人数(人次)	Winners of Youth Science Competition (person-time)	58 630	6 459	34 775	17 396
青少年参加国际及港澳台科技交流活动(次)	International and Hong Kong, Macao and Taiwan Technology Exchange Activities (time)	9	4	3	2
青少年参加国际及港澳台科技交流活动人数(人次)	Participants in International and Hong Kong, Macao and Taiwan Technology Exchange Activities(person-time)	88	28	50	10
举办青少年科学营(次)	Youth Science Camp (time)	17	1	1	15
青少年科学营参加人数(人次)	Participants in Youth Science Camp(person-time)	2 331	1 280	80	971
举办青少年科技教育培训(次)	Youth Science and Technology Education and Training (time)	398	35	218	145
青少年科技教育培训参加人数(万人次)	Trainees of Youth Science and Technology Education and Training(10 000 person-times)	18.31	0.36	16.66	1.30

表 19.11 各级科协机构和人员(2021)
INSTITUTIONS AND PERSONNEL OF SCIENCE AND TECHNOLOGY ASSOCIATIONS AT VARIOUS LEVELS

指标	Indicators	市级科协及直属机构 Municipal Level Associations and Their Directly Subordinate Institutions	区级科协及直属机构 District Level Associations and Their Directly Subordinate Institutions
机构数(个)	Institutions(unit)	6	25
人员(人)	Personnel(person)	223	245
各级学会在册个数(个)	All Levels Societies Registered(unit)	205	252

表 19.11 续表 continued

指标	Indicators	机构数(个) Quantity of Institutions (unit)	个人会员(万人) Individual Members (10 000 persons)	团体会员数(个) Organization Members (unit)	所属分科学会(个) Attached Associations (unit)
市级学会	Prefectural Societies	205	31.51	22 998	1 904

表 19.12 科协系统学术交流情况(2021)
ACADEMIC EXCHANGES OF SCIENCE AND TECHNOLOGY ASSOCIATIONS

指 标	Indicators	合 计 Total	其中 of which #市级科协 Municipal Level Associations	市级学会 Municipal Level Academies
国内学术会议	**Domestic Academic Conferences**			
举办次数(次数)	Times(time)	1 328	5	1 264
参加人数(人次)	Participants (person-times)	779 845	1 000	763 376
交流论文(篇)	Papers Exchanged (piece)	26 873	39	26 403
境内国际学术会议	**International Academic Conferences**			
举办次数(次数)	Times(time)	46	3	38
参加人数(人次)	Participants (person-times)	235 113	430	186 501
交流论文及报告(篇)	Papers and Reports Exchanged (piece)	2 275	31	1 915
港澳台地区学术会议	**Quantity of Academic Meeting Related with Hong Kong, Macao and Taiwan**			
举办次数(次数)	Times(time)	3	2	1
参加人数(人次)	Participants (person-times)	715	700	15
交流论文及报告(篇)	Papers and Reports Exchanged (piece)	60	57	3
参加大陆境外科技活动人数(人次)	**Participants in Scientific and Technological Activities Outside the Mainland (person-time)**	**83**		
接待大陆境外专家学者(人次)	**Reception of Experts and Scholars Outside the Mainland (person-time)**	**68**	**12**	
#接待港澳台地区专家学者	Reception of Hong Kong, Macao and Taiwan Experts and Scholars	6	4	

表 19.13 主要年份规模以上工业企业研究与试验发展(R&D)活动情况
BASIC STATISTICS OF RESEARCH AND DEVELOPMENT(R&D) OF INDUSTRIAL ENTERPRISES ABOVE THE SET SCALE IN MAIN YEARS

指标	Indicators	2000	2010	2020	2021
有 R&D 活动单位数(个)	**Quantity of Science and Technology Institutions (unit)**	**327**	**1 193**	**2 498**	**2 722**
R&D 人员投入情况	**Personnel Investment on R&D**				
R&D 人员(人)	R&D Personnel(person)	26 253	82 095	117 886	136 693
R&D 人员全时当量(人年)	Full-time Equivalent of R&D Personnel (person-year)	20 576	69 077	87 957	93 966
基础研究	Basic Research			145	97
应用研究	Applied Research	764	244	1 740	1 979
试验发展	Experimental Development	19 812	68 833	86 072	91 890
R&D 经费投入情况	**Expenditure on R&D**				
R&D 经费内部支出(亿元)	Intramural Expenditure on R&D (100 million yuan)	31.15	274.05	635.01	698.33
按活动类型分	By Activity Types				
基础研究	Basic Research			0.84	1.00
应用研究	Applied Research	1.33	2.00	7.20	9.80
试验发展	Experimental Development	29.82	272.05	626.97	687.52
按经费来源分	By Source of Funds				
政府资金	Government Funds	0.37	16.77	38.12	39.51
企业资金	Self-raised Funds by Enterprises	20.19	253.75	592.46	656.79
境外资金	Offshore Funds		2.37	3.51	1.77
R&D 项目(课题)情况	**R&D project**				
R&D 项目(课题)数(项)	Quantity of Projects (item)	2 412	9 240	14 903	16 590
R&D 项目(课题)人员全时当量(人年)	Personnel Engaged in Projects (person-year)		60 232	80 482	93 512
R&D 项目(课题)经费内部支出(亿元)	Inner Expenditure on Projects (100 million yuan)	28.14	247.29	695.27	709.24
科技产出及成果情况	**Output of Science and Technic Activities**				
新产品销售收入(亿元)	Sales Revenue of New Products (100 millon yuan)	1 351.69	6 543.07	10 159.22	10 574.88
发表科技论文数(篇)	Quantity of Science and Technic Papers Published(case)		2 846	3 095	2 769
形成国家或行业标准数(项)	Becoming The Formation of National or Industry Standards (item)		630	718	984
专利申请受理数(件)	Number of Patents Applications Accepted(piece)	1 455	14 967	40 630	41 431
#发明专利	Inventions	221	6 474	17 544	16 786
有效发明专利数(件)	Effective Invention Patents(piece)	468	9 822	62 147	66 509

注：本表 2000 年数据统计范围为大中型工业企业。
Note: Statistics range of data of 2000 is large and medium-sized industrial enterprises.

表 19.14 主要年份规模以上工业企业 R&D 人员情况
PERSONNEL FOR RESEARCH AND DEVELOPMENT(R&D) ACTIVITIES OF INDUSTRIAL ENTERPRISES ABOVE THE SET SCALE IN MAIN YEARS

单位:万人(10 000 persons)

类别	Types	2010	2020	2021
总　计	**Total**	**8.21**	**11.79**	**13.67**
按隶属关系分	**By Subordination**			
中央单位	Central Units	1.41	1.29	1.11
地方单位及其他	Local Units and Others	6.80	10.50	12.56
按登记注册类型分	**By Registration Categories**			
内　资	Domestic Funded	3.81	6.95	8.21
#国　有	State-owned	0.37	0.01	0.04
有限责任公司	Companies with Limited Liabilities	1.05	2.51	2.42
股份有限公司	Share-holding Companies with Limited Liabilities	0.91	1.30	1.79
港澳台商投资	Hong Kong, Macao and Taiwan Funded	0.98	1.22	1.48
外商投资	Foreign Funded	3.42	3.62	3.99
按企业规模分	**By Size**			
#大型企业	Large	3.35	4.88	5.43
中型企业	Medium	3.30	2.93	3.46
小型企业	Small	1.56	3.93	4.73
按行业分	**By Sectors**			
#高技术产业	High Technology Industry	2.54	3.68	4.13
信息化学品制造	Information Chemical Product Manufacturing	0.02	0.00	0.00
医药制造业	Medicine Manufacturing	0.36	0.56	0.72
航空航天器制造	Aviation and Aircraft Manufacturing	0.13	0.37	0.16
电子及通信设备制造业	Electronic and Communicantion Equipment Manufacturing	1.60	1.88	2.21
电子计算机及办公设备制造业	Electronic Computer and Office Equipment Manufacturing	0.16	0.25	0.29
医疗设备及仪器仪表制造业	Medical Machinery amd Measuring Instrument Manufacturing	0.27	0.63	0.75
#六个重点发展工业行业	Six Key Industries	6.50	8.72	10.03
电子信息产品制造业	Electronic Information Product Manufacturing	2.09	2.61	3.12
汽车制造业	Automobile Manufacturing	1.13	1.92	2.29
石油化工及精细化工制造业	Petrochemical and Fine Chemical Products Manufacturing	0.50	0.66	0.79
精品钢材制造业	Fine Steel Manufacturing	0.29	0.25	0.27
成套设备制造业	Equipment Complex Manufacturing	1.98	2.33	2.33
生物医药制造业	Bio-medicine Manufacturing	0.51	0.95	1.23

表 19.15 规模以上工业企业 R&D 经费内部支出来源构成(2021)

STRUCTURE OF R&D INNER EXPENDITURE SOURCE OF INDUSTRIAL ENTERPRISES ABOVE THE SET SCALE

单位:亿元(100 million yuan)

类别	Types	R&D 经费内部支出合计 Total of R&D Inner Expenditure	其中 of which		
			#政府资金 Government Funds	企业资金 Enterprise Funds	境外资金 Foreign Funds
总 计	**Total**	**698.33**	**39.51**	**656.79**	**1.77**
按隶属关系分	**By Subordination**				
中央单位	Central Units	63.53	9.04	54.42	0.01
地方单位及其他	Local Units	634.80	30.47	602.36	1.76
按登记注册类型分	**By Registration Categories**				
内 资	Domestic Funded	420.95	21.78	398.32	0.70
#国 有	State-owned	3.92		3.92	
有限责任公司	Companies with Limited Liabilities	189.26	11.60	177.20	0.39
股份有限公司	Share-holding Companies with Limited Liabilities	112.88	9.12	103.73	0.01
港澳台商投资	Hong Kong, Macao and Taiwan Funded	63.52	0.95	62.51	0.06
外商投资	Foreign Funded	213.86	16.78	195.96	1.02
按企业规模分	**By Size**				
#大型企业	Large	439.63	32.34	406.44	0.81
中型企业	Medium	125.63	2.44	122.34	0.75
小型企业	Small	131.62	4.72	126.58	0.22
按行业分	**By Sectors**				
#高技术产业	High Technology Industry	280.64	33.50	245.79	1.23
医药制造业	Medicine Manufacturing	40.00	0.82	38.42	0.71
航空航天器制造	Aviation and Aircraft Manufacturing	9.65	8.63	1.02	
电子及通信设备制造业	Electronic and Communication Equipment Manufacturing	192.42	22.19	169.79	0.38
电子计算机及办公设备制造业	Electronic Computer and Office Equipment Manufacturing	9.31	0.03	9.13	0.14
医疗设备及仪器仪表制造业	Medical Machinery amd Measuring Instrument Manufacturing	29.26	1.83	27.43	
#六个重点发展工业行业	Six Key Industries	597.30	38.24	557.28	1.60
电子信息产品制造业	Electronic Information Product Manufacturing	222.72	22.92	199.09	0.64
汽车制造业	Automobile Manufacturing	162.5	2.06	160.32	0.07
石油化工及精细化工制造业	Petrochemical and Fine Chemical Products Manufacturing	26.68	0.18	26.50	
精品钢材制造业	Fine Steel Manufacturing	28.33	0.46	27.86	0.01
成套设备制造业	Equipment Complex Manufacturing	95.98	11.01	84.80	0.17
生物医药制造业	Bio-medicine Manufacturing	61.09	1.61	58.71	0.71

表 19.16 规模以上工业企业办科技机构情况(2021)
SCIENCE AND TECHNIC RESEARCH INSTITUTIONS FUNDED BY INDUSTRIAL ENTERPRISES ABOVE THE SET SCALE

类别	Types	科技机构数（个）Technological Development Institutions (unit)	机构人员数（万人）Quantity of Personnel (10 000 persons)	机构经费支出（亿元）Expenditure of Institutions (100 million yuan)	机构仪器设备原价（亿元）Original Value of Equipment (100 million yuan)
总 计	**Total**	**850**	**7.51**	**608.58**	**367.31**
按隶属关系分	**By Subordination**				
中央单位	Central Units	44	0.44	55.54	31.04
地方单位及其他	Local Units and Others	806	7.07	553.04	336.27
按登记注册类型分	**By Registration Categories**				
内 资	Domestic Funded	581	4.45	320.18	202.69
#国 有	State-owned	3	0.09	5.02	1.06
有限责任公司	Companies with Limited Liabilities	166	1.48	119.04	123.75
股份有限公司	Share-holding Companies with Limited Liabilities	59	1.39	141.31	48.73
港澳台商投资	Hong Kong, Macao and Taiwan Funded	89	0.72	40.53	40.82
外商投资	Foreign Funded	180	2.33	247.86	123.80
按企业规模分	**By Size**				
#大型企业	Large	97	3.68	436.94	223.18
中型企业	Medium	216	2.10	98.17	88.50
小型企业	Small	527	1.73	73.22	55.18
按行业分	**By Sectors**				
#高技术产业	High Technology Industry	198	1.83	131.45	109.17
#医药制造业	Medicine Manufacturing	45	0.47	30.10	16.13
航空航天器制造	Aviation and Aircraft Manufacturing	4	0.06	0.42	1.24
电子及通信设备制造业	Electronic and Communication Equipment Manufacturing	95	1.10	89.48	85.65
电子计算机及办公设备制造业	Electronic Computer and Office Equipment Manufacturing	8	0.07	3.93	2.68
医疗设备及仪器仪表制造业	Medical Machinery amd Measuring Instrument Manufacturing	46	0.13	7.52	3.47
#六个重点发展工业行业	Six Key Industries	536	6	526	297
电子信息产品制造业	Electronic Information Product Manufacturing	137	1.31	100.42	92.14
汽车制造业	Automobile Manufacturing	86	2.17	271.84	111.89
石油化工及精细化工制造业	Petrochemical and Fine Chemical Products Manufacturing	80	0.40	20.23	15.48
精品钢材制造业	Fine Steel Manufacturing	4	0.07	37.36	14.43
成套设备制造业	Equipment Complex Manufacturing	150	1.22	58.75	43.91
生物医药制造业	Bio-medicine Manufacturing	79	0.63	37.30	18.76

表 19.17 规模以上工业企业其他技术活动费用支出情况(2021)
SPECIAL TECHNICAL PROJECT FUNDS OF INDUSTRIAL ENTERPRISES ABOVE THE SET SCALE

单位:亿元 (100 million yuan)

类别	Types	技术改造经费支出 Expenditures of Technical Transformation	技术引进经费支出 Expenditures of Technical Introduction	购买国内技术支出 Expenditures of Buying Domestic Technology
总　计	**Total**	**150.17**	**147.28**	**35.66**
按隶属关系分	**By Subordination**			
中央单位	Central Units	78.84	6.53	30.64
地方单位及其他	Local Units and Others	71.32	140.75	5.03
按登记注册类型分	**By Registration Categories**			
内　资	Domestic Funded	97.91	7.71	32.56
#国　有	State-owned			
有限责任公司	Companies with Limited Liabilities	25.65	2.13	5.62
股份有限公司	Share-holding Companies with Limited Liabilities	67.19	5.38	26.70
港澳台商投资	Hong Kong, Macao and Taiwan Funded	3.59	0.12	0.71
外商投资	Foreign Funded	48.66	139.45	2.40
按企业规模分	**By Size**			
#大型企业	Large	122.83	143.13	30.92
中型企业	Medium	15.89	3.49	2.35
小型企业	Small	11.18	0.67	2.17
按行业分	**By Sectors**			
#高技术产业	High Technology Industry	6.77	0.25	1.48
医药制造业	Medicine Manufacturing	1.55	0.05	0.35
航空航天器制造	Aviation and Aircraft Manufacturing			
电子及通信设备制造业	Electronic and Communicantion Equipment Manufacturing	4.53	0.20	1.12
电子计算机及办公设备制造业	Electronic Computer and Office Equipment Manufacturing	0.02		
医疗设备及仪器仪表制造业	Medical Machinery amd Measuring Instrument Manufacturing	0.67		0.01
#六个重点发展工业行业	Six Key Industries	122.52	146.08	31.70
电子信息产品制造业	Electronic Information Product Manufacturing	6.15	0.20	1.56
汽车制造业	Automobile Manufacturing	44.82	138.79	2.08
石油化工及精细化工制造业	Petrochemical and Fine Chemical Products Manufacturing	5.64	0.04	0.07
精品钢材制造业	Fine Steel Manufacturing	60.86	4.03	26.7
成套设备制造业	Equipment Complex Manufacturing	2.78	2.96	0.93
生物医药制造业	Bio-medicine Manufacturing	2.27	0.06	0.36

表 19.18 规模以上工业企业新产品产出情况(2021)
OUTPUT OF NEW PRODUCTS OF INDUSTRIAL ENTERPRISES ABOVE THE SET SCALE

单位:亿元 (100 million yuan)

类别	Types	新产品销售收入 Sales Revenue of New Products	其中 of which #新产品出口 Exports of New Products
总计	**Total**	**10 574.88**	**1 365.04**
按隶属关系分	**By Subordination**		
中央单位	Central Units	706.31	124.27
地方单位及其他	Local Units and Others	9 868.57	1 240.76
按登记注册类型分	**By Registration Categories**		
内资	Domestic Funded	4 919.28	686.71
#国有	State-owned	49.58	1.38
有限责任公司	Companies with Limited Liabilities	1 608.97	412.50
股份有限公司	Share-holding Companies with Limited Liabilities	1 308.20	66.48
港澳台商投资	Hong Kong, Macao and Taiwan Funded	1 039.14	290.81
外商投资	Foreign Funded	4 616.46	387.52
按企业规模分	**By Size**		
#大型企业	Large	6 088.17	735.44
中型企业	Medium	2 373.67	415.06
小型企业	Small	2 095.35	213.66
按行业分	**By Sectors**		
#高技术产业	High Technology Industry	1 810.84	737.26
信息化学品制造	Information Chemical Product Manufacturing	0.37	0.02
医药制造业	Medicine Manufacturing	136.27	14.72
航空航天器制造	Aviation and Aircraft Manufacturing	102.25	0.20
电子及通信设备制造业	Electronic and Communicantion Equipment Manufacturing	1 242.40	530.63
电子计算机及办公设备制造业	Electronic Computer and Office Equipment Manufacturing	187.72	171.64
医疗设备及仪器仪表制造业	Medical Machinery amd Measuring Instrument Manufacturing	141.83	20.05
#六个重点发展工业行业	Six Key Industries	8 479.51	1 088.05
电子信息产品制造业	Electronic Information Product Manufacturing	1 758.79	719.28
汽车制造业	Automobile Manufacturing	4 002.26	91.77
石油化工及精细化工制造业	Petrochemical and Fine Chemical Products Manufacturing	490.57	40.97
精品钢材制造业	Fine Steel Manufacturing	323.89	28.05
成套设备制造业	Equipment Complex Manufacturing	1 645.17	181.27
生物医药制造业	Bio-medicine Manufacturing	258.83	26.71

注：新产品既包括经政府有关部门认定并在有效期内的新产品，也包括企业自行研制开发，未经政府有关部门认定，从投产之日起一年之内的新产品。

Note: New Products include new products certified by relevant government agencies within the period of certification, as well as new products designed and produced by enterprises within a year without certification by government agencies.

表 19.19 主要年份大中型工业企业科技活动情况
SCIENTIFIC AND TECHNOLOGICAL ACTIVITIES OF LARGE AND MEDIUM INDUSTRIAL ENTERPRISES IN MAIN YEARS

指 标	Indicators	2000	2010	2020	2021
企业办科技机构数（个）	**Science and Technic Institutions Funded by Enterprises (unit)**	**264**	**638**	**324**	**313**
从事 R&D 活动人员数（万人）	**R&D Personnel(10 000 persons)**	**2.63**	**6.64**	**7.81**	**8.89**
#研究人员	Researchers		2.26	3.57	3.76
科技活动经费支出情况(亿元)	**Expenditures on Science and Technic Activities (100 million yuan)**				
#R&D 经费支出	R&D Expenditures	30.98	237.75	503.56	565.26
#新产品开发经费支出	Expenditures on New Products Development	47.56	302.45	658.61	824.19
其他技术活动费用支出(亿元)	**Other Expenditures on Technic Activities (100 million yuan)**	**117.47**	**235.63**	**368.15**	**381.89**
技术改造经费支出	Expenditures on Technological Transformation	75.31	123.21	185.79	138.72
技术引进经费支出	Expenditures on Technological Introduction	39.00	61.09	96.97	146.62
用于消化吸收的经费	Expenditures on Technological Digesting and Absorbing	2.41	28.68	56.02	63.28
购买国内技术支出	Expenditures on Buying Domestic Technology	0.75	22.65	29.37	33.27
科技项目情况	**Science and Technic Project**				
项目数（项）	Quantity of Projects (item)	5 140	11 384	6 892	7 065
项目人员折合全时当量（人）	Full-time Equivalent of Personnel of Project Groups (10 000 person-years)	4.53	9.42	5.45	6.20
项目经费内部支出(亿元)	Intramural Expenditure on Projects(100 million yuan)	63.72	309.75	570.20	567.81
科技活动产出情况	**Output of Science and Technic Activities**				
新产品销售收入(亿元)	New Products Sales Revenue (100 million yuan)	1 351.69	6 180.81	8 362.92	8 461.85
#新产品出口	New Products Exported	197.41	1 023.11	1 282.43	1 150.50

注：本表 2016 年起科技项目为 R&D 项目。
Note: The Science and Technic Project is R&D Project since 2016.

上 / 海 / 统 / 计 / 年 / 鉴

主要统计指标解释

■ 科技活动

指在自然科学、农业科学、医药科学、工程与技术科学、人文与社会科学领域(简称科学技术领域)中,与科技知识的产生、发展、传播和应用密切相关的有组织的活动。可分为研究与试验发展(R&D)、研究与试验发展成果应用及相关的科技服务三类活动。

■ R&D

R&D是"科学研究与试验发展"的英文缩写。指在科学技术领域,为增加知识总量,以及运用这些知识去创造新的应用进行的系统的创造性的活动。R&D包括基础研究、应用研究、试验发展三类活动。

■ 基础研究

指为了获得关于现象和可观察事实的基本原理的新知识(揭示客观事物的本质、运动规律,获得新发现、新学说)而进行的实验性或理论性研究,它不以任何专门或特定的应用或使用为目的。其成果以科学论文和科学著作为主要形式。用来反映知识的原始创新能力。

■ 应用研究

指为获得新知识而进行的创造性研究,主要针对某一特定的目的或目标。应用研究是为了确定基础研究成果可能的用途,或是为达到预定的目标探索应采取的新方法(原理性)或新途径。其成果形式以科学论文、专著、原理性模型或发明专利为主。

■ 试验发展

指利用从基础研究、应用研究和实际经验所获得的现有知识,为产生新的产品、材料和装置,建立新的工艺、系统和服务,以及对已产生和建立的上述各项作实质性的改进而进行的系统性工作。其成果形式主要是专利、专有技术、具有新产品基本特征的产品原型或具有新装置基本特征的原始样机等。在社会科学领域,试验发展是指把通过基础研究、应用研究获得的知识转变成可以实施的计划(包括为进行检验和评估实施示范项目)的过程。人文科学领域没有对应的试验发展活动。

■ 科技活动人员

指直接从事科技活动以及专门从事科技活动管理和为科技活动提供直接服务,累计从事科技活动的时间占全年制度工作时间10%及以上的人员。(1)直接从事科技活动的人员,包括:在独立核算的科学研究与技术开发机构、高等学校、各类企业及其他事业单位内设的研究室、实验室、技术开发中心及中试车间(基地)等机构中从事科技活动的研究人员、工程技术人员、技术工人及其他人员;虽不在上述机构工作,但编入科技活动项目(课题)组的人员;科技信息与文献机构中的专业技术人员;从事论文设计的研究生等。(2)专门从事科技活动管理和为科技活动提供直接服务的人员包括:独立核算的科学研究与技术开发机构、科技信息与文献机构、高等学校、各类企业及其他事业单位主管科技工作的负责人,专门从事科技活动的计划、行政、人事、财务、物资供应、设备维护、图书资料管理等工作的各类人员,但不包括保卫、医疗保健人员、司机、食堂人员、茶炉工、水暖工、清洁工等为科技活动提供间接服务的人员。

■ R&D人员

R&D人员一般用折合全时当量来表示。即参加R&D项目人员的全时当量及应分摊在R&D项目的管理和直接服务人员的全时当量两部分相加计算。一个折合全时当量是一人年。例如,一个人在R&D活动上花费了30%的正常工作时间而70%的时间用于其他工作,则其折合全时当量为0.3。

■ 科技活动经费支出

指企事业单位实际支出的全部科技活动费用,包括来自科研渠道的经费、教育事业费、基本建设投资、技术改造投资等实际用于科技活动支出的费用。科技活动经费支出分为内部支出和外部支出。

■ R&D经费内部支出

指企事业单位用于内部开展R&D活动(包括基础研究、应用研究、试验发展)的实际支出。包括用于R&D项目(课题)活动的直接支出,以及间接用于R&D活动的管理费、服务费、与有关的基本建设支出以及外协加工费等。不包括生产性活动支出、归还贷款支出

主要统计指标解释

以及与外单位合作或委托外单位进行R&D活动而转拨给对方的经费支出。

■ 专　利

是专利权的简称，是对发明人的发明创造经审查合格后，由专利局依据专利法授予发明人和设计人对该项发明创造享有的专有权。专利包括发明、实用新型和外观设计三种类型。

■ 发　明

指对产品、方法或者其改进所提出的新的技术方案。是国际通行的反映拥有自主知识产权技术的核心指标。

■ 实用新型

指对产品的形状、构造或者其结合所提出的适于实用的新的技术方案。反映具有一定技术含量的技术成果情况。

■ 外观设计

指对产品的形状、图案、色彩或者其结合所作出的富有美感并适于工业上应用的新设计。反映拥有自主知识产权的外观设计成果情况。

■ 新产品

指采用新技术原理、新设计构思研制、生产的全新产品，或在结构、材质、工艺等某一方面比原有产品有明显改进，从而显著提高了产品性能或扩大了使用功能的产品。新产品既包括政府有关部门认定并在有效期内的新产品，也包括企业自行研制开发，未经政府有关部门认定，从投产之日起一年之内的新产品。

■ 独立研究与开发机构

指有明确的任务和研究方向，有一定学术水平的业务骨干和一定数量的研究人员，具有研究、开发、开展学术工作的基本条件，主要进行科学研究与技术开发活动，并且在行政上有独立的组织形式，财务上独立核算盈亏，有权与其他单位签订合同，在银行有单独户头的单位。

SHANGHAI STATISTICAL YEARBOOK

EXPLANATORY NOTES TO MAJOR STATISTICAL INDICATORS

□ Scientific and Technological Activities (S&T Activities)

Scientific and Technological Activities (S&T Activities) refer to organized activities which are closely related with the creation, development, dissemination and application of the scientific and technical knowledge in the fields of natural sciences, agricultural sciences, medical sciences, engineering and technological sciences, humanities and social sciences (referred to as scientific and technological fields). S&T activities can be classified into 3 categories: research and development (R&D) activities, application of R&D results, and related S&T services.

□ R&D

R&D is an abbreviation which stands for ′ Science Research and Experimental Development′, which means systematic and creative endeavors aimed at expanding the overall volume of knowledge and applying the knowledge in systematic creation. R&D includes basic studies, application research and experimental development.

□ Basic Research

Basic Research refers to empirical or theoretical research aiming at obtaining new knowledge on the fundamental principles of phenomena of observable facts to reveal the nature and law of movement of objects and to acquire new discoveries or new theories. Basic research takes no specific or designated application as the aim of the research. Results of basic research are mainly released or disseminated in the form of scientific papers or monographs. This indicator reflects the original innovation capacity of knowledge.

□ Applied Research

Applied Research refers to creative research aiming at obtaining new knowledge on a specific objective or target. Purpose of the applied research is to identify the possible use of results from basic research, or to explore new (fundamental) methods or new approaches. Results of applied research are expressed in the form of scientific papers, monographs, fundamental models or invention patents.

□ Experimental Development

Experimental Development refer to systematic activities aiming at using the knowledge from basic and applied researches or from practical experience to develop new products, materials and equipment, to establish new production process, systems and services, or to make substantial improvement on the existing products, process or services. Results of experiment and development activities are embodied in patents, exclusive technology, and monotype of new products or equipment. In social sciences, experiment and development activities refer to the process of converting the knowledge from basic or applied researches into feasible programmes (including conduct of demonstration projects for assessment and evaluation). There are no experiment and development activities in the science of humanities.

□ Personnel Engaged in S&T Activities

Personnel Engaged in S&T Activities refer to personnel directly engaged in S&T activities, in the management of S&T activities, and in providing direct service to S&T activities, who spend over 10% of the total working hours in a year in S&T activities. (1) Personnel directly engaged in S&T activities include researchers, engineers, technicians and other related personnel engaged in S&T activities in independent- accounting R&D institutions, institutions of higher learning, and in research institutes, laboratories, technology development centers and central experiment workshops under enterprises and institutions. Also included are people working in S&T information archiving institutes, and graduate students working on the design of their thesis. (2) Personnel engaged in the management of S&T activities and in providing direct service to S&T activities include senior management people responsible for S&T activities in independent-accounting R&D institutions, S&T information archiving institutes, institutions of higher learning, and in enterprises and institutions where S&T activities are undertaken. Also included are people responsible for the planning, administration, personnel management, financial management, logistics supply, equipment maintenance, information and library management that are related with S&T activities. People providing indirect services are excluded, such as security, medical ser-

EXPLANATORY NOTES TO
MAJOR STATISTICAL INDICATORS

vice, drivers, plumbers, cleaners and those providing catering and related service.

□ R&D Personnel

R&D Personnel generally amount to the full-time equivalent. It equals the full-time equivalent of personnel engaged in the R&D projects plus the full-time equivalent of personnel directly manage and service the allocated R&D projects. A full-time equivalent refers to a person year. For example, a person spent thirty percent of common working time on R&D activities and seventy percent on other jobs, then the full-time equivalent is 0.3.

□ Expenditures on Science and Technical Activities

Expenditures on Science and Technical Activities refers to the total expenditures that the enterprises actually spent on science and technical activities. It includes expenditures on scientific research, education expenses, basic construction investment, investment on technical transformation. It is divided into internal expenditure and external expenditure.

□ Internal Expenditure on R&D

Internal Expenditure on R&D refers to the actually expense on R&D activities inside enterprises. It includes the direct expense on R&D projects, and indirect expense, such as management fees, service fees, basic construction investment and processing fees, on R&D activities. But it does not include the expenditures for productive activities, expenditures on repay the loans and the expenditures pay for the R&D activities entrusted to other enterprises.

□ Patent

Patent is an abbreviation for the patent right and refers to the exclusive right of ownership by the inventors or designers for the creation or inventions, given from the patent offices after due process of assessment and approval in accordance with the Patent Law. Patents are granted for inventions, utility models and designs.

□ Invention

Inventions refer to the new technical proposals to the products or methods or their modifications. This is universal core indicator reflecting the technologies with independent intellectual property.

□ Utility Models

Utility Models refer to the practical and new technical proposals on the shape and structure of the product or the combination of both. This indicator reflects the condition of technological results with certain technical content.

□ Exterior Designs

Exterior Designs refer to the aesthetics and industrially applicable new designs for the shape, pattern and color of the product, or their combinations. This indicator reflects the appearance design achievements with independent intellectual property.

□ New Products

New Products refer to new products produced with new technology and new design, or products that represent noticeable improvement in terms of structure, material, or production process so as to improve significantly the character or function of the older versions. They include new products certified by relevant government agencies within the period of certification, as well as new products that are not certified by relevant government agencies and are designed and produced by enterprises within one year since they are put into production.

□ Independent Research and Development Institutions

Independent Research and Development Institutions refer to the state-owned institutions which have direct mission and research purpose, a certain research level and quantities of personnel, favorable conditions for R&D and engaging in scientific research and technological development. The institutions also have their own independent organization, accounting system authority to sign contract with other units, and their own accounts in banks.

第二十篇

CHAPTER 20

教 育

EDUCATION

简要说明

一、本篇资料的主要内容

教育统计资料包括公办教育和民办教育、学历教育和非学历教育。具体有高等教育(研究生教育、普通高等教育和成人高等教育)、中等教育(高中阶段教育、初中阶段教育和成人中等教育)、初等教育(小学)、学前教育(幼儿园)、特殊教育(特殊教育学校和工读学校等)和留学生教育等资料。主要指标包括学校数、在校学生数、招生数、毕业生数、教职工数和专任教师数等。

二、本篇资料的来源

教育统计资料由上海市教育委员会提供。

BRIEF INTRODUCTION

I. Main Contents

Data on education cover the situations on education funded by government and non-government agencies, and the education with and without academic credentials including higher education (education of postgraduates, general higher education and adult education), secondary education (senior and junior high schools), elementary education (primary schools), preschool education, special education (special education schools and reformatory schools) and overseas education. The main indicators include the number of schools, the number of students enrolled, the number of new students enrolled, the number of graduates, the number of staff and workers, the number of full-time teachers.

II. Sources of Data

Data on education are provided by Shanghai Municipal Education Commission.

表 20.1 主要年份教育事业基本情况
BASIC STATISTICS OF EDUCATION IN MAIN YEARS

指 标	Indicators	2000	2010	2020	2021
学校数(所)	**Quantity of Schools (unit)**	**2 225**	**1 730**	**1 719**	**1 733**
普通高等学校	Regular Institutions of Higher Education	37	66	63	64
普通中等学校	Secondary Schools	1 133	869	941	958
中等专业学校	Specialized Secondary Schools	84	65	50	50
职业中学	Vocational Secondary Schools	60	26	23	23
技工学校	Technical Worker Schools	115	10	6	6
普通中学	Regular Secondary Schools	861	755	850	867
工读学校	Reformatory	13	13	12	12
普通小学	Regular Primary Schools	1 021	766	684	680
特殊教育学校	Special Education Schools	34	29	31	31
教职工数(万人)	**Quantity of Teachers and Staff (10 000 persons)**	**22.73**	**21.42**	**24.02**	**24.96**
普通高等学校	Regular Institutions of Higher Education	6.01	7.42	7.90	8.39
普通中等学校	Secondary Schools	10.43	8.26	9.13	9.38
中等专业学校	Specialized Secondary Schools	1.27	0.91	0.69	0.70
职业中学	Vocational Secondary Schools	0.66	0.43	0.35	0.36
技工学校	Technical Worker Schools	0.77	0.13	0.08	0.08
普通中学	Regular Secondary Schools	7.66	6.73	7.97	8.20
工读学校	Reformatory	0.07	0.06	0.04	0.04
普通小学	Regular Primary Schools	6.13	5.58	6.81	7.01
特殊教育学校	Special Education Schools	0.16	0.16	0.18	0.18
专任教师(万人)	**Quantity of Full-time Teachers (10 000 persons)**	**12.83**	**14.52**	**18.25**	**18.72**
普通高等学校	Regular Institutions of Higher Education	2.05	3.92	4.77	4.87
普通中等学校	Secondary Schools	6.26	5.97	7.19	7.36
中等专业学校	Specialized Secondary Schools	0.53	0.50	0.46	0.47
职业中学	Vocational Secondary Schools	0.39	0.29	0.28	0.28
技工学校	Technical Worker Schools	0.30	0.07	0.05	0.05
普通中学	Regular Secondary Schools	5.01	5.07	6.38	6.54
高 中	Senior Secondary Schools	1.42	1.67	1.90	1.94
初 中	Junior Secondary Schools	3.59	3.40	4.47	4.6
工读学校	Reformatory	0.03	0.04	0.03	0.02
普通小学	Regular Primary Schools	4.43	4.52	6.15	6.33
特殊教育学校	Special Education Schools	0.09	0.11	0.14	0.16

注：2021 年，普通中学学校数中，完全中学 88 所，高级中学 143 所，初级中学 375 所，九年一贯制学校 230 所，十二年一贯制学校 31 所。
Note: In regular secondary schools in 2021, there are 88 whole secondary schools, 143 senior high schools, 375 junior high schools, 230 system schools of 9 years and 31 system schools of 12 years.

表 20.1 续表 continued

指 标	Indicators	2000	2010	2020	2021
毕业生数(万人)	**Graduates (10 000 persons)**	**55.67**	**47.14**	**45.50**	**45.69**
普通高等学校	Regular Institutions of Higher Education	4.09	13.37	13.56	13.57
普通中等学校	Secondary Schools	32.76	21.24	17.64	17.15
中等专业学校	Specialized Secondary Schools	3.86	3.34	1.87	1.49
职业中学	Vocational Secondary Schools	3.99	1.38	0.66	0.81
技工学校	Technical Worker Schools	1.86	0.31	0.24	0.30
普通中学	Regular Secondary Schools	22.92	16.13	14.83	14.53
高 中	Senior Secondary Schools	7.18	6.24	5.23	5.17
初 中	Junior Secondary Schools	15.74	9.89	9.60	9.36
工读学校	Reformatory	0.13	0.08	0.04	0.03
普通小学	Regular Primary Schools	18.73	12.44	14.23	14.89
特殊教育学校	Special Education Schools	0.09	0.09	0.07	0.09
招生数(万人)	**New Student Enrollment (10 000 persons)**	**52.23**	**50.66**	**56.97**	**57.12**
普通高等学校	Regular Institutions of Higher Education	8.13	14.46	15.33	15.25
普通中等学校	Secondary Schools	33.71	21.07	22.78	23.01
中等专业学校	Specialized Secondary Schools	3.00	2.99	2.23	1.61
职业中学	Vocational Secondary Schools	2.44	1.23	0.74	0.85
技工学校	Technical Worker Schools	1.68	0.42	0.33	0.28
普通中学	Regular Secondary Schools	26.46	16.33	19.45	20.24
高 中	Senior Secondary Schools	7.84	5.39	5.97	6.05
初 中	Junior Secondary Schools	18.62	10.94	13.48	14.19
工读学校	Reformatory	0.13	0.10	0.03	0.03
普通小学	Regular Primary Schools	10.28	15.05	18.77	18.77
特殊教育学校	Special Education Schools	0.11	0.08	0.09	0.10
在校学生(万人)	**Student Enrollment (10 000 persons)**	**207.61**	**197.70**	**213.18**	**220.52**
普通高等学校	Regular Institutions of Higher Education	22.68	51.57	54.07	54.87
普通中等学校	Secondary Schools	105.53	75.47	72.51	75.83
中等专业学校	Specialized Secondary Schools	11.89	10.91	6.03	5.03
职业中学	Vocational Secondary Schools	8.48	3.77	2.01	2.65
技工学校	Technical Worker Schools	5.37	1.08	0.95	0.87
普通中学	Regular Secondary Schools	79.54	59.44	63.45	67.20
高 中	Senior Secondary Schools	23.94	16.89	16.64	17.45
初 中	Junior Secondary Schools	55.60	42.55	46.81	49.75
工读学校	Reformatory	0.25	0.27	0.07	0.08
普通小学	Regular Primary Schools	78.86	70.16	86.10	89.28
特殊教育学校	Special Education Schools	0.54	0.50	0.50	0.53

表 20.2 每万人口在校学生数、每个教师负担学生数(1978~2021)
STUDENTS ENROLLMENT PER 10 000 PERSONS AND STUDENTS TAUGHT BY EACH TEACHER

单位:人(person)

年 份 Year	平均每万人口在校学生数 Students Enrollment per 10 000 Persons				平均每个教师负担学生数 Students Taught by Each Teacher		
	大学生 Colleges and Universities	中专生 Speciallized Secondary Schools	中学生 Secondary Schools	小学生 Primary Schools	普通高等学校 Institutions of Higher Education	普通中等学校 Regular Secondary Schools	普通小学 Primary Schools
1978	46	14	908	789	3	17	18
1979	60	21	719	774	4	16	19
1980	67	24	544	742	4	13	18
1981	78	25	427	713	5	11	17
1982	71	28	451	665	4	12	16
1983	66	30	433	665	4	10	16
1984	74	37	404	686	4	11	17
1985	88	48	391	683	4	12	17
1986	94	55	387	693	5	11	17
1987	97	55	381	706	5	11	17
1988	100	51	355	764	5	11	18
1989	96	49	351	809	5	11	19
1990	90	46	362	826	5	11	19
1991	87	45	379	825	5	12	19
1992	88	47	401	830	5	13	22
1993	95	54	417	845	6	14	21
1994	100	66	468	815	6	15	21
1995	101	76	512	776	7	16	20
1996	102	68	525	734	7	16	20
1997	103	75	500	688	8	16	20
1998	108	81	483	630	8	17	19

表 20.2 续表 continued

单位：人(person)

年 份 Year	平均每万人口在校学生数 Students Enrollment per 10 000 Persons				平均每个教师负担学生数 Students Taught by Each Teacher		
	大学生 Colleges and Universities	中专生 Speciallized Secondary Schools	中学生 Secondary Schools	小学生 Primary Schools	普通高等学校 Institutions of Higher Education	普通中等学校 Regular Secondary Schools	普通小学 Primary Schools
1999	119	83	489	556	9	17	19
2000	141	74	494	490	11	17	18
2001	168	73	481	433	13	16	17
2002	194	74	461	393	14	17	17
2003	214	78	427	367	16	16	17
2004	227	77	451	293	15	17	14
2005	234	72	407	283	14	16	14
2006	237	70	362	272	14	15	14
2007	235	62	318	258	14	14	14
2008	235	56	289	276	14	13	14
2009	232	52	273	304	13	13	15
2010	224	47	258	305	13	13	16
2011	218	44	252	311	13	12	16
2012	213	42	248	319	13	12	16
2013	209	38	246	328	13	12	16
2014	209	32	241	331	12	11	16
2015	212	30	246	331	12	11	15
2016	213	28	236	326	12	10	15
2017	213	26	236	325	12	10	14
2018	214	25	244	330	12	10	14
2019	217	23	251	340	11	10	14
2020	217	24	255	346	11	10	14
2021	220	20	270	359	11	10	14

表 20.3 各级各类学校在校学生数(1978~2021)
STUDENTS ENROLLMENT BY VARIOUS SCHOOLS

单位:万人 (10 000 persons)

年 份 Year	普通高等学校 Institutions of Higher Education	普通中等学校 Secondary Schools	其中 of which: 中等专业学校 Specialized Secondary Schools	普通中学 Regular Secondary Schools	职业中学 Secondary Vocational Schools	技工学校 Technical Worker Schools	普通小学 Regular Primary Schools	特殊教育学校 Special Education Schools
1978	5.06	101.81	1.55	100.26			87.06	0.18
1979	6.74	90.80	2.42	81.72		6.66	88.00	0.18
1980	7.67	71.68	2.81	62.71	0.29	5.87	85.47	0.18
1981	9.11	58.82	2.94	49.93	0.45	5.50	83.22	0.16
1982	8.39	61.69	3.30	53.53	0.85	4.01	78.88	0.16
1983	7.87	60.53	3.61	52.04	1.71	3.17	79.82	0.23
1984	8.99	61.01	4.48	49.18	3.07	4.28	83.47	0.21
1985	10.79	63.50	5.92	48.23	4.69	4.66	84.18	0.23
1986	11.77	64.82	6.86	48.31	4.71	4.94	86.56	0.25
1987	12.25	64.50	7.03	48.21	4.08	5.18	89.35	0.28
1988	12.82	61.20	6.52	45.68	3.69	5.31	98.39	0.30
1989	12.61	61.01	6.45	46.10	3.54	4.92	106.02	0.32
1990	12.13	62.59	6.17	48.31	3.66	4.45	110.19	0.33
1991	11.69	65.92	6.01	51.24	3.97	4.70	111.38	0.35
1992	11.95	70.84	6.41	54.77	4.90	4.76	113.37	0.38
1993	13.10	76.54	7.58	57.69	6.39	4.88	116.70	0.44
1994	14.04	87.23	9.23	65.56	7.54	4.90	113.98	0.52
1995	14.41	96.38	10.85	72.40	8.64	4.49	109.78	0.57
1996	14.79	99.97	9.95	76.23	9.12	4.67	106.46	0.62
1997	15.38	100.81	11.10	74.43	10.29	4.99	102.44	0.63
1998	16.51	102.53	12.38	73.85	10.72	5.58	96.14	0.52

注：本表中普通中等学校在校学生数中不包括工读学校在校学生。
Note: Quantity of students enrollment of secondary schools in this table doesn't include those of reformatory schools.

表 20.3 续表 continued

单位:万人 (10 000 persons)

年份 Year	普通高等学校 Institutions of Higher Education	普通中等学校 Secondary Schools	其中 of which 中等专业学校 Specialized Secondary Schools	普通中学 Regular Secondary Schools	职业中学 Secondary Vocational Schools	技工学校 Technical Worker Schools	普通小学 Regular Primary Schools	特殊教育学校 Special Education Schools
1999	18.63	105.66	13.06	76.69	10.21	5.70	87.16	0.53
2000	22.68	105.28	11.89	79.54	8.48	5.37	78.86	0.54
2001	28.00	104.37	12.12	80.23	7.48	4.54	72.28	0.48
2002	33.16	103.59	12.66	78.97	7.56	4.40	67.24	0.55
2003	37.85	100.71	13.69	75.47	7.04	4.51	64.83	0.55
2004	41.57	106.94	14.05	82.78	6.43	3.68	53.74	0.54
2005	44.26	99.24	13.67	77.02	5.76	2.79	53.50	0.52
2006	46.63	92.25	13.70	71.17	5.33	2.05	53.37	0.50
2007	48.49	85.17	12.81	65.60	5.20	1.56	53.33	0.50
2008	50.29	79.97	12.08	61.77	4.80	1.32	59.06	0.51
2009	51.28	77.07	11.50	60.37	4.14	1.06	67.12	0.50
2010	51.57	75.20	10.91	59.44	3.77	1.08	70.16	0.50
2011	51.13	73.96	10.22	59.17	3.52	1.05	73.11	0.49
2012	50.66	73.45	9.88	59.04	3.55	0.98	76.04	0.49
2013	50.48	72.63	9.23	59.35	3.24	0.81	79.25	0.47
2014	50.66	69.67	7.74	58.42	2.72	0.79	80.30	0.46
2015	51.16	67.39	7.24	57.05	2.32	0.78	79.87	0.45
2016	51.47	66.67	6.68	57.11	2.04	0.84	78.97	0.43
2017	51.49	66.15	6.31	57.06	1.97	0.81	78.49	0.43
2018	51.78	67.97	5.98	59.07	1.99	0.93	80.02	0.44
2019	52.65	69.70	5.70	61.04	1.97	0.99	82.63	0.48
2020	54.07	72.44	6.03	63.45	2.01	0.95	86.10	0.50
2021	54.87	75.75	5.03	67.20	2.65	0.87	89.28	0.53

表 20.4 主要年份各阶段教育实施情况
BASIC STATISTICS OF VARIOUS PHASES EDUCATION IN MAIN YEARS

单位:%

	指 标 Indicators	2000	2010	2020	2021
小 学	**Primary Schools**				
小学学龄儿童净入学率	Enrollment Rate of School-age Children	99.9	99.9	99.9	99.9
初 中	**Junior Schools**				
初中学生净入学率	Enrollment Rate of Students in Junior Secondary School Phase	99.9	99.9	99.9	99.9
高 中	**Senior Schools**				
高中阶段新生入学率	Enrollment Rate of Students in Senior Secondary School Phase	97.0	96.5	99.7	99.1
普通高中招生比例	Recruit Students Rate of Regular Senior Secondary Schools	51	51	62	61

表 20.5 主要年份各级民办学校基本情况
BASIC STATISTICS OF CIVIL SCHOOLS IN MAIN YEARS

	类 别 Types	2000	2010	2020	2021
民办高等学校	**Civil Institutions of Higher Education**				
学校数(所)	Schools (unit)	3	20	19	19
在校学生(万人)	Students Enrollment(10 000 persons)	0.67	9.37	12.59	13.00
专任教师(人)	Full-time Teachers(person)	304	3 906	5 876	6 253
民办中学	**Civil Secondary Schools**				
学校数(所)	Schools (unit)	155	109	131	130
班级数(个)	Classes(unit)	1 842	2 103	2 649	2 811
在校学生(万人)	Students Enrollment(10 000 persons)	8.48	7.87	8.87	9.33
高 中	Senior	4.54	1.68	1.37	1.50
初 中	Junior	3.94	6.19	7.50	7.83
专任教师(人)	Full-time Teachers(person)	2 400	4 583	8 338	8 759
民办小学	**Civil Primary Schools**				
学校数(所)	Schools (unit)	35	184	78	68
班级数(个)	Classes(unit)	987	3 747	3 108	3 086
在校学生(万人)	Students Enrollment(10 000 persons)	3.95	16.42	10.56	10.38
专任教师(人)	Full-time Teachers(person)	831	7 181	7 308	7 188
民办幼儿园	**Civil Kindergarten**				
学校数(所)	Schools (unit)	92	396	644	662
班级数(个)	Classes(unit)	636	3 584	6 007	5 947
在校学生(万人)	Students Enrollment(10 000 persons)	1.77	9.91	15.34	14.61
专任教师(人)	Full-time Teachers(person)	1 056	7 161	11 587	11 334

表 20.6 民办学校(园)基本情况(2021)
BASIC STATISTICS OF CIVIL SCHOOLS

单位:人(person)

指 标	Indicators	学校数(所) Schools (unit)	毕业生数 Graduates	招生数 Students Recruited	在校生数 Students Enrollment	专任教师数 Full-time Teachers
普通高等学校	Institutions of Higher Education	19	32 617	39 405	129 979	6 253
普通中学	Regular Secondary Schools	130	20 398	25 576	93 286	8 759
高 中	Senior Schools	59	3 832	5 282	15 029	1 833
初 中	Junior Schools	71	16 566	20 294	78 257	6 926
普通小学	Primary Schools	68	18 793	20 869	103 791	7 188
幼儿园	Kindergartens	662	51 975	45 610	146 079	11 334

注：根据《民办教育促进法》的新规定，民办中、小学统计口径中扣除了公立转制学校。
Note：According to new provision of Civil Education Advance Law, the scope of civil secondary and primary school excluded public schools transformed.

表 20.7 主要年份外国留学生情况
STATISTICS OF FOREIGN STUDENT IN MAIN YEARS

指 标	Indicators	2005	2010	2020	2021
外国留学生人数(人)	**Quantity of Foreign Students(person)**	**13 691**	**17 340**	**25 196**	**18 176**
按地区来源分	By District				
亚 洲	Aisa	10 490	11 689	14 852	11 536
非 洲	Africa	289	969	2 515	2 076
欧 洲	Europe	1 927	3 023	4 797	2 372
北美洲	North America	766	983	1 846	1 410
南美洲	South America	129	477	744	580
大洋洲	Oceania	90	199	442	202

表 20.8　主要年份研究生人数
QUANTITY OF POSTGRADUATE STUDENTS IN MAIN YEARS

单位：人(person)

年 份 Year	获博士学位人数 Quantity of Doctor's Degrees Obtained	获硕士学位人数 Quantity of Master's Degrees Obtained	研究生 Postgraduates					
			毕业生数 Graduates		招生数 New Students Enrollment		在读人数 Students Enrollment	
			普通高等学校 Institutions of Higher Education	研究所(院) Research Institutions (Academies)	普通高等学校 Institutions of Higher Education	研究所(院) Research Institutions (Academies)	普通高等学校 Institutions of Higher Education	研究所(院) Research Institutions (Academies)
1978			9		1 072		1 253	
1980			6		410		2 696	
1985	57	1 371	1 543	37	4 264	83	8 163	170
1990	300	2 746	2 953	369	2 803	324	8 533	1 035
1991	342	2 739	2 936	320	2 717	302	8 020	949
1992	343	2 124	2 262	264	3 323	345	8 858	997
1993	368	2 489	2 569	315	3 919	363	10 037	1 008
1994	442	2 363	2 608	251	4 665	465	11 905	1 185
1995	606	2 742	3 038	317	4 776	525	13 378	1 335
1996	627	3 233	3 537	323	5 915	592	15 307	1 528
1997	890	3 585	4 117	358	6 163	562	16 841	1 619
1998	1 090	3 552	4 253	389	7 281	593	19 499	1 663
1999	1 323	4 288	5 196	415	8 758	655	22 656	1 764
2000	1 307	4 546	5 435	433	11 796	856	28 582	2 032
2001	1 487	5 330	6 380	437	14 751	1 075	36 528	2 515
2002	1 655	6 067	7 481	445	17 848	1 363	45 713	3 183
2003	1 994	7 683	9 501	578	20 767	1 757	55 092	3 998
2004	2 678	10 580	12 788	681	23 545	1 789	64 747	4 690
2005	3 119	13 245	15 857	884	25 845	1 847	73 557	5 171
2006	3 772	15 957	18 833	1 098	28 250	1 849	81 487	5 419
2007	4 355	19 250	22 691	1 235	28 748	1 862	86 177	5 586
2008	4 483	20 734	24 431	1 322	30 195	1 947	89 778	5 720
2009	4 661	23 622	26 949	1 342	35 418	2 007	97 639	5 853
2010	4 749	23 458	26 843	1 364	36 619	2 024	105 711	6 006
2011	4 610	25 568	29 431	1 385	37 971	2 109	112 902	6 115
2012	4 913	29 270	33 189	1 417	41 899	2 330	120 503	6 511
2013	5 077	30 311	34 148	1 521	43 659	2 564	127 803	6 996
2014	4 516	32 056	36 013	559	43 353	577	131 806	1 748
2015	4 490	33 378	37 289	579	45 400	605	136 539	1 748
2016	5 009	34 724	39 181	552	48 450	626	143 172	1 806
2017	5 513	34 912	40 425	557	58 906	613	151 536	1 785
2018	5 412	37 018	42 462	619	62 971	657	176 905	1 885
2019	5 677	40 559	45 427	613	66 664	824	194 116	2 150
2020	6 213	46 146	51 587	615	74 235	754	213 794	2 142
2021	6 623	49 453	55 427	661	77 141	738	231 074	2 194

①2001 年前的获博士学位和获硕士学位的人数为当年毕业生人数。
②2014 学年起，中科院、煤炭院所属科研机构不纳入本市研究生培养机构统计。
❶Quantity of Doctor's and Master's Degrees obtained refer to Quantity of graduates in this year before 2001.
❷Since 2014 school year, subsidiary institutions of Chinese Academy of Science and Coal Research Institute are not included in the statistics of postgraduate training mechanism.

表 20.9 普通高等学校基本情况(2021)
BASIC STATISTICS OF INSTITUTIONS OF HIGHER EDUCATION

类别 Types		学校(所) Institutions (unit)	毕业生数(人) Graduates (person)	招生数(人) New Students Enrollment (person)	在校学生人数(人) Students Enrollment (person)	教职员工(人) Staff and Workers (person)	其中 of which	
							#专任教师 Full-time Teacher	其中 of which #正、副高级 Senior and Associate Title
总 计	**Total**	**64**	**135 655**	**152 453**	**548 733**	**83 911**	**48 692**	**25 670**
综合大学	Comprehensive Universities	4	15 704	16 911	70 862	29 002	12 531	8 905
理工院校	Science and Engineering	25	51 988	58 668	208 180	23 505	15 812	7 241
农业院校	Agriculture and Forestry	2	3 941	4 619	16 400	1 717	1 095	526
医药院校	Medical	2	3 895	4 236	15 604	2 237	1 368	568
师范院校	Teacher Training	2	8 362	8 750	35 293	7 349	4 405	3 002
语文院校	Linguistics and Literacy	3	4 336	3 906	14 680	2 087	1 321	509
财经院校	Economics and Finance	17	36 069	42 235	143 882	12 214	8 512	3 340
政法院校	Politics and Law	3	6 304	7 608	24 739	2 641	1 883	762
体育院校	Physical Culture	1	1 053	1 218	4 513	829	540	305
艺术院校	Art Schools	5	4 003	4 302	14 580	2 330	1 225	512

注：学生数中未包括在读研究生人数，在分类院校学生数中未包括成人高等学校中的普通本专科学生。

Note: Post-graduates are not included in the students enrollment. Undergraduates and junior college students in adult education schools are not included in the students enrollment by types of colleges enrollment by types of colleges.

表 20.10 普通高等学校分科专任教师数(2021)
FULL-TIME TEACHERS IN INSTITUTIONS OF HIGHER EDUCATION BY SUBJECTS

单位:人(person)

类别 Types		专任教师数 Full-time Teachers	其中 of which				
			正高级 Senior Title	副高级 Associate Title	中级 Junior Title	初级 Primary Title	无职称 Non-Title
总 计	**Total**	**43 001**	**9 508**	**14 699**	**15 764**	**2 001**	**1 029**
哲 学	Philosophy	1 206	242	333	476	89	66
经济学	Economics	2 429	474	864	980	52	59
法 学	Law	3 683	611	1 024	1 490	357	201
教育学	Education	3 132	351	963	1 344	380	94
文 学	Literature	5 650	739	1 657	2 884	260	110
历史学	History	571	195	178	181	8	9
理 学	Science	5 130	1 859	1 958	1 192	51	70
工 学	Engineering	12 273	3 354	4 712	3 824	212	171
农 学	Agriculture	269	78	107	56	6	22
医 学	Medical	2 577	646	877	841	149	64
管理学	Administration	3 433	634	1 234	1 333	143	89
艺术学	Art	2 648	325	792	1 163	294	74

表 20.11 普通高等学校本科分科学生数(2021)
UNDERGRADUATE STUDENTS IN INSTITUTIONS OF HIGHER EDUCATION BY SUBJECTS

单位:人(person)

类 别	Types	毕业生人数 Graduates	招生人数 New Students Enrollment	在校学生人数 Students Enrollment
总 计	**Total**	**92 227**	**103 529**	**405 818**
哲 学	Philosophy	153	397	880
经济学	Economics	9 998	9 358	38 821
法 学	Law	5 652	5 918	24 110
教育学	Education	2 258	2 958	11 116
文 学	Literature	9 329	10 303	39 170
历史学	History	226	568	1 698
理 学	Science	5 250	6 385	24 690
工 学	Engineering	30 510	34 949	139 928
农 学	Agriculture	466	647	2 411
医 学	Medical	3 932	5 303	20 924
管理学	Administration	17 104	17 148	68 119
艺术学	Art	7 349	9 595	33 951

表 20.12 中等专业学校基本情况(2021)
BASIC STATISTICS OF SPECIALIZED SECONDARY SCHOOLS

单位:人(person)

类 别	Types	毕业生数 Graduates	招生数 New Students Enrollment	在校学生 Students Enrollment	专任教师 Full-time Teachers in Professional Course	其中 of which #正副高级 Senior and Associate Title	中 级 Junior Title
总 计	**Total**	**31 894**	**38 730**	**108 907**	**8 051**	**1 792**	**3 998**
#土木建筑	Civil Construction	1 607	1 698	5 189	189	58	88
装备制造	Equipment Manufacturing	6 444	5 953	19 102	808	189	351
交通运输	Transport	3 554	3 433	10 155	420	64	232
电子与信息	Electronics and Information	3 243	4 411	12 879	701	162	350
医药卫生	Health	1 333	2 825	5 231	283	75	150
财经商贸	Trade and Tour	4 471	5 073	14 623	816	195	421
旅游服务	Finance and Economics	2 370	2 303	6 977	250	57	118
文化艺术	Culture and Art	1 749	2 238	7 316	1 172	255	529
教育与体育	Sports and Fitness	2 341	2 734	7 957	2 851	589	1 485
公共管理与服务	Society Commonality Business	1 801	4 489	8 035	153	28	79

表 20.13 各区普通中学基本情况(2021)
BASIC STATISTICS OF REGULAR SECONDARY SCHOOLS BY DISTRICTS

地 区 District		学 校 (所) Schools (unit)	毕业生数 (人) Graduates (person)	招生数 (人) New Students Enrollment (person)	在校学生 (人) Students Enrollment (person)	教职员工 (人) Staff and Workers (person)	其 中 of which #专任教师 Full-time Teachers
总 计	**Total**	**867**	**145 264**	**202 367**	**672 004**	**81 960**	**65 443**
浦东新区	Pudong New Area	172	33 911	48 680	159 138	16 291	13 887
黄 浦 区	Huangpu	33	6 059	7 484	25 570	3 493	2 795
徐 汇 区	Xuhui	42	9 611	13 004	44 089	5 045	4 181
长 宁 区	Changning	26	4 108	5 378	18 667	2 850	2 027
静 安 区	Jing'an	51	8 643	10 948	38 166	5 199	3 947
普 陀 区	Putuo	51	6 875	9 833	33 166	4 435	3 585
虹 口 区	Hongkou	35	5 264	6 486	22 621	3 274	2 867
杨 浦 区	Yangpu	50	8 227	11 045	36 820	4 323	3 804
闵 行 区	Minhang	83	13 805	22 738	73 748	8 430	6 449
宝 山 区	Baoshan	77	10 439	15 077	50 138	5 067	4 487
嘉 定 区	Jiading	48	7 870	11 396	36 955	4 081	3 372
金 山 区	Jinshan	37	6 128	6 683	23 566	3 432	2 613
松 江 区	Songjiang	49	8 829	13 595	43 195	6 146	4 046
青 浦 区	Qingpu	35	5 757	7 524	24 899	3 308	2 647
奉 贤 区	Fengxian	48	5 884	8 079	25 686	3 230	2 801
崇 明 区	Chongming	30	3 854	4 417	15 580	3 356	1 935

表 20.14　各区普通中学初、高中学生基本情况(2021)
BASIC STATISTICS OF REGULAR JUNIOR AND SENIOR SCHOOLS' STUDENTS BY DISTRICTS

单位:人 (person)

地　区	District	毕业生数 Graduates 初　中 Junior	毕业生数 Graduates 高　中 Senior	招生数 New Students Enrollment 初　中 Junior	招生数 New Students Enrollment 高　中 Senior	在校学生 Students Enrollment 初　中 Junior	在校学生 Students Enrollment 高　中 Senior
总　计	**Total**	**93 572**	**51 692**	**141 905**	**60 462**	**497 550**	**174 454**
浦东新区	Pudong New Area	22 336	11 575	34 273	14 407	118 308	40 830
黄 浦 区	Huangpu	2 980	3 079	4 195	3 289	15 857	9 713
徐 汇 区	Xuhui	5 879	3 732	8 741	4 263	31 645	12 444
长 宁 区	Changning	2 707	1 401	3 773	1 605	14 036	4 631
静 安 区	Jing'an	5 303	3 340	7 028	3 920	26 944	11 222
普 陀 区	Putuo	4 481	2 394	6 908	2 925	24 964	8 202
虹 口 区	Hongkou	3 269	1 995	4 250	2 236	16 143	6 478
杨 浦 区	Yangpu	4 752	3 475	7 151	3 894	25 416	11 404
闵 行 区	Minhang	9 377	4 428	17 112	5 626	58 060	15 688
宝 山 区	Baoshan	7 073	3 366	11 186	3 891	38 967	11 171
嘉 定 区	Jiading	5 413	2 457	8 387	3 009	28 352	8 603
金 山 区	Jinshan	3 781	2 347	4 530	2 153	16 777	6 789
松 江 区	Songjiang	6 090	2 739	10 165	3 430	33 256	9 939
青 浦 区	Qingpu	3 836	1 921	5 446	2 078	18 662	6 237
奉 贤 区	Fengxian	3 779	2 105	5 906	2 173	19 164	6 522
崇 明 区	Chongming	2 516	1 338	2 854	1 563	10 999	4 581

表 20.15 各区普通小学基本情况(2021)
BASIC STATISTICS OF REGULAR PRIMARY SCHOOLS BY DISTRICTS

地 区	District	学 校 (所) Schools (unit)	毕业生数 (人) Graduates (person)	招生数 (人) New Students Enrollment (person)	在校学生 (人) Students Enrollment (person)	教职员工 (人) Staff and Workers (person)	其 中 of which #专任教师 Full-time Teachers
总 计	**Total**	**680**	**148 862**	**187 739**	**892 789**	**70 057**	**63 336**
浦东新区	Pudong New Area	134	37 406	45 472	217 367	15 255	14 584
黄 浦 区	Huangpu	27	3 845	4 548	22 591	2 240	1 933
徐 汇 区	Xuhui	44	8 551	10 672	49 974	3 681	3 218
长 宁 区	Changning	23	4 181	4 576	22 900	1 965	1 674
静 安 区	Jing'an	44	6 573	7 531	37 831	3 578	2 942
普 陀 区	Putuo	25	7 375	8 872	43 639	3 529	3 331
虹 口 区	Hongkou	34	4 231	4 898	23 994	2 271	2 113
杨 浦 区	Yangpu	43	7 185	9 202	43 509	3 512	3 393
闵 行 区	Minhang	63	18 309	22 381	107 106	7 627	6 881
宝 山 区	Baoshan	69	12 279	15 693	75 920	5 812	5 584
嘉 定 区	Jiading	41	8 610	13 276	58 837	4 072	3 666
金 山 区	Jinshan	23	4 466	5 692	27 431	2 415	2 053
松 江 区	Songjiang	38	11 160	15 584	72 203	5 719	4 852
青 浦 区	Qingpu	28	5 443	8 826	37 700	3 140	2 774
奉 贤 区	Fengxian	23	6 299	7 798	36 573	2 782	2 663
崇 明 区	Chongming	21	2 949	2 718	15 214	2 459	1 675

表 20.16　主要年份实验性示范性中学基本情况
BASIC STATISTICS OF SECONDARY CAMPUS SCHOOL IN MAIN YEARS

指　标	Indicators	2000	2010	2020	2021
学　校(所)	Schools (unit)	84	128	147	148
班级数(个)	Classes (unit)	2 584	4 063	4 484	4 595
在校学生(万人)	Students Enrollment(10 000 persons)	12.10	14.67	16.06	16.77
教职员工(万人)	Staff and Workers (10 000 persons)	1.40	1.88	2.15	2.17
#专任教师	Full-time Teachers	0.88	1.42	1.77	1.79

注：实验性示范性中学包括重点中学和寄宿制高级中学。
Note: Secondary campus school includes important secondary school and boarding high school.

表 20.17　主要年份幼儿园基本情况
BASIC STATISTICS OF KINDERGARTENS IN MAIN YEARS

指　标	Indicators	2000	2010	2020	2021
幼儿园(所)	Kindergartens (unit)	958	1 252	1 678	1 699
幼儿数(万人)	Children Enrollment (10 000 persons)	24.12	40.03	57.15	56.01
教职员工(万人)	Staff and Workers(10 000 persons)	2.52	4.09	8.08	8.46
#教　师	Teachers	1.50	2.67	4.40	4.55

表 20.18　主要年份特殊教育基本情况
BASIC STATISTICS OF SPECIAL EDUCATION IN MAIN YEARS

指　标	Indicators	2000	2010	2020	2021
学　校(所)	Schools (unit)	34	29	31	31
毕业生数(人)	Graduates(person)	868	918	1 429	857
招生数(人)	New Students Enrollment(person)	1 141	776	1 323	989
在校学生(人)	Students Enrollment(person)	5 407	5 036	5 020	5 317
教职员工(人)	Staff and Workers(person)	1 584	1 596	1 768	1 845
#专任教师	Full-time Teachers	943	1 143	1 415	1 584

表 20.19 网络教育本科学生情况(2021)
BASIC STATISTICS OF UNDERGRADUATE STUDENTS OF NETWORK EDUCATION BY SUBJECT

单位:人(person)

类 别	Types	毕业生人数 Graduates	招生人数 New Students Enrollment	在校学生人数 Students Enrollment
总 计	**Total**	**19 238**	**32 850**	**76 023**
经济学	Economics	218	203	897
法 学	Law	447	1 817	2 525
教育学	Education	1 989	4 326	6 828
文 学	Literature	586	1 472	2 564
理 学	Science	174		266
工 学	Engineering	2 041	3 862	10 724
医 学	Medical	1 569	3 515	7 706
管理学	Administration	12 015	16 957	42 842
艺术学	Art	199	698	1 671

表 20.20 各级各类成人学校基本情况(2021)
BASIC STATISTICS OF ADULT SCHOOLS AT VARIOUS LEVELS

类 别	Types	学校数(所) Schools (unit)	毕业生人数(人) Graduates (person)	招生数(人) New Students Enrollment (person)	在校学生人数(人) Students Enrollment (person)	教职员工人数(人) Staff and Workers (person)	其中 of which #专任教师 Full-time Teachers
成人高等教育	**Adult Higher Education**	**12**	**42 847**	**46 377**	**136 322**	**1 203**	**561**
广播电视大学	Broadcasting and TV Universities	1				350	114
职工高等学校	Staff Higher Education Schools	10	1 873	2 422	7 339	853	447
管理干部学院	Institutes for Administrative Officials	1					
普通高等学校办	Run by Regular Higher Education Institutions	54	40 974	43 955	128 983		
函 授	Correspondence Programs	7	1 056	1 334	3 467		
业 余	Spare Time	47	39 918	42 621	125 516		
成人网络本、专科	**Adult Network Education**		**46 266**	**60 516**	**146 043**		
成人中等专业学校	**Specialized Secondary Schools**	**8**	**5 918**	**10 358**	**21 147**	**181**	**88**
职业技术培训机构	**Adult Technical Secondary Schools**	**548**	**848 900**		**837 380**	**944**	**5 278**

①普通高等学校办的函授、业余学校数是指举办这类教育的学校点数，括号内是点数之和。
②成人职业技术学校毕业生及在校学生数为培训半年以上人次数。
❶The number of correspondence school and amateur school that regular institutions of higher education runs refers to teaching centers. It is the sum of number inside.
❷Graduates and Students Enrollment of adult technical secondary schools refers to accumulative total number of students registered at schools who has been trained more than half a year.

上 / 海 / 统 / 计 / 年 / 鉴

主要统计指标解释

学　校

指按国家规定的设置标准和审批程序批准设立的，招收适龄人口实施各级各类教育活动的教育机构。

普通高等学校

指按照国家规定的设置标准和审批程序批准举办的，通过全国普通高等学校统一招生考试，招收高中毕业生为主要培养对象，实施高等教育的全日制大学、独立设置的学院和高等专科学校、高等职业学校和其他机构。

大学、独立设置的学院主要实施本科层次以上教育，高等专科学校、高等职业学校实施专科层次教育，其他机构是承担国家普通招生计划任务不计校数的机构。包括普通高等学校分校和批准筹建的普通高等学校等。

成人高等学校

指按国家规定的设置标准和审批程序举办的，通过全国成人高等教育统一招生考试，招收高中毕业或同等学历的人员为主要培养对象，利用函授、业余、脱产的多种形式对其实施高等学历教育的学校。包括：职工高等学校、农民高等学校、管理干部学院、教育学院、独立函授学院、广播电视大学、其他机构等。

中等专业学校

指经县或县以上教育行政部门批准设立，招收初中毕业生实施中等专业课程教育的教学机构。

职业中学（职业高中、职业初中）

指经县或县以上教育行政部门批准设立，招收小学或初中毕业生实施中等职业技术教育的教学机构。按学校性质类别可分为：独立设置的职业中学（包括：职业初中、职业高中、职业初高中合设学校）；附设有普通中学班的职业中学。

普通中学（普通高中、普通初中）

普通中学分为普通高级中学和普通初级中学两个阶段。普通初级中学是指独立设置的招收小学毕业的适龄人口进行初级中等基础教育的机构；普通高级中学是指独立设置的招收初中毕业的适龄人口进行高级中等基础教育的机构；完全中学是指普通初、高中合设的教育机构；一贯制学校是指在一所学校连续实施中小学教育的机构。其中包括实施九年义务教育的九年一贯制学校和实施高中教育的十二年一贯制学校。（说明：一贯制学校的办学条件如能划分为小学、初中、高中，则分开填报；如不能划分清楚，可按就高不就低的方法填入初中、高中报表中，不能重复填写。）

普通小学

指由区或区以上教育行政部门批准，招收学龄儿童实施初等教育的教学机构。

幼儿园

指招收三周岁以上（含三周岁）学龄前幼儿，对其进行保育和教育的单位。

特殊教育学校

指本市独立设置的招收盲聋哑和智残儿童，以及其他特殊需要的儿童、青少年进行普通或职业初、中等教育的教学机构。

小学学龄儿童净入学率

小学学龄人口中正在接受小学教育人数所占比重。

初中学生净入学率

是指初中阶段教育（接受普通初中教育和职业初中教育）在校学生总数占初中阶段教育学龄人口数的比重。

SHANGHAI STATISTICAL YEARBOOK

EXPLANATORY NOTES TO MAJOR STATISTICAL INDICATORS

□ School Institutions

School Institutions refer to education establishments set up according to the government evaluation and approval procedures, enrolling population of the right age, providing various phase education activity.

□ Regular Institutions of Higher Education

Regular Institutions of Higher Education refer to educational establishments set up according to the government evaluation and approval procedures, enrolling graduates from senior secondary schools and providing higher education courses and training for senior professionals. They include full-time universities, colleges, high professional schools, high professional vocational schools and others.

Universities and colleges are mainly providing undergraduate courses; those high professional schools and high professional vocational schools are mainly providing professional trainings; and others refer to educational establishments, which are responsible for enrolling students but not covered in the total number of schools, including: branch schools of universities and colleges, and universities and colleges that have been proved and prepared to construct.

□ Institutions of Higher Education for Adults

Institutions of Higher Education for Adults refer to educational establishments, set up in line with relevant rules approved by the government, enrolling personnel with senior secondary schools or equivalent education, and providing higher education courses in many forms of correspondence, spare time, or full time for adults. Institutions of higher schools for adults include schools of higher educations for staff and workers, schools of higher education for peasants, colleges for management cadres, pedagogical colleges, independent correspondence colleges, Radio and TV universities and other educational establishments, etc.

□ Specialized Secondary Schools

Specialized Secondary schools refer to educational establishments set up according to approval and permission by educational administration department of district and above government, enrolling graduates from junior secondary schools and providing secondary professional education courses.

□ Vocational Secondary Schools (senior secondary schools and junior secondary schools)

Vocational Secondary Schools (senior secondary schools and junior secondary schools) refer to educational establishments set up according to approval and permission by educational administration department of district and above government, enrolling graduates from primary schools and junior secondary schools and providing secondary vocational education courses.

□ Regular Secondary Schools (senior secondary schools and junior secondary schools)

Regular Secondary Schools (senior secondary schools and junior secondary schools) are classified as senior secondary schools and junior secondary schools. Junior Secondary Schools refer to educational establishments enrolling graduates from primary schools and providing junior secondary educational courses. Senior Secondary Schools refer to educational establishments enrolling graduates from junior secondary schools and providing higher secondary educational courses.

□ Regular Primary Schools

Regular Primary Schools refer to educational establishments set up according to approval and permission by educational administration department of district and above government, enrolling graduates from children of school age and providing primary educational courses.

□ Kindergartens

Kindergartens refer to nursery and education establishments, enrolling children in 3 years old and above.

□ Special Education Schools

Special Education Schools refer to educational establishments set up independently, enrolling blind, deaf, dumb, amentia or other special children, and educational establishment, providing regular or vocational junior and senior secondary education for hobbledehoy.

EXPLANATORY NOTES TO
MAJOR STATISTICAL INDICATORS

□ Enrollment Rate of School-age Children

Enrollment Rate of School-age Children refers to the proportion of school age children enrolled at schools to the total number of school age children both in and outside schools.

□ Enrollment Rate of Students in Junior Secondary School Phase

It refers to the proportion of total quantity of student in junior secondary school to the population of junior school age.

第二十一篇

CHAPTER 21

卫生、社会保障和社会福利业

HEALTH, SOCIAL SECURITY AND SOCIAL WELFARE

简要说明

一、本篇资料的主要内容

本篇主要反映卫生、社会保障和社会福利的发展情况。

卫生部分主要包括卫生机构、卫生技术人员、卫生机构床位、医疗机构诊疗入院、疾病死亡原因、婴儿死亡原因、三大死亡率、防病工作、家庭病床、妇幼卫生工作、公民献血用血、卫生总费用等情况。

社会保障部分主要包括城乡基本养老保险、城镇职工基本医疗保险、城乡居民基本医疗保险、城镇职工失业保险、城镇职工生育保险、城镇职工工伤保险、少儿住院基金等参保人数情况。

社会福利部分主要包括社会保障标准、社会福利事业机构、民间组织、养老服务、医疗服务和红十字会等情况。

二、本篇资料的来源

卫生部分资料由上海市卫生健康委员会提供。社会保障资料由上海市人力资源和社会保障局、上海市医疗保障局提供。社会福利资料中,社会保障标准、社会福利事业机构、民间组织、养老服务资料由上海市民政局、上海市退役军人事务局提供;医疗服务资料由上海市卫生健康委员会提供;红十字会资料由上海市红十字会提供。

BRIEF INTRODUCTION

I. Main Contents

Data in this chapter mainly reflect the development of public health, social security, and social welfare.

Data on public health include mainly the number of medical and healthcare institutions, medical personnel, beds available at such institutions, in-patients medical treatment and death-causing diseases, infant death-causing diseases and composition, top three death-causing diseases, disease prevention, family sickbeds, work of gynecology and pediatrics, blood offered and used by citizens, total expenditure on health.

Data on social security include mainly the numbers of participants in urban basic pension insurance, urban employee basic medical care insurance, urban basic medical care insurance, unemployment insurance, maternity insurance, work injury insurance, rural social medical care insurance, and medical fund of children.

Data on social welfare include social security standards, social welfare institutions, civil organizations, services for aged people, medical services and basic statistics about the Red Cross Society of China Shanghai Municipal Branch.

II. Sources of data

Data on public health are provided by Shanghai Municipal Health Commission. Data on social security are provided by Shanghai Municipal Human Resources and Social Security Bureau, and Shanghai Municipal Healthcare Security Administration. Of data on social welfare, data on social security standards, social welfare institutions, civil organizations, and services for aged people are provided by Shanghai Civil Affairs Bureau, and Shanghai Municipal Veterans Affairs Bureau; data on medical services are provided by Shanghai Municipal Health Commission; data on Red Cross are provided by the Red Cross Society of China Shanghai Municipal Branch.

表 21.1　卫生事业基本情况(1978~2021)
BASIC STATISTICS OF PUBLIC HEALTH

年 份 Year	卫生机构数（个） Health Care Institutions (unit)	其中 of which #医院 Hospitals	卫生技术人员（万人） Medical Professionals (10 000 persons)	其中 of which #执业(助理)医师 Licensed (Assistant) Doctors	卫生机构床位数（万张） Beds in Health Care Institutions (10 000 beds)	其中 of which #医院 Hospitals	每万人口医生数(人) Doctors per 10 000 Persons (person)	每万人口医院床位数(张) Hospital Beds per 10 000 Persons (bed)
1978	4 823	388	8.50	3.35	5.47	4.68	30	42
1979	5 627	394	8.88	3.58	5.56	4.78	31	42
1980	6 067	399	9.41	3.92	5.80	4.94	34	43
1981	6 337	403	9.57	4.37	5.84	4.99	37	43
1982	6 445	408	9.88	4.72	5.93	5.11	40	43
1983	6 451	415	10.09	4.87	6.00	5.20	41	43
1984	6 318	420	10.24	4.84	6.16	5.34	40	44
1985	7 245	405	10.42	4.85	6.02	5.32	39	43
1986	7 306	419	10.71	4.91	6.22	5.47	39	44
1987	7 330	431	11.00	5.05	6.38	5.60	40	44
1988	7 471	444	11.46	5.40	6.79	5.89	42	46
1989	7 550	460	11.65	5.73	6.87	6.04	44	46
1990	7 690	462	11.84	5.82	6.96	6.21	44	47
1991	7 554	463	11.92	5.89	7.01	6.31	44	47
1992	7 363	454	11.82	5.88	7.07	6.42	43	47
1993	6 077	486	11.53	5.75	7.12	6.75	42	49
1994	5 606	497	11.20	5.52	7.20	6.81	39	49
1995	5 286	485	11.06	5.37	7.10	6.69	38	47
1996	5 200	477	10.95	5.24	7.00	6.73	36	46
1997	5 028	474	10.89	5.13	7.00	6.78	34	46
1998	4 637	473	10.84	5.03	7.02	6.83	33	45

①2002 年开始，卫生指标按照新的《中国卫生统计调查制度》统计。
②2007 年开始，医院统计范围按照新的《2007 国家卫生统计调查制度》统计，不再包括社区卫生服务中心、妇幼保健院和专科防治院。
③2013 年开始，卫生机构，卫生技术人员和床位数中包含村卫生室相关数据。
❶Since 2002, statistics of health care has been based on "China Health Care Statistical Investigation System".
❷Since 2007, statistics of hospital has been based on "2007 National Health Care Statistical Investigation System", not including the community health care service center, maternity and child care hospital and special disease hospital.
❸Since 2013, data of health institutions, health technology personnel and beds contain the related data of village health rooms.

表 21.1 续表 continued

年 份 Year	卫生机构数（个）Health Care Institutions (unit)	其中 of which #医 院 Hospitals	卫 生 技术人员（万人）Medical Professionals (10 000 persons)	其中 of which #执 业（助理）医师 Licensed (Assistant) Doctors	卫生机构床位数（万张）Beds in Health Care Institutions (10 000 beds)	其中 of which #医 院 Hospitals	每万人口医生数（人）Doctors per 10 000 Persons (person)	每万人口医院床位数（张）Hospital Beds per 10 000 Persons (bed)
1999	4 620	465	10.81	5.06	7.24	7.06	32	45
2000	4 400	459	10.71	4.99	7.53	7.31	31	45
2001	3 813	432	10.51	4.85	7.88	7.63	30	47
2002	2 422	436	10.16	4.38	8.15	8.13	27	50
2003	2 319	452	10.22	4.41	8.44	8.11	26	47
2004	2 577	489	10.17	4.38	8.64	8.50	25	49
2005	2 527	487	10.35	4.40	9.08	8.93	25	50
2006	2 519	505	10.90	4.55	9.44	9.28	25	51
2007	2 646	288	12.24	4.88	9.59	7.54	26	41
2008	2 809	301	12.77	5.12	9.78	7.78	27	41
2009	3 013	296	13.09	5.11	9.97	7.95	27	41
2010	3 270	306	13.54	5.13	10.51	8.48	22	37
2011	3 358	308	13.91	5.21	10.71	8.75	22	37
2012	3 465	317	14.61	5.42	10.96	9.00	23	38
2013	4 929	328	15.64	5.81	11.43	9.47	24	39
2014	4 987	332	16.40	6.13	11.75	9.83	25	41
2015	5 016	338	17.02	6.31	12.28	10.35	26	42
2016	5 011	349	17.82	6.55	12.92	11.01	27	46
2017	5 144	363	18.80	6.83	13.46	11.59	28	48
2018	5 298	364	20.65	7.49	14.72	12.90	31	53
2019	5 610	387	21.33	7.77	15.46	13.67	32	56
2020	5 905	405	22.64	8.23	16.15	14.36	33	58
2021	6 317	432	23.96	8.70	16.85	15.08	35	61

表 21.2 各类卫生机构、床位及人员数(2021)
VARIOUS HEALTH CARE INSTITUTIONS, BEDS AND PERSONNEL

机构类别	Type of Institutions	机构数(个) Health Care Institutions (unit)	床位数(张) Beds (bed)	从业人员数(人) Personnel (person)
总 计	**Total**	**6 317**	**168 463**	**293 353**
#医 院	Hospitals	432	150 815	192 237
综合医院	Comprehensive Hospitals	183	78 925	126 466
中医医院	Hospitals of Traditional Chinese Medicine	23	6 817	11 430
中西医结合医院	Hospitals of Traditional Chinese and Western Medicine	10	4 642	7 103
专科医院	Special Diseases Hospitals	133	36 203	40 142
护理院	Nursing Homes	83	24 228	7 096
基层医疗卫生机构	Basic Medical and Health Institutions	5 656	15 537	82 090
社区卫生服务中心(站)	Community Health Care Centers	1 159	15 537	37 897
村卫生室	Village Health Rooms	1 147		1 531
门诊部	Policlinics	1 397		24 877
诊所、卫生所、医务室、护理站	Clinics, Health Centers and Infirmaries	1 953		17 785
专业公共卫生机构	Professional Medical and Health Institutions	103	1 346	14 326
疾病预防控制中心	Disease Prevention and Control Centers	19		3 279
专科疾病防治院(所、站)	Special Disease Hospitals and Institutions	16	204	1 578
健康教育所(站、中心)	Health Education Institutions	1		158
妇幼保健院(所、站)	Maternity and Child Care Hospitals and Institutions	19	1 142	2 932
急救中心(站)	First-aid Centers	12		4 088
采供血机构	Blood Collection and Supply Institutions	8		825
卫生监督所(中心)	Health Supervision Centers	17		1 351
计划生育技术服务机构	The Family Planning Technical Service Institutions	11		115
其他卫生机构	Other Health Care Institutions	126	765	4 700
疗养院	Sanatoriums	4	765	515
卫生监督检验(监测、检测)所(站)	Health Supervision and Inspection Institutions			
医学科学研究机构	Institutions of Medical Science	8		571
医学在职培训机构	Medical In-service Training Institutions	7		193
临床检验中心(所、站)	Clinical Test Centers	58		2 136
其 他	Others	49		1 285

表 21.2 续表 continued

机构类别	Type of Institutions	#卫生技术人员 Medical Professionals	其中 of which #执业(助理)医师 Licensed (Assistant) Doctors	注册护士 Registered Nurses
总　计	**Total**	**239 571**	**87 004**	**108 677**
#医　院	Hospitals	163 662	53 580	80 545
综合医院	Comprehensive Hospitals	108 665	36 191	53 732
中医医院	Hospitals of Traditional Chinese Medicine	9 735	3 824	4 078
中西医结合医院	Hospitals of Traditional Chinese and Western Medicine	6 313	2 398	2 899
专科医院	Special Diseases Hospitals	33 438	9 918	16 940
护理院	Nursing Homes	5 511	1 249	2 896
基层医疗卫生机构	Basic Medical and Health Institutions	63 644	28 818	25 497
社区卫生服务中心(站)	Community Health Care Centers	32 997	14 062	12 451
村卫生室	Village Health Rooms	1 531	959	28
门诊部	Policlinics	21 229	9 886	9 619
诊所、卫生所、医务室、护理站	Clinics, Health Centers and Infirmaries	7 887	3 911	3 399
专业公共卫生机构	Professional Medical and Health Institutions	9 804	4 017	2 270
疾病预防控制中心	Disease Prevention and Control Centers	2 549	1 502	33
专科疾病防治院(所、站)	Special Disease Hospitals and Institutions	1 311	637	487
健康教育所(站、中心)	Health Education Institutions	58	28	
妇幼保健院(所、站)	Maternity and Child Care Hospitals and Institutions	2 532	991	1 166
急救中心(站)	First-aid Centers	1 551	829	207
采供血机构	Blood Collection and Supply Institutions	619	22	375
卫生监督所(中心)	Health Supervision Centers	1 166		
计划生育技术服务机构	The Family Planning Technical Service Institutions	18	8	2
其他卫生机构	Other Health Care Institutions	2 461	589	365
疗养院	Sanatoriums	376	155	137
卫生监督检验(监测、检测)所(站)	Health Supervision and Inspection Institutions			
医学科学研究机构	Institutions of Medical Science	314	94	6
医学在职培训机构	Medical In-service Training Institutions	30	11	12
临床检验中心(所、站)	Clinical Test Centers	1 221	110	28
其　他	Others	520	219	182

表 21.3 各区卫生机构基本情况(2021)
STATISTICS OF HEALTH CARE INSTITUTIONS BY DISTRICTS

地 区 District		机构数(个) Health Care Institutions(unit)	床位数(张) Hospital Beds (bed)	卫生技术人员(人) Medical Professionals (person)	其 中 of which	
					# 执业(助理)医师 Licensed (Assistant) Doctors	注册护士 Registered Nurses
总 计	**Total**	**6 317**	**168 463**	**239 571**	**87 004**	**108 677**
浦东新区	Pudong New Area	1 316	22 524	33 096	13 158	14 025
黄浦区	Huangpu	319	16 163	28 546	10 124	13 336
徐汇区	Xuhui	380	17 931	29 347	10 152	13 690
长宁区	Changning	328	8 412	12 282	4 408	5 768
静安区	Jing'an	393	14 211	22 460	7 746	10 585
普陀区	Putuo	225	7 689	11 345	4 044	5 344
虹口区	Hongkou	183	8 897	12 046	4 432	5 577
杨浦区	Yangpu	259	13 455	17 824	5 946	8 714
闵行区	Minhang	512	13 271	15 999	5 721	7 295
宝山区	Baoshan	354	10 735	11 158	4 005	5 149
嘉定区	Jiading	392	8 832	11 022	4 206	5 004
金山区	Jinshan	307	5 492	7 363	2 644	3 236
松江区	Songjiang	254	5 390	8 341	3 033	3 352
青浦区	Qingpu	399	6 375	7 010	2 726	2 926
奉贤区	Fengxian	334	5 343	6 707	2 676	2 726
崇明区	Chongming	362	3 743	5 025	1 983	1 950

表 21.4 医疗机构病床使用情况(2021) STATISTICS OF HOSPITAL BED USAGE IN MEDICAL TREATMENT INSTITUTION

机构类别	Types	平均开放床位数(张) Average Beds Opened(bed)	病床周转次数(次) Turnover Times of Beds(time)	病床使用率(%) Usage Rate of Beds(%)	出院者平均住院日(日) Average Days to Inpatient in Hospital(day)
总　计	**Total**	**162 594.82**	**29.24**	**86.64**	**10.51**
卫生部门	Medical Institutions	108 493.64	38.09	89.41	8.63
#医　院	Hospital	92 056.32	31.57	88.48	9.84
#综合医院	Comprehensive Hospitals	56 057.81	48.44	91.59	6.95
中(西)医医院	Hospitals of Chinese (Western) Medicine	10 324.97	41.86	87.33	7.67
护理院	Nursing Hospitals	1 513.69	0.97	97.83	180.48
社区卫生服务中心(站)	Community Health Care Centers	14 889.92	1.80	72.73	160.91
其他部门	Other Departments	54 101.18	11.47	81.08	23.01

表 21.5 医疗机构诊疗人次和入院人数(2021) PATIENTS TREATED AND INPATIENTS IN MEDICAL TREATMENT INSTITUTION

机构类别	Types	诊疗人次(万人次) Total Patients Treated(10 000 person-times)	其中 of which #门、急诊 Outpatients and Emergency Patients	入院人数(万人) Inpatients (10 000 persons)	每百诊次的入院人数(人) Inpatients per 100 Patient-times (person)
总　计	**Total**	**27 249.09**	**25 785.43**	**476.26**	**1.75**
医　院	Hospitals	17 675.47	17 506.38	460.69	2.61
综合医院	Comprehensive Hospitals	12 421.77	12 340.35	314.05	2.53
中(西)医医院	Hospitals of Chinese(Western) Medicine	2 576.19	2 499.74	43.95	1.71
传染病医院	Infectious Diseases Hospitals	57.68	57.68	3.12	5.40
精神病医院	Mental Hospitals	207.31	201.65	1.53	0.74
结核病医院	Tuberculosis Hospitals	133.48	133.48	11.84	8.87
肿瘤医院	Tumor Hospitals	191.44	191.44	15.98	8.35
儿童医院	Children's Hospitals	639.51	639.51	14.21	2.22
其他专科医院	Other Specialized Hospitals	1 366.90	1 361.50	52.57	3.85
护理院	Nurse Hospitals	81.18	81.03	3.45	4.25
社区卫生服务中心(站)	Community Health-care Service Centers (Stations)	7 103.63	6 967.54	2.56	0.04
妇幼保健院(所、站)	Maternity and Child Care Hospital	191.59	184.77	5.92	3.09
其他医疗机构	Other Medical Facilities	2 278.40	1 126.75	7.10	0.31

表 21.6 前十位疾病死亡原因和构成(2021)
THE TOP 10 DEATH-CAUSING DISEASES AND COMPOSITION

死亡原因	Cause of Death	死亡专率(1/10 万) Death Rate(1/100 000)	占死亡总数(%) Percentage of Total Death(%)
循环系病	Circulation Diseases	391.50	43.55
肿　瘤	Tumor	266.41	29.64
呼吸系病	Respiratory System Diseases	60.35	6.71
内分泌营养代谢病	Endocrine-Immunity-Metabolic Diseases	54.44	6.06
损伤中毒	Damnification and Poisoning	44.95	5.00
消化系病	Digestive System Diseases	20.97	2.33
神经系病	Nervous System Disease	15.83	1.76
传染病及寄生虫病	Infectious & Parasitic Diseases	7.68	0.85
泌尿生殖系病	Genitourinary Diseases	7.47	0.83
精神障碍	Mental Disorder	7.26	0.81

表 21.7 婴儿前五位疾病死亡原因和构成(2021)
THE TOP 5 INFANT DEATH-CAUSING DISEASES AND COMPOSITION

死亡原因	Cause of Death	死亡专率(1/10 万) Death Rate(1/100 000)	占死亡总数(%) Percentage of Total Death(%)
新生儿病	Neonatal Disease	70.98	50.00
先天异常	Congenital Anomaly	39.27	27.66
损伤中毒	Damnification and Poisning	9.06	6.38
内分泌营养代谢病	Endocrine-Immunity-Metabolic Diseases	9.06	6.38
神经系病	Nervous System Disease	6.04	4.26

表 21.8 婴儿死亡率、新生儿死亡率、孕产妇死亡率(2018~2021)
DEATH RATE OF INFANT, NEW BORN, PREGNANT AND LYING-IN WOMAN

指　标	Indicators	2018	2019	2020	2021
婴儿死亡率(‰)	Death Rate of Infant(‰)	3.52	3.06	2.66	2.30
新生儿死亡率(‰)	Death Rate of New Born(‰)	2.17	1.67	1.12	1.30
孕产妇死亡率(1/10 万)	Death Rate of Pregnant and Lying-in Woman(1/100 000)	1.15	3.51	3.66	1.60

注：2016 年起，婴儿死亡率和孕产妇死亡率调整为上海地区口径，不再包含本市户籍妇女在外省市生育的数据。
Note: Since 2016, the statistic coverage of infant mortality rate and the maternal mortality rate has been adjusted to the Shanghai region, and no longer include data on the births of women in other provinces and cities.

表 21.9 主要年份防病工作情况
BASIC STATISTICS OF DISEASE PREVENTION IN MAIN YEARS

指 标	Indicators	2000	2010	2020	2021
传染病发病总例数（甲、乙）(万例)	**Cases of Contagious Diseases Reported (A,B) (10 000 cases)**	**3.58**	**2.22**	**1.48**	**1.70**
发病率(1/10 万)	Disease Rate(1/100 000)	271.66	161.17	102.16	118.12
传染病死亡总人数(人)	Quantity of Deaths Caused by Contagious Diseases (person)	179	127	101	89
死亡率(1/10 万)	Death Rate (1/100 000)	1.36	0.92	0.70	0.62
结核病登记病人数(千例)	T.B. Patients Registered (1 000 cases)	3.09	3.26	3.17	3.07
登记患病率(‰)	Registered Disease Rate(‰)	0.23	0.23	0.21	0.21
结核病新发病人数(千例)	Newly Reported T.B. Cases(1 000 cases)	5.18	3.76	3.25	3.18
登记新发病率(1/万)	Registered Newly Diseased Rate (1/10 000)	3.94	2.67	2.20	2.14
结核病死亡人数(人)	Quantity of Deaths Caused By T.B (person)	293	112	165	180
死亡率(1/10 万)	Death Rate (1/100 000)	2.22	0.80	1.12	1.21
牙病受检人数(万人)	Quantity of People Undergoing Tooth Disease Check (10 000 persons)	51.89	54.85	34.34	77.32
龋牙患病率(%)	Rate of Caries Patients (%)	28.28	38.61	29.16	30.55
小学生视力不良率(%)	Nearsight Rate of Students in Primary School (%)	26.0	36.1	53.9	52.3
初中生视力不良率(%)	Nearsight Rate of Students in Junior High School (%)	55.0	70.0	78.7	78.6
高中生视力不良率(%)	Nearsight Rate of Students in Senior High School (%)	78.5	85.7	88.7	87.9
免疫规划疫苗常规免疫接种率(%)	Conventional Vaccines of Vaccine Immunization Programmes Recipients Rate	99.7	99.8	99.8	99.8
乙肝疫苗全程接种率(%)	Hepatitis-B Inoculation Rate(%)	99.9	99.8	99.8	99.9

表 21.10 家庭病床情况(2021)
FAMILY SICKBEDS

机构类别	Types	开展工作机构数(个) Running Institutions (unit)	上门诊疗总次数(次) Total Times of Family Call (time)	年底实有病床数(张) Year-end Sickbeds (bed)	年内开设总病床数(张) Sickbeds Set up in 2020 (bed)
总 计	**Total**	**267**	**766 852**	**18 491**	**63 728**
医 院	Hospitals	4	4 053	372	666
社区卫生服务中心(站)	Community Health-care Centers	263	762 799	18 119	63 062

表 21.11 主要年份妇幼卫生工作情况
BASIC STATISTICS OF GYNAECOLOGY AND PAEDIATRICS IN MAIN YEARS

指 标	Indicators	2000	2010	2020	2021
妇女病普查人数(万人)	**Quantity of People Surveyed for Female Diseases (10 000 persons)**	**40.27**	**86.54**	**60.85**	**68.39**
患病率(%)	Sufferers Rate(%)	35.0	33.3	34.7	36.9
治疗率(%)	Patients Treated Rate(%)	91.1	98.7	89.6	89.3
胎儿娩出顺产数(万人)	Quantity of Smooth Delivery (10 000 persons)	4.05	8.81	7.03	6.34
顺产率(%)	Smooth Delivery Rate(%)	47.5	45.1	51.6	50.7
出生低体重儿(人)	Quantity of Low-weight Newborns (person)	2 567	6 961	6 800	6 841
占活产总数(%)	Proportion in All Deliveries (%)	3.0	3.6	5.0	5.5
出生缺陷人数(人)	Quantity of Newborns with Innate Problems (person)	764	2 496	1 946	2 294
出生缺陷率(‰)	Disabled Among All Deliveries Rate (‰)	8.96	12.80	14.27	18.35
0~6 岁儿童保健管理率(%)	Children of 0-6 Years Old under Health Programm Rate(%)	94.3	97.0	99.4	99.5
婚前检查人数(万人)	Quantity of People Undergoing Pre-marriage Checkup (10 000 persons)	17.36	8.53	2.36	2.82
婚检率(%)	Pre-marriage Checkup Recipients Rate(%)	98.4	35.4	13.2	16.0

表 21.12 主要年份公民献血、用血情况
BLOOD OFFER AND USE OF CITIZENS IN MAIN YEARS

指 标	Indicators	2000	2010	2020	2021
无偿(义务)献血(万人份)	Volunteer or Compulsory Blood Offer (10 000 person unit)	35.19	46.27	33.09	37.93
临床用血量(万人份)	Clinic Blood Use Volum (10 000 person unit)	34.70	42.02	51.59	57.87

表 21.13 主要年份社会保险参保人数
QUANTITY OF PARTICIPANTS IN SOCIAL INSURANCE IN MAIN YEARS

单位:万人(10 000 persons)

指 标	Indicators	2000	2010	2020	2021
城镇职工基本养老保险	**Urban Basic Pension Insurance**				
在职职工	Urban Staff and Workers	431.27	522.44	1 051.96	1 081.58
个体工商户和自由职业人员	Individual Businessmen	9.82	20.43	42.94	44.43
领取养老金的离退休人员	Retired Veteran Cadres and Retired Staff and Workers with Pensions	234.23	352.02	521.77	528.35
城镇职工基本医疗保险	Basic Medical Insurance for Urban Staff and Workers				
在职职工	Urban Staff and Workers	364.59	608.41	1 064.86	1 084.74
享受医保的离退休人员	Retired Veteran Cadres and Retired Staff and Workers with Medicare	202.14	391.33	523.39	529.64
城乡居民基本医疗保险	Basic Medical Insurance for Urban Residents		259.17	355.99	365.05
城镇职工失业保险	Unemployment Insurance of Urban Staff and Workers	434.86	556.20	987.64	1 021.26
城镇职工生育保险	Generational Insurance of Urban Staff and Workers		657.30		
城镇职工工伤保险	Injured Insurance of Urban Staff and Workers		555.36	1 082.23	1 097.33
少儿住院基金	Medicare Fund of Children	212.47	197.19	231.23	234.95

①根据《中华人民共和国保险法》,2011 年对社会保险政策进行了调整。 原参加“小城镇社会保险”和“来沪从业人员综合保险”的从业人员被纳入城镇职工保险范围内,并对养老、医疗、工伤、失业、生育保险的相关政策作出了调整。

②根据 2016 年 1 月发布的《国务院关于整合城乡居民基本医疗保险制度的意见》,对城镇居民基本医疗保险和新型农村合作医疗两项制度进行整合,建立统一的城乡居民基本医疗保险制度。

❶According to Insurance Law of the People's Republic of China, the social insurance policy has been adjusted since 2011. Employees, who have participated in Town Social Insurance and General Insurance of Employment of Migratory Population before, are now within the range of insurance for urban staff and workers. Relative policies of pension, medical, injured, unemployment and generational insurances have also been adjusted.

❷According to Opinions of the State Council on the Integration of Basic Medical Insurance System for Urban and Rural Residents which is issued on January 2016, the two basic medical insurance systems of urban residents and the new rural cooperative medical service are integrated to establish a unified basic medical insurance system for urban and rural residents.

表 21.14 主要年份社会保障标准
SOCIAL SECURITY STANDARD IN MAIN YEARS

单位:元/月(yuan/month)

指 标	Indicators	2000	2010	2020	2021
职工工资最低标准	Minimum Standard of Wages of Staff and Workers	445	1 120	2 480	2 590
城镇居民生活保障最低标准	Minimum Standard of Urban Living Security	280	450	1 240	1 330

表 21.15 主要年份民政事业机构数和职工人数
QUANTITY OF SOCIAL WELFARE INSTITUTIONS AND STAFF AND WORKERS IN MAIN YEARS

指 标	Indicators	2000	2010	2020	2021
机构数(个)	**Total Institutions (unit)**				
提供住宿的社会工作机构	Social work insititutions with accommodations			696	713
社会救助中心	Social Assistance Centers	16	22	6	6
婚姻登记服务单位	Marriage Register Service Institutions		16	17	16
殡仪服务单位	Funeral and Interment Service Institutions	68	79	72	74
福利彩票发行单位	Issue Institutions of Welfare Lottery	16	19	17	17
职工人数(人)	**Staff and Workers (person)**				
提供住宿的社会工作机构	Social work insititutions with accommodations			30 841	32 992
社会救助中心	Social Assistance Centers	472	403	75	66
婚姻登记服务单位	Marriage Register Service Institutions		110	176	181
殡仪服务单位	Funeral and Interment Service Institutions	2 577	3 201	3 441	3 576
福利彩票发行单位	Issue Institutions of Welfare Lottery	86	87	197	207

表 21.16 主要年份民间组织情况
STATISTICS OF CIVIL ORGANIZATIONS AND CHARITY IN MAIN YEARS

指 标	Indicators	2005	2010	2020	2021
民间组织数(个)	**Quantity of Civil Organizations (unit)**	**7 556**	**10 104**	**17 048**	**17 368**
社会团体	Social Organizations	2 952	3 634	4 242	4 304
民办非企业	Civil Non-Enterprises	4 537	6 353	12 273	12 490
基金会	Foundations	67	117	533	574

表 21.17 主要年份养老服务
ENDOWMENT SERVICE IN MAIN YEARS

指 标	Indicators	2005	2010	2020	2021
机构养老服务	**Endowment Service of Institutions**				
机构数(家)	Quantity of Institutions (unit)	474	625	729	730
床位数(万张)	Quantity of Beds (10 000 beds)	4.95	9.78	15.70	15.86
#新增养老床位	Newly Added Endowmet Beds	1.01	1.08	0.76	0.57
养老床位占 60 周岁及以上老年人口比例(%)	Ratio of Endowment Bed in Population above 60 (%)	1.9	3.1	3.0	2.9
社区托养服务	**Household Endowment Service**				
社区老年人日间照护机构机构数(家)	Community Daytime Service Institutions for Aged People Quantity of Institutions (unit)	83	303	758	831
日均服务人数(万人)	Population of Daytime Service Aged People (10 000 persons)	0.21	0.90	1.50	1.05
获得政府补贴的老年人(万人)	Population of Aged People Gained Governmental Subsidy (10 000 persons)	3.94	13.00	7.48	7.91

表 21.18 主要年份老年医疗服务
MEDICARE SERVICE FOR AGED PEOPLE IN MAIN YEARS

指 标	Indicators	2005	2010	2020	2021
独立老年护理院	**Independent Nursing Home for Aged People**				
机构数(所)	Quantity of Institutions (unit)	13	14	64	83
建筑面积(平方米)	Structure Area (sq.m)	59 742	101 048	446 961	626 375
床位数(张)	Beds (bed)	2 353	3 285	19 597	24 228
出院人数(人次)	Person-time in Hospital (person-time)			28 571	31 926
老年医院	**Hospital for Aged People**				
机构数(所)	Quantity of Institutions(unit)	3	4	3	3
出院人数(人次)	Person-time in Hospital (person-time)			1 573	2 221
家庭病床总数(张)	**Total Quantity of bed in home (bed)**	**40 745**	**43 880**	**55 204**	**63 728**

表 21.19 主要年份红十字会基本情况
BASIC STATISICS ON RED CROSS SOCIETY OF CHINA SHANGHAI MUNICIPAL BRANCH IN MAIN YEARS

	指 标 Indicators	2005	2010	2020	2021
红十字会组织机构	**Institutions**				
基层组织(个)	Primary Instituntions(unit)	2 934	3 042	1 499	1 495
冠名红十字会医疗机构(个)	Medical Institutions(unit)	67	72	75	75
红十字会团体会员单位(个)	Team Members(unit)	970	969	771	822
红十字会会员人数(万人)	**Quantity of Members(10 000 persons)**	**61.62**	**86.52**	**83.75**	**81.00**
#青少年会员(万人)	Hobbledehoy Members(10 000 persons)	37.16	58.64	39.18	38.30
组织各种宣传活动	**Times of Publicizing Activity**				
在报刊登载宣传文章(篇)	Articles on Newspaper and Periodical (piece)	831	609	420	89
电视台播报宣传节目(条/次)	Programs on Television (piece/time)	459	200	7	3
卫生救护工作	**Sanitation Rescue**				
应急救护知识普及(万人次)	Rescue Popularization Training (10 000 person-time)	24.72	37.35	29.51	49.98
造血干细胞捐献工作	**Contributing Trunk Cell**				
参加造血干细胞捐献库人数(万人)	Quantity of Subscribers (10 000 persons)	5.60	10.42	15.34	15.94
遗体捐献工作	**Contributing Reliquiae**				
遗体捐献登记站(个)	Register Centers(unit)	27	25	26	26
遗体捐献接收站(个)	Accepting Centers(unit)	8	7	10	6
全年接受捐献遗体登记(人)	Quantity of Contributing Reliquiae(Person)	1 284	1 170	2 376	2 926
全年接受角膜捐献登记(人)	Quantity of Contributing Cornea(Person)	133	73	931	1 362
社会救灾和救助工作	**Working on Social Relieving**				
救灾投入(万元)	Relieve Devotion (10 000 yuan)	10 635.36	19 267.76	368.59	2 398.68
救助款物投入(万元)	Salvation Devotion (10 000 yuan)	1 538.12	4 780.71	17 470.15	2 048.30
救助受益人次(万人次)	Quantity of Beneficiaries (10 000 persons-times)	2.87	4.11	3.24	3.20

①社区救助受益人次不包含外省市受益人次。
②2013 年起,“参加普及宣传无偿献血活动人次数”口径调整为红十字会主办活动人次数。
③根据 2017 年 5 月 8 日新修订实施的《中华人民共和国红十字会法》第七条“县级以上地方按行政区域建立地方各级红十字会”的有关规定,自 2017 年起“基层组织”的统计口径不再包含“居村红十字小组”。
❶Persons benefited from community salvation devotion do not contain people from other provinces and cities.
❷The statistical caliber of Person-time Attended Publicizing Volunteer Blood Donation Activities was adjusted to Person-time of participating in the activities organized by the Red Cross since 2013.
❸According to the relevant provisions of Article 7 of the “Red Cross Society Law of the People's Republic of China”, “Local Red Cross Societies at the County Level and Above by Administrative Regions”, which was implemented on May 8, 2017, the statistical caliber of “Basic Organizations” will no longer includes the “Village Red Cross Group” since 2017.

表 21.20 全市残疾人各残疾类别人数情况(2021)
THE NUMBER OF CASES OF EACH TYPE OF DISABILITY

单位:人(person)

地 区	District	总 计 Total	视 力 Vision	听 力 Hearing	言 语 Speech	肢 体 Limb	智 力 Intelligence	精 神 Spirit	多 重 Multiple
全 市	**Total**	**605 601**	**95 946**	**83 542**	**5 521**	**294 047**	**56 794**	**53 971**	**15 780**
浦东新区	Pudong New Area	112 055	19 731	17 488	1 229	47 211	13 043	10 539	2 814
黄 浦 区	Huangpu	33 765	8 254	5 547	274	13 083	2 335	3 346	926
徐 汇 区	Xuhui	26 119	6 028	3 784	199	9 987	2 278	3 100	743
长 宁 区	Changning	25 148	3 853	3 539	196	13 142	1 298	2 202	918
静 安 区	Jing'an	42 272	7 226	7 153	325	19 922	2 570	4 012	1 064
普 陀 区	Putuo	41 835	5 617	5 003	312	23 743	2 627	3 264	1 269
虹 口 区	Hongkou	27 812	4 969	3 650	158	13 663	1 739	2 976	657
杨 浦 区	Yangpu	51 524	6 790	6 264	346	30 327	2 745	3 595	1 457
闵 行 区	Minhang	38 476	6 518	5 714	284	17 764	3 791	3 514	891
宝 山 区	Baoshan	41 723	7 120	5 429	373	20 234	3 544	4 037	986
嘉 定 区	Jiading	31 813	3 286	4 644	254	16 572	2 926	3 099	1 032
金 山 区	Jinshan	18 951	2 307	1 819	623	8 223	3 399	2 005	575
松 江 区	Songjiang	25 045	3 345	2 109	188	14 174	3 242	1 722	265
青 浦 区	Qingpu	24 882	2 237	3 112	184	14 377	2 096	2 495	381
奉 贤 区	Fengxian	20 843	1 958	2 369	321	9 907	3 629	2 072	587
崇 明 区	Chongming	43 338	6 707	5 918	255	21 718	5 532	1 993	1 215

注：本表数据由市残疾人联合会提供。
Note: Data in this table are provided by Shanghai Disabled Persons'Federation.

表 21.21 卫生总费用(来源法)(2001~2020) TOTAL HEALTH EXPENDITURE BY SOURCE

年 份 Year	卫生总费用(亿元) Total Health Expenditure (100 million yuan)	其 中 of which			构 成(%)			人均卫生费用(元) Per Capita Health Expenditure (yuan)
		政府卫生支出 Government Health Expenditure	社会卫生支出 Social Health Expenditure	个人现金卫生支出 Personal Out-of-Pocket Health Expenditure	政府卫生支出 Government Health Expenditure	社会卫生支出 Social Health Expenditure	个人卫生支出 Personal Health Expenditure	
2001	202.63	45.70	98.01	58.93	22.6	48.4	29.0	1 233
2002	220.31	40.65	121.14	58.52	18.5	55.0	26.5	1 356
2003	266.19	51.30	151.60	63.29	19.3	56.9	23.8	1 556
2004	315.48	59.54	170.14	85.80	18.9	53.9	27.2	1 811
2005	362.13	70.30	199.44	92.39	19.4	55.1	25.5	2 036
2006	401.46	77.13	226.39	97.94	19.2	56.4	24.4	2 212
2007	485.67	99.39	278.50	107.79	20.5	57.3	22.2	2 614
2008	559.83	135.82	314.97	109.04	24.2	56.3	19.5	2 965
2009	656.66	141.30	366.90	148.45	21.5	55.9	22.6	3 418
2010	751.99	177.20	419.82	154.96	23.6	55.8	20.6	3 266
2011	931.00	215.70	521.62	193.68	23.2	56.0	20.8	3 966
2012	1 092.35	232.49	646.51	213.35	21.3	59.2	19.5	4 589
2013	1 248.68	250.82	740.42	257.44	20.1	59.3	20.6	5 170
2014	1 347.79	275.29	792.51	279.99	20.4	58.8	20.8	5 556
2015	1 536.60	319.94	882.39	334.27	20.8	57.4	21.8	6 362
2016	1 838.00	430.73	1 061.74	345.53	23.4	57.8	18.8	7 596
2017	2 087.09	449.64	1 209.53	427.92	21.5	58.0	20.5	8 611
2018	2 301.60	507.92	1 326.42	467.26	22.0	57.6	20.3	9 496
2019	2 532.68	564.16	1 439.66	528.86	22.3	56.8	20.9	10 183
2020	2 634.22	633.70	1 491.95	508.57	24.1	56.6	19.3	10 592

表 21.22 卫生总费用构成(机构法)(2001~2020) THE STRUCTURE OF TOTAL HEALTH EXPENDITURE BY INSTITUTION

单位:%

年 份 Year	卫生总费用 Total Health Expenditure	医 院 Hospitals	基层医疗卫生机构 Basic Medical and Health Institutions	药品零售机构 Drug Retailers	公共卫生机构 Public Health Institutions	卫生行政管理机构 Health Administrative Organization	其 他 Others
2001	100	62.9	18.3	10.1	5.3	0.3	3.1
2002	100	65.9	15.7	8.9	5.2	0.3	4.0
2003	100	65.6	13.7	8.1	5.1	0.4	7.1
2004	100	65.1	14.1	8.4	5.8	0.5	6.1
2005	100	63.6	14.6	8.4	5.8	0.5	7.1
2006	100	65.3	14.8	8.4	6.1	0.3	5.1
2007	100	66.5	14.8	7.5	5.2	1.7	4.3
2008	100	62.5	17.8	10.0	6.2	1.2	2.3
2009	100	64.9	17.3	8.1	6.3	1.1	2.3
2010	100	65.8	14.6	8.0	5.6	1.6	4.4
2011	100	68.1	13.0	7.4	3.2	1.9	6.4
2012	100	69.8	12.9	7.2	3.2	2.3	4.6
2013	100	70.7	13.1	7.2	3.5	2.6	2.9
2014	100	71.7	12.9	7.3	3.1	2.8	2.2
2015	100	71.8	13.4	7.1	3.2	2.4	2.0
2016	100	68.8	12.2	7.2	3.5	7.0	1.4
2017	100	69.3	12.8	8.5	3.9	4.1	1.4
2018	100	69.2	13.2	8.9	3.7	3.5	1.5
2019	100	69.6	13.7	8.1	2.9	3.6	2.1
2020	100	68.0	14.0	6.8	3.1	4.3	3.8

上/海/统/计/年/鉴

主要统计指标解释

■ 卫生机构

是指从卫生行政部门取得《医疗机构执业许可证》，或从民政、工商行政、机构编制管理部门取得法人单位登记证书，为社会提供医疗保健、疾病控制、卫生监督服务或从事医学研究和医学在职培训等工作的单位。

■ 医疗机构

指从卫生行政部门取得《医疗机构执业许可证》的机构，包括医院、疗养院、社区卫生服务中心（站）、卫生院、门诊部、诊所（卫生所、医务室）、妇幼保健院（所、站）、专科疾病防治院（所、站）、急救中心（站）和临床检验中心，但不包括村卫生室（单纯统计）。

■ 医　院

包括综合医院、中医医院、中西医结合医院、民族医院、各类专科医院和护理院，不包括专科疾病防治院、妇幼保健院和疗养院。

■ 卫生技术人员

包括执业医师、执业助理医师、注册护士、药师（士）、检验技师、影像技师（士）、卫生监督员和见习医（药、护、技）师（士）等卫生专业人员。不包括从事管理工作的卫生技术人员（如院长、副院长、党委书记等）。

■ 执业（助理）医师

一律按领取医师执业证书且实际从事临床工作的人数统计，不包括从事管理工作的医师。

■ 优抚对象

优抚指政府对革命烈士家庭、病故残疾工作人员以及参战负伤致残的民兵、民工的抚恤和人民群众对其的优待。优抚对象包括革命烈士家属、因公牺牲和病故军人家属、革命伤残人员、现役军属、退伍红军老战士、红军失散人员、复员军人、退伍军人、在职退役军人、在乡退役军人、带病回乡退伍军人、复退军人精神病员、孤老优抚对象等。

■ 社会福利事业单位

指集中收养社会孤老、残、幼的机构。包括由民政部门管理的社会福利院、儿童福利院、精神病人福利院和城镇集体办的福利院，以及农村集体办的敬老院。

■ 基本养老保险

1.（参保）职工人数：指报告期末按照国家法律、法规和有关政策规定参加基本养老保险并在社保经办机构已建立缴费记录档案的职工人数，包括中断缴费但未终止养老保险关系的职工人数，不包括只登记未建立缴费记录档案的人数。

2.（参保）离退休人员人数：指报告期末参加基本养老保险的离休、退休和退职人员的人数。

3. 基本养老保险基金收入：指根据国家有关规定，由纳入基本养老保险范围的缴费单位和个人按国家规定的缴费基数和缴费比例缴纳的养老保险基金，以及通过其他方式取得的形成基金来源的收入。包括单位和职工个人缴纳的基本养老保险费、基本养老保险基金利息收入、上级补助收入、下级上解收入、转移收入、财政补贴和其他收入。

4. 基本养老保险基金支出：指按照国家政策规定的开支范围和开支标准从养老保险基金中支付给参加基本养老保险的离休、通休、退职人员个人的养老金、丧葬抚恤补助，以及由于保险关系转移、上下级之间调剂资金等原因而发生的支出。包括离休金、退休金、退职金、各种补贴、医疗费、死亡丧葬补助费、抚恤救济费、社会保险经办机构管理费、补助下级支出、上解上级支出、转移支出、其他支出等。

5. 基本养老保险基金累计结余：指截至报告期末基本养老保险基金收支相抵后的累计余额。

■ 基本医疗保险

1. 参保人数：指报告期末按国家有关规定参加基本医疗保险的人数。包括参加保险的职工人数和退休人员人数。

2. 基金收入：指根据国家有关规定，由纳入基本医疗保险范围的缴费单位和个人，按国家规定的缴费基数和缴费比例缴纳的基金，以及通过其他方式取得的形成基金来源的款项，包括：单位缴纳的社会统筹基金收入、个人缴纳的个人账户基金收入、财政补贴收入、利息收入、其他收入。

3. 基金支出：指按照国家政策规定的开支范围和开

主要统计指标解释

支标准从社会统筹基金中支付给参加基本医疗保险的职工和退休人员的医疗保险待遇支出，和从个人帐户基金中支付给参加基本医疗保险的职工和退休人员的医疗费用支出，以及其他支出。包括：住院医疗费用支出、门急诊医疗费用支出、个人账户基金支出、其他支出。

4. 基金累计结余：指截至报告期末基本医疗保险的社会统筹和个人帐户基金累计结余金额。包括银行存款、财政专户、债券投资和其他。

■ 失业保险

1. 参保人数：指报告期末按照国家法律、法规和有关政策规定参加了失业保险的城镇企业事业单位的职工及地方政府规定参加失业保险的其他人员的人数。

2. 失业保险基金收入：指按照规定从企业、事业及其他单位筹集的失业保险费及其他并入失业保险基金收入的总额。包括单位和个人缴纳的失业保险费、失业保险基金利息收入、上级补助收入、下级上解收入、转移收入、财政补贴和其他收入。

3. 失业保险基金支出：指报告期内为保障失业人员和下岗职工基本生活、促进其再就业等支出的基金总额。包括失业救济金、医疗费、死亡丧葬补助费、抚恤救济费、转业训练费支出、失业保险经办机构管理费、补助下级支出、上解上级支出、转移支出和其他支出。

4. 基金累计结余：指截至报告期末失业保险基金收支相抵后的累计余额。

■ 工伤保险

1. 参加保险人数: 指报告期末依据国家有关规定参加工伤保险的职工人数。

2. 享受保险待遇人数: 指劳动者因工负伤致残、死亡或因患职业病致残，根据有关规定享受工伤保险待遇职工或供养直系亲属人数。包括伤残人数、职业病人数、因工死亡人数、供养直系亲属人数。

3. 基金收入: 指根据国家有关规定，由参加工伤保险的单位按国家规定的缴费基数和缴费比例缴纳的工伤保险基金，以及通过其他形式取得的形成基金来源的款项。包括：单位缴纳的社会统筹基金收入、财政补贴收入、利息收入、其他收入。

4. 基金支出: 指按照国家政策规定的开支范围和开支标准从工伤保险基金中支付给参加工伤保险的人员及供养直系亲属工伤保险待遇支出及其他支出。包括工伤医疗费、伤残补助金、工亡补助金、护理费、丧葬补助费、工伤预防费用、职业康复费用和其他支出。

5. 基金累计结余: 指截至报告期末工伤保险基金累计结余金额。包括银行存款、财政专户、债券投资和其他。

■ 生育保险

1. 参保人数: 指报告期末依据有关规定参加生育保险的职工人数。

2. 基金收入: 指根据国家有关规定，由参加生育保险的单位按照国家规定的缴费基数和缴费比例缴纳的生育保险基金，以及通过其他方式取得的形成基金来源的款项，包括：单位缴纳的基金收入、利息收入和其他收入。

3. 基金支出: 指按照国家政策规定的开支范围和开支标准，从生育保险基金中支付给参加生育保险的职工，因妊娠、分娩和计划生育手术而享受的待遇及其他支出。包括：生育津贴、医疗费用支出及其他支出。

4. 基金累计结余: 指截至报告期末生育保险基金累计结余金额。包括银行存款、财政专户、债券投资和其他。

SHANGHAI STATISTICAL YEARBOOK

EXPLANATORY NOTES TO MAJOR STATISTICAL INDICATORS

□ Health Care Institutions

Health Care Institutions refer to the units which have been qualified the Certification of Health Care Institution by the administration of public health, or qualified the Certification of Corporate Unit by the civil affairs, administration for industry and commerce, commission office for public sector reform, and engaging in medical care, disease prevention and control, health supervision and inspection, medicine research and health professional education, etc.

□ Medical Organizations

Medical Organizations refer to the institutions which have been qualified the Certification of Health Care Institution by the administration of public health, including: hospitals, health centers, community health service centers (stations), health centers, clinics (health stations and infirmaries), women and children care agencies (centers and stations), special disease prevention and curing agencies (centers and stations), first-aid centers (stations) and clinic inspection centers, but excluding village health care rooms.

□ Hospitals

Hospitals includes comprehensive hospitals, traditional Chinese medicine hospitals, traditional Chinese and western medicine hospitals, ethnic minority medicine hospitals, various special disease hospitals and nursing homes, but excludes special disease prevention and curing agencies, women and children care agencies and health centers.

□ Medical Technical Personnel

Medical Technical Personnel includes licensed doctors, licensed assistant doctors, pharmacists (assistant pharmacists), inspection technicians, image technicians (assistant image technicians), health care inspectors and practice doctors (pharmacists, nurses, and technicians), excludes medical technical personnel engaging in administrative jobs.

□ Licensed Doctors (Assistant Doctors)

It refers to the medical workers who have obtained the license of qualified doctors (assistant doctors) and are employed by medical institutions, but excludes the doctors engaging in administrative jobs.

□ Special Care

Special Care is offered by the government to the family member of the martyrs, disabled or demobilized servicemen or laborers who were injured on duty. Entitled to the special care are family members of the revolutionary martyrs, family members of servicemen who dies on duty or died of an illness, disabled servicemen, family members of servicemen on active service, retired veteran Red Army soldiers, scattered Red Army soldiers, demobilized servicemen, ex-servicemen, servicemen who were demobilized while on duty, ex-servicemen back to their rural homes, ex-servicemen who were demobilized because of an illness and have gone back to their rural homes, ex-servicemen who suffer from mental illness and elderly persons with no family.

□ Social Welfare Institutions

Social Welfare Institutions refer to institutions taking care of old people without children, handicapped people and orphans. They include social welfare institutions run by civil affairs departments, children's welfare institutions, welfare institutions for mental patients, and collectively-run old people's homes in rural areas.

□ Basic Pension Insurance

1. Number of staff and workers covered refer to staff and workers participating in basic pension insurance programme in line with national laws, regulations and related policies by the end of reference period, who have already had payment records in social security management agencies, including those who interrupt payment without terminating the insurance programme. Those who have registered in the programme with no payment records are not included.

2. Number of retirees participating in basic pension insurance programme refer to number of retirees participating in basic pension insurance programme by the end of reference period.

3. Revenue of basic pension insurance refer to payments made by employers and individuals participating in pension in-

EXPLANATORY NOTES TO MAJOR STATISTICAL INDICATORS

surance programs in accordance with the basis and proportion stipulated in state regulations, and income from other sources that become source of pension insurance fund, including the premium paid by employers and individuals, interest income, subsidies from higher level agencies, income as transfer from subordinate agencies, transferred income, government financial subsidies and other income.

4. Expenses of basic pension insurance refer to payment made to those retired and resigned people covered in pension insurance program in terms of pension or compensation within the scope and standards of expenditure according to related national policies, and expenditure occurred due to shift of the insurance relationship or adjustment of funds among agencies, including pension for resigned people, pension for retired people, pension for people quitting jobs, various subsidies, medical fees, funeral subsidies, compensation pension, management fees for social security agencies, expenses on subsidies to lower subordinates, expenses as transfer to agencies at higher level, transferred expenditure and other expenditure.

5. Balance of basic pension insurance refers to the balance of basic pension insurance at the end of the reference period after deducting expenses from revenue.

□ Basic Medical Care Insurance

1. Number of people participating in the insurance programme refers to people participating in the basic medical care insurance programme according to related regulations by the end of reference period, including number of staff and workers and retirees participating in this insurance programme.

2. Revenues of insurance programme refer to payments made by employers and individuals participating in medical care insurance programs in accordance with the basis and proportion stipulated in state regulations, and income from other sources that become source of medical insurance fund, including income of social comprehensive funds paid by employers, income from individual accounts, government financial subsidies, interest income and other income.

3. Expenses of insurance programme refer to payments made from social comprehensive funds to those retired and resigned people covered in basic medical care insurance within the scope and standards of expenditure according to related national policies, and medical care payment made from individual accounts to staff and workers and retirees, and other expenses, including medical expenses of hospital inpatients, medical expenses for outpatients and emergency patients, payment from individual accounts and other expenditure.

4. Balance of basic medical care insurance refer to the balance of medical care insurance of social comprehensive funds and individual accounts at the end of the reference period, including bank savings, special fiscal accounts, investment in bonds and others.

□ Unemployment Insurance

1. Number of people covered refers to staff and workers in urban enterprises or institutions who have participated in unemployment insurance programme in line relevant policies and regulations, and other people who have participated according to local government regulations, by the end of reference period.

2. Revenue of unemployment insurance refer to payments made by employers and individuals participating in unemployment insurance programme in accordance with relevant regulations and other income contributed to this programme, including unemployment insurance premium made by employers and individuals, interest income, subsidies from higher level agencies, income as transfer from subordinate agencies, transferred income, government financial subsidies and other income.

3. Expenses of unemployment insurance refers to total expenses during the reference period to guarantee the basic livelihood of unemployed people and laid-off staff and workers and to encourage their re-employment. Included are unemployment relief, medical fees, funeral subsidies, compensation pension, training expenses, management fees for unemployment insurance agencies, subsidies to lower level agencies, expenses as transfer to higher level agencies, transferred expenditure and other expenditure.

4. Balance of unemployment insurance refer to the balance of unemployment revenue deducting unemployment expenses at the end of the reference period.

□ Work Injury Insurance

1. Number of people covered refers to staff and workers who have participated in work injury insurance programme in line with relevant national regulations.

2. Number of beneficiaries refers to staff and workers and their direct dependents who can, in line with relevant regulations, benefit from work injury insurance, as a result of work injury leading to disability or death of the staff/worker, or occupational disease leading to disability. Included in this category are

EXPLANATORY NOTES TO MAJOR STATISTICAL INDICATORS

number of injured and disabled people, number of people with occupational diseases, number of deaths at work places, and number of direct dependents.

3. Revenues of work injury insurance refer to payments made by employers participating in work injury insurance programs in accordance with the basis and proportion stipulated in state regulations, and income from other sources that become source of work injury insurance fund, including income of social comprehensive funds paid by employers, government financial subsidies, interest income and other income.

4. Expenses of work injury insurance refer to payments made from work injury insurance funds to those who participated in the work injury insurance programme and their direct dependents within the scope and standards of expenditure according to related national policies, and other expenditure, including medical fees for work injury, injury and disability subsidies, death subsidies, nursing fees, funeral subsidies, injury prevention fees, rehabilitation fees for occupational diseases and other expenditure.

5. Balance of work injury insurance refers to the balance of the work injury funds at the end of the reference period, including bank savings, special fiscal account, investment in bonds and others.

□ Maternity Insurance

1. Number of people covered refers to staff and workers who have participated in maternity insurance programme according to relevant regulation at the end of the reporting period.

2. Revenues of maternity insurance refer to payments made by employers participating in maternity insurance programs in accordance with the basis and proportion stipulated in state regulations, and income from other sources that become source of maternity insurance fund, including income of funds paid by employers, interest income and other income.

3. Expenses of maternity insurance refer to payments made from maternity insurance funds to staff and workers who participated in maternity insurance programme within the scope and standards of expenditure according to related national policies, expenses paid for pregnancy, child delivery or surgeries related to family planning, and other expenditure, including allowance for child bearing, medical fees and other expenditure.

4. Balance of the maternity insurance refers to the balance of the maternity insurance funds at the end of reference period, including bank savings, special fiscal account, investment in funds and others.

第二十二篇

CHAPTER 22

文化和体育

CULTURE AND SPORTS

简要说明

一、本篇资料的主要内容

本篇主要反映文化、文物、广电、新闻出版、档案、体育事业发展情况。

内容包括全市艺术表演团体、艺术表演场馆、群艺馆、文化馆(站)、文物机构、文化娱乐机构、公共图书馆、新闻出版机构、档案机构等单位的机构、人员、经费和业务活动情况;全市广播电视机构设施、制作播出节目时间情况;全市电影摄制、译制和发行放映情况;全市图书、期刊、报纸、音像电子出版数量情况;全市优秀运动员、教练员、体育系统职工、社会体育指导员发展情况。

二、本篇资料的来源

文化、广电资料由上海市文化和旅游局、上海市广播电视局提供;文物资料由上海市文物局提供;新闻出版资料由上海市新闻出版局提供;档案机构资料由上海市档案局提供;体育资料由上海市体育局提供。

BRIEF INTRODUCTION

I. Main Contents

Data mainly reflect the development of culture; cultural relics; radio broadcasting, films and television; news and publication; archives and sports undertakings.

Data mainly include: data on institutions and employed persons, funds and activities of art troupes, art venues, mass artcenter, cultural center (station), heritage institutions, cultural entertainment institutions, public libraries, press and publications, archival institutions, etc; data and playing hours of television stations and broadcasting stations, data on production, dubbing and showing of films, data on books, periodicals, newspaper, electronic audio and video products published, data on excellent athletes, coaches, staff and workers in sports sectors, social sports instructors.

II. Sources of data

Data on culture, television and broadcasting are from Shanghai Municipal Administration of Culture and Tourism, Shanghai Municipal Administration of Radio and Television; data on historical relics are from Shanghai Municipal Administration of Cultural Heritage; data on news and publishing are from Shanghai Municipal Press and Publication Bureau; data on archive institutions are from Shanghai Municipal Archives; data on sports are from Shanghai Municipal Sports Bureau.

表 22.1　主要年份文化机构数
QUANTITY OF CULTURAL INSTITUTIONS IN MAIN YEARS

单位：个（unit）

年　份 Year	图书馆 Libraries	群艺馆、文化馆（站） Mass Art Center， Culture Center（Station）	艺术教育 机　构 Art Education	文艺科研 机　构 Research	文物机构 Agency of Historic Relics	档案机构 Archives Institutions
1978	23	364	3		7	
1980	21	367	2	2	8	
1985	46	369	3	2	9	
1990	51	410	3	2	18	137
1991	31	397	3	2	18	671
1992	31	394	3	2	20	745
1993	31	376	3	2	21	720
1994	31	371	3	2	23	
1995	31	332	3	2	23	768
1996	32	348	4	2	24	674
1997	32	352	4	2	24	681
1998	32	355	4	2	23	643
1999	32	349	4	2	24	994
2000	31	340	4	2	24	792
2001	32	276	3	2	23	614
2002	32	270	1	2	26	652
2003	35	261	1	2	26	656
2004	28	251	1	2	99	513
2005	28	248	1	2	106	545
2006	28	250	1	2	106	439
2007	30	247	1	2	111	524
2008	29	245	1	2	111	524
2009	29	242	1	2	112	533
2010	28	240	1	2	115	707
2011	25	241	1	2	125	677
2012	25	240	1	2	115	734
2013	25	239	1	2	112	743
2014	25	238	1	2	114	818
2015	25	237	1	2	110	760
2016	24	237	1	2	135	725
2017	24	238	1	2	135	730
2018	23	239	1	2	142	727
2019	23	242	1	2	127	651
2020	23	242			151	544
2021	22	241			176	538

注：自 2004 年起文物保护机构中包括系统外的机构数。
Note：From 2004，Agency of Historic Relics Preservation refers to total quantity of Agency Bureau.

表 22.2 影剧院、艺术表演场馆、艺术表演团体数(1978~2021)
QUANTITY OF CINEMAS, THEATRES AND ART PERFORMANCE TROUPES

单位:个(unit)

年 份 Year	电影放映单位 Film Projection Units	其 中 of which #电影院 Cinemas and Theatres	艺术表演场馆 Art Performance Places	其 中 of which #剧 院 Theatres	书场、曲艺场 Storytelling and Quyi Places	艺术表演团体 Art Performance Troupes
1978	803	109	31	26	4	17
1979	799	115	46	32	5	45
1980	770	119	47	43	6	48
1981	804	127	60	56	6	49
1982	815	134	31	48	6	46
1983	822	140	54	49	8	46
1984	815	146	54	48	8	44
1985	847	156	52	47	8	44
1986	859	169	53	49	9	42
1987	890	199	51	48	8	42
1988	734	215	53	50	8	40
1989	579	213	52	49	8	37
1990	577	211	49	46	8	38
1991	548	229	51	47	9	38
1992	530	249	51	47	9	37
1993	462	254	49	40	9	34
1994	462	254	47	39	8	35
1995	452	249	43	35	7	31
1996	488	280	45	38	7	31
1997	466	263	45	38	7	31
1998	445	242	44	39	5	29
1999	445	242	44	41	4	29
2000	445	242	44	39	5	29
2001	370	273	41	35	3	28
2002	370	273	37	31		28
2003	328	238	180	174	4	72
2004	311	225	177	163	7	75
2005	236	193	160	150	5	85
2006	245	186	148	137	2	97
2007	233	175	150	140	6	103
2008	235	172	139	134	5	107
2009	226	169	104	100		77
2010	152	136	97	86	2	89
2011	161	146	103	90	4	102
2012	153	140	111	99	3	138
2013	169	151	127	116	3	148
2014	189	172	93	81	4	158
2015	209	202	50	34	1	180
2016	245	238	47	27	7	205
2017	320	302	49	31	1	199
2018	360	339	45	31	1	254
2019	400	359	50	35	1	311
2020	374	342	61	41	1	315
2021	389	389	83	68	2	298

注：自 2003 年起文化统计范围扩大到全行业。
Note: The scope of statistics to culture expands to total sectors since 2003.

表 22.3 主要年份主要文化机构从业人员数
QUANTITY OF EMPLOYEES IN MAJOR CULTURAL INSTITUTIONS IN MAIN YAERS

单位：人(person)

机构类别	Category of Institution	2000	2010	2020	2021
总　计	**Total**	**21 1642**	**259 240**	**189 004**	**175 339**
图书馆	Libraries	2 513	2 180	2 112	2 158
档案机构	Archives Institutions	2 330	3 822	2 113	2 201
群艺馆、文化馆(站)	Mass Art Center, Cultural Center(Station)	3 874	4 702	4 862	4 819
文物机构	History Relic	1 136	2 558	4 338	5 124
文化市场经营机构	Cultural Market Operation Institutions	63 297	60 358	45 309	23 727
新闻出版机构	Institutions Engaged in News and Publishing	138 492	185 620	127 808	137 310
其他文化机构	Other Cultural Institutions	1 171	5 545	2 462	3 498

表 22.4 主要文化机构和人员数(2021)
MAJOR CULTURAL INSTITUTIONS AND PERSONNEL

机构类别	Category of Institution	机构数(个) Institutions(unit)	从业人数(人) Employees(person)
艺术机构	**Art**	**403**	**14 883**
艺术表演团体	Art Performance Troupes	298	10 546
艺术表演场馆	Art Centers	83	3 807
艺术展览创作机构	Art Education Creation Organization	22	530
图书馆	**Libraries**	**22**	**2 158**
#少儿图书馆	Libraries for Children	4	100
档案机构	**Archives Institution**	**538**	**2 201**
群艺馆、文化馆(站)	**Mass Art Center, Cultural Center(Station)**	**241**	**4 819**
群众艺术馆、文化馆	Mass Art Centers	23	911
文化站	Cultural Stations	218	3 908
文物机构	**Historical Relic**		
文物保护管理机构	Heritage management agencies	5	98
博物馆	Museums	116	4 178
其他文物机构	Other Historical Relic	38	716
文化市场经营机构	**Cultural Market Operation Institutions**	**2 720**	**23 727**
新闻出版机构	**Institutions Engaged in News and Publishing**	**6 896**	**13 731**
其他文化和旅游机构	**Other Cultural Institutions**	**95**	**2 498**

注：2018 年起，档案机构不再统计兼职人员数。
Note: Since 2018, the number of part-time employees will not be counted by the archives organizations.

表 22.5 艺术馆和文化馆(站)情况(2021)
MASS ART AND CULTURAL CENTERS

指 标	Indicators	合 计 Total	群众艺术馆、文化馆 Mass Art and Cultural Centers	文化站 Cultural Stations
单位数（个）	Quantity of Units (unit)	241	23	218
从业人员(人)	Employees (person)	4 819	911	832
组织活动	Organizing Activity			
文艺活动（次）	Literary Activity(time)	54 652	6 421	48 231
理论研讨和讲座（次）	Theoretics Conference and Chair(time)	748	748	
举办训练班(次)	Conducting Training Courses(time)	68 778	15 423	53 355
举办展览个数（个）	Exhibitions Conducted (unit)	3 845	376	3 469
场地面积(万平方米)	Floor Space(10 000 sq.m)	148.84	20.42	128.42

表 22.6 艺术表演团体情况(2021)
BASIC STATISTICS OF ART TROUPES

类 别	Types	剧团数（个） Troupes (unit)	从业人员（人） Employees (person)	国内演出场次(万场) Times of Domestic Performance (10 000 times)	观众人数（万人次） Spectators (10 000 person-times)
总 计	**Total**	**298**	**10 546**	**2.80**	**1 410.94**
按隶属关系分	**By Administrative Relationship**				
市 级	Perfectural level	18	3 199	0.69	219.53
区 级	District and County level	280	7 347	2.11	1 191.41
按剧种分	**By Type of Drama**				
话剧、儿童剧、滑稽剧团	Drama, Children´s Play & Comedy Troupes	17	949	0.25	92.34
歌舞、音乐类	Opera, Dance Drama,Opera and Dance Troupes	56	3 168	0.55	699.02
京剧、昆曲类	Song and Dances Troupeand Light Music Orchestras	9	729	0.09	34.05
地方戏曲类	Orchestras and Chorus	121	3 230	0.91	304.24
杂技、魔术、马戏类	Drama Troupes	2	220	0.04	19.88
曲艺类	Quyi, Acrobatics, Puppet, and Shadow Play Troupes	21	439	0.22	53.39
综合艺术表演团体	Comprehensive Art Performance Groups	72	1 811	0.74	208.03

表 22.7　博物馆情况(2021)
STATISTICS OF MUSEUMS

类　别 Types		机构数(个) Quantity of Institutions (unit)	馆内藏品实际数量 Real Quantity of Collections (件/套) (piece/set)	#一至三级藏品 Collections of Class One to Three	展览活动(个) Exhibit Activity (unit)	参观人次(万人次) Visiting Person-times (10 000 person-times)
总　计	**Total**	**116**	**440 470**	**234 657**	**736**	**2 003.91**
综合性	Comprehensive	14	19 570	4 951	114	257.48
历史类	Historical	41	205 096	75 143	231	849.14
艺术类	Art	7	144 803	144 715	73	128.25
自然科技类	Natural Science and Technology	3	7 782	7 782	43	547.31
其　他	Others	51	63 219	2 066	275	221.73

注：2019 年起博物馆统计不再包括无独立法人资格的单位。
Note: Since 2019, the museum statistics no longer include the units without independent legal personality.

表 22.8　主要年份文物保护维修情况
PRESERVATION AND MAINTAIN OF HISTORICAL RELICS IN MAIN YEARS

指　标	Indicators	2005	2010	2020	2021
保护维修项目数(个)	Items of Preservation and Maintaining (item)	44	45	44	49
#国家级	National	4	10	6	12
市　级	Municipal	18	6	25	24

表 22.9 主要年份广播电台、电视台情况
TELEVISION STATIONS AND BROADCASTING STATIONS IN MAIN YEARS

类别	Types	2005	2010	2020	2021
广播电台	**Broadcasting Stations**				
中、短波发射台(座)	Relaying Stations of Medium and Short Wave Broadcast (uint)	4	4	3	3
发射功率(千瓦)	Transmited Power (kw)	390	240	236	201
公共广播节目套数(套)	Public Radio Programs (set)	21	21	21	21
付费广播节目套数(套)	Pay Radio Programs(set)	1	1	1	1
日均播音时间(小时)	Broadcasting Time a day (hour)	347	360	415	372
全年制作节目时间(小时)	Length of Programs Produced (hours)	83 665	85 262	92 360	100 134
电视台	**Television Stations**				
发射台(座)	Realying Stations (unit)	11	11	20	12
发射功率(千瓦)	Transmitted Power (kw)	170	172	68	13
公共电视节目套数(套)	Public TV Programs (set)	25	25	21	21
付费电视节目套数(套)	Pay TV Programs (set)	15	16	15	15
周均播放时间(小时)	Broadcast Time a week (hour)	2 871	3 361	2 678	2 492
全年制作节目时间(小时)	Length of Programs Produced (hours)	62 819	49 507	37 623	40 120

注：2015 年起，电视发射台与调频发射台合并统计，不再单独统计。
Note: Since 2015, the statistics of television transmitting station have merged with FM transmitting station, and are no longer separate.

表 22.10 电视和广播公共节目播出时间(2021)
PLAYING HOURS OF TELEVISION AND BROADCASTING PUBLIC PROGRAMS

单位:小时(hour)

类别	Types	电视台 Television Stations			广播电台 Broadcasting Stations		
		合计 Total	市级 Municipal Level	区级 District Level	合计 Total	市级 Municipal Level	区级 District Level
总计	**Total**	**129 943**	**84 968**	**44 974**	**135 818**	**85 549**	**50 269**
新闻资讯类节目	News Program	18 467	12 957	5 511	20 476	10 934	6 542
专题服务类节目	Subject Service Program	32 776	21 879	10 897	40 729	23 773	16 956
综艺益智类节目	Variety and Quiz Show	7 932	8 175	355	44 327	32 908	11 419
广播剧/电视剧	Radio Drama /TV Play	44 382	21 064	23 318	4 980	1 219	3 761
广告类节目	Advertising Program	13 122	9 567	3 554	8 800	6 408	2 392
其他类节目	Others	13 264	12 010	1 340	16 506	10 307	6 199

表 22.11 主要年份有线电视基本情况
BASIC STATISTICS ON CABLE TELEVISION IN MAIN YEARS

指标	Indicators	2000	2010	2020	2021
有线电视总用户数(万户)	Quantity of Cable TV Users (10 000 households)	303	573	872	899
#数字电视用户	Digital TV Users		236	733	755
有线广播电视传输干线总长(公里)	Lines Total Length (kilometer)	604	36 211	90 840	93 566

表 22.12 电影摄制、译制和放映情况(1978~2021)
PRODUCTION, DUBBING AND SHOWING OF FILMS

年 份 Year	摄制和译制电影片 Production and Dubbing		电影放映 Film Showing	
	故事片 (部) Feature Films (film)	动画电影 (本) Animated Film(reel)	放映场次 (万场) Showing (10 000 times)	观众人次 (万人次) Spectators (10 000 person-times)
1978	10	24	35	27 405
1979	14	25	40	32 763
1980	17	30	39	29 304
1981	17	32	38	26 823
1982	19	35	38	25 828
1983	19	34	37	25 204
1984	19	40	36	24 149
1985	15	43	34	21 885
1986	19	38	36	23 220
1987	17	38	37	21 985
1988	13	29	38	20 461
1989	17	29	37	20 776
1990	16	47	38	19 351
1991	17	37	36	15 766
1992	17	42	29	9 145
1993	16	35	16	3 862
1994	14	13	22	4 001
1995	17	37	23	4 419
1996	10	58	27	4 420
1997	11	17	25	3 670
1998	4	16	23	2 924

表 22.12 续表 continued

年 份 Year	摄制和译制电影片 Production and Dubbing 故事片 (部) Feature Films (film)	动画电影 (本) Animated Film (reel)	电影放映 Film Showing 放映场次 (万场) Showing (10 000 times)	观众人次 (万人次) Spectators (10 000 person-times)
1999	17	10	20	2 055
2000	10	20	18	1 794
2001	12	2	18	1 553
2002	10	2	20	1 198
2003	9	10	20	971
2004	12	1	24	1 364
2005	13		28	1 509
2006	9		27	1 254
2007	9		33	1 385
2008	17	8	35	1 456
2009	11		44	1 938
2010	19	2	55	2 288
2011	25		76	2 792
2012	22	6	96	3 154
2013	27		132	3 793
2014	28	8	158	4 678
2015	34	10	190	6 810
2016	32	2	252	7 307
2017	67	6	337	8 306
2018	75	2	403	8 728
2019	75	7	472	8 649
2020	64	4	200	2 545
2021	56	13	422	4 986

注：2012 年起，译制片的统计口径发生变化，单位由过去的“本”改为“部”。
Note：Since 2012, the statistical calibre of dubbed films has been changed from reel to set.

表 22.13　主要年份电影发行放映情况
BASIC STATISTICS OF FILM DISTRIBUTION AND PROJECTION IN MAIN YEARS

指　标	Indicators	2005	2010	2020	2021
电影放映机构(个)	Movie Projection Agencies(unit)		117	374	389
放映场次(万场)	Projection Times (10 000 times)	27.60	54.63	199.91	421.90
观众人次数(万人次)	Quantity of Audience (10 000 person-times)	1 509.31	2 287.84	2 544.94	4 986.00
放映收入(万元)	Projection Revenue (10 000 yuan)	27 192.03	93 875.11	116 468.14	254 443.61
平均每一放映场次	Average on per Projection Time				
观众人数(人)	Quantity of Audience (Person)	55	42	13	12
放映收入(元)	Returns (yuan)	985	1 718	583	603
日均放映场次(场)	Projection Time a Day (time)	756	1 497	5 477	11 559
日均观众人次(万人次)	Average Audience a Day (10 000 person-times)	4.14	6.27	6.97	13.66

注：电影放映机构数为正在活动的单位数。
Note: The number of movie projection agencies is the number of units being active.

表 22.14 文化娱乐机构基本情况 (2021)
BASIC STATISTICS OF CULTURE AND ENTERTAINMENT INSTITUTIONS

类 别	Types	机构数 (个) Quantity of Institutions (unit)	从业人员 (人) Employees (person)	主营业务收入 (万元) Major Business Revenue (10 000 yuan)	主营业务利润 (万元) Major Business Profits (10 000 yuan)
总 计	**Total**	**980**	**14 430**	**317 038.2**	**19 543.0**
按城乡分	**By City and District**				
城 市	Municipal Level	774	12 042	291 248.3	17 468.5
县 城	County Level	101	1 098	15 966.6	1 278.0
县以下	County and Below	105	1 290	9 823.3	796.5
机构分类	**Classification of Mechanisms**				
歌舞厅	Dance Hall	238	3 440	55 317.7	1 293.7
卡拉 OK 厅	Karraoke Lounge	636	8 794	148 754.8	5 583.9
游艺娱乐场所	A Place of Entertainment	87	1 597	93 156.7	8 866.8
其 他	Others	19	599	19 809.0	3 798.6

注：文化娱乐机构未包括互联网上网服务营业场所及经营性互联网文化单位。
Note: Culture and Entertainment Institutions do not include internet service business places and commercial internet cultural units.

表 22.15 公共图书馆情况(2021)
PUBLIC LIBRARIES

指 标	Indicators	合 计 Total	市 级 Municipal Level	区 级 District Level
机构数 (个)	Institutions (unit)	22	2	20
从业人员 (人)	Employees (person)	2 158	923	1 235
总藏量 (万册、件)	Collection (10 000 copies)	8 222.16	5 922.87	2 299.29
#图 书	Books	3 901.06	1 762.73	2 138.33
报 刊	Newspaper and Magzines	409.45	383.66	25.79
本年新购藏量 (万册、件)	Publications Newly Bought (10 000 copies)	187.29	88.22	99.07
建筑面积 (万平方米)	Floor Space of Buildings (10 000 sq.m)	44.29	14.49	29.80
#书 库	Stack Room	9.18	5.58	3.60
阅览室	Reading Room	11.13	1.29	9.84
阅览座位 (个)	Seats in Reading Room (unit)	22 565	1 686	20 879
书刊文献外借情况	Books Lending			
人 次 (万人次)	Readers (10 000 person-times)	275.66	55.05	220.61
册 数 (万册次)	Books (10 000 copy-times)	1 536.38	257.20	1 279.18
信息化装备	Information Equipment			
计算机 (台)	Computer(unit)	6 713	2 834	3 879
#电子阅览室终端数	E-reading Room Terminals	2 697	712	1 985
为读者举办各种活动	Activities Held for Readers			
组织各类讲座次数 (次)	All Kinds of Lectures (time)	1 632	143	1 489
参加人次 (万人次)	Participants (10 000 person-times)	29.92	3.35	26.57

表 22.16 图书出版数量(1978~2021)
BOOKS PUBLISHED

年 份 Year	种 数 (种) Quantity of Publications (type)	其 中 of which #新出版 Newly Published	总印数 (亿册) Total Printed (100 million copies)	总印张数 (亿印张) Total Printed Signatures (100 million signatures)
1978	1 666	1 332	3.92	12.19
1979	2 040	1 563	4.58	15.54
1980	2 338	1 804	5.62	17.73
1981	2 801	1 949	6.01	22.89
1982	3 395	2 057	6.07	21.76
1983	3 653	2 254	4.65	21.31
1984	3 848	2 328	5.37	25.58
1985	4 176	2 634	4.96	23.95
1986	4 531	3 045	3.66	17.81
1987	5 103	3 151	4.26	19.84
1988	5 538	3 658	4.33	19.04
1989	6 765	4 960	3.28	14.52
1990	7 767	4 887	2.98	14.66
1991	8 141	4 756	3.11	17.30
1992	8 095	4 179	2.75	17.19
1993	7 721	4 272	2.26	15.34
1994	7 812	4 382	2.35	17.01
1995	8 338	4 185	2.44	17.92
1996	9 234	4 445	2.79	20.10
1997	9 928	4 844	2.70	18.00
1998	10 718	5 083	2.83	18.69

表 22.16 续表 continued

年 份 Year	种 数 (种) Quantity of Publications (type)	其 中 of which #新出版 Newly Published	总印数 (亿册) Total Printed (100 million copies)	总印张数 (亿印张) Total Printed Signatures (100 million signatures)
1999	11 381	5 880	2.68	18.69
2000	12 682	6 936	2.54	19.05
2001	14 000	7 947	2.68	21.24
2002	14 537	8 156	2.59	21.38
2003	15 636	8 726	2.74	23.27
2004	16 449	9 391	2.67	23.54
2005	16 504	9 286	2.59	23.65
2006	17 283	9 338	2.54	24.86
2007	16 958	9 085	2.40	24.05
2008	17 780	9 945	2.64	24.97
2009	18 873	10 615	2.74	25.46
2010	19 519	11 241	2.89	26.34
2011	22 056	12 542	2.89	27.37
2012	23 792	13 142	3.35	31.35
2013	24 969	13 665	3.37	32.09
2014	24 676	13 193	3.26	30.47
2015	25 954	13 626	3.53	33.83
2016	27 462	13 905	4.17	36.26
2017	27 772	13 261	4.23	37.56
2018	30 009	14 227	4.81	44.90
2019	30 876	14 017	5.33	51.81
2020	28 056	12 779	4.95	44.51
2021	30 080	12 885	4.94	42.84

表 22.17　期刊出版数量(1978~2021)
PERIODICALS PUBLISHED

年 份 Year	种 数 (种) Quantity of Publications (type)	每期平均印数 (万册、份) Average Publications Issued (10 000 copies)	总印数 (亿册) Total Printed (100 million copies)	总印张数 (亿印张) Total Printed Signatures (100 million signatures)
1978	42	459	0.47	1.12
1979	90	721	0.73	2.08
1980	126	1 061	1.22	3.37
1981	266	1 873	2.03	5.95
1982	308	2 203	2.31	6.37
1983	349	2 572	2.51	7.07
1984	402	3 502	3.10	8.56
1985	491	3 424	3.45	9.21
1986	541	3 073	3.03	8.17
1987	546	3 058	3.13	8.05
1988	535	2 624	2.66	6.63
1989	527	1 793	1.86	4.58
1990	522	1 735	1.73	4.24
1991	504	1 749	1.79	4.44
1992	527	1 794	1.84	4.59
1993	535	1 668	1.82	4.95
1994	556	1 569	1.72	4.87
1995	565	1 583	1.78	5.30
1996	582	1 530	1.66	5.14
1997	587	1 513	1.66	5.35
1998	591	1 503	1.65	5.81

表 22.17 续表 continued

年 份 Year	种 数 （种） Quantity of Publications (type)	每期平均印数 （万册、份） Average Publications Issued (10 000 copies)	总印数 （亿册） Total Printed (100 million copies)	总印张数 （亿印张） Total Printed Signatures (100 million signatures)
1999	606	1 493	1.78	6.87
2000	613	1 489	1.85	7.38
2001	616	1 413	1.85	7.58
2002	621	1 332	1.80	7.77
2003	626	1 335	1.83	8.51
2004	612	1 184	1.93	8.94
2005	612	1 130	1.90	8.96
2006	616	1 125	1.83	8.76
2007	624	1 117	1.83	8.75
2008	623	1 105	1.90	9.27
2009	621	1 039	1.79	9.02
2010	632	1 019	1.78	9.04
2011	632	1 023	1.82	9.42
2012	626	938	1.76	9.67
2013	625	875	1.62	9.00
2014	627	804	1.45	8.10
2015	628	715	1.28	7.23
2016	628	653	1.12	6.37
2017	630	579	0.94	5.23
2018	630	528	0.85	4.56
2019	632	477	0.74	3.87
2020	633	419	0.62	3.48
2021	633	401	0.59	3.08

表22.18　报纸出版数量(1978~2021)
NEWSPAPER PUBLISHED

年　份 Year	种　数 (种) Quantity of Publications (type)	每期平均印数 (万份) Average Publication Issued (10 000 copies)	总印数 (亿份) Total Printed (100 million copies)	总印张数 (亿印张) Total Printed Signatures (100 million signatures)
1978	5	257	6.41	6.20
1979	8	349	7.32	7.08
1980	12	464	8.55	8.20
1981	15	640	10.28	9.77
1982	31	936	14.93	13.13
1983	34	1 185	18.13	15.49
1984	41	1 429	19.63	16.57
1985	89	1 656	19.54	17.07
1986	93	1 750	19.94	18.37
1987	90	2 003	22.45	20.49
1988	83	1 958	21.38	22.07
1989	81	1 477	15.85	16.25
1990	81	1 510	16.16	16.76
1991	75	1 506	18.48	19.16
1992	77	1 506	24.76	24.76
1993	81	1 506	32.27	32.27
1994	87	1 369	30.43	30.43
1995	86	1 358	19.04	34.00
1996	87	1 357	18.93	36.96
1997	87	1 397	19.34	43.19
1998	80	1 441	19.73	49.84

表 22. 18 续表 continued

年 份 Year	种 数 (种) Quantity of Publications (type)	每期平均印数 (万份) Average Publication Issued (10 000 copies)	总印数 (亿份) Total Printed (100 million copies)	总印张数 (亿印张) Total Printed Signatures (100 million signatures)
1999	75	1 311	18.42	46.26
2000	103	1 135	16.77	44.57
2001	101	1 060	16.98	47.67
2002	101	983	16.46	51.42
2003	101	886	17.05	66.13
2004	103	939	19.71	83.66
2005	102	903	19.06	89.94
2006	101	850	17.89	87.33
2007	101	815	17.04	86.75
2008	100	787	17.24	88.29
2009	100	741	16.33	77.94
2010	100	752	15.90	78.65
2011	100	734	15.61	79.38
2012	100	686	14.54	68.03
2013	101	605	13.16	58.86
2014	100	537	11.45	48.96
2015	98	505	10.80	44.59
2016	98	478	10.09	37.97
2017	97	441	9.13	35.99
2018	97	396	8.17	32.08
2019	97	371	7.84	30.36
2020	94	320	6.94	20.84
2021	94	310	6.66	20.90

表 22.19 主要年份新闻出版机构和人员数
NUMBER OF INSTITUTIONS AND EMPLOYEES ENGAGED IN NEWS AND PUBLISHING IN MAIN YEARS

指 标	Indicators	2000	2010	2020	2021
图书出版机构	**Publishing Houses**				
机构数（个）	Institutions（unit）	37	40	40	40
从业人员（人）	Employee（person）	3 666	3 949	3 783	3 814
印刷机构	**Printing Houses**				
机构数（个）	Institutions（unit）	4 543	4 606	2 509	2 346
从业人员（万人）	Employee（10 000 persons）	11.54	16.02	10.38	10.62
发行机构	**Issuing Houses**				
机构数（个）	Institutions（unit）	6 743	9 327	3 712	4 510
从业人员（万人）	Employee（10 000 persons）	1.94	2.14	2.03	2.73

注：发行机构数中包括发行网点数。
Note：Issuing Houses include quantity of net places.

表 22.20 图书出版数量(2021)
BOOKS PUBLISHED

类 别	types	种 数（种）Number of Publications（type）	其中 of which #新出版 Newly Published	总印数（万册）Total Printed（10 000 copies）	总印张数（万印张）Total Printed Signatures（10 000 signatures）
总 计	**Total**	**30 080**	**12 885**	**49 418.93**	**428 405.42**
书 籍	Books				
社科人文类	Humanities and Social Sciences	26 135	10 969	42 714.48	402 061.07
科学技术类	Science and Technology	3 797	1 828	2 478.01	24 227.71
综合类	Complex	148	88	226.44	2 116.64

表 22.21 期刊出版数量(2021)
PERIODICALS PUBLISHED

类 别 Types		种 数 (种) Quantity of Publications (type)	出版期数 (期) Quantity of Issue (issue)	总印数 (万册) Total Printed (10 000 copies)	总印张数 (万印张) Total Printed Signatures (10 000 signatures)
总 计	**Total**	**633**	**5 328**	**5 914.49**	**30 847.55**
综 合	Comprehensive	14	80	43.29	293.78
哲学、社会科学	Philosophy and Social Science	145	1 393	2 489.93	11 783.42
自然科学、科技	Natural Science and Technology	354	2 783	1 114.25	8 111.47
文化教育	Culture and Education	78	725	1 180.64	5 571.96
文学艺术	Literature and Art	42	347	1 086.38	5 086.91

表 22.22 报纸出版数量(2021)
NEWSPAPER PUBLISHED

类 别 Types		种 数 (种) Quantity of Publications (type)	期 数 (期) Issue (issue)	每期平均印数 (万份) Average Publication Per Issue (10 000 copies)	总印数 (万份) Total Printed (10 000 copies)	总印张数 (万印张) Total Printed Signatures (10 000 signatures)
总 计	**Total**	**94**	**7 986**	**310.41**	**66 603.01**	**208 982.87**
综合报	Comprehensive	11	2 597	112.73	40 231.26	150 335.90
专业报	Specialized	83	5 389	197.68	26 371.75	58 646.97

表 22.23 音像电子出版数量(2021)
AUDIO, VIDEO AND ELECTRON PUBLISHED

类 别 Types		种 数 (种) Quantity of Publications (type)	出版数量 (万张、万盒) Quantity of Publications (10 000 piece box)	发行数量 (万张、万盒) Quantity of Issued (10 000 piece box)	发行总金额 (万元) Total Values (10 000 yuan)
总 计	**Total**	**1 518**	**2 322.85**	**2 311.90**	**8 891.42**
电子出版物	Electronic Publication	448	953.42	965.92	5 061.01
数码激光视盘	DVD	28	13.61	14.00	13.00
高密度激光视盘	EVD	231	795.41	790.54	214.82
激光唱盘	CD	651	511.07	488.84	2 692.20
录音带	Tape	64	44.51	44.51	327.57
其 他	Others	96	4.83	8.09	582.82

表 22.24 档案机构基本情况(2021)
BASIC STATISTICS OF ARCHIVE INSTITUTIONS

指　标	Indicators	合　计 Total	档案行政管理部门 Archival Administrative Department	档案馆 Archives Library	档案室(处、科) Archives
机构数(个)	**Quantity of Institutions(unit)**	**538**	**17**	**41**	**480**
从业人员(人)	**Employees(person)**	**2 201**	**193**	**837**	**1 171**
馆藏档案	**Archives Collected**				
全　宗(个)	Overall Rolls(unit)	6 428		6 428	
案　卷(万卷)	Rolls(10 000 rolls)	4 880.4		1 513.8	3 366.6
以件为保管单位档案(万件)	Archives(10 000 pieces)	2 283.5		820.2	1 463.2
录音、录像、影片档案(万盘)	Record,Video and Film(10 000 disks)	118.4		3.5	114.9
照片档案(万张)	Photo Records(10 000 pieces)	283.3		184.7	98.6
底　图(万张)	Base Maps(10 000 pieces)	2 000.1		11.1	1 988.9
微缩胶片(万幅)	Microfilm(10 000 pieces)	3 970.8		2 912.0	1 058.9
档案利用	**Records Utilized**				
卷　次(万卷次)	Roll-times(10 000 roll-times)	176.9		99.2	77.7
人　次(万人次)	Person-times(10 000 person-times)	135.3		114.2	21.2
档案开放	**Records Openness**				
已开放档案	Records Opened				
案　卷(万卷)	Rolls(10 000 rolls)	232.4		232.4	
案　件(万件)	Cases(10 000 cases)	5.2		5.2	
开放档案目录(万条)	Catalog of Records Opened(10 000 pieces)				
案卷级	Roll Grade	145.5		145.5	
文件级	Document Grade	530.7		530.7	

注：2018 年起，档案机构不再统计兼职人员数。
Note： Since 2018, the number of part-time employees will not be counted by the archives organizations.

表 22.25 主要年份裁判员、优秀运动员、教练员情况
BASIC STATISTICS ON PEFEREES, EXCELLENT ATHLETES AND COACHES IN MAIN YEARS

单位：人（person）

指 标	Indicators	2000	2010	2020	2021
优秀运动员	Excellent Athletes	899	771	1 092	1 277
# 女运动员	Women	402	371	552	621
专职教练员	Full-time Coaches			1 200	1 173
# 女专职教练员	Women			403	390

表 22.26 体育系统从业人员(2021)
EMPLOYEES IN SPORTS SECTORS

单位：人（person）

指 标	Indicators	总 计 Total	其中 of which # 优秀运动队 Excellent Sports Teams	体育运动学校 Physical Education and Sports Schools	业余体校 Sparetime Sports School	体育场馆 Stadiums and Gymnasiums
总 计	**Total**	**5 100**	**1 679**	**517**	**1 138**	**615**
# 专职教练	Full-time Coaches	1 173	238	101	691	38
管理人员	Administraive Staff	1 384	198	80	177	403
文化教师	Culture Teachers	138		104	32	2
科研人员	Scientific and Technical Personnel	100	9	2	12	

表 22.27 社会体育指导员发展情况(2021)
DEVELOPMENT OF SOCIAL SPORTS INSTRUCTORS

指 标	Indicators	总 计 Total	获得技术等级称号的人数 Number of People Obtaining Technical Grade Title	获得职业资格的人数 Number of People with Professional Qualifications
累计审批人数	Cumulative Number of Approvers	98 268	67 968	30 300
# 本年度审批人数	Number of Approvers This Year	7 666	5 082	2 584

上/海/统/计/年/鉴

主要统计指标解释

■ 文化机构

是指专门从事文化工作具有法人资格，独立核算的事业、企业单位，以及单独核算，附属于事业单位的经营性专业文化活动单位。包括从事艺术、图书馆、档案馆、群众文化、文物保护、艺术教育、艺术研究、文化娱乐、新闻出版等机构，以及其他文化机构。

■ 电影放映单位

指具有放映机器设备、固定或不固定的放映场所与专职或兼职的放映技术人员，经有关部门登记批准，经常为一定的观众对象放映电影的机构。包括电影院、影剧院、开放礼堂、俱乐部、放映队、对内礼堂俱乐部。

■ 艺术表演团体

指从事戏曲、音乐、舞蹈、杂技等专业艺术表演，有独立账户的单位，不包括半工半艺、半农半艺和民间职业剧团。该指标主要反映上海专业艺术表演团体发展规模水平。

■ 艺术表演观众人次

指售票、包场演出或民族地区免费演出的艺术表演观众人次数，不包括彩排审查和内部观摩演出的观看人次数。该指标主要反映上海观看专业艺术表演团体演出的效益规模。

■ 社会体育指导员

指在群众性体育活动中从事技能传授、锻炼指导和组织管理并获得社会体育指导员技术等级称号的工作人员。等级称号分为一级、二级、三级社会体育指导员。

■ 专职教练员

指专门从事运动训练的教练员，其中包括未聘用待岗的教练员。不包括有教练员职称但从事其他工作的人员。专职教练员的技术职称按人事部门批准的技术等级填写。

SHANGHAI STATISTICAL YEARBOOK

EXPLANATORY NOTES TO MAJOR STATISTICAL INDICATORS

□ Cultural Institutions

Cultural Institution refers to undertaking and business institutions which specialize in cultural work and have legal personality and independent accounting system, and those professional cultural institutions attached to undertaking institutions and have independent accounting system. It includes institutions specialize in art, library, archives, mass culture, historical relic protection, art education, art research, entertainment, news and publication and other cultural institutions.

□ Film Projection Units

Film Projection Units refer to units with film projection equipments, full or part-time projectionists, permanent or non-permanent places, approved by related administrative departments to show films regularly for certain groups of audience, including cinemas, theaters, public auditoriums, clubs, film projection teams, and interior auditorium clubs.

□ Art Troupe

Art Troupe refers to the troupe which is engaged in drama, opera, music, dance, acrobatics or other art performance, opens independent accounts with banks and has self-supporting accounting system; excluding the troupes which are engaged partly in industrial or agricultural activities, partly in art performance and the professional troupes organized by the people. This indicator reflects the development of Shanghai's professional art troupes.

□ Quantity of Spectators at Art Performance

Number of Spectators at Art Performance refers to the number of attendants at commercial shows, completely booked shows or free shows given in minority national areas, and does not include the number of spectators at rehearsals for examination and internal shows for study. This indicator reflects beneficial results of spectators at Professional Art Performance.

□ Social Sports Instructor

Refers to the staff who are engaged in skill teaching, exercise guidance, organization and management in mass sports activities and have obtained the title of technical grade of social sports instructor. The grade titles are divided into the first, second and third level social sports instructors.

□ Full Time Coaches

Refer to coaches specialized in sports training, including coaches who are not employed. Those who have the title of coach but are engaged in other work are not included. The technical titles of full-time coaches shall be filled in according to the technical grades approved by the personnel department.

第二十三篇

CHAPTER 23

法律、公证和其他

LAWS, NOTARY AND OTHERS

简要说明

一、本篇资料的主要内容

本篇主要包括公检法司的情况。

内容主要包括律师机构、公证机构、人民调解委员会的机构、人员、主要业务活动情况;公安机关立案的刑事案件及查处的治安案件情况;交通事故和火灾事故的次数、伤亡人数和损失折款情况;检察院直接立案侦查案件、民事行政案件办理、申诉案件处理情况;法院各类案件办理、执行案件和各类案件结案情况。

二、本篇资料的来源

律师、公证和人民调解等资料由上海市司法局提供;刑事案件、治安案件、交通事故等资料由上海市公安局提供;火灾事故资料由上海市消防救援总队提供;检察院相关案件资料由上海市检察院提供;法院相关案件资料由上海市高级人民法院提供。

BRIEF INTRODUCTION

I. Main Contents

Data in this chapter reflect statistics on public security,procuratorial,legal and judicial affairs.

Data include mainly general information, personnel, and main activities of law firms, notarizations and meditations; criminal cases registered and offense cases handled by the public security agencies; casualties, and losses in traffic or fire accidents, cases under direct investigation by procurator′s office, civil cases, administrative cases and appeals handled by procurator's offices; cases handled, executed, and closed by courts.

II. Sources of Data

Data on law firms, notarizations, and meditations are provided by Shanghai Municipal Bureau of Justice; data on criminal cases, offense cases, and traffic accidents are provided by Shanghai Municipal Public Security Bureau; Data on fire accidents are provided by Shanghai Municipal Fire and Rescue Corps. Data on procurators are provided by Shanghai Municipal People's Procurator's Offices; data on courts are provided by Shanghai Municipal Senior People's Court.

表 23.1 主要年份律师、公证及调解工作基本情况
BASIC STATISTICS OF LAWYERS, NOTARIZATIONS AND MEDIATIONS IN MAIN YEARS

指标	Indicators	2000	2010	2020	2021
律师工作	Lawyers				
律师事务所（个）	Law Offices (unit)	415	1 064	1 709	1 776
律师人数（人）	Lawyers (person)	4 642	13 027	31 679	35 252
#专职律师	Full-time Lawyers	3 522	11 749	28 135	30 860
兼职律师	Part-time Lawyers	731	549	779	809
全年办理	Total Transacted				
民事案件诉讼代理（万件）	Civil Lawsuit (10 000 cases)	7.05	7.69	29.76	33.76
刑事诉讼辩护及代理（万件）	Criminal Lawsuit and Vindication (10 000 cases)	1.13	1.49	4.39	4.68
非诉讼法律事务（万件）	Non-litigation Action (10 000 cases)	2.65	3.32	17.52	16.10
公证工作	Notarizations				
公证处（个）	Notarial Offices (unit)	22	22	22	26
公证人员（人）	Notarial Personnel (person)	366	821	1 164	1 233
#公证员	Notaries	243	359	439	513
办理公证文书（万件）	Documents Notarized (10 000 cases)	47.72	40.76	28.79	31.65
国内公证	Domestic	12.79	18.54	18.97	20.64
涉外公证	Foreign	19.93	20.98	9.08	10.07
涉港澳台公证	Hong Kong, Macao and Taiwan		1.24	0.74	0.94
公证费收入（亿元）	Revenue of Notarial Fees (100 million yuan)	1.13	4.70	4.72	5.67
人民调解工作	People's Mediation				
专职司法助理员（人）	Full-time Judicial Assistants (person)	416	734	814	1 146
人民调解委员会（万个）	People's Mediation Committees (10 000 units)	0.89	0.63	0.65	0.66
调解人员（万人）	Mediators (10 000 persons)	3.55	3.41	1.78	1.83
调解民间纠纷（万件）	Civil Disputes Mediated (10 000 cases)	6.37	23.24	37.24	45.56
#调解成功	Successfully Mediated		22.81	37.23	37.09
#婚姻家庭	Family Disputes	1.97	3.63	6.31	8.80
邻　里	Neighbor Disputes	2.51	5.12	7.13	7.44
赔　偿	Compensation	0.25	3.02	0.88	1.12
房屋宅基地	Housing and Housing Sites	1.04	1.29	0.46	0.36

注：办理公证文件中包括涉及港、澳、台公证文件。
Note: The notarized documents handled include Hong Kong, Macao and Taiwan's.

表 23.2 公证工作情况(2019~2021)
STATISTICS OF NOTARIZATION WORK

指 标	Indicators	2019	2020	2021
公证处(个)	**Notarial Offices(unit)**	**22**	**22**	**26**
公证人员(人)	**Notarial Personnel(person)**	**1 190**	**1 164**	**1 233**
#公证员	Notaries	431	439	513
公证文书总计(件)	**Documents Notarized(case)**	**410 687**	**288 015**	**316 492**
#合同(协议)	Contract (agreement)	12 414	13 368	10 463
继 承	Inheritance	35 494	41 139	44 690
委 托	Entrustment	30 261	29 157	38 158
声 明	Statement	21 332	10 853	12 193
赠 与	Presentation	42	67	97
遗 嘱	Will	10 468	7 263	6 543
现场监督	Field Supervision	1 277	8 756	9 728
婚姻状况、亲属关系、收养关系	Marital Status, Kinship, Adoption	27 182	6 533	5 990
出生、生存、死亡	Birth, Existence, Death	18 420	8 705	9 291
身份、经历、学历、学位、职务、职称	Identity, Experience, Education Background, Degree, Job Title, Professional Technical Title	253	82	92
有无违法犯罪记录	Having or Not Having Illegal and Criminal Record	25 854	17 307	19 238
公司章程	Articles of Association	167	112	116
保全证据	Preservation Evidence	27 354	34 720	39 072
证书、证照	Certificate and License	92 485	42 423	48 774
签名、印鉴	Signature and Seal	8 879	6 985	9 055
文本相符	Text Consistency	55 000	29 281	31 303
赋予强制执行效力	Compulsory Execution Effect	25 511	22 222	23 559
执行证书	Grant Compulsory Enforcement Force	285	601	254
国内公证文书出证数(件)	**Number of Domestic Notarial Documents Issued(case)**	**184 272**	**189 735**	**206 419**
国外公证文书出证数(件)	**Number of Foreign Notarial Documents Issued(case)**	**216 400**	**90 846**	**100 695**
涉港澳台公证文书出证数(件)	**Number of Notarial Documents Issued Involving Hong Kong, Macao and Taiwan(case)**	**10 015**	**7 434**	**9 378**
涉台公证文书出证数(件)	**Number of Taiwan related Notarial Documents Issued(case)**	**8 191**	**5 852**	**6 897**
公证费收入(亿元)	**Notarization Fee Income(billion yuan)**	**4.88**	**4.72**	**5.67**

表 23.3 主要年份公安机关立案刑事案件情况
CRIMINAL CASES REGISTERED IN PUBLIC SECURITY ORGANS IN MAIN YEARS

单位:起(time)

类 别	Types	2000	2010	2020	2021
总 计	**Total**	**104 946**	**119 691**	**101 579**	**94 753**
杀 人	Homicide	252	174	120	130
伤 害	Injury	1 553	2 545	1 544	1 195
抢 劫	Robbery	3 033	1 558	72	47
强 奸	Rape	396	448	461	438
诈 骗	Fraud	8 425	16 598	52 543	49 203
盗 窃	Larceny	77 912	78 322	17 508	10 510
其 他	Others	13 375	20 046	29 331	33 230

表 23.4 主要年份公安机关查处治安案件情况
OFFENSE CASES AGAINST PUBLIC ORDER HANDLED BY PUBLIC SECURITY ORGANS IN MAIN YEARS

单位:起(time)

类 别	Types	2000	2010	2020	2021
总 计	**Total**	**194 141**	**566 607**	**229 059**	**127 129**
#扰乱公共秩序	Disturbing Work and Public Order	23 568	25 787	9 520	7 885
寻衅滋事	Gang Fighting or Picking Quarrels and Making Trouble	3 373	3 315	1 189	1 066
阻碍国家工作人员执行职务	Obstructing the Government Workers to Perform Their Duty	1 029	658	708	660
殴打他人	Beating Other Body	16 973	59 876	39 670	32 367
诈骗、抢夺、敲诈勒索财物	Defrauding, Snatching or Extoring and Racketeering Valuables	2 936	24 510	77 024	18 208
伪造、变造、倒卖有价票证、凭证	Forging and Fraudulently Selling Bills or Certificates	5 551	524	106	9
卖淫、嫖娼	Prostitution or Going Whoring	4 631	7 281	6 727	5 216
赌 博	Gambling	17 464	21 760	12 491	6 321

表 23.5 交通事故和火灾情况(1980~2021)
BASIC STATISTICS OF TRAFFIC ACCIDENTS AND FIRES

年 份 Year	交通事故 Traffic Accidents				火 灾 Fires			
	发生数(万起) Number (10 000 cases)	死亡人数(人) Death (person)	受伤人数(万人) Injuries (10 000 persons)	损失折款(万元) Losses Converted -into Cash (10 000 yuan)	发生数(万起) Number (10 000 cases)	死亡人数(人) Death (person)	受伤人数(人) Injuries (person)	损失折款(万元) Losses Converted -into Cash (10 000 yuan)
1980	1.10	445	1.01	96	0.08	17	126	457
1981	1.18	507	1.06	119	0.09	33	81	202
1982	0.83	434	0.77	98	0.07	33	76	255
1983	0.73	443	0.70	99	0.06	24	67	533
1984	0.83	503	0.75	123	0.05	21	71	177
1985	0.71	687	0.57	318	0.05	30	74	374
1986	0.84	678	0.62	576	0.06	25	54	790
1987	1.01	811	0.67	959	0.06	51	56	575
1988	0.84	707	0.56	1 117	0.06	58	53	460
1989	0.75	652	0.49	1 137	0.03	30	30	394
1990	0.76	608	0.47	1 345	0.21	45	137	1 868
1991	0.75	594	0.45	1 530	0.17	38	112	937
1992	0.45	591	0.18	2 029	0.17	40	57	2 742
1993	0.81	699	0.29	4 652	0.14	73	128	2 252
1994	1.26	722	0.33	8 337	0.11	51	95	2 378
1995	1.67	788	0.38	12 077	0.11	47	86	2 100
1996	2.01	783	0.44	13 462	0.09	87	96	2 206
1997	2.16	780	0.58	13 682	0.74	51	138	2 639
1998	2.40	781	0.65	15 186	0.72	42	114	2 205
1999	2.61	726	0.78	15 924	0.66	43	90	1 487
2000	4.13	1 492	1.61	20 391	0.52	40	57	1 919

表 23.5 续表 continued

年 份 Year	交通事故 Traffic Accidents 发生数（万起）Number (10 000 cases)	死亡人数（人）Death (person)	受伤人数（万人）Injuries (10 000 persons)	损失折款（万元）Losses Converted into Cash (10 000 yuan)	火 灾 Fires 发生数（万起）Number (10 000 cases)	死亡人数（人）Death (person)	受伤人数（人）Injuries (person)	损失折款（万元）Losses Converted into Cash (10 000 yuan)
2001	4.21	1 503	1.57	23 883	0.32	31	65	966
2002	4.71	1 400	1.57	30 052	0.60	39	58	1 313
2003	5.42	1 406	1.12	39 721	0.58	47	85	1 724
2004	2.71	1 543	1.13	19 149	0.51	30	47	1 681
2005	0.92	1 393	0.88	7 961	0.43	54	84	1 731
2006	0.66	1 231	0.67	3 292	0.45	45	54	2 292
2007	0.40	1 171	0.38	1 943	0.42	50	45	2 650
2008	0.27	1 100	0.26	1 469	0.35	50	57	14 523
2009	0.28	1 042	0.27	1 226	0.61	63	41	3 990
2010	0.22	1 011	0.19	967	0.57	101	125	22 949
2011	0.21	944	0.18	1 349	0.58	43	46	11 000
2012	0.23	916	0.21	1 488	0.45	39	45	6 924
2013	0.20	914	0.15	988	0.96	73	79	12 417
2014	0.12	902	0.06	463	0.58	59	55	7 428
2015	0.10	868	0.05	470	0.46	52	41	14 000
2016	0.08	759	0.02	371	0.45	44	47	10 763
2017	0.07	676	0.02	363	0.42	54	50	7 823
2018	47.28	647	8.57	27 487	0.39	44	43	6 367
2019	43.29	1 130	7.95	15 969	0.40	44	43	13 820
2020	43.66	818	9.19	31 495	1.05	62	54	6 546
2021	52.29	797	16.21	75 477	1.47	65	125	17 672

注：2018 年起，交通事故统计口径扩大范围，包含走简易程序处理的事故，以前只包含走一般程序处理的事故。

Note: Since 2018, the scope of traffic accident statistics which only including accidents handled by general procedures before has been expanded, and the accidents handled by simple procedures are also included.

表 23.6 交通事故情况(2021)
BASIC STATISTICS OF TRAFFIC ACCIDENTS

类 别	Types	发生数(起) Number (case)	死亡人数(人) Death (person)	受伤人数(人) Injuries (person)	损失折款(万元) Losses Converted -into Cash (10 000 yuan)
总 计	**Total**	**522 878**	**797**	**162 056**	**75 477**
#死亡事故	Death Accident	780	797	157	492
伤人事故	Injury Accident	146 023		167 645	17 246
#机动车	Motor-driven Vehicles	430 501	503	89 812	70 158
#汽 车	Automobiles	426 904	472	87 991	69 728
摩托车	Motorcycles	2 573	24	1 564	320
非机动车	Non-motor-driven Vehicles	88 471	237	69 119	5 075
行 人	Pedestrians	3 030	56	2 751	169

注：2018 年起，交通事故统计口径扩大范围，包含走简易程序处理的事故，以前只包含走一般程序处理的事故。
Note: Since 2018, the scope of traffic accident statistics which only including accidents handled by general procedures before has been expanded, and the accidents handled by simple procedures are also included.

表 23.7 交通违法情况(2019~2021)
BASIC STATISTICS ON TRAFFIC VIOLATIONS

单位:万人次(10 000 person-times)

指 标	Indicators	2019	2020	2021
处理违法人次	**Dealing with Illegal Activities**	**2 238.91**	**2 066.69**	**2 140.28**
教育人次	Education	34.94	18.6	42.67
处罚人次	Punishment	2 203.96	2 048.09	2 097.61
#罚 款	Fine	2 186.19	2 045.03	2 039.38
机动车	Motor Vehicle	1 483.85	1 464.46	1 519.42
非机动车	Non-Motor Vehicle	711.48	567.51	558.17
行人和行车人	Pedestrians and Drivers	43.58	34.72	62.69

表 23.8 火灾事故情况(2021)
BASIC STATISTICS OF FIRES

指 标	Indicators	发生数(起) Number (case)	死亡人数(人) Death (person)	受伤人数(人) Injuries (person)	损失折款(万元) Losses Converted -into Cash (10 000 yuan)
总 计	**Total**	**14 685**	**65**	**125**	**17 671.61**
电气火灾	Electrical Fire	5 518	28	56	9 038.84
生产作业类火灾	Production Operations	349		26	2 580.71
生活用火不慎	Careless Use of Fire	4 199	5	17	513.35
吸 烟	Smoking	2 449	18	5	2 411.83
玩 火	Play with Fire	63		1	51.49
自 燃	Spontaneous Combustion	195			521.33
雷 击	Lightning	15			3.65
静 电	Static Electricity	14		3	5.14
不明确原因	Unexplained	179	5	8	1 016.78
放 火	Set Fire	56	3	2	455.94
其 他	Others	1 648	6	7	1 072.55

表 23.9 检察院民事、行政案件办理情况(2021)
CIVIL CASES AND ADMINISTRATIVE CASES HANDLED BY PROCURATOR'S OFFICES

单位:件(case)

类 别	Types	受 案 Cases Accepted	结案处理 Cases Settled	其中 of which: 提出抗诉 Appeals Rejected	不支持监督申请 pervision Application not Supported	终止审查 Censorship Terminaled
总 计	**Total**	**4 332**	**4 213**	**57**	**1 629**	**1 781**
民事案	Civil Cases	2 076	1 994	54	1 058	377
婚姻家庭	Marriages Disputes	50	44	1	36	2
继承纠纷	Inheritance Disputes	59	48	2	36	7
物权保护	Property Rights Protection	85	86	2	74	4
所有权争议	Ownership Disputes	80	76		72	3
合同纠纷	Contract Disputes	775	771	45	436	82
劳动人事争议	Labor and Personnel Disputes	191	187		137	17
其 他	Others	836	782	4	267	262
行政案	Administrative Cases	2 256	2 219	3	571	1 404

表 23.10 检察院申诉案件处理情况(2021)
APPEALS HANDLED BY PROCURATOR'S OFFICES

单位:件(case)

类 别	Types	受 案 Cases Accepted	审查处理 Cases Investigated	其 中 of which 分送本院其他部门 Delivering to Other Department of Such Procurator's Offices
总 计	**Total**	**2 320**	**2 285**	**2 047**
# 首次申诉	**Appeals First Time**	**2 288**	**2 253**	**2 022**
# 不服不起诉	Appeals Against Non-prosecution	42	35	30
不服不立案	Appeals Against Rejection of the Case	22	16	8
不服逮捕	Appeals Against Arrest	1	1	
不服刑事判决	Appeals Against Judgment of Criminal Case	317	306	123
不服民事行政裁决	Appeals Against Administration Arbitrament of Civil Case	1 499	1 497	1 480

表 23.10 续表 continued

单位:件(case)

类 别	Types	其 中 of which 移送其他检察院 Removing to Other Procurator's Offices
总 计	**Total**	**16**
# 首次申诉	**Appeals First Time**	**16**
# 不服不起诉	Appeals Against Non-prosecution	
不服不立案	Appeals Against Rejection of the Case	1
不服逮捕	Appeals Against Arrest	1
不服刑事判决	Appeals Against Judgment of Criminal Case	1
不服民事行政裁决	Appeals Against Administration Arbitrament of Civil Case	12

表 23.11 法院各类案件办理情况(2021)
CASES HANDLED BY COURTS

单位:件(case)

类别	Types	收案 Cases Accepted	结案 Cases Settled	其中 of which 判决 Judgement	裁定 Arbitration	调解 Mediation
一审刑事案件	**First Trial Criminal Cases**	**27 489**	**27 815**	**27 658**	**106**	
#侵犯公民人身权利、民主权利罪	Offences Against Citizens' Personal and Democratic Rights	1 999	2 005	1 967	31	
侵犯财产罪	Offences Against Properties	6 909	7 012	6 968	27	
妨碍社会管理秩序罪	Offences Against Social Management of Order	10 499	10 386	10 337	33	
一审民事案件	**First Trial Civil Cases**	**585 379**	**577 341**	**218 308**	**239 405**	**82 818**
人格权纠纷	Personality Right Disputes	7 079	7 276	2 698	1 588	2 825
婚姻家庭、继承纠纷	Marriage and Family, Inheritance Disputes	33 082	32 734	8 723	7 210	16 046
婚姻家庭纠纷	Marriage and Family Disputes	22 451	22 296	6 926	5 461	9 326
继承纠纷	Inheritance Disputes	10 631	10 438	1 797	1 749	6 720
物权纠纷	Property Rights Disputes	16 149	15 000	5 857	5 396	3 027
合同、无因管理、不当得利纠纷	Contract, Non-management, Unjust Enrichment Disputes	394 859	393 112	168 168	172 519	44 971
合同纠纷	Contract Disputes	393 462	391 755	167 700	171 822	44 837
不当得利纠纷	Unjust Enrichment Disputes	1 369	1 327	457	680	132
无因管理纠纷	Non-management Disputes	28	30	11	17	2
知识产权与竞争纠纷	Intellectual Property Rights and Competition Disputes	51 122	47 035	5 175	32 915	1 841
劳动争议、人事纠纷	Labor Disputes and Personnel Disputes	13 597	14 174	7 584	2 431	3 269
劳动争议	Labor Disputes	13 551	14 131	7 564	2 409	3 268
人事纠纷	Personnel Disputes	46	43	20	22	1
与公司、证券、保险、票据等有关的民事纠纷	Civil Disputes Related to Companies, Securities, Insurance, Negotiable Instruments, etc.	22 590	22 275	8 632	7 916	3 264
侵犯责任纠纷	Infringement Liability Disputes	23 342	22 670	10 644	4 344	7 347
其他民事案由	Other Civil Cases	23 559	23 065	827	5 086	228
一审行政案件	**First Trial Administrative Cases**	**5 829**	**5 786**	**3 346**	**2 286**	**153**

表 23.12 法院执行案件情况(2021) CASES EXECUTED BY COURTS

单位:件(case)

类 别 Types		收 案 Cases Accepted	结 案 Cases Settled	其中 of which 执行完毕 Execution Completed	终结执行 Execution Terminated	终结本次执行程序 Execution Procedure Terminated
总 计	**Total**	**189 487**	**188 525**	**55 871**	**50 793**	**78 914**
刑 事	Criminal Cases	6 672	6 521	3 558	542	2 394
民 事	Civil Cases	163 389	162 276	45 152	47 066	68 434
行政与行政赔偿	Administrative Cases	380	336	100	105	129
行政非诉审查与执行	Non-litigious Investigation and Execution of Administration	759	767	314	30	421
仲 裁	Arbitration	17 311	17 615	6 486	2 878	6 966
公证债权文书	Notary Creditor's Rights	361	390	45	140	198
其 他	Others	615	620	216	32	372

表 23.13 主要年份法院各类案件结案情况 CASES ENDED BY COURTS IN MAIN YEARS

单位:起(time)

类 别 Types		2005	2010	2020	2021
总 计	**Total**	**283 230**	**406 582**	**868 843**	**870 108**
#刑事案件	Criminal Cases	17 353	22 137	32 639	31 314
婚姻家庭、继承案件	Marriages and Inheritance Cases	28 563	31 114	30 279	34 533
合同纠纷案件	Contract Disputes Cases	128 118	180 459	395 060	412 443
行政案件	Administrative Cases	3 016	2 135	7 771	8 566
申诉、申请再审	Second Trial on Appeals and Requisition	4 023	4 120	6 670	7 805
司法赔偿	Justice Compensation	6	1	71	60
执行案件	Executed Cases	70 998	102 221	162 071	188 525

上 / 海 / 统 / 计 / 年 / 鉴

主要统计指标解释

律　师

指依法取得律师执业证书，担任法律顾问，民事（刑事、行政）案件代理人、刑事案件辩护人、办理非诉讼业务，解答法律询问，代写法律事务文书等，为社会提供法律服务的人员。

公证人员

指在国家机关依法办理公证事务的司法人员。包括公证员、助理公证员和在公证处工作的其他人员。

公证文书

指公证处根据当事人申请，依照事实和法律，按照法定程序制作的，具有法律效力的司法证明文书。根据公证书用途和使用地，公证书分为国内公证书、国内经济公证书、涉外民事公证书、涉外经济公证书四类。

调解民间纠纷

指调解委员会按照法律规定，根据自愿原则，用说服教育的方法调解民间发生的有关民事权利和义务争执的件数，包括调解成功数和调解未成功数。该指标主要反映人民调解委员会的工作量。

立　案

指人民检察院对受理的报案、控告、举报或自首及自行发现的犯罪线索、犯罪嫌疑人进行初步调查后，认为存在职务犯罪事实和应追究刑事责任，并决定作为刑事案件进行侦查的诉讼活动，是追究犯罪的开始。该指标主要反映人民检察院依法将职务犯罪线索作为刑事案件进行侦查的诉讼活动。

申　诉

指经检察机关信访部门审查处理后，移送到检察机关申诉部门的申诉案件，包括不服检察机关处理决定和不服法院刑事判决和裁定的申诉的案件。

SHANGHAI STATISTICAL YEARBOOK

EXPLANATORY NOTES TO MAJOR STATISTICAL INDICATORS

□ Lawyers

Lawyers are certified legal workers according to law, and who are employed by legal counseling firms to act as legal advisers, agents in criminal or civil lawsuits, or defenders in criminal lawsuits, or to handle non-litigious legal affairs, to advise on matters of law or to write legal papers for others, and provide service to the public.

□ Notary Personnel

Notary Personnel are judicial workers of the state notary organs handling notarization work according to law. They include notaries, assistant notaries, and other people working in notary firms.

□ Notary Documents

Notary Documents refer to the judicatory notary documents drawn up by the request of the party and are in accordance with facts and laws and following certain legal proceedings. According to usage and locality, the notary documents are divided into following 4 types: domestic notary documents, domestic economic notary documents, foreign- related civil notary documents and foreign-related economic notary documents.

□ Mediation of Civil Disputes

Mediation of Civil Disputes refers to number of cases made by mediation committees in mediating in civil disputes concerning civil rights and duties through persuasion and education in accordance with the provisions of law on a voluntary basis, so as to solve disputes by helping the parties involved come to an agreement and understanding, including those unsuccessful ones. This indicator reflects the workload of the mediation committees.

□ Acceptance of Case

Acceptance of Case refers to the decision made by the people's procuratorate office on reported cases, prosecution, impeachment, surrender, self-found criminal clues or suspects after initial investigation to confirm the act of crime and to start legal proceedings of the case as criminal case.

□ Appeals

Appeals refer to cases transferred to the appeal departments of procurator's offices after initial review by departments dealing with complaint letters and calls of the public. Included are appeals against decisions made by procurator's offices and appeals against court rules and verdicts.